MARKETING STRATEGY

A DECISION-FOCUSED APPROACH

FOURTH EDITION

McGraw-Hill/Irwin Series in Marketing

MARKETING STRATEGY
A DECISION-FOCUSED APPROACH

FOURTH EDITION

ORVILLE C. WALKER, JR.
James D. Watkins Professor of Marketing
University of Minnesota

HARPER W. BOYD, JR.
Donaghey Distinguished Professor of Marketing
University of Arkansas—Little Rock

JOHN MULLINS
Associate Professor of Marketing
Daniels College of Business
University of Denver
Visiting Associate Professor of Entrepreneurship
London Business School

JEAN-CLAUDE LARRÉCHÉ
Alfred H. Heineken Professor of Marketing
European Institute of Business Administration
INSEAD

Boston   Burr Ridge, IL   Dubuque, IA   Madison, WI   New York   San Francisco   St. Louis
Bangkok   Bogotá   Caracas   Kuala Lumpur   Lisbon   London   Madrid   Mexico City
Milan   Montreal   New Delhi   Santiago   Seoul   Singapore   Sydney   Taipei   Toronto

McGraw-Hill Higher Education

A Division of The McGraw-Hill Companies

MARKETING STRATEGY: A DECISION-FOCUSED APPROACH
Published by McGraw-Hill/Irwin, a business unit of The McGraw-Hill Companies, Inc., 1221
Avenue of the Americas, New York, NY, 10020. Copyright © 2003, 1999, 1996, 1992 by The
McGraw-Hill Companies, Inc. All rights reserved. No part of this publication may be reproduced
or distributed in any form or by any means, or stored in a database or retrieval system, without
the prior written consent of The McGraw-Hill Companies, Inc., including, but not limited to, in
any network or other electronic storage or transmission, or broadcast for distance learning.
Some ancillaries, including electronic and print components, may not be available to customers
outside the United States.

This book is printed on acid-free paper.

domestic 2 3 4 5 6 7 8 9 0 DOW/DOW 0 9 8 7 6 5 4 3 2
international 1 2 3 4 5 6 7 8 9 0 DOW/DOW 0 9 8 7 6 5 4 3 2

ISBN: 0-07-246670-7

Publisher: *John E. Biernat*
Executive editor: *Linda Schreiber*
Editorial assistant: *Sarah Crago*
Marketing manager: *Kim Kanakes Szum*
Project manager: *Laura Griffin*
Senior production supervisor: *Michael R. McCormick*
Senior designer: *Jennifer McQueen*
Media producer: *Craig Atkins*
Supplement producer: *Vicki Laird*
Photo research coordinator: *David A. Tietz*
Cover design: *JoAnne Schopler*
Cover image: *Alan Kearney/Getty Images, Inc.*
Typeface: *10/12 Times Roman*
Compositor: *ElectraGraphics, Inc.*
Printer: *R. R. Donnelley & Sons Company*

Library of Congress Cataloging-in-Publication Data

Marketing strategy : a decision-focused approach / Orville C. Walker . . . [et al.].—4th ed.
    p. cm.
    Rev. ed. of: Marketing strategy / Orville C. Walker, Jr., Harper Boyd, Jr., Jean-Claude
Larréché. 3rd ed. c1999.
    Includes bibliographical references and indexes.
    ISBN 0-07-246670-7 (alk. paper)—ISBN 0-07-115117-6 (International ed.)
    1. Marketing—Management. I. Walker, Orville C. II. Walker, Orville C. Marketing
strategy.
    HF5415.13.W249 2003
    658.8'02—dc21   2002020042

INTERNATIONAL EDITION ISBN 0-07-115117-6
Copyright © 2003. Exclusive rights by The McGraw-Hill Companies, Inc. for manufacture and
export. This book cannot be re-exported from the country to which it is sold by McGraw-Hill.
The International Edition is not available in North America.

www.mhhe.com

BRIEF CONTENTS

CONTENTS

SECTION THREE
FORMULATING MARKETING STRATEGIES 190

9 Marketing Strategies for New Market
Entries 192

10 Strategies for Growth Markets 214

11 Strategies for Mature and Declining
Markets 238

SECTION FOUR
IMPLEMENTATION AND CONTROL   300

PREFACE

WHY THIS COURSE?

THE BEST OF THE LEADING BUSINESS SCHOOLS and other executive education programs offer capstone or other elective courses in marketing whose strategic perspective challenges students to "pull it all together" and integrate what they have learned in earlier courses—including those in marketing and other disciplines—in making strategic marketing decisions. Whether called Marketing Strategy, Strategic Market Planning, Strategic Brand Management, Marketing in the New Economy, or something else, such courses typically ask students to apply what they learn to decision making in cases that bring alive real marketing situations. Many also ask students to complete a term-long project of some kind, such as the development of a marketing plan for a new or existing product or a new venture. We have written this text to serve exactly these kinds of capstone and advanced elective courses.

WHY THIS BOOK?

Why did your instructor choose this book? Chances are, it was for one or more of the following reasons:

- Among your instructor's objectives is to give you the necessary tools and frameworks to enable you to be an effective contributor to marketing **decision making,** whether as an entrepreneur or in an established firm. This book's focus on decision making sets it apart from other texts that place greater emphasis on *description* of marketing phenomena than on the strategic and tactical marketing *decisions* that marketing managers and entrepreneurs must make each and every day.
- Your instructor prefers a tightly written text whose strategic perspectives serve as a **concise foundation** around which a broader set of materials, such as case studies or supplementary readings that fit the specific theme of the course, are

assembled. Thus, this text assumes student familiarity with—and thus does not repeat—the basics of buyer behavior, the four Ps, and other marketing fundamentals typically covered in earlier courses.

- Your instructor wants to use the most current and most **Web-savvy** book available. We integrate the latest new-economy developments into each chapter, and we devote an entire chapter—Chapter 12—to the development of marketing strategies for the new economy. In addition, we supplement the book with an interactive website to help you learn and to help your instructor choose the best case and other materials and in-class activities. Our goal—and probably that of your instructor, as well—is to make both the latest Web-based tools as well as time-tested marketing principles relevant to those of you who will work in either old- or new-economy companies.
- Your instructor appreciates and believes you will benefit from the **real-world, global perspectives** offered by the authors of this book. Our combined entrepreneurial, marketing management, and consulting experience spans a broad variety of manufacturing, service, software, and distribution industries and has taken us—and thereby you, the reader—around the world many times over.

As the reader will see from the outset in Chapter 1, marketing decision making is a critical activity in every firm, including start-ups—not just in big companies with traditional marketing departments. Further, it is not just marketing managers who make marketing decisions. People in nearly every role in every company can have powerful influence on how happy its customers are—or are not—with the goods and services the company provides. Stockbrokers must attract new customers. Accounting and consulting firms must find ways to differentiate their services from other providers so their customers have reasons to give them their business. Software engineers developing the next great Internet or other technology must understand how their technology can benefit the intended customer, for without such benefits, customers will not buy. Thus, we have written this book to meet the marketing needs of readers who hope to make a difference in the long-term strategic success of their organizations—whether their principal roles are in marketing or otherwise.

In this brief preface, we want to say a bit more about each of the four distinctive benefits—bulleted above—that this book offers its readers. We also point out the key changes in this edition compared to previous ones; and we thank our many students, colleagues, and others from whom we have learned so much, without whom this book would not have been possible.

A FOCUS ON DECISION MAKING

This fourth edition of *Marketing Strategy: A Decision-Focused Approach* retains the strategic perspectives that have marked the earlier editions, while providing, in each chapter, specific tools and frameworks for **making marketing decisions** that take best advantage of the conditions in which the firm finds itself—both internally, in terms of the firm's mission and competencies, and externally, in terms of the market and competitive context in which it operates.

This decision-focused approach is important to students and executives who are our readers, because, in most advanced marketing management classes and executive courses, the students or participants will be asked to make numerous decisions—decisions in case studies about what the protagonist in the case should do; decisions in a course project, such as those entailed in developing a marketing plan; or decisions in a marketing simulation such as Gamar, included with this book.

Our decision-focused approach is also important to employers, who tell us they want today's graduates to be prepared to "hit the ground running" and contribute to the firm's decision making from day one. The ability to bring thoughtful and disciplined tools and frameworks—as opposed to seat-of-the-pants hunches or blind intuition—to marketing decision making is one of the key assets today's business school graduates offer their employers. This book puts the tools in the toolbox to make this happen. In the end, employers want to know what their new hires can *do,* not just what they *know.*

A CONCISE STRATEGIC FOUNDATION

This fourth edition serves as a **concise foundation** for a capstone or advanced elective course in marketing whose focus is on strategic issues. By combining this book with supplemental readings and/or cases, instructors can design a rich and varied course in which students learn experientially, as they focus on the various strategic decisions that define contemporary marketing theory and practice.

Because the book is concise, students learn the key strategic principles quickly, so they can devote most of their reading and prep time to the *application* of those principles to cases or a course project. The book's concise strategic focus also helps instructors build specialized elective courses—in Strategic Brand Management or in Marketing in the New Economy, for example—that draw on supplemental readings to complete the thematic picture.

WEB-SAVVY INSIGHTS

Because this book has been written by authors who teach at Web-savvy institutions and work with Web-savvy companies, it brings a realistic, informed, and **Web-savvy perspective** to an important question many students are asking: "Has the advent of the Internet changed all the rules?" Our answer is, "Well, yes and no." On one hand, the Internet has made available a host of new marketing tools—from banner ads to e-mail marketing to delivery of digital goods and services over the Internet—many of which are available to companies in the so-called old and new economies alike. On the other hand, time-tested marketing fundamentals—such as understanding one's customers and competitors and meeting customer needs in ways that are differentiated from the offerings of those competitors—have become even more important in the fast-moving, dot-com world, as the many dot-com failures over the last few years attest.

Thus, throughout the book, we integrate examples of new-economy companies—both successful and otherwise—to show how both yesterdays' and today's marketing tools and decision frameworks can most effectively be applied. Because the advent of the Internet, mobile telephony, and other new-economy technologies is so important in its own right, however, we also devote an entire chapter—Chapter 12—to new-economy strategies, in order to provide for marketers in all kinds of companies a roadmap for decisions about where, when, and how to deploy new-economy tools.

A REAL-WORLD, GLOBAL PERSPECTIVE

Theory is important, because it enhances our understanding of business phenomena and helps managers think about what they should do. It is in the *application* of theory—the world of marketing practice—where we believe this book excels. Our decision focus is all about application. But we don't just bring an academic perspective to the party, important as that perspective is.

Two of us on the author team, Jean-Claude Larréché and John Mullins, have started successful entrepreneurial companies. One of these firms has "gone public." Two of us, Orville Walker and John, have worked for many years in the United States, at the University of Minnesota and University of Denver, respectively. Two, Jean-Claude and John, work in Europe, Jean-Claude at INSEAD and John as a visiting professor at the London Business School. All of us, including Harper Boyd, who passed away in 1999 but whose legacy lives on in this edition, have contributed the fruits of our research to the growing body of knowledge in the marketing management, marketing strategy, new products, and entrepreneurship arenas. The result of our collective and varied experience and expertise is a book marked by its **real-world, global perspective.** The book's many examples of real people from around the world making real strategic marketing decisions include examples of start-ups and high-growth companies as well as examples of larger, more established firms.

WHAT'S NEW IN THIS EDITION?

Aside from our extensive treatment of the new economy in this edition—as we've already noted—we've also made a few other important changes worth noting to those familiar with previous editions.

- We've brought forward, to Chapter 1, the material that outlines what a marketing plan is and does, to better support students who are asked, as part of the capstone or elective course in which

this book is used, to develop marketing plans for either real or hypothetical products, whether existing ones or new. The balance of the book then provides the detail that enables students to make the necessary decisions to complete, and even implement, such a plan.

- We've added new material in Chapter 2 on brands and brand management, to reflect the growing strategic importance of these topics. The addition of this new material also provides support for instructors who wish to give their capstone or elective course a brand management emphasis.

- We've added a chapter, Chapter 6, to provide the necessary tools and frameworks to enable students to prepare evidence-based forecasts of demand for products whose marketing plans they may be asked to prepare. We've also included in Chapter 6 references to enough marketing research basics to enable them to conduct primary research for a marketing plan project and—perhaps more importantly—to make every reader of this book a better informed and more critical user of marketing research studies. This enhanced decision support for student projects—inherent in our decision-focused approach—is, we believe, a major strength of this revised edition.

- We've added an interactive website—at **www.mhhe.com/walker**—to complement the book, one we believe will be helpful to students and instructors alike. For students, the website offers a series of self-diagnostic questions to enable them to self-test their understanding of the tools and decision frameworks covered in each chapter. For instructors, the website offers suggested activities and assignments for each chapter, in order to aid instructors who seek to build interactive classroom environments. The website also suggests the "best of the best" decision-focused cases—including international ones, dot-coms, and companies in services and manufacturing industries—and other supplemental readings to help instructors find the best teaching materials to train graduates for the local economies in which they are likely to work and to most effectively nail down the learning in each chapter.

In reality, though, no chapter has escaped untouched. All have been updated, although the basic flow, sequence, and strategic focus of the book have remained unchanged.

THANKS!

Simply put, this book is not solely our work—far from it. Many of our students, colleagues, and those with whom we work in industry have made contributions that have significantly shaped our perspectives on marketing decision making. We are grateful to all of them.

We also thank a small army of talented people at Irwin/McGraw-Hill for their work that has turned our rough manuscript into an attractive and readable book. In particular, our editors, Linda Schreiber and Sarah

Crago, have been instrumental in giving birth to this edition. Without them, we'd probably still be writing!

Finally, we thank Harper Boyd, without whom this book would not exist, and our parents, without whom, of course, none of us would be here. To all of you we extend our love, our respect, and our gratitude for passing on to us your curiosity and your passion for learning. We therefore dedicate this book to Harper Boyd, to Jeannette and Orville Walker, Sr., to Jack and Alice Mullins, and to Odette and Pierre Larréché.

Orville C. Walker, Jr.
John Mullins
Jean-Claude Larréché
Minneapolis, London, and Fontainebleau:
Spring 2002

About the Authors

Orville C. Walker, Jr.

Orville C. Walker, Jr. is the James D. Watkins Professor of Marketing, and Director of the PhD Program, in the University of Minnesota's Carlson School of Management. He holds a Master's degree in social psychology from the Ohio State University and a PhD in marketing from the University of Wisconsin–Madison.

Orville is the co-author of three books and has published more than 50 research articles in scholarly and business journals. He has won several awards for his research, including the O'Dell award from the *Journal of Marketing Research,* the Maynard award from the *Journal of Marketing,* and a lifetime achievement award from the Sales Management Interest Group of the American Marketing Association.

Orville has been a consultant to a number of business firms and not-for-profit organizations, and he has taught in executive development programs around the world, including programs in Poland, Switzerland, Scotland, and Hong Kong. Perhaps his biggest business challenge, however, is attempting to turn a profit as the owner-manager of a small vineyard in western Wisconsin.

Harper W. Boyd, Jr.

The late **Harper W. Boyd, Jr.** was the Donaghey Distinguished Professor Emeritus of Marketing at the University of Arkansas at Little Rock. He was internationally known in the areas of marketing strategy and marketing research. He authored, co-authored, or edited more than 50 books and monographs and 100 articles, cases, and other teaching materials, and served as editor of the *Journal of Marketing Research.* He taught on the faculties of several prominent business schools around the world, including Stanford, Northwestern, Tulane, and INSEAD; and he received an honorary Doctorate of Letters from the Edinburgh Business School in Scotland. He also consulted extensively with both consumer and industrial products companies around the world.

John Mullins

John Mullins is Visiting Associate Professor of Entrepreneurship at London Business School and Associate Professor of Marketing at the Daniels College of Business of the University of Denver. He earned his MBA at the Stanford Graduate School of Business and, considerably later in life, his PhD in marketing from the University of Minnesota. An award-winning teacher, John brings to his teaching and research 20 years of executive experience in high-growth firms, including two ventures he founded, one of which he took public. Since becoming a business school professor in 1992, John has published more than 30 articles in a variety of outlets, including *Harvard Business Review,* the *Journal of Product Innovation Management,* and the *Journal of Business Venturing.* His research has won national and international awards from the Marketing Science Institute, the American Marketing Association, and the Richard D. Irwin Foundation. He is also co-author of *Marketing Management: A Strategic-Decision Making Approach,* 4th edition.

Jean-Claude Larréché

Jean-Claude Larréché is Alfred H. Heineken Professor of Marketing and Director of the Competitiveness Fitness of Global Firms Initiative at the European Institute of Business Administration, INSEAD, in Fontainebleau,

France. He holds an MBA from INSEAD and a PhD in marketing from the Stanford University Graduate School of Business. A consultant to several major international firms, Jean-Claude has worked with top management teams in Europe, North America, and Asia. He is chairman and founder of StratX, a publisher of marketing simulations and other tools for strategic marketing. An award-winning teacher, Jean-Claude is also a two-time winner of the overall case competition of the European Case Clearing House. He is co-author of *Marketing Management: A Strategic Decision-Making Approach,* 4th edition.

Section One

Introduction to Strategy

MARKET-ORIENTED PERSPECTIVES UNDERLIE SUCCESSFUL CORPORATE, BUSINESS, AND MARKETING STRATEGIES

IBM Switches Strategies[1]

FOR DECADES International Business Machines focused most of its efforts on the hardware side of the computer industry: first on large mainframe computers, then on personal computers (PCs), and then, as the Internet began to take off in the mid-1990s, on servers and related equipment. Its target customers for that hardware were typically organizations rather than individual consumers and usually large organizations that needed lots of data-processing capacity and had the financial resources to afford it. The firm did not ignore consumers or small businesses, but it relied on independent retailers, such as Circuit City, and value-added resellers to reach those segments while focusing much of its own marketing and sales effort on large organizations.

IBM's competitive strategy was also quite consistent over the years. Given that the firm was never the lowest-cost producer in the industry, it did not try to compete with low prices. Instead, the firm pursued a quality differentiation strategy by offering superior products backed up by excellent technical service and selling them at premium prices.

To implement its strategy, the company tried to ensure a steady stream of cutting-edge products by allocating vast resources to R&D and product development. IBM also generally followed an "open architecture" policy. In its PC business, for instance, the firm licensed its PC-DOS operating system (developed in collaboration with Microsoft) to other manufacturers and software developers. This helped expand the number of PC-DOS users, thereby providing incentives for IBM's licensees to develop more innovative applications software to run on PC-DOS systems, which in turn enhanced the usefulness and customer value of IBM's hardware.

On the marketing side, the firm maintained substantial advertising and promotion budgets to keep potential customers informed about its constantly evolving product lines and to burnish the identity of the IBM brand. More important, though, were the millions spent recruiting, training, and compensating one of the world's largest and most technically competent salesforces.

For decades IBM's corporate, business, and marketing strategies were all very successful. Within two years of entering the personal computer business in 1981, for instance, IBM had captured more than 40 percent of the U.S. PC market. More importantly, the firm's strategies were instrumental in spurring the rapid growth of the U.S. market from 3.5 million units per year in 1983 to over 20 million in 1996 and stimulating adoption of PCs in other countries as well.

TECHNOLOGY CHANGES AND COMPETITOR ACTIONS REQUIRE A SHIFT IN STRATEGY

By the mid-1990s, however, several of IBM's traditional businesses were in trouble. The company's share of the worldwide PC market fell to about 8 percent in 1999, third behind Dell and Compaq. Worse, the firm's PC business was projected to lose $400 million, on top of a $1 billion loss in 1998. Similarly, while server sales, made up mostly of UNIX-based computers, were growing rapidly around the world, IBM was able to capture only a small share of that business. Its growth rate in the server market during the late 1990s was only about one-third as fast as that of major competitors such as Sun Microsystems. Even its venerable mainframe business, which had been a low-growth but highly profitable market throughout the 1980s and early 1990s, suffered a profit squeeze due to falling prices and declining demand.

IBM's performance problems can be traced to a variety of factors, which all worked to make the firm's tried-and-true corporate, competitive, and marketing strategies less effective than they once were. For one thing, major technological changes in the macroenvironment—such as the rapid increase

in power of desktop PCs, the emergence of the Internet, and the development of internal, organizationwide computer networks (or intranets)—greatly contributed to the declining demand for large mainframe computers and centralized data-processing systems.

Also, IBM's quality differentiation strategy became less effective as some of its product-markets began to mature and customers' purchase criteria changed. Technical and performance differences among competing brands became less pronounced as the PC industry matured, for example, and later buyers tended to be less technically sophisticated, more price-conscious, and more interested in buying equipment that was easy to use. IBM's premium price position put it at a disadvantage in attracting such customers. Worse, a number of competitors, notably Dell, provided more benefits at lower prices by offering custom-designed systems, convenient direct purchasing over the Web, and user-friendly service and support programs.

Even IBM's traditional focus on large organizational customers contributed to the firm's problems in the newly emerging markets for servers and related equipment and software. It was slow to pursue the many small start-up businesses at the forefront of the dot.com revolution, leaving an open field for Sun, Hewlett-Packard, and other competitors. "We've had to adapt our [strategy] model to them," concedes Lou Gerstner, IBM's CEO. "We were late."

A NEW CORPORATE STRATEGY

When Lou Gerstner took over as IBM's chief executive in 1994, he and a task force of other executives, including many from the marketing and sales ranks, reexamined all the firm's businesses, customer segments, competitors, and potential competitors. Their conclusion: The Internet would change everything. They foresaw that "[t]he real leadership in the [information technology] industry was moving away from the creation of the technology to the application of the technology," says Gerstner. "The explosive growth is in services."

Further, "[w]e concluded that this [the Internet] was not an information superhighway. This was all about business, doing transactions, not looking up information."

Consequently, IBM's top executives began to refocus the corporate mission, de-emphasizing the development and manufacture of high-tech hardware while increasing the emphasis on providing customers with e-business engineering, design, and outsourcing services. To leverage the firm's existing competencies and its long-term relationships with its traditional customers, many of the new services the firm developed concentrate on helping large, bricks-and-mortar firms (1) hook old corporate databases (often on mainframes) into new online systems, (2) integrate Web technology into their internal business processes to improve efficiency, and (3) develop and run company websites. For instance, Lego, the Danish toy manufacturer, pays IBM to run its entire Web operation, including contracting with the Danish post office to handle shipping.

But the corporation also has expanded the scope of both its new service and old hardware businesses to embrace smaller customers, especially Web start-ups and dot.com organizations. For example, one of the 20 new Internet-related service businesses IBM launched in 1999 offered to provide all the hardware, software, and services that small businesses need to get online for as little as $99 a month.

New Business and Marketing Strategies

IBM's new corporate emphasis on e-business services as its primary path toward future growth also has forced some changes in the firm's competitive and marketing strategies. At the business level, the

Exhibit 1.1

A Print Advertisement for IBM's E-Business Services

www.yamaha.com is an IBM e-business.
Yamaha Global Jukebox Technology puts digital music on the Web. IBM technology puts it at your fingertips.

firm still seeks to differentiate itself from competitors on the basis of superior quality and to charge premium prices for that quality. But in its new service businesses, competitive superiority depends on the knowledge, experience, and expertise of its consultants—and their familiarity with a customer's operations that comes from continuing interaction—rather than the technical quality of its products. Therefore, to implement its new service-based differentiation strategy effectively, the company reorganized and reallocated many of its internal resources. For example, the firm created a new Internet division with responsibility for ensuring that all company products work with the Web and for developing and coordinating a continuing stream of e-business services. It has also shifted over 50 percent of its $5 billion R&D budget into projects aimed at creating new Internet-based services and software. And like Intel and Cisco Systems, IBM quietly invests about $60 million a year of venture capital backing Web start-ups, mostly to provide "headlights" into cutting-edge technologies.

Given that the success of IBM's competitive strategy depends heavily on the knowledge and expertise of its personnel and their ability to forge beneficial relationships with customers, the firm's salesforce is even more crucial than ever. Many salespeople who used to spend a portion of their time selling the company's hardware have been given additional training and turned into full-time e-business consultants. The 50,000 consultants in the firm's Global Services unit dwarf the workforces of all its competitors and generated over $10 billion in revenue in 2000.

The superior expertise and experience of IBM's people—and the firm's ability to satisfy the e-commerce needs of customers in a variety of industries—also were effectively communicated via an advertising campaign featuring a series of ads such as that shown in Exhibit 1.1. The ads identified firms in different industries that relied on IBM to design and implement their websites and were placed in a variety of media directed at managers and entrepreneurs.

THE BOTTOM LINE

At the time of this writing, IBM's new strategies had not yet resolved all the firm's problems. But the company estimates that more than 25 percent of its revenues in 2000—some $22 billion—came from e-business products and services. That was more than the revenues of the top 25 dot.coms (i.e., AOL, Amazon, eBay, E*Trade, etc.) combined. More important, revenues from its new service businesses were growing more than 30 percent annually, compared to a 9 percent growth rate for the company as a whole. And the firm was gaining market share relative to Oracle and other competitors in crucial segments, such as database software. As one e-business competitor conceded, "They get it. Every day they tell a better story."

STRATEGIC CHALLENGES ADDRESSED IN CHAPTER 1

IBM's experiences in the information technology industry illustrate some important points about the nature of business strategy and the interrelationships among different levels of strategy in an organization, points that will recur as major themes throughout this book. They also demonstrate the importance of timely and accurate insights into customer desires, environmental trends, and competitors' actions in formulating successful strategies at every level.

Most firms, particularly larger corporations with multiple divisions or business units like IBM, pursue a hierarchy of interdependent strategies. Each strategy is formulated at different levels in the organization and deals with different sets of issues. For example, IBM's goals of becoming a leading Internet service provider and seeking future growth primarily through the development of new e-commerce engineering, design, and outsourcing services reflect its new **corporate strategy.** This level of strategy provides direction on the company's mission, the kinds of businesses it should be in, and its growth policies.

On the other hand, attempts to differentiate its offerings by providing superior quality based on the expertise, experience, and customer knowledge of its huge contingent of consultants while avoiding cut-throat price competition reflect IBM's **business-level strategy** in its new Internet division. This level of strategy primarily addresses how a business will compete in its industry.

Finally, interrelated functional decisions about how to divide the market into segments, which segments to target, what goods and services to offer each segment, what promotional tools and appeals to employ, and what prices to charge all reflect the **marketing strategies** for each of IBM's various product-market entries.

Because a major part of the marketing manager's job is to monitor and analyze the needs and desires of potential customers, emerging challenges posed by competitors, and opportunities and threats related to trends in the external environment, they often play a crucial role in influencing strategies formulated at higher levels in the firm. While the need for new corporate and competitive strategies at IBM became obvious because of stagnating sales and declining profits in some of the firm's most venerable businesses, decisions about the content of those new strategies were influenced by information and analyses supplied by the firm's marketing and sales personnel. Marketing executives were key members of the task force appointed by CEO Gerstner to analyze the firm's strengths and weaknesses and develop new directions for growth and profitability. And Gerstner himself was recruited, in part, because of his experience working for customer-oriented package goods and financial services firms of Nabisco and American Express.

Some firms systematically incorporate such market and competitive analyses into their planning processes. They also coordinate their activities around the primary goal of satisfying unmet customer needs. Such firms are *market-oriented* and follow a business philosophy commonly called the *marketing concept.* Market-oriented firms have been shown to be among the more profitable and successful at maintaining strong competitive positions in their industries over time. As we shall see later in this chapter, however, companies do not always embrace a market orientation—nor rely as heavily on inputs from their marketing and sales personnel—in developing their strategies. Some firms' strategies are driven more by technology, production, or cost concerns.

Regardless of their participation or influence in formulating corporate and business-level strategies, marketing managers' freedom of action is ultimately constrained by those higher-level strategies. The objectives, strategies, and action plans for a specific product-market are but one part of a hierarchy of strategies within the firm. Each level of strategy must be consistent with—and therefore influenced and constrained by—higher levels within the hierarchy. For example, not only the new services developed by IBM, but also their advertising appeals, prices, and other aspects of the marketing plans, were shaped by the shift in corporate strategy toward emphasizing Web-based services as the primary avenue for future growth.

These interrelationships among the various levels of strategy raise several questions of importance to marketing managers as well as managers in other functional areas and top executives. What do strategies consist of, and do they have similar or different components at the corporate, business, and functional levels? While marketing managers clearly bear the primary responsibility for developing strategic marketing plans for individual product offerings, what role do they play in formulating strategies at the corporate and divisional or business unit level? Why do some organizations pay much more attention to customers and competitors when formulating their strategies (i.e., why are some firms more market-oriented) than others, and does it make any dif-

STRATEGIC ISSUE

Why do some organizations pay much more attention to customers and competitors when formulating their strategies (i.e., why are some firms more market-oriented) than others, and does it make any difference in their performance?

ference in their performance? What specific decisions and analytical processes underlie the formulation and implementation of effective marketing strategies? These are the questions tackled in the rest of this chapter.

THREE LEVELS OF STRATEGY: SIMILAR COMPONENTS BUT DIFFERENT ISSUES

What Is a Strategy?

Although *strategy* first became a popular business buzzword during the 1960s, it continues to be the subject of widely differing definitions and interpretations. The following definition, however, captures the essence of the term:

> A **strategy** is a fundamental pattern of present and planned objectives, resource deployments, and interactions of an organization with markets, competitors, and other environmental factors.[2]

Our definition suggests that a strategy should specify (1) *what* (objectives to be accomplished), (2) *where* (on which industries and product-markets to focus), and (3) *how* (which resources and activities to allocate to each product-market to meet environmental opportunities and threats and to gain a competitive advantage).

The Components of Strategy

A well-developed strategy contains five components, or sets of issues:

1. *Scope.* The scope of an organization refers to the breadth of its strategic domain—the number and types of industries, product lines, and market segments it competes in or plans to enter. Decisions about an organization's strategic scope should reflect management's view of the firm's purpose or *mission.* This common thread among its various activities and product-markets defines the essential nature of what its business is and what it should be.
2. *Goals and objectives.* Strategies also should detail desired levels of accomplishment on one or more dimensions of performance—such as volume growth, profit contribution, or return on investment—over specified time periods for each of those businesses and product-markets and for the organization as a whole.
3. *Resource deployments.* Every organization has limited financial and human resources. Formulating a strategy also involves deciding how those resources are to be obtained and allocated, across businesses, product-markets, functional departments, and activities within each business or product-market.
4. *Identification of a sustainable competitive advantage.* One important part of any strategy is a specification of *how the organization will compete* in each business and product-market within its domain. How can it position itself to develop and sustain a differential advantage over current and potential competitors? To answer such questions, managers must examine the market opportunities in each business and product-market and the company's distinctive competencies or strengths relative to its competitors.
5. *Synergy.* Synergy exists when the firm's businesses, product-markets, resource deployments, and competencies complement and reinforce one another. Synergy enables the total performance of the related businesses to be greater than it would otherwise be: The whole becomes greater than the sum of its parts.

The Hierarchy of Strategies

Explicitly or implicitly, these five basic dimensions are part of all strategies. However, rather than a single comprehensive strategy, most organizations have a hierarchy of interrelated strategies, each formulated at a different level of the firm. The three major levels of strategy in most large, multiproduct organizations are (1) **corporate strategy,** (2) **business-**

level strategy, and (3) **functional strategies** focused on a particular product-market entry. These three levels of strategy are diagrammed in Exhibit 1.2. In small single-product-line companies or entrepreneurial start-ups, however, corporate and business-level strategic issues merge.

Our primary focus is on the development of marketing strategies and programs for individual product-market entries, but other functional departments—such as R&D and production—also have strategies and plans for each of the firm's product-markets. Throughout this book, therefore, we examine the interfunctional implications of product-market strategies, conflicts across functional areas, and the mechanisms that firms use to resolve those conflicts.

Strategies at all three levels contain the five components mentioned earlier, but because each strategy serves a different purpose within the organization, each emphasizes a different

Exhibit 1.2

THE HIERARCHY OF STRATEGIES

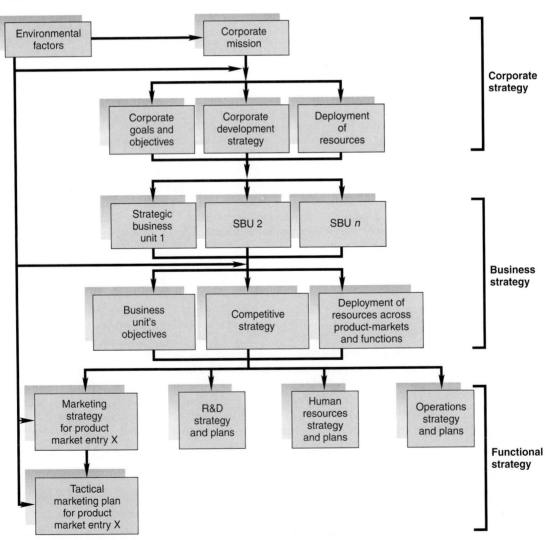

Exhibit 1.3

KEY COMPONENTS OF CORPORATE, BUSINESS, AND MARKETING STRATEGIES

Strategy components	Corporate strategy	Business strategy	Marketing strategy
Scope	• Corporate domain—"Which businesses should we be in?" • Corporate development strategy Conglomerate diversification (expansion into unrelated businesses) Vertical integration Acquisition and divestiture policies	• Business domain—"Which product-markets should we be in within this business or industry? • Business development strategy Concentric diversification (new products for existing customers or new customers for existing products)	• Target market definition • Product-line depth and breadth • Branding policies • Product-market development plan • Line extension and product elimination plans
Goals and objectives	• Overall corporate objectives aggregated across businesses Revenue growth Profitability ROI (return on investment) Earnings per share Contributions to other stakeholders	• Constrained by corporate goals • Objectives aggregated across product-market entries in the business unit Sales growth New product or market growth Profitability ROI Cash flow Strengthening bases of competitive advantage	• Constrained by corporate and business goals • Objectives for a specific product-market entry Sales Market share Contribution margin Customer satisfaction
Allocation of resources	• Allocation among businesses in the corporate portfolio • Allocation across functions shared by multiple businesses (corporate R&D, MIS)	• Allocation among product-market entries in the business unit • Allocation across functional departments within the business unit	• Allocation across components of the marketing plan (elements of the marketing mix) for a specific product-market entry
Sources of competitive advantage	• Primarily through superior corporate financial or human resources; more corporate R&D; better organizational processes or synergies relative to competitors across all industries in which the firm operates	• Primarily through competitive strategy, business unit's competencies relative to competitors in its industry	• Primarily through effective product positioning; superiority on one or more components of the marketing mix relative to competitors within a specific product-market
Sources of synergy	• Shared resources, technologies, or functional competencies across businesses within the firm	• Shared resources (including favorable customer image) or functional competencies across product-markets within an industry	• Shared marketing resources, competencies, or activities across product-market entries

set of issues. Exhibit 1.3 on the previous page summarizes the specific focus and issues dealt with at each level of strategy; we discuss them in the next sections.

CORPORATE STRATEGY

At the corporate level, managers must coordinate the activities of multiple business units and, in the case of conglomerates, even separate legal business entities. Decisions about the organization's scope and resource deployments across its divisions or businesses are the primary focus of corporate strategy. The essential questions at this level include, What business(es) are we in? What business(es) *should* we be in? and What portion of our total resources should we devote to each of these businesses to achieve the organization's over-all goals and objectives? Thus, new CEO Gerstner and other top-level managers at IBM decided to pursue future growth primarily through the development of Web-based services and software rather than computer hardware. They shifted substantial corporate resources—including R&D expenditures, marketing and advertising budgets, and vast numbers of salespeople—into the corporation's service and software businesses to support the new strategic direction.

Attempts to develop and maintain distinctive competencies at the corporate level focus on generating superior human, financial, and technological resources; designing effective organization structures and processes; and seeking synergy among the firm's various businesses. Synergy can provide a major competitive advantage for firms where related businesses share R&D investments, product or production technologies, distribution channels, a common salesforce, and/or promotional themes—as in the case of IBM.[3]

Business-Level Strategy

How a business unit competes within its industry is the critical focus of business-level strategy. A major issue in a business strategy is that of sustainable competitive advantage. What distinctive competencies can give the business unit a competitive advantage? And which of those competencies best match the needs and wants of the customers in the business's target segment(s)? For example, a business with low-cost sources of supply and efficient, modern plants might adopt a low-cost competitive strategy. One with a strong marketing department and a competent salesforce may compete by offering superior customer service.[4]

Another important issue a business-level strategy must address is appropriate scope: how many and which market segments to compete in, and the overall breadth of product offerings and marketing programs to appeal to these segments. Finally, synergy should be sought across product-markets and across functional departments within the business.

Marketing Strategy

The primary focus of marketing strategy is to effectively allocate and coordinate marketing resources and activities to accomplish the firm's objectives within a specific product-market. Therefore, the critical issue concerning the scope of a marketing strategy is specifying the target market(s) for a particular product or product line. Next, firms seek competitive advantage and synergy through a well-integrated program of marketing mix elements (primarily the 4 Ps of product, price, place, promotion) tailored to the needs and wants of potential customers in that target market.

WHAT IS MARKETING'S ROLE IN FORMULATING AND IMPLEMENTING STRATEGIES?

The essence of strategic planning at all levels is identifying threats to avoid and opportunities to pursue. The primary strategic responsibility of any manager is to look outward continuously to keep the firm or business in step with changes in the environment. Because they occupy positions at the boundary between the firm and its customers, distributors, and competitors, marketing managers are usually most familiar with conditions and trends in the market environment. Consequently, they not only are responsible for developing strategic plans for their own product-market entries, but also are often primary participants and contributors to the planning process at the business and corporate levels as well.

The wide-ranging influence of marketing managers on higher-level strategic decisions is clearly shown in a recent survey of managers in 280 U.S. and 234 German business units of firms in the electrical equipment, mechanical machinery, and consumer package goods industries.[5] The study examined perceptions of marketing managers' influence relative to managers from sales, R&D, operations, and finance on a variety of strategic and tactical decisions within their businesses. Exhibit 1.4 summarizes the results.

The study found that, on average, marketing and sales executives exerted significantly more influence than managers from other functions on strategic decisions concerning traditional marketing activities, such as advertising messages, pricing, distribution, customer

Exhibit 1.4

INFLUENCE OF FUNCTIONAL UNITS OVER VARIOUS BUSINESS DECISIONS

Decisions	Marketing	Sales	R&D	Operations	Finance
Business strategy decisions					
Strategic direction of the business	38	29**	11**	9**	14**
Expansion into new geographic markets	39	45**	3**	3**	10**
Choices of strategic partners	33	38*	7**	9**	12**
New product development	32	23**	29**	9**	7**
Major capital expenditures	13	11**	13	29**	35**
Marketing strategy decisions					
Advertising messages	65	29**	3**	1**	2**
Customer satisfaction measurement	48	35**	5**	8**	4**
Customer satisfaction improvement	40	37*	7**	10**	6**
Distribution strategy	34	52**	1**	6**	6**
Customer service and support	31	47**	5**	10**	7**
Pricing	30	41**	4**	9**	16**

The number in each cell is the mean of the amount of points given by responding managers to each function, using a constant-sum scale of 100. A t-test was performed to compare column 2 (mean of relative influence of marketing) with columns 3 through 6 (relative influence of sales, R&D, operations, and finance). Statistically significant differences with marketing are indicated by asterisks, where: * $p < .05$; ** $p < .01$.

Source: Christian Homburg, John P. Workman Jr., and Harley Krohmer, "Marketing's Influence Within the Firm," *Journal of Marketing 63* (April 1999), p. 9. Reprinted with permission from the *Journal of Marketing,* published by the American Marketing Association.

service and support, and measurement and improvement of customer satisfaction. Interestingly, though, the influence of sales executives was perceived to be even greater than that of marketing managers on some of these decisions. One reason—particularly in the industrial goods firms selling electronic equipment and machinery—may be that sales managers have more detailed information about customer needs and desires because they have direct and continuing contact with existing and potential buyers.

More surprisingly, marketing managers also were perceived to wield significantly more influence than managers from other functional areas on cross-functional, business-level strategic decisions. While the views of finance and operations executives carry more weight in approving major capital expenditures, marketing and sales managers exert more influence on decisions concerning the strategic direction of the business unit, expansion into new geographic markets, the selection of strategic business partners, and new product development.

Might the relative influence of the different functions become more similar as firms adopt more integrative organizational forms, such as cross-functional work teams? The study's results suggest not. Marketing's influence was not significantly reduced in companies that had instituted cross-functional structures and processes.

But marketing managers may not play as pervasive a strategic role in other cultures as they do in the United States. The study found that marketers' influence on both tactical and strategic issues was significantly lower in German firms. As one of the study's authors points out, "Germany has traditionally stressed technology and operations more than the softer, customer-oriented aspects central to marketing. So even when the environment changes, a signal to top-level German managers that marketing should be playing a greater role, they are reluctant to give it that role."[6]

Market-Oriented Management

Even within the United States, however, marketing managers do not play an equally extensive strategic role in every firm because not all firms are equally market-oriented. Not surprisingly, marketers tend to have a greater influence on all levels of strategy in organizations that embrace a market-oriented philosophy of business. More critically, managers in other functional areas of market-oriented firms incorporate more customer and competitor information into their decision-making processes as well.

Market-oriented organizations tend to operate according to the business philosophy known as the marketing concept. As originally stated by General Electric four decades ago, the **marketing concept** holds that the planning and coordination of all company activities around the primary goal of satisfying customer needs is the most effective means to attain and sustain a competitive advantage and achieve company objectives over time.

Thus, market-oriented firms are characterized by a consistent focus by personnel in all departments and at all levels on customers' needs and competitive circumstances in the market environment. They also are willing and able to quickly adapt products and functional programs to fit changes in that environment. Such firms pay a great deal of attention to customer research *before* products are designed and produced. They embrace the concept of market segmentation by adapting product offerings and marketing programs to the special needs of different target markets.

Market-oriented firms also adopt a variety of organizational procedures and structures to improve the responsiveness of their decision making, including using more detailed environmental scanning and continuous, real-time information systems; seeking frequent feedback from and coordinating plans with key customers and major suppliers; decentralizing strategic decisions; encouraging entrepreneurial thinking among lower-level managers; and

Exhibit 1.5

GUIDELINES FOR MARKET-ORIENTED MANAGEMENT

1. Create customer focus throughout the business.
2. Listen to the customer.
3. Define and nurture your distinctive competence.
4. Define marketing as market intelligence.
5. Target customers precisely.
6. Manage for profitability, not sales volume.
7. Make customer value the guiding star.
8. Let the customer define quality.
9. Measure and manage customer expectations.
10. Build customer relationships and loyalty.
11. Define the business as a service business.
12. Commit to continuous improvement and innovation.
13. Manage culture along with strategy and structure.
14. Grow with partners and alliances.
15. Destroy marketing bureaucracy.

Source: Frederick E. Webster Jr., "Executing the New Marketing Concept," *Marketing Management* 3, no. 1 (1994), p. 10.

using interfunctional management teams to analyze issues and initiate strategic actions outside the formal planning process.[7] For example, IBM formed a high-level cross-functional task force to reevaluate its market environment, develop a new strategic focus, and map new avenues toward future growth. The company also has formed alliances with enterprise software developers, such as PeopleSoft and Great Plains Software, to improve its ability to help customers integrate Web technology into their business processes. These and other actions recommended to make an organization more market-driven and responsive to environmental changes are summarized in Exhibit 1.5.

Do Customers Always Know What They Want?

Some managers—particularly in high-tech firms—question whether a strong focus on customer needs and wants is always a good thing. They argue that customers cannot always articulate their needs and wants, in part because they do not know what kinds of products or services are technically possible. As Akio Morita, the late visionary CEO of Sony, once said:

> Our plan is to lead the public with new products rather than ask them what kind of products they want. The public does not know what is possible, but we do. So instead of doing a lot of marketing research, we refine our thinking on a product and its use and try to create a market for it by educating and communicating with the public.[8]

Others have pointed out that some very successful new products, such as the Chrysler mini-van and Compaq's pioneering PC network server, were developed with little or no market research. On the other hand, some famous duds, like Ford's Edsel, New Coke, and McDonald's McLean low-fat hamburger, were developed with a great deal of customer input.[9]

The laws of probability dictate that some new products will succeed and more will fail regardless of how much is spent on marketing research. But the critics of a strong customer focus argue that paying too much attention to customer needs and wants can stifle innovation and lead firms to produce nothing but marginal improvements or line extensions of products and services that already exist. How do marketers respond to this charge?

While many consumers may lack the technical sophistication necessary to articulate their needs or wants for cutting-edge technical innovations, the same is not true for industrial purchasers. About half of all manufactured goods in most countries are sold to other organizations rather than individual consumers. Many high-tech industrial products are initiated at the urging of one or more major customers, developed with their cooperation (perhaps in the form of an alliance or partnership), and refined at customer beta sites.

As for consumer markets, one way to resolve the conflict between the views of technologists and marketers is to consider the two components of R&D. First there is basic research and then there is development—the conversion of technical concepts into actual salable products or services. Most consumers have little knowledge of scientific advancements and emerging technologies. Therefore, they usually don't—and probably shouldn't—play a role in influencing how firms allocate their basic research dollars.

However, a customer focus is critical to development. Someone within the organization must have either the insight and market experience or the substantial customer input necessary to decide what product to develop from a new technology, what benefits it will offer to customers, and whether customers will value those benefits sufficiently to make the product a commercial success. Iomega's experiences in developing the Zip drive into a commercially successful product—as described in Exhibit 1.6—illustrate this point.

Often, as was the case with the Zip drive, a new technology must be developed into a concrete product concept before consumers can react to it and its commercial potential can be assessed. In other cases, consumers can express their needs or wants for specific benefits

Exhibit 1.6   Iomega's Zip Drive—Helping Customers Store Their "Stuff"

In the late 1980s Iomega Corporation pioneered a nifty technological innovation. The Bernoulli Box was a portable, add-on storage unit for personal computers (PCs). Resembling a gray shoebox with a hole in the front, it could hold 150 megabytes of data on one disk—the equivalent of 107 floppy disks.

But by late 1993 the product was in trouble. Its $600 unit price and $100 disk price had proven too high to attract many individual PC users, the 52-page user's manual was hard for customers to decipher, and a competitor had already introduced a cheaper, faster alternative. Consequently, the firm reported an $18 million loss for the year and its stock price was at an all-time low.

The struggling company brought in a new CEO whose first priority was to convert the Bernoulli Box technology into a product line that would succeed in the marketplace. He appointed a cross-functional development team with representatives from engineering, marketing, operations, and other areas. The team, together with designers from Fitch PLC, an industrial design firm, started by conducting exhaustive interviews with over 1,000 people who used computers in large companies, in small organizations, or at home. Based on the information gathered, they created several generations of prototype products that were subsequently further refined in response to reactions from additional samples of potential customers.

Based on the extensive customer feedback received, the development team greatly streamlined the old Bernoulli Box, reducing its weight to about a pound so it could fit in a briefcase. To appeal to different segments of individual and business users, they designed three different models with different storage capacities and different prices. All three were given bright colors to make them stand out from their environment and to signal that they were different from the "gray" competition. The most basic model—the Zip drive—held 100 megabytes and was initially priced at $200 per unit and $20 per disk (prices that have fallen substantially since) to appeal to individual PC owners for their personal use. Finally, a promotional campaign was crafted around the theme that Zip could help people organize their "stuff" to make it more accessible and portable.

Within three years of its introduction, more than three million Zip drives were sold. Consequently, Iomega's share price soared from $2 to $150 (before stock splits), and the firm made it into the top 50 of *Fortune*'s list of fastest-growing companies.

Source: "The Right Stuff," *Journal of Business and Design* 2 (Fall 1996), pp. 6–11; "America's Fastest Growing Companies," *Fortune*, October 14, 1996, pp. 90–104; and Paul Eng, "What to Do When You Need More Space," *Business Week*, November 4, 1996, p. 126.

even though they do not know what is technically feasible. They can tell you what problems they are having with current products and services and what additional benefits they would like from new ones. For instance, before Sony introduced the Walkman, few consumers would have asked for such a product because they were unfamiliar with the possibilities of miniaturization in the electronics industry. But if they had been asked whether they would buy a battery-driven product small enough to hook on their belt that could produce sound nearly as good as the full-sized stereo system in their home, many probably would have said, "Sure!"

A strong customer focus is not inconsistent with the development of technically innovative products, nor does it condemn a firm to concentrate on satisfying only current, articulated customer wants. More important, while firms can sometimes succeed in the short run even though they ignore customer desires, a strong customer focus usually pays big dividends in terms of market share and profit over the long haul. As Iomega's CEO points out, "I don't know how else you can sell in a consumer marketplace without understanding product design and usage. You have to know what the end user wants."[10]

Does Being Market-Oriented Pay?

Since an organization's success over time hinges on its ability to provide benefits of value to its customers—and to do that better than its competitors—it seems likely that market-oriented firms should perform better than others. By paying careful attention to customer needs and competitive threats—and by focusing activities across all functional departments on meeting those needs and threats effectively—organizations should be able to enhance, accelerate, and reduce the volatility and vulnerability of their cash flows.[11] And that should enhance their economic performance and shareholder value. Indeed, profitability is the third leg, together with a customer focus and cross-functional coordination, of the three-legged stool known as the marketing concept.

Sometimes the marketing concept is interpreted as a philosophy of trying to satisfy all customers' needs regardless of the cost. That would be a prescription for financial disaster. Instead, the marketing concept is consistent with the notion of focusing on only those segments of the customer population that the firm can satisfy both effectively *and* profitably. Firms might offer less extensive or costly goods and services to unprofitable segments or avoid them. For example, the Buena Vista Winery website (**www.buenavistawinery.com**) does not accept orders of less than a half case because they are too costly to process and ship.

Substantial evidence supports the idea that being market-oriented pays dividends, at least in a highly developed economy such as the United States. A number of studies involving more than 500 firms or business units across a variety of industries indicate that a market orientation has a significant positive effect on various dimensions of performance, including return on assets, sales growth, and new product success.[12]

STRATEGIC ISSUE

A market orientation has a significant positive effect on various dimensions of performance, including return on assets, sales growth, and new product success.

Factors That Mediate Marketing's Strategic Role

Despite the evidence that a market-orientation boosts performance, many companies around the world are not very focused on their customers or competitors. Among the reasons firms are not always in close touch with their market environments are these:

- Competitive conditions may enable a company to be successful in the short run without being particularly sensitive to customer desires.
- Different levels of economic development across industries or countries may favor different business philosophies.

- Firms can suffer from strategic inertia—the automatic continuation of strategies successful in the past, even though current market conditions are changing.

Competitive Factors Affecting a Firm's Market Orientation   The competitive conditions some firms face enable them to be successful in the short term without paying much attention to their customers, suppliers, distributors, or other organizations in their market environment. Early entrants into newly emerging industries, particularly industries based on new technologies, are especially likely to be internally focused and not very market-oriented. This is because there are likely to be relatively few strong competitors during the formative years of a new industry, customer demand for the new product is likely to grow rapidly and outstrip available supply, and production problems and resource constraints tend to represent more immediate threats to the survival of such new businesses.

Businesses facing such market and competitive conditions are often **product-oriented** or **production-oriented.** They focus most of their attention and resources on such functions as product and process engineering, production, and finance in order to acquire and manage the resources necessary to keep pace with growing demand. The business is primarily concerned with producing more of what it wants to make, and marketing generally plays a secondary role in formulating and implementing strategy. Such firms commonly rely on financial or long-range planning systems and base their strategies on extrapolations of the current situation. Other functional differences between production-oriented and market-oriented firms are summarized in Exhibit 1.7.

As industries grow, they become more competitive. New entrants are attracted and existing producers attempt to differentiate themselves through improved products and more-efficient production processes. As a result, industry capacity often grows faster than demand and the environment shifts from a seller's market to a buyer's market. Firms often respond to such changes with aggressive promotional activities—such as hiring more salespeople, increasing advertising budgets, or offering frequent price promotions—to maintain market share and hold down unit costs.

Unfortunately, this kind of **sales-oriented** response to increasing competition still focuses on selling what the firm wants to make rather than on customer needs. Worse, competitors

Exhibit 1.7

DIFFERENCES BETWEEN PRODUCTION-ORIENTED AND MARKET-ORIENTED ORGANIZATIONS

Business activity or function	Production orientation	Marketing orientation
Product offering	Company sells what it can make; primary focus on functional performance and cost.	Company makes what it can sell; primary focus on customers' needs and market opportunities.
Product line	Narrow.	Broad.
Pricing	Based on production and distribution costs.	Based on perceived benefits provided.
Research	Technical research; focus on product improvement and cost cutting in the production process.	Market research; focus on identifying new opportunities and applying new technology to satisfy customer needs.
Packaging	Protection for the product; minimize costs.	Designed for customer convenience; a promotional tool.
Credit	A necessary evil; minimize bad debt losses.	A customer service; a tool to attract customers.
Promotion	Emphasis on product features, quality, and price.	Emphasis on product benefits and ability to satisfy customers' needs or solve problems.

can easily match such aggressive sales tactics. Simply spending more on selling efforts usually does not create a sustainable competitive advantage.

As industries mature, sales volume levels off and technological differences among brands tend to disappear as manufacturers copy the best features of each other's products. Consequently, a firm must seek new market segments or steal share from competitors by offering lower prices, superior services, or intangible benefits other firms cannot match. At this stage, managers can most readily appreciate the benefits of a market orientation, and marketers are often given a bigger role in developing competitive strategies.[13] It is not surprising, then, that many of America's most market-oriented firms—and those working hardest to become market-oriented—are well-established competitors in relatively mature industries. For such firms, customer-focused total quality management (TQM) programs aimed at improving product or service quality and reducing costs—with the ultimate objective of improving customer satisfaction and loyalty—can be crucial for remaining a viable competitor in global markets. Witness, for example, the desperate efforts by the U.S. auto manufacturers to improve quality, reduce costs, and increase customer satisfaction and retention in order to stave off the advance of Japanese and European competitors.[14]

The Influence of Different Stages of Development across Industries and Global Markets

The previous discussion suggests that the degree of adoption of a market orientation varies not only across firms but also across entire industries. Industries that are in earlier stages of their life cycles, or that benefit from barriers to entry or other factors reducing the intensity of competition, are likely to have relatively fewer market-oriented firms. For instance, in part because of governmental regulations that restricted competition, many service industries—including banks, airlines, physicians, lawyers, accountants, and insurance companies—were slow to adopt the marketing concept. But with the trend toward deregulation and the increasingly intense global competition in such industries, many service organizations are working much harder to understand and satisfy their customers.[15]

Given that entire economies are in different stages of development around the world, the popularity—and even the appropriateness—of different business philosophies also may vary across countries. A production orientation was the dominant business philosophy in the United States, for instance, during the industrialization that occurred from the mid-1800s through World War I.[16] Similarly, a primary focus on developing product and production technology may still be appropriate in developing nations that are in the midst of industrialization.

International differences in business philosophies can cause some problems for the globalization of a firm's strategic marketing programs, but it can create some opportunities as well, especially for alliances or joint ventures. Consider, for example, General Electric's joint venture with the Mexican appliance manufacturer Organization Mabe. The arrangement benefits GE by providing direct access to Mexico's rapidly growing market for household appliances and its low-cost supply of labor. But it also benefits Mabe—and the Mexican economy—by giving the firm access to cutting-edge R&D and production technology and the capital necessary to take advantage of its newfound know-how.[17]

Strategic Inertia

In some cases, a firm that achieved success by being in tune with its environment loses touch with its market because managers become reluctant to tamper with strategies and marketing programs that worked in the past. They begin to believe there is one best way to satisfy their customers. Such strategic inertia is dangerous because customers' needs and competitive offerings change over time. IBM's traditional focus on large organizational customers, for instance, caused the company to devote too little effort to the much faster-growing segment of small dot.com start-ups. And its emphasis on computer technology and hardware made it slow to respond to the explosive growth in demand for Web-based applications and services. Thus, in environments where such changes happen frequently, the strategic planning process needs to be ongoing and adaptive. All the participants, whether from marketing or other functional departments, need to pay constant attention to what is happening with their customers and competitors.

Recent Developments Affecting the Strategic Role of Marketing

In the future, strategic inertia will be even more dangerous in many industries because they are facing increasing magnitudes and rates of change in their environments. These changes are rapidly altering the context in which marketing strategies are planned and carried out and the information and tools that marketers have at their disposal. These developments include (1) the increased globalization of markets and competition, (2) the growth of the service sector of the economy and the importance of service in maintaining customer satisfaction and loyalty, (3) the rapid development of new information and communications technologies, and (4) the growing importance of relationships for improved coordination and increased efficiency of marketing programs and for capturing a larger portion of customers' lifetime value. Some recent impacts of these four developments on marketing management are briefly summarized below and will be continuing themes throughout this book. We will also speculate from time to time about how these ongoing trends may reshape the tasks, tools, and techniques of marketing in the future. It is impossible to predict exactly how these trends will play out. Consequently, new business school graduates who both understand the marketing management process and are savvy with respect to one or more of these ongoing developments can play an important role—and gain a potential competitive advantage—within even the largest firms. Such newly minted managers can bring fresh perspectives and valuable insights concerning how these emerging trends are likely to impact their organizations' customers, competitors, and marketing strategies.

 Globalization   International markets account for a large and growing portion of the sales of many organizations. The 100 largest U.S.-based multinationals generate nearly $1 trillion in revenues from foreign markets, and many smaller firms rely heavily on international sales as well. For example, Petrofsky's—a St. Louis manufacturer of frozen bagel dough—reformulated its product to fit the preferences of Japanese consumers (a bigger, softer bagel offered in some unique flavors). The results were so successful that the firm sold its domestic business to Quaker Oats in order to concentrate on sales to Japan and other Asian markets.

While global markets represent promising opportunities for additional sales growth and profits, differences in market and competitive conditions across country boundaries can require firms to adapt their competitive strategies and marketing programs to be successful. Even when similar marketing strategies are appropriate for multiple countries, international differences in infrastructure, culture, legal systems, and the like often mean that one or more elements of the marketing program—such as product features, promotional appeals, or distribution channels—must be tailored to local conditions for the strategy to be effective.

Increased Importance of Service   A service can be defined as "any activity or benefit that one party can offer another that is essentially intangible and that does not result in the ownership of anything. Its production may or may not be tied to a physical product."[18] Service businesses such as airlines, hotels, restaurants, and consulting firms account for roughly two-thirds of all economic activity in the United States, and services are the fastest-growing sector of most other developed economies around the world. While many of the decisions and activities involved in marketing services are essentially the same as those for marketing physical goods, the intangible nature of many services can create unique challenges for marketers. We will discuss these challenges—and the tools and techniques firms have developed to deal with them—throughout this book.

As the definition suggests, services such as financing, delivery, installation, user training and assistance, and maintenance often are provided in conjunction with a physical product. Such ancillary services have become more critical to firms' continued sales and financial success in many product-markets. As markets have become crowded with global competitors offering similar products at ever-lower prices, the creative design and effective delivery of supplemental services have become crucial means by which a company may differentiate its offering and generate additional benefits and value for customers. Those additional benefits, in turn, can justify higher prices and margins in the short term and help improve customer satisfaction, retention, and loyalty over the long term.[19] This is particularly true in organizational markets. Office Depot was able to win many of the purchases that MIT had previously spread over 20,000 separate vendors by offering superior service in the form of computerized ordering and timely delivery direct to the purchaser's desk.

Information Technology   The computer revolution and related technological developments are changing the nature of marketing management in two important ways. First, new technologies are making it possible for firms to collect and analyze more detailed information about potential customers and their needs, preferences, and buying habits. For instance, Fingerhut—the $2 billion catalog retailer—stores more than 500 pieces of information about personal characteristics, past purchases, and payment patterns for each of more than 50 million active and potential customers. It uses that information to tailor personalized catalogs and mail them to customers when they are most likely to buy. The firm's database also has helped uncover opportunities for new products and services, such as a credit card designed for Fingerhut's mostly low-income customers.[20] Thus, information technology is making it possible for many firms to identify and target smaller and more precisely defined market segments—sometimes segments consisting of only one or a few customers—and to customize product features, promotional appeals, prices, and financing arrangements to fit such segments.

A second impact of information technology has been to open new channels for communications and transactions between suppliers and customers. As Exhibit 1.8 suggests, one simple way of categorizing these new channels is based on whether the suppliers and customers involved are organizations or individual consumers.

 An estimated $657 billion in sales were transacted over the World Wide Web in 2000, and that figure is expected to grow to around $4 trillion by 2003.[21] Roughly 80 percent of those sales were business-to-business transactions, such as those in the upper-left quadrant of Exhibit 1.8. Many high-tech firms such as Oracle Corp. and Cisco Systems, and even some low-tech companies such as General Motors, conduct all or a large portion of their purchasing activities over the Web. And many firms rely on their websites to communicate product information to potential customers, make sales, and deal with customer problems.

Perhaps even more important, though, new information and communications technologies are enabling firms to forge more cooperative and efficient relationships with their suppliers and distribution channel partners. For example, Procter & Gamble and 3M have formed alliances with major retailers—such as Kroger and Wal-Mart—to develop automatic restocking systems. Sales information from the retailer's checkout scanners is sent directly to the supplier's computers, which figure out automatically when to replenish each

Exhibit 1.8

CATEGORIES OF E-COMMERCE

	Business	Consumer
Business	**Business-to-Business (B2B)** Examples: • Purchasing sites of Ford, Oracle, Cisco • Supply chain networks linking producers and distribution channel members, such as 3M and Wal-Mart	**Business-to-Consumer (B2C)** Examples: • E-tailers, such as E*Trade, Amazon, RedEnvelope • Producers' direct sales sites, such as Dell, American Airlines • Websites of traditional retailers, such as Sears, Lands' End
Consumer	**Consumer-to-Business (C2B)** Examples: • Sites that enable consumers to bid on unsold airline tickets and other goods and services, such as Priceline	**Consumer-to-Consumer (C2C)** Examples: • Auction sites, such as eBay, QXL

Source: Adapted from "A Survey of E-Commerce: Shopping Around the Web," *The Economist,* February 26, 2000, p. 11.

product and schedule deliveries direct to each of the retailer's stores. Such paperless exchanges reduce mistakes and billbacks, minimize inventory levels, improve cash flow, and increase customer satisfaction and loyalty.

In contrast, Internet sales from businesses to consumers (the upper-right quadrant in Exhibit 1.8) accounted for less than $120 billion in 2000. However, sales volumes of firms such as Amazon, Dell Computer, and RedEnvelope are expanding rapidly, and many traditional retailers are expanding their marketing efforts on the Web as well. Information available over the Internet is affecting consumer purchase patterns even when the purchases are made in traditional retail outlets. For instance, while fewer than 3 percent of car sales were actually made over the Web in 1999, an estimated 40 percent of all car buyers used the Web to compare prices or gather information about brands.[22]

Clearly, the Web is presenting marketers with new strategic options—as well as new competitive threats and opportunities—regardless of what or to whom they are selling. Therefore, we will devote all of Chapter 12 to marketing strategies for e-commerce. However, the changes being wrought by these new technologies are so extensive and profound we will discuss specific examples and their implications in every chapter.

Relationships across Functions and Firms New information technologies and the ongoing search for greater marketing efficiency and customer value in the face of increasing competition are changing the nature of exchange between companies. Instead of engaging in a discrete series of arm's-length, adversarial exchanges with customers, channel members, and suppliers on the open market, more firms are trying to develop and nurture long-term relationships and alliances, such as the one between 3M and Wal-Mart. Such cooperative relationships are thought to improve each partner's ability to adapt quickly to environmental changes or threats, to gain greater benefits at lower costs from its exchanges, and to increase the lifetime value of its customers.[23]

Similar kinds of cooperative relationships are emerging inside companies as firms seek mechanisms for more effectively and efficiently coordinating across functional departments the various activities necessary to identify, attract, service, and satisfy customers. In many firms, the planning and execution that used to be the responsibility of a product or marketing manager are now coordinated and carried out by cross-functional teams.

The Future Role of Marketing

In light of such changes, it is apparent that firms in most, if not all, industries will have to be market-oriented, tightly focused on customer needs and desires, and highly adaptive to succeed and prosper in the future. In turn, this suggests that the effective performance of marketing activities—particularly those associated with tracking, analyzing, and satisfying customers' needs—will become even more critical for the successful formulation and implementation of strategies at all organizational levels.

It is important to note, however, that such marketing activities may not always be carried out by marketing managers located in separate functional departments. As more firms embrace the use of multifunctional teams or network structures, the boundaries between functions are likely to blur and the performance of marketing tasks will become everybody's business. Similarly, as organizations become more focused and specialized in developing unique core competencies, they will rely more heavily on suppliers, distributors, dealers, and other partners to perform activities—including marketing and sales tasks—that fall outside those areas of competence. All of this suggests that the ability to create, manage, and sustain exchange relationships with customers, vendors, distributors, and others will become a key strategic competence for firms in the future—and that is what marketing is all about.

FORMULATING AND IMPLEMENTING MARKETING STRATEGY—AN OVERVIEW OF THE PROCESS

This book examines the development and implementation of marketing strategies for individual product-market entries, whether goods or services. Exhibit 1.9 briefly diagrams the activities and decisions involved in this process, and it also serves as the organizational framework for the rest of this book. For that reason, it is important to note the basic focus of this framework and the sequence of events within it.

A Decision-Making Focus

The framework has a distinct decision-making focus. Planning and executing a marketing strategy involves many interrelated decisions about what to do, when to do it, and how. Those decisions are the primary focus of this book. Every chapter details either the decisions to be made and actions taken when designing and implementing strategies for various market situations, or the analytical tools and frameworks you will need to make those decisions intelligently.

Analysis Comes First

Exhibit 1.9 suggests that a substantial amount of analysis of customers, competitors, and the company itself should occur *before* designing a marketing strategy. This reflects our view that successful strategic decisions usually rest on an objective, detailed, and evidence-based understanding of the market and the environmental context. Of course, most marketing

Exhibit 1.9

THE PROCESS OF FORMULATING AND IMPLEMENTING MARKETING STRATEGY

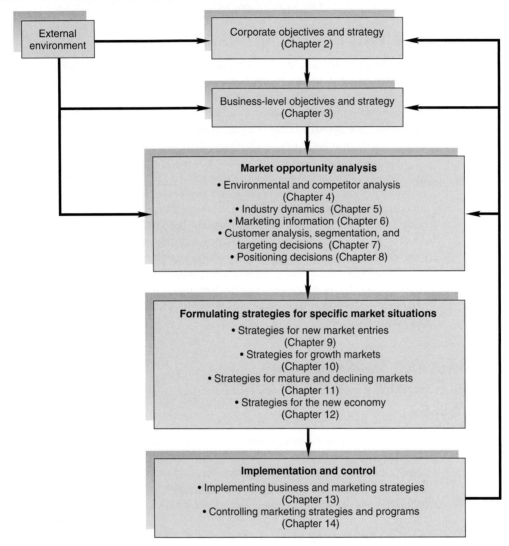

strategies never get implemented in quite the same way as they were drawn on paper. Adjustments are made and new activities undertaken in response to rapid changes in customer demands, competitive actions, and shifting economic conditions. But a thorough and ongoing analysis of the market and the broader environment enables managers to make such adjustments in a well-reasoned and consistent way rather than by the seat of their pants.

The analysis necessary to provide the foundation for a good strategic marketing plan should focus on four elements of the overall environment that may influence its appropriateness and ultimate success: (1) the *company's* internal resources, capabilities, and strategies; (2) the environmental *context*—such as broad social, economic, and technology trends—in which the firm will compete; (3) the relative strengths and weaknesses of *competitors* and trends in the competitive environment; and (4) the needs, wants, and characteristics of current and potential *customers*. Marketers refer to these elements as **the 4Cs.** They are the focus of a *market opportunity analysis* and are discussed in more detail below.

Integrating Marketing Strategy with the Firm's Other Strategies and Resources

A major part of the marketing manager's job is to monitor and analyze customers' needs and wants and the emerging opportunities and threats posed by competitors and trends in the external environment. Therefore, because all levels of strategy must consider such factors, marketers often play a major role in providing inputs to—and influencing the development of—corporate and business strategies. Conversely, general managers and senior managers in other functions need a solid understanding of marketing in order to craft effective organizational strategies.

Marketing managers also bear the primary responsibility for formulating and implementing strategic marketing plans for individual product-market entries or product lines. But as we have seen, such strategic marketing programs are not created in a vacuum. Instead, the marketing objectives and strategy for a particular product-market entry must be achievable with the company's available resources and capabilities and consistent with the direction and allocation of resources inherent in the firm's corporate and business-level strategies. In other words, there should be a good fit—or internal consistency—among the elements of all three levels of strategy.

Chapters 2 and 3 describe in more detail the components of corporate and business strategies and the roles marketers and other functional managers play in shaping the strategic direction of their organizations and business units.

STRATEGIC ISSUE

The marketing objectives and strategy for a particular product-market entry must be achievable with the company's available resources and capabilities and consistent with the direction and allocation of resources inherent in the firm's corporate and business-level strategies.

Market Opportunity Analysis

A major factor in the success or failure of strategies at all three levels is whether the strategy elements are consistent with the realities of the firm's external environment. Thus, the next step in developing a strategic marketing plan is to monitor and analyze the opportunities and threats posed by factors outside the organization. This is an ongoing responsibility for marketing managers.

Environmental and Competitor Analysis   To understand potential opportunities and threats over the long term, marketers first must monitor and analyze broad trends in the economic and social environment. These include demographic, economic, technological, political/legal, and social/cultural developments. Of particular concern within an organization's economic environment are the actions and capabilities of its current and potential competitors. Chapter 4 identifies a number of macroenvironmental factors to which marketing managers should pay attention. It discusses methods for monitoring, analyzing, and perhaps even influencing the impact of those factors on the future performance of their product-market entries.

Industry Dynamics and Strategic Change   The competitive and market environments of an industry are not static, but can change dramatically over time. For example, Iomega's initial product, the Bernoulli Box, lost much of its early momentum when SyQuest entered the market with a faster, cheaper alternative. Chapter 5 explores the competitive dynamics of an industry, emphasizing how competition and customers' buying patterns are likely to change as an industry or product-market moves through various life cycle stages.

Marketing Research and Market Measurements   Marketing managers must obtain objective information about potential customers, the satisfaction and loyalty of current customers, the firm's wholesale and retail partners, and the strengths and weaknesses of competitors. Consequently, even relatively small organizations such as Iomega and RedEnvelope often expend substantial financial and personnel resources studying the needs and preferences of potential customers, developing new products, and tracking the sales patterns and satisfaction of existing customers and channel members.

If managers are to make informed decisions, however, research information must be converted into estimates of the sales volume and profit the firm might reasonably expect a particular marketing program to generate within a given market segment. Chapter 6 discusses techniques and methods for collecting and analyzing marketing research information and for measuring the market potential and likely sales volumes of particular market segments.

Market Segmentation, Targeting, and Positioning Decisions   Not all customers with similar needs seek the same products or services to satisfy those needs. Their purchase decisions may be influenced by individual preferences, personal characteristics, social circumstances, and so forth. On the other hand, customers who do purchase the same product may be motivated by different needs, seek different benefits from the product, rely on different sources of information about products, and obtain the product from different distribution channels. Thus, one of the manager's most crucial tasks is to divide customers into **market segments**—distinct subsets of people with similar needs, circumstances, and characteristics that lead them to respond in a similar way to a particular product or service offering or to a particular strategic marketing program. Chapter 7 examines dimensions for measurement and analytical techniques that can help managers identify and define market segments in both consumer and organizational markets.

After defining market segments and exploring customer needs and the firm's competitive strengths and weaknesses within segments, the manager must decide which segments represent attractive and viable opportunities for the company, that is, on which segments to focus a strategic marketing program. Iomega, for instance, targeted two market segments with its new line of data storage drives. The Zip drive was aimed at individual PC owners for their personal use, while larger capacity and more expensive drives were aimed at organizational buyers. Chapter 7 discusses some of the considerations in *selecting a target segment.*

Finally, the manager must decide how to **position** the product or service offering within a target segment, that is, to design the product and its marketing program so as to emphasize attributes and benefits that appeal to customers in the target segment and at once distinguish the company's offering from those of competitors. Issues and analytical techniques involved in marketing positioning decisions are discussed in Chapter 8.

Formulating Marketing Strategies for Specific Situations

The strategic marketing program for a product should reflect market demand and the competitive situation within the target market. But demand and competitive conditions change over time as a product moves through its life cycle. Therefore, different strategies are typically more appropriate and successful for different market conditions and at different life cycle stages. Chapter 9 examines some marketing strategies for introducing new goods or services to the market. Chapter 10 discusses strategies appropriate for building or maintaining a product's share of a growing market in the face of increasing competition. Chapter 11 considers strategies a manager might adopt in mature or declining markets. And Chapter 12 explores how all of the above strategies might be influenced or modified by the rapidly evolving conditions being created by e-commerce and the new economy.

Implementation and Control of the Marketing Strategy

A final critical determinant of a strategy's success is the firm's ability to implement it effectively. And this depends on whether the strategy is consistent with the resources, the organizational structure, the coordination and control systems, and the skills and experience of company personnel.[24] Managers must design a strategy to fit the company's existing resources, competencies, and procedures—or try to construct new structures and systems to fit the chosen strategy. For example, Iomega's attempt to develop a new generation of data storage products would not have been so successful without its substantial investments in R&D and marketing research and a team structure that encouraged communication and cooperation across functional areas throughout the development process. Chapter 13 discusses the structural variables, planning and coordination processes, and personnel and corporate culture characteristics related to the successful implementation of various marketing strategies.

The final tasks in the marketing management process are determining whether the strategic marketing program is meeting objectives and adjusting the program when performance is disappointing. This evaluation and control process provides feedback to managers and serves as a basis for a market opportunity analysis in the next planning period. Chapter 14 examines ways to evaluate marketing performance and develop contingency plans when things go wrong.

The Marketing Plan—A Blueprint for Action

The results of the various analyses and marketing program decisions discussed above should be summarized periodically in a detailed formal marketing plan.[25]

> A **marketing plan** is a written document detailing the current situation with respect to customers, competitors, and the external environment and providing guidelines for objectives, marketing actions, and resource allocations over the planning period for either an existing or a proposed product or service.

While some firms—particularly smaller ones—do not bother to write their marketing plans, most organizations believe that "unless all the key elements of a plan are written down . . . there will always be loopholes for ambiguity or misunderstanding of strategies and objectives, or of assigned responsibilities for taking action."[26] This suggests that even small organizations with limited resources can benefit from preparing a written plan, however brief. Written plans also provide a concrete history of a product's strategies and performance over time, which aids institutional memory and helps educate new managers assigned to the product. Written plans are necessary in most larger organizations because a marketing manager's proposals usually must be reviewed and approved at higher levels of management and because the approved plan provides the benchmark against which the manager's performance will be judged. Finally, the discipline involved in producing a formal plan helps ensure that the proposed objectives, strategy, and marketing actions are based on rigorous analysis of the 4Cs and sound reasoning.

Because a written marketing plan is such an important tool for communicating and coordinating expectations and responsibilities throughout the firm, we will say more about it in Chapter 13 when we discuss the implementation of marketing programs in detail. But because the written plan attempts to summarize and communicate an overview of the marketing management process we have been examining, it is worthwhile to briefly examine the contents of such plans here.

Marketing plans vary in timing, content, and organization across companies. In general, marketing plans are developed annually, though planning periods for some big-ticket industrial products such as commercial aircraft may be longer, and in some highly volatile industries such as telecommunications or e-commerce they can be shorter. Plans typically follow a format similar to that outlined in Exhibit 1.10.

There are three major parts to the plan. First, the marketing manager details his or her assessment of the current situation. This is the homework portion of the plan where the manager summarizes the results of his or her analysis of current and potential customers, the company's relative strengths and weaknesses, the competitive situation, the major trends in the broader environment that may affect the product and, for existing products,

Exhibit 1.10

CONTENTS OF A MARKETING PLAN

Section	Content
I. Executive summary	Presents a short overview of the issues, objectives, strategy, and actions incorporated in the plan and their expected outcomes for quick management review.
II. Current situation and trends	Summarizes relevant background information on the market, competition and the macroenvironment, and trends therein, including size and growth rates for the overall market and key segments.
III. Performance review (for an existing product or service only)	Examines the past performance of the product and the elements of its marketing program (e.g., distribution, promotions, etc.).
IV. Key issues	Identifies the main opportunities and threats to the product that the plan must deal with in the coming year, and the relative strengths and weaknesses of the product and business unit that must be taken into account in facing those issues.
V. Objectives	Specifies the goals to be accomplished in terms of sales volume, market share, and profit.
VI. Marketing strategy	Summarizes the overall strategic approach that will be used to meet the plan's objectives.
VII. Action plans	This is the most critical section of the annual plan for helping to ensure effective implementation and coordination of activities across functional departments. It specifies • The **target market** to be pursued. • **What** specific actions are to be taken with respect to each of the 4 Ps. • **Who** is responsible for each action. • **When** the action will be engaged in. • **How** much will be budgeted for each action.
VIII. Projected profit-and-loss statement	Presents the expected financial payoff from the plan.
IX. Controls	Discusses how the plan's progress will be monitored; may present contingency plans to be used if performance falls below expectations or the situation changes.
X. Contingency plans	Describes actions to be taken if specific threats or opportunities materialize during the planning period.

past performance outcomes. This section typically also includes forecasts, estimates of sales potential, and other assumptions underlying the plan, which are especially important for proposed new products or services. Based on these analyses, the manager also may call attention to several key issues—major opportunities or threats that should be dealt with during the planning period.

The second part of the plan details the strategy for the coming period. This part usually starts by detailing the objectives (e.g., sales volume, market share, profits, customer satisfaction levels, etc.) to be achieved by the product or service during the planning period. It then outlines the overall marketing strategy, the actions associated with each of the 4 Ps (the product, price, promotion, and "place" or distribution) necessary to implement the strategy, and the timing and locus of responsibility for each action.

Finally, the plan details the financial and resource implications of the strategy and the controls to be employed to monitor the plan's implementation and progress over the period. Some plans also specify some contingencies: how the plan will be modified if certain changes occur in the market, competitive, or external environments.

TAKE AWAYS

- Marketing perspectives lie at the heart of strategic decision making, whether at the corporate, business-unit, or product-market levels. All managers who aspire to general management roles need marketing concepts and tools in their repertoire.

- Market-oriented firms—those that plan and coordinate company activities around the primary goal of satisfying customer needs—tend to outperform other firms on a variety of dimensions, including sales growth, return on assets, and new product success.

- A focus on satisfying customer needs and wants is not inconsistent with being technologically innovative.

- Formulating a successful marketing strategy requires an understanding of the 4Cs: the company and its mission, strategies, and resources; the macroenvironmental context in which it operates; customer segments and their needs and wants; and competitors. Obtaining an objective, detailed, evidence-based understanding of these factors is critical to effective marketing decision making.

- Self-diagnostic questions to test your ability to apply the concepts in this chapter can be found at this book's website at **www.mhhe.com/walker.**

ENDNOTES

1. This opening case example is based on material found in Jim Kerstetter and Spencer E. Ante, "IBM vs. Oracle: It Could Get Bloody," *Business Week,* May 28, 2001, pp. 65–66; Ira Sager, "Inside IBM: Internet Business Machines," *Business Week,* E-BIZ Section, December 13, 1999, pp. EB20–EB38; Raju Narisetti, "IBM to Revamp Struggling Home-PC Business," *The Wall Street Journal,* October 14, 1997, p. B1; Raju Narisetti, "How IBM Turned Around Its Ailing PC Division," *The Wall Street Journal,* March 12, 1998, p. B1; and IBM's website at **www.ibm.com.** Also, some historical background information is based on Das Narayandas and V. Kasturi Rangan, "Dell Computer Corporation," Harvard Business School case #9-596-058 (Cambridge, MA: Harvard Business School, 1995).

2. For a summary of the definitions offered by a number of other authors, see Roger Kerin, Vijay Mahajan, and P. Rajan Varadarajan, *Contemporary Perspectives on Strategic Market Planning* (Boston: Allyn and Bacon, 1990), pp. 8–9. Our definition differs from some others, however, in that we view the setting of objectives as an integral part of strategy formulation, whereas they see objective setting as a separate process. Because a firm's objectives are influenced and constrained by many of the same environmental and competitive factors as the other elements of strategy, however, it seems logical to treat both the determination of objectives and the resource allocations aimed at reaching those objectives as two parts of the same strategic planning process.

3. However, while such corporate-level synergies often are used to justify mergers, acquisitions, and forays into new businesses, they sometimes prove elusive. For example, see Laura Landro, "Giants Talk Synergy but Few Make It Work," *The Wall Street Journal,* September 25, 1995, p. B1.

4. C. K. Prahalad and Gary Hamel, "The Core Competence of the Corporation," *Harvard Business Review* 68 (May–June 1990), pp. 79–91.

5. Christian Homburg, John P. Workman Jr., and Harley Krohmer, "Marketing's Influence within the Firm," *Journal of Marketing* 63 (April 1999), pp. 1–17.

6. Quoted in Katherine Z. Andrews, "Still a Major Player: Marketing's Role in Today's Firms," *Insights from MSI,* Winter 1999, p. 2.

7. Frederick E. Webster Jr., "Executing the New Marketing Concept," *Marketing Management* 3 (1994), pp. 9–16.

8. Quoted in Gary Hamel and C. K. Prahalad, *Competing for the Future* (Cambridge, MA: Harvard Business School Press, 1994).

9. Justin Martin, "Ignore Your Customer," *Fortune,* May 1, 1995, pp. 121–26.

10. "The Right Stuff," *Journal of Business and Design* 2 (Fall 1996), p. 11.

11. Rajendra K. Srivastava, Tasadduq A. Shervani, and Liam Fahey, "Marketing, Business Processes, and Shareholder Value: An Organizationally

Embedded View of Marketing Activities and the Discipline of Marketing," *Journal of Marketing* 63 (Special Issue 1999), pp. 168–79.

12. For example, see John C. Narver and Stanley F. Slater, "The Effect of a Market Orientation on Business Profitability," *Journal of Marketing* 54 (April 1990), pp. 1–18; Bernard J. Jaworski and Ajay Kohli, "Market Orientation: Antecedents and Consequences," *Journal of Marketing* 57 (July 1993); and Stanley F. Slater and John C. Narver, "Market Orientation, Performance, and the Moderating Influence of Competitive Environment," *Journal of Marketing* 58 (January 1994), pp. 46–55.

13. Stanley F. Slater and John C. Narver, "Market Orientation, Performance, and the Moderating Influence of Competitive Environment," *Journal of Marketing* 58 (January 1994), pp. 46–55; and John P. Workman Jr., "When Marketing Should Follow Instead of Lead," *Marketing Management* 2 (1993), pp. 8–19.

14. Kathleen Kerwin and Joann Muller, "Reviving GM," *Business Week,* February 1, 1999, pp. 114–22.

15. For many examples, see Valarie A. Zeithaml and Mary Jo Bitner, *Services Marketing* (New York: McGraw-Hill, 1996).

16. E. Jerome McCarthy and William D. Perreault Jr., *Basic Marketing: A Global Managerial Approach,* 11th ed. (Burr Ridge, IL: Richard D. Irwin, 1993), chap. 2.

17. "GE's Brave New World," *Business Week,* November 8, 1993, pp. 64–70.

18. Philip Kotler and Gary Armstrong, *Principles of Marketing* (Englewood Cliffs, NJ: Prentice Hall, 1989), p. 575.

19. For examples, see Terry G. Vavra, *Aftermarketing* (Burr Ridge, IL: Richard D. Irwin, 1995).

20. Susan Chandler, "Data Is Power, Just Ask Fingerhut," *Business Week,* June 3, 1996, p. 69.

21. Estimate by Forrester Research, as reported in "The 2001 Marketing Factbook," *Marketing News,* July 2, 2001, p. 18.

22. "A Survey of E-Commerce: Shopping Around the Web," *The Economist,* February 26, 2000, p. 5.

23. Ravi S. Achrol and Philip Kotler, "Marketing in the Network Economy," *Journal of Marketing* 63 (Special Issue 1999), pp. 146–63.

24. C. K. Prahalad and Gary Hamel, "The Core Competence of the Corporation," *Harvard Business Review* 68 (May–June 1990), pp. 79–91; and George S. Day, "The Capabilities of Market-Driven Organizations," *Journal of Marketing* 58 (October 1994), pp. 37–52.

25. For a more detailed discussion of formal marketing plans, see Donald R. Lehmann and Russell S. Winer, *Analysis for Marketing Planning,* 4th ed. (New York: Irwin/McGraw-Hill, 1997).

26. David S. Hopkins, *The Marketing Plan* (New York: The Conference Board, 1981), p. 2.

Chapter Two

Corporate Strategy Decisions and Their Marketing Implications

---

RedEnvelope—Marketing Upscale Gifts Online[1]

IN 1997 TWO GRADUATES of the University of California's Haas Business School started a company called 911Gifts. The firm combined a website and a toll-free customer service center with gifts provided by two established merchants to cater to last-minute crisis shoppers. Although the new company attracted gift-givers, it also had some weaknesses: The company name, with its connotation of wailing ambulances, turned off many potential customers; the firm's suppliers provided an uninspired assortment of gifts; and a lack of capital inhibited the company's ability to grow. As a result, by early 1999 the firm was treading water. The site had managed only about $1 million in sales the previous year. Consequently, the owners decided to reinvent the company.

A New Mission and Corporate Strategy

The owners' first move was to hire a marketing-savvy chief executive officer. They attracted Hilary Billings, a 36-year-old manager, away from Williams-Sonoma where she had successfully developed the firm's Pottery Barn catalog operation.

After analyzing 911Gifts' strengths and weaknesses, she crafted a new mission and competitive strategy for the company. Instead of positioning itself as a center for emergency gifts, the firm would aim for upscale elegance. Further, it would try to broaden the definition of gift-giving opportunities. "Most online retailers are inherently self-purchase," Ms. Billings says. They "repurpose themselves just before Christmas as gift companies. There's a big difference between that and a company that thinks only about gifts."

Within six weeks of becoming CEO, Ms. Billings had developed marketing and business plans detailing how the firm would accomplish its new strategic mission and had hired the core of a new management team. She then made the rounds of Silicon Valley's venture capitalists with a slide show detailing the company's new plans and subsequently obtained $21 million in new financing from Sequoia Capital and $10 million from Weston Presidio in exchange for approximately a one-third ownership of the company.

The New Marketing Plan

The Target Market Consistent with the firm's new strategic mission, it targeted its marketing efforts at a more selective segment of potential customers. The new target market was similar to the one Ms. Billings knew from her days at Williams-Sonoma: high income (over $85,000 per year), well-educated professionals, including both men and women. The focus was also on people who were connected to the Internet and had a history of buying online.

To understand the needs and preferences of the firm's target customers, managers did a little qualitative marketing research, informally interviewing some prospective customers and analyzing past sales patterns. But initially the firm relied more heavily on the customer knowledge its managers had gained through past experience. "We talked about our [target] customer in a very intimate way," one manager recalls. "What kind of clothes they wore, what kind of car they drove. We put up a poster labeled 'him' and 'her' and we'd put Post-it Notes under each with products we thought they'd want to buy."

The New Product Line and Company Brand Armed with information and intuition concerning the desires of the target market, company managers set about upgrading the product line. A variety of suppliers were contracted to provide products that reflected a high-quality, upscale point of view: things such as amber heart necklaces, old-fashioned thermometers, and boxes of pistachios and caramels (10 ounces of each for $40). The firm also partnered with suppliers to develop its first wave of exclusive merchandise: a series of gift baskets that might be described as "lifestyle kits." For instance, for fishing fanatics they developed a fishing creel filled with 12 hand-cut fish-shaped cookies for $48.

Another criterion the firm used to reorganize its product offerings was a high gross margin. Most of the firm's products carry margins of 50 percent or more, a necessary offset for lavish spending on customer service, which Ms. Billings says is un-avoidable in view of the company's strategy of pursuing future growth, in part, by building customer loyalty and repeat purchases. "You have to own your customer's experience—and that comes at a price." About half of the 450 stockkeeping units (SKUs) that 911Gifts had been selling were dropped, and more than 300 items were added.

To simplify a customer's search for the perfect gift, the company also redesigned its website. The new website allowed customers to navigate through the offerings by type of recipient, by gift-giving occasion, or by product category.

Finally, to more clearly reflect the firm's new upscale positioning, the company name was changed to RedEnvelope Gifts Online. The name derives from an Asian custom of marking special occasions by giving cash or small presents enclosed in a red envelope. It also suggested a distinctive packaging approach: all RedEnvelope gifts are delivered in a red gift box with a hand-tied bow.

Advertising and Promotion With only a few weeks to go before the peak holiday selling season, RedEnvelope decided to devote a third of its new capital to advertising aimed at building customer awareness of the site. Rather than costly TV ads, the firm concentrated its money on a series of print ads to be run in newspapers and magazines, such as the *New York Times*, with readerships similar to RedEnvelope's target market. The company also paid to establish partnerships with a number of online hubs such as America Online, web portals such as Yahoo! and Excite, and a select group of more narrowly focused websites such as iVillage.com. It devoted $2 million to these partnerships—paid for through either a flat fee or a percentage of sales—for a simple reason: "To be where people are shopping online means being on the portals," says RedEnvelope's vice president for business development. Finally, the firm pursues people who prefer a more traditional form of nonstore shopping by developing a series of print catalogs.

Distribution and Order Fulfillment RedEnvelope owns its own inventory, marketing, systems management, and customer service operations. But it does not yet have sufficient capital to develop its own physical logistics and order fulfillment operation. Consequently, the company contracted with ComAlliance, a fulfillment firm in Ohio, to provide warehouse space and everything that goes with it, including the workers expected to produce scads of smartly wrapped packages. The ComAlliance facility is located at the end of an Airborne Express runway. Thus, merchandise that leaves the warehouse by 2 A.M. can be in the air by 4:30 and to its destination by noon. This setup allowed RedEnvelope to make a promise that was the core of its early brand-building efforts: Christmas Eve delivery of gifts ordered by midnight on December 23.

Customer Feedback   Once the site was up and running, managers were able to track purchases hourly and quickly reformulate the product mix. For example, a line of wines was not selling as quickly as expected, generating only six purchases an hour. It was replaced with a Zen fountain that sold reliably at a rate of one every five minutes.

THE RESULTS

RedEnvelope's new management team brought the new operation online 60 days before Christmas in 1999. In two months the company shipped 20,000

packages and generated more revenue than the firm had managed in the preceding two years. Its Web alliances and ads were particularly effective. According to Nielsen NetRatings, 17.4 percent of those who saw the firm's banner clicked on it; the typical click-through rate for banner ads is about 2 percent. And nearly 6 percent of those who visited the site made purchases, compared to an industry average conversion rate of about 2 percent. Most important, the firm lived up to its promises. It filled 98 percent of its orders accurately, shipped 99 percent of its packages on time, and only 2 percent of recipients wanted to return their gifts.

On the minus side, during the first months of its existence the company shelled out nearly $4 in marketing for every $1 in gross sales. Thus, the future profitability of RedEnvelope—just as with many other new Internet retailers—will depend on the firm's ability to build a loyal customer base and reap repeat purchases to recoup its marketing investments. The good news is that the high margins the firm earns on its products may make future profitability a more attainable goal than it has been for some low-margin Internet marketers. And as of this writing, at least, RedEnvelope has managed to dodge the dot.com debacle of 2001 and continues to pursue its revenue growth and profitability goals.

STRATEGIC CHALLENGES ADDRESSED IN CHAPTER 2

The corporate strategy crafted by Hillary Billings after joining RedEnvelope provides a clear sense of direction and useful guidance for the firm's managers when developing competitive, marketing, and other functional strategies because it speaks to the dimensions of strategy we discussed in Chapter 1. First, it defines the overall mission and scope of the firm by clearly focusing on marketing elegant and unique gifts for all occasions to an upscale segment of on-line consumers. It also lays out goals and objectives for the company—particularly concerning revenue growth and the rapid attainment of profitability—and specifies a corporate development strategy for achieving those objectives. Specifically, RedEnvelope seeks growth primarily through increased penetration of its target customer segment, and profitability by focusing on high-margin merchandise and lowering customer acccquisition costs by improving their loyalty and repeat purchases.

RedEnvelope's objectives and development strategy, in turn, influence the way it allocates its resources and leverages its core competencies in order to build and maintain a competitive advantage. The firm hired experienced managers with extensive knowledge of the target segment, allocated substantial resources to tracking customers' purchase patterns and preferences, formed alliances with suppliers to develop exclusive and unique products that fit those preferences, and invested heavily in the people and systems necessary to provide excellent service and build customer loyalty. Finally, the firm seeks synergy across the various products it offers by investing in advertising and promotion activities aimed at building a strong corporate identity and awareness of the RedEnvelope brand, and by developing the necessary capabilities—both internally or through alliances—to provide superior service and timely order fulfillment regardless of what the customer buys.

The successful reformulation of RedEnvelope's corporate strategy illustrates the importance of a detailed understanding of target customers, potential competitors, and the market environment when developing strategies at any level. Indeed, Hillary Billings was hired as the firm's CEO partly because of her extensive experience in marketing high-margin merchandise to a similar target segment at Williams-Sonoma. As we pointed out in Chapter 1, marketers' close contact with customers and the external environment often means they play a crucial role in influencing strategies formulated at higher levels in the firm, even when they're not appointed CEO.

On the other hand, a well-defined corporate strategy also influences and constrains the strategic decisions that marketers and other functional managers can make at lower organizational levels. RedEnvelope's mission of offering elegant and unique gifts for all occasions clearly influences the kinds of items the firm's marketers can—and cannot—add to the product line. And its objective of achieving profitability by maintaining high margins rules out aggressive pricing policies and frequent sales promotions.

In view of the interactions and interdependences between corporate-level strategy decisions and strategic marketing programs for individual product-market entries, this chapter examines the five components of a well-defined corporate strategy in more detail: (1) the overall scope and mission of the organization, (2) company goals and objectives, (3) a development strategy for future growth, (4) the allocation of corporate resources across the firm's various businesses, and (5) the search for synergy via the sharing of corporate resources, competencies, or programs across businesses or product lines. Exhibit 2.1 summarizes some of the crucial questions that need to be addressed by each of these five components.

While a market orientation—and the analytical tools that marketing managers use to examine customer desires and competitors' strengths and weaknesses—can provide useful insights to guide decisions concerning all five elements of corporate strategy, they are particularly germane for revealing the most attractive avenues for future growth and for determining which businesses or product-markets are likely to produce the greatest returns on the company's resources. In turn, all five components of corporate strategy have major implications for the strategic marketing plans of the firm's various products or services. Together, they define the general stategic direction, objectives, and resource constraints within which those marketing plans must operate. We examine the marketing implications involved in both formulating and implementing the five components of corporate strategy in the following sections.

CORPORATE SCOPE—DEFINING THE FIRM'S MISSION

A well-thought-out mission statement guides an organization's managers as to which market opportunities to pursue and which fall outside the firm's strategic domain. A clearly stated mission can help instill a shared sense of direction, relevance, and achievement among employees, as well as a positive image of the firm among customers, investors, and other stakeholders.

Exhibit 2.1   Corporate Strategy Components and Issues

Strategy component	Key issues
Scope, mission, and intent	• What business(es) should the firm be in?
	• What customer needs, market segments, and/or technologies should be focused on?
	• What is the firm's enduring strategic purpose or intent?
Objectives	• What performance dimensions should the firm's business units and employees focus on?
	• What is the target level of performance to be achieved on each dimension?
	• What is the time frame in which each target should be attained?
Development strategy	• How can the firm achieve a desired level of growth over time?
	• Can the desired growth be attained by expanding the firm's current businesses?
	• Will the company have to diversify into new businesses or product-markets to achieve its future growth objectives?
Resource allocation	• How should the firm's limited financial resources be allocated across its businesses to produce the highest returns?
	• Of the alternative strategies that each business might pursue, which will produce the greatest returns for the dollars invested?
Sources of synergy	• What competencies, knowledge, and customer-based intangibles (e.g., brand recognition, reputation) might be developed and shared across the firm's businesses?
	• What operational resources, facilities, or functions (e.g., plants, R&D, salesforce) might the firm's businesses share to increase their efficiency?

To provide a useful sense of direction, a corporate mission statement should clearly define the organization's strategic scope. It should answer such fundamental questions as the following: What is our business? Who are our customers? What kinds of value can we provide to these customers? and What should our business be in the future? For example, several years ago PepsiCo, the manufacturer of Pepsi-Cola, broadened its mission to focus on "marketing superior quality food and beverage products for households and consumers dining out." That clearly defined mission guided the firm's managers toward the acquisition of several related companies, such as Frito-Lay, Taco Bell, and Pizza Hut, and the divestiture of operations that no longer fit the company's primary thrust.

More recently, in response to a changing global competitive environment, PepsiCo narrowed its scope to focus primarily on *package* foods (particularly salty snacks) and beverages distributed through supermarket and convenience store channels. This new, narrower mission led the firm to (1) divest all of its fast-food restaurant chains; (2) acquire complementary beverage businesses, such as Tropicana juices and Lipton's iced teas; and (3) develop new brands targeted at rapidly growing beverage segments, such as Aquafina bottled water.[2]

Market Influences on the Corporate Mission

Like any other strategy component, an organization's mission should fit both its internal characteristics and the opportunities and threats in its external environment. Obviously, the firm's mission should be compatible with its established values, resources, and distinctive competencies. But it also should focus the firm's efforts on markets where those resources and competencies will generate value for customers, an advantage over competitors, and synergy across its products. Thus, PepsiCo's new mission reflects the firm's package goods marketing, sales, and distribution competencies and its perception that substantial synergies can be realized across snack foods and beverages within supermarket channels via shared logistics, joint displays and sales promotions, cross-couponing, and the like.

Criteria for Defining the Corporate Mission

Several criteria can be used to define an organization's strategic mission. Many firms specify their domain in *physical* terms, focusing on *products* or *services* or the *technology* used. The problem is that such statements can lead to slow reactions to technological or customer-demand changes. For example, Theodore Levitt argues that Penn Central's view of its mission as being "the railroad business" helped cause the firm's failure. Penn Central did not respond to major changes in transportation technology, such as the rapid growth of air travel and the increased efficiency of long-haul trucking. Nor did it respond to consumers' growing willingness to pay higher prices for the increased speed and convenience of air travel. Levitt argues that it is better to define a firm's mission as *what customer needs are to be satisfied and the functions the firm must perform to satisfy them.*[3] Products and technologies change over time, but basic customer needs tend to endure. Thus, if Penn Central had defined its mission as satisfying the transportation needs of its customers rather than simply being a railroad, it might have been more willing to expand its domain to incorporate newer technologies.

One problem with Levitt's advice, though, is that a mission statement focusing only on basic customer needs can be too broad to provide clear guidance and can fail to take into account the firm's specific competencies. If Penn Central had defined itself as a transportation company, should it have diversified into the trucking business? Started an airline? As the upper-right quadrant of Exhibit 2.2 suggests, the most useful mission statements focus on the customer need to be satisfied and the functions that must be performed to satisfy that need, and they are *specific* as to the customer groups and the products or technologies on which to concentrate. Thus, instead of seeing itself as being in the railroad business or as satisfying the transportation needs of all potential customers, Burlington Northern Santa Fe Railroad's mission is to provide long-distance transportation for large-volume producers of low-value, low-density products, such as coal and grain.

Social Values and Ethical Principles

 An increasing number of organizations are developing mission statements that also attempt to define the social and ethical boundaries of their strategic domain. The annual reports of firms such as Borden and 3M, for example, often include sections on "Social Responsibility,"

Exhibit 2.2

CHARACTERISTICS OF EFFECTIVE CORPORATE MISSION STATEMENTS

	Broad	Specific
Functional Based on customer needs	Transportation business	Long-distance transportation for large-volume producers of low-value, low-density products
Physical Based on existing products or technology	Railroad business	Long-haul, coal-carrying railroad

Source: From *Strategy Formulation: Analytical Concepts,* 1st edition, by © 1978. Reprinted with permission of South-Western College Publishing, a division of Thomson Learning. Fax 800-730-2215.

which outline the ethical principles the firm tries to follow in dealings with customers, suppliers, and employees, and its policies concerning such social issues as charitable contributions and environmental protection. Roughly two-thirds of U.S. firms have formal codes of ethics, and one in five large firms has formal departments dedicated to encouraging compliance with company ethical standards. At United Technologies, a global defense contractor and engineering firm, 160 business ethics officers monitor the firm's activities and relations with customers, suppliers, and governments around the world.[4]

Outside America, fewer firms have formal ethics bureaucracies. To some extent, this reflects the fact that in other countries governments and organized labor both play a bigger role in corporate life. In Germany, for instance, workers' councils often deal with issues such as sexual equality, race relations, and workers' rights.[5]

Ethics is concerned with the development of moral standards by which actions and situations can be judged. It focuses on those actions that may result in actual or potential harm of some kind (e.g., economic, mental, physical) to an individual, group, or organization.

Particular actions may be legal but not ethical. For instance, extreme and unsubstantiated advertising claims, such as "Our product is far superior to Brand X," might be viewed as simply legal puffery engaged in to make a sale, but many marketers (and their customers) view such little white lies as unethical. Thus, ethics is more proactive than the law. Ethical standards attempt to anticipate and avoid social problems, whereas most laws and regulations emerge only after the negative consequences of an action become apparent.[6]

Why Are Ethics Important? The Marketing Implications of Ethical Standards

One might ask why a corporation should take responsibility for providing moral guidance to its managers and employees. While such a question may be a good topic for philosophical debate, there is a compelling, practical reason for a firm to impose ethical standards to guide employees. Unethical practices can damage the trust between a firm and its suppliers or customers, thereby disrupting the development of long-term exchange relationships and resulting in the likely loss of sales and profits over time. For example, one survey of 135 purchasing managers from a variety of industries found that the more unethical a supplier's sales and marketing practices were perceived to be, the less eager were the purchasing managers to buy from that supplier.[7]

Unfortunately, not all customers or competing suppliers adhere to the same ethical standards. As a result, marketers sometimes feel pressure to engage in actions that are inconsistent with what they believe to be right—either in terms of personal values or formal company standards—in order to close a sale or stay even with the competition. This point was illustrated by a survey of 59 top marketing and sales executives concerning commercial bribery—attempts to influence a potential customer by giving gifts or kickbacks. While nearly two-thirds of the executives considered bribes unethical and did not want to pay them, 88 percent also felt that *not* paying bribes might put their firms at a competitive disadvantage.[8] Such dilemmas are particularly likely to arise as a company moves into global markets involving different cultures and levels of economic development where economic exigencies and ethical standards may be quite different.

Such inconsistencies in external expectations and demands across countries and markets can lead to job stress and inconsistent behavior among marketing and sales personnel, which in turn can risk damaging long-term relationships with suppliers, channel partners, and customers. A company can reduce such problems by spelling out formal social policies and ethical standards in its corporate mission statement and communicating and enforcing those

Exhibit 2.3

ISSUES ADDRESSED BY COMPANY ETHICS STATEMENTS

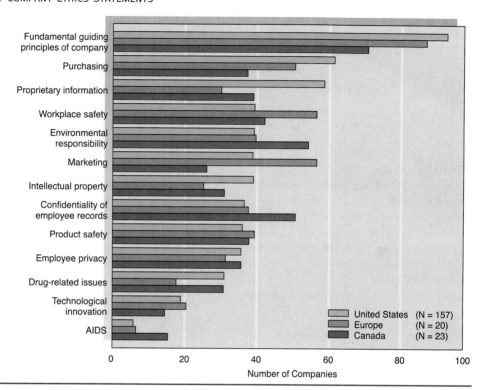

Source: Ronald E. Berenbeim, *Corporate Ethics Practices* (New York: The Conference Board, 1992).

standards. Unfortunately, it is not always easy to decide what those policies and standards should be. There are multiple philosophical traditions or frameworks that managers might use to evaluate the ethics of a given action. Consequently, different firms or managers can pursue somewhat different ethical standards, particularly across national cultures. Exhibit 2.3 displays a comparison (across three geographic regions) of the proportion of company ethical statements that address a set of specific issues. Note that a larger number of companies in the United States and Europe appear to be more concerned with the ethics of their purchasing practices than those of their marketing activities. Comparing firms across regions, U.S. companies are more concerned about proprietary information. Canadian firms are more likely to have explicit guidelines concerning environmental responsibility, and European companies more frequently have standards focused on workplace safety. Since many ethical issues in marketing are open to interpretation and debate, we will examine such issues and their implications individually as they arise throughout the remainder of this book.

CORPORATE OBJECTIVES

Confucius said, "For one who has no objective, nothing is relevant." Formal objectives provide decision criteria that guide an organization's business units and employees toward specific dimensions and performance levels. Those same objectives provide the benchmarks against which actual performance can be evaluated.

To be useful as decision criteria and evaluative benchmarks, corporate objectives must be specific and measurable. Therefore, each objective contains four components:

- A *performance dimension* or attribute sought.
- A *measure or index* for evaluating progress.
- A *target or hurdle* level to be achieved.
- A *time frame* within which the target is to be accomplished.

Exhibit 2.4 lists some common performance dimensions and measures used in specifying corporate as well as business-unit and marketing objectives.

Exhibit 2.4

COMMON PERFORMANCE CRITERIA AND MEASURES THAT SPECIFY CORPORATE, BUSINESS-UNIT, AND MARKETING OBJECTIVES

Performance criteria	Possible measures or indexes
• Growth	$ sales Unit sales Percent change in sales
• Competitive strength	Market share Brand awareness Brand preference
• Innovativeness	$ sales from new products Percentage of sales from product-market entries introduced within past five years Percentage cost savings from new processes
• Profitability	$ profits Profit as percentage of sales Contribution margin* Return on investment (ROI) Return on net assets (RONA) Return on equity (ROE)
• Utilization of resources	Percent capacity utilization Fixed assets as percentage of sales
• Contribution to owners	Earnings per share Price/earnings ratio
• Contribution to customers	Price relative to competitors Product quality Customer satisfaction Customer retention Customer loyalty Customer lifetime value
• Contribution to employees	Wage rates, benefits Personnel development, promotions Employment stability, turnover
• Contribution to society	$ contributions to charities or community institutions Growth in employment

*Business-unit managers and marketing managers responsible for a product-market entry often have little control over costs associated with corporate overhead, such as the costs of corporate staff or R&D. It can be difficult to allocate those costs to specific strategic business units (SBUs) or products. Consequently, profit objectives at the SBU and product-market level are often stated as a desired *contribution margin* (the gross profit prior to allocating such overhead costs).

Enhancing Shareholder Value: The Ultimate Objective

In recent years a growing number of executives of publicly held corporations have concluded that the organization's ultimate objective should be to increase its shareholders' economic returns as measured by dividends plus appreciation in the company's stock price.[9] To do so management must balance the interests of various corporate constituencies, including employees, customers, suppliers, debtholders, and stockholders. The firm's continued existence depends on a financial relationship with each of these parties. Employees want competitive wages. Customers want high quality at a competitive price. Suppliers and debtholders have financial claims that must be satisfied with cash when they fall due. And shareholders, as residual claimants, look for cash dividends and the prospect of future dividends reflected in the stock's market price.

If a company does not satisfy its constituents' financial claims, it ceases to be viable. Thus, a going concern must strive to enhance its ability to generate cash from the operation of its businesses and to obtain any additional funds needed from debt or equity financing.

The firm's ability to attain debt financing (its ability to borrow) depends in turn on projections of how much cash it can generate in the future. Similarly, the market value of its shares, and therefore its ability to attain equity financing, depends on investors' expectations of the firm's future cash-generating abilities. People willingly invest in a firm only when they expect a better return on their funds than they could get from other sources without exposing themselves to any greater risks. Thus, management's primary objective should be to pursue capital investments, acquisitions, and business strategies that will produce sufficient future cash flows to return positive value to shareholders. Failure to do so not only will depress the firm's stock price and inhibit the firm's ability to finance future operations and growth, but also it could make the organization more vulnerable to a takeover by outsiders who promise to increase its value to shareholders.

Given this rationale, many firms set explicit objectives targeted at increasing shareholder value. These are usually stated in terms of a target return on shareholder equity, increase in the stock price, or earnings per share. Recently, though, some executives have begun expressing such corporate objectives in terms of *economic value added* or *market value added (MVA)*. A firm's MVA is calculated by combining its debt and the market value of its stock, then subtracting the capital that has been invested in the company. The result, if positive, shows how much wealth the company has created.[10]

Unfortunately, such broad shareholder-value objectives do not always provide adequate guidance for a firm's lower-level managers or benchmarks for evaluating performance. For one thing, standard accounting measures, such as earnings per share or return on investment, are not always reliably linked to the true value of a company's stock.[11] And as we shall see later in this chapter, tools are available to evaluate the future impact of alternative strategic actions on shareholder value, but those valuation methods have inherent pitfalls and can be difficult to apply at lower levels of strategy such as trying to choose the best marketing strategy for a particular product-market entry.[12]

STRATEGIC ISSUE

In the long term, customer value and shareholder value converge; a firm can continue to provide attractive returns to shareholders only so long as it satisfies and retains its customers.

Finally, there is a danger that a narrow focus on short-term financial, shareholder-value objectives may lead managers to pay too little attention to actions necessary to provide value to the firm's customers and sustain a competitive advantage.[13] In the long term, customer value and shareholder value converge; a firm can continue to provide attractive returns to shareholders only so long as it satisfies and retains its customers. But some managers may overlook this in the face of pressures to achieve aggressive short-term financial objectives, as illustrated by the experience of Schlitz Brewing discussed in Exhibit 2.5.

Exhibit 2.5   **Schlitz: An Example of Increasing Stock Price at the Expense of Competitive Position**

In the early 1970s Schlitz Brewing made the mistake of boosting its share price at the expense of its competitive position. The firm shortened its brewing process by 50 percent, reduced labor cost, and switched to less costly ingredients. As a result, it became the lowest-cost producer in the industry, its profits soared, and its stock price rose to a high of $69 by 1974. Unfortunately, however, Schlitz's aggressive cost-cutting campaign also degraded the quality of its beer. By 1976 the firm was receiving constant customer and dealer complaints and its market share was slipping badly. In 1978 a new management team attempted to get product quality back on track, but by then consumers had such a low opinion of Schlitz beer that the company could not recover. By 1981 Schlitz's market share position had slipped from number two to number seven, and its share price had dropped to a mere $5.

Source: George S. Day and Liam Fahey, "Putting Strategy into Shareholder Value Analysis," *Harvard Business Review,* March–April 1990, pp. 156–62. Reprinted with permission. Copyright 1990 by the President and Fellows of Harvard College, all rights reserved.

The Marketing Implications of Corporate Objectives

Most organizations pursue multiple objectives. This is clearly demonstrated by a study of the stated objectives of 82 large corporations. The largest percentage of respondents (89 percent) had explicit profitability objectives: 82 percent reported growth objectives; 66 percent had specific market-share goals. More than 60 percent mentioned social responsibility, employee welfare, and customer service objectives, and 54 percent of the companies had R&D/new product development goals.[14] These percentages add up to more than 100 percent because most firms had several objectives.

Trying to achieve many objectives at once leads to conflicts and trade-offs. For example, the investment and expenditure necessary to pursue growth in the long term is likely to reduce profitability and ROI in the short term.[15] Managers can reconcile conflicting goals by prioritizing them. Another approach is to state one of the conflicting goals as a constraint or **hurdle.** Thus, a firm attempts to maximize growth subject to meeting some minimum ROI hurdle.

In firms with multiple business units or product lines, however, the most common way to pursue a set of conflicting objectives is to first break them down into subobjectives, then assign subobjectives to different business units or products. Thus, subobjectives often vary across business units and product offerings depending on the attractiveness and potential of their industries, the strength of their competitive positions, and the resource allocation decisions made by corporate managers. For example, PepsiCo's managers likely set relatively high volume and share-growth objectives but lower ROI goals for the firm's Aquafina brand, which is battling for prominence in the rapidly growing bottled water category, than for Lay's potato chips, which hold a commanding 40 percent share of a mature product category. Therefore, two marketing managers responsible for different products may face very different goals and expectations—requiring different marketing strategies to accomplish—even though they work for the same organization.

As firms emphasize developing and maintaining long-term customer relationships, *customer-focused objectives*—such as satisfaction, retention, and loyalty—are being given greater importance. Such market-oriented objectives are more likely to be consistently pursued across business units and product offerings. There are several reasons for this. First, given the huge profit implications of a customer's lifetime value, maximizing satisfaction and loyalty tends to make good sense no matter what other financial objectives are being pursued in the short term. Second, satisfied, loyal customers of one product can be leveraged to provide synergies for other company products or services. For instance, IBM hopes that satisfied customers of its website development services for small businesses will eventually become customers for the company's servers and software products as they grow. Finally, customer satisfaction and loyalty are determined by factors other than the product itself or the activities of the marketing department. A study of one industrial paper company, for example, found that about 80 percent of customers' satisfaction scores were accounted for by nonproduct factors, such as order processing, delivery, and postsale services.[16] Since such factors are influenced by many functional departments within the corporation, they are likely to have a similar impact across a firm's various businesses and products.

CORPORATE GROWTH STRATEGIES

Often, the projected combined future sales and profits of a corporation's business units and product-markets fall short of the firm's long-run growth and profitability objectives. There is a gap between what the firm expects to become if it continues on its present course and what it would like to become. This is not surprising because some of its high-growth markets are likely to slip into maturity over time and some of its high-profit mature businesses may decline to insignificance as they get older. Thus, to determine where future growth is coming from, management must decide on a strategy to guide corporate development.

STRATEGIC ISSUE

A firm can go in two major directions in seeking future growth: expansion of its current businesses and activities or diversification into new businesses.

Essentially, a firm can go in two major directions in seeking future growth: **expansion** of its current businesses and activities or **diversification** into new businesses, either through internal business development or acquisition. Exhibit 2.6 outlines some specific options a firm might pursue while seeking growth in either of these directions.

Expansion by Increasing Penetration of Current Product-Markets

One way for a company to expand is by increasing its share of existing markets. This typically requires actions such as making product or service improvements, cutting costs and prices, or outspending competitors on advertising or promotions. Amazon.com pursued a combination of all these actions—as well as forming alliances with Web portals, affinity groups, and the like—to expand its share of Web shoppers, even though the expense of such activities postponed the firm's ability to become profitable.

Even when a firm holds a commanding share of an existing product-market, additional growth may be possible by encouraging current customers to become more loyal and concentrate their purchases, use more of the product or service, use it more often, or use it in new ways. In addition to its promotional efforts, Amazon.com spent hundreds of millions of dollars on warehouses and order fulfillment activities, investments that earned the loyalty of its customers. As a result, by the year 2000 more than three-quarters of the firm's sales were coming from repeat customers.[17] Other examples include museums that sponsor special exhibitions to encourage patrons to make repeat visits and the recipes that Quaker Oats includes on the package to tempt buyers to include oatmeal as an ingredient in other foods, such as cookies and desserts.

Exhibit 2.6

ALTERNATIVE CORPORATE GROWTH STRATEGIES

	Current products	New products
Current markets	Market penetration strategies • Increase market share • Increase product usage 　Increase frequency of use 　Increase quantity used 　New applications	Product development strategies • Product improvements • Product-line extensions • New products for same market
New markets	Market development strategies • Expand markets for existing 　products 　Geographic expansion 　Target new segments	Diversification strategies • Vertical integration 　Forward integration 　Backward integration • Diversification into related 　businesses 　(concentric diversification) • Diversification into unrelated 　businesses 　(conglomerate diversification)

Expansion by Developing New Products for Current Customers

A second avenue to future growth is through a product-development strategy emphasizing the introduction of product-line extensions or new product or service offerings aimed at existing customers. For example, Arm & Hammer successfully introduced a laundry detergent, an oven cleaner, and a carpet cleaner. Each capitalized on baking soda's image as an effective deodorizer and on a high level of recognition of the Arm & Hammer brand. Similarly, RedEnvelope's managers are constantly searching for unique new items to add to its line of gifts.

Expansion by Selling Existing Products to New Segments or Countries

Perhaps the growth strategy with the greatest potential for many companies is the development of new markets for their existing goods or services. This may involve the creation of marketing programs aimed at nonuser or occasional-user segments of existing markets. Thus, theaters, orchestras, and other performing arts organizations often sponsor touring companies to reach audiences outside major metropolitan areas and promote matinee performances with lower prices and free public transportation to attract senior citizens and students.

Exhibit 2.7

NUMBER OF ONLINE SHOPPERS IN THE EUROPEAN UNION (USERS IN MILLIONS)

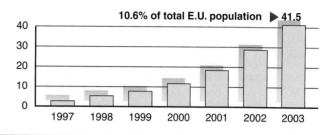

Source: Jupiter Communications, as reported in Jennifer L. Schenker, "The Future Is Now," *Time,* April 10, 2000, p. 85. © 2000 Time Inc. Reprinted by permission.

Expansion into new geographic markets, particularly new countries, is also a primary growth strategy for many firms. For example, General Electric announced a growth strategy that shifts the firm's strategic center of gravity from the industrialized West to Asia and Latin America.[18]

While developing nations represent attractive growth markets for basic industrial and infrastructure goods and services, growing personal incomes and falling trade barriers are making them attractive potential markets for many consumer goods and services as well. Even developed nations can represent growth opportunities for products or services based on newly emerging technologies or business models. For instance, while the rapid growth of e-retailers such as Amazon.com is likely to slow in the United States over the next few years, growth in the number of online shoppers is expected to expand rapidly in Europe,[19] as shown in Exhibit 2.7.

Expansion by Diversifying

Firms also seek growth by diversifying their operations. This is typically riskier than the various expansion strategies because it often involves learning new operations and dealing with unfamiliar customer groups. Nevertheless, the majority of large U.S., European, and Asian firms are diversified to one degree or another.

Vertical integration is one way for companies to diversify. **Forward vertical integration** occurs when a firm moves downstream in terms of the product flow, as when a manufacturer integrates by acquiring or launching a wholesale distributor or retail outlet. For example, IBM recently withdrew its Aptiva desktop PCs from independent computer retailers such as CompUSA and made them available only over the company's own retail website in order to improve customer service and reduce costs. **Backward integration** occurs when a firm moves upstream by acquiring a supplier.

Integration can give a firm access to scarce or volatile sources of supply or tighter control over the marketing, distribution, or servicing of its products. But it increases the risks inherent in committing substantial resources to a single industry. Also, the investment required to vertically integrate often offsets the additional profitability generated by the integrated operations, resulting in little improvement in return on investment.[20]

Related (or concentric) diversification occurs when a firm internally develops or acquires another business that does not have products or customers in common with its current businesses but that might contribute to internal synergy through the sharing of production facilities, brand names, R&D know-how, or marketing and distribution skills. Thus, PepsiCo acquired Cracker Jack to complement its salty snack brands and leverage its distribution strengths in grocery stores.

The motivations for **unrelated (or conglomerate) diversification** are primarily financial rather than operational. By definition, an unrelated diversification involves two businesses that have no commonalities in products, customers, production facilities, or functional areas of expertise. Such diversification mostly occurs when a disproportionate number of a firm's current businesses face decline because of decreasing demand, increased competition, or product obsolescence. The firm must seek new avenues of growth. Other, more fortunate, firms may move into unrelated businesses because they have more cash than they need in order to expand their current businesses, or because they wish to discourage takeover attempts.

Unrelated diversification tends to be the riskiest growth strategy in terms of financial outcomes. Most empirical studies report that related diversification is more conducive to capital productivity and other dimensions of performance than is unrelated diversification.[21] This suggests that the ultimate goal of a corporation's strategy for growth should be to develop a compatible portfolio of businesses to which the firm can add value through the application of its unique core competencies. The corporation's marketing competencies can be particularly important in this regard, as evidenced by the success of firms like PepsiCo.

Expansion by Diversifying through Organizational Relationships or Networks

Recently, firms have attempted to gain some benefits of market expansion or diversification while simultaneously focusing more intensely on a few core competencies. They try to accomplish this feat by forming relationships or organizational networks with other firms instead of acquiring ownership.[22]

Perhaps the best models of such organizational networks are the Japanese *keiretsu* and the Korean *chaebol*—coalitions of financial institutions, distributors, and manufacturing firms in a variety of industries that are often grouped around a large trading company that helps coordinate the activities of the various coalition members and markets their goods and services around the world. Compaq is a Western firm that is attempting to develop a similar network of organizational alliances. While Compaq concentrates on its core competencies in marketing and servicing computer hardware and software, it depends increasingly on partnerships with other firms for other functions and for expertise in new markets and product lines. For instance, Compaq relies heavily on Accenture for assistance in designing computer networks for its largest customers and on a number of Asian suppliers and assemblers for the manufacture of its products. Such relationships allow Compaq to concentrate on its core competencies while simultaneously expanding its product and service offerings and reducing its costs and assets employed.[23]

ALLOCATING CORPORATE RESOURCES

Diversified organizations have several advantages over more narrowly focused firms. They have a broader range of areas in which they can knowledgeably invest, and their growth and profitability rates may be more stable because they can offset declines in one business with gains in another. To exploit the advantages of diversification, though, corporate managers must make intelligent decisions about how to allocate financial and human resources across the firm's various businesses and product-markets. Two sets of analytical tools have proven useful in making such decisions: **portfolio models** and **value-based planning.**

Portfolio Models

One of the most significant developments in strategic management during the 1970s and 1980s was the widespread adoption of portfolio models to help managers allocate corporate resources across multiple businesses. These models enable managers to classify and review their current and prospective businesses by viewing them as portfolios of investment opportunities and then evaluating each business's competitive strength and the attractiveness of the markets it serves.

The Boston Consulting Group's (BCG) Growth-Share Matrix   One of the first—and best known—of the portfolio models is the growth-share matrix developed by the Boston Consulting Group in the late 1960s. It analyzes the impact of investing resources in different businesses on the corporation's future earnings and cash flows. Each business is positioned within a matrix, as shown in Exhibit 2.8. The vertical axis indicates the industry's growth rate and the horizontal axis shows the business's relative market share.

The growth-share matrix assumes that a firm must generate cash from businesses with strong competitive positions in mature markets. Then it can fund investments and expenditures in industries that represent attractive future opportunities. Thus, the **market growth rate** on the vertical axis is a proxy measure for the maturity and attractiveness of an industry. This model represents businesses in rapidly growing industries as more attractive investment opportunities for future growth and profitability.

Exhibit 2.8

BCG'S MARKET GROWTH RELATIVE SHARE MATRIX

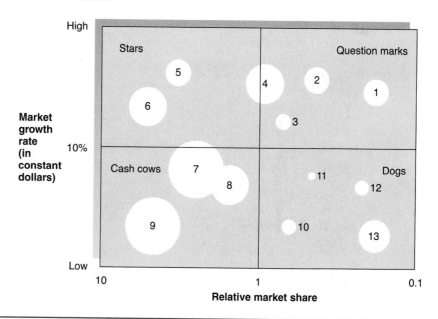

Source: Reprinted from *Long Range Planning*, Volume 10 (February 1977), Barry Hedley, "Strategy and the Business Portfolio," Copyright 1977, with the permission from Elsevier Science.

Similarly, a business's **relative market share** is a proxy for its competitive strength within its industry. It is computed by dividing the business's absolute market share in dollars or units by that of the leading competitor in the industry. Thus, in Exhibit 2.8 a business is in a strong competitive position if its share is equal to, or larger than, that of the next leading competitor (i.e., a relative share of 1.0 or larger). Finally, in the exhibit, the size of the circle representing each business is proportional to that unit's sales volume. Thus, businesses 7 and 9 are the largest-volume businesses in this hypothetical company, while business 11 is the smallest.

Resource Allocation and Strategy Implications   Each of the four cells in the growth-share matrix represents a different type of business with different strategy and resource requirements. The implications of each are discussed below and summarized in Exhibit 2.9.

- *Question marks.* Businesses in high-growth industries with low relative market shares (those in the upper-right quadrant of Exhibit 2.9) are called *question marks* or *problem children.* Such businesses require large amounts of cash, not only for expansion to keep up with the rapidly growing market, but also for marketing activities (or reduced margins) to build market share and catch the industry leader. If management can successfully increase the share of a question mark business, it becomes a star. But if managers fail, it eventually turns into a dog as the industry matures and the market growth rate slows.
- *Stars.* A *star* is the market leader in a high-growth industry. Stars are critical to the continued success of the firm. As their industries mature, they move into the bottom-left quadrant and become cash cows. Paradoxically, while stars are critically important, they often are net users rather than suppliers of cash in the short run (as indicated by the possibility of a negative cash flow shown in Exhibit 2.9). This is because the firm must continue to invest in such businesses to keep up with rapid market growth and to support the R&D and marketing activities necessary to maintain a leading market share.
- *Cash cows.* Businesses with a high relative share of low-growth markets are called *cash cows* because they are the primary generators of profits and cash in a corporation. Such businesses

Exhibit 2.9

CASH FLOWS ACROSS BUSINESSES IN THE BCG PORTFOLIO MODEL

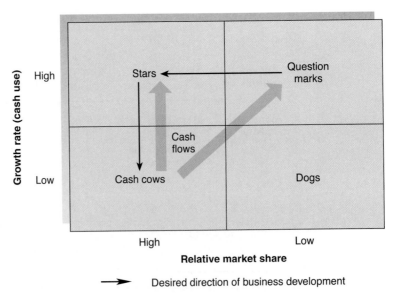

do not require much additional capital investment. Their markets are stable, and their share leadership position usually means they enjoy economies of scale and relatively high profit margins. Consequently, the corporation can use the cash from these businesses to support its question marks and stars (as shown in Exhibit 2.9). However, this does not mean the firm should necessarily maximize the business's short-term cash flow by cutting R&D and marketing expenditures to the bone—particularly not in industries where the business might continue to generate substantial future sales.

- *Dogs.* Low-share businesses in low-growth markets are called *dogs* because although they may throw off some cash, they typically generate low profits, or losses. Divestiture is one option for such businesses, although it can be difficult to find an interested buyer. Another common strategy is to harvest dog businesses. This involves maximizing short-term cash flow by paring investments and expenditures until the business is gradually phased out.

Limitations of the Growth-Share Matrix

Because the growth-share matrix uses only two variables as a basis for categorizing and analyzing a firm's businesses, it is relatively easy to understand. But while this simplicity helps explain its popularity, it also means the model has limitations:

- *Market growth rate is an inadequate descriptor of overall industry attractiveness.* Market growth is not always directly related to profitability or cash flow. Some high-growth industries have never been very profitable because low entry barriers and capital intensity have enabled supply to grow even faster, resulting in intense price competition. Also, rapid growth in one year is no guarantee that growth will continue in the following year.

- *Relative market share is inadequate as a description of overall competitive strength.* Market share is more properly viewed as an outcome of past efforts to formulate and implement effective business-level and marketing strategies than as an indicator of enduring competitive strength.[24] If the external environment changes, or the SBU's managers change their strategy, the business's relative market share can shift dramatically.

- *The outcomes of a growth-share analysis are highly sensitive to variations in how growth and share are measured.*[25] Defining the relevant industry and served market (i.e., the target-market segments being pursued) also can present problems. For example, does Pepsi Cola compete only for a share of the cola market, or for a share of the much larger market for non-alcoholic beverages, such as iced tea, bottled water, and fruit juices?

- *While the matrix specifies appropriate investment strategies for each business, it provides little guidance on how best to implement those strategies.* While the model suggests that a firm should invest cash in its question mark businesses, for instance, it does not consider whether there are any potential sources of competitive advantage that the business can exploit to successfully increase its share. Simply providing a business with more money does not guarantee that it will be able to improve its position within the matrix.

- *The model implicitly assumes that all business units are independent of one another except for the flow of cash.* If this assumption is inaccurate, the model can suggest some inappropriate resource allocation decisions. For instance, if other SBUs depend on a dog business as a source of supply—or if they share functional activities, such as a common plant or salesforce, with that business—harvesting the dog might increase the costs or reduce the effectiveness of the other SBUs.

Alternative Portfolio Models

In view of the above limitations, a number of firms have attempted to improve the basic portfolio model. Such improvements have focused primarily on developing more detailed, multifactor measures of industry attractiveness and a business's competitive strength and on making the analysis more future-oriented. Exhibit 2.10 shows some factors managers might use to evaluate industry attractiveness and a business's competitive position. Corporate managers must first select factors most appropriate for their firm and weight them according to their relative importance. They then rate each business and its industry on the two sets of factors. Next, they combine the weighted evaluations into summary measures

Exhibit 2.10

THE INDUSTRY ATTRACTIVENESS-BUSINESS POSITION MATRIX

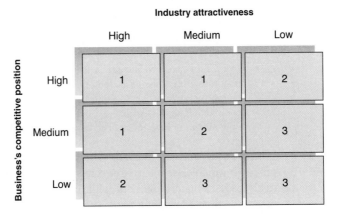

1 Invest/grow
2 Selective investment/maintain position
3 Harvest/divest

Variables that might be used to evaluate:

Business's competitive position		Industry attractivement	
Size	Distribution	Size	Profitability
Growth	Technology	Growth	Technological sophistication
Relative share	Marketing skills	Competitive intensity	Government regulations
Customer loyalty	Patents	Price levels	
Margins			

used to place each business within one of the nine boxes in the matrix. Businesses falling into boxes numbered 1 (where both industry attractiveness and the business's ability to compete are relatively high) are good candidates for further investment for future growth. Businesses in the 2 boxes should receive only selective investment with an objective of maintaining current position. Finally, businesses in the 3 boxes are candidates for harvesting or divestiture.

These multifactor models are more detailed than the simple growth-share model and consequently provide more strategic guidance concerning the appropriate allocation of resources across businesses. They are also more useful for evaluating potential new product-markets. However, the multifactor measures in these models can be subjective and ambiguous, especially when managers must evaluate different industries on the same set of factors. Also, the conclusions drawn from these models still depend on the way industries and product-markets are defined.[26]

Value-Based Planning

As mentioned, one limitation of portfolio analysis is that it specifies how firms should allocate financial resources across their businesses without considering the competitive strategies those businesses are, or should be, pursuing. Portfolio analysis provides little guidance, for instance, in deciding which of two question mark businesses—each in attractive markets but following different strategies—is worthy of the greater investment or in choosing which of several competitive strategies a particular business unit should pursue.

Value-based planning is a resource allocation tool that attempts to address such questions by assessing the shareholder value a given strategy is likely to create. Thus, value-based planning provides a basis for comparing the economic returns to be gained from investing in different businesses pursuing different strategies or from alternative strategies that might be adopted by a given business unit.

A number of value-based planning methods are currently in use, but all share three basic features.[27] First, they assess the economic value a strategy is likely to produce by examining the cash flows it will generate, rather than relying on distorted accounting measures, such as return on investment.[28] Second, they estimate the shareholder value that a strategy will produce by discounting its forecasted cash flows by the business's risk-adjusted cost of capital. Finally, they evaluate strategies based on the likelihood that the investments required by a strategy will deliver returns greater than the cost of capital. The amount of return a strategy or operating program generates in excess of the cost of capital is commonly referred to as its **economic value added,** or EVA.[29] This approach to evaluating alternative strategies is particularly appropriate for use in allocating resources across business units because most capital investments are made at the business-unit level, and different business units typically face different risks and therefore have different costs of capital.

Discounted Cash Flow Model   Perhaps the best-known and most widely used approach to value-based planning is the discounted cash flow model proposed by Alfred Rappaport and the Alcar Group, Inc. In this model, as Exhibit 2.11 indicates, shareholder value created by a strategy is determined by the cash flow it generates, the business's cost of capital (which is used to discount future cash flows back to their present value), and the market value of the debt assigned to the business. The future cash flows generated by the strategy are, in turn,

Exhibit 2.11

FACTORS AFFECTING THE CREATION OF SHAREHOLDER VALUE

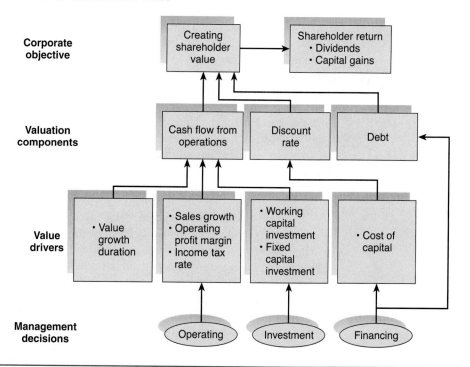

affected by six "value drivers": the rate of sales growth the strategy will produce, the operating profit margin, the income tax rate, investment in working capital, fixed capital investment required by the strategy, and the duration of value growth.

The first five value drivers are self-explanatory, but the sixth requires some elaboration. The duration of value growth represents management's estimate of the number of years over which the strategy can be expected to produce rates of return that exceed the cost of capital. This estimate, in turn, is tied to two other management judgments. First, the manager must decide on the length of the planning period (typically three to five years); he or she must then estimate the residual value the strategy will continue to produce after the planning period is over. Such decisions are tricky, for they involve predictions of what will happen in the relatively distant future.[30]

Some Limitations of Value-Based Planning[31]   Value-based planning is not a substitute for strategic planning; it is only one tool for evaluating strategy alternatives identified and developed through managers' judgments. It does so by relying on forecasts of many kinds to put a financial value on the hopes, fears, and expectations managers associate with each alternative. Projections of cash inflows rest on forecasts of sales volume, product mix, unit prices, and competitors' actions. Expected cash outflows depend on projections of various cost elements, working capital, and investment requirements.

While good forecasts are notoriously difficult to make, they are critical to the validity of value-based planning. Once someone attaches numbers to judgments about what is likely to happen, people tend to endow those numbers with the concreteness of hard facts. Therefore, the numbers derived from value-based planning can sometimes take on a life of their own, and managers can lose sight of the assumptions underlying them.

Consequently, inaccurate forecasts can create problems in implementing value-based planning. For one thing, there are natural human tendencies to overvalue the financial projections associated with some strategy alternatives and to undervalue others. For instance, managers are likely to overestimate the future returns from a currently successful strategy. Evidence of past success tends to carry more weight than qualitative assessments of future threats. Managers may pay too little attention to how competitive behavior, prices, and returns might change if, for example, the industry were suddenly beset by a slowdown in market growth and the appearance of excess capacity.

On the other hand, some kinds of strategy alternatives are consistently undervalued. Particularly worrisome from a marketing viewpoint is the tendency to underestimate the value of keeping current customers. Putting a figure on the damage to a firm's competitive advantage from *not* making a strategic investment necessary to maintain the status quo is harder than documenting potential cost savings or profit improvements that an investment might generate. For example, a few years ago Cone Drive Operations, a small manufacturer of heavy-duty gears, faced a number of related problems. Profits were declining, inventory costs were climbing, and customers were unhappy because deliveries were often late. Cone's management thought that a $2 million computer-integrated manufacturing system might help solve these problems; but a discounted cash flow analysis indicated the system would be an unwise investment. Because the company had only $26 million in sales, it was hard to justify the $2 million investment in terms of cost savings. However, the financial analysis underestimated intangibles such as improved product quality, faster order processing, and improved customer satisfaction. Management decided to install the new system anyway, and new business and nonlabor savings paid back the investment in just one year. More important, Cone retained nearly all of its old customers, many of whom had been seriously considering switching to other suppliers.

> **STRATEGIC ISSUE**
>
> *Some kinds of strategy alternatives are consistently undervalued. Particularly worrisome from a marketing viewpoint is the tendency to underestimate the value of keeping current customers.*

Finally, another kind of problem involved in implementing value-based planning occurs when management fails to consider all the appropriate strategy alternatives. Since it is only an analytical tool, value-based planning can evaluate alternatives, but it cannot create them. The best strategy will never emerge from the evaluation process if management fails to identify it. To realize its full benefits, then, management must link value-based planning to sound strategic analysis that is rigorous enough to avoid the problems associated with undervaluing certain strategies, overvaluing others, and failing to consider all the options.

SOURCES OF SYNERGY

A final strategic concern at the corporate level is to increase synergy across the firm's various businesses and product-markets. As mentioned, synergy exists when two or more businesses or product-markets, and their resources and competencies, complement and reinforce one another so that the total performance of the related businesses is greater than it would be otherwise.

Knowledge-Based Synergies

Some potential synergies at the corporate level are knowledge-based. The performance of one business can be enhanced by the transfer of competencies, knowledge, or customer-related intangibles—such as brand-name recognition and reputation—from other units within the firm. For instance, the technical knowledge concerning image processing and the quality reputation that Canon developed in the camera business helped ease the firm's entry into the office copier business.

In part, such knowledge-based synergies are a function of the corporation's scope and mission—or how its managers answer the question, What businesses should we be in? When a firm's portfolio of businesses and product-markets reflects a common mission based on well-defined customer needs, market segments, or technologies, the company is more likely to develop core competencies, customer knowledge, and strong brand franchises that can be shared across businesses. However, the firm's organization structure and allocation of resources also may enhance knowledge-based synergy. A centralized corporate R&D department, for example, is often more efficient and effective at discovering new technologies with potential applications across multiple businesses than if each business unit bore the burden of funding its own R&D efforts. Similarly, some argue that strong corporate-level coordination and support are necessary to maximize the strength of a firm's brand franchise, and to glean full benefit from accumulated market knowledge, when the firm is competing in global markets.

Corporate Identity and the Corporate Brand as a Source of Synergy

Corporate identity—together with a strong corporate brand that embodies that identity—can help a firm stand out from its competitors and give it a sustainable advantage in the market. *Corporate identity* flows from the communications, impressions, and personality projected by an organization. It is shaped by the firm's mission and values, its functional competencies, the quality and design of its goods and services, its marketing communications, the actions of its personnel, the image generated by various corporate activities, and other factors.[32]

In order to project a positive, strong, and consistent identity, firms as diverse as Caterpillar, Walt Disney, and The Body Shop have established formal policies, criteria, and guidelines to help ensure that all the messages and sensory images they communicate reflect their unique values, personality, and competencies. One rationale for such corporate identity programs is that they can generate synergies that enhance the effectiveness and efficiency of the firm's marketing efforts for its individual product offerings. By focusing on a common core of corporate values and competencies, every impression generated by each product's design, packaging, advertising, and promotional materials can help reinforce and strengthen the impact of all the other impressions the firm communicates to its customers, employees, shareholders, and other audiences, and thereby generate a bigger bang for its limited marketing bucks. For example, by consistently focusing on values and competencies associated with providing high-quality family entertainment, Disney has created an identity that helps stimulate customer demand across a wide range of product offerings—from movies to TV programs to licensed merchandise to theme parks and cruise ships.

Corporate Branding Strategy—When Does a Strong Corporate Brand Make Sense?

Before a company's reputation and corporate image can have any impact—either positive or negative—on customers' purchase decisions, those customers must be aware of which specific product or service offerings are sponsored by the company. This is where the firm's corporate branding strategy enters the picture. Essentially, a firm might pursue one of three options concerning the corporate brand:[33]

1. The corporate brand (typically the company's own name and logo) might serve as the brand name of all or most of the firm's products in markets around the world, as is the case with many high-tech (e.g., Cisco Systems, Siemens, IBM, Caterpillar) and service (e.g., British Airways, Amazon.com, McDonald's, Hilton hotels) companies.

2. The firm might adopt a dual branding strategy in which each offering carries both a corporate identifier and an individual product brand. Examples include Microsoft software products (e.g., Microsoft Windows, Microsoft Word, etc.) and Ford automobiles (Ford Taurus, Ford Explorer, etc.)

3. Finally, each product offering might be given a unique brand and identity—perhaps even different brands across different global markets—while the identity of the source company is de-emphasized or hidden. This is the strategy pursued by Procter and Gamble and many other consumer package goods firms.

The question is, When does it make sense to emphasize—and seek to gain synergy from—a strong corporate identity and brand name in a company's branding strategy? Surprisingly, this question has not been subjected to much empirical research. However, some of the conditions favoring a dominant corporate brand are rather obvious. For instance, the corporate brand will not add much value to the firm's offerings unless the company has a strong and favorable image and reputation among potential customers in at least most of its target markets. Thus, the 3M Company features the 3M logo prominently on virtually all of its 70,000 products because the firm's reputation for innovativeness and reliability is perceived positively by many of its potential customers regardless of what they are buying.

A related point is that a strong corporate brand makes most sense when company-level competencies or resources are primarily responsible for generating the benefits and value customers receive from its various individual offerings. For example, many service organizations (e.g., McDonald's, Disney, Marriott, etc.) emphasize their corporate brands. This is due, in part, to the fact that services are relatively intangible and much of their value is directly generated by the actions of company personnel and facilitated by other firm-specific resources, such as its physical facilities, employee training and reward programs, quality control systems, and the like.

Finally, a recent exploratory study based on interviews with managers in 11 Fortune 500 companies suggests that a firm is more likely to emphasize a strong corporate brand when its various product offerings are closely interrelated, either in terms of having similar positionings in the market or cross-product elasticities that might be leveraged to encourage customers to buy multiple products from the firm.[34] The study also found that firms with strong corporate brands tended to have more centralized decision-making structures where top management made more of the marketing strategy decisions. The obvious question, of course, is whether a firm's decision-making structure influences brand strategy, or vice versa. We will explore such organization design issues and their marketing strategy implications in more detail later in Chapter 13.

Synergy from Shared Resources

A second potential source of corporate synergy is inherent in sharing operational resources, facilities, and functions across business units. For instance, two or more businesses might produce products in a common plant or use a single salesforce to contact common customers. When such sharing helps increase economies of scale or experience-curve effects, it can improve the efficiency of each of the businesses involved. However, the sharing of operational facilities and functions may not produce positive synergies for all business units. Such sharing can limit a business's flexibility and reduce its ability to adapt quickly to changing market conditions and opportunities. Thus, a business whose competitive strategy is focused on new-product development and the pursuit of rapidly changing markets may be hindered more than helped when it is forced to share operating resources with other units.[35] For instance, when Frito-Lay attempted to enter the packaged cookie market with its Grandma's line of soft cookies, the company relied on its 10,000 salty-snack route salespeople to distribute the new line to grocery stores. The firm thought its huge and well-established snack salesforce would give its cookies a competitive advantage in gaining shelf space and retailer support. But because those salespeople were paid a commission on their total sales revenue, they were reluctant to take time from their salty-snack products to push the new cookies. The resulting lack of a strong sales effort contributed to Grandma's failure to achieve a sustainable market share.

As we shall see in the next chapter, the type of competitive strategy a business unit chooses to pursue can have a number of implications for corporate-level decisions concerning organizational structure and resource allocation as well as for the marketing strategies and programs employed within the business.

TAKE AWAYS

- A clearly defined corporate mission answers the question "What business(es) should we be in?" It provides guidance to a firm's managers concerning what alternative product categories and market segments fit best with the firm's competencies, resources, and objectives. Mission statements are most useful, therefore, when they are relatively specific concerning *both* the customer groups and the products or technologies on which the firm will concentrate.

- Unethical behavior by a firm's employees can damage the trust between a firm and its suppliers and customers, thereby disrupting the development of long-

term relationships and reducing sales and profits over time.

- In the long term, the value a firm generates for its shareholders and the value it delivers to its customers converge. A firm can continue to provide attractive returns to shareholders only so long as it satisfies and retains its customers.

- The four major paths to corporate growth—market penetration, market development, product development, and diversification strategies—imply differences in a firm's strategic scope, require different competencies and marketing actions, and involve different types and amounts of risk. Decisions about which path(s) to pursue should consider all of these factors.

- A strong corporate brand can create synergy across a firm's various product offerings, but only if potential customers are aware that the company possesses competencies or values that (1) are likely to enhance the

value they receive from the firm's goods and services and (2) differentiate the company from its competitors.

- Self-diagnostic questions to test your ability to apply the concepts in this chapter can be found at this book's website at **www.mhhe.com/walker.**

ENDNOTES

1. This case example is based on information found in Dan Brekke, "The Future Is Now—or Never," *New York Times Magazine,* January 23, 2000, pp. 30–33, and at the company's website, **www.redenvelope.com.**

2. John A. Byrne, "PepsiCo's New Formula," *Business Week,* April 10, 2000, pp. 172–84.

3. Theodore Levitt, "Marketing Myopia," *Harvard Business Review,* July–August 1960, pp. 455–56.

4. "Good Grief," *The Economist,* April 8, 1995, p. 57; and "Doing Well by Doing Good," *The Economist,* April 22, 2000, pp. 65–67.

5. "Doing Well by Doing Good," p. 66.

6. Robert A. Cooke, *Ethics in Business: A Perspective* (Chicago: Arthur Andersen, 1988).

7. I. Fredrick Trawick, John E. Swan, Gail W. McGee, and David R. Rink, "Influence of Buyer Ethics and Salesperson Behavior on Intention to Choose a Supplier," *Journal of the Academy of Marketing Science* 19 (Winter 1991), pp. 17–23.

8. Dawn Bryan, "Using Gifts to Make the Sale," *Sales & Marketing Management,* September 1989, pp. 48–53. See also "The Destructive Cost of Greasing Palms," *Business Week,* December 6, 1993, pp. 133–38.

9. Alfred Rappaport, *Creating Shareholder Value: The New Standard for Business Performance* (New York: Free Press, 1986), chap. 1; and Shawn Tully, "America's Best Wealth Creators," *Fortune,* November 28, 1994, pp. 143–62.

10. Tully, "America's Best Wealth Creators," p. 143.

11. Bradley T. Gale and Donald J. Swire, "The Tricky Business of Measuring Wealth," *Planning Review,* March–April 1988, pp. 14–17, 47.

12. Patrick Barwise, Paul R. Marsh, and Robin Wensley, "Must Finance and Strategy Clash?" *Harvard Business Review,* September–October 1989, pp. 85–90; and George S. Day and Liam Fahey, "Putting Strategy into Shareholder Value Analysis," *Harvard Business Review,* March–April 1990, pp. 156–62.

13. "Debate: Duking It Out over EVA," *Fortune,* August 4, 1997, p. 232.

14. Y. K. Shetty, "New Look at Corporate Goals," *California Management Review* 12 (Winter 1979), pp. 71–79; see also Robert S. Kaplan and David P. Norton, "Using the Balanced Scorecard as a Strategic Management System," *Harvard Business Review* 74 (January–February 1996), pp. 75–85.

15. Gordon Donaldson, *Managing Corporate Wealth* (New York: Praeger, 1984). See also Kaplan and Norton, "Using the Balanced Scorecard," and Rajendra K. Srivastava, Tasadduq A. Shervani, and Liam Fahey, "Marketing, Business Processes, and Shareholder Value: An Organizationally Embedded View of Marketing Activities and the Discipline of Marketing," *Journal of Marketing* 63 (Special Issue 1999), pp. 168–79.

16. Daniel P. Finkelman, "Crossing the 'Zone of Indifference,' " *Marketing Management* 2, no. 3 (1993), pp. 22–31.

17. Heather Green, "Shakeout: E–tailers," *Business Week,* May 15, 2000, pp. EB102–108.

18. "GE's Brave New World," *Business Week,* November 8, 1993, pp. 64–70.

19. Jennifer L. Schenker, "The Future Is Now," *Time,* April 10, 2000, pp. 85–86.

20. Robert D. Buzzell and Bradley T. Gale, *The PIMS Principles: Linking Strategy to Performance* (New York: Free Press, 1987), chap. 8.

21. For a more comprehensive review of the evidence concerning the effects of diversification on firm performance, see Roger A. Kerin, Vijay Mahajan, and P. Rajan Varadarajan, *Contemporary Perspectives on Strategic Market Planning* (Boston: Allyn and Bacon, 1990), chap. 6.

22. For example, see Ravi S. Achrol and Philip Kotler, "Marketing in the Network Economy," *Journal of Marketing* 63 (Special Issue 1999), pp. 146–63.

23. Garry McWilliams, "Compaq at the Crossroads," *Business Week,* July 22, 1996, pp. 70–72.

24. Robert Jacobson argues that market share and profitability are joint outcomes from successful strategies and, further, that management skills likely have the greatest impact on profitability. See "Distinguishing Among Competing Theories of the Market Share Effect," *Journal of Marketing* 52 (October 1988), pp. 68–80.

25. Yoram Wind, Vijay Mahajan, and Donald J. Swire, "An Empirical Comparison of Standardized Portfolio Models," *Journal of Marketing* 47 (Spring 1983), pp. 89–99.

26. For a more detailed discussion of the uses and limitations of multifactor portfolio models, see Kerin, Mahajan, and Varadarajan, *Contemporary Perspectives on Strategic Market Planning,* chap. 3.

27. The discounted cash flow model is the approach focused on in this chapter. It is detailed in Alfred Rappaport, *Creating Shareholder Value: A New Standard for Business Performance* (New York: Free Press, 1986).

28. For a detailed discussion of the shortcomings of accounting data for determining the value created by a strategy, see Rappaport, *Creating Shareholder Value,* chap. 2.

29. For a more detailed discussion of EVA and some practical examples, see Shawn Tully, "The Real Key to Creating Wealth," *Fortune,* September 20, 1993, pp. 38–50; and Terrence P. Pare, "The New Champ of Wealth Creation," *Fortune,* September 18, 1995, pp. 131–32.

30. A more in-depth discussion of the forecasts and other procedures used in value-based planning can be found in Rappaport, *Creating Shareholder Value,* or Kerin, Mahajan, and Varadarajan, *Contemporary Perspectives on Strategic Market Planning,* chap. 9.

31. The limitations of value-based planning are discussed in more detail in George S. Day and Liam Fahey, "Putting Strategy into Shareholder Value Analysis," *Harvard Business Review,* March–April, 1990, pp. 156–62.

32. Wally Olins, *Corporate Identity* (Cambridge, MA: Harvard Business School Press, 1993).

33. For a more detailed typology of brand strategies or "architectures," see David A. Aaker and Erich Joachimsthaler, *Brand Leadership* (New York: Free Press, 2000).

34. Gabriel J. Biehal and Daniel A. Sheinin, *Building Corporate Brands: An Exploratory Study,* Report 01–100 (Cambridge, MA: Marketing Science Institute, 2001). See also Aaker and Joachimthaler, *Brand Leadership.*

35. Robert W. Ruekert and Orville C. Walker Jr., *Shared Marketing Programs and the Performance of Different Business Strategies,* Report 91–100 (Cambridge, MA: Marketing Science Institute, 1991).

CHAPTER THREE

BUSINESS STRATEGIES AND THEIR MARKETING IMPLICATIONS

Business Strategies and Marketing Programs at 3M[1]

THE MINNESOTA MINING AND Manufacturing Company, better known as 3M, began manufacturing sandpaper nearly a century ago. Today it is the leader in dozens of technical areas from fluorochemistry to fiber optics. The firm makes more than 60,000 different products, which generated $16.7 billion in global sales in 2000. The company produced $3.1 billion in operating income, for more than a 19 percent return on invested capital.

As you might expect of a firm with so many products, 3M is organized into a large number of strategic business units (SBUs). The company contains more than 40 such SBUs or product divisions organized into six market sectors:

- The Industrial Sector makes a variety of tapes, abrasives, and adhesives for industrial applications ranging from electronics to the auto industry.

- The Transportation, Graphics, and Safety Sector produces such things as reflective materials for traffic signs, respirators for worker safety, and materials for commercial graphics.

- The Health Care Sector markets a variety of medical, surgical, pharmaceutical, and dental products and services.

- The Consumer and Office Sector offers products for homes and offices, such as Post-it brand repositionable notes and Scotch brand tapes.

- The Electro and Communications Sector supplies connecting, splicing, and protective products for electronics and telecommunications markets.

- The Specialty Materials Sector provides fluorothermoplastics and fluorothermopolymers for a variety of applications from packaging to electronics.

While 3M has acquired many smaller firms over the years, its growth strategy has focused primarily on internal new product development, emphasizing both improved products for existing customers and new products for new markets. One formal objective assigned to every business unit is to obtain at least 30 percent of annual sales from products introduced within the past four years. The company supports its growth strategy with an

R&D budget of more than $1 billion, almost 7 percent of total revenues.

The company also pursues growth through the aggressive development of foreign markets for its many products. A seventh organizational sector is responsible for coordinating the firm's marketing efforts across countries. In 2000, 3M attained $9 billion in sales—53 percent of its total revenue—from outside the United States.

Differences in customer needs and life-cycle stages across industries, however, lead 3M's various business units to pursue their growth objectives in different ways. The Industrial Tape Division within the Industrial Sector, for example, operates in an industry where both the product technologies and the customer segments are relatively mature and stable. Growth in this group results from extending the scope of adhesive technology (for instance, attaching weather-stripping to auto doors), product improvements and line extensions targeted at existing customers, and expansion into global markets.

In contrast, the firm's Drug Delivery Systems Division within the Health Care Sector develops new medical applications for emerging technologies developed in 3M's many R&D labs. It sells a variety of technologies for the delivery of medications that are inhaled or absorbed through the skin. Most of the unit's growth comes from developing new products, often through alliances with other pharmaceutical firms, aimed at new markets.

The competitive strategies of 3M's various business units also differ. For instance, the industrial tape unit is primarily concerned with maintaining its commanding market share in existing markets while preserving or even improving its profitability. Its competitive strategy is to differentiate itself from competitors on the basis of product quality and excellent customer service.

But the drug delivery systems unit's strategy is to avoid head-to-head competitive battles by being the technological leader and introducing a stream of unique new products. To be successful, though, the unit must devote substantial resources to R&D and to the stimulation of primary demand. Thus, its main objective is volume growth; and it must sometimes sacrifice short-run profitability to fund the product development and marketing efforts needed to accomplish that goal.

These differences in competitive strategy, in turn, influence the strategic marketing programs within the various business units. For instance, the firm spends little on advertising or sales promotion for its mature industrial tape products. However, it does maintain a large, well-trained technical salesforce that provides valuable problem-solving assistance and other services to customers and informed feedback to the firm's R&D personnel about potential new applications and product improvements.

In contrast, the pioneering nature of the drug delivery unit's technologies calls for more extensive promotion to attract potential alliance partners, develop awareness among prescribing physicians, and stimulate primary demand. Consequently, the unit devotes a relatively large portion of its revenues to advertising in technical journals aimed at the pharmaceutical industry, physicians, and other medical professionals. It also supports a well-trained salesforce, but those salespeople spend much of their time demonstrating new technologies and building relationships with drug manufacturers who are prospective customers and partners.

STRATEGIC CHALLENGES ADDRESSED IN CHAPTER 3

The situation at 3M illustrates that large firms with multiple businesses usually have a hierarchy of strategies extending from the corporate level down to the individual product-market entry. As we saw in Chapter 2, corporate strategy addresses such issues as the firm's mission and scope and the directions it will pursue for future growth. Thus, 3M's corporate growth strategy focuses primarily on developing new products and new applications for emerging technologies.

The major strategic question addressed at the business-unit level is, How should we compete in this business? For instance, 3M's industrial tape unit attempts to maintain its commanding market share and high profitability by differentiating itself on the basis of high product quality and good customer service. The drug delivery unit, on the other hand, seeks high growth via aggressive new product and market development.

Finally, the strategic marketing program for each product-market entry within a business unit attempts to allocate marketing resources and activities in a manner appropriate for accomplishing the business unit's objectives. Thus, most of the strategic marketing programs within 3M's drug delivery unit involve relatively large expenditures for marketing research and introductory advertising and promotion campaigns aimed at achieving sales growth.

One key reason for 3M's continuing success is that all three levels of strategy within the company have usually been characterized by good internal and external consistency, or **strategic fit.** The company's managers have done a good job of monitoring and adapting their strategies to the market opportunities, technological advances, and competitive threats in the company's external environment. The firm's marketing and sales managers play critical roles both in developing market-oriented strategies for individual products and in influencing and helping to formulate corporate and business-level strategies that are responsive to environmental conditions. At the same time, those strategies are usually internally compatible. Each strategy fits with those at other levels as well as with the unique competitive strengths and competencies of the relevant business unit and the company as a whole.[2]

Recent empirical evidence shows that when there is a good fit between a business's competitive strategy and the strategic marketing programs of its various product or service offerings, the business will achieve better results in terms of sales growth, market share, and profitability than when the two levels of strategy are inconsistent with one another.[3] Therefore, this chapter focuses on what marketing decision makers can and should do to help ensure that the strategic marketing plans they develop are appropriate in light of the available resources and competitive thrust of the business that is their organizational home.

STRATEGIC ISSUE

When there is a good fit between a business's competitive strategy and the strategic marketing programs of its various product or service offerings, the business will achieve better results.

First, we briefly examine the strategic decisions that must be made at the business level, including how business units should be designed. We'll pay particular attention to the question of how a business might choose to compete. What generic competitive strategies might a business pursue, and in what environmental circumstances is each strategy most appropriate? We'll also explore whether the same kinds of competitive strategies are relevant for small, single-business organizations and entrepreneurial start-ups as for large multi-SBU firms such as 3M and whether technological shifts, such as the growth of e-commerce, are likely to give birth to new competitive strategies or make some old ones obsolete.

Next, we examine the interrelationships between different business competitive strategies and elements of the strategic marketing programs for the various products within the business. How does—or should—a particular competitive strategy influence or constrain marketing programs for the business's product offerings? And what happens if the market positioning or specific marketing actions that would be most effective for appealing to a product's target customers do not fit very well with the competitive strategy of the larger business unit? For example, as some of the products made by the drug delivery unit at 3M—such as the inhalers they make for delivering asthma medications—become well-established and mature, they may require marketing actions (e.g., more competitive pricing) that are not consistent with the aggressive product development strategy of the business unit. What should 3M and the marketing manager responsible for inhalers do under such circumstances?

STRATEGIC DECISIONS AT THE BUSINESS-UNIT LEVEL

The components of a firm engaged in multiple industries or businesses are typically called **strategic business units,** or **SBUs.** Managers within each of these business units decide which objectives, markets, and competitive strategies to pursue. Top-level corporate managers typically reserve the right to review and approve such decisions to ensure their overall consistency with the company's mission, objectives, and the allocation of resources across SBUs in its portfolio. However, SBU-level managers, particularly those in marketing and sales, bear the primary responsibility for collecting and analyzing relevant information and generating appropriate strategies for their businesses. Those managers are more familiar with a given SBU's products, customers, and competitors and are responsible for successfully implementing the strategy. The rationale for breaking larger firms into semi-autonomous SBUs usually stems from a market-oriented desire to move strategic decision making closer to the customers the business is trying to reach.

The first step in developing business-level strategies, then, is for the firm to decide how to divide itself into SBUs. The managers in each SBU must then make recommendations about (*a*) the unit's objectives, (*b*) the scope of its target customers and offerings, (*c*) which broad competitive strategy to pursue to build a competitive advantage in its product-markets, and (*d*) how resources should be allocated across its product-market entries and functional departments.

How Should Strategic Business Units Be Designed?

Ideally, strategic business units have the following characteristics:

- *A homogeneous set of markets to serve with a limited number of related technologies.* Minimizing diversity across an SBU's product-market entries enables the unit's manager to better formulate and implement a coherent and internally consistent business strategy.

- *A unique set of product-markets,* in the sense that no other SBU within the firm competes for the same customers with similar products. Thus, the firm avoids duplication of effort and maximizes economies of scale within its SBUs.

- *Control over those factors necessary for successful performance,* such as production, R&D and engineering, marketing, and distribution. This does not mean an SBU should not share resources, such as a manufacturing plant or a salesforce, with one or more other business units. But the SBU should determine how its share of the joint resource is used to effectively carry out its strategy.

- *Responsibility for their own profitability.*

As you might expect, firms do not always meet all of these ideals when designing business units. There are usually trade-offs between having many small homogeneous SBUs versus large but fewer SBUs that managers can more easily supervise.

What criteria should managers use to decide how product-markets should be clustered into a business unit? The three dimensions that define the scope and mission of the entire corporation also define individual SBUs:

1. *Technical compatibility,* particularly with respect to product technologies and operational requirements, such as the use of similar production facilities and engineering skills.

2. Similarity in the *customer needs* or the product benefits sought by customers in the target markets.

3. Similarity in the *personal characteristics* or behavior patterns of customers in the target markets.

In practice, the choice is often between technical/operational compatibility on the one hand and customer homogeneity on the other. Frequently management defines SBUs by product-markets requiring similar technologies, production facilities, and employee skills. This minimizes the coordination problems involved in administering the unit and increases its ability to focus on one or a few critical competencies.

In some firms, however, the marketing synergies gained from coordinating technically different products aimed at the same customer need or market segment outweigh operational considerations. In these firms, managers group product-market entries into SBUs based on similarities across customers or distribution systems. For instance, 3M's Medical Products unit includes a wide range of products involving very different technologies and production processes. They are grouped within the same business unit, though, because all address health needs, are marketed to physicians and other health professionals, and can be sold through a common salesforce and distribution system.

Business-Unit Objectives

Companies break down corporate objectives into subobjectives for each SBU. In most cases, those subobjectives vary across SBUs according to the attractiveness of their industries, the strength of their competitive positions within those industries, and resource allocation decisions by corporate management. For example, managers may assign an SBU in a rapidly growing industry relatively high volume and share-growth objectives but lower ROI objectives than an SBU with a large share in a mature industry.

A similar process of breaking down overall SBU objectives into a set of subobjectives should occur for each product-market entry within the unit. Those subobjectives obviously must reflect the SBU's overall objectives; but once again they may vary across product-market entries according to the attractiveness and growth potential of individual market segments and the competitive strengths of the company's product in each market. For example, when 3M's consumer products group first introduced its Scotch-Brite Never Rust soap pads—a new form of scouring pad that will never rust or splinter because it is made from recycled plastic beverage bottles—its objective was to capture a major share of the $100 million soap pad market from well-entrenched competitive brands such as SOS and Brillo. 3M wanted to maximize Never Rust's volume growth and market share even if the new line did not break even for several years. Consequently, the firm's top managers approved a major investment in a new plant and a substantial introductory advertising budget. At the same time, though, the consumer group maintained high profitability goals for its other established products—such as Scotch brand Magic Transparent Tape and Post-it brand notes—to provide the cash required for Never Rust's introduction and preserve the group's overall profit level.[4]

Allocating Resources within the Business Unit

Once an SBU's objectives and budget have been approved at the corporate level, its managers must decide how the available resources should be allocated across the unit's various product-market entries. Because this allocation process is quite similar to allocating corporate resources across SBUs, many firms use similar economic value, value-based planning, or portfolio analysis tools for both. Of course, at the SBU level managers must determine the attractiveness of individual target markets, the competitive position of their products within those markets, and the cash flows each product entry will likely generate rather than analyzing industry attractiveness and the overall competitive strengths of the firm.

Unfortunately, value-based planning is not as useful a tool for evaluating alternative resource allocations across product-market entries as it is for evaluating allocations across SBUs. This is because the product-market entries within a business unit often share the benefits of common investments and the costs of functional activities, as when multiple products are produced in the same plant or sold by the same salesforce. The difficulty of deciding what portion of such common investments and shared costs should be assigned to specific products increases the difficulty of applying a discounted cash flow analysis at the product-market level. As we shall see in Chapter 14, some firms have adopted activity-based costing systems in an attempt to resolve such problems,[5] but many difficulties remain.

HOW DO BUSINESSES COMPETE?

As mentioned, the essential strategic question at the SBU level is, How are we going to compete in this business? Thus, business strategies are primarily concerned with allocating resources across functional activities and product-markets to give the unit a sustainable advantage over its competitors. Of course, the unit's core competencies and resources, together with the customer and competitive characteristics of its industry, determine the viability of any particular competitive strategy.[6] The 3M drug delivery unit's strategy of gaining revenue growth via technological leadership and aggressive new product and market development, for instance, will continue to work only if the firm's R&D, engineering, and marketing competencies and resources continue to outweigh those of its competitors. Consequently, most SBUs pursue a single competitive strategy—one that best fits their market environments and competitive strengths—across all or most of the product-markets in which they compete. The question is, What alternative strategies are available to a business unit? What are the basic, or generic, competitive strategies most SBUs choose to pursue?

Generic Business-Level Competitive Strategies

Researchers have identified general categories of business-level competitive strategies based on overall patterns of purpose, practice, and performance in different businesses. Michael Porter distinguishes three strategies—or competitive positions—that businesses pursue to gain and maintain competitive advantages in their various product-markets: (1) *overall cost leadership;* (2) *differentiation*—building customer perceptions of superior product quality, design, or service; and (3) *focus,* in which the business avoids direct confrontation with its major competitors by concentrating on narrowly defined market niches. Porter describes firms that lack a distinctive strategy as being "stuck in the middle" and predicts that they will perform poorly.[7]

Robert Miles and Charles Snow identified another set of business strategies based on a business's intended rate of product-market development (new product development, penetration of new markets).[8] They classify business units into four strategic types: *prospectors, defenders, analyzers,* and *reactors.* Exhibit 3.1 describes each of these business strategies briefly. As you can see, businesses pursuing a *prospector strategy* focus on growth through the development of new products and markets. 3M's drug delivery business unit illustrates this. *Defender businesses* concentrate on maintaining their positions in

Exhibit 3.1

DEFINITIONS OF MILES AND SNOW'S FOUR BUSINESS STRATEGIES

Prospector

- Operates within a broad product-market domain that undergoes periodic redefinition.
- Values being a "first mover" in new product and market areas, even if not all of these efforts prove to be highly profitable.
- Responds rapidly to early signals concerning areas of opportunity, and these responses often lead to new rounds of competitive actions.
- Competes primarily by stimulating and meeting new market opportunities, but may not maintain strength over time in all markets it enters.

Defender

- Attempts to locate and maintain a secure position in relatively stable product or service areas.
- Offers relatively limited range of products or services compared with competitors.
- Tries to protect its domain by offering lower prices, higher quality, or better service than competitors.
- Usually not at the forefront of technological/new product development in its industry; tends to ignore industry changes not directly related to its area of operation.

Analyzer

- An intermediate type; makes fewer and slower product-market changes than prospectors, but is less committed to stability and efficiency than defenders.
- Attempts to maintain a stable, limited line of products or services, but carefully follows a selected set of promising new developments in its industry.
- Seldom a first mover, but often a second or third entrant in product-markets related to its existing market base—often with a lower cost or higher-quality product or service offering.

Reactor

- Lacks any well-defined competitive strategy.
- Does not have as consistent a product-market orientation as its competitors.
- Not as willing to assume the risks of new product or market development as its competitors.
- Not as aggressive in marketing established products as some competitors.
- Responds primarily when it is forced to by environmental pressures.

Source: Adapted from R. E. Miles and C. C. Snow, *Organizational Strategy, Structure, and Process* (New York: McGraw-Hill, 1978).

established product-markets while paying less attention to new product development, as is the case with 3M's industrial tape business unit. The *analyzer strategy* falls in between these two. An analyzer business attempts to maintain a strong position in its core product-market(s) but also seeks to expand into new—usually closely related—product-markets. Finally, *reactors* are businesses with no clearly defined strategy.

Even though both the Porter and Miles and Snow typologies have received popular acceptance and research support, neither is complete by itself. For example, a *defender business unit* could pursue a variety of competitive approaches to protect its market position, such as offering the lowest cost or differentiating itself on quality or service. Thus, we have combined the two typologies in Exhibit 3.2 to provide a more comprehensive overview of business strategies. Exhibit 3.2 classifies business strategies on two primary dimensions: the unit's desired rate of product-market development (expansion) and the unit's intended method of competing in its established product-markets.

Each of our strategic categories could be further subdivided according to whether a business applies the strategy across a broadly defined product-market domain or concentrates

Exhibit 3.2

COMBINED TYPOLOGY OF BUSINESS-LEVEL COMPETITIVE STRATEGIES

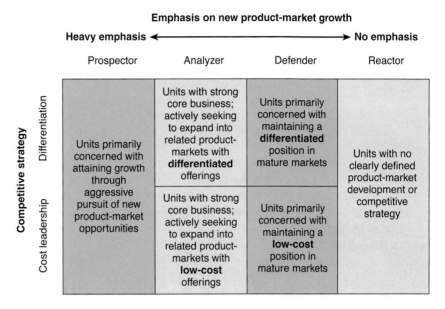

on a narrowly defined segment where it hopes to avoid direct confrontation with major competitors (the *focus* strategy of Porter). Although this distinction is useful, it is more germane to a discussion of the business's target market strategy (as discussed in Chapter 7) than to its competitive strategy. Most businesses compete in a reasonably consistent way across all of their product-markets, whether their domain is broad or narrow.

Exhibit 3.2 describes only six business strategies, rather than the eight that one might expect. We view reactor and prospector business units as two homogeneous categories.

Evidence suggests that a substantial portion of businesses fall into the reactor category. One study, for instance, found that 50 out of 232 businesses examined could be classified as reactors.[9] By definition, however, such businesses do not have well-defined or consistent approaches either to new product development or to ways of competing in existing product-markets. In other words, reactors have no clear competitive strategy. Therefore, we will largely ignore them during the rest of this discussion.

Prospectors are also shown as a single strategic category in Exhibit 3.2 because the desire for rapid new product or market development is the overriding aspect of their strategy. There is little need for a prospector business to consider how it will compete in the new product-markets it develops because it will face little or no competition—at least not until those markets become established and other firms begin to enter.

Do the Same Competitive Strategies Work for Single-Business Firms and Start-ups?

Even small firms with a single business and only a few related product offerings or start-ups with a single product must decide how they will compete. And just like an SBU in a major corporation such as 3M, their competitive strategies should be tailored to their unique resources and competencies and aimed at securing a sustainable advantage over existing or potential competitors. Therefore, the same set of generic competitive strategies is just as appropriate for small firms as for business units within larger ones. For example, Jack Daniels defends its commanding share of the prestige segment of the very mature North American whiskey market by stressing the long tradition of its production process and the superior quality of its Kentucky bourbon: in other words, by pursuing a very effective differentiated defender strategy.

However, there is one important difference between single-business and multi-SBU organizations. In smaller single-business firms the distinction between business-level competitive strategy and marketing strategy tends to blur and the two strategies blend into one. Jack Daniels' competitive strategy, for instance, is essentially the same as the market positioning for its primary product: a product that offers higher quality than competing brands because it is made with old-fashioned methods and ingredients that have not changed for more than a century. And the elements of its marketing strategy all flow from that competitive/market positioning: a premium price, advertising that stresses the product's long history and traditional production practices, old-fashioned packaging, and the like.

Another difference applies to entrepreneurial start-ups. Most start-ups do not have the resources to succeed by competing as a "me-too" competitor in a well-established and highly competitive product market. By definition they do not have an established market position to defend. Therefore, while the taxonomy of competitive strategies is still relevant to entrepreneurial firms, in reality most of them—at least those that stand a reasonable chance of success— begin life as prospectors. They compete primarily by developing a unique product or service that meets the needs and preferences of a customer segment that is not being well served by established competitors.

STRATEGIC ISSUE

While the taxonomy of competitive strategies is still relevant to entrepreneurial firms, in reality most of them—at least those that stand a reasonable chance of success— begin life as prospectors.

The critical question for a start-up firm, though, is, What happens when the new product matures and competitors arrive on the scene? Should the firm continue to focus on developing a stream of new products to stay a step ahead of the competition, even though such a strategy would mean paying less attention to its successful first entry? Should the firm switch to a defender strategy to leverage its initial success, even though that would mean competing head to head with other, probably bigger, competitors? Should the firm create two separate SBUs with different competitive strategies, even though it is small and resources are limited? These are the kinds of questions that arise when the market and competitive conditions facing a product entry change. The entry's marketing strategy should be adjusted in response to such changes, but that may make it less compatible with the overall competitive strategy of the business, which is typically harder to change in the short term. These and similar issues related to strategic change are examined in more detail later in this chapter.

Do the Same Competitive Strategies Work for Service Businesses?

What is a service? Basically, *services* can be thought of as **intangibles** and *goods* as **tangibles.** The former can rarely be experienced in advance of the sale, while the latter can be experienced, even tested, before purchase.[10] Using this distinction, a **service** can be defined as "any activity or benefit that one party can offer to another that is essentially intangible and that does not result in the ownership of anything. Its production may or may not be tied to a physical product."[11]

We typically associate services with nonmanufacturing businesses, even though service is often an indispensable part of a goods producer's offering. Services such as applications engineering, system design, delivery, installation, training, and maintenance can be crucial for building long-term relationships between manufacturers and their customers, particularly in consumer durable and industrial products businesses. Thus, almost all businesses are engaged in service to some extent.

Many organizations are concerned with producing and marketing a service as their primary offering rather than as an adjunct to a physical product. These organizations include public-sector and not-for-profit service organizations, such as churches, hospitals, universities, and arts organizations. The crucial question is this: To be successful, must service organizations employ different competitive strategies than goods manufacturers?

The framework we used to classify business-level competitive strategies in Exhibit 3.2 is equally valid for service businesses. Some service firms, such as Super 8 or Days Inn in the lodging industry, attempt to minimize costs and compete largely with low prices. Other firms, like Marriott, differentiate their offerings on the basis of high service quality or unique benefits. Similarly, some service businesses adopt prospector strategies and aggressively pursue the development of new offerings or markets. For instance, American Express's Travel Related Services Division has developed a variety of new services tailored to specific segments of the firm's credit-card holders. Other service businesses focus narrowly on defending established positions in current markets. Still others can best be described as analyzers pursuing both established and new markets. For instance, Cable & Wireless Communications, a long-distance carrier whose competitive strategy is discussed in Exhibit 3.3, might best be described as a differentiated analyzer.

A study of the banking industry provides empirical evidence that service businesses actually do pursue the same types of competitive strategies as goods producers. The 329 bank CEOs who responded to the survey had little trouble categorizing their institution's competitive strategies into one of Miles and Snow's four types. Fifty-four of the executives reported that their banks were prospectors, 87 identified their firms as analyzers, 157 as defenders, and 31 as reactors.[12]

Exhibit 3.3   Cable & Wireless Communications—Differentiation through Customer Relationships

Cable & Wireless Communications, the U.S. subsidiary of a British telecommunications firm, competes in the relatively mature and highly competitive business of providing long-distance services to business customers. Company executives knew long ago that their operation could not compete on price with larger competitors like AT&T or MCI. So they sought to differentiate themselves—and to defend their established customer base—by providing the best customer support in the industry. As a result, Cable & Wireless turned itself from a mundane commodity business into a sophisticated telemanager and partner with its customers.

Part of Cable & Wireless's success was the result of good target market selection. The firm focused on winning and holding on to small or medium-sized business clients with monthly billings of $500 to $15,000. For such small businesses, the company's 500 U.S. salespeople, working out of 36 regional offices, acted like telecommunications managers. Corporations too small to hire their own telecom specialists valued the advice and expertise Cable & Wireless people could offer, and top management gave those salespeople substantial autonomy to tailor their offerings and advice to each customer's needs.

Within its target small-business segment, however, Cable & Wireless was not content to merely maintain relationships with established customers. The firm pursued a differentiated analyzer strategy by also devoting substantial effort and resources to developing and pitching specialized services aimed at attracting new customers from new industry segments. For example, the company gained substantial business from smaller firms within the legal profession by developing functions that appealed specifically to lawyers, such as innovative ways to track and bill calls linked to specific client accounts.

Source: From *The Discipline of Market Leaders* by Michael Treacy and Fred Wiersema. Copyright 1995 by Michael Treacy and Fred Wiersema. Reprinted by permission of Perseus Books Publishers, a member of Perseus Books, L.L.C.

Do the Same Competitive Strategies Work for Global Competitors?

In terms of the strategies described in Exhibit 3.2, businesses that compete in multiple global markets almost always pursue one of the two types of analyzer strategy. They must continue to strengthen and defend their competitive position in their home country—and perhaps in other countries where they are well established—while simultaneously pursuing expansion and growth in new international markets.

When examined on a country-by-country basis, however, the same business unit might be viewed as pursuing different competitive strategies in different countries. For instance, while 3M's industrial tape group competes like a differentiated defender in the United States, Canada, and some European countries where it has established large market shares, it competes more like a prospector when attempting to open and develop new markets in emerging economies such as China and Mexico. This suggests that a single SBU may need to engage in different functional activities (including different strategic marketing programs)—and perhaps even adopt different organizational structures to implement those activities—across the various countries in which it competes. McDonald's faces this kind of situation across the 94 countries in which it operates, as discussed in Exhibit 3.4.

Will the Internet Change Everything?

Some analysts argue that the Internet will change the way firms compete. The Internet makes it easier for buyers and sellers to compare prices, reduces the number of middlemen necessary between manufacturers and end users, cuts transaction costs, improves the functioning of the price mechanism, and thereby increases competition.[13] One possible outcome of all these changes is that it will be harder for firms to differentiate themselves on any basis other than low price. All the business-level competitive strategies focused on differentiation will become less viable, while firms pursuing low-cost strategies will be more successful.

While we agree that the Internet has increased both efficiency and competitiveness in many product-markets, we doubt that competition will focus exclusively on price. For one thing, innovation is likely to continue—and probably accelerate—in the future. Unique new products and services will continue to emerge and provide a way for the innovator to gain a competitive advantage, at least in the short term. Thus, firms with the resources and competencies necessary to produce a continuing stream of new product or service offerings that appeal to one or more customer segments—that is, to effectively implement a prospector strategy—should be successful regardless of whether they are the lowest-cost producers in their industries. Amazon.com, the largest e-tailer as of early 2001, is generally not the lowest priced.

In addition, the Internet is primarily a communications channel. While it facilitates the dissemination of information, including price information, the goods and services themselves will continue to offer different features and benefits. As customers gather more information from the Internet and become better informed, they are less likely to be swayed by superficial distinctions between brands. But if a firm offers unique benefits that a segment of customers perceive as *meaningful,* it should still be able to differentiate its offering and command a premium price, at least until its competitors offer something similar.

STRATEGIC ISSUE

The Internet will make it easier for firms to customize their offerings and personalize their relationships with their customers.

Finally, the Internet will make it easier for firms to customize their offerings and personalize their relationships with their customers. Such personalization should differentiate the firm from its competitors in the

Exhibit 3.4   McDonald's—Different Strategies in Different Countries

McDonald's now has nearly 29,000 retail outlets serving customers around the world. As you can see from the chart, in 1985 more than three-quarters of all McDonald's restaurants were inside the United States, but by 1999 more than half were outside America.

McDonald's is growing faster overseas in part because the fast-food market is more mature and much more competitive in the United States than in most other nations. Consequently, the firm's competitive strategies—and therefore its prices, marketing costs, and operating margins—tend to be different in other countries than in the United States.

McDonald's holds a commanding 42 percent share of the domestic burger market. The firm's competitive strategy in the United States, then, is that of a differentiated defender intent on preserving its market share position and profitability in the face of slowing demand and increasing competition. Among other things, the company has begun an aggressive campaign to reduce its operating costs by simplifying its restaurant designs, reducing the number of items on the menu, and so on. Some of those cost savings will be reflected in lower prices, while the rest will be plowed back into aggressive advertising and promotion programs. Finally, the firm is attempting to gain more sales and profits from older adults—a segment where McDonald's has not been very strong—by improving product quality via a new "made for you" food preparation system.

Outside the United States, on the other hand, McDonald's faces less organized competition (Pizza Hut is its nearest rival), but the demand for fast food is just beginning to grow. Consequently, the firm must often pursue a prospector strategy focused on building demand among new customers. This helps explain

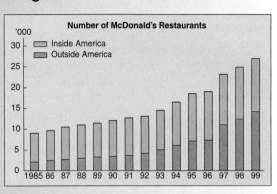

the rapid rate of new restaurant construction outside of the United States. The firm built about 1,800 new outlets in 1999, but only 150 were in the United States. Unfortunately, infrastructure problems in developing markets such as China and Eastern Europe mean that, on average, new restaurants cost much more to build. And to attract new customers in such markets, McDonald's initially has to price its burgers very low. While demand growth and economies of scale usually help individual units turn a profit relatively soon after opening, at the national level McDonald's is often making a rather long-term bet—a bet with the risk of political or economic upheaval.

To help managers in each country adjust to local market and environmental differences, McDonald's gives them great flexibility and autonomy. In every country the pace of expansion—and the strategy for achieving it—is decided locally. And so far those locally developed strategies have been quite successful.

Source: *McDonald's 2000 Annual Report,* found on the company's website at www.mcdonalds.com; and "McWorld," *The Economist,* June 29, 1996, pp. 61–62.

customer's eyes and improve customer loyalty and retention. For instance, over the past few years, the Internet has played a major role in developing logistical alliances among organizational buyers and their suppliers. Consumer goods and services firms, and even Internet portals, also are using the Internet's interactive capabilities to acquire and communicate information and build customer relationships. For example, the My Yahoo! website allows individual consumers to personalize their Web portal in exchange for some basic demographic information. An optional section enables the customer to make choices that enable Yahoo! to customize the kind of news, websites, and information displayed on that person's screen. Such customization helps differentiate Yahoo! in the customer's eyes and increases switching costs.[14]

HOW DO COMPETITIVE STRATEGIES DIFFER FROM ONE ANOTHER?

In Chapter 1 we said that all strategies consist of five components or underlying dimensions: scope (or breadth of strategic domain), goals and objectives, resource deployments, a basis for achieving a sustainable competitive advantage, and synergy. But the generic strategies summarized in Exhibit 3.2 are defined largely by their differences on only one dimension: the nature of the competitive advantage sought. Each strategy also involves some important differences on the other four dimensions—differences that are outlined in Exhibit 3.5 and discussed below. Those differences provide insights concerning the conditions under which each strategy is most appropriate and about the relative importance of different marketing actions in implementing them effectively.

Differences in Scope

Both the breadth and stability of a business's domain are likely to vary with different strategies. This, in turn, can affect the variables the corporation uses to define its various businesses. At one extreme, defender businesses, whether low-cost or differentiated, tend

Exhibit 3.5

HOW BUSINESS STRATEGIES DIFFER IN SCOPE, OBJECTIVES, RESOURCE DEPLOYMENTS, AND SYNERGY

Dimensions	Low-cost defender	Differentiated defender	Prospector	Analyzer
• *Scope*	Mature/stable/ well-defined domain; mature technology and customer segments	Mature/stable/well-defined domain; mature technology and customer segments	Broad/dynamic domains; technology and customer segments not well-established	Mixture of defender and prospector strategies
• *Goals and objectives* Adaptability (new product success)	Very Little	little	Extensive	Mixture of defender and prospector strategies
Effectiveness (increase in market share)	Little	Little	Large	Mixture of defender and prospector strategies
Efficiency (ROI)	High	High	Low	Mixture of defender and prospector strategies
• *Resource deployment*	Generate excess cash (cash cows)	Generate excess cash (cash cows)	Need cash for product development (question marks or stars)	Need cash for product development but less so than do prospectors
• *Synergy*	Need to seek operating synergies to achieve efficiencies	Need to seek operating synergies to achieve efficiencies	Danger in sharing operating facilities and programs— better to share technology/marketing skills	Danger in sharing operating facilities and programs— better to share technology/marketing skills

to operate in relatively well-defined, narrow, and stable domains where both the product technology and the customer segments are mature.

At the other extreme, prospector businesses usually operate in broad and rapidly changing domains where neither the technology nor customer segments are well established. The scope of such businesses often undergoes periodic redefinition. Thus, prospector businesses are typically organized around either a core technology that might lead to the development of products aimed at a broad range of customer segments or a basic customer need that might be met with products based on different technologies. The latter is the approach taken by 3M's drug delivery systems business. Its mission is to satisfy the health needs of a broad range of patients with new products developed from technologies drawn from other business units within the firm.

Analyzer businesses, whether low-cost or differentiated, fall somewhere in between the two extremes. They usually have a well-established core business to defend, and often their domain is primarily focused on that business. However, businesses pursuing this intermediate strategy are often in industries that are still growing or experiencing technological changes. Consequently, they must pay attention to the emergence of new customer segments and/or new product types. As a result, managers must review and adjust the domain of such businesses from time to time.

Differences in Goals and Objectives

Another important difference across generic business-level strategies with particular relevance for the design and implementation of appropriate marketing programs is that different strategies often focus on different objectives. SBU and product-market objectives might be specified on a variety of criteria, but to keep things simple, we focus on only three performance dimensions of major importance to both business-unit and marketing managers:

1. *Effectiveness.* The success of a business's products and programs relative to those of its competitors in the market. Effectiveness is commonly measured by such items as *sales growth* relative to competitors or *changes in market share.*
2. *Efficiency.* The outcomes of a business's programs relative to the resources used in implementing them. Common measures of efficiency are *profitability* as a percent of sales and *return on investment.*
3. *Adaptability.* The business's success in responding over time to changing conditions and opportunities in the environment. Adaptability can be measured in a variety of ways, but the most common ones are the *number of successful new products* introduced relative to those competitors or the *percentage of sales accounted for by products introduced within the last five years.*

However, it is very difficult for any SBU, regardless of its competitive strategy, to simultaneously achieve outstanding performance on even this limited number of dimensions, because they involve substantial trade-offs. Good performance on one dimension often means sacrificing performance on another.[15] For example, developing successful new products or attaining share growth often involves large marketing budgets, substantial up-front investment, high operating costs, and a shaving of profit margins—all of which reduce ROI. This suggests that managers should choose a competitive strategy with a view toward maximizing performance on one or two dimensions, while expecting to sacrifice some level of performance on the others, at least in the short term. Over the longer term, of course, the chosen strategy should promise discounted cash flows that exceed the business's cost of capital and thereby increase shareholder value.

As Exhibit 3.5 indicates, prospector businesses are expected to outperform defenders on both new product development and market-share growth. On the other hand, both defender strategies should lead to better returns on investment. Differentiated defenders likely produce higher returns than low-cost defenders, assuming that the greater expenses involved in maintaining their differentiated positions can be more than offset by the higher margins gained by avoiding the intense price competition low-cost competitors often face. Once again, both low-cost and differentiated analyzer strategies are likely to fall between the two extremes.[16]

Differences in Resource Deployment

Businesses following different strategies also tend to allocate their financial resources differently across product-markets, functional departments, and activities within each functional area. Prospector—and to a lesser degree, analyzer—businesses devote a relatively large proportion of resources to the development of new product-markets. Because such product-markets usually require more cash to develop than they produce short term, businesses pursuing these strategies often need infusions of financial resources from other parts of the corporation. In portfolio terms, they are "question marks" or "stars."

Defenders, on the other hand, focus the bulk of their resources on preserving existing positions in established product-markets. These product-markets are usually profitable; therefore, defender businesses typically generate excess cash to support product and market development efforts in other business units within the firm. They are the "cash cows."

Resource allocations among functional departments and activities within the SBU also vary across businesses pursuing different strategies. For instance, marketing budgets tend to be the largest as a percentage of an SBU's revenues when the business is pursuing a prospector strategy; they tend to be the smallest as a percentage of sales under a low-cost defender strategy. We discuss this in more detail later in this chapter.

Differences in Sources of Synergy

Because different strategies emphasize different methods of competition and different functional activities, a given source of synergy may be more appropriate for some strategies than for others.

At one extreme, the sharing of operating facilities and programs may be an inappropriate approach to gaining synergy for businesses following a prospector strategy. And to a lesser extent, this also may be true for both types of analyzer strategies. Such sharing can reduce an SBU's ability to adapt quickly to changing market demands or competitive threats. Commitments to internally negotiated price structures and materials, as well as the use of joint resources, facilities, and programs, increase interdependence among SBUs and limit their flexibility. It is more appropriate for such businesses to seek synergy through the sharing of a technology, engineering skills, or market knowledge—expertise that can help improve the success rate of their product development efforts. Thus, 3M's drug delivery systems business attempts to find medical applications for new technologies developed in many of the firm's other business units.

At the other extreme, however, low-cost defenders should seek operating synergies that will make them more efficient. Synergies that enable such businesses to increase economies of scale and experience curve effects are particularly desirable. They help reduce unit costs and strengthen the strategy's basis of competitive advantage. The primary means of gaining such operating synergies is through the sharing of resources, facilities, and functional activities across product-market entries within the business unit or across related business units. Emerson Electric, for instance, formed an "operating group" of several otherwise autonomous business units that make different types of electrical motors and tools. By sharing production facilities, marketing activities, and a common salesforce, the group was able to reduce the costs of both per-unit production and marketing.

Deciding When a Strategy Is Appropriate: The Fit between Business Strategies and the Environment

Because different strategies pursue different objectives in different domains with different competitive approaches, they do not all work equally well under the same environmental circumstances. The question is, Which environmental situations are most amenable to the successful pursuit of each type of strategy? Exhibit 3.6 outlines some major market, technological, and competitive conditions—plus a business unit's strengths relative to its competitors—that are most favorable for the successful implementation of each generic business strategy. We next discuss the reasons each strategy fits best with a particular set of environmental conditions.

Appropriate Conditions for a Prospector Strategy

A prospector strategy is particularly well suited to unstable, rapidly changing environments resulting from new technology, shifting customer needs, or both. In either case, such industries, like many involving e-commerce, tend to be at an early stage in their life cycles and offer many opportunities for new product-market entries. Industry structure is often unstable because few competitors are present and their relative market shares can shift rapidly as new products are introduced and new markets develop.

Because they emphasize the development of new products and/or new markets, the most successful prospectors are usually strong in, and devote substantial resources to, two broad areas of competence: first, R&D, product engineering, and other functional areas that identify new technology and convert it into innovative products; second, marketing research, marketing, and sales—functions necessary for the identification and development of new market opportunities.

In some cases, however, even though a prospector business has strong product development and marketing skills, it may lack the resources to maintain its early lead as product-markets grow and attract new competitors. For example, Minnetonka was the pioneer in several health and beauty-aid product categories with brands such as Softsoap liquid soap and Check-Up plaque-fighting toothpaste. However, because competitors such as Procter & Gamble and Colgate-Palmolive introduced competing brands with advertising and promotion budgets much larger than Minnetonka could match, the firm was eventually forced to change its strategy and concentrate on manufacturing products under licenses from larger firms.

Appropriate Conditions for an Analyzer Strategy

The analyzer strategy is a hybrid. On one hand, analyzers are concerned with defending—via low costs or differentiation in quality or service—a strong share position in one or more established product-markets. At the same time, the business must pay attention to new product development to avoid being leapfrogged by competitors with more technologically

Exhibit 3.6

ENVIRONMENTAL FACTORS FAVORABLE TO DIFFERENT BUSINESS STRATEGIES

External factors	Prospector	Analyzer	Differentiated defender	Low-cost defender
Industry and market	Industry in introductory or early growth stage of life cycle; many potential customer segments as yet unidentified and/or undeveloped.	Industry in late growth or early maturity stage of life cycle; one or more product offerings currently targeted at major customer segments, but some potential segments may still be undeveloped.	Industry in maturity or decline stage of life cycle; current offerings targeted at all major segments; sales primarily due to repeat purchases/ replacement demand.	Industry in maturity or decline stage of life cycle; current offerings targeted at all major segments; sales primarily due to repeat purchases/ replacement demand.
Technology	Newly emerging technology; many applications as yet undeveloped.	Basic technology well developed but still evolving; product modifications and improvements—as well as emergence of new competing technologies—still likely.	Basic technology fully developed and stable; few major modifications or improvements likely.	Basic technology fully developed and stable; few major modifications or improvements likely.
Competition	Few established competitors; industry structure still emerging; single competitor holds commanding share of major market segments.	Large number of competitors, but future shakeout likely; industry structure still evolving; one or more competitors hold large shares in major segments but continuing growth may allow rapid changes in relative shares.	Small to moderate number of well-established competitors; industry structure stable, though acquisitions and consolidation possible; maturity of markets means relative shares of competitors tend to be reasonably stable over time.	Small to moderate number of well-established competitors; industry structure stable, though acquisitions and consolidation possible; maturity of markets means relative shares of competitors tend to be reasonably stable over time.
Business's relative strengths	SBU (or parent) has strong R&D, product engineering, and marketing research and marketing capabilities.	SBU (or parent) has good R&D, product engineering, and marketing research capabilities, but not as strong as some competitors'; has either low-cost position or strong sales, marketing, distribution, or service capabilities in one or more segments.	SBU has no outstanding strengths in R&D or product engineering; costs are higher than at least some competitors'; SBU's outstanding strengths are in process engineering and quality control and/or in marketing, sales, distribution, or customer services.	SBU (or parent) has superior sources of supply and/or process engineering and production capabilities that enable it to be low-cost producer; R&D, product engineering, marketing, sales, or service capabilities may not be as strong as some competitors'.

advanced products or being left behind in newly developing application segments within the market. This dual focus makes the analyzer strategy appropriate for well-developed industries that are still experiencing some growth and change as a consequence of evolving customer needs and desires or continuing technological improvements.

Commercial aircraft manufacturing is an example of such an industry. Both competitors and potential customers are few and well established. But technology continues to improve, the increased competition among airlines since deregulation has changed the attributes those firms look for when buying new planes, and mergers have increased the buying power of some customers. Thus, Boeing's commercial aircraft division has had to work harder to maintain a nearly 50 percent share of worldwide commercial plane sales. Although the firm continues to enjoy a reputation for producing high-quality and reliable planes, it had to make price concessions and increase customer services during the late 1980s and early 1990s to stave off threats from competitor European Airbus. At the same time, Boeing's commercial aircraft division had to engage in a major development effort aimed at producing the next generation of aircraft, including its 757, 767, and 777 models. Unfortunately, the proliferation of new models contributed to substantial production and delivery problems in the late 1990s, which produced some customer dissatisfaction.

Boeing's experience illustrates one problem with an analyzer strategy. Few businesses have the resources and competencies needed to successfully defend an established core business while generating new products at the same time. Success on both dimensions requires strengths across virtually every functional area, and few businesses (or their parent companies) have such universal strengths relative to competitors. Therefore, analyzers are often not as innovative in new product development as prospectors. And they may not be as profitable in defending their core businesses as defenders.

Appropriate Conditions for a Defender Strategy

A defender strategy makes sense only when a business has something worth defending. It is most appropriate for units with a profitable share of one or more major segments in a relatively mature, stable industry. Consistent with the "constant improvement" principles of total quality management, most successful defenders initiate process improvements, product improvements, or line extensions to help protect and strengthen their established positions. But they devote relatively few resources to basic R&D or the development of innovative new products. Thus, a defender strategy works best in industries where the basic technology is not very complex or where it is well developed and unlikely to change dramatically over the short term. For instance, Pillsbury's prepared-dough products SBU has pursued a differentiated defender strategy for years. The unit generates substantial profits from well-established refrigerated dough products such as Pillsbury Crescent rolls and Hungry Jack biscuits. But while it has introduced a number of line extensions over the years, most have been reconfigurations of the same basic dough-in-a-can technology, such as Soft Breadsticks.

Differentiated Defenders   To effectively defend its position by differentiation, a business must be strong in those functional areas critical for maintaining its particular competitive advantages over time. If a business's differentiation is based on superior product quality, those key functional areas include production, process engineering, quality control, and perhaps product engineering to develop product improvements. The effort to develop and maintain a quality differentiation can be worthwhile, though, because evidence suggests that superior product quality has a strong impact on a business's return on investment—an important performance objective for defenders.[17]

Regardless of the basis for differentiation, marketing is also important for the effective implementation of a differentiated defender strategy. Marketing activities that track changing customer needs and competitive actions and communicate the product offering's unique advantages through promotional and sales efforts to maintain customer awareness and loyalty are particularly important.

Low-Cost Defenders   Successful implementation of a low-cost defender strategy requires the business to be more efficient than its competitors. Thus, the business must establish the groundwork for such a strategy early in the growth stage of the industry. Achieving and maintaining the lowest per-unit cost usually means that the business has to seek large volume from the beginning—through some combination of low prices and promotional efforts—to gain economies of scale and experience. At the same time, such businesses must also invest in more plant capacity in anticipation of future growth and in state-of-the-art equipment to minimize production costs. This combination of low margins and heavy investment can be prohibitive unless the parent corporation can commit substantial resources to the business or unless extensive sharing of facilities, technologies, and programs with other business units is possible.

The low-cost defender's need for efficiency also forces the standardization of product offerings and marketing programs across customer segments to achieve scale effects. Thus, such a strategy is usually not so effective in fragmented markets desiring customized offerings as it is in commodity industries such as basic chemicals, steel, or flour, or in industries producing low-technology components such as electric motors or valves.

While low-cost defenders emphasize efficiency and low price as the primary focus of their competitive strategy, it is important to keep in mind that businesses pursuing other strategies should also operate as efficiently as possible given the functional activities necessary to implement those strategies. Some of the most effective businesses are those that work *simultaneously* to lower costs and improve quality and service.[18] And operating efficiency is likely to become even more critical as the Internet makes it easier for customers to compare prices across alternative suppliers or to obtain low-price bids via "buyers' auction" sites, such as **www.FreeMarkets.com** or **www.MetalSite.com.**

HOW DIFFERENT BUSINESS STRATEGIES INFLUENCE MARKETING DECISIONS

Business units typically incorporate a number of distinct product-markets. A given entry's marketing manager monitors and evaluates the product's environmental situation and develops a marketing program suited to it. However, the manager's freedom to design such a program may be constrained by the business unit's competitive strategy. This is because different strategies focus on different objectives and seek to gain and maintain a competitive advantage in different ways. As a result, different functions within the SBU—and different activities within a given functional area, such as marketing—are critical for the success of different strategies.

There are, therefore, different functional key factors for success inherent in the various generic business strategies. This constrains the individual marketing manager's freedom of action in two basic ways. First, because varying functions within the business unit are more important under different strategies, they receive different proportions of the SBU's total resources. Thus, the SBU's strategy influences *the amount of resources committed to marketing* and ultimately the budget available to an individual marketing manager within the business unit. Second, the SBU's choice of strategy influences both the kind of *market and competitive situation* that individual product-market entries are likely to face and the *objectives* they are asked to attain. Both constraints have implications for the design of marketing programs for individual products within an SBU.

It is risky to draw broad generalizations about how specific marketing policies and program elements might fit within different business strategies. While a business strategy is a general statement about how an SBU chooses to compete in an industry, that unit may comprise a number of product-market entries facing different competitive situations in various markets. Thus, there is likely to be a good deal of variation in marketing programs, and in the freedom individual marketing managers have in designing them, across products within a given SBU. Still, a business's strategy does set a general direction for the types of target markets it will pursue and how the unit will compete in those markets. And it does have some influence on marketing policies that cut across product-markets. Exhibit 3.7 outlines differences in marketing policies and program elements that occur across businesses pursuing different strategies, and those differences are discussed below.

Product Policies

One set of marketing policies defines the nature of the products the business will concentrate on offering to its target markets. These policies concern the *breadth or diversity of product lines,* their *level of technical sophistication,* and the target *level of product quality* relative to competitors.

Exhibit 3.7

DIFFERENCES IN MARKETING POLICIES AND PROGRAM COMPONENTS ACROSS BUSINESSES PURSUING DIFFERENT STRATEGIES

Marketing policies and program components	STRATEGY		
	Prospector	Differentiated defender	Low-cost defender
Product policies			
• Product-line breadth relative to competitors	+	+	−
• Technical sophistication of products relative to competitors	+	+	−
• Product quality relative to competitors	?	+	−
• Service quality relative to competitors	?	+	−
Price policies			
• Price levels relative to competitors	+	+	−
Distribution policies			
• Degree of forward vertical integration relative to competitors	−	+	?
• Trade promotion expenses as percent of sales relative to competitors	+	−	−
Promotion policies			
• Advertising expenses as percent of sales relative to competitors	+	?	−
• Sales promotions expenses as percent of sales relative to competitors	+	?	−
• Salesforce expenses as percent of sales relative to competitors	?	+	−

Key: Plus sign (+) = greater than the average competitor.
        Minus sign (−) = smaller than the average competitor.
        Question mark (?) = uncertain relationship between strategy and marketing policy or program component.

Because prospector businesses rely heavily on the continuing development of unique new products and the penetration of new markets as their primary competitive strategy, policies encouraging broader and more technically advanced product lines than those of competitors should be positively related to performance on the critical dimension of share growth. The diverse and technically advanced product offerings of 3M's drug delivery systems SBU are a good example of this.

Whether a prospector's products should be of higher quality than competitors' products is open to question. Quality is hard to define; it can mean different things to different customers. Even so, it is an important determinant of business profitability.[19] Thus, Hambrick suggests that in product-markets where technical features or up-to-the-minute styling are key attributes in customers' definitions of quality, high-quality products may play a positive role in determining the success of a prospector strategy. In markets where the critical determinants of quality are reliability or brand familiarity, the maintenance of relatively high product quality is likely to be more strongly related to the successful performance of defender businesses, particularly differentiated defenders.[20]

Differentiated defenders compete by offering more or better choices to customers than do their competitors. For example, 3M's commercial graphics business, a major supplier of sign material for truck fleets, has strengthened its competitive position in that market by developing products appropriate for custom-designed signs. Until recently, the use of film for individual signs was not economical. But the use of computer-controlled knives and a new Scotch-brand marking film produce signs of higher quality and at lower cost than those that are hand-painted. This kind of success in developing relatively broad and technically sophisticated product lines should be positively related to the long-term ROI performance of most differentiated defender businesses.

However, broad and sophisticated product lines are less consistent with the efficiency requirements of the low-cost defender strategy. For one thing, maintaining technical sophistication in a business's products requires continuing investments in product and process R&D. For another, broad, complex lines can lead to short production runs and larger inventories. Some of the efficiency problems associated with broader, more-customized product lines may disappear, however, with continuing improvements in computer-assisted design and manufacturing, process reengineering, and the like.[21]

Instead of, or in addition to, competing on the basis of product characteristics, businesses can distinguish themselves relative to competitors on the *quality of service* they offer. Such service might take many forms, including engineering and design services, alterations, installation, training of customer personnel, or maintenance and repair services. A policy of high service quality is particularly appropriate for differentiated defenders because it offers a way to maintain a competitive advantage in well-established markets.

The appropriateness of an extensive service policy for low-cost defenders, though, is more questionable if higher operating and administrative costs offset customer satisfaction benefits. Those higher costs may detract from the business's ability to maintain the low prices critical to its strategy, as well as lowering ROI—at least in the short term. On the other hand, even low-cost defenders may have difficulty holding their position over the long term without maintaining at least competitive parity with respect to critical service attributes.[22]

Pricing Policies

Success in offering low prices relative to those of competitors should be positively related to the performance of low-cost defender businesses—for low price is the primary competitive weapon of such a strategy. However, such a policy is inconsistent with both differentiated defender and prospector strategies. The higher costs involved in differentiating a business's products on either a quality or service basis require higher prices to maintain profitability. Differentiation also provides customers with additional value for which higher prices can be charged. Similarly, the costs and benefits of new product and market development by prospector businesses require and justify relatively high prices. Thus, differentiated defenders and prospectors seldom adhere to a policy of low competitive prices.

Distribution Policies

Some observers argue that prospector businesses should show a greater degree of *forward vertical integration* than defender businesses.[23] The rationale for this view is that the prospector's focus on new product and market development requires superior market intelligence and frequent reeducation and motivation of distribution channel members. This can best be accomplished through tight control of company-owned channels. However, these arguments seem inconsistent with the prospector's need for flexibility in constructing new channels to distribute new products and reach new markets.

Attempting to maintain tight control over the behavior of channel members is a more appropriate policy for defenders who are trying to maintain strong positions in established markets. This is particularly true for defenders who rely on good customer service to differentiate themselves from competitors. Thus, it seems more likely that a relatively high degree of forward vertical integration is found among defender businesses, particularly differentiated defenders, while prospectors rely more heavily on independent channel members—such as manufacturer's representatives or wholesale distributors—to distribute their products.[24]

Because prospectors focus on new products where success is uncertain and sales volumes are small in the short run, they are likely to devote a larger percentage of sales to *trade promotions* than are defender businesses. Prospectors rely on trade promotion tools such as quantity discounts, liberal credit terms, and other incentives to induce cooperation and support from their independent channel members.

Promotion Policies

Extensive marketing communications also play an important role in the successful implementation of both prospector and differentiated defender strategies. The form of that communication, however, may differ under the two strategies. Because prospectors must constantly work to generate awareness, stimulate trial, and build primary demand for new and unfamiliar products, high advertising and sales promotion expenditures are likely to bear a positive relationship to the new product and share-growth success of such businesses. The drug delivery SBU at 3M, for instance, devotes substantial resources to advertising in professional journals and distributing samples of new products, as well as to maintaining an extensive salesforce.

Differentiated defenders, on the other hand, are primarily concerned with maintaining the loyalty of established customers by adapting to their needs and providing good service. These tasks can best be accomplished—particularly in industrial goods and services industries—by an extensive, well-trained, well-supported salesforce.[25] Therefore, differentiated defenders are likely to have higher salesforce expenditures than are competitors.

Finally, low-cost defenders appeal to their customers primarily on price. Thus, high expenditures on advertising, sales promotion, or the salesforce would detract from their basic strategy and may have a negative impact on their ROI. Consequently, such businesses are likely to make relatively low expenditures as a percentage of sales on those promotional activities.

WHAT IF THE BEST MARKETING PROGRAM FOR A PRODUCT DOES NOT FIT THE BUSINESS'S COMPETITIVE STRATEGY?

What should a marketing manager do if the market environment facing a particular product or service demands marketing actions that are not consistent with the overall competitive strategy of the business to which it belongs? What if, for example, the product's target market is rapidly becoming more mature and competitive, but it is housed in a prospector business unit that does not have the cost structure or the personnel to allow the aggressive pricing or excellent customer service that may be needed for the product to compete successfully? Or what if newly emerging technology demands that a mature product category undergo an innovative redesign even though the defender SBU does not have extensive R&D and product development capabilities?

If a business unit is focused on a single product category or technological domain—as is the case with 3M's industrial tape unit—the ideal solution might be for the whole SBU to change its strategy in response to shifting industry circumstances. As the product category matures, for instance, the SBU might switch from a prospector to an analyzer strategy, and ultimately to one of the defender strategies.

The problem is that—as we shall see in Chapter 13—effective implementation of different business strategies requires not only different functional competencies and resources but also different organizational structures, decision-making and coordination processes, reward systems, and even personnel. Because such internal structures and processes are hard to change quickly, it can be very difficult for an entire SBU to make a successful transition from one basic strategy to another.[26] For example, many of Emerson Electric's SBUs historically were successful low-cost defenders, but accelerating technological change in their industries caused the corporation to try to convert them to low-cost analyzers that would focus more attention on new product and market development. Initially, however, this attempted shift in strategy resulted in some culture shock, conflict, and mixed performance outcomes within those units.

In view of the implementation problems involved, some firms do not try to make major changes in the basic competitive strategies of their existing business units. Instead, they might form new prospector SBUs to pursue emerging technologies and industries rather than expecting established units to handle extensive new product development efforts.

Similarly, as individual product-market entries gain successful positions in growing markets, some firms move them from the prospector unit that developed them into an existing analyzer or defender unit, or even into a newly formed SBU, better suited to reaping profits from them as their markets mature. For example, a number of innovative products developed at 3M, such as Post-it repositionable notes, have enjoyed sufficient success that new divisions were formed to concentrate on defending them as their markets matured. Many successful entrepreneurial start-ups eventually reorganize into two or more business units, one to continue prospecting new products and markets and another to defend the firm's initial product offering as its market matures.

Finally, some firms that are technological leaders in their industries may divest or license individual product-market entries as they mature rather than defend them in the face of increasing competition and eroding margins. This approach is relatively common at firms such as 3M and DuPont.

Because the marketing manager responsible for a given product-market entry is usually most closely tuned-in to changes in the market environment, he or she bears the responsibility

Exhibit 3.8   Jim Watkins Takes a Hike

When he was a product manager at the Pillsbury Company in the early 1970s, James D. Watkins became convinced that microwave technology represented a major opportunity for the packaged food industry. Consequently, he developed a marketing plan that proposed the pioneering development and aggressive introduction of a line of microwavable food products, starting with microwave popcorn. However, the business unit he worked for—and the entire Pillsbury Company at that time—was focused on defending strong positions in established markets, largely through incremental line extensions and product improvements. In other words, it was pursuing more of an analyzer strategy. As a result, top management rejected Watkins's proposal as being too risky and requiring resources and capabilities that were in short supply.

Watkins subsequently quit Pillsbury, founded a new firm called Golden Valley Microwave, attracted venture capital, hired some food scientists to do the necessary R&D, and began to market ActII microwave popcorn through large mass merchandisers such as Wal-Mart. As Watkins had predicted in his original marketing plan, the availability of microwavable foods spurred a rapid increase in consumer demand for microwave ovens, which in turn increased demand for more microwavable foods. His new company grew rapidly, and a few years later he sold it to Conagra for many millions of dollars.

But don't be too critical of Pillsbury. Like a good analyzer, the company avoided playing the risky role of the pioneer, but it eventually responded to the growing potential of microwave technology and successfully launched its own line of microwavable foods, including popcorn.

for pointing out any mismatches between what is best for the product and the capabilities of the organizational unit to which it belongs. The marketer should develop a marketing strategy that makes the most sense in light of a detailed analysis of the available customer and competitive information and present a strong case for the resources necessary to implement the plan. If those resources are not available within the business unit, or if the marketing strategy is inconsistent with the SBU's objectives or competitive strategy, top management faces a choice of moving the product to a more benign unit of the firm or rejecting the recommended strategy. If the strategy is rejected, the marketer will likely have to make compromises to the strategy to make it fit better with the competitive thrust of the SBU, even though an attractive opportunity may be lost. But if the marketer has great confidence in the recommended strategy, he or she might opt to quit the firm and pursue the opportunity elsewhere, as was the case with Jim Watkins, as discussed in Exhibit 3.8.

TAKE AWAYS

- Research suggests that a business is likely to achieve superior revenue growth, market share, and profitability when there is a good fit between its competitive strategy and the strategic marketing programs of its various product or service offerings.

- Business-level competitive strategies can be usefully categorized into (1) prospector strategies focused on growth via the development of new products and markets, (2) defender strategies primarily concerned with defending strong positions in established markets through either low prices or offering customers superior value in terms of product quality or service, and (3) analyzer strategies, which are hybrids of the other two strategies.

- The generic competitive strategies described in the previous point apply equally well to services and physical products, single-product start-ups and multi-divisional corporations, and global and domestic operations, and they are unlikely to change dramatically due to the rise of e-commerce.

- Because the various business-level strategies focus on different objectives and seek to gain a competitive advantage in different ways, marketing may play a different role under each of the strategies, and varying marketing actions may be called for.

- The marketing decision-maker's job is to develop a sound, evidence-based marketing strategy for his or her offering and to make a persuasive case for its support. If that strategy does not fit the objectives or available resources and competencies of the business unit in which the product is housed, top management may choose to move the product to a more amenable unit or require adjustments to the strategy.

- Self-diagnostic questions to test your ability to apply the analytical tools and concepts in this chapter to marketing decision making may be found at this book's website at **www.mhhe.com/walker.**

ENDNOTES

1. Material for this example was obtained from *The 3M Company 2000 Annual Report* and other information found on the company's website, www.3m.com; and Shawn Tully, "Why to Go for Stretch Targets," *Fortune,* November 14, 1994, pp. 145–58.

2. For a more detailed discussion of the concept of strategic fit and the role of various external and internal variables in influencing the effectiveness of a firm's strategies, see N. Venkatraman and James Camillus, "The Concept of 'Fit' in Strategic Management," *Academy of Management Review* 9 (1984), pp. 513–24.

3. Stanley F. Slater and Eric M. Olson, "Marketing's Contribution to the Implementation of Business Strategy: An Empirical Analysis," working paper (Bothell, WA: University of Washington at Bothell, 2000).

4. Tulley, "Why to Go for Stretch Targets," p. 150.

5. For example, see Robin Cooper and Robert S. Kaplan, "Measure Costs Right: Make the Right Decisions," *Harvard Business Review,* September–October 1988, pp. 96–103; and Terrence P. Pare, "A New Tool for Managing Costs," *Fortune,* June 14, 1993, p. 124.

6. C. K. Prahalad and Gary Hamel, "The Core Competence of the Corporation," *Harvard Business Review* 68 (May–June 1990), pp. 79–91.

7. Michael E. Porter, *Competitive Strategy* (New York: Free Press, 1980). Also see Michael E. Porter, *Competitive Advantage: Creating and Sustaining Superior Performance* (New York: Free Press, 1985).

8. Robert E. Miles and Charles C. Snow, *Organizational Strategy, Structure, and Process* (New York: McGraw-Hill, 1978). For another taxonomy of business-level competitive strategies that incorporates elements of both the Porter and Miles and Snow frameworks, see Michael Treacy and Fred Wiersema, *The Discipline of Market Leaders* (Reading, MA: Addison-Wesley, 1995).

9. Charles C. Snow and Lawrence G. Hrebiniak, "Strategy, Distinctive Competence, and Organizational Performance," *Administrative Science Quarterly* 25 (1980), pp. 317–35.

10. Theodore Levitt, *The Marketing Imagination* (New York: Free Press, 1986), pp. 94–95.

11. Philip Kotler and Gary Armstrong, *Principles of Marketing* (Englewood Cliffs, NJ: Prentice Hall, 1989), p. 575.

12. Daryl O. McKee, P. Rajan Varadarajan, and William M. Pride, "Strategic Adaptability and Firm Performance: A Market-Contingent Perspective," *Journal of Marketing,* July 1989, pp. 21–35.

13. For example, see "Internet Economics: A Thinker's Guide," *The Economist,* April 1, 2000, pp. 64–66.

14. Larry Chiagouris and Brant Wansley, "Branding on the Internet," *Marketing Management* 9 (Summer 2000), pp. 35–38.

15. Gordon Donaldson, *Managing Corporate Wealth* (New York: Praeger, 1984).

16. Donald C. Hambrick, "Some Tests of the Effectiveness and Functional Attributes of Miles and Snow's Strategic Types," *Academy of Management Journal* 26 (1983), pp. 5–26; and McKee, Varadarajan, and Pride, "Strategic Adaptability and Firm Performance."

17. Robert D. Buzzell and Bradley T. Gale, *The PIMS Principles: Linking Strategy to Performance* (New York: Free Press, 1987), chap. 6.

18. For example, see Ronald Henkoff, "Cost Cutting: How to Do It Right," *Fortune,* April 9, 1990, pp. 40–49.

19. Buzzell and Gale, *The PIMS Principles,* chap. 6.

20. Hambrick, "Some Tests of Effectiveness."

21. B. Joseph Pine II, Bart Victor, and Andrew C. Boynton, "Making Mass Customization Work," *Harvard Business Review* 71 (September–October 1993), pp. 108–19.

22. For additional arguments in the debate about the relative costs and competitive benefits of superior customer service, see Rahul Jacob, "Beyond Quality and Value," *Fortune,* Special Issue, Autumn–Winter 1993, pp. 8–11; and Valarie A. Zeithaml and Mary Jo Bitner, *Services Marketing* (New York: McGraw-Hill, 1996), chap. 2.

23. Miles and Snow, *Organizational Strategy, Structure, and Process;* and Hambrick, "Some Tests of Effectiveness."

24. Although Hambrick argues for the reverse relationship, data from his study of 850 SBUs actually support our contention that defenders have more vertically integrated channels than do prospectors. See Hambrick, "Some Tests of Effectiveness."

25. Leonard A. Schlesinger and James L. Heskett, "The Service-Driven Service Company," *Harvard Business Review* 69 (September–October 1991), pp. 71–81; and Jaclyn Fierman, "The Death and Rebirth of the Salesman," *Fortune,* July 25, 1994, pp. 80–91.

26. Connie J. G. Gersick, "Revolutionary Change Theories: A Multilevel Exploration of the Punctuated Equilibrium Paradigm," *Academy of Management Review* 16 (1991), pp. 10–36; and Michael L. Tushman, William H. Newman, and Elaine Romanelli, "Convergence and Upheaval: Managing the Unsteady Pace of Organizational Evolution," *California Management Review* 29 (1986), pp. 29–44.

SECTION TWO

OPPORTUNITY ANALYSIS

CHAPTER FOUR

IDENTIFYING ATTRACTIVE MARKETS

The Changing American Menswear Market[1]

FROM JEANS TO KHAKIS, from tailored suits to "business casual," clothing preferences among American men have been changing. A trend toward casual dress in the workplace that got its start during the 1980s in high-tech firms in Silicon Valley in California became pervasive throughout the business world during the dot-com boom of the late 1990s. One day in early 2000, some 350 lawyers and staffers from the old-line New York law firm of Cadwalader, Wickersham, and Taft crowded into the Polo mansion on New York's posh upper east side to get some advice on how to enter the "business casual" era.

THE IMPACT OF UNFAVORABLE MACROENVIRONMENTAL TRENDS

For companies serving the men's tailored clothing market, the challenges brought about by the business casual trend have been daunting. Manufacturers of tailored men's clothing have stumbled, and some have attempted to reposition themselves as purveyors of more casual attire. Retailers of men's suits also have struggled, and some, like the Kuppenheimer chain, a unit of Hartmarx, the leading manufacturer of tailored menswear in the United States, have closed their doors entirely.

What happens when unexpected unfavorable trends, like that toward more casual dress in the workplace, cause demand for a category of goods or services to shrink, as has happened with tailored men's clothing? First, providers of such goods feel a softening in their sales. As sales grow softer, firms find themselves having excess capacity and expense levels that cannot be supported by reduced levels of revenue. Often, the performance figures that result paint a picture that is anything but pretty. By 1999, Hartmarx, which had struggled with the changing menswear market for a decade, found its pretax profit margins in its men's apparel group languishing at 2 percent of sales, while its stock had fallen to less than $4 per share, from an already depressed $10 in 1997. Hartmarx was far from the only menswear firm to feel the heat. In 1999 the bankrupt retailer Edison Brothers liquidated its 295 Riggings stores because not a single buyer out of 250 interested parties was willing to buy the ailing chain. Today's Man, a 25-store menswear chain in the eastern United States, was forced to reorganize under bankruptcy protection in 1998. Numerous other chains and independent men's clothiers suffered similar fates.

The widespread troubles experienced by menswear retailers and manufacturers in the 1990s are typical of what can happen when unforeseen trends—whether social trends, as in this case, or others—cause consumer demand to drop rapidly. Simply put, the market for tailored men's apparel shrank like a cheap suit and the ensuing competitive pressures in the menswear manufacturing and retailing industries made this market and these industries far less attractive than they had once been.

Is Success Impossible in the Face of Unfavorable Trends?

Most observers of the men's apparel market in the 1990s would have concluded that success would have been difficult to achieve for *any* player serving that market. At least one tailored clothing retailer, however, continued to prosper in spite of adverse market conditions. The Men's Wearhouse, whose first store opened in Houston, Texas, in 1973, went public in 1992 and grew consistently throughout the 1990s, opening as many as 50 stores per year in the late 1990s. The chain's same-store sales grew as well, including a 10.4 percent same-store sales increase in 1998. How did Men's Wearhouse thrive where others failed? It offered a mix of branded and private-label merchandise in low-cost but nicely appointed strip center locations. It spent heavily on employee training to build a customer-oriented, team-selling culture. It

spent its marketing money largely in broadcast media, instead of the more traditional print advertising used by other menswear retailers, making founder George Zimmer, its radio spokesman, a celebrity in the process. As President David Edwab noted in 1999, "If you look at this company, we've taken the most difficult part of the apparel business, added marketing, training, the right real estate, and store strategies to sell men what they like the least. As a result, we've gained market share in a consolidating industry."

What's Next? Will Suits Come Back?

When the dot-com bubble burst in 2000, the time seemed right for a return to more formal business attire. The logic was that laid-off dot-com workers would be interviewing again, and those who had kept their jobs would begin dressing better out of fear. So far, however, according to Neal Fox, vice chairman of Today's Man, the menswear retailer, "Right now there's more spin out there, but not a massive upsurge in suit sales." Will suits come back, or will they simply be one option, to be worn when appropriate, for client meetings or to make one's employer think you have a job interview? Time will tell. For marketing strategists in the menswear industry, it's a question not to be ignored.

Strategic Challenges Addressed in Chapter 4

As the story of the changing menswear market shows, unfavorable sociocultural or other trends that negatively influence market demand can have a devastating effect on the performance of firms serving that market. Similarly, favorable trends exert positive forces that make it easier for firms to perform well. As discussed in Exhibit 4.1, retailers and manufacturers of casual clothing suitable for today's workplace have fared well in the late 1990s. Entrepreneurs seeking to start new firms, investors in search of favorable returns, and managers in existing firms are therefore well advised to consider the presence and strength of such trends in deciding where to place their bets.

In this chapter, we address the second of the 4 Cs—the **environmental context** in which the business operates—that were identified in Chapter 1 as the analytical foundation

Exhibit 4.1　Khakis Conquer the Workplace

With suits passé, what are up-and-coming young professionals wearing to work? For many, the answer is khakis and sportshirts. In the young men's sportswear category in 1999, the khaki business more than doubled over 1998, as, in traditional department stores, khakis' share of the young men's apparel business grew from 6 percent in 1998 to 15 percent in 1999. Levi's, a leading brand in the khakis category, increased its young men's market share to 25 percent and maintained its number one position in the young men's category.

Casual clothing retailers happily rode the wave, as well. Gap, Inc., and its family of stores enjoyed increased demand for its casual clothing in 1999, resulting in a 29 percent increase in worldwide sales and a 38 percent increase in earnings per share. An important part of Gap's growth was its broadened focus on Internet retail-

ing. "We also reached new customers and expanded market share by opening more than 500 stores worldwide and broadening our brands online. Our passion for serving customers better every day will continue to drive quality growth for Gap, Banana Republic, and Old Navy," said Millard S. Drexler, president and CEO.

Gap's ability to stay in tune with fashion trends proved less than infallible, however. From late 1999 into 2002, Gap struggled to find the right mix of merchandise for its stores, and same-store sales and company profits tumbled. Will Gap successfully tune in to what its customers want in the new millennium? Time will tell.

Source: "Khakis Sales Up, Jeans Sales Down for 1999," *DNR*, February 11, 2000, p. 18; Gap, Inc., website, www.gap.com; Calmetta Coleman, "Gap, Inc. Stumbles as Respected CEO Loosens Reins," *The Wall Street Journal*, September 7, 2000, p. B4.

of the marketing management process. We provide a framework to help managers, entrepreneurs, and investors comprehensively assess the environment in which they operate or propose to operate, in order to assess market attractiveness and enhance their likelihood of achieving success. Thus, this chapter addresses three important questions for marketing strategists: Does it really matter whether we swim upstream or downstream? How can we be sure we've identified and understood the key trends? And finally, how does macro trend analysis play out in assessing markets and in making marketing decisions?

SWIMMING UPSTREAM OR DOWNSTREAM: AN IMPORTANT STRATEGIC CHOICE

Casual dress in the workplace is a social trend. The graying of America is a demographic one. Global warming is a trend in our physical environment. All these trends influence the fortunes of some companies, but not others. As we have seen, the influence of **macro-environmental trends**—or **macro trends,** for short—like these can be pervasive and powerful. In general, life is better swimming downstream, accompanied by favorable trends, than upstream, running counter to such trends.

Like mosquitoes or cooling breezes on a humid summer evening, trends will always be present, whether marketing managers like them or not. The question is what managers can do about them. For some trends, marketers and other managers can do little but react and adapt. In the 1990s, manufacturers of products sold in spray containers were required to find new propellants less harmful to the ozone layer. Governments concerned about global warming mandated this change. For other trends, like the shift toward casual dress in the workplace for Gap, favorable moves can be reinforced through effective marketing. Similarly, sometimes, unfavorable ones can be mitigated. But doing these things requires that important trends be noticed and understood. The sociocultural, demographic, and physical environments are but three of six major

STRATEGIC ISSUE

Like mosquitoes or cooling breezes on a humid summer evening, trends will always be present, whether marketing managers like them or not. The question is what managers can do about them.

components of the **macroenvironment.** The other three are the political/legal, economic, and technological components. We deal with the competitive environment in Chapter 5.

MACRO TREND ANALYSIS: A FRAMEWORK FOR ASSESSING MARKET ATTRACTIVENESS

Each of the six macroenvironmental components will be examined in terms of how the dynamics of change affect the attractiveness of particular markets and influence marketing strategies and programs.

The Demographic Environment

The world's population in 1994 was 5.63 billion persons versus 2.52 billion in 1950. It is expected to grow to 7.47 billion by 2015. Some 80 percent of the world's population lives in the less-developed countries, where 95 percent of the increase in population takes place. Africa and Asia represent nearly 90 percent of the increase. Africa's population is expected to double by 2025—from 728 million to 1.49 billion—while that of Asia is expected to grow by 40 percent—from 3.46 billion to 4.96 billion. China and India will account for most of this increase. Europe over the next 20 years is expected to have a declining population. The United States is the only major developed country projected to show a population increase—from 263 million (current) to 331 million by 2025.[2]

A major trend is the aging of the world's population caused primarily by declining mortality rates. The developing nations are experiencing dramatic changes in their over-65 age group—a severalfold increase over the next 20 years is expected. Another important global trend is the rapid shift in the populations of the less-developed countries from rural to urban. By 2025 nearly 60 percent of the population of the less-developed countries is expected to be urban versus 37 percent currently. In contrast 75 percent of the population of developed countries is currently urban, but is expected to grow very slowly in the future.[3] By the year 2015, seven cities will have populations in excess of 20 million (see Exhibit 4.2).

Exhibit 4.2

POPULATIONS OF THE 10 LARGEST URBAN AREAS—1994 VERSUS 2015 (IN MILLIONS)

Urban area	1994	Urban area	2015
1. Tokyo	26.5	1. Tokyo	28.4
2. New York	16.3	2. Bombay	27.4
3. São Paulo	16.1	3. Lagos	24.4
4. Mexico City	15.5	4. Shanghai	23.4
5. Shanghai	14.7	5. Jakarta	21.2
6. Bombay	14.5	6. São Paulo	20.8
7. Los Angeles	12.2	7. Karachi	20.6
8. Beijing	12.0	8. Beijing	19.4
9. Calcutta	11.5	9. Dhaka	19.0
10. Seoul	11.5	10. Mexico City	18.8

Source: Review of Population Trends, Policies, and Programs: Monitoring of World Population Trends and Policies (New York: United Nations, January 1996), table 9. The United Nations is the author of the original material. Reprinted by permission.

U.S. Demographics[4]   The U.S. population grew by 20 million persons during the 1990s—the largest increase of any developed country—and is expected to grow by about 2 million a year well into the 21st century. Four major shifts are occurring in the U.S. population: the changing family structure, aging, geographic distribution, and ethnic composition. Each of these trends is discussed briefly below.

Family Structure   The traditional husband-dominated, closely structured family is less and less typical of American society. Today's households because of divorce (about half of all marriages end in divorce) and remarriage have evolved into a number of different kinds of households populated by single individuals; adults of the same sex or both sexes (married or not) living together; unmarried adults living with children, both related and unrelated; single-parent families; and married couples with children. The situation is further complicated because a substantial number of these households have two or more wage earners. These different types of households vary in their income and in their purchases of various products and services. For example, households with two wage earners are apt to have more than one car and spend more money on eating out.

Aging   Baby boomers (those born between 1946 and 1964) who now constitute nearly 80 million persons continue to dominate growth in the age groups they pass through en route to old age. And the number of people over 65 has increased by 13 percent since 1990 to nearly 35 million. Those over 85 have increased 40 percent to over 4.2 million during this timespan. In the years ahead we can expect the over-65 age group to increase substantially. As boomers age, they increasingly affect the purchase of goods and services. Households age 45 to 54 are the single most affluent U.S. consumer segment. For a description of what these households are buying, see Exhibit 4.3.

Geographic Distribution   Immigrants account for nearly one-third of U.S. annual growth and end up residing mostly in the large metropolitan areas in California, New York, Texas, Florida, New Jersey, and Illinois. The South and West continue to gain population at the expense of the Midwest and Northeast. California, Texas, and Florida accounted for over half the U.S. growth in the 1980s, and the latter two states continued to have strong growth during the 90s. Yet another trend is the migration of jobs and people to suburban cities—farther and farther from central cities.

Ethnic Composition   Another major trend is that the United States is becoming more diverse ethnically. At present, more than 25 percent of the population is composed of racial minorities. The Hispanic population is the fastest-growing segment and is expected to increase from 22.5 million in 1990 to nearly 90 million, rising from 9 percent to a 22 percent share of the total population by 2050. The African-American population is forecasted to double by 2050—from 30.6 to 62 million—while Asians will increase from 7.6 million

---

Exhibit 4.3   **What Boomers Age 50–64 Buy**

As boomers fight aging, they consume large quantities of skin creams, suntan lotions, hair coloring, cosmetics, vitamins, and nutritional supplements. This segment spends more than any other on books, women's clothing, home computers, entertainment, new cars and trucks, and restaurant meals. By 2000 they accounted for the largest share of purchasing a majority of most categories of goods and services.

Source: Cheryl Russell, "The Baby Boomers Turn 50," *American Demographics*, December 1995, p. 22. Reprinted by permission.

to 41 million. The three groups, over the next 50 or so years, will account for nearly 50 percent of the total U.S. population. Such growth will further internationalize the United States—especially in such major cities as Los Angeles, Miami, and New York. Products with high ethnic appeal, in such areas as food and clothing, should be in high demand in such cities.

Implications of Demographic Trends for Market Attractiveness   The demographic trends discussed in this section have resulted in rapidly growing markets for a diverse array of products and services. Rapid economic development and a growing middle class in Asia have been a boon for capital goods manufacturers in the United States and Europe, as they export capital equipment to the Asian factories seeking to satisfy Asia's growing demand for manufactured goods for local as well as export markets.

Aging populations in developed countries have created growing demand for senior housing of many types and for in-home, home repair, and home modification services to enable older persons to stay in their homes.[5] Demographic trends also have led marketers to develop products and special marketing programs targeted at minority and other demographic groups whose numbers are growing.

On the downside, demographic trends have made other markets less attractive than they once were. Migration of jobs and people from some Northeast and Midwest cities to suburbs or cities elsewhere in the United States has led to stagnant real estate and employment markets there, while cities in the West and South thrive.

The Sociocultural Environment

This environment represents the values, attributes, and general behavior of the individuals in a given society. Compared with economic, political, and technological changes, the sociocultural environment evolves slowly. People grow up in a system of values they tend to carry throughout their lifetimes. Transformation in the structure of society, in its institutions, and in the distribution of wealth occurs gradually in democratic countries. Even so, we have in recent years seen a substantial change in individual values, family structure, minority rights, leisure-time activities, and conservation.

The Evolution of Individual Values   North American society has been characterized by the traditional values of hard work, thriftiness, and faith in others and in institutions. In the 60s, however, new social values emerged. Instead of leaving the destiny of their country in the hands of their elders and institutions, the young—particularly college students—collectively fought for what they perceived to be good causes, such as civil rights, the end of the Vietnam war, and nonconformism. The young emerged as a new social force—sharing and defending a common set of new values even across national borders. This era is often referred to as the "Age of Us."

More recently, individual values have shifted again, particularly in the younger generation (20–29 years of age), often referred to as Generation X.[6] During their formative years they have been exposed to dire predictions about the economic health of America, many public scandals, the advent of the knowledge society, the electronic/computer revolution, the changing structure of the American family, and the growing influence of minority groups.

Because of these experiences, members of this generation are greatly concerned with simplifying their lives, with obtaining a college education, with their relations with their families and the opposite sex, and with economic security. Their coping includes living at home (particularly men), postponing marriage, and delaying having children. They are realistic and pragmatic about surviving yet do not define success solely in terms of money. They place considerable emphasis on the family life they missed as children. While generally turned off by big government, they care a great deal about such issues as AIDS, abortion, and the environment.[7] For one professional's list of the shifting values in Western societies, see Exhibit 4.4.

The Evolution of Family Structure   The traditional husband-dominated, closely structured family is less and less typical of our North American society. Children are becoming more autonomous and participate at an earlier age in many family decisions. A more balanced allocation of power between husband and wife also has emerged. In part this has resulted from the fact that many women are more independent economically. Working parents' absence from the home has substantially reduced the interactions among family members and family cohesiveness. The increasing divorce rate has made one-parent households more common. All these factors have considerably changed the buying process for many goods, including which family members are involved in the purchase of certain goods.

Implications of Sociocultural Trends for Market Attractiveness   Along with broader sociocultural trends come changes in consumer tastes and behavior. Natural foods are in. Exercise for both genders is in. Fat and cholesterol are out. Thus, sociocultural changes, such as those described in this section and at the beginning of the chapter, influence the markets for a broad array of consumer products such as natural foods, exercise equipment and sports beverages, low-fat food products, and men's apparel. Sociocultural trends also have influenced how marketing activities are carried out in some markets. For example, advertising programs now accommodate more joint decision making in households.

Exhibit 4.4

SHIFTING VALUES IN WESTERN SOCIETIES

Traditional values	New values
Self-denial ethic	Self-fulfillment ethic
Higher standard of living	Better quality of life
Traditional sex roles	Blurring of sex roles
Accepted definition of success	Individualized definition of success
Traditional family life	Alternative families
Faith in industry, institutions	Self-reliance
Live to work	Work to live
Hero worship	Love of ideas
Expansionism	Pluralism
Patriotism	Less nationalistic
Unparalleled growth	Growing sense of limits
Industrial growth	Information/service growth
Receptivity to technology	Technology orientation

Developed Western societies are gradually moving away from traditional values and toward the emerging new values being embraced on an ever-widening scale, says author Joseph Plummer.

Source: "Changing Values: The New Emphasis on Self-Actualization," originally published in the January–February 1989 issue of *The Futurist,* p. 15. Used with permission from World Future Society, 7910 Woodmont Avenue, Suite 450, Bethesda, Maryland 20814. Telephone: 301-656-8274; Fax: 301-951-0394; http://www.wfs.org.

The Economic Environment

The economic performance of a country is measured by **gross domestic product (GDP)**—usually on a per-capita basis after accounting for inflation. To realistically compare incomes across countries, it is necessary to use a **purchasing power parity (PPP)** approach that considers the cost of a standard basket of products (expressed in U.S. dollars) for each country. Thus, using a PPP analysis helps to compare the relative purchasing power of a given country for goods with what these same goods would cost in the United States. If GDP per capita is calculated on the basis of exchange rates, then Japan has the world's highest average. But America has the highest if purchasing power parity is used to calculate per capita GDP.[8]

Using PPP values typically produces lower GDP per capita income for the wealthier countries and higher ones for the poorer nations. Despite this "leveling," the gap in real GDP (less inflation) has increased between rich and poor countries—mainly because of higher population growth.[9] But PPP does not take into account the subsidies provided by many countries for such essentials as food, utilities, shelter, transportation, education, and medical care, which account for about half of the average household expenditures in developed countries.

The world's economic growth continues to increase as measured by total gross national product (GDP). In the years ahead, the developing countries are expected to have substantially higher rates of economic growth than the developed ones. Asia has experienced the strongest growth—over 8 percent (primarily because of China's explosive growth)—and is expected to continue at a 7 percent rate near-term. In South America, Argentina and Brazil are forecasted to continue their strong growth rates while Ecuador is still suffering from economic difficulties. Some countries in Central Europe will have difficulty avoiding negative growth.[10]

America seems to have regained its competitiveness because of a powerful surge in productivity triggered by low interest rates, flat unit labor costs, low inflation, and heavy capital investments, especially in high-tech equipment. The more-open U.S. market has made its companies more competitive as compared with Europe and, to some extent, Japan.[11]

In the United States, growth will come largely from the large number of baby boomers moving into their peak earning years (age 44–54). Overall, the forecast calls for increased spending on personal insurance and pensions, owned homes, appliances, home furnishings, food at home, utilities, health insurance, entertainment, and education. Expected to decline are expenditures for food away from home, alcoholic beverages, rental units, apparel, vehicles, gasoline, reading, and tobacco products.[12] Of considerable concern is the growing gap between the classes. An average American middle-class household experienced a 4.6 percent decline in its inflation-adjusted annual income over a 15-year period versus a 7.9 percent increase for the top one-third group. The richest 5 percent of American families had an increase of 29.1 percent in their annual income.[13]

International Trade   Increasingly countries have become more economically interdependent as have many of their industries. Free-trade agreements in various stages of completion embrace a high percentage of the industrialized nations, including a single European market (EC); a merging of the European Community (EC) with the European Free Trade Area (EFTA) to form the European Economic Area (EEA); and the North American Free Trade Agreement (NAFTA) between the United States, Canada, and Mexico, which will eventually embrace most Latin American countries.

The United States is by far the largest **national market,** representing about 25 percent of the total world market for goods and services (Japan is second with 10 percent). As such, the U.S. market is a high priority target for the business firms of most countries, especially those of Japan and Europe. Inevitably, the United States is a highly competitive market for many goods and services. It is not only the biggest importer of goods and services, but also the biggest exporter, with Germany a close second. Even small companies are now significant players in the export game.[14]

Today nearly one-third of all automobiles sold in the United States are of Japanese origin. A large percentage of all TVs, radios, calculators, motorcycles, binoculars, robots, cameras, VCRs, tape players, and digital watches sold in the United States are foreign-made. Many U.S. companies are foreign-owned—for example, Pillsbury (English), Carnation (Swiss), Firestone (Japanese), and CBS Records (Japanese).

Fluctuating exchange rates can significantly change the relative price competitiveness of firms manufacturing in different countries. For example, the devaluation of the yen versus the U.S. dollar (from 108.95 in June 1996 to 122.78 in February 1997) enabled Japanese automakers to offer better deals in selling and leasing their cars in the United States, especially those made in Japan. The big three U.S. automakers (General Motors, Ford, and DaimlerChrysler) complained about the U.S. policy of strengthening the value of the dollar against the yen and the German mark and forecast lower profits—even a decline in market share.

Implications of Economic Trends for Market Attractiveness   Economic trends influence the level of demand in most markets, but they are particularly important in capital goods markets, real estate, and other markets where sensitivity to interest rates and the level of household or corporate income can be extreme. Economic trends often combine with other macro trend categories, with powerful effects. For example, the growth of the baby boomers, a demographic trend, together with the strong American economy and low interest rates in the late 1990s, both economic trends, resulted in rapidly growing demand for condominiums and second homes in resort areas. Some who foresaw these trends made a killing during this period. If these trends continue, rising resort real estate prices are likely also to continue, unless the supply of resort properties outpaces demand.

STRATEGIC ISSUE

Economic trends often combine with other macro trend categories, with powerful effects.

The Political/Legal Environment

In every country there is a legislative or **regulatory environment** within which both local and foreign firms must operate. As with any other external force, the political/legal environment presents a firm with strategic opportunities as well as threats. The business regulations in a country reflect its economic maturity and political philosophy. At the extreme, political risk for the firm includes confiscation (seizure without compensation as happened in Iran several years ago), expropriation (seizure with some compensation), and domestication (requiring transfer of ownership to the host country and local management and sourcing).

Other risks include changes in exchange control (which can take a variety of forms), local content laws, import restrictions, taxes, and price controls—all of which usually operate to the advantage of local industry. Clearly, many third world countries present an array of political risks to companies seeking to do business in them. (See Exhibit 4.5 for a discussion of the risks of investing in China.) On the other hand, governments can encourage foreign investment through policies such as tax concessions and tariff protection. Indeed, countries commonly encourage certain kinds of investments while simultaneously restricting others. For example, governments may encourage local firms to export to countries that have considerable political risk by providing insurance against losses from such risk (for instance, the U.S. Export-Import Bank).

Exhibit 4.5 — China—A Risky Investment

In but a few years China has emerged as a powerful economic force with the world's largest potential market. Because of its longer-term attractiveness, it has attracted substantial investments by a diverse group of multinational firms despite high inflation rates, widespread corruption, the growing power of the military, and the possible turmoil following the death of its aging leader. Examples of the poor treatment accorded foreign investors include the eviction of McDonald's from a prime location in Beijing, even though its lease had 17 years to run; Lehman Brothers' having to sue two state corporations to pay $100 million for losses in foreign exchange trading; and a group of Japanese, German, and Italian banks begging Beijing to reimburse them for $400 million of defaulted loans made to state enterprises.

Source: Louis Kraar, "The Risks Are Rising in China," *Fortune,* March 6, 1995. See also Pete Engardio and Dexter Roberts, "Rethinking China," *Business Week,* March 4, 1995, p. 57.

Controversies over copyright infringement involve the highest stakes. In China, pirate factories often under the protection of senior politicians and high-ranking military officials engage in counterfeiting such items as videos, compact disks, computer software, prescription drugs, herbicides, and Rolex watches. Such counterfeiting costs U.S. companies an estimated $1 to $2 billion a year.[15]

Government Regulation   The number and intricacy of laws and regulations make it difficult to understand regulatory elements affecting marketing. Most countries have regulations concerning food and drugs, as well as price, products, promotion, and distribution, but these vary considerably in their applicability to marketing. For example, the European Community (EC) is phasing in thousands of rules to provide uniform safety, health, and environmental standards for its member countries. These rules now favor companies producing a variety of products for several countries, but in the future some exporters will be required to make costly design changes, to substantially retool, and to add new quality control systems.

It has long been argued that regulations cripple the economy and stifle innovation. This is often true, but effects are frequently overstated since business will strive to find innovative ways to adhere to regulations at less than the anticipated costs. For example, when the U.S. Occupational Safety and Health Administration issued a higher standard for avoiding worker exposure to the toxic chemical formaldehyde, industry costs were expected to be $10 million yearly. But by modifying the resins and reducing the amount of formaldehyde, costs were negligible. Further, the changes enhanced the global competitiveness of the U.S. foundry supply and equipment industry.[16]

Government Deregulation   Government, business, and the general public throughout much of the world have become increasingly aware that overregulation protects inefficiencies, restricts entry by new competitors, and creates inflationary pressures. In the United States, airlines, trucking, railroads, telecommunications, and banking have been deregulated. Markets also are being liberated in Western and Eastern Europe, Asia, and many of the developing countries. Trade barriers are crumbling due to political unrest and technological innovation.

Deregulation has typically changed the structure of the affected industries as well as lowered prices. For example, in the decade following deregulation of the U.S. airline industry (1978–1985), over 200 new air carriers entered the market, and prices were estimated to be 40 percent cheaper than they would have been under regulation. Also, some 900 monopoly routes were made more competitive.[17] The early actions of firms following deregulation include improving pricing capabilities, finding new ways to differentiate their services, increasing their marketing skills, and conserving capital to maintain flexibility. Later, the strategies of the surviving companies center on fine-tuning their pricing capabilities, preempting competitors via strategic alliances, and developing their marketing skills.[18]

Implications of Regulation and Deregulation for Market Attractiveness

As regulatory practices wax and wane, the attractiveness of markets often follows suit. For example, the deregulation of telecommunications in Europe, following earlier deregulation in the United States, is opening markets to firms seeking to offer new services and take market share from the established monopolies. The rise of Internet retailing and Internet telephony has policy makers arguing over the degree to which these Internet activities should be subject to state and federal tax in the United States. The outcome of these arguments may have considerable effect on consumers' interest in buying and calling on the Web. Further, the U.S. government's effort to force a breakup of Microsoft has left high-tech firms wondering about the extent to which their successful innovations will cause them to run afoul of government antitrusters.[19]

The Technological Environment

Technology can have a substantial impact on an industry's performance. Consider the effect of genetic engineering on pharmaceuticals, of transistors on telecommunications, and of plastics on metals. Identification of the commercial potential of technological developments has dramatically accelerated, and the lag between ideas, invention, and commercialization has decreased.

In the past three decades, an amazing number of new technologies have brought forth such products as video recorders, compact disks, ever-more-powerful and ever-smaller computers, fax machines, new lightweight materials, and highly effective genetically engineered drugs. Technological progress over the next 10 years is predicted to be several times that experienced during the past 10 years; much of it will be spurred by the need to find solutions to our environmental problems. Major technological innovations can be expected in a variety of fields, especially in biology and electronics/telecommunications.[20]

Trends in Biology   The biological revolution is of fairly recent origin, especially gene therapy. There are some 60,000 to 80,000 genes in each human cell, which, by instructing cells to make proteins, can dictate not only our physical characteristics (the color of our eyes), but also our susceptibility to certain diseases. A single gene can trigger creation of a protein that, if it works like a drug, can lead to the development of a drug worth $500 million annually, such as Amgen's anemia-fighting Epogen. Research to discover faulty genes, if successful, may lead to the development of therapeutic treatments for such diseases as cystic fibrosis and colon cancer, which would be worth billions of dollars.[21]

Drug companies around the world are investing vast sums in R&D in their continued search for new problem-solving agents. Anticipated results in the pharmaceutical and agricultural areas include such exciting prospects as these:[22]

- *Pharmaceuticals:* production of human growth hormones to cure dwarfism and prevent muscle wasting, the introduction of powerful genetically engineered vaccines to treat certain kinds of cancers, and replacing defective genes that cause a variety of diseases (such as cystic fibrosis). A gene has been discovered that holds the promise of successfully treating obesity.[23] Scientists are also making good progress in the development of mass-produced tissue cultures for growing skin (for treating severe burn patients) and other organs (livers). This technology could reduce the need for donated transplants and plastic implants.[24]

- *Agriculture:* production of more disease-resistant livestock and plants, nonpolluting biological pesticides and insecticides, and a solution to the crop losses from salty soil.[25] Farmers are beginning to plant commercial crops of engineered corn, cotton, soybeans, and potatoes. The biotech seeds are targeted at making crops resistant to popular weed killers as well as viruses and fungal diseases. The danger is that cotton-munching boll worms and other pests will develop resistance to the toxins produced by the engineered plants.[26]

Trends in Electronics/Telecommunications   Electronics have played an important role in our society since the 1950s. They were first used primarily in radio and television and lately in digital watches, automatic cameras, video games, and microcomputers. Probably nothing has changed the workplace more in recent years than the personal computer, now numbering nearly 200 million worldwide. See Exhibit 4.6 for a description of Intel's new supercomputer on a chip.

Technology is also changing the nature and scope of the telecommunications industry. The changes are revolutionizing how businesses operate (banks, airlines, retail stores, and marketing research firms), how goods and services as well as ideas are exchanged, and how individuals learn and earn as well as interact with one another. Consumers today enjoy check-free banking, the death of the invoice, and ticketless air travel.

These innovations are the result not only of changes in computing systems but also of reduced costs in communicating (voice or data). For example, the cost of processing an additional telephone call is so small it might as well be free. And distance is no longer a factor—it costs about the same to make a trans-Atlantic call as one to your next-door neighbor.[27] The major events responsible for fueling the information revolution are[28]

- The development of fiber-optic cables in which a single fiber can carry 30,000 messages simultaneously. Such cables can be used by both telephone and cable operators, and they cost less to develop and maintain than copper wire systems.
- Storage devices developed to handle the increasing volume of data required to make the modern corporation competitive. Information about a firm's customers accounts for much of the increase. Over the next several years the storage market is expected to grow an average of 98 percent a year.[29]
- Breakthroughs leading to the use of flexible low-cost wireless transmissions, which provide mobility to the user and can provide inexpensive access to homes, versus the use of fixed systems.
- Development of low-cost multimedia chips (microprocessors).

 At the dawn of the new millennium, developments in telecommunications and computing have led to the rapid convergence of the telecommunications, computing, and entertainment industries. Music-hungry college students with personal computers now download music from legal sites, such as **mp3.com,** and perhaps illegal ones.[30] For them,

Exhibit 4.6   Present and Future Supercomputers

Intel's new dream computer will break the barrier of 1.6 trillion calculations per second—the previous record was 281 thousand per second. But that's nothing compared with what's likely to happen in the future. By 2005 the rate of calculations per second could increase to 100, and possibly 500, trillion. Such incredibly powerful machines would be especially important in areas such as modeling the atomic make-up of new materials and their performance under a variety of conditions, biological modeling, and simulating the effects on humans of air and car crashes.

Source: Reprinted from Otis Port, "Speed Gets a Whole New Meaning," *Business Week,* April 29, 1996, p. 90, with special permission. Copyright © 1996 by The McGraw-Hill Companies, Inc.

brick-and-mortar music stores may soon be a thing of the past. Cell phone users in Europe check sports scores, breaking news, stock quotes, and more using wireless application protocol, or WAP.[31] Savvy marketers and entrepreneurs who follow technological trends are able to foresee new and previously unheard of applications such as these and thereby place themselves and their firms at the forefront of the innovation curve, sometimes earning entrepreneurial fortunes in the process.

Implications of Technological Trends for Market Attractiveness   Changes in technology have always created attractive new markets. Think of all the markets created or made more attractive by Henry Ford's invention of the automobile. Such changes also have swept away old ones, such as the market for buggy whips. Today's venture capital investors monitor such changes, and many seek to invest their funds to serve markets that are growing exponentially as a result of technological developments, such as providing services for e-commerce firms. Some would say that choosing attractive markets or industries for investment is one of the most important criteria for venture capital success.[32]

In addition to creating attractive new markets, technological developments are having a profound impact on all aspects of marketing practice, including marketing communication (ads on the Web or via e-mail), distribution (books and other consumer and industrial goods bought and sold via the Web), packaging (use of new materials), and marketing research (monitoring supermarket purchases with scanners or Internet activity with digital "cookies"). We explore the most important of these changes in later chapters in this book.

The Physical Environment

Beyond the depletion of many of the earth's valuable resources, there are indications that the earth's overall health is declining. Deserts are growing while forests are shrinking, lakes are dying, the quality and quantity of groundwater are declining, and the planet may be experiencing a rising temperature.

One of the more frightening environmental scenarios concerns the buildup of carbon dioxide in the atmosphere that has resulted from heavy use of fossil fuels. This carbon dioxide "blanket" traps the sun's radiation, which leads to an increase in the earth's average temperature. One computer model of the climate predicts a cooling of Europe; Africa, East Asia, and South America warming a lot; and less rain in East Asia, Southern Africa, most of South America, Mexico, and parts of the United States. While the evidence is increasing that greenhouse gases are changing the climate, there is considerable disagreement over the details of the warming effects. Still, various concerned groups (including insurance companies) are demanding that governments take strong remedial action.[33] Among other undesirable eventualities, the greenhouse effect might trigger the infection of nontropical populations with such diseases as malaria, hepatitis, yellow fever, cholera, and meningitis.[34]

Worldwide, there are inadequate supplies of municipal water, which has forced European cities to use tertiary sewage treatments to purify water for household use. California has recently begun to use reclaimed sewage water for parks, golf courses, and roadside landscaping, but not for drinking.[35] Poor water quality causes Americans to spend $7 billion annually for bottled water and for tap-water purification. Americans drink three times as much bottled water as they did a decade ago.[36]

Pollution problems exist throughout the world, especially in Eastern Europe, China, and the developing countries. Germany is spending tens of billions of dollars to clean up eastern Germany, where under communist rule forests were blighted, drinking water badly polluted, and the air fouled such that motorists were forced to use their headlights during the day. China is the world's worst polluter, dumping billions of tons of industrial pollutants into waterways and hundreds of millions of tons of carbon emissions into the atmosphere. It is encouraging to note that pollution regulations are becoming stricter throughout the world, including China, where authorities are considering making serious pollution punishable by death.[37] And recycling programs are increasing in popularity throughout the world.[38]

Development of Green Products as a Response to Environmental Problems

In general, discussion of the problems in the physical environment has stressed the threats and penalties facing business throughout the world. But business can do a number of things to turn problems into opportunities. One is to invest in research to find ways to save energy in heating and lighting. Another is to find new energy sources such as low-cost wind farms and hydroelectric projects. Businesses also have seen opportunities in developing hundreds of **green products** (those that are environmentally friendly) such as phosphate-free detergents, recycled motor oil, tuna caught without netting dolphins, organic fertilizers, high-efficiency light bulbs, recycled paper, and men's and women's casual clothes made from 100 percent organic cotton and colored with nontoxic dyes.[39] Other innovations include using smaller packages for many consumer goods (such as compact containers for superconcentrated soaps and collapsible pouches for cleaners once packed in plastic jugs), discontinuing the use of cardboard packages for deodorants, and selling teabags without tags and strings.[40] For the public, prices of eco (green) products are in line with ordinary products, especially when the quantity offered (tissues per roll of toilet tissue and loads of laundry per liter of concentrated detergent) is considered.[41]

Implications of Trends in the Physical Environment for Market Attractiveness

Global warming can create attractive opportunities for green products that are earth-friendly. On the other hand, if global warming continues, it may play havoc with markets for winter vacationers, snowmobiles, and other products and services whose demand depends on the reliable coming of Old Man Winter. Other physical trends such as the depletion of natural resources and fresh groundwater may significantly impact firms in many industries serving a vast array of markets. Tracking such trends and understanding their effects are important tasks.

ENVIRONMENTAL ANALYSIS GUIDES MARKETING DECISION MAKING

Macro trends can have powerful influence on the attractiveness of markets, as well as on marketing practice. What should managers charged with strategic responsibilities do to take advantage of or cope with such trends? First, they need to prioritize trend categories, so they know what to watch for. Second, they need to identify, and then monitor, sources of relevant information about macro trends. Third, as key developments are noted, they need to anticipate impacts and be prepared to change strategies if necessary.

Prioritizing Trend Categories

Apparel marketers closely watch sociocultural trends so as to provide garments in tune with today's changing lifestyles. For example, specialized undergarments for female athletes have become a growing market, as more and more women participate in athletic pursuits. To the delight of sports apparel marketers like Nike, Brandi Chastain's shirtless torso and sports bra won front-page and front-cover positions in numerous publications following her successful penalty kick that won for the United States the coveted World Cup women's soccer title in 1999.

Real estate investors closely monitor economic trends, because changes in interest rates or income can dramatically impact demand for both commercial and residential properties. Venture capitalists and high-tech entrepreneurs watch technological trends. Food marketers study demographic and sociocultural trends to provide new food products that fit modern lifestyles and satisfy rapidly growing demand for ethnic foods. The list goes on and on. What's important is for businesspeople to understand which macro trend categories are likely to have the most impact on their fortunes and monitor those categories accordingly. Similarly, managers need to monitor changes in ethical standards and expectations, so they do not run afoul of their customers' expectations. Ethical Perspective 4.1 discusses ethical issues that have arisen in this arena.

STRATEGIC ISSUE

What's important is for businesspeople to understand which macro trend categories are likely to have the most impact on their fortunes and monitor those categories accordingly.

Information Sources and Outputs of Macro Trend Analysis

There is an endless supply of information about macro trends, including the popular and business press, the Internet, supplier and customer contacts, and so on. Thus, gathering relevant data is not difficult, but it does take time and effort. A good place to start is with trade associations and trade magazines, both of which typically track and report on trends relevant to the industries they serve. Most local, state, and federal governments provide demographic data easily accessible at their websites, such as **www.census.gov** in the United States. Government sources and the business press are good places to look for economic

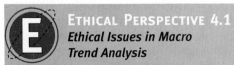

ETHICAL PERSPECTIVE 4.1
Ethical Issues in Macro Trend Analysis

Because there are myriad ways in which business and the environment interact, it is not surprising that firms find it difficult to cope with environmental issues. More and more companies, however, are taking an active role in dealing with the environmental issues that face society today, not only making sure they are in compliance with environmental regulations, but also taking a strong proenvironmental stance that includes abandoning products that are environmentally harmful.

Most companies make an effort to develop a proenvironment attitude among their employees, customers, and the general public—a substantial majority have ethical codes of behavior to guide their employees regarding the environment. Many support green organizations such as the National Wildlife Federation, the Sierra Club, and the Environmental Defense Fund. Since the public demands it, more and more resource conservation and recycling receive

considerable support from many members of the business community. McDonald's, for example, has switched from plastic and styrofoam packaging to cardboard and paper.

Another ethical problem area lies in treatment of third world countries. Concern for such countries has a long history; witness the campaigns against South Africa's apartheid and, more recently, for civil rights in China. U.S. companies have come under severe criticism for contracting with suppliers that use child labor or that provide unhealthy working environments and for charging high prices in third world countries for goods such as pharmaceutical drugs.

Dealing with environmental problems can seem intractable because of difficulty in defining their severity (e.g., the greenhouse effect), let alone knowing how to solve them (replenishing underground water supplies). When we think we have found a solution, we are not sure of its long-term versus short-term effects and the extent to which the solution may be dysfunctional. In some areas, however, the picture is clearer, and a positive response may even be good business.

trend data. Various books, such as one called *Find It Fast,* provide guidance on where to look online and offline for various kinds of such information.[42]

The key outputs of a competent macro trend analysis for any market should include both quantitative and qualitative data. Quantitative data should provide evidence of the market's size and growth rate, for the overall market as well as for key segments. Qualitative data should include factors that will likely influence these figures in the future, whether favorably or unfavorably.

Anticipating and Responding to Environmental Change

Critical changes in macroenvironmental conditions often call for changes in the firm's strategy. Such changes can be proactive or reactive, or both. To the extent that a firm identifies and effectively deals with key trends before its competitors do, it is more likely to win and retain competitive advantage. In any case, management needs systems to help identify, evaluate, and respond to environmental events that may affect the firm's longer-term profitability and position. One such approach uses an opportunity/threat matrix to better assess the impact and the timing of an event, followed by the development of an appropriate response strategy. This approach is discussed below.

Impact and Timing of Event   In any given period, many environmental events that could have an impact on the firm—either positively or negatively—may be detected. Somehow, management must determine the probability of their occurrence and the degree of impact (profitability and/or market share) of each event. One relatively simple way to accomplish these tasks is to use a 2 × 2 dimensional **opportunity/threat matrix** such as that shown in Exhibit 4.7. This example contains four potential environmental events that a large U.S. telecommunications company might have identified as worthy of concern in the early 2000s. The probability of each occurring by the year 2010 was rated as was the impact on the company in terms of profitability or market share. The event likely both to occur by 2010 and to have the greatest impact appears in the upper left-hand box. At the

Exhibit 4.7

OPPORTUNITY/THREAT MATRIX FOR A TELECOMMUNICATIONS COMPANY

Level of Impact on Company*	Probability of Occurrence (2010)	
	High	Low
High	4	1
Low	2	3

1. Wireless communications technology will make networks based on fiber and copper wires redundant.
2. Technology will provide for the storage and accessing of vast quantities of data at affordable costs.
3. The prices of large-screen (over 36-inch) digitalized TV sets will be reduced by 50 percent (constant dollars).
4. Telephone companies will emerge as the dominant force in the telecommunications industry as well as the operators of telecommunications systems.

*Profits or market share or both.

very least, such an event should be examined closely, including estimating with as much precision as possible its impact on profitability and market share.

The opportunity/threat matrix enables the examination of a large number of events in such a way that management can focus on the most important ones. Thus, events such as number 4 in the exhibit with a high probability of occurring and having a high impact should be closely monitored. Those with a low probability of occurrence and low impact, such as number 3 in the exhibit, should probably be dropped, at least for the moment. Events with a low probability/high impact (number 1) should be reexamined less frequently to determine whether the impact rating remains basically sound.

TAKE AWAYS

- Trends can and often will profoundly influence the success of any business. Serving attractive markets, where trends are favorable—swimming with the current—is likely to yield more success than serving those where trends are unfavorable—swimming against the current. Thus, context, the second of the 4 Cs, matters and is central to the assessment of any opportunity.

- Taken together, the six macro trend categories constitute a useful analytical framework to ensure that all bases are covered when scanning environmental conditions.

- Paying regular and systematic attention to the highest priority macro trend categories permits timely decision making, perhaps ahead of competitors.

- Gathering hard data on macro trends is not difficult. Trade associations and trade magazines provide a good place to start.

- Self-diagnostic questions to test your ability to apply the analytical tools and concepts in this chapter to marketing decision making may be found at this book's website at **www.mhhe.com/walker.**

ENDNOTES

1. This section on the changing men's apparel market is based on information found in Lisa Munoz, "The Suit Is Back—or Is It?" *Fortune,* June 25, 2001, p. 202; AnnMarie Dodd, "Clothing Consultation Addresses the Variable Dress Code," *DNR,* April 7, 2000, p. 16; Melanie Kletter, "Tough 4th Quarter for Three Men's Merchants," *DNR,* March 19, 1999, p. FC; Jean Palmieri, "George Zimmer Is Gradually Zeroing in on $10B for Men's Wearhouse," *DNR,* June 23, 1999, p. 24; Vicki M. Young, "Edison Bros. to Liquidate Riggins, JeansWest," *DNR,* April 26, 1999, p. A1; and the 1999 annual reports of Hartmarx Corp. and The Men's Wearhouse, Inc.

2. *Review of Population Trends, Policies, and Programs: Monitoring of World Population Trends and Policies* (New York: United Nations, January 1996), table 9. The data contained in the remainder of this section are based largely on the contents of this report.

3. Ibid.

4. This section is based on data contained in the following: Kevin E. Deardorff and Patricia Montgomery, *National Population Trends* (Washington, DC: U.S. Census Bureau, June 1996); Carl Haub, "Global and U.S. National Population Trends," *Consequences* (1995), funded by NOAA, NASA, and NSF, produced by Saginaw Valley State University, Michigan 48710; Cheryl Russell, "The Baby Boom Turns 50," *American Demographics,* December 1995, p. 22; and Cyndee Miller, "Boomers Come of Old Age," *American Demographics,* January 15, 1996, p. 1. For an interesting discussion on U.S. teenagers as a market, see Peter Zollo, "Talking to Teens," *American Demographics,* November 1995, p. 22.

5. For a closer look at the implications of America's graying population, see Ken Dychtwald, *The Age Wave* (New York: Bantam Books, 1990), and Ken Dychtwald, *Age Power* (New York: J. P. Tarcher, 1999).

6. Early research on this group reported their behavior as being strange and unexplainable and hence the name "Generation X," which derived from a

novel of that name written by Douglas Copeland (New York: St. Martin's Press, 1991). Subsequent research reveals this stereotype to be highly inaccurate in describing this generation's values and beliefs.

7. Material summarized in this section comes from "A Trend Analysis Report on Youth," *Nachus Ov Realities,* no. 1 (New York: BKG Young, n.d.); Chiat/Day, "Notes from the Emerging Media Frontier," *Fame and Flame,* January 6, 1994; "The New Femininity," *Mademoiselle,* Spring 1994; Karen Ritchie, "Marketing to Generation X," *American Demographics,* April 1995, p. 34; Karen Cooperman, "Marketing to Generation X—A Special Report," *Advertising Age,* February 6, 1994, p. 27; John Naisbitt's *Trendletter* 14, no. 9 (April 27, 1995); and Diedre R. Schwieslow, "Sixties Legacy: This Monstrous Bureaucracy," *USA Today,* July 26, 1995, p. 1.

8. See Chip Walker, "The Global Middle Class," *American Demographics,* September 1995, p. 40.

9. Ibid.

10. *U.S. Trade Outlook* (Columbus, OH: Trade Point USA, 1995). Also see "Economic Growth: The Poor and the Rich," *The Economist,* May 25, 1996.

11. Christopher Farrell, Michael J. Mandel, and Joseph Weber, "Riding High," *Business Week,* October 9, 1995, p. 134.

12. "The Future of Spending," *American Demographics,* January 1995, p. 12.

13. John Cassidy, "Who Killed the Middle Class?" *New Yorker,* October 16, 1995, p. 113.

14. Amy Barrett, "It's a Small (Business) World," *Business Week,* April 17, 1995, p. 96.

15. Bill Montague, "China Deal Unlikely to Halt Piracy," *USA Today,* June 18, 1996, p. A1.

16. John Carey and Mary Beth Regan, "Are Regs Bleeding the Economy," *Business Week,* June 17, 1995, p. 75. Also, see Michael E. Porter and Clas Van der Linde, "Green and Competitive," *Harvard Business Review,* September–October 1995, p. 123. American companies have long insisted they were overregulated. For a discussion of why this may not be true—at least as far as Germany and Japan are concerned—see "To All U.S. Managers Upset by Regulations: Try Germany or Japan," *The Wall Street Journal,* December 14, 1995, p. A5.

17. Peter R. Dickson, *Marketing Management* (Ft. Worth, TX: The Dryden Press, 1994), p. 92.

18. Joel A. Bleeke, "Strategic Choices for Newly Opened Markets," *Harvard Business Review,* September–October 1990, p. 163.

19. N. Gregory Mankiw, "D.C., Stay Out of the Economy," *Fortune,* May 15, 2000, p. 70.

20. These were among the top technologies in importance ranked by scientists at a leading research institute. Others include those concerned with high-density energy sources (fuel cells), miniaturization (supercomputer that fits in a pocket), antiaging products (making the process less traumatic), and sensors that can detect diseases at an early stage (lung cancer from breath measurements). See Douglas E. Olesen, "The Top Technologies for the Next 10 Years," *The Futurist,* September–October 1995, p. 9.

21. John Carey, Joan O. C. Hamilton, Julia Flynn, and Geoffery South, "The Gene Kings," *Business Week,* May 8, 1995, p. 72.

22. For a discussion of the validity of the hype that surrounds gene therapy, see "A Triumph of Hype over Experience," *The Economist,* December 16, 1995, p. 77.

23. Laura Johnannes, "Scientists Clone Gene Said to Be Curb on Weight," *The Wall Street Journal,* December 29, 1995, p. B6.

24. "Sowing Cells, Growing Organs," *The Economist,* January 6, 1996, p. 65.

25. "A Sweeter Life for Crops in Salty Soil," *Business Week,* January 15, 1996, p. 90.

26. Rhonda L. Rundle, "Bright Future Is Predicted for Pest-Resistant Seeds," *The Wall Street Journal,* August 31, 1995, p. B4.

27. "The Death of Distance," *The Economist,* September 30, 1995, p. 5; and Bill Gates, *The Road Ahead* (New York: Viking Penguin, 1995), p. 6.

28. "Death of Distance"; and Gates, *Road Ahead.*

29. Audrey Choi, "Storage Devices Take Spotlight in Computer Industry," *The Wall Street Journal,* April 22, 1996, p. B4.

30. Alex Salkever, "Ultimate Jukebox: The ABC's of MP3," *Business Week,* June 5, 2000, p. 135.

31. "Room to Roam," *Fortune Technology Guide,* Summer 2000, p. 174.

32. Bob Zider, "How Venture Capital Works," *Harvard Business Review,* November–December 1998, p. 133.

33. "Science and Technology: Reading the Patterns," *The Economist,* April 1, 1995, p. 65.

34. George F. Sanderson, "Climate Change: The Threat to Human Health," *The Futurist,* March–April 1992, p. 34.

35. "California Water—Want Some More?" *The Economist,* October 8, 1994, p. 30.

36. Carole R. Hedder, "Water Works," *American Demographics,* January 1996, p. 46.

37. Jane H. Lii, "Boom at a Glance," *New York Times Magazine,* February 18, 1995, p. 27.

38. In some countries, voluntary recycling programs have been so successful that systems cannot keep up with the supply. See "Austria Has Recycling Problems," *Business Europe,* March 7, 1994, p. 6.

39. Pat Sloan, "Where-O-Where Can You Get 'Green' Garb?" *Advertising Age,* June 5, 1992, p. 3.

40. Gary Strauss, "Big Trend: Smaller Packaging," *USA Today,* April 1, 1993, p. B1.

41. Kristen Clark, "The Frugal Environmentalist," *The Environmental Magazine,* May–June 1994. For a discussion of how concern for the environment has affected exporting products to Europe, see Kristen Bergstrom, "The Eco-Label and Exporting to Europe," *Business America,* November 29, 1993, p. 21.

42. Robert I. Berkman, *Find It Fast,* 4th ed. (New York: HarperPerennial, 1997).

CHAPTER FIVE

INDUSTRY ANALYSIS AND COMPETITIVE ADVANTAGE

The Cellular Telephone Business: Increasing Competition in a Growing Market[1]

FROM LONDON TO TOKYO TO CHICAGO, cell phones have become a "Can't do without it" tool of time-pressed businesspeople, hip teenagers, and just about anyone else who wants to stay in touch. There is little doubt that the market for mobile telephone service is growing rapidly. In 1983, when the first cellular phone system began operations, it was projected that by 2000, less than one million people would subscribe. As a result of dramatic growth among both business and household users, however, the number of cell phone users has reached more than 100 million worldwide! In Finland, the world's most cell-phone-crazy country, cell phone penetration has passed 70 percent; in South Korea and Hong Kong, 60 percent.

The market for mobile telephony is served by two principal industries: cell phone manufacturers and cell phone service providers. How attractive are these apparently booming industries?

CELL PHONE MANUFACTURING

Rapid-fire technological advances from Qualcomm, Ericsson, Nokia, and others have brought countless new features to the market, including software to access the World Wide Web. In Europe, new phones enable mobile users to check the weather forecast, their e-mail, stock quotes, and more. Finland's Nokia has rocketed to world leadership in cell phones, leaving early and longtime leader Motorola in the dust. From year to year, though, market share figures for leading cell phone manufacturers can double or be halved, depending on whose latest technology catches the fancy of users. To investors' joy or dismay, stock prices follow suit. Qualcomm's shares soared 2,600 percent in 1999, only to fall back by more than 60 percent by mid 2000. Nokia, too, saw its share price tumble in 2001.

This recent history in the hotly competitive cell phone manufacturing industry suggests that a rapidly growing market does not necessarily provide a smooth path to success. Growing markets are one thing, but turbulent industries serving those markets are quite another.

CELL PHONE SERVICE PROVIDERS

Industry conditions for service providers have run wild as well. The race to win global coverage has led to mergers of large players, such as Europe's

Vodaphone with America's AirTouch, in 1999. Vodaphone did not stop there, however, going on to acquire Germany's Mannesmann in 2000. Other marketers with well-known brands also have jumped into the fray. Richard Branson's Virgin Group bought idle capacity from a British also-ran and launched Virgin Telecom, picking up 150,000 customers in his first six weeks. All over Europe, where cell phone penetration is far higher than in the United States, market-by-market battles for market share are raging. Prices for cell phone service have slid, given the competitive pressures. To make matters worse, the cost of obtaining new government licenses to support new third-generation (3G) services has skyrocketed. Britain's auction in early 2000 of 3G licenses wound up raising some $35 billion in license fees, roughly 10 times what was expected. Other European governments have taken notice. Thus, the rapidly growing market for cell phone service has attracted so much interest from competing firms and some governments eager to get their hands on a share of the money that the long-term future profitability of the industry has been put into question. By 2001, the result was a severely depressed market for the shares of wireless providers and other telecom companies as well.

STRATEGIC CHALLENGES ADDRESSED IN CHAPTER 5

As the examples of the cellular phone manufacturing and service industries show, serving a growing market hardly guarantees smooth sailing. Equally or more important are industry conditions and the degree to which specific players in the industry can establish and sustain competitive advantage. Thus, as entrepreneurs and marketing decision makers ponder an **opportunity** to enter or attempt to increase their share of a growing market like that for mobile phones, they also must carefully examine a host of other issues, including the conditions that are currently prevailing in the industry in which they would compete and the likelihood that favorable conditions will prevail in the future.

In this chapter, we provide analytical frameworks to enable prospective entrepreneurs and marketing strategists in established firms to address four critical questions pertinent to such an examination: How can we assess the attractiveness of an industry? If we aim to compete on the basis of innovation, how can we determine how quickly our innovation is likely to win market acceptance? What does the overall attractiveness of the market and industry context imply for chances for future success? Finally, how can we establish and then sustain competitive advantage over the duration of our product's life cycle? First, however, we clarify the difference between two oft-confused terms: **market** and **industry.**

MARKETS AND INDUSTRIES: WHAT'S THE DIFFERENCE?

In Chapter 1, we defined a market as being comprised of individuals and organizations who are interested and willing to buy a good or service to obtain benefits that will satisfy a particular need or want and who have the resources to engage in such a transaction. One such market consists of college students who get hungry in the middle of the afternoon and have a few minutes and enough spare change to buy a snack between classes.

An industry is a group of firms that offer a product or class of products that are similar and are close substitutes for one another. What industries serve the student snack market? At the producer level, there are the salty snack industry (makers of potato and corn chips and similar products); the candy industry; the fresh produce industry (growers of apples, oranges, bananas, and other easy-to-eat fruits); and others too numerous to mention. Distribution channels for these products include the supermarket industry, the food service industry, the coin-operated vending industry, and so on. Clearly, these industries are different and offer varying bundles of benefits to hungry students.

The distinction between markets and industries is an important one. Sellers who look only to others in their own industry as competitors are likely to overlook other very real rivals and risk having their markets undercut by innovators from other industries. Should Kodak be more concerned with Fuji, Agfa, and other longtime players in the film and photoprocessing industries, or should it be worrying about Hewlett-Packard, Sony, and others whose digital technologies may make photography's century-old silver halide chemistry go the way of the buggy whip? Only time will tell.

STRATEGIC ISSUE

The distinction between markets and industries is an important one. Sellers who look only to others in their own industry as competitors are likely to overlook other very real rivals.

Defining Markets and Industries: Levels of Analysis

Assessing the attractiveness of markets and industries requires clarity about which consumers and which of their needs or which sellers of which products are to be included in the assessment. Confusion between market and industry can result since consumer needs are often thought of in product terms—"I'm hungry. I need a candy bar."—in the same way that industries are typically described by the products they sell. Thus, *markets* are often defined both in demographic and/or geographic terms (who and/or where the customers are) and in terms of a particular good or service demanded by the consumer, expressed at the industry, product class, or product type level.

Challenges in Market and Industry Definition

Markets and industries can be defined at several **levels of analysis: industry, product class,** and **product type** are most common. The level chosen for a particular analysis can have important implications for strategic and marketing planning. Defining a market or industry at too broad a level can cause the analyst to overlook important market–industry interactions in a particular market segment or for a particular product class or type. But defining the market or industry too narrowly can cause the analyst to miss potentially important competitive developments.

The problem with using the **industry level** is that it typically includes an array of noncompeting products. For example, within the automotive market, is a Toyota Echo in competition with a BMW or a Mack truck? Within chemical markets, do polymers that substitute for natural materials compete with gasoline additives, dyestuffs, and industrial coatings? Probably not. For an entrepreneur seeking to market a new chemical compound that enhances the depth of color when cotton yarns are dyed, understanding the state of the overall chemical industry is probably less important than understanding dyestuffs competitors.

Using **product class** as one's level of analysis suffers from this same type of problem since the products involved may serve diverse markets or market segments. The more generic the definition of a product class, the higher the aggregation level of products (for instance, all cars versus sport utility vehicles) and the more stable is market demand, as well as the product life cycle curve, a concept we explore later in this chapter. Thus, basic needs for automobiles (at least, in developed countries) typically change slowly, though demand patterns for SUVs or pickup trucks or compact cars may be more volatile. The more generically the product class is defined, the less useful it is for strategic planning, which seeks to identify opportunities and threats for specific product-market relationships.

Product types are subsets of a product class and contain items that are technically similar, although they may vary in such aspects as appearance and price. In the case of cereals, for example, the product types could be defined as hot or cold cereals. Hot cereals would include at least two subtypes: regular and instant. Cold cereals would include regular, presweetened, natural, and fortified. Regular could be broken down into such categories as corn flakes, raisin brans, and shredded wheat. Other examples of product hierarchies abound, especially when different processing technologies are involved—frozen, canned, fresh, dehydrated, and freeze-dried fruits and vegetables, for example. Most marketers select product type as their level of analysis for marketing planning because, while products within a product type may serve different subsets of needs, they are typically close substitutes for one another. The product-type level of aggregation is considerably more sensitive than the other levels to environmental changes—such as those driven by macro trends, as discussed in Chapter 4—that create opportunities or threats for individual product-market entries. The danger in restricting one's market and competitive analysis to a particular product type is that other product types, such as bagels or a trip through the drive-through at McDonald's in the breakfast market, may be overlooked. Focusing on the true **consumer need** (i.e., a fast breakfast, rather than cereal, a product) can help avoid this problem.

Doing so appears to be uncommon, however. A recent study found that managers tended to rely on supply-based attributes (i.e., what companies sell) in identifying competitors, rather than demand- or customer need-based attributes (i.e., what customers need).[2] Further, managers tend to identify too few firms as competitors and are especially likely to omit new firms or potential competitors. Stories of experienced managers who "know their business" and are surprised by the sudden emergence of a new competitor that operates in a different way are legion.[3] For an example of how firms create new market space not bound by old industry definitions, see Exhibit 5.1.

Exhibit 5.1   Creating New Market Space

W. Chan Kim and Reneé Mauborgne argue that one way to avoid cutthroat, head-to-head competition, in rapidly growing markets as well as those that are flat or growing slowly, is to find new "market space," as they call it, that defies conventional boundaries of industry competition. By looking across substitute industries or to complementary product and service offerings that go beyond what an industry has traditionally offered, companies can rethink the functional and emotional orientation of their industry and help shape industry trends to their own advantage. Cisco Systems created new market space in this way when it recognized that the doubling of the number of Internet users every 100 days was creating demand for high-speed data exchange that was not being adequately served by existing industries. Today, more than 80 percent of all traffic on the Internet flows through Cisco's routers, switches, and other network devices, on which Cisco earns margins in the 60 percent range. Creating new market space can be attractive, indeed!

Source: W. Chan Kim and Reneé Mauborgne, "Creating New Market Space," *Harvard Business Review*, January–February 1999, pp. 83–93.

THE MARKET IS ATTRACTIVE: WHAT ABOUT THE INDUSTRY?

As consumers and businesspeople have become hooked on cell phones, the market for mobile communication has grown rapidly. By most measures, this is a large, growing, and attractive *market*. But are cell phone manufacturing and cellular services attractive *industries?* An industry's attractiveness at a point in time can best be judged by analyzing its driving forces, its critical success factors and the degree to which a management team can perform on these factors, and especially the five major competitive forces: rivalry among present competitors, potential competitors, the bargaining power of suppliers, the bargaining power of buyers, and the threat of substitute products.

Driving Forces

Just as macroenvironmental trends are important in shaping market attractiveness, so, too, are they important in shaping the attractiveness of industries. Michael Porter calls these trends driving forces.[4] These include (1) changes in the industry's long-term growth rate, which directly affect investment decisions and intensity of competition; (2) changes in key buyer segments, which affect demand and strategic marketing programs; (3) diffusion of proprietary knowledge, which controls both the rate at which products become more alike and the entry of new firms; (4) changes in cost and efficiency, derived from scale and learning effects, which have the potential of making entry more difficult; and (5) changes in government regulations, which can affect entry, costs, bases of competition, and profitability. Collecting and examining trend data in each of these areas helps an entrepreneur or marketer determine whether an industry is sufficiently attractive to enter or remain in and helps shape strategic marketing decisions that enable the firm to compete effectively. The profusion of data now available on the Internet has made the gathering of these data much easier than was true several years ago.

Porter's Five Competitive Forces[5]

Five interactive competitive forces collectively determine an industry's long-term attractiveness: present competitors, potential competitors, the bargaining power of suppliers, the bargaining power of buyers, and the threat of substitute products (see Exhibit 5.2). This mix of forces explains why some industries are consistently more profitable than others and provides further insights into which resources are required and which strategies should be adopted to be successful.

The strength of the individual forces varies from industry to industry and, over time, within the same industry. In the fast-food industry the key forces are present competitors (for example, Wendy's versus Burger King versus McDonald's), substitute products (neighborhood delis, salad bars, all-you-can-eat buffet restaurants, and frozen meals), and buyers who are concerned about health and nutrition and who see fast foods as a symbol of a throw-away society.

STRATEGIC ISSUE

Five interactive competitive forces collectively determine an industry's long-term attractiveness: present competitors, potential competitors, the bargaining power of suppliers, the bargaining power of buyers, and substitute products.

Rivalry among Present Competitors   Rivalry occurs among firms that produce products that are close substitutes for each other, especially when one competitor acts to improve its standing or protect its position. Thus, firms are mutually dependent: What one firm does affects others, and vice versa. Ordinarily, profitability decreases as rivalry increases. Rivalry is greater under the following conditions:

Exhibit 5.2

THE MAJOR FORCES THAT DETERMINE INDUSTRY ATTRACTIVENESS

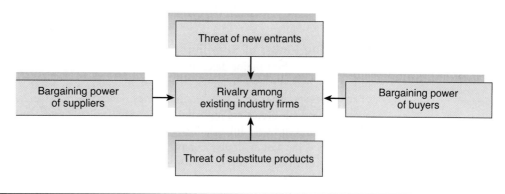

- *There is high investment intensity; that is, the amount of fixed and working capital required to produce a dollar of sales is large.* High intensity requires firms to operate at or near capacity as much as possible, thereby putting strong downward pressure on prices when demand slackens. Thus, high investment–intensity businesses are, on average, much less profitable than those with a lower level of investment. Bob Crandall, the CEO of American Airlines, once described the airline business as being "intensely, vigorously, bitterly, savagely competitive."[6]

- *There are many small firms in an industry or no dominant firms exist.* In recent years, hundreds of pharmaceutical companies have started up, all hoping to produce new wonder drugs. In such crowded segments as neurosciences, inflammatory diseases, and drug delivery, competition is keen, and some companies are considering preemptive steps in an effort to dominate their niches.[7]

- *There is little product differentiation*—for example, major appliances, TV sets, and passenger-car tires.

- *There is a high cost to changing suppliers (switching costs)* as would be the case in changing a major computer software system.[8]

The greater the competitive rivalry in an industry, the less attractive it is to current players or would-be entrants. Though the cellular service industry is capital intensive, there are several dominant firms whose products are differentiated through rapid technological change, and switching costs to change cell phone suppliers are low. Thus, rivalry in this industry might be judged as moderately favorable.

Threat of New Entrants   A second force affecting industry attractiveness is the threat of new entrants. New competitors add capacity to the industry and bring with them the need to gain market share, thereby making competition more intense. The threat of new entrants, such as firms using new packet-switching technology that allows the user to always be connected, is a very real concern to present cellular industry players.[9] The greater the threat of new entrants, the less will be an industry's attractiveness. Entry is more difficult under the following conditions:

- *When strong economies of scale and learning effects are present,* since it takes time to obtain the volume and learning required to yield a low relative cost per unit. If firms already present are vertically integrated, entry becomes even more expensive. Also, if the existing firms share their output with their related businesses, the problem of overcoming the cost disadvantage is made even more difficult.

- *If the industry has strong capital requirements at the outset.*
- *When strong product differentiation exists.*
- *If gaining distribution is particularly difficult.*
- *If a buyer incurs switching costs in moving from one supplier to another.*

Bargaining Power of Suppliers   The bargaining power of suppliers over firms in an industry is the third major determinant of industry attractiveness. It is exercised largely through increased prices. Its impact can be significant, particularly when a limited number of suppliers service several different industries. Their power is increased if switching costs and prices of substitutes are high and they can realistically threaten forward integration.[10] Suppliers are especially important when their product is a large part of the buyer's value added—as is the case with metal cans, where the cost of tin plate is over 60 percent of the value added. In recent years, the bargaining power of suppliers in many industries has changed dramatically as more companies seek a partnership (just-in-time) relationship with their suppliers. What was once an arm's-length adversarial relationship has turned into a cooperative one resulting in lower transaction costs, improved quality derived primarily from using a supplier's technological skills to design and manufacture parts, and decreased transaction time in terms of inventory replenishments.

The greater the bargaining power of the key suppliers to an industry, the less will be the overall attractiveness of the industry. The newly discovered power that European governments have begun to exert by auctioning bandwidth for new cellular services has raised the bargaining power of the suppliers of bandwidth to the cellular industry. This change has reduced the attractiveness of this industry.

Bargaining Power of Buyers   An industry's customers constantly look for reduced prices, improved product quality, and added services and thus can affect competition within an industry. Buyers play individual suppliers against one another in their efforts to obtain these and other concessions. This is certainly the case with some large retailers in their dealings with many of their suppliers.

The extent to which buyers succeed in their bargaining efforts depends on (1) the extent of buyer concentration, as when a few large buyers that account for a large portion of industry sales can gain concessions; (2) switching costs that reduce the buyer's bargaining power; (3) the threat of backward integration, thereby alleviating the need for the supplier; (4) the product's importance to the performance of the buyer's product—the greater the importance, the lower their bargaining power; and (5) buyer profitability—if buyers earn low profits and the product involved is an important part of their costs, then bargaining will be more aggressive.

The greater the power of the high-volume customers served by an industry, the less attractive will be that industry. One attractive dimension of the cellular phone service industry is that its customers have relatively little power to set terms and conditions for cellular phone service. Buyers are numerous and not very concentrated and their cell phone costs are typically not of great importance or expense, relatively speaking.

Threat of Substitute Products   Substitutes are alternative product types (not brands) that perform essentially the same functions, as tin versus aluminum cans, oleomargarine versus butter, and the faxing of documents versus overnight express delivery. Substitute products put a ceiling on the profitability of an industry by limiting the price that can be charged, especially when supply exceeds demand. Thus, in the metal container industry, aluminum is a substitute for tinplate and constrains the prices charged by tinplate producers (see Exhibit 5.3). For cellular phone service providers, possible substitutes include personal digital assistants (PDAs) such as 3Com's Palm Pilot,[11] possible new multimedia devices from the likes of Sony, Matsushita, and Samsung,[12] or new mobile digital products not yet imagined.

Exhibit 5.3	Steel versus Aluminum in the Automotive Industry

Experimental aluminum cars accelerate faster, shift gears more smoothly, and stop more quickly than a steel car—but the latter is sturdier and safer, thereby keeping the competition between the two metals a draw. Steel, which makes up 55 percent of the weight of the average car, is feeling seriously threatened since the car industry is mandated to produce a more fuel-efficient vehicle (getting up to 80 miles per gallon) that meets the consumers' needs for performance and safety—all at a reasonable price. Aluminum has a substantial weight advantage and is easier to mold. Steel, however, is cheaper and easier to recycle as well as safer. And neither industry can afford to ignore competition from plastics. Given the billions of dollars at stake, small wonder that scientists, engineers, and CEOs around the world are spending tens of millions of dollars to increase their share of the materials used to produce a car.

Source: Erle Norton and Gabriella Stern, "Steel and Aluminum Vie over Every Ounce in a Car's Construction," *Wall Street Journal,* May 9, 1995, p. A1. Copyright 1995 by Dow Jones & Co. Inc. Reproduced with permission of Dow Jones & Co. Inc. via Copyright Clearance Center.

A Five Forces Analysis of the Cellular Phone Service Industry

A useful way to summarize a five forces industry analysis is to construct a chart like that shown in Exhibit 5.4. There, we summarize one analyst's judgment of the favorability of the five forces for the cellular phone service industry in the year 2001. This analysis indicates that, compared to earlier in the industry's history when there were fewer players (thus, less rivalry), no threatening substitutes on the horizon, and a cozier relationship with governments to provide bandwidth, the industry today is probably less attractive than some industries, for which four or five of the forces might be favorable. Thus, strategists who must decide whether to enter or continue to invest in this industry must make a judgment as to whether the rapid growth of the *market—a favorable* **environmental context**—is sufficient to offset the deteriorating attractiveness of the *industry—the not-so-favorable* **competitive situation.** Given this mixed outlook, strategists will no doubt consider other factors, including the degree to which they believe they are likely to be able to establish and sustain competitive advantage. We further develop this theme later in this chapter.

Changing Competition and Industry Evolution

As we shall see later in this chapter, most products and product categories pass through a series of stages in their life cycles: introduction, growth, shakeout, maturity, and decline. All five competitive forces just discussed are affected by the passage of time; therefore, their strength varies as the industry passes from its introductory stage to its growth stage and on to maturity, followed by decline. Competitive forces are apt to be weakest during the fast-growth period; thus, there are substantial opportunities for gaining market share. During the shakeout period, competitive forces are at their strongest, and many competitors are forced to exit the industry. During maturity, competition typically slackens, but only if the industry leader holds a strong relative share position. An industry will experience more price competition during maturity if the leader holds a weak *relative* share position. Kellogg and General Mills hold two-thirds of the U.S. domestic cereal market, but because Kellogg does not hold a dominant relative share, the industry experiences considerable price competition. A declining industry usually witnesses considerable rivalry, the extent of which depends on the strength of the exit barriers and the rate of decline.

Exhibit 5.4

FIVE FORCES ANALYSIS OF THE WORLDWIDE CELL PHONE SERVICE INDUSTRY IN LATE 2001

Five forces	Score	Rationale
Rivalry among present competitors	Rivalry is low to moderate: moderately favorable	Products are differentiated through new features and services; customer switching costs are low.
Threat of new entrants	Threat of new entrants is high: moderately unfavorable	Rapid pace of technological change may bring new entrants based on new technologies: packet switching, satellites.
Supplier power	Supplier power is high: moderately unfavorable	Governments have raised the price of additional bandwidth through auctions.
Buyer power	Buyer power is low: very favorable	Even large customers have little power to set terms and conditions in this oligopolistic industry.
Threat of substitutes	Threat of substitutes is high: moderately unfavorable	PDAs or new multimedia devices could replace cell phones.

Overall conclusion: Only two of the five forces are favorable, while three are unfavorable. Thus, the cellular phone service industry is not particularly attractive at this time.

Critical Success Factors

The **critical success factors** that differentiate between the success and failure of firms *within* an industry differ from industry to industry. These factors often are concerned with one or more of the elements in the marketing mix—product (e.g., the capability to generate successful new products), price (be a low-cost producer), place (obtain widespread product distribution), and promotion (strong relationships with large customers). As the old saying goes in the retailing industry, only three things are critical to success: location, location, and location. Thus, location, a potentially powerful source of competitive advantage, often makes the difference between which retailers are successful and which are not.

Assessing the fit between an industry's critical success factors and the presence of those factors in a firm or a proposed management team is a good way to assess whether an industry is attractive to that particular firm or management team and to determine whether that firm or team is likely to be attractive to investors or other suppliers of resources. Thus, before deciding whether or not to invest in a start-up, most venture capitalists want to know whether the start-up team has the necessary competencies to be successful in the industry it proposes to enter.

INDUSTRY ANALYSIS LOCALLY: HOW INTENSE IS THE IMMEDIATE COMPETITION?

As we have seen, assessing an industry's driving forces and Porter's five forces and understanding its critical success factors are important to industry analysis. These are macro-level issues, similar to the macro trends we examined in Chapter 4. To most firms, immediate and local competitive conditions are equally if not more important. Such conditions are particularly

ETHICAL PERSPECTIVE 5.1
SCIP: Setting Standards for Gathering Competitive Intelligence

SCIP, the Society of Competitive Intelligence Professionals (**www.scip.org**), is an organization of consultants and businesspeople whose job it is to monitor the competitive environment for their firms. Competitive intelligence (CI) enables senior managers in companies of all sizes to make informed decisions about everything from marketing, R&D, and investing tactics to long-term business strategies. Effective CI is a continuous process involving the legal and ethical collection of information, analysis that doesn't avoid unwelcome conclusions, and controlled dissemination of actionable intelligence to decision makers. SCIP's code of ethics provides a useful guide for anyone charged with gathering information about competitors.

SCIP Code of Ethics for CI Professionals

To continually strive to increase the recognition and respect of the profession.

To comply with all applicable laws, domestic and international.

To accurately disclose all relevant information, including one's identity and organization, prior to all interviews.

To fully respect all requests for confidentiality of information.

To avoid conflicts of interest in fulfilling one's duties.

To provide honest and realistic recommendations and conclusions in the execution of one's duties.

To promote this code of ethics within one's company, with third-party contractors, and within the entire profession.

To faithfully adhere to and abide by one's company policies, objectives, and guidelines.

Source: www.scip.org. Reprinted by permission.

---

salient for firms, such as retailers, that operate on a local basis. If an entrepreneur wants to open a fly-fishing shop near a blue-ribbon trout stream in Montana, he or she will be pleased that fly-fishing is on the rise, that consumers have adequate income to pursue such a sport, and that leisure activities are becoming more important to many people. But it also matters if there are already a couple of fly-fishing shops serving the local market, and whether those shops serve their customers effectively. If so, the overall trends and industry conditions probably do not matter much, for the local fly-fishing pie can be sliced only so many ways! Thus, assessing an industry must typically be done locally, as well as more globally, and relevant information about specific competitors must be obtained.

In Chapter 6, we address the market knowledge systems that many firms use to gather competitive information, as well as other relevant market and industry data. As we shall see, gathering this information is important, and ethical issues having to do with how competitive information is obtained are likely to arise. For a discussion of ethical issues in gathering information to perform competitive analyses, see Ethical Perspective 5.1.

RATE OF DIFFUSION OF INNOVATIONS: ANOTHER FACTOR IN ASSESSING OPPORTUNITY ATTRACTIVENESS

Before entrepreneurs or established marketers invest in the development and introduction of an innovation, they should evaluate how rapidly the innovation is likely to be adopted by the target market. The faster the adoption rate, the more attractive an innovative good or service is to the marketer, as competitors are caught short while consumers build loyalty to the new product. **Diffusion of innovation** theory seeks to explain the adoption of a product or service over time among a group of potential buyers. Lack of awareness typically limits early adoption. As positive word

STRATEGIC ISSUE

Diffusion theory is useful to managers in predicting the likely adoption rate for new and innovative goods or services.

about the product spreads, the product is adopted by additional consumers. Diffusion theory is useful to managers in predicting the likely adoption rate for new and innovative goods or services.

The Adoption Process

The **adoption process** involves the attitudinal changes experienced by individuals from the time they first hear about a new product, service, or idea until they adopt it. Not all individuals respond alike; some tend to adopt early, some late, and some never. Thus, the market for a new product tends to be segmented over time.

The five stages in the adoption process are awareness, interest, evaluation, trial, and adoption:

1. *Awareness.* In this stage, the person is only aware of the existence of the new product and is insufficiently motivated to seek information about it.

2. *Interest.* Here the individual becomes sufficiently interested in the new product but is not yet involved.

3. *Evaluation.* This is sometimes referred to as the *mental rehearsal* stage. At this point, the individual is mentally applying the new product to his or her own use requirements and anticipating the results.

4. *Trial.* Here the individual actually uses the product, but, if possible, on a limited basis to minimize risk. Trial is not tantamount to adoption; only if the use experience is satisfactory will the product stand a chance of being adopted.

5. *Adoption.* In this stage, the individual not only continues to use the new product but also adopts it in lieu of substitutes.

The Rate of Adoption

If plotted on a cumulative basis, the percentage of people adopting a new product over time resembles an S curve. Although the curve tends to have the same shape regardless of the product involved, the length of time required differs among products—often substantially.

The time dimension is a function of the rate at which people in the target group (those ultimately adopting) move through the five stages in the adoption process. Generally, the speed of the adoption process depends on the following factors: (1) the risk (cost of product failure or dissatisfaction), (2) the relative advantage over other products, (3) the relative simplicity of the new product, (4) its compatibility with previously adopted ideas, (5) the extent to which its trial can be accomplished on a small-scale basis, and (6) the ease with which the central idea of the new product can be communicated.[13] Some new products move quickly through the adoption process (a new breakfast cereal), while others take years. Risk minimization via guarantees and reliable and prompt service is critical as is the ability to demonstrate the product's uniqueness in meeting the customer's needs. Source credibility is also important.

The rate at which a product passes through the adoption process is also a function of the actions taken by the product's supplier. Thus, the diffusion process is faster when there is strong competition among members of the supplier group, when they have favorable reputations, and when they allocate substantial sums to R&D (to improve performance) and marketing (to build awareness).[14] The cellular phone industry should score high on these adoption factors.

Adopter Categories

Early adopters differ from later adopters. Using time of adoption as a basis for classifying individuals, five major groups can be distinguished: innovators, early adopters, early majority, late majority, and laggards. (Note that these are different from the five stages of adoption for a given individual just discussed.) See Exhibit 5.5 for the approximate size

Exhibit 5.5

SIZE AND CHARACTERISTICS OF INDIVIDUAL ADOPTER GROUP

- **Innovators** represent the first 2.5 percent of all individuals who ultimately adopt a new product. They are more venturesome than later adopters, more likely to be receptive to new ideas, and tend to have high incomes, which reduces the risk of a loss arising from an early adoption.

- **Early adopters** represent the next 13 to 14 percent who adopt. They are more a part of the local scene, are often opinion leaders, serve as vital links to members of the early majority group (because of their social proximity), and participate more in community organizations than do later adopters.

- The **early majority** includes 34 percent of those who adopt. These individuals display less leadership than early adopters, tend to be active in community affairs (thereby gaining respect from their peers), do not like to take unnecessary risks, and want to be sure that a new product will prove successful before they adopt it.

- The **late majority** represents another 34 percent. Frequently, these individuals adopt a new product because they are forced to do so for either economic or social reasons. They participate in community activities less than the previous groups and only rarely assume a leadership role.

- **Laggards** comprise the last 16 percent of adopters. Of all the adopters, they are the most "local." They participate less in community matters than members of the other groups and stubbornly resist change. In some cases, their adoption of a product is so late it has already been replaced by another new product.

and characteristics of each group.[15] Because each category comprises individuals who have similar characteristics and because individuals differ substantially across categories, these adopter groups can be considered market segments. Thus, one would use a different set of strategies to market a new product to the early adopter group than to market it to the late majority group. For a discussion of the challenges in transitioning marketing efforts from group to group, see Exhibit 5.6.

The differences cited in Exhibits 5.5 and 5.6 are important because they help in the development of strategic marketing programs. In organizational markets, suppliers can identify innovative firms by reputation, profitability, size, and the suppliers' experiences in dealing with them. As evident from earlier discussion, information alone about the product or service is not usually a sufficient reason to adopt. Commercial sources of information (such as salespeople and mass media advertising) are important at the outset, but less-commercial and more-professional sources are sought to validate the proclaimed merits of the new product, especially during the evaluation stage. Advice from opinion leaders is more critical as a legitimizing agent than as a source of information. A classic study of how doctors reacted to the introduction of a new "miracle drug" found that only 10 percent adopted on the basis of data provided by their initial source of information, indicating that data alone will not cause adoption.[16]

Thus, commercial sources are most important at the awareness stage in the adoption process, while personal influence is most important at the evaluation stage. In the interest stage, both are important. In the trial stage, marketers should attempt to make it relatively easy for a prospect to try a product under conditions that minimize risk. Therefore, strategic marketing programs should accommodate the various stages in the adoption process as well as the different adoption audiences.

Implications of Diffusion of Innovation Theory for Forecasting Sales of New Products and New Firms

Optimistic entrepreneurs or new product managers sometimes wax euphoric about the prospects for the innovations they plan to bring to market. They naively forecast that their innovations will capture 10 percent or 20 percent of the market in its first year. How likely

Exhibit 5.6   Crossing the Chasm: A Difficult Transition in the Diffusion Process

In his classic book on the marketing of high-technology products, Geoffrey Moore explores the challenges of crossing the "chasm," as he calls it, in the diffusion process between the early adopters and the early majority. For many high-tech products, innovators and early adopters have quite different needs from early majority customers. Innovators and early adopters are often willing to adopt a revolutionary new product that is not yet very user-friendly or whose product features have not yet been fully developed. Their own technical skill enables them to adapt such a product to their needs and resolve some of the uncertainties inherent in the product's perhaps still-unclear potential. Their self-perception as an innovator gives them comfort in trying new products before others do. Early majority buyers, on the other hand, typically require easier-to-use products, whose benefits are clearly defined, and for which there is proof that the product will perform. Taking a product from the first group of buyers to the second is a difficult challenge, one that is compounded by the fact that buyers in the innovator and early adopter groups are not likely to associate or talk with buyers in the early majority group.

Source: Geoffrey Moore, *Crossing the Chasm* (New York: Harper-Business, 1995).

is it that a truly innovative new product, even a compellingly attractive one, will win all of the innovators plus most of the early adopters in its first year on the market? History suggests that such penetration levels are rare at the outset. More typically, first-year penetration levels include some but not all of the innovators, well under 2½ percent of those who, it is hoped, will ultimately adopt!

A good way to estimate how quickly an innovation is likely to move through the diffusion process is to construct a chart that rates the adoption on the six key factors influencing adoption speed, as shown in Exhibit 5.7. An innovation that is risky for the prospective user to try or buy, has little competitive advantage, is complex or incompatible with current user behavior, and is difficult or expensive to try or to understand its benefits is likely to face tough sledding, regardless of the attractiveness of the industry. Personal robots, introduced in the early 1980s with great fanfare following the introduction of personal computers, were such an innovation. Thus, introducing a new product that delivers no real benefits or lacks competitive advantage into *any* industry, regardless of its high-tech profile, is likely to be an unpleasant experience!

SUSTAINING COMPETITIVE ADVANTAGE OVER THE PRODUCT LIFE CYCLE

STRATEGIC ISSUE

The PLC concept is extremely valuable in helping management look into the future and better anticipate what changes will need to be made in strategic marketing programs.

The product life cycle is concerned with the sales history of a product or product class. The concept holds that a product's sales change over time in a predictable way and that products go through a series of five distinct stages: introduction, growth, shakeout, maturity, and decline (see Exhibit 5.8). Each of these stages provides distinct opportunities and threats, thereby affecting the firm's strategy as well as its marketing programs. Despite the fact that many new products do not follow such a prescribed route because of failure, the concept is extremely valuable in helping management look into the future and better anticipate what changes will need to be made in strategic marketing programs.

At the beginning (the **introductory stage**), a new product's purchase is limited because members of the target market are insufficiently aware of its existence; also, the product often lacks easy availability. As more people learn about the product and it becomes more

Exhibit 5.7

COMPARISON OF RATE OF ADOPTION OF CELLULAR PHONES AND PERSONAL COMPUTERS FOR HOME USE

Adoption factor	Cell phones	Home computers
Risk	+/– Moderate risk: Cell phones were given away to attract early adopters who agreed to one year's usage.	– An expensive investment wasted, if it turned out not to be useful.
Relative advantage	+ Enabled people to make and receive phone calls from anywhere—in the car or at the beach!	– It was not clear, in the early days of personal computing, what the advantages of a PC were in the home.
Relative simplicity	+ Early cell phones were easy to use.	– Early PCs were inordinately complex to use.
Compatibility with current behavior	+ Just like making or receiving a phone call at home or office.	– Lots of learning required to use.
Ease of small-scale trial	+ Contracts required only modest minutes of use.	+/– One could visit a store for hands-on trial, but couldn't understand the "bits, bytes, and RAM."
Ease of communication of benefits	+ "Make or receive calls anywhere" is easy to understand.	– Benefits were not clear, thus not communicable.

Key:

+ Favorable for rapid adoption

– Unfavorable for rapid adoption

readily available, sales increase at a progressively faster rate (the **growth stage**). Growth slows as the number of buyers nears the maximum and repeat sales become increasingly more important than trial sales. As the number of both buyers and their purchases stabilizes, growth becomes largely a function of population growth in the target market. At the end of the growth period—just before the advent of maturity—the **shakeout or competitive turbulence stage** occurs. This is characterized by a decreasing growth rate that results in strong price competition, forcing many firms to exit the industry or sell out. The **mature stage** is reached when the net adoption rate holds steady—that is, when adopters approximate dropouts. When the latter begin to exceed new first-time users, the sales rate declines and the product is said to have reached its final or **decline stage.**[17]

Life Cycle Curves

Many products do not go through the product life cycle curve shown in Exhibit 5.8 because a high percentage are aborted after an unsatisfactory introductory period. Other products seemingly never die (Scotch whiskey, TVs, automobiles). The shape of the life cycle curve varies considerably between and within industries but is typically described as "S"-shaped. One study identified 12 different types of curves.[18]

In general, however, only one or a very few curves typify an industry (see Exhibit 5.9 for the common types). The growth-decline plateau is probably the most common since a majority of products are in their mature stage (color TVs and most household appliances). This is followed by the cycle/recycle type, which is characteristic of many pharmaceutical products that receive heavy promotions at the outset and again when sales begin to falter. The innovative-maturity curve goes through several life cycles because new innovative characteristics as well as new uses are discovered. A classic illustration is 3M's Scotch

Exhibit 5.8

GENERALIZED PRODUCT LIFE CYCLE

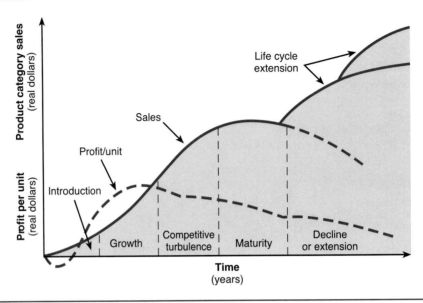

Source: From *Analysis for Strategic Marketing Decisions,* 1st edition, by G. S. Day © 1986. Reprinted with permission of South-Western College Publishing, a division of Thomson Learning. Fax 800-730-2215.

tape, which initially expanded to a line of colored and patterned items for gift wrapping. Next, a low-price commercial line was added, and finally 3M developed a coated type to compete with reflective tape. All of these tapes are still doing *very* well.[19] The classic S-shaped curve occurs only when the product passes through all stages to its death (steam engines and many prescription drugs). Where is the Web in its life cycle?

Fads, such as Beanie Babies, pet rocks, and hula hoops, enter suddenly, experience strong and quick enthusiasm, peak early, and enter the decline stage shortly thereafter. Thus, even when successful, their life cycle is unusually short and is typically depicted in the form of an inverted V.[20]

Market and Competitive Implications of Product Life Cycle Stages

The various stages of the product life cycle present different opportunities and threats to the firm. By understanding the characteristics of the major stages, a firm can do a better job of setting forth its objectives and formulating its strategies as well as developing its action plans (see Exhibit 5.10). Our discussion here is generalized; in Chapters 10, 11, and 12 we present a comprehensive examination of specific marketing-strategy programs and do so for both leaders and followers.

Introductory Stage   There is a vast difference between pioneering a product class and a product type. The former is more difficult, time-consuming, expensive, and risky, as must have been the case when the telephone was introduced versus the introduction of the cellular phone. The introductory period, in particular, is apt to be long, even for relatively simple product classes such as packaged food products. Because product type and subtype

Exhibit 5.9

COMMON PRODUCT LIFE CYCLE CURVES

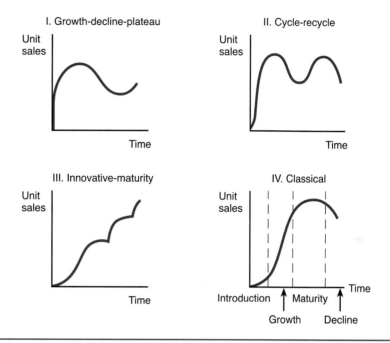

Source: J. E. Swan and D. R. Rink, "Effective Use of Industrial Product Life Cycle Trends," in *Marketing in the '80s*, 1980, pp. 198–99. Reprinted by permission from the publisher, American Marketing Association.

entries usually emerge during the late-growth and maturity stages of the product class, they have shorter introductory and growth periods. Once the product is launched, the firm's goal should be to move it through the introductory stage as quickly as possible. Research, engineering, and manufacturing capacity are critical to ensure the availability of quality products. Where service is important, the firm must be able to provide it promptly (as in postpurchase service and spare-parts availability). The length of the product line should be relatively short to reduce production costs and hold down inventories.

For sophisticated industrial products, the initial market consists mainly of large companies with enough resources to risk adoption, the technical capabilities to objectively evaluate the merits of the new product, and the most to gain if it works out well. To encourage trial and repeat buying, marketers of consumer products use a combination of methods, including heavy demonstration-oriented TV advertising, in-store displays, free samples, coupons, and special introductory prices. The firm also must obtain distribution and ample shelf space to provide product availability—particularly in self-service outlets such as supermarkets.

Marketing Mix in the Introductory Stage The length of the product line typically should be relatively short to reduce production costs and hold down inventories. Efforts to establish competitive advantage are typically focused on differentiating the new product or product line from solutions customers previously employed to satisfy the targeted want or need. Many early PCs were purchased to perform spreadsheet analyses on the computer, instead of running the calculations by hand, with all the potential for error and difficulty

Exhibit 5.10

EXPECTED CHARACTERISTICS AND RESPONSES BY MAJOR LIFE CYCLE STAGES

STAGES IN PRODUCT LIFE CYCLE

Stage characteristics	Introduction	Growth	Shakeout	Mature	Decline
Market growth rate (constant dollars)	Moderate	High	Leveling off	Insignificant	Negative
Technical change in product design	High	Moderate	Limited	Limited	Limited
Segments	Few	Few to many	Few to many	Few to many	Few
Competitors	Few	Many	Decreasing	Limited	Few
Profitability	Negative	High	Low	High for market-share leaders	Low
Firm's normative responses					
Strategic marketing objectives	Stimulate primary demand	Build share	Build share	Hold share	Harvest
Product	Quality	Continue quality improvements	Rationalize	Concentrate on features	No change
Product line	Narrow	Broad	Rationalize	Hold length of line	Reduce length of line
Price	Skimming or penetration	Reduce	Reduce	Hold or reduce selectively	Reduce
Channels	Selective	Intensive	Intensive	Intensive	Selective
Communications	High	High	High	High to declining	Reduce

in making changes that the previous manual procedures entailed. Where service is important, the firm must be able to provide it promptly (as in postpurchase service and spare-parts availability).

The firm's pricing is strongly affected by a variety of factors: the product's value to the end user; how quickly it can be imitated by competitors; the presence of close substitutes; and the effect of price on volume (elasticity) and, in turn, on costs. Basic strategy choices involve skimming and penetration. **Skimming** is designed to obtain as much margin per unit as possible. This enables the company to recover its new product investments more quickly. Such a strategy is particularly appropriate in niche markets and where consumers are relatively insensitive to price, as was the case in the sale of cellular phones to business executives early in the product life cycle. **Penetration pricing** enables the firm to strive for quick market development and makes sense when there is a steep experience curve, which lowers costs; a large market; and strong potential competition.

The importance of **distribution** and channel intermediaries varies substantially from consumer to industrial goods. The latter are often sold direct, but with few exceptions consumer goods use one or more channel intermediaries. Product availability is particularly important with consumer goods because of the large amounts spent on promotion to make consumers aware of the product and to induce usage. Distribution is easier if the company uses the same channels for its other products and has a successful track record with new product introductions.

During the introductory period, **promotion** expenditures involving advertising and salesforce are a high percentage of sales, especially for a mass-market, small-value product. Some dot-coms spent themselves to failure for promotional purposes. For industrial goods, personal selling costs are apt to be much higher than advertising costs.

The communications task at the outset is to build awareness of the new product's uniqueness, which is typically an expensive undertaking. Further, the promotional expenditures (such as in-store displays, premiums, coupons, samples, and off-list pricing) required to obtain product availability and trial are substantial. For industrial products, the time required to develop awareness of the product's uniqueness is often extensive due to the number of people in the buying center and the complexity of the buying systems.

Growth Stage   This stage starts with a sharp increase in sales. Important product improvements continue in the growth stage, but at a slower rate. Increased brand differentiation occurs primarily in product features. The product line expands to attract new segments. It does so by offering an array of prices and different product features. During the latter part of the growth stage, the firm—especially the dominant one—makes every effort to extend the growth stage by adding new segments, lowering costs, improving product quality, adding new features, and trying to increase product usage among present users.

Marketing Mix Changes   The *product line* expands to attract new market segments. It does so by offering an array of prices and different product features. The quest for competitive advantage now shifts to differentiation from other entrants in the product class. *Prices* tend to decline during the growth period (the average cost of servicing cellular subscribers has been dropping by about 20 percent annually), and price differences between brands decrease. The extent of the decline depends on cost—volume relationships, industry concentration, and the volatility of raw material costs. If growth is so strong it outpaces supply, there is little or no pressure on price; indeed, it may enable sellers to charge premium prices.

During this period sellers of both industrial and consumer goods strive to build a channel or a direct-sales system that provides maximum product availability and service at the lowest cost. If this can be accomplished, rivals are placed at a disadvantage, even to the extent of being excluded from some markets. This is particularly the case with some industrial goods for which the number of intermediaries in any one market is limited. A brand must attain some degree of distribution success in advance of the mature stage, because channel members then tend to disinvest in less-successful brands.

Promotion costs (advertising and personal selling) become more concerned with building demand for a company's brand (selective demand) than demand for the product class or type (primary demand). Firms strive to build favorable attitudes toward their brand on the basis of its unique features. Communications are also used to cultivate new segments. Even though promotion costs remain high, they typically decline as a percentage of sales.

Shakeout Stage   The advent of this period is signaled by a drop in the overall growth rate and is typically marked by substantial price cuts. As weaker competitors exit the market, the stronger firms gain shares. Thus, major changes in the industry's competitive structure occur. During shakeout the firm must *rationalize* its product line by eliminating weaker items, emphasize creative promotional pricing, and strengthen its channel relationships. The personal computer industry is now mired in a global price war in its efforts to adjust to a slowing market. The entire industry is experiencing higher inventories and simultaneously intensifying competitive environment. Several firms have dropped out of the retail computer market. And Apple has gone through serious financial problems. To a considerable extent, what happens during the shakeout has been predetermined by how well each brand has been positioned in relation to its targeted segments, its distribution system, and its relative costs per unit.

Marketing Mix Changes In addition to entering into more direct *price* competition, firms make every effort to maintain and enhance their *distribution* system. Channel intermediaries use this downturn in industry sales to reduce the number of products carried and, hence, their inventories. Weaker competitors often have to offer their intermediaries substantial inducements to continue stocking all or even part of their line. *Promotion costs* may increase, particularly for low-share firms, as companies attempt to maintain their distribution by offering consumers buying incentives. This is particularly the case for sellers of consumer goods.

Mature Stage When sales plateau, the product enters the mature stage, which typically lasts for some time. Most products now on the market are in the mature stage. Stability in terms of demand, technology, and competition characterizes maturity. Strong market leaders, because of lower per-unit costs and the lack of any need to expand their facilities, should enjoy strong profits and high positive cash flows. But there is always the possibility of changes in the marketplace, the product, the channels of distribution, the production processes, and the nature and scope of competition. The longer the mature stage lasts, the greater the possibility of change. If the firm does not respond successfully to a change but its competitors do, then a change in industry structure may occur.

Marketing Mix Changes Because of technical maturity, the various brands in the marketplace become more similar; therefore, any significant breakthroughs by R&D or engineering that help to differentiate the product or redirect its cost can have a substantial payout (see Exhibit 5.11). One option is to add value to the product that benefits the customer by improving the ease of use (voice-activated dialing with cellular phones), by incorporating labor-saving features, or by selling systems rather than single products (adding extended service contracts). Increasingly, *service* becomes a way of differentiating the offering. *Promotion* expenditures and *prices* tend to remain stable during the mature stage. But the nature of the former is apt to change; media advertising for consumer goods declines and in-store promotions, including price deals, increase. The price premium attainable by the high-quality producer tends to erode. The effect of experience on costs and prices becomes smaller and smaller. Competition may force prices down, especially when the two leading competitors hold similar shares. For consumer goods, distribution and in-store displays (shelf facings) become increasingly important, as does effective cost management.

Exhibit 5.11   What the Bicycle Industry Needs Is Innovation

In the early 80s mountain bikes gave the bicycle industry a much-needed boost in sales. But the demand for such bikes has peaked and most firms in the industry are experiencing flat or declining sales. Clearly what the industry needs, and is attempting, to do is reinvent the bike. An attempt to do so via the use of a battery-powered motor to propel the bike failed, but one entrepreneur is working on a foldable bike that weighs less than 3.5 pounds.

Source: "Reinventing the Bicycle," *The Economist*, November 18, 1995, p. 76.

Exhibit 5.12   GM Sinks Its Big Boats

General Motors decided in 1995 to stop producing its Chevrolet Caprice Classic—a large, rear-wheel-drive car that has long been the favorite of police departments and taxis—and its gargantuan Cadillac Fleetwood, which is the model of choice for stretch limos and hearses. The factory where the cars are built is now used to assemble a more trendy line of cars and pickup trucks. In dropping this duo, GM turned their markets over to Ford, which had been considering abandoning its big rear-wheel-drive Crown-Victoria, but no doubt will reconsider its decision. Not everyone at GM agrees with the company's decision. Some want to continue these models "as is," while others argue for small-volume production, even if it requires an outside contractor.

Source: Gabriella Stern and Neal Timplin, "GM Turns Away from Cop-Car, Limo Markets," *Wall Street Journal,* May 16, 1995, p. B1. Copyright 1995 by Dow Jones & Co. Inc. Reproduced with permission of Dow Jones & Co. Inc. via Copyright Clearance Center.

Decline Stage   Eventually most products enter the decline stage, which may be gradual (canned vegetables/hot cereals) or extremely fast (some prescription drugs). The sales pattern may be one of decline and then petrification as a small residual segment still clings to the use of the product (tooth powder versus toothpaste). Products enter this stage primarily because of technologically superior substitutes (jet engines over piston engines) and a shift in consumer tastes, values, and beliefs (cholesterol-free margarine over butter).

As sales decline, costs increase, and radical efforts are needed to reduce costs and the asset base. Even so, if exit barriers are low, many firms vacate the market, which increases the sales of remaining firms, thereby delaying their exit (see Exhibit 5.12). Stronger firms may even prosper for a time. If the curve is a steep decline followed by a plateau, then some firms can adjust. If the firm is strong in some segments vacated by its competitors, then it may experience a sufficient increase in market share to compensate for loss of sales elsewhere.

Marketing Mix Changes   Marketing expenditures, especially those associated with *promotion,* usually decrease as a percentage of sales in the decline stage. *Prices* tend to remain stable if the rate of decline is slow, there are some enduring profitable segments and low exit barriers, customers are weak and fragmented, and there are few single-product competitors. Conversely, aggressive pricing is apt to occur when decline is fast and erratic, there are no strong unique segments, there are high exit barriers, a number of large single-product competitors are present, and customers have strong bargaining power. For consumer goods, marketing activity centers on distribution—persuading intermediaries to continue to stock the item even though they may not promote it. For industrial products the problem may center around maintaining the interest of the salesforce in selling the item.

Harvesting or withdrawal has as its objective an increase in cash flow that can be accomplished by milking (making only the essential investments), internal transfer of assets, and sales of the business or its assets. In any milking operation, management looks for ways to reduce assets, costs, and the number of items in the product line.

Strategic Implications of the Product Life Cycle

The product life cycle model is a framework that signals the occurrence of opportunities and threats in the marketplace and the industry, thereby helping the business better anticipate change in the product's strategic market objective, its strategy, and its marketing program. By matching the entry's market position objective with the investment level required and the profits and cash flows associated with each stage in the product life cycle, we can better visualize the interrelationships (see Exhibit 5.13). As would be expected, there is a

Exhibit 5.13

RELATIONSHIP OF STRATEGIC MARKET POSITION OBJECTIVE, INVESTMENT LEVELS, PROFITS, AND CASH FLOW TO INDIVIDUAL
STAGES IN THE PRODUCT LIFE CYCLE

STAGES IN THE PRODUCT LIFE CYCLE

Stage	Strategic market objective	Investments	Profits	Cash flow
Introduction	For both innovators and followers, accelerate overall market growth and product acceptance through awareness, trial, and product availability	Moderate to high for R&D, capacity, working capital, and marketing (sales and advertising)	Highly negative	Highly negative
Growth	Increase competitive position	High to very high	High	Negative
Shakeout	Improve/solidify competitive position	Moderate	Low to moderate	Low to moderate
Mature	Maintain position	Low	High	Moderate

high correlation between the market and industry characteristics of each stage, the market
share objectives, and the level of investment, which, in turn, strongly affect cash flow.

 Introductory and Growth Stages   Because the introduction of a new product
requires large investments, most firms sustain a rather sizable short-term loss. For many dot-
coms, these losses have been especially sizable! As the product moves into the growth stage,
sales increase rapidly; hence, substantial investments continue. Profitability is depressed
because facilities have to be built in advance to ensure supply. The firm with the largest
share during this period should have the lowest per-unit costs due to scale and learning
effects. If it chooses to decrease its real price proportionate to the decline in its costs, it dries
up the investment incentives of would-be entrants and lower-share competitors. The inno-
vating firm's share is likely to erode substantially during the growth stage. Nevertheless, it
must still make large investments, for even though it is losing share, its sales are increasing.
New entrants and low-share sellers are at a substantial disadvantage here. They must not
only invest to accommodate market growth, but also to gain market share.

Mature and Declining Stages   As the product enters the mature stage, the larger-
share sellers should be able to reap the benefits of their earlier investments. Given that the
price is sufficient to keep the higher-cost sellers in business, that growth investments are no
longer needed, and that most competitors may no longer be striving to gain share, the
leader's profitability and positive cash flow can be substantial. But the leader needs to continue making investments to improve its product and to make its manufacturing, marketing,
and physical logistics more efficient. The generalized product life cycle model portrays a
profitability peak during the latter part of the growth stage. But one study of over 1,000
industrial businesses found that despite declining margins, overall profitability did not
decline during maturity mainly because less money was spent on marketing and R&D.[21]

Limitations of the Product Life Cycle Framework

The product life cycle model's major weakness lies in its normative approach to prescribing strategies based on assumptions about the features or characteristics of each stage. It
fails to take into account that the product life cycle is, in reality, driven by market forces

expressing the evolution of consumer preferences (the market), technology (the product), and competition (the supply side).[22] Mary Lambkin and George Day argue strongly that greater emphasis on competitive issues helps to better understand the evolution of a product-market. This is especially the case in understanding the dynamics of competitive behavior in evolving market structures.[23]

Strategic Value of Product-Market Evolution

As illustrated by the cellular phone industry, products and markets are constantly evolving. On the product side, the growing commonality of technology increases the difficulty of maintaining strong product differentiation. Over time, costs per unit tend to decline because of scale and learning effects leading to lower prices. On the market side, demand eventually slows, and consumers become more knowledgeable about the product, forming attitudes about the attractiveness of competing brands. And over time, industry structure and rivalry among established companies change.

These evolutionary forces interact to affect not only a market's or an industry's attractiveness but also the success requirements for a firm's various product-market entries. The management implications of this evolutionary process are as follows:

At the *corporate* and *business-unit levels,* the firm must generate new products or enter new markets to sustain its profitability. This has been the case in the American beer industry, where overall demand is down, but the sales of microbrews have experienced rapid growth over the past 10 years. The younger generation finds such beers particularly attractive.[24]

At the *product level,* objectives and strategy change as the product passes through various evolutionary stages. For example, PC sales to the American home market—the fastest-growing segment of the PC market—have slowed substantially. Firms once serving this segment such as Packard Bell, IBM, and Digital have suffered substantial losses or exited the market. Low-cost machines designed to service consumers who want to use only the Internet are now available. In an effort to accommodate change, industry players are dropping prices, downsizing, accelerating their R&D, and even selling parts of their companies.[25]

At the *marketing program level,* the evolutionary process typically generates significant changes. For example, when the sales of camcorders (lightweight video cameras) plateaued, the industry realized it had to find new markets beyond young parents. In an effort to reach new customers, camcorder firms downplayed the high-tech nature of their product by simplifying its design, cutting prices, and changing advertising appeals and media vehicles.[26]

Anticipating change is a very difficult undertaking and requires a systematic framework to help managers better understand the product-market evolutionary process. This is especially the case as more and more markets become international. Chapters 4 and 5 have provided a series of tools and analytical frameworks to guide managers in addressing the critical decisions that these changes bring about.

TAKE AWAYS

- Companies are more likely to be successful in generating sales and profits if the opportunities they pursue are blessed with the following conditions:
  - Driving forces for the industry are favorable.
  - The industry's five forces are, on balance, favorable.

- The capabilities of the firm and/or the management team are sufficient to perform with respect to the industry's critical success factors.
- Local competitive conditions are favorable.
- In other words, choosing an attractive industry, as well as a growing market, is important!

- An innovation is more likely to be successful if it will diffuse at a rate rapid enough to quickly establish customer loyalty and advantage over competitors. This chapter provides a framework for assessing this likelihood.

- Regardless of the nature of the playing field, developing and regularly updating winning marketing strategies are important, too! In developing strategies to build and sustain competitive advantage, marketing decision makers are more likely to win the competitive war by adjusting their strategies as the markets and industries in which they compete evolve through the stages of the product life cycle. Specific tools and frameworks for managing this task are provided in the balance of this book.

- Self-diagnostic questions to test your ability to apply the analytical tools and concepts in this chapter to marketing decision making may be found at this book's website at **www.mhhe.com/walker**.

ENDNOTES

1. Information on the cellular telephone business at the turn of the 21st century comes from the following sources: Moon Ihlwan, "Asia Gets Hooked on Wireless," *Business Week,* June 19, 2000, p. 109; "Commentary: Europe Shouldn't Squander This Telecom Windfall," *Business Week,* May 22, 2000; Stephen Baker, "The Race to Rule Mobile," *Business Week* International Edition, February 21, 2000; Stephen Baker, "Smart Phones," *Business Week* International Edition, October 18, 1999; "Online Overseas," *New York Times,* June 7, 2000, p. H8; Steve Frank, "Darling to Dog to . . . ," *Wall Street Journal Sunday,* June 18, 2000; and Peter Elstrom, "More Americans Are Packing Finnish Phones," *Business Week,* December 21, 1998.

2. Bruce H. Clark and David B. Montgomery, "Managerial Identification of Competitors," *Journal of Marketing* 63 (July 1999), pp. 67–83.

3. Adrian J. Slywotzky, *Value Migration* (Boston: Harvard Business School Press, 1996).

4. Michael Porter, *Competitive Strategy* (New York: Free Press, 1980).

5. Ibid., chap. 3.

6. Wendy Zellner, Andrea Rothman, and Eric Schine, "The Airlines Mess," *Business Week,* July 6, 1992.

7. Vdayan Gupta, "Consolidation in Biotechnology Industry Accelerates," *The Wall Street Journal,* July 27, 1992, p. B2.

8. Myron Magnet, "Meet the New Revolutionaries," *Fortune,* February 24, 1992, pp. 98–99.

9. Baker, "The Race to Rule Mobile."

10. For an interesting case study involving a PC chip-maker and its strategy to forward integrate by entering the PC business, see P. B. Campbell, "Chip-Maker Cyrex Plans to Enter Tough PC Business," *The Wall Street Journal,* March 6, 1996, p. B4.

11. Baker, "Smart Phones."

12. Ibid.

13. Everett M. Rogers, *Diffusion of Innovations* (New York: Free Press, 1983).

14. Thomas S. Robertson and Hubert Gatignon, "Competitive Effects on Technological Diffusion," *Journal of Marketing,* July 1986, pp. 1–12.

15. Rogers, *Diffusion of Innovations.*

16. Frederick E. Webster Jr., *Industrial Marketing Strategy* (New York: John Wiley & Sons, 1991), pp. 158–74.

17. For an interesting discussion of the application of the life cycle concept to almost anything besides products (e.g., the fall of the Berlin Wall, the unification of Europe, and the demise of communism), see Theodore Modes, "Life Cycles," *The Futurist,* September–October 1994, p. 20.

18. J. E. Swan and D. R. Rink, "Effective Use of Industrial Life Cycle Trends," in *Marketing in the '80s* (New York: American Marketing Association, 1980), pp. 198–99.

19. Theodore Levitt, "Exploit the Life Cycle," *Harvard Business Review,* November–December 1963, p. 93.

20. For an interesting discussion of fads versus trends, see Martin G. Letscher, "How to Tell Fads from Trends," *American Demographics,* December 1994, p. 38.

21. Hans B. Thorelli and Stephen C. Burnett, "The Nature of Product Life-Cycles for Industrial Goods Businesses," *Journal of Marketing,* Fall 1981, p. 108.

22. Webster, *Industrial Marketing Strategy,* p. 128.

23. Mary Lambkin and George S. Day, "Evolutionary Processes in Competitive Markets beyond the Product Life Cycle," *Journal of Marketing,* July 1989, pp. 8–9.

24. John Student, "True Brew," *American Demographics,* May 1995, p. 32.

25. "The End of Good Times," *The Economist,* December 9, 1995, p. 61; Andy Serwer, "Dell Does Domination," *Fortune,* January 21, 2002, at www.fortune.com/indext.jhtml?channel=print_article.jhtml&doc_id=205940.

26. Patrick M. Reilly, "Camcorder Makers, with Growth Easing, Try to Bring New Markets into the Picture," *The Wall Street Journal,* December 26, 1991, p. B1.

Chapter Six

Measuring Market Opportunities

African Communications Group: Bringing Modern Telecommunications to Tanzania[1]

IN TANZANIA IN THE EARLY 1990S, many towns and villages had no access whatsoever to telecommunications services. Even in the capital, Dar es Salaam, a city of almost two million people, on average only one telephone line had been installed per hundred residents. The waiting list to obtain service from the Tanzania Telecommunications Company Limited (TTCL) was 7 to 10 years. Monique Maddy and Côme Laguë, two recent MBA graduates from a leading U.S. business school, saw in these and other market and industry data an opportunity not only to bring telecommunications services to Tanzania, but long term to bring a variety of telecommunications services—including pay phones, paging, voice-mail, and other voice and data communications services—to sub-Saharan Africa. After three months of on-site research in late 1993, Maddy and Laguë decided that building a pay phone network in Tanzania was the most promising opportunity for entering this market. They knew that, in order to obtain financing as well as the necessary licenses to operate in Tanzania, they would have to prepare a credible business plan. They also knew that among the most critical elements of any business plan was the sales forecast. Not only would the

sales number be the starting point from which all the other numbers in the plan would be developed, but it would be a key litmus test for prospective investors. If the sales forecast were well supported and credible, Maddy and Laguë believed the rest of the pieces would fall into place. But how could such a forecast be prepared with any confidence for a largely new and underdeveloped market?

Market Analysis

As a result of their research, Maddy and Laguë had concluded that the market for building a pay phone system in Tanzania was extremely attractive. Beyond those on the waiting list for phone service, there was huge "unofficial" demand from individuals who had not bothered to apply for service. Maddy and Laguë estimated that, by 1996, there would be 500,000 potential subscribers for telephone service, and that even with a planned doubling of its capacity, TTCL could satisfy only perhaps half this demand. Moreover, on most Tanzanian phones, it took several minutes to receive a dial tone. Once dial tone was received it could take 40 minutes to connect with cities in Africa, or 20 minutes with Europe. Of the 300 coin-operated pay phones in Tanzania, many were inoperative, and some only took coins that no longer were in circulation and were virtually worthless due to Tanzania's high rate of inflation. The market for phone service looked promising, indeed.

INDUSTRY ANALYSIS

TTCL, Tanzania's central telephone company, was state-owned, though it was expected that TTCL would be privatized at some point. TTCL offered neither paging, fax, cellular, nor data services. There were several small private telecommunications companies, including one radio-calling service with 105 subscribers, and two high-end cellular phone companies. New licenses were likely to be issued in the next couple of years for cellular services, paging, and pay phones; and Maddy and Laguë hoped to be among those who would win these licenses.

Maddy and Laguë's analysis told them that industry conditions overall were attractive. Though new competitors would likely enter the market, Maddy and Laguë's head start would put them in good position; there were numerous suppliers eager to expand in the African market, and buyers currently had few options to obtain phone service of any kind. There were no substitutes other than cellular service, which was extremely expensive, due to the high cost of building the infrastructure, and the bureaucratic TTCL did not seem likely to be a very vigorous competitor.

CONSUMER NEEDS AND BEHAVIOR

Not only was Tanzania's telecommunications infrastructure poorly developed, but the same was true for its electricity and water services and its roads.

It took three days to travel from Dar es Salaam to Mwanza, Tanzania's second-largest city, only 751 miles away. Most telephone calls in cities were made by businesspeople, who accounted for 70 percent of telecommunications revenue. Since most residences had no phones, misuse of business phones was common. Employees were generally required to use pay phones for all types of long-distance calls. Most retail shops—known as *dukas,* which were makeshift open-air stalls made of wood and tin—had no phones. Maddy and Laguë believed their pay phone network, together with the voice-mail and paging services they planned to offer, would provide more efficient ways of doing business to these small merchants who constituted the backbone of the Tanzanian economy. The biggest challenge they would face would probably be to educate Tanzanians on how to use their proposed system. Since the literacy rate in Tanzania was 90 percent, they felt optimistic about their ability to do so.

THE BUSINESS IDEA

The idea for African Communications Group (ACG), their proposed venture, was innovative but simple. Maddy and Laguë would build a network of pay phones based on wireless radio technology, with a central platform for routing calls and connecting with the TTCL network. The phones would be card-operated, with prepaid cards sold in retail establishments located near the phone booths. The retailers would get a margin on the sale of the phone cards, and might help watch over the phones to discourage vandalism. Paging and voice-mail would soon be added to the system at low incremental cost. These features would provide quick communication to parties that did not have regular phone service. Subscribers could receive voice-mail messages and leave messages for other voice-mail subscribers. The pagers could be used to signal the subscriber that a message had been received.

MEASURING THE OPPORTUNITY: DETERMINING MARKET POTENTIAL AND PREPARING A SALES FORECAST

Maddy and Laguë liked the opportunity that lay before them, and they felt their business skills and contacts made them a good team to pursue it. But how could they translate all the market and industry data they had gathered into a credible estimate of market potential and an evidence-based sales forecast? Proving that the market and industry were attractive and that consumers would see benefits from using their network was one thing. Coming up with hard numbers for market potential and sales revenue was quite another.

STRATEGIC CHALLENGES ADDRESSED IN CHAPTER 6

Entrepreneurs like Maddy and Laguë and managers in established firms need to develop knowledge about their market and industry and synthesize that knowledge into tangible plans that their organizations can act on. These plans can take many forms. For Maddy and Laguë, a business plan was needed to raise the necessary capital and obtain the operating licenses to start the venture. For new product managers in established firms, marketing plans must be developed to win support and resources to permit the product's launch. Elsewhere in organizations of all kinds, annual budgets are prepared to guide decision making for the coming year.[2] These decisions determine staffing, investments in productive capacity, levels of operating expense, and so on. In almost every case, these planning and budgeting activities begin with a sales forecast. Once a sales figure is agreed to, the various activities and investments needed to support the planned sales level are budgeted.

In Chapter 6, we deal with two key issues that enable managers and entrepreneurs to bring life to their dreams. First, we address the challenges in estimating **market potential** and **forecasting** sales, for both new and existing products or businesses. We provide a menu of evidence-based forecasting methods, each of which is useful in some situations, but not others, and we discuss their limitations. Second, we briefly address the informational needs of the forecasting task—as well as the tasks addressed in the earlier chapters of this book that enable managers and entrepreneurs to understand their market and competitive contexts—to provide guidance on where to gather, collect, and report data relevant to strategic marketing decision making, that is, **marketing research.** In this second portion of the chapter, we assume the reader already has learned the basics of planning and conducting marketing research. Such research is essential in strategic decision making— to provide evidence on which to base the various corporate-level and business-level decisions discussed in Chapter 2. Depending solely on hunches—instead of more carefully thought-out research inquiries, even modest ones done quickly—can be a risky proposition indeed.

EVERY FORECAST IS WRONG!

We know of no manager who has ever seen a forecast that came in *exactly* on the money. Some forecasts turn out too high; others too low. Forecasting is an inherently difficult task, because no one has a perfect crystal ball. The future is inherently uncertain, especially in today's rapidly changing markets. Consumer wants and needs shift, buffeted by the winds of ever-changing macro trends. Competitors come and go. New technologies sweep away

STRATEGIC ISSUE

Given the stakes and the risks entailed in being very wrong with a forecast, some effort to prepare an evidence-based forecast, instead of a wild guess, is almost always called for, even if time and money are scarce. So forecast we must, but how?

old ones. Some forecasts are based on extensive and expensive research, others on small-scale inquiries, still others on uninformed hunches. As we have seen, however, forecasting plays a central role in all kinds of planning and budgeting in all kinds of businesses and other organizations.[3] Given the stakes and the risks entailed in being *very* wrong with a forecast, some effort to prepare an **evidence-based forecast,** instead of a wild guess, is almost always called for, even if time and money are scarce. So forecast we must, but how?

A FORECASTER'S TOOLKIT: A TOOL FOR EVERY FORECASTING SETTING

Before choosing a method to prepare a forecast, one first must know what is to be estimated or forecasted. First, there's the size of the potential market, that is, the likely demand from all actual and potential buyers of a product or product class. An estimate of **market potential** often serves as a starting point for preparing a sales forecast, which we explore in more detail later in this chapter. For Maddy and Laguë's venture in Tanzania, prospective investors will want to know how large the potential market for telephone services will be in the coming years, measured perhaps in several ways: in numbers of telephone users, in numbers and/or minutes of calls, and in dollars or Tanzanian shillings. This market is comprised of those consumers who are likely to have both the willingness and ability to buy and use a phone card or one of ACG's other services at one of ACG's pay phones. There's also the size of the currently **penetrated market,** those who are actually using pay phones in Tanzania at the time of the forecast. Investors also will want to know these figures—the size of the potential and penetrated markets for the market segments Maddy and Laguë intend to serve, their **target market.** They also will need a **sales forecast,** in which they predict sales revenues for ACG, for five years or so. How might they do these things?

Established organizations employ two broad approaches for preparing a sales forecast: top-down and bottom-up. Under the top-down approach, a central person or persons take the responsibility for forecasting and prepare an overall forecast, perhaps using aggregate economic data, current sales trends, or other methods we describe shortly.[4] Under the bottom-up approach, common in decentralized firms, each part of the firm prepares its own sales forecast, and the parts are aggregated to create the forecast for the firm as a whole. For an example of how managers at Gap Inc. retailing divisions combine both methods to forecast next-year sales, see Exhibit 6.1.

The bottom-up logic also applies to Maddy and Laguë's task. They can break their anticipated demand into pieces and sum the components to create the summary forecast. These pieces could be market segments, such as small retailers, mobile businesspeople, consumers, and so on, or product lines, such as revenue from phone cards or individual pay phones, voice-mail fees, pager fees, and the like. Using the bottom-up approach presents numerous advantages. First, this approach will force them to think clearly about the drivers of demand for each market segment or product line, and thus better understand the real potential of their business and its parts.[5] Second, they will be forced to make explicit assumptions about the drivers of demand in each category, assumptions they can debate—and support with evidence gathered from their research—with prospective investors and they can later verify as the business unfolds. Third, such an approach facilitates "what if" planning. Various combinations of market segments and/or product lines can be combined to build a business plan that looks viable.

Exhibit 6.1   Forecasting Next Year's Sales at Old Navy

At rapidly growing retailer Gap Inc., forecasting sales for the next year for each of its divisions—Gap, Banana Republic, and Old Navy—is an important process that drives a host of decisions, including how much merchandise to plan to buy for the coming year. Both top-down and bottom-up approaches are used. At Old Navy, for example, each merchandiser generates a forecast of what level of sales his or her category—women's knit tops, men's jeans, and so on—can achieve for the next year. Group merchandise managers then provide their input and sum these numbers to create a total forecast from a merchandising perspective. A second bottom-up forecast is generated by the store operations organization, summing stores and groups of stores. Simultaneously, a top-down figure is prepared at headquarters in California, using macroeconomic data, corporate growth objectives, and other factors. The three forecasts are then compared, differences debated, and a final figure on which to base merchandise procurement and expense budgets is determined. Though the effort to prepare such a forecast is considerable, the broad involvement in the process helps to ensure both knowledgeable input to the forecast as well as subsequent commitment to "make the numbers." Most important, Old Navy finds that the different processes together with the ensuing discussion lead to substantially better forecasts.

Source: Marshall L. Fisher, Ananth Raman, and Anna Sheen McClelland, "Rocket Science Retailing Is Almost Here: Are You Ready?" *Harvard Business Review,* July–August 2000, pp. 115–24.

From what forecasting methods, or tools, can Maddy and Laguë choose? There are six major evidence-based methods for estimating market potential and forecasting sales: statistical methods, observation, surveys, analogy, judgment, and market tests.[6] A seventh method, not evidenced-based—the SWAG method (Silly Wild-@*# Guess)—is not condoned here, though there is little else to support some forecasts!

Statistical and Other Quantitative Methods

Statistical methods use past history and various statistical techniques, such as multiple regression or time series analysis, to forecast the future based on an extrapolation of the past.[7] This method is typically not useful for ACG or other entrepreneurs or new product managers charged with forecasting sales for a really new product or new business. There is no history in their venture on which to base a statistical forecast.

In established firms, for established products, statistical methods are extremely useful. When Michelin, the tire maker, wants to forecast demand for the replacement automobile tire market in Asia for the next year, it can build a statistical model using such factors as the number and age of vehicles currently on the road in Asia, predictions of GDP for the region, the last few years' demand, and other relevant factors to forecast market potential as well as Michelin's own replacement tire sales for the coming year. Such a procedure is likely to result in a more accurate forecast than other methods, especially if Michelin has years of experience with which to calibrate its statistical model.

As with all forecasting methods, statistical methods have important limitations. Most important of these is that statistical methods generally assume that the future will look very much like the past. Sometimes this is not the case. US WEST, the regional Bell telephone company serving the Rocky Mountain and Northwest regions of the United States, ran into trouble in the 1990s when its statistical models used to predict needs for telephone capacity failed to allow for rapidly increasing use of computer modems, faxes, and second lines for teenagers in American homes. Suddenly, the average number of lines per home skyrocketed, and there was not enough physical plant—cable in the ground, switches, and so on—to accommodate the growing demand. Consumers had to wait, sometimes for months, to get additional lines, and they were not happy about it! Similarly, if product or market characteristics change, statistical models used without adequate judgment may not keep pace. When tire makers produce automobile tires that last 80,000 miles instead of 30,000 to 50,000 miles, the annual demand for replacement tires is reduced. If automobile manufacturers were to change the number of wheels on the typical car from four, the old statistical models also would be in trouble.

Other quantitative forecasting methods, especially for new product forecasting, also have been developed. These include methods to mathematically model the diffusion of innovation process for consumer durables[8] (discussed in Chapter 5) and conjoint analysis,[9] a method to forecast the impact on consumer demand of different combinations of attributes that might be included in a new product.

Observation

Another method for preparing an evidence-based forecast is to directly observe or gather existing data about what real consumers do in the product-market of interest. Maddy and Laguë conducted a study of pay phone use in Tanzania to find out how many minutes per day the typical pay phone was used. Their study showed that an average of 150 three-minute calls were made per day at the 60 working pay phones then provided by other companies in Dar es Salaam. Revenue for most pay phones fell into the US$100 to $150 range.[10]

Like statistical methods, **observation-based forecasting** is attractive because it is based on what people actually *do.* If behavioral or usage data can be found from existing secondary sources—in company files, at the library, or on the Internet—data collection is both faster and cheaper than if a new study like the one Maddy and Laguë conducted must be designed and carried out. For new-to-the-world products, however, observation is typically not possible and secondary data are not available, since the product often does not yet exist, except in concept form. Had there been no pay phones in Tanzania or a similar country, observation would not have been possible. Market tests, which we discuss later in this section, are one way to get real purchase data about new-to-the-world products.

Surveys

Another common way to forecast sales or estimate market potential is to conduct surveys. These surveys can be done with different groups of respondents. Consumers, after being shown a statement of the product concept[11] or a prototype or sample of the product, can be asked how likely they are to buy, creating a **survey of buyers' intentions.** Buyers also can be asked about their current buying behavior: what they currently buy, how often, or how much they use. The salespeople can be asked how much they are likely to sell, completing a **survey of salesforce opinion.** Experts of various kinds—members of the distribution channel, suppliers, consultants, trade association executives, and so on—also can be surveyed.

As part of their research in Dar es Salaam, Maddy and Laguë surveyed pay phone customers to find out more about them. A whopping 65 percent were using a pay phone because they lacked access to another working phone—good news for the ACG concept! Sixty-three percent were business customers, 20 percent were students or teachers, and 17 percent were other nonbusiness customers. Business customers spent an average of US$10 per week for 14 pay phone calls, and nonbusiness customers spent US$6 per week for 12 calls.[12] By combining these data with demographic data on the Tanzanian population, Maddy and Laguë now had what they needed to prepare an evidence-based, bottom-up forecast of market potential, market segment by market segment.

Exhibit 6.2

A SURVEY OF BUYERS' INTENTIONS: WHAT PEOPLE SAY IS NOT WHAT THEY *DO*

When Nestlé's refrigerated foods division in the United States was considering whether to acquire Lambert's Pasta and Cheese, a fresh pasta maker, it wanted to forecast the likely first-year sales volume if the acquisition were completed. To do so, Nestlé used a concept test in which consumers were asked, among other things, how likely they were to *try* the fresh pasta product. The results were as shown in the first two columns in the table below:

Purchase intent	% response	Rule of thumb reduction for forecasting purposes	Percentage of market deemed likely to actually buy
Definitely would buy	27%	Multiply by .8	27% × **.8** = 21.6%
Probably would buy	43%	Multiply by .3	43% × **.3** = 12.9%
Might or might not buy	22%	Count as zero	
Probably or definitely would not buy	8%	Count as zero	
Totals	100%		21.6% + 12.9% = 34.5%

Even though 70% of consumers surveyed indicated they were likely to buy, Nestlé's experience indicated that these "top two box" percentages should be cut sharply: "Definitely" responses were reduced by 20%, while "Probably" responses were reduced by 70%. "Maybe" responses were considered as "No." These adjustments, shown in columns three and four, reduced the 70% figure by more than half, to 34.5%. Most consumer product manufacturers who employ concept tests use similar rules of thumb when interpreting purchase intent data for forecasting purposes, because they have learned that what people *say* they will buy exceeds what they will *actually* buy. Similar logic is useful in a variety of forecasting situations.

Source: Marie Bell and V. Kasturi Rangan, *Nestlé Refrigerated Foods: Contadina Pasta and Pizza.* Boston: Harvard Business School, 1995. Copyright © 1995 by the President and Fellows of Harvard College. Reprinted by permission.

Surveys possess important limitations, however. For one, what people *say* is not always what people *do.* Consumer surveys of buyer intention are always heavily discounted to allow for this fact. For one common approach to doing so, see Exhibit 6.2. Second, the persons who are surveyed may not be knowledgeable, but if asked for their opinion, they will probably provide it! Third, what people imagine about a product concept in a survey may not be what is actually delivered once the product is launched. If consumers are asked if they will buy an "old world spaghetti sauce with homemade flavor," they will surely provide a response. Whether they will actually *like* the taste and texture of the sauce that the lab develops is another story! In general, statistical and observational methods, where adequate data or settings are available in which to apply them, are superior to survey methods of forecasting, because such methods are based, at least in part, on what people have *actually done* or bought (e.g., the number of old cars actually on the road, or the length of pay phone calls in Tanzania), while survey methods (Are you likely to buy replacement tires this year? How often are you likely to use a pay phone?) are based on what people *say*, a less reliable indicator of their future behavior.

Analogy

An approach often used for new product forecasting where neither statistical methods nor observations are possible is to forecast the sales or market potential for a new product or product class by **analogy.** Under this method, the product is compared with similar products for which historical data *are* available. When Yoplait, the leading marketer of yogurt in the United States, plans to introduce a new flavor, its managers likely will look at the sales history of earlier introductions to forecast the sales for the newest flavor. This method also is used for new-to-the-world high-technology products, for which product prototypes are often either not available or extremely expensive to produce. Rather than conduct surveys to ask consumers about their likelihood to buy a product they can hardly imagine (What would someone have said in 1978 about his or her likelihood to buy a personal computer?), forecasters consider related product introductions with which the new product may be compared. Early forecasts for high-definition television (HDTV) were done this way, comparing HDTV with historical penetration patterns for color TV, videocassette recorders (VCRs), camcorders, and other consumer electronic products.[13]

As always, there are limitations. First, the new product is never exactly like that to which the analogy is drawn. Early VCRs penetrated American households at a much faster rate than did color TV. Which analogy should be used for HDTV? Why? Second, market and competitive conditions may differ considerably from when the analogous product was launched. Such conditions need to be taken into account.

Judgment

While we hesitate to call this a forecasting method of its own, since capable and informed judgment is required for *all* methods, sometimes forecasts are made *solely* on the basis of experienced **judgment,** or intuition. Some decision makers are intuitive in their decision processes and cannot always articulate the basis for their judgments. Said a footwear buyer at Nine West Group, "Trend forecasting is a visceral thing that cannot be trained. I rely on my sense of color and texture, but at times I cannot explain why I feel a certain way . . . I just know."[14] Those with sufficient forecasting experience in a market they know well may be quite accurate in their intuitive forecasts. Unfortunately, it is often difficult for them to defend their forecasts against those prepared by evidence-based methods when the two differ. Nonetheless, the importance of experienced judgment in forecasting, whether it is used solely and intuitively or in concert with evidence-based methods, cannot be discounted.

Market Tests

Market tests of various kinds are the last of our most commonly used methods. Used largely for new products, market tests such as **experimental test markets** may be done under controlled experimental conditions in research laboratories, or in live **test markets** with real advertising and promotion and distribution in stores. Use of test markets has declined over the past two decades for two reasons. First, they are expensive to conduct because significant quantities of the new product must be produced and marketing activities of various kinds must be paid for. More importantly, in today's data-intensive environment, especially for consumer products sold through supermarkets and mass merchants, competitors can buy the data collected through scanners at the checkout and learn the results of the test market without bearing the expense. More diabolically, competitors can engage in marketing tactics to mislead the company conducting the test, by increasing sampling programs, offering deep discounts or buy-one-get-one-free promotions, or otherwise distorting normal purchasing patterns in the category. Experimental test markets, on the other hand, are still commonly used.

The coming of the Internet has made possible a new kind of market test: an offer directly to consumers on the Web. Offers to chat rooms, interest groups, or e-mail lists of current customers are approaches that have been tried. Use of such techniques likely will increase, due to companies' ability to carry out such tests quickly and at low cost. We explore these and other Internet marketing strategies in greater detail in Chapter 9.

Mathematics Entailed in Forecasting

Regardless of the method used, the ultimate purpose of the forecasting exercise is to end up with numbers that reflect what the forecaster believes is the most likely outcome, or sometimes a range of outcomes under different assumptions, in terms of future market potential or for the sales of a product or product line. The combination of judgment and other methods often leads to the use of either of two mathematical approaches to determine the ultimate numbers: the chain ratio calculation or the use of indices. See Exhibits 6.3 and 6.4 for examples applying these mathematical calculations to arrive at sales forecasts. Both mathematical approaches begin with an estimate of market potential (the number of households in the target market in Exhibit 6.3; the national market potential for a product category in Exhibit 6.4). The market potential is then multiplied by various fractional factors that, taken together, predict the portion of the overall market potential that one firm or product can expect to obtain. In Exhibit 6.3, which shows the more detailed of the two approaches, the factors reflect the appeal of the product to consumers, as measured by marketing research data, and the company's planned marketing program.

CAUTIONS AND CAVEATS IN FORECASTING

Keys to Good Forecasting

There are two important keys to improve the credibility and accuracy of forecasts of sales and market potential. The first of these is to make explicit the **assumptions** on which the forecast is based. This way, if there is debate or doubt about the forecast, the *assumptions* can be

Exhibit 6.3

CHAIN RATIO FORECAST: TRIAL OF FRESH PASTA

Once Nestlé's research on fresh pasta had been completed (see Exhibit 6.2), it used the chain ratio method to calculate the total number of households who would try their fresh pasta. The chain ratio calculation went like this:

Research results for	Data from research	Chain ratio calculation	Result
Number of households in target market	77.4 million		
Concept purchase intent: adjusted figure from Exhibit 6.2	34.5% will try the product	77.4 million × 34.5%	26.7 million households will try *if aware*
Awareness adjustment: based on planned advertising level	48% will be aware of the product	26.7 million × 48%	12.8 million households will try *if they find product at their store*
Distribution adjustment: based on likely extent of distribution in supermarkets, given the introductory trade promotion plan	The product will obtain distribution reaching 70% of U.S. households	12.8 million × 70%	9.0 million will try the product

Similar chain ratio logic is useful in a variety of forecasting settings.

Source: Marie Bell and V. Kasturi Rangan, *Nestlé Refrigerated Foods: Contadina Pasta and Pizza.* Boston: Harvard Business School, 1995. Copyright © 1995 by the President and Fellows of Harvard College. Reprinted by permission.

Exhibit 6.4   Estimating Market Potential Using Indices

There are several published indices of buying behavior, including the "Annual Survey of Buying Power" published by *Sales and Marketing Management*. The Buying Power Index (BPI) is a weighted sum of a geographical area's percentage of national buying power for the area, based on census income data (weight = .5), plus the percentage of national retail sales for the area (weight = .3), plus the percentage of national population located in the area (weight = .2). If this calculation comes to 3.50 for a given state or region, one might expect 3.5 percent of sales in a given category (toys, power tools, or whatever) to come from that geographical area.

Category development indices (CDIs) are similar indices that report the ratio of consumption in a certain *category* (say, restaurant sales) to population in a defined geographical area. Trade associations or trade magazines relevant to the category typically publish such indices. Ratios greater than 1.0 for a particular geographic area, say metropolitan Chicago, indicate that the area does more business than average (compared to the country as a whole) in that category. **Brand development indices** (BDIs) compare sales for a given *brand* (say, Macaroni Grill restaurants) to population. Companies that use BDI indices typically calculate them for their own use. The ratio of the BDI to the CDI for a given area is an indicator of how well a brand is doing, compared to its category overall, in that area. These various indices are useful for estimating market potential in defined geographic areas. They are, however, crude numbers, in that they do not consider differences in consumer behavior from region to region. The CDI or BDI for snowmobiles in Minnesota is far higher than in Texas, for example. Attempting to rectify this imbalance by increasing the snowmobile advertising budget in Texas would be difficult!

debated, and data to support the assumptions can be obtained. The resulting conversation is far more useful than stating mere opinions about whether the forecast is too high or too low.

STRATEGIC ISSUE

There are two important keys to improve the credibility and accuracy of forecasts of sales and market potential.

For ACG, the combination of observational and survey forecasting methods enabled Maddy and Laguë to articulate the assumptions on which their revenue forecasts were based, and to support those assumptions with data. Their evidence-based forecast was instrumental in their obtaining US$3.5 million in start-up capital to get their venture off the ground.[15]

The second key to effective forecasting is to use multiple methods. When forecasts obtained by different methods converge near a common figure, greater confidence can be placed in that figure. The procedure used at Gap Inc. to forecast next-year sales (see Exhibit 6.1) is an example of such an approach. Where forecasts obtained by multiple methods diverge, the assumptions inherent in each can be examined to determine which set of assumptions can best be trusted. Ultimately, however, any forecast is almost certainly wrong. Contingency plans should be developed to cope with the reality that ultimately unfolds.[16]

Biases in Forecasting

Several sources of potential bias in forecasts should be recognized. First, forecasters are subject to anchoring bias, where forecasts are perhaps inappropriately "anchored" in recent historical figures, even though market conditions have markedly changed, for better or worse.[17] Second, capacity constraints are sometimes misinterpreted as forecasts. Someone planing to open a car wash that can process one car every seven minutes would probably be amiss in assuming sufficient demand to actually run at that rate all the time. A restaurant chain that is able to turn its tables 2.5 times each night, on average, must still do local market research to ascertain how much volume a new restaurant will really produce. Putting similar 80-table restaurants in two trade areas with different population makeup and density, with different levels of competition, will result in varying sales levels.

Another source of bias in forecasting is incentive pay. Bonus plans can cause managers to artificially inflate or deflate forecasts, whether intentionally or otherwise. "Sandbagging"—setting the forecast or target at an easily achievable figure in order to earn bonuses when that figure is beaten—is common.

Finally, unstated but implicit assumptions can overstate a well-intentioned forecast. While 34.5 percent of those surveyed (after adjustments, as shown in Exhibit 6.2) may indicate their willingness to buy a new grocery product, such as fresh pasta, for such a forecast to pan out requires that consumers actually are *made aware* of the new product when it is introduced, and that the product *can actually be found* on supermarket shelves. Assumptions of **awareness** and **distribution coverage** at levels less than 100 percent, depending on the nature of the planned marketing program for the product, should be applied to such a forecast, using the chain ratio method (see Exhibit 6.3).

WHY DATA? WHY MARKETING RESEARCH?

In the first portion of this chapter, we provided several approaches to forecasting, each of which requires that data be collected. Similarly, the first five chapters of this book provided frameworks for gaining a better understanding of market and competitive conditions and of what buyers in a given market want and need—what we call **market knowledge**.[18] Obtaining market knowledge also requires data, and so far we've provided little discussion of exactly how one might best find the necessary data. Without relevant and timely data, market knowledge is generally incomplete and often ill-informed, based perhaps on hunches or intuition that may or may not be correct.

Without adequate market knowledge, strategic marketing decisions are likely to be misguided. Products for which there is little demand may be introduced, only to subsequently fail. New markets may be entered, despite market or industry conditions that make success unlikely. Attractive product-markets may be overlooked. Products may be marketed to the wrong target market, when consumers in another market segment would like the product better. Pricing may be too high, reducing sales, or too low, leaving money on the table. Advertising and promotion monies may be poorly spent. Second-best distribution channels may be chosen. These outcomes are all too common. Most often, they result from ill- or under-informed marketing decisions. Thoughtfully designed, competently executed marketing research can mitigate the chances of such unpleasant outcomes.

Thus, in the remainder of this chapter we address the challenge of obtaining market knowledge, including the development of systems to track pertinent market information inside and outside the firm, as well as the design and implementation of more targeted studies intended to collect information about a particular marketing problem. We begin by discussing the principal kinds of **market knowledge systems** used in companies large and small, and we show how such systems can improve the timeliness and quality of marketing decisions.

MARKET KNOWLEDGE SYSTEMS: CHARTING A PATH TOWARD COMPETITIVE ADVANTAGE

Marketing is rapidly becoming a game where information, rather than raw marketing muscle, wins the race for competitive advantage. There are four commonly used market knowledge systems on which companies rely to keep pace with daily developments: internal records regarding marketing performance in terms of sales and the effectiveness and efficiency of marketing programs, marketing databases, competitive intelligence systems, and systems to organize client contact. Effective use of such systems is likely to result in happier, higher-volume, more loyal customers. Few of these systems existed in their current form until developments in data processing and data transmission made them cost effective.

Internal Records Systems

Every Monday morning, each retail director at the headquarters of Nine West Retail Stores, a leading operator of shoe specialty stores, receives the "Godzilla Report," a tabulation of detailed sales and inventory information about the fastest-selling items in Nine West stores from the prior week.[19] By style and color, each director learns which items in his or her stores are selling fast and need to be reordered. A similar report provides information about all other styles currently in Nine West's stores, so that slow sellers can be marked down or transferred to stores where those styles are in higher demand. Additional reports aggregate sales information by style and color; by merchandise category (e.g., dress or casual); by store, area, or region; and for various time periods. The information provided by these reports constitutes the backbone of Nine West's decision making about which shoes to offer in which of its stores. Imagine how much more difficult the retail director's job would be without today's point-of-sale systems to collect and report such data! Imagine the potential advantage Nine West has over shoe retailers who lack such information.

Every marketer, not just retailers, needs information about "what's hot, what's not." Unfortunately, accounting systems generally do not collect such data. Typically, such systems just track dollars of revenue, with no information about *which* goods or services were sold. Thus, marketers need **internal records systems** to track what is selling, how fast, in which locations, to which customers, and so on. Providing input on the design of such systems so that the right data are provided to the right people at the right time is a critical marketing responsibility in any company. In some cases, such systems constitute a significant competitive advantage.

But what constitutes critical marketing information varies from company to company and industry to industry. Nine West retail directors need to know which styles and colors are selling, in which stores, at what rate. Wal-Mart believes its key suppliers need to know its store-by-store item and category sales data, so it provides password-protected online access to such data to those suppliers. Telemarketers need to know which callers are producing sales, at what times of day, for which products. Marketers of kitchen gadgets through infomercials on late-night television need to know which ads on which stations in which cities are performing, in order to place media dollars where they will be most productive. Companies selling their wares to industrial markets through outside salesforces need to know not only which products are selling to which customers but also which salespeople are selling how much, at what margins and expense rates, to whom. The salesforce, too, needs information about status of current orders, customer purchasing history, and so on. For an example of how **salesforce automation software** is helping modern salespeople to be more productive and more able to satisfy customer needs, see Exhibit 6.5. For those charged with developing or updating internal record systems in their companies, we provide, in Exhibit 6.6, a series of questions to help marketing decision makers specify what internally generated sales data are needed, when, for whom, in what sequence, at what level of aggregation.

Exhibit 6.5   **How Salesforce Automation Software Places Internal Records at the Salesforce's Fingertips**

In many companies, an outside salesforce bears the principal responsibility for customer contact and for producing revenue. The use of intranets combined with salesforce automation software now gives traveling salespeople instant access to whatever information they or their customers need. At Ascom Timeplex, Inc., a marketer of telecommunications equipment, sales reps use their laptop computers to access price lists, order status, e-mail, and a host of other customer-relevant information from the company's worldwide data network. When orders are placed anywhere, they are sent electronically from the sales rep's laptop to headquarters in New Jersey. Rarely does an Ascom Timeplex salesperson say to a customer, "I don't know. I'll have to get back to you on that."

Source: Reprinted from John W. Verity, "Taking a Laptop on a Call," *Business Week,* October 25, 1993, pp. 124–25, with special permission. Copyright © 1993 by The McGraw-Hill Companies, Inc.

Marketing Databases

Many companies have become quite sophisticated about keeping track of their customers' purchases using marketing databases. Catalog marketers such as Lands' End and L.L Bean know who are their best customers and what categories they tend to buy. Online marketers like Amazon.com use "cookies," electronic signatures placed at a customer's personal computer, so they not only keep track of what each customer has bought, but they also recognize the customer when he or she logs on to their site. Airlines track members of their frequent flyer programs and target some with special promotions. Supermarket chains such as Safeway encourage their customers to obtain cards that give the user "clipless coupon" savings when they shop, and that permit Safeway to better understand the purchasing patterns of its customers.

Designing marketing databases that take effective advantage of customer data that companies are in a position to collect requires that several major issues be considered: the cost of collecting the data, the economic benefits of using the data, the ability of the company to keep the data current in today's mobile society, and the rapid advances in technology that permit the data to be used to maximum advantage.

Collecting information, then storing and maintaining it, always costs money. If a company wants to know more about the demographics and lifestyles of its best customers, in addition to their purchasing histories, it must obtain demographic and lifestyle data about them. Doing so is more difficult than it sounds; most people are unwilling to spend much time filling out forms that ask nosy questions about education, income, whether they play tennis, and what kind of car they drive. The cost of collecting such information must be weighed against its value. What will be done with the information once it is in hand?

Various commercial marketing databases are available, with varying depth and quality of information. For example, the Polk Company (**www.polk.com**) sells data compiled from state driver's license records in the United States, as well as a demographic and lifestyle database compiled from questionnaires returned with warranty cards for consumer durables such as toasters, stereos, and the like. Donnelley's DQI database (**www.donnelley.com**) covers more than 150 million individual U.S. consumers and 90 million U.S. households and includes more than 1,600 demographic, lifestyle, purchasing power, and creditworthiness variables, among others. Claritas's PRIZM service (Potential Rating Index for Zip Markets, **www.claritas.com**) classifies U.S. consumers into one of 62 distinct demographic and behavioral clusters according to the Zip code and postal carrier route where they live. Claritas and others offer a range of database marketing products

Exhibit 6.6

DESIGNING AN INTERNAL RECORDS SYSTEM FOR MARKETING DECISION MAKERS

Questions to ask	Implications for a chain footwear retailer	Implications for an infomercial marketer of kitchen gadgets
What information is key to providing our *customers* with what they want?	Need to *know* which shoes sell, in which stores and markets, at what rate	Need to *know* which gadgets sell, in what markets, at what rate
What regular marketing decisions are critical to our profitability?	*Decide* which shoes and shoe categories to buy more of, which to buy less of or get rid of, in which stores and markets to sell them	*Decide* on which specific TV stations, programs, and times of day to place infomercials for which gadgets
What data are critical to managing profitability?	Inventory turnover and gross margin	Contribution margin (gross margin less media cost) per gadget sold
Who needs to know?	Buyers and managers of merchandise categories	Media buyers, product managers
When do they need to know, for competitive advantage?	For hottest sellers, need to know before competitors, to beat them to the reorder market. For dogs, need to know weekly, to mark them down.	Need to know daily, for prior night's ads, to reallocate media dollars
In what *sequence* and at what *level of aggregation* should data be reported?	Sequence of report: hot sellers first, in order of inventory turnover	Sequence of report: hot stations/programs first, in order of contribution margin per gadget sold
	Aggregation: by style and color for buyers, by category for merchandise managers	Aggregation: By stations/programs for media buyers, by gadget for product managers

and services in Europe and other developed regions. Virtually every credit-card issuer, magazine publisher, affinity group (e.g., United Airlines Mileage Plus members), and others who sell to or deal directly with consumers sell their customer databases. Marketers who consider buying lists or other services from any of these commercial database providers need to inquire exactly how and where the data are collected and when (Have 20 percent of the people on the list moved?). They also should compare the costs of databases containing names about which more is known (higher cost, but of higher value to targeted marketers, since response rates will be higher for names chosen on the basis of more relevant information) to the extra value, compared to simpler **compiled databases,** such as those taken from telephone directories or automobile registrations. Marketers planning to build their own databases need also to consider several increasingly important ethical issues, as discussed in Ethical Perspective 6.1.

For firms with deep pockets, advances in computing power and database technology, including new **data-mining** technology,[20] are permitting firms to combine databases from different sources to permit a more complete understanding of any member of the database. Keeping current with what is possible in database technology is important, as technological advances often make possible that which was only a dream a short time ago.

Competitive Intelligence Systems[21]

In today's fast-paced business climate, keeping up with competitors and the changing macroenvironment is no easy task. Competitive intelligence (CI) is a systematic and ethical approach for gathering and analyzing information about competitors' activities and related business trends. It is based on the idea that more than 80 percent of all information

ETHICAL PERSPECTIVE 6.1
Ethical Issues in Database Marketing, Internet Marketing, and Marketing Research

New technologies relating to the gathering and use of information about consumers and their behavior, interests, and intentions raise a host of legal and ethical questions. These new technologies have the potential to harm individuals when such information "is used without their knowledge and/or consent, leading them to be *excluded from* or *included in* activities in such a way that they are harmed economically, psychologically, or physically. Examples include the improper disclosure of a person's credit rating, denying medical insurance to an individual based on confidential information, and a person's being placed on target lists for direct mail and telemarketing. The depth of privacy concerns varies from country to country, a critical issue for Internet marketers, given their global reach.

Ethical issues in marketing research stem, in large part, from the interaction between the researcher and respondents, clients, and the general public. For instance, respondents should not be pressured to participate, should have the right to remain anonymous, and should not be deceived by fake sponsorship.

Client issues involve the confidentiality of the research findings and the obligation to strive to provide unbiased and honest results regardless of client expectations. The public is very much involved when they are exposed to a sales solicitation disguised as a marketing research study or issuing from data obtained from "volunteer surveys" using write-ins or call-ins.

In discussing the reliability of, and ethical issues involved with, marketing research studies, a *Wall Street Journal* article noted that many studies "are little more than vehicles for pitching a product or opinion." An examination of hundreds of recent studies indicated that the business of research has become pervaded by bias and distortion. More studies are being sponsored by companies or groups with a financial interest in the results. This too often leads to a bias in the way questions are asked.

Because of shortages in time and money, sample sizes are being reduced to the point that, when groups are further broken into subgroups, the margin of error becomes unacceptable—assuming a probability sample was used. In addition to sample size, the way the sampling universe is defined can bias the results. Thus, in a Chrysler study showing that people preferred Chrysler's cars to Toyota's, a sample of only 100 respondents was used in each of two tests, and none owned a foreign car. Thus, the respondents may well have been biased in favor of U.S. cars.

In addition to the problems noted above, subjective sampling procedures often are used, data analysis may be flawed, or only the best conclusions are reported. Frequently researchers are hired whose views on the subject area being researched are known to be similar to those of the client. In an attempt to regulate the marketing research industry, several codes of conduct and ethics have been developed. These include published codes by the American Marketing Association, the American Association for Public Opinion Research, the Marketing Research Association, and the Council of American Survey Research Organizations.

Source: Paul N. Bloom, Robert Adler, and George R. Milne, "Identifying the Legal and Ethical Risks and Costs of Using New Information Technologies to Support Marketing Programs," in *The Marketing Information Revolution*, Robert C. Blattberg, Rashi Glazer, and John D. C. Little, eds. (Boston: Harvard Business School Press, 1994), p. 294; Cynthia Crossen, "Studies Galore Support Products and Positions, But Are They Reliable?" *The Wall Street Journal*, November 14, 1991, pp. A1 and A8; and Thomas E. Weber, "Europe and U.S. Reach Truce on Net Privacy, But What Comes Next?" *The Wall Street Journal*, June 19, 2000, p. B1.

is public knowledge. The most important sources of CI information include companies' annual and other financial reports, speeches by company executives, government documents, online databases, trade organizations, as well as the popular and business press. The challenge is to find the relevant knowledge, analyze it, and share it with the decision makers in the organization, so they can use it. The critical questions that managers setting up a CI system should ask are

- How rapidly does the competitive climate in our industry change? How important is it that we keep abreast of such changes?
- What are the objectives for CI in our company?

- Who are the best internal clients for CI? To whom should the CI effort report?
- What budget should be allocated to CI? Will it be staffed full- or part-time?

In companies that operate in industries with dynamic competitive contexts, the use of full-time CI staff is growing.

Client Contact Management Systems

Several low-cost software applications that run on PCs are available to keep track of client lists and the various kinds of contacts that are made with each client. ACT and Goldmine are two of the best-known programs in this arena. These programs keep track of clients' names, addresses, phone and fax numbers, and so on—along with all kinds of personal tidbits, such as their spouse's and children's names and the kind of wine the client likes to drink—and they also provide an organized way to make notes about each contact with the customer. They also can remind the user when it is time to follow up with the customer on a topic left pending. Most whose livelihood depends on face-to-face selling now use such systems to keep themselves organized.

Other Kinds of Market Knowledge Systems

We have covered but a few of the most common market knowledge systems, most of which are computer applications in today's increasingly sophisticated data-driven age. These tools make marketers better informed about their customers, potential customers, and competitors and help them be more productive, both of which help establish and sustain competitive advantage. New applications are being developed every day. Ultimately, the potential that many of these systems share is to enable marketers to serve target markets of one; that is, to know enough about any given customer and the competitive context that an offering can be tailored to fit each customer so well that the customer's needs are met perfectly. Doing so is many a marketer's dream!

MARKETING RESEARCH: A FOUNDATION FOR STRATEGIC DECISION MAKING

We now turn briefly to the **marketing research** task: the design, collection, analysis, and reporting of research intended to gather data pertinent to a *particular* marketing challenge or situation. The word *particular* is very important. Marketing research is intended to address carefully defined marketing problems or opportunities. Research carried out without carefully thought-out objectives usually means time and money down the tubes! Some marketing problems commonly addressed through marketing research include tracking customer satisfaction from unit to unit or year to year (**tracking studies**); testing consumer responses to elements of marketing programs, such as prices or proposed advertising campaigns; and assessing the likelihood that consumers will buy proposed new products.

The steps in the marketing research process are shown in Exhibit 6.7. As this exhibit shows, the marketing research process is fraught with numerous opportunities for error. That's why it's so important that all who play influential roles in setting strategy for their firms or who use marketing research results for decision making be well-informed and critical users of the information that results from market research studies.

It is beyond the scope of this book, however, to instruct the reader in how to design

Exhibit 6.7

STEPS IN THE MARKETING RESEARCH PROCESS: WHAT CAN GO WRONG?

Steps	What frequently goes wrong?
1. Identify managerial problem and establish research objectives	Management identifies no clear objective, no decision to be made based on the proposed research.
2. Determine data sources (primary or secondary) and types of data and research approaches (qualitative or quantitative) required	Primary data are collected when cheaper and faster secondary data will do. Quantitative data are collected without first collecting qualitative data.
3. Design research: type of study, data collection approach, sample, etc.	These are technical issues best managed by skilled practitioners. Doing these steps poorly can generate misleading or incorrect results.
4. Collect data	Collector bias: hearing what you want to hear.
5. Analyze data	Tabulation errors or incorrect use or interpretation of statistical procedures may mislead the user.
6. Report results to the decision maker	Some users do not really want objective information—they want to prove what they already believe to be true.

marketing research studies. For those wishing to read more on this topic, numerous textbooks on marketing research are available.[22] In Exhibit 6.8, we do suggest a variety of sources where secondary data may be obtained to assess the attractiveness of markets and industries, two important tasks for any strategic marketing decision maker.

WHAT USERS OF MARKETING RESEARCH SHOULD ASK

The research process described in Exhibit 6.7 makes clear where many of the potential stumbling blocks are in designing and conducting marketing research. The informed and critical user of marketing research should ask the following questions, ideally before implementing the research or, if necessary, subsequent to its completion, to ensure that the research is unbiased and the results are reliable.

1. What are the objectives of the research? Will the data to be collected be sufficient to meet those objectives?

2. Are the data sources appropriate? Are cheaper, faster secondary data used where possible? Is qualitative research planned to ensure that quantitative research, if any, is on target?

3. Are the planned qualitative and/or quantitative research approaches suited to the objectives of the research? Qualitative research is better for deep insights into consumer behavior, while quantitative research is better for measurement of a population's attitudes and likely responses to products or marketing programs.

4. Is the research designed well? Will questionnaire scales permit the measurement necessary to meet the research objectives? Are the questions on a survey or in an interview or focus group unbiased? ("Isn't this a great new product? Do you like it?") Do the contact method and sampling plan entail any known bias? Is the sample size large enough to meet the research objectives?

5. Are the planned analyses appropriate? They should be specified *before* the research is conducted.

Exhibit 6.8

SOME INFORMATION SOURCES FOR MARKET AND INDUSTRY ANALYSIS

Type of information	Library sources	Internet sources
To find trade associations and trade magazines	*Gale Directory of Publications; Encyclopedia of Associations*	www.gale.com www.instat.com
Information on specific companies	*Hoover's Handbook of American Business; Ward's Business Directory; Dun and Bradstreet Million Dollar Directory; Moody's Industrial Manual*	www.hoovers.com www.sec.gov/edgarhp.htm
U.S. demographic and lifestyle data	*Lifestyle Market Analyst*	www.census.gov
Demographic data on a specific region or local trade area in the United States	*Sourcebook of County Demographics; Sourcebook of Zip Code Demographics; Survey of Buying Power* in *Sales and Marketing Management;* National Decision Systems, 1-800-866-6520 (fee); Urban Decision Systems, 1-800-364-4837 (fee)	
International demographics and world trade	*Predicasts F&S Index United States, Europe and International*	www.stat-usa.gov www.cia.gov/cia/publications www.census.gov/ftp/pub/ipc/www/ idbnew.html www.i-trade.com
Macro trends	*Statistical Abstract of the United States; Business Periodicals Index*	www.stat-usa.gov
E-commerce	*Red Herring* magazine	www.cyberatlas.com www.ecommercetimes.com www.mediametrix.com www.emarketer.com
Proprietary providers of research reports		www.forrester.com www.gartner.com www.scarborough.com www.findsvp.com
Market share information	*Market Share Reporter*	
Clearinghouse of business information sites		www.dis.strath.ac.uk/business
Average financial statements by industry	*Annual Statement Studies,* Risk Management Association, formerly Robert Morris and Associates	www.rmahq.org/ann_studies/asstudies.html

Given the rate of change on the Web, some Internet addresses may change, and some print sources may add websites.

Source: Robert I. Berkman, *Find It Fast: How to Uncover Expert Information on Any Subject in Print or Online* (New York: HarperCollins, 1997); various Web addresses as listed above.

TAKE AWAYS

- Every forecast and estimate of market potential is wrong! *Evidence-based* forecasts and estimates, prepared using the tools provided in this chapter, are far more credible—and generally more accurate—than hunches or wild guesses. A menu of evidence-based forecasting approaches is provided in this chapter.

- Forecasts have powerful influence on what companies do, through budgets and other planning procedures. Thus, forecasting merits significant management attention and commitment.

- Superior market knowledge is not only an important source of competitive advantage, but it also results in happier, higher-volume, and more loyal customers. Thus, the systematic development of market knowledge is a critically important activity in any organization.

- Much can go wrong in marketing research and often does. Becoming an informed and critical user of marketing research is an essential skill for anyone who seeks to contribute to strategic decision making.

- Self-diagnostic questions to test your ability to apply the analytical tools and concepts in this chapter to marketing decision making may be found at this book's website at **www.mhhe.com/walker.**

ENDNOTES

1. Information to prepare this section was taken from Anita M. McGahan, *African Communications Group (Condensed)* (Boston: Harvard Business School Publishing, 1999); and Dale O. Coxe, *African Communications Group* (Boston: Harvard Business School Publishing, 1996).

2. Charles Wardell, "High-Performance Budgeting," *Harvard Management Update,* January 1999.

3. Ibid.

4. Peter L. Bernstein and Theodore H. Silbert, "Are Economic Forecasters Worth Listening to," *Harvard Business Review,* July–August 1982.

5. F. William Barnett, "Four Steps to Forecast Total Market Demand," *Harvard Business Review,* July–August 1988.

6. For a more detailed look at forecasting methods, see David M. Georgeoff and Robert G. Murdick, "Manager's Guide to Forecasting," *Harvard Business Review,* January–February 1986; and John C. Chamber, Satinder K. Mullick, and Donald D. Smith, *Harvard Business Review,* July–August 1971.

7. Arthur Schleifer Jr., *Forecasting with Regression Analysis* (Boston: Harvard Business School Publishing, 1996).

8. See Frank M. Bass, "A New Product Growth Model for Consumer Durables," *Management Science,* January 1969, pp. 215–27; and Trichy V. Krishnan, Frank M. Bass, and V. Kumar, "Impact of a Late Entrant on the Diffusion of a New Product/Service," *Journal of Marketing Research,* May 2000, pp. 269–78.

9. For more on conjoint analysis, see Robert J. Dolan, *Conjoint Analysis: A Manager's Guide* (Boston: Harvard Business School Publishing, 1990).

10. McGahan, *African Communications Group (Condensed).*

11. For more on concept testing, see Robert J. Dolan, *Concept Testing* (Boston: Harvard Business School Publishing, 1990).

12. McGahan, *African Communications Group (Condensed).*

13. Fareena Sultan, *Marketing Research for High Definition Television* (Boston: Harvard Business School Publishing, 1991).

14. Colin Welch and Ananth Raman, *Merchandising at Nine West Retail Stores* (Boston: Harvard Business School Publishing, 1998).

15. Coxe, *African Communications Group.*

16. A key challenge for manufacturers is to be able to quickly adjust production schedules to adapt to demand that differs from the forecast. To read more about how to enable production to respond quickly in the face of unforeseen changes in demand, see Marshall L. Fisher, Janice H. Hammond, Walter R. Obermeyer, and Ananth Raman, "Making Supply Meet Demand in an Uncertain World," *Harvard Business Review,* May–June 1994.

17. Amos Tversky and Daniel Kahneman, "Judgment under Uncertainty," *Science* 185 (1974), pp. 1124–31.

18. Li and Calantone define market knowledge as "organized and structured information about the market." See Tiger Li and Roger J. Calantone, "The Impact of Market Knowledge Competence on New Product Advantage: Conceptualization and Empirical Examination," *Journal of Marketing,* October 1998, pp. 13–29.

19. Welch and Raman, *Merchandising at Nine West Retail Stores.*

20. For more on data mining and related topics, see Peter Jacobs, "Data Mining: What General Managers Need to Know," *Harvard Management Update,* October 1999; and Jeff Papows, *Enterprise.com: Market Leadership in the Information Age* (Cambridge, MA: Perseus Publishing, 1998).

21. Information in this section comes from the Society of Competitive Intelligence Professionals website at www.scip.org/images/education/ci.htm.

22. For more on marketing research, see any business school marketing research text, such as Dillon, Madden, and Firtle, *Marketing Research in a Marketing Environment* (Burr Ridge, IL: Irwin/McGraw-Hill, 1993). Also see Pamela L. Alreck and Robert B. Settle, *The Survey Research Process* (Burr Ridge, IL: Irwin/McGraw-Hill, 1994). The survey research methods section of the American Statistical Association offers useful guides to conducting focus groups and surveys. Downloadable PDF files may be found at www.stat.ncsu.edu/info/srms/srms.html.

CHAPTER SEVEN

TARGETING ATTRACTIVE MARKET SEGMENTS

OurBeginning.com Bets $5 Million on Super Bowl Ads[1]

MICHAEL BUDOWSKI likes living on the edge. In September 1999, it occurred to him that the Super Bowl offered an opportunity to "Put a turbocharger in this company," as he put it. In early 1999, Budowski had convinced his wife Susan, who ran a small business as a wedding consultant out of their home, to expand into cyberspace. They soon launched the OurBeginning website, where customers could order wedding invitations, birth announcements, thank you notes, and other printed matter. Now, in September, with the Super Bowl looming, Budowski saw an opportunity to put his company on the map and quickly establish his brand. The Super Bowl was the top-rated TV show of the year, with an expected viewing audience of 135 million people.

A SIGNIFICANT INVESTMENT

A successful entrepreneur with interests in the restaurant industry and the exterminating business, CEO Budowski and investor and COO Michael Brandenburg spent three weeks obtaining loans and selling equity to fund their $5 million gamble. They would need $1 million to beef up the site so it could handle an anticipated two million users a day, far beyond its average of only 10,000 per day. They would pay Disney i.d.e.a.s., a unit of the Walt Disney Company, another $1 million to create a series of funny ads out of the seemingly staid topic of stationery and wedding invitations. And they would spend $3 million to run three pregame ads and a fourth spot during the game. For his $5 million, Budowski hoped to create a database of five million customers (many of whom would have heard about the site while watching the big game), establish brand recognition, and jumpstart his sales.

Budowski was not the only dot-com entrepreneur who saw the Super Bowl as a path to riches. Two dot-com companies, Monster.com and HotJobs.com, had made big splashes the year before with clever Super Bowl ads, and HotJobs had, in August, successfully completed a successful initial public offering of its stock. After a month of trading, the stock had tripled. For the upcoming game on January 30, 2000, more than a dozen dot-com companies had made plans similar to Budowski's, notwithstanding the $2.2 million average cost to run a single 30-second TV commercial.

Measuring the Results

So, what happened? Did the flurry of Super Bowl ads take these companies where they wanted to go? According to a study by Nielsen/NetRatings, the dot-com Super Bowl ads did not necessarily translate into sustained increases in Web traffic. For established Web brands, the ads seemed to have helped hold and increase their Web traffic. Comparing traffic in January and March, Monster.com traffic was up 6 percent, to 2.6 million unique visitors in March; E-Trade.com was up 18 percent; and Pets.com was up 7 percent (see Exhibit 7.1). For Britannica, an established offline brand still new to the Web, traffic was up 68 percent to just over one million unique visitors in March. For unknown newcomers like OurBeginnings, however, the story was mostly dismal. While AutoTrader.com had done well, with a traffic increase of 45 percent to almost 1.6 million unique visitors, most newcomers, as a lot, had generated small numbers of new visitors, especially in light of the spending it took to generate them. For most of them, including OurBeginning.com, the Super Bowl–generated spike in February traffic had fallen off sharply in March.

Exhibit 7.1

TRAFFIC AT WEBSITES OF DOT-COM ADVERTISERS: SUPER BOWL 2000

Site	Unique Audience		
	January	February	March
Monster.com	2,465,104	2,477,203	2,604,519
E-Trade.com	1,877,011	1,810,694	2,223,285
AutoTrader.com	1,099,489	1,508,672	1,593,865
WebMD.com	1,041,583	969,586	1,331,850
LifeMinders.com	1,207,055	1,413,347	1,104,164
Britannica.com	594,468	779,927	1,003,216
Pets.com	592,029	532,442	636,319
HotJobs.com	794,933	731,085	598,112
OnMoney.com	NA	217,284	349,632
Kforce.com	167,355	247,705	156,399
Netpliance.com	38,395*	100,536	119,185
OurBeginning.com	284,049	510,730	92,292*
LastMinuteTravel.com	50,474*	77,869*	50,965*
Computer.com	68,468*	89,910*	31,669*
Epidemic.com	77,131*	31,263*	NA
Agillion.com	NA	NA	NA

NA—Fewer than 10 visitors.

* Below statistically stable total. From: Nielsen/NetRatings survey of 50,000 Web surfers.

Source: Greg Farrell, "Bailing Out from the Super Bowl Ad Binge," *USA Today,* June 7, 2000. Copyright 2000, *USA Today.* Reprinted with permission.

Of course, some would argue that traffic counts only tell part of the story. Huge media coverage of the dot-com phenomenon placed many of these companies' names in the popular and business press, in both print and broadcast media. OurBeginning.com received more than 450 print mentions and 100 broadcast hits. Others would say that the Super Bowl exposure would make it easier for them to raise venture capital, a task growing more difficult by the day in 2000, as the dot-com financing window nearly slammed shut. These advertisers and their agencies used these explanations to put a brave face on the results.

But those who would assess the effectiveness of these Super Bowl ads in consumer marketing terms would prefer to use as metrics either the relationships between ad spending and the revenue dollars they generated—never mind *margin* dollars—or the per-customer cost of acquiring new customers. Let's look at OurBeginning.com's results. First, traffic. In the first quarter, January through March, their site had, according to their own reports, one million unique visitors, a figure not dramatically dissimilar to the Nielsen figure of 882,000 visitors (see Exhibit 7.1). At two million total hits, this traffic represented an average of just over 20,000 hits per day, up from 10,000 per day in the fall of 1999. While traffic was indeed up, the Super Bowl effort seemed to have fallen well short of Budowski's goal of building a five-million-customer database. What about sales, you ask? The one million visitors spent a total of $510,000 in the first quarter, a figure equal to approximately *one-tenth* of the marketing expense it took to generate these sales. If a typical customer spent $50 to $100—an educated guess—OurBeginning.com acquired perhaps 5,000 to 10,000 customers, at a cost of $5 million. These figures translate into a customer acquisition cost of $500 to $1,000 per customer.

Was it worth it? Are new customers worth this cost? Did Budowski's $5 million bet pay off? Time will tell whether those who learned of his site from the Super Bowl ads and the attendant publicity will buy enough wedding invitations, birth announcements, and other things OurBeginning.com sells to make the effort worthwhile. What if they don't? "It doesn't fold the company," he says. "I like living on the edge, but not that close to the edge."

STRATEGIC CHALLENGES ADDRESSED IN CHAPTER 7

OurBeginning.com's Super Bowl advertising is but one example of the many cases where naïve marketers fail to clearly identify the target market most likely to purchase their goods or services. In doing so, they risk wasting enormous resources by paying to deliver promotional messages to customers who are unlikely to buy what they have to sell. While some Super Bowl viewers undoubtedly fell into the demographic group most likely to need wedding invitations, birth announcements, and related products, most in that very broad audience did not. The problem for Budowski was that each set of eyeballs had to be paid for, whether they fell into the target market or not.

In Chapter 7, we draw on the foundation of market knowledge and customer understanding that the reader of the first six chapters is now able to assemble to introduce what are probably the most important and fundamental tools in the marketer's toolkit: **market segmentation** and **target marketing.** Together with product positioning, which we address in Chapter 8, these tools provide the platform upon which most effective marketing programs are built. Learning to apply these tools effectively, however, requires that several important questions be addressed. Why do market segmentation and target marketing make sense; why not pitch our wares to the widest possible audience, as did Michael Budowski during Super Bowl 2000? Second, how can potentially attractive market segments be identified and defined? Finally, how can these segments be prioritized so that the most attractive ones are pursued? Answering these questions should enable any

STRATEGIC ISSUE

The most important and fundamental tools in the marketer's toolkit—market segmentation and target marketing—provide the platform upon which most effective marketing programs are built.

entrepreneur, a venture capital investor in Silicon Valley, or a marketing manager in an established firm to decide which market segments should be targeted and which investments should be made.

WHY DO MARKET SEGMENTATION AND TARGET MARKETING MAKE SENSE?

Market segmentation is the process by which a market is divided into distinct subsets of customers with similar needs and characteristics that lead them to respond in similar ways to a particular product offering and marketing program. Target marketing requires evaluating the relative attractiveness of various segments (in terms of market potential, growth rate, competitive intensity, and other factors) and the firm's mission and capabilities to deliver what each segment wants, in order to choose which segments it will serve. Product positioning entails designing product offerings and marketing programs that collectively establish an enduring competitive advantage in the target market by creating a unique image, or position, in the customer's mind. Arguably, OurBeginning.com would have been better served by examining its early customer base, or other customers it sought to serve, to determine who comprised its target market and how that market could best be reached—in terms of effectiveness and efficiency—with promotional strategies intended to win new customers.

These three decision processes—market segmentation, target marketing, and positioning—are closely linked and have strong interdependence. All must be well considered and implemented if the firm is to be successful in managing a given product-market relationship. More often than not, successful companies have been able to manage this relationship and, in so doing, distance themselves from their competitors. Consider the following international example.[2]

> In England, Japanese companies have outperformed their British rivals across a range of industries. A major reason for this was that the Japanese were better at managing the segmentation, targeting, and positioning relationships. Thus, only 13 percent of the Japanese firms versus 47 percent of the British were unclear about their target segment of customers and their special needs.
>
> All too often the marketing directors of the British companies remarked that they see their target market as being the whole market and since their products had wide appeal, there was no need to segment the market. As a consequence, the Japanese concentrated their resources in specific high-potential segments while the British tended to spread theirs thinly across the entire market. When British companies did segment, they did so at the lower, cheaper end of the market. This resulted in customers increasingly perceiving the Japanese, in contrast to the British, as offering quality and status.

However large the firm, its resources are usually limited compared with the number of alternative market segments available for investment. Thus, a firm must make choices. Even in the unusual case where a firm can afford to serve all market segments, it must determine the most appropriate allocation of its marketing effort *across* segments. But are all these analyses and conscious choices about which segments to serve really necessary?

Most Markets Are Heterogeneous

Because markets are rarely homogeneous in benefits wanted, purchase rates, and price and promotion elasticities, their response rates to products and marketing programs differ. Variation among markets in product preferences, size and growth in demand, media habits, and competitive structures further affect the differences and response rates. Thus, markets are complex entities that can be defined (segmented) in a variety of ways. The critical issue is to find an appropriate segmentation scheme that will facilitate target marketing, product positioning, and the formulation of successful marketing strategies and programs. Many dot-com advertisers who invested considerable sums in Super Bowl ads in 2000, only to win minimal consumer response, now recognize that broadly targeted advertising that fails to identify and reach a properly focused target market is a roadmap to bankruptcy. Of course, some of these advertisers would say that their real purpose was to reach venture capital investors or others who might eventually buy their stock in a hoped-for IPO. Was the Super Bowl a cost-effective way to reach these target markets with their message? History—not to mention sound marketing practice—suggests otherwise.

Today's Market Realities Often Make Segmentation Imperative

Market segmentation has become increasingly important in the development of marketing strategies for several reasons. First, population growth has slowed, and more product-markets are maturing. This sparks more intense competition as firms seek growth via gains in market share (the situation in the automobile industry) as well as in an increase in brand extensions (Starbucks coffee ice cream, Colgate toothbrushes, Visa traveler's checks).

Second, such social and economic forces as expanding disposable incomes, higher educational levels, and more awareness of the world have produced customers with more varied and sophisticated needs, tastes, and lifestyles than ever before. This has led to an outpouring of goods and services that compete with one another for the opportunity of satisfying some group of consumers.

Third, there is an increasingly important trend toward microsegmentation in which extremely small market segments are targeted.[3] This trend has been accelerated in some industries by new technology such as computer-aided design, which has enabled firms to mass-customize many products as diverse as designer jeans and cars. For example, many automobile companies are using a flexible production system that can produce different models on the same production line. This enables the company to produce cars made to order and soon, perhaps, sell them on the Internet.[4]

Finally, many marketing organizations have made it easier to implement sharply focused marketing programs by more sharply targeting their own services. For example, many new media have sprung up to appeal to narrow interest groups. These include special interest magazines, such as *Backpacker* and *Working Mother;* radio stations with formats targeted to different demographic groups, such as classical music, rock, country, and jazz, not to mention talk shows of various kinds; and cable TV channels, such as Nickelodeon and the Filipino Channel. Also, more broad-based magazines such as *Newsweek, Sports Illustrated,* and *People* offer advertisers the opportunity to target specific groups of people within their subscription base. An advertiser can target specific regions, cities, or Zip codes, or even selected income groups.

In addition to forcing firms to face the realities of the marketplace, market segmentation offers the following benefits:

- *It identifies opportunities for new product development.* Often a careful analysis of various segments of potential customers reveals one or more groups whose specific needs and concerns are not being well-satisfied by existing competitive offerings. Such uncovered segments may represent attractive opportunities for development of new products or innovative marketing approaches: for example, the laptop computer.

- *It helps in the design of marketing programs that are most effective for reaching homogeneous groups of customers.*

- *It improves the strategic allocation of marketing resources.* The strategic benefits of segmentation are sometimes overlooked. Well-defined segments, when coupled with specific products, serve as potential investment centers for a business. Most successful business strategies are based on market segmentation and a concentration of resources in the more attractive segments. Segmentation should focus on subdividing markets into areas in which investments can gain a long-term competitive advantage.

HOW ARE MARKET SEGMENTS BEST DEFINED?

There are several important objectives entailed in the market segmentation process:

- The process should identify one or more relatively homogeneous groups of prospective buyers with regard to their wants and needs and/or their likely responses to differences in the elements of the marketing mix—the 4 Ps (product, price, promotion, and place). For marketers of athletic shoes, such as Nike and Adidas, for example, high-performance distance runners is such a segment.

- Differences within one market segment should be small compared to differences across various segments (most high-performance distance runners probably have athletic footwear needs that are quite similar to one another, but quite different from, say, the needs of basketball players).

- The segmentation criteria should measure or describe the segments clearly enough so that members can be readily identified and accessed, in order for the marketer to know whether a given prospective customer is or is not in the target market and in order to reach the prospective customer with advertising or other marketing communication messages. Nike or Adidas might have defined their initial target market as being comprised of members of running clubs or distance runners on collegiate track and cross-country teams.

- Finally, the segmentation process should determine the size and market potential of each segment for use in prioritizing which segments to pursue, a topic we address in more detail later in this chapter. Nike, for example, could easily ascertain how many such runners there were in the United States, and they probably knew how many pairs of shoes per year the typical distance runner bought, at what average price.

Given these objectives, what kinds of segmentation criteria, or descriptors, are most useful? Marketers divide segmentation descriptors into three major categories for both consumer and organizational markets: **demographic descriptors** (which reflect *who* the target customers are), **geographic descriptors** (*where* they are), and **behavioral descriptors** of various kinds (*how* they behave with regard to their use and/or purchases of a given category of goods or services). We examine each of these categories next.

Demographic Descriptors

While firm demographics (age of firm, size of firm, industry, etc.) are useful in segmenting organizational markets, we usually think of demographics in terms of attributes of individual consumers, as shown in Exhibit 7.2. Some examples of demographic descriptors used to segment consumer markets are as follows:

Age: "Thanks to a demographic trend that is being called 'invasion of the stroller people,' babies are hot, both as consumers and marketing tools." There are nearly 24 million children under five in the United States—20 percent more than in 1980. Aside from medical costs, new parents spend on average $7,000 on a baby's first year. Nike has announced a new line of toddler clothes.[5]

Exhibit 7.2

SOME OF THE MORE COMMONLY USED DEMOGRAPHIC DESCRIPTORS*

Demographic descriptors	Examples of categories
Age	Under 2, 2–5, 6–11, 12–17, 18–24, 25–34, 35–49, 50–64, 65 and over
Sex	Male, female
Household life cycle	Young, single; newly married, no children; youngest child under 6; youngest child 6 or over; older couples with dependent children; older couples without dependent children; older couples retired; older, single
Income	Under $15,000, $15,000–24,999; $25,000–74,999, etc.
Occupation	Professional, manager, clerical, sales, supervisor, blue collar, homemaker, student, unemployed
Education	Some high school, graduated high school, some college, graduated college
Events	Birthdays, graduations, anniversaries, national holidays, sporting events
Race and ethnic origin	Anglo-Saxon, African-American, Italian, Jewish, Scandinavian, Hispanic, Asian

*Others include marital status, home ownership, and presence and age of children.

Sex: Recently General Motors' Chevrolet division spent considerable funds on advertising and events to convince women that its cars are made with them in mind. Chevrolet's efforts recognize that women spend $85 billion annually in buying half of all the new cars purchased in the United States.[6]

Household life cycle: Formerly known as family life cycle, this concept has been "modernized" by incorporating nontraditional households such as single-parent and never-married singles households. Essentially it describes the stages in the formation, growth, and decline in a household unit. Each stage differs in its expenditure patterns. Thus, young marrieds are heavy buyers of small appliances, furniture, and linens. With the arrival of children, purchases include insurance, washers and dryers, medical care, and an assortment of child-oriented products. A recent study confirmed that transitions in household situations are related to meaningful changes in spending behavior, but that it is often difficult to relate these changes to the purchase of specific products.[7]

Income: Higher-income households purchase a disproportionate number of cellular phones, expensive cars, and theater tickets. The circulation and advertising of magazines targeting the rich have increased dramatically in recent years—for example, *The Robb Report,* a monthly magazine whose readers have an average income of $755,000.[8]

Occupation: The sales of certain kinds of products (e.g., work shoes, automobiles, uniforms, and trade magazines) are tied closely to occupational type. The increase in the number of working women has created needs for specialized goods and services including financial services, business wardrobes, convenience foods, automobiles, and special-interest magazines.

Education: There is a strong positive correlation between the level of education and the purchase of travel, books, magazines, insurance, theater tickets, and photographic equipment.

Events: These include a varied set of activities ranging from national holidays, sports, and back-to-school week, to personal events such as birthdays, anniversaries, and weddings. Each requires a specific marketing program.

Race and ethnic origin: More and more companies are targeting these segments via specialized marketing programs. Motorola has run separate advertising campaigns for its pagers and cellular phones to African-Americans, Asian-Americans, and Hispanics. Spiegel and *Ebony* magazine have combined to produce a direct-mail catalog designed to provide apparel that meets the style, color, and fit needs of African-Americans. Efforts, so far, have been successful.[9]

Demographic descriptors are also important in the segmentation of industrial markets, which are segmented in two stages. The first, *macrosegmentation,* divides the market according to the characteristics of the buying organization using such descriptors as age of firm, firm size, and industry affiliation (SIC code). The international counterpart of SIC is the trade-category code.

The second stage, *microsegmentation,* groups customers by the characteristics of the individuals who influence the purchasing decision—for instance, age, sex, and position within the organization. International markets are segmented in a similar hierarchical fashion, starting with countries, followed by groups of individuals or buying organizations.

Geographic Descriptors

Different locations vary in their sales potential, growth rates, customer needs, cultures, climates, service needs, and competitive structures, as well as purchase rates for a variety of goods. For example, more pickup trucks are sold in the southwest United States, more vans in the Northeast, and more high-priced imports in the West. Uni-Marts, Inc., a convenience store operator of over 400 stores, focuses on small towns and rural areas, thereby avoiding big competitors. In its 23-year history, it has yet to record a loss.[10]

Geographic segmentation is used in both consumer and organizational markets and is particularly important in retailing and many services businesses, where customers are unwilling to travel very far to obtain the goods or services they require. Thus, one way to segment retail markets is by distance or driving time from a particular location. The area included within such a geographically defined region is called a **trade area.**

In the brave new world of electronic commerce, geographic segmentation issues can be very important, given the global reach of the Internet. For an example of how one online auction site is segmenting and targeting the European market country by country, see Exhibit 7.3.

Exhibit 7.3   QXL's Segmented Approach Expands across Europe, Country by Country

From Jim Rose's office in London, more than 5,000 miles from Silicon Valley, eBay doesn't look so invincible. Rose, chief executive officer of QXL.com, believes that thinking global means thinking local. Unlike eBay, QXL lets established retailers as well as ordinary consumers pitch their wares, to make relatively inexperienced European net surfers more comfortable with the online auction game.

Rather than fielding a single website for the European continent, QXL moved from its 1997 start in the United Kingdom to a dozen countries by 2000. In some, it launched a new site; in others it bought an already established player. Says Rose, "We're operating in 12 different languages. That means 12 different currencies, too." Though the QXL logo looks identical on each country's site, the merchandise featured on the sites' front pages varies substantially. On its German site, for example, a travel agency might be auctioning a vacation package to Majorca, a destination popular with German travelers. "You would never find that on the list for a U.K. promotion," says Stanislaus

Laurent, a 31-year-old Frenchman and QXL's senior vice president of sales and marketing. "In the U.K. it would be Madrid, or maybe St. Lucia." To ensure that each site effectively targets local preferences and needs, each one has its own office and staff that customizes what QXL offers and oversees local marketing efforts.

Is QXL's segmented, targeted approach working? "QXL is painfully slow and antiquated compared with eBay," says Heather Gardner, a British bank clerk who sells antiques and collectibles online. But she points out that her merchandise sells better on QXL than it does on eBay's U.K. site. "For some reason, I get the sales there," she says. Whether QXL's targeted, segmented approach will win the war against eBay has yet to be determined. As Jim Rose says, "The issue is how you execute."

Source: Thomas E. Weber, "EBay's European Rival Expands Methodically, Country by Country," *Wall Street Journal,* June 26, 2000, p. B1. Copyright 2000 by Dow Jones & Co. Inc. Reproduced with permission of Dow Jones & Co. Inc. via Copyright Clearance Center.

Geodemographic Descriptors

Many segmentation schemes involve *both* demographic and geographic factors. Thus, retailers usually want to know something about the people who live within, say, a two-mile or five-mile radius of their proposed new store. Neiman Marcus, the upscale department store, might target one demographic group within a given trade area, and Wal-Mart, a discounter, might target another. National Decision Systems (**www.ends.com**) and other sources offer low-cost reports based on census data that show the demographic profile of the population residing within any given radius of a particular street corner or shopping center location. These reports are useful in assessing the size and market potential of a market segment defined by a particular trade area. Geodemographics also attempts to predict consumer behavior by making demographic, psychographic, and consumer information available at the block and Zip code levels. Claritas's PRIZM service classifies all U.S. households into 62 demographically and behaviorally distinct clusters, each of which, in turn, is assigned to one of 15 social groups.[11]

Behavioral Descriptors

There is no limit to the number of insightful ways successful marketers have segmented markets in behavioral terms. Nike originally targeted high-performance distance runners. Specialized and Gary Fisher target bicyclists who wish to ride on single-track trails or back-country terrain. Europe's EasyJet airline targets leisure travelers. Gatorade's original target market consisted of athletes who needed to replenish water and salts lost through perspiration. This simple segmentation scheme created a whole new category of "sports beverages," which now includes entries from Coke (Powerade) and Pepsi (All Sport), though Gatorade still dominates the category with an 80 percent market share. This one-time niche market has grown into a $2.2 billion market in the United States alone.[12] These examples all demonstrate the power of highly specific behavioral descriptors in defining sharply focused market segments, based not on *who* the target consumers are or *where* they live, but based on what they *do*. In virtually every consumer and organizational market there are probably segments like these just waiting to be identified and targeted by insightful marketers. Behavioral descriptors can take many forms, including those based on consumer needs; on more general behavioral patterns, including lifestyle or social class; and, in organizational markets, on the structure of firms' purchasing activities and the types of buying situations they encounter.

Consumer Needs   Customer needs are expressed in **benefits sought** from a particular product or service. Individual customers do not have identical needs and thus attach different degrees of importance to the benefits offered by different products. In the end, the product that provides the best bundle of benefits—given the customer's particular needs—is most likely to be purchased.

Since purchasing is a problem-solving process, consumers evaluate product or brand alternatives on the basis of desired characteristics and how valuable each characteristic is to the consumer—**choice criteria.** Marketers can define segments according to these different choice criteria in terms of the presence or absence of certain characteristics and the importance attached to each. Firms typically single out a limited number of benefit segments to target. Thus, for example, different automobile manufacturers have emphasized different benefits over the years, such as safety (presence of side door airbags), reliability, and high mileage versus styling, quickness, and status.

In organizational markets, customers consider relevant benefits that include product performance in different use situations. For example, some super computers are bought because they meet the high-speed computational requirements of a small group of customers such as governments, universities, and research labs. Other considerations in the purchase of industrial products/services include on-time delivery, credit terms, economy, spare parts availability, and training.

Product-Related Behavioral Descriptors   In addition to highly specific behavioral descriptors such as those just discussed, there are more general product-related descriptors as well. They include product usage, loyalty, purchase predisposition, and purchase influence, all of which can be used to segment both consumer and industrial markets. **Product usage** is important because in many markets a small proportion of potential customers makes a high percentage of all purchases. In organizational markets, the customers are better known, and heavy users (often called *key accounts*) are easier to identify.

With respect to **loyalty**—as reflected by the numbers of successive purchases made over time—current users can vary considerably in their purchases of a given brand or patronage of a particular supplier. In organizational markets, sellers can often observe this directly; in consumer markets, identifying loyal customers requires marketing research.[13]

Consumers hold different predispositions toward the purchase of a product. A market segmentation scheme based on product knowledge (are they aware of it?) and **purchase predisposition** can identify the nonusers who are most likely to become future buyers. For example, knowledgeable nonusers who state intentions to buy, say, a high-fiber cereal are the most likely to become future users. Knowledgeable nonusers who do not intend to buy, on the other hand, would probably represent a low potential.

Market segmentation based on sources of **purchase influence** is relevant for both consumer and organizational markets. Many products used by various family members are purchased by the wife, but joint husband–wife decisions are becoming more common. Children's products, prescription drugs, and gifts are clearly influenced by a variety of individuals. In organizational markets, several individuals or units with varying degrees of influence participate in the buying center.

General Behavioral Descriptors   More general behavioral descriptors, including lifestyle and social class, are also commonly used in consumer markets. In organizational markets, prospective customers differ in how they structure their purchasing activities and in the nature of the buying situations they are engaged in.

Lifestyle   Segmentation by lifestyle, or psychographics, groups consumers on the basis of their activities, interest, and opinions. From such information it is possible to infer what types of products and services appeal to a particular group, as well as how best to communicate with individuals in the group.

Various segmentation approaches based on lifestyle have been developed, either by companies seeking to segment their own markets or by service providers whose tools are available to anyone. For example, Goodyear Tire and Rubber and Ogilvy and Mather (an advertising agency), working separately, have developed several classifications for global lifestyle segments. The Goodyear effort consists of six groups: the prestige buyer, the comfortable conservative, the value shopper, the pretender, the trusting patron, and the bargain hunter. Ogilvy and Mather proposes 10 global segments based on lifestyle characteristics: basic needs, fairer deal, traditional family life, conventional family life, look-at-me, somebody better, real conservatism, young optimist, visible achiever, and socially aware.[14]

Stanford Research Institute (SRI) has created an improved U.S. segmentation service (called VALS 2), which builds on the concept of self-orientation and resources for the individual. *Self-orientation* is based on how consumers pursue and acquire products and services that provide satisfaction and shape their identities. In doing so, they are motivated by the orientations of principle, status, and action. Principle-oriented consumers are motivated by abstract and idealized criteria, while status-oriented consumers shop for products that demonstrate the consumer's success. Action-oriented consumers are guided by the need for social or physical activity, variety, and risk taking.

Resources include all of the psychological, physical, demographic, and material means consumers have to draw on. They include education, income, self-confidence, health, eagerness to buy, intelligence, and energy level—on a continuum from minimal to abundant.

Based on these two dimensions, VALS 2 defines eight segments that exhibit distinctive behavior and decision making: actualizers, fulfillers, achievers, experiencers, believers, strivers, makers, and strugglers. The segments are approximately the same size so as to represent viable market targets. Claritas and similar commercial organizations identify each of the respondents as to their VALS type, thereby permitting a cross-classification of VALS type with the product usage and personal information collected by such companies. Thus, users can determine what each VALS segment bought, what their media habits are, and similar data. The VALS system has been further developed in Europe and Asia.[15] Those interested in the VALS segmentation scheme can complete a short survey on the VALS website (log onto **http://future.sri.com/VALS/VALSindex.shtml**) and discover the VALS segment to which they belong.

Social Class Every society has its status groupings based largely on similarities in income, education, and occupation.[16] Because researchers have long documented the values of the various classes, it is possible to infer certain behavior concerning a given product. For example, the middle classes tend to place more value on education, family activities, cleanliness, and being up-to-date than do lower-class families. In the international field, one has to be careful in using social class as a segmentation variable since the differences among classes can become blurred, as they do in the Scandinavian countries.[17] In America many of the criteria used to define class status seem to some to be no longer applicable as the nation becomes increasingly fragmented into dozens of distinct subcultures, each with its own unique tastes and ambitions. As noted earlier, Claritas, Inc., has identified 62 distinct classes in the United States, each with its own set of beliefs and aspirations.[18]

Organizational or Firm Behavioral Descriptors   Purchasing structure and buying situation segmentation descriptors are unique to organizational markets. **Purchasing structure** is the degree to which the purchasing activity is centralized. In such a structure the buyer is likely to consider all transactions with a given supplier on a global basis, to emphasize cost savings, and to minimize risk. In a decentralized situation, the buyer is apt to be more sensitive to the user's need, to emphasize product quality and fast delivery, and to be less cost-conscious.

The **buying situation** descriptor includes three distinct types of situations: straight rebuy, a recurring situation handled on a routine basis; modified rebuy, which occurs when some element, such as price or delivery schedules, has changed in a client–supplier relationship; and a new buying situation, which may require the gathering of considerable information and an evaluation of alternative suppliers.

Global Market Segmentation

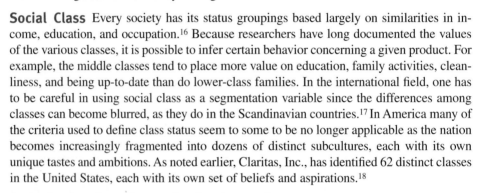

The traditional approach to global market segmentation has been to view a country or a group of countries as a single segment comprising all consumers. This approach is seriously flawed because it relies on country variables rather than consumer behavior, assumes homogeneity *within* the country segment, and ignores the possibility of the existence of homogeneous groups of consumers *across* country segments.[19]

More and more companies are approaching global market segmentation by attempting to identify consumers with similar needs and wants reflected in their behavior in the marketplace in a range of countries. This intercountry segmentation enables a company to develop reasonably standardized programs requiring little change across local markets, thereby resulting in scale economies. Star TV's launch of a Pan-Asian satellite television service broadcasting throughout Asia in English and Chinese is an example of such a strategy.[20]

Theodore Levitt has long been a proponent of globalization of a homogeneous marketplace for certain goods (for instance, consumer durables) based on price and high quality. He argues that similar segments have emerged in different countries at the same time because of technological developments affecting communications, transportation, and travel.[21] Others, using the same reasoning, believe there are two emerging intercountry global segments: the **global elite** consumer and the **global teenage** segment. The former is targeted by producers of products and services with an image of exclusivity (cellular phones, personal computers, luxury cars, expensive perfumes). The growing number of reasonably affluent groups in Latin America offer considerable potential for a variety of goods including automobiles, compact disc players, children's clothing, and health and beauty aids.[22]

The global teenage segment assumes a minimum of differences in cultural norms and lifestyles for teenagers across countries. Empirical evidence exists for this view for certain kinds of products, such as Swatch watches, Sony's line of audio products for children, and Benetton's colorful knitwear. Even in Japan, typed as a homogeneous culture featuring the "Japan First" sentiment, there is considerable evidence that younger generations are becoming more positive about U.S. and European products.[23]

Clearly, many global trends are influencing the behavior of consumers, including increased per-capita GNP, increased literacy and education, growth in urbanization, greater availability of TV and the Internet, and more travel. Many consumer products are becoming more common (automobiles, major home appliances, TVs). Thus, the global market for many products can be thought of as in transition. This development will require global marketers to continuously monitor their markets to identify emerging segments.

Innovative Segmentation: A Key to Marketing Breakthroughs

At the beginning of this section (see How Are Market Segments Best Defined? on page 153), we identified four objectives of the market segmentation process. Effective marketers, such as the creators of Nike athletic shoes, Gatorade, and other highly successful products, know that meeting these objectives through insightful and innovative market segmentation schemes is often the key to marketing breakthroughs. Often, combinations of different descriptors are used to more precisely target an attractive segment: perhaps some behavioral dimension together with a carefully defined demographic profile within some geographic region. Generally, it is useful to know the demographic profile of the target market to be pursued, even if the driving force behind the segmentation scheme is geographical and/or behavioral in nature. Understanding the demographic profile of a target market enables the marketer to better choose targeted advertising media or other marketing communication vehicles, unlike many Super Bowl advertisers in January 2000.

As is the case for many kinds of marketing decision making, computer-based decision support systems have been developed to aid marketers as they wrestle with market segmentation decisions. Some widely used systems are identified in Exhibit 7.4.

As several examples in this section have shown, at the foundation of many marketing breakthroughs one often finds an insightful segmentation scheme that is sharply focused in a *behavioral* way. Marketers with superior market knowledge are probably more likely

Exhibit 7.4   Software Tools for Market Segmentation

Two broad kinds of software applications are used in segmenting markets. **Data mining** applications enable the marketer to examine a customer database to identify patterns of variables that predict which customers buy or don't buy, as well as how much they buy. CART® and MARS™ from Salford Systems, Inc. (**www.salford-systems.com**) are two such applications. Various tools for analyzing the demographic makeup of a proposed target market are also available. National Decision Systems (**www.ends.com**) is one such supplier. Various analytical procedures in SPSS MR or other statistical software packages also are useful for market segmentation

Source: "Directory of Marketing Technology: Software & Internet Services." Reprinted with permission from *Marketing News,* published by the American Marketing Association, July 17, 2000.

---

to generate the insights necessary to define market segments in these innovative and meaningful ways. Phil Knight and Bill Bowerman, the founders of Nike, as runners themselves, had the necessary market knowledge to see how distance runners, as a market segment, were underserved.[24] Their insight, together with the development of innovative products and the creation of effective marketing programs, led the growth of the athletic footwear market, as consumers purchased different shoes for their different athletic pursuits, and ultimately revolutionized the athletic footwear industry.

CHOOSING ATTRACTIVE MARKET SEGMENTS: A FIVE-STEP PROCESS

Most firms no longer aim a single product and marketing program at the mass market. Instead, they break that market into homogeneous segments on the basis of meaningful differences in the benefits sought by different groups of customers. Then they tailor products and marketing programs to the particular desires and idiosyncrasies of each segment. *But not all segments represent equally attractive opportunities for the firm.* To prioritize target segments by their potential, marketers must evaluate their future attractiveness and their firm's strengths and capabilities relative to the segments' needs and competitive situations.

Within an established firm, rather than allowing each business unit or product manager to develop an approach to evaluate the potential of alternative market segments, it is often better to apply a common analytical framework across segments. With this approach, managers can compare the future potential of different segments using the same set of criteria and then prioritize them to decide which segments to target and how resources and marketing efforts should be allocated. One useful analytical framework managers or entrepreneurs can use for this purpose is the **market-attractiveness/competitive-position matrix.** As we saw in Chapter 2, managers use such models at the corporate level to allocate resources across businesses, or at the business-unit level to assign resources across product-markets. We are concerned with the second application here.

Exhibit 7.5 outlines the steps involved in developing a market-attractiveness/competitive-position matrix for analyzing current and potential target markets. Underlying such a matrix is the notion that managers can judge the attractiveness of a market (its profit potential) by examining market, competitive, and environmental factors that may influence profitability. Similarly, they can estimate the strength of the firm's competitive position by

Exhibit 7.5

STEPS IN CONSTRUCTING A MARKET-ATTRACTIVENESS/COMPETITIVE-POSITION MATRIX FOR EVALUATING POTENTIAL TARGET MARKETS

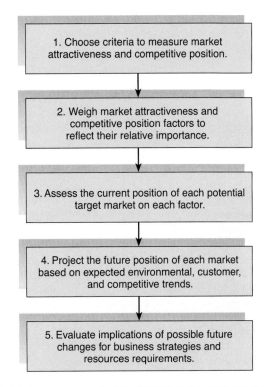

looking at the firm's capabilities or shortcomings *relative* to the needs of the market and the competencies of likely competitors. By combining the results of these analyses with other considerations, including risk, the mission of the firm, and ethical issues (see Ethical Perspective 7.1), conclusions about which markets and market segments should be pursued can be reached.

The first steps in developing a market-attractiveness/competitive-position matrix, then, are to identify the most relevant variables for evaluating alternative market segments and the firm's competitive position regarding them and to weight each variable in importance. Note, too, that Exhibit 7.5 suggests conducting a forecast of future changes in market attractiveness or competitive position in addition to, but separately from, an assessment of the current situation. This reflects the fact that a decision to target a particular segment is a strategic choice that the firm will have to live with for some time.

Step 1: Select Market-Attractiveness and Competitive-Position Factors

An evaluation of the attractiveness of a particular market or market segment and of the strength of the firm's current or potential competitive position in it builds naturally on the kind of opportunity analysis developed in Chapters 4 through 6. Managers can assess both

Over the years, marketing managers have confronted a number of ethical problems relating to the selection of target markets. Problems can rise from targeting consumers who because of their *inclusion* in the targeted group may be influenced to make decisions thought by some to be not in their best interest. Some would argue that advertising $150 sneakers to inner-city teenagers is ethically dubious; others say the advertising of snack foods and soft drinks to children is questionable. In other cases, *exclusion* issues are raised because the firm's marketing efforts did not include a particular group.

In the area of inclusion issues, advertisers often resort to undesirable stereotypes in an effort to simplify advertising messages. These include sex-role, race, or age stereotypes. Thus, the portrayal of women as sex objects (bikini-clad models in beer ads) or, in general, subordinate to male authority figures is thought by many to be dehumanizing and offensive. Reverse sexism with men shown as sex objects also has been on the increase to the dismay of some groups.

In recent years the targeting of minority or other groups for cigarettes and alcohol has increased. In some cases, a backlash against such targeting has prompted individual firms (and whole industries) to abandon or modify their targeting practices (brewers who have reduced their marketing programs that target students during spring break) and/or to emphasize moderation (responsible drinking). But one still can question the ethics of using sports heroes as role models in the advertising of products that may prove harmful to people's health. Indeed, the mass marketing of alcohol and tobacco products raises serious ethical questions.

For exclusion issues, the concern is not only that certain groups are deprived of products and services but also that they may pay more for those they do receive. There is considerable evidence to support the latter claim. A survey in New York City found that food prices are highest in neighborhoods that can least afford them. Low-income shoppers (family of four) paid 8.8 percent more for their groceries—$350 per year. Further, inner-city stores were on average poorly stocked, had inferior foodstuffs, and offered poorer service.

Companies often face the ethical problem of whether they may exclude certain groups they would rather not serve. For example, insurance companies want only low-risk policyholders, credit-card companies only low-risk cardholders, and hospitals only patients with insurance.

Source: N. Craig Smith and John A. Quelch, *Ethics in Marketing* (Burr Ridge, IL: Richard D. Irwin, 1993), pp. 183–95; and Felix M. Freedman, "The Poor Pay More for Food in New York, Survey Finds," *The Wall Street Journal,* April 15, 1991.

dimensions on the basis of information obtained from analyses of the environment, industry and competitive situation, market potential estimates, and customer needs. To make these assessments, they need to establish criteria, such as those shown in Exhibit 7.6, against which prospective markets or market segments can be evaluated. Both market and competitive perspectives are necessary.

Market-Attractiveness Factors   As we showed in Chapter 4, assessing the attractiveness of markets or market segments involves determining the market's size and growth rate and assessing various trends—demographic, sociocultural, economic, political/legal, technological, and physical—that influence demand in that market. An even more critical factor in determining whether to *enter* a new market or market segment, however, is the degree to which *unmet customer needs,* or needs that are currently not being well served, can be identified. In the absence of unmet or underserved needs, it is likely to be difficult to win customer loyalty, regardless of how large the market or how fast it is growing. "Me-too" products often face difficult going in today's highly competitive markets.

Competitive-Position Factors   As we showed in Chapter 5, understanding the attractiveness of the industry in which one competes is also important. Entering a segment

Exhibit 7.6

FACTORS UNDERLYING MARKET ATTRACTIVENESS AND COMPETITIVE POSITION

Market-attractiveness factors	Competitive-position factors
Customer needs and behavior	**Opportunity for competitive advantage**
• Are there unmet or underserved needs we can satisfy?	• Can we differentiate?
	• Can we perform against critical success factors?
	• Stage of competing products in product life cycle: Is the timing right?
Market or market segment size and growth rate	**Firm and competitor capabilities and resources**
• Market potential in units, dollars, number of prospective customers	• Management strength and depth
• Growth rate in units, dollars, number of prospective customers	• Financial and functional resources: marketing, distribution, manufacturing, R&D, etc.
• Might the target segment constitute a platform for later expansion into related segments in the market as a whole?	• Brand image
	• Relative market share
Macro trends: Are they favorable, on balance?	**Attractiveness of industry in which we would compete**
• Demographic	• Threat of new entrants
• Sociocultural	• Threat of substitutes
• Economic	• Buyer power
• Political/legal	• Supplier power
• Technological	• Competitive rivalry
• Physical	• Industry capacity
	• Driving forces: are they favorable, on balance?

that would place the firm in an unattractive industry or increase its exposure in an unattractive industry in which it already competes may not be wise. Of more immediate and salient concern, however, is the degree to which the firm's proposed product entry into the new market or segment will be sufficiently *differentiated* from competitors, given the critical success factors and product life cycle conditions already prevalent in the category. Similarly, decision makers need to know whether their firm has or will be able to acquire the resources it will take—human, financial, and otherwise—to effectively compete in the new segment. Simply put, most new goods or services need to be either better from a consumer point of view or cheaper than those they hope to replace. Entering a new market or market segment without a source of competitive advantage is a trap.

Step 2: Weight Each Factor

Next, a numerical weight is assigned to each factor to indicate its relative importance in the overall assessment. Let's imagine that we are Phil Knight or Bill Bowerman in 1964, before Nike even existed, and we are considering starting a venture to market new and better athletic shoes specifically designed for distance runners. Weights that Knight and Bowerman might have assigned to the major factors in Exhibit 7.6 are shown in Exhibit 7.7. Some users would rate each bullet point in Exhibit 7.6 independently, assigning a weight to each one.

Exhibit 7.7

ASSESSING THE DISTANCE RUNNER MARKET SEGMENT IN 1964

	Weight	Rating (0–10 scale)	Total
Market-attractiveness factors			
Customer needs and behavior: unmet needs?	.5	10	5.0
Segment size and growth rate	.3	7	2.1
Macro trends	.2	8	1.6
Total: Market attractiveness	**1.0**		**8.7**
Competitive-position factors			
Opportunity for competitive advantage	.6	7	4.2
Capabilities and resources	.2	5	1.0
Industry attractiveness	.2	7	1.4
Total: Competitive position	**1.0**		**6.6**

Step 3: Rate Segments on Each Factor; Plot Results on Matrices

This step requires that evidence—typically both qualitative and quantitative data—be collected to objectively assess each of the criteria identified in Step 1. For Knight and Bowerman in 1964, the assessment of the various factors might have looked such as those shown in Exhibit 7.7. While more detailed evidence than we discuss here should have been, and no doubt was, gathered, Knight and Bowerman might have reached the following conclusions:[25]

Market-attractiveness factors

- Unmet customer needs for lateral stability, cushioning, and lightweight shoe have been identified. Score: 10.
- The distance runner segment is quite small, though growing, but it might lead to other segments in the future. Score: 7.
- Macro trends are largely favorable: fitness is "in," number of people in demographic groups likely to run is growing, global trade is increasing. Score 8.

Competitive-position factors

- Opportunity for competitive advantage is somewhat favorable; proposed shoes will be differentiated, but shoe category seems mature, and their new firm has no track record. Score: 7.
- Resources are extremely limited, though management knows runners and distance running; Bowerman has strong reputation. Score: 5.
- Five forces are largely favorable (low buyer and supplier power, little threat of substitutes, low rivalry among existing firms), driving forces attractive. Score: 7.

Mere armchair judgments about each criterion are not very credible and run the risk of taking the manager or entrepreneur into a market segment that may turn out not to be viable. It is especially important to undertake a detailed analysis of key competitors, especially with regard to their objectives, strategy, resources, and marketing programs, as was discussed in Chapter 5. Similarly, compelling evidence that a proposed entry into a new

Exhibit 7.8

MARKET-ATTRACTIVENESS/COMPETITIVE-POSITION MATRIX

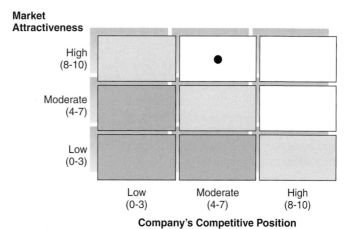

● = Market attractiveness and competitive position of distance runners segment in 1964

segment will satisfy some previously unmet needs, and do so in a way that can bring about sustainable competitive advantage, is called for. Both qualitative and quantitative marketing research results are typically used for this purpose. Once these assessments have been made, the weighted results can be plotted on a **market-attractiveness/competitive-position matrix** like the one shown in Exhibit 7.8.

Step 4: Project Future Position for Each Segment

Forecasting a market's future is more difficult than assessing its current state. Managers or entrepreneurs should first determine how the market's attractiveness is likely to change over the next three to five years. The starting point for this assessment is to consider possible shifts in customer needs and behavior, the entry or exit of competitors, and changes in their strategies. Managers also must address several broader issues, such as possible changes in product or process technology, shifts in the economic climate, the impact of social or political trends, and shifts in the bargaining power or vertical integration of customers.

Managers next must determine how the business's competitive position in the market is likely to change, assuming that it responds effectively to projected environmental changes but the firm does not undertake any initiatives requiring a change in basic strategy. The expected changes in both market attractiveness and competitive position can then be plotted on the matrix in the form of a vector (arrow) that reflects the direction and magnitude of the expected changes. Anticipating such changes may be critically important in today's Internet age.

Step 5: Choose Segments to Target; Allocate Resources

Managers should consider a market to be a desirable target only if it is strongly positive on at least one of the two dimensions of market attractiveness and potential competitive position and at least moderately positive on the other. In Exhibit 7.8 this includes markets positioned in any of the three cells in the upper right-hand corner of the matrix. However, a business may decide to enter a market that currently falls into one of the middle cells under these conditions: (1) managers believe that the market's attractiveness or their competitive strength is likely to improve over the next few years; (2) they see such markets as stepping-stones to entering larger, more attractive markets in the future; or (3) shared costs are present, thereby benefiting another entry.

The market-attractiveness/competitive position matrix offers general guidance for strategic objectives and allocation of resources for segments currently targeted and suggests which new segments to enter. Thus, it also can be useful, especially under changing market conditions, for assessing markets or market segments from which to withdraw or to which allocations of resources, financial and otherwise, might be reduced. Exhibit 7.9 summarizes generic guidelines for strategic objectives and resource allocations for markets in each of the matrix cells. The general thrust of these guidelines is that managers should concentrate resources in attractive markets where the business is securely positioned, use them to improve a weak competitive position in attractive markets, and disengage from unattractive markets where the firm enjoys no competitive advantage.

DIFFERENT TARGETING STRATEGIES SUIT DIFFERENT OPPORTUNITIES

Most successful entrepreneurial ventures target narrowly defined market segments at the outset, as OurBeginning.com might have done, and as Phil Knight and Bill Bowerman did,

Exhibit 7.9

IMPLICATIONS OF ALTERNATIVE POSITIONS WITHIN THE MARKET-ATTRACTIVENESS/COMPETITIVE-POSITION MATRIX FOR TARGET MARKET SELECTION, STRATEGIC OBJECTIVES, AND RESOURCE ALLOCATION

	Competitive Position		
	Weak	**Medium**	**Strong**
High	Build selectively: • Specialize around limited strengths • Seek ways to overcome weaknesses • Withdraw if indications of sustainable growth are lacking	DESIRABLE POTENTIAL TARGET Invest to build: • Challenge for leadership • Build selectively on strengths • Reinforce vulnerable areas	DESIRABLE POTENTIAL TARGET Protect position: • Invest to grow at maximum digestible rate • Concentrate on maintaining strength
Medium	Limited expansion or harvest: • Look for ways to expand without high risk; otherwise, minimize investment and focus operations	Manage for earnings: • Protect existing strengths • Invest to improve position only in areas where risk is low	DESIRABLE POTENTIAL TARGET Build selectively: • Emphasize profitability by increasing productivity • Build up ability to counter competition
Low	Divest: • Sell when possible to maximize cash value • Meantime, cut fixed costs and avoid further investment	Manage for earnings: • Protect position • Minimize investment	Protect and refocus: • Defend strengths • Seek ways to increase current earnings without speeding market's decline

(Market Attractiveness on the vertical axis)

Source: Adapted from George S. Day, *Analysis for Strategic Market Decisions* (St. Paul: West, 1986), p. 204; D. F. Abell and J. S. Hammond, *Strategic Market Planning Problems and Analytical Approaches* (Englewood Cliffs, NJ: Prentice Hall, 1979); and S. J. Robinson, R. E. Hitchens, and D. P. Wade, "The Directional Policy Matrix: Tool for Strategic Planning," *Long Range Planning* 11 (1978), pp. 8–15.

for two reasons. One, doing so puts the nascent firm in a position to achieve early success in a market segment that it understands particularly well. Second, such a strategy conserves precious resources, both financial and otherwise. But segmenting the market into narrow niches and then choosing one niche to target is not always the best strategy, particularly for established firms having substantial resources. Three common targeting strategies are **niche-market, mass-market,** and **growth-market** strategies.

Niche-Market Strategy

This strategy involves serving one or more segments that, while not the largest, consist of substantial numbers of customers seeking somewhat-specialized benefits from a product or service. Such a strategy is designed to avoid direct competition with larger firms that are pursuing the bigger segments. For example, overall coffee consumption is down substantially, but the sales of gourmet coffees have boomed in recent years.

Mass-Market Strategy

A business can pursue a mass-market strategy in two ways. First, it can ignore any segment differences and design a single product-and-marketing program that will appeal to the largest number of consumers. The primary object of this strategy is to capture sufficient volume to gain economies of scale and a cost advantage. This strategy requires substantial resources, including production capacity, and good mass-marketing capabilities. Consequently, it is favored by larger business units or by those whose parent corporation provides substantial support. For example, when Honda first entered the American and European motorcycle markets, it targeted the high-volume segment consisting of buyers of low-displacement, low-priced cycles. Honda subsequently used the sales volume and scale economies it achieved in that mass-market segment to help it expand into smaller, more-specialized segments of the market.

A second approach to the mass market is to design separate products and marketing programs for the differing segments. This often is called **differentiated marketing.** For example, Marriott does this with its various hotel chains. Although such a strategy can generate more sales than an undifferentiated strategy, it also increases costs in product design, manufacturing, inventory, and marketing, especially promotion.

Growth-Market Strategy

Businesses pursuing a growth-market strategy often target one or more fast-growth segments, even though they may not currently be very large. It is a strategy often favored by smaller competitors to avoid direct confrontations with larger firms while building volume and share. Most venture capital firms invest only in firms pursuing growth-market strategies, because doing so is the only way they can earn the 30 percent to 60 percent annual rates of return on investment that they seek for portfolio companies. Such a strategy usually requires strong R&D and marketing capabilities to identify and develop products appealing to newly emerging user segments, plus the resources to finance rapid growth. The problem, however, is that fast growth, if sustained, attracts large competitors. This happened to DEC when IBM entered the minicomputer business. The goal of the early entrant is to have developed an enduring competitive position via its products, service, distribution, and costs by the time competitors enter.

SELECTING TARGET MARKETS IN THE INTERNATIONAL ARENA

Some companies go international to defend their home position against global competitors who are constantly looking for vulnerability. This forces the firm to target major developed countries (the United States, Japan, and Western European countries). A global competitor can attack the home market by reducing price, the cost of which is subsidized by profits generated elsewhere in the world. If the defending company is solely a domestic player, it has to respond by cutting price on its entire volume, while the aggressor has to do so on only part of its total sales.

To prevent such attacks, or minimize their impact, a firm must have the capacity to strike back in markets where the aggressor is vulnerable. For example, Caterpillar, through a joint venture with Mitsubishi Heavy Industries, has for the past 30 years made a substantial investment in Japan to deny its Japanese competitor, Komatsu, strength at home, thereby taking away its profit sanctuary. Had Cat not been successful in doing so, Komatsu would have been able to compete more aggressively with Cat, not only in the United States but also in other major world markets.[26]

Another reason a firm may go overseas and target a specific country is to service customers who also are engaging in global expansion. In recent years Japanese automobile companies that have created U.S. manufacturing facilities have encouraged some of their parts suppliers to do the same. Firms also enter overseas markets to earn foreign exchange and, in some cases, are subsidized by their governments to do so.

The selection of one or more target countries may be dictated by the availability of an appropriate partner. For example, Kellogg has had a European presence since the 1920s and controls about half the market. General Mills, which is Kellogg's major U.S. competitor, has long wanted to enter the European market, but to do so on its own would have been an extremely expensive undertaking, given Kellogg's high market share. The solution was to enter into a joint venture (Cereal Partners Worldwide) with Nestlé, which has no cereals but does have a powerful distribution system.[27] France, Spain, and Portugal constituted the initial target markets for General Mills' Honey Nut Cheerios and Golden Grahams.

In general, with the exception of these strategic special circumstances, the selection of overseas target markets follows essentially the same patterns as for domestic markets, although given the magnitude of economic, social, and political change in the world today, companies are paying considerably more attention to political risk.

TAKE AWAYS

- Marketers and entrepreneurs who find new and insightful ways to segment mature markets often uncover opportunities for uncontested market entry and rapid growth.

- Sharply focused target marketing enables marketers to differentiate from mass-market leaders by giving consumers in a narrowly defined market segment what they want.

- Focused market entry strategies conserve resources and facilitate early success.

- The five-step procedure provided in this chapter identifies segments having the highest potential.

- The market-attractiveness/competitive-position matrix is a useful analytical framework for deciding which markets or market segments to enter and from which to withdraw.

- Self-diagnostic questions to test your ability to apply the analytical tools and concepts in this chapter to marketing decision making may be found at this book's website at **www.mhhe.com/walker**.

ENDNOTES

1. Based on articles by Greg Farrell, "Bailing Out from the Super Bowl Ad Binge," *USA Today,* June 7, 2000, at http://www.usatoday.com/life/cyber/tech/cth780.htm; Mark Hyman, "Inside a Dot.com Betting on a Super Bowl, *BusinessWeek,* January 31, 2000, at http://222.businessweek.com/2000/00_/05/b3666136.htm; and a May 25, 2000 OurBeginning.com press release at http://www.ourbeginning.com/home.nsf/

2. Peter Doyle, "Managing the Marketing Mix," in *The Marketing Book,* Michael J. Baker, ed. (Oxford, England: Butterworth-Heinemann, 1992), p. 273.

3. Laurie Hays, "Using Computers to Divine Who Might Buy a Gas Grill," *The Wall Street Journal,* August 16, 1994, p. B1. The article notes that American Express has a data bank of 500 billion bytes of data describing not only the purchases made by 35 million buyers worth some $350 billion since 1991 but their demographics as well.

4. Joseph Pine II, Bart Victor, and Andrew C. Boynton, in the article "Making Mass Customization Work," *Harvard Business Review,* September–October 1993, pp. 108–19, discuss some of the problems involved in the implementation of a highly segmented, customized strategy.

5. Ellen Newborne, "Marketers Tap Growth Market," *USA Today,* May 8, 1995, p. B1.

6. Julie Ralston, "Chevy Targets Women," *Advertising Age,* August 7, 1995, p. 24.

7. Robert E. Wilkes, "Household Life-Cycle Stages, Transitions and Product Expenditures," *Journal of Consumer Research,* June 1995, p. 27.

8. Anita Sharpe, "Magazines for the Rich Rake in Readers," *The Wall Street Journal,* February 2, 1996, p. B1.

9. Michael Wilke and Todd Preizan, "Motorola Puts Ethnic Marketing to Work for Cellular Phones, Pagers," *Advertising Age,* June 24, 1996, p. 16; and Cyndi Miller, "Catalogers Learn to Take Blacks Seriously," *Marketing News,* March 3, 1995, p. 8.

10. Mora Somassundarm, "Uni-Marts Inc.'s Small Town Strategy for Convenience Stores Is Paying Off," *The Wall Street Journal,* November 20, 1995, p. B5A.

11. Jon Goss, "We Know Who You Are and We Know Where You Live: The Instrumental Rationality of Geodemographics," *Economic Geography* 71, no. 2 (1995), p. 171.

12. Michael Arndt, "Quaker Oats Is Thirsty for Even More Gatorade Hits," *www.businessweek.com/bwdaily/dnflash/feb2000/nf202c.htm,* February 2, 2000.

13. For a detailed discussion of the implications of customer loyalty for both market share leaders and challengers, see Adrian J. Slywotzky and Benson P. Shapiro, "Levering to Beat the Odds: The New Marketing Mind-Set," *Harvard Business Review,* September–October 1993, pp. 97–107.

14. Salah S. Hassan and Lea P. Kataris, "Identification of Global Consumer Segments: A Behavioral Framework," *Journal of International Consumer Marketing 3,* no. 2 (1991), p. 16.

15. From information provided by Stanford Research Institute.

16. The relative weight of these vary across countries. In China, for example, more weight is given to occupation and education, whereas Western countries emphasize residence, income, and family background. See John D. Daniels and Lee H. Radebaugh, *International Dimensions of Contemporary International Business* (Boston: PWS-Kent, 1993), p. 136.

17. Simon Majaro, "International Marketing—the Major Issues" in *The Marketing Book,* Michael J. Baker, ed. (Oxford, England: Butterworth-Heinemann, 1992), p. 430.

18. Kenneth Labech, "Class in America," *Fortune,* February 7, 1994, p. 14.

19. Hassan and Kataris, "Identification of Global Consumer Segments," p. 16.

20. Henry Laurence, Michael Y. Yoshino, and Peter Williamson, *STAR TV* (A) (Boston: Harvard Business School Publishing, 1994).

21. Theodore Levitt, "The Globalization of Markets," *Harvard Business Review,* May–June 1983, pp. 92–102. Also, see Sundar G. Bharadway and P. Rajan Varadarajar, "Standardization versus Adaptation of International Marketing Strategy: An Empirical Investigation," *Journal of Marketing,* October 1993.

22. Ignacio Galeeran and Jon Berry, "A New World of Consumers," *American Demographics,* March 1995, p. 26.

23. Marte J. Rhea, Barbara C. Garland, and John C. Crawford, "International Market Segmentation: The U.S.-Japanese Markets," *Journal of International Consumer Marketing 2,* no. 2 (1989), pp. 75–90. Also see Robert M. March, *The Honorable Consumer* (London, England: Pitman, 1990), p. 150.

24. Nike, Inc. website at *www.nikebiz.com.*

25. Ibid.

26. Douglas Lamont, *Winning Worldwide* (Burr Ridge, IL: Business One Irwin, 1991), pp. 59–69.

27. Christopher Knowlton, "Europe Cooks Up a Cereal Brawl," *Fortune,* June 3, 1991, p. 175.

CHAPTER EIGHT

DIFFERENTIATION AND POSITIONING

Dell's Direct Business Model Wins Customers and Competitive Advantage[1]

FROM 1994 TO 1998, Dell Computer Corporation grew from $3.5 to $18.2 billion in revenue and from $149 million to $1.5 billion in profits. During this period, Dell grew more than twice as fast as its major rivals and tripled its market share. Michael Dell, its founder, ranked as the fourth richest American, with an estimated worth of $13 billion. Clearly, Dell Computer was doing something right.

GIVING CUSTOMERS WHAT THEY WANT

From its origins in Michael Dell's dorm room at the University of Texas, Dell Computer sold personal computers directly to end users, in contrast to most other leading manufacturers, who sold through distributors, resellers, and retailers. By **differentiating** from other computer makers—selling direct, first over the telephone, and later via the Internet—Dell enabled customers, especially corporate customers, to specify exactly the features they wanted. Dell then quickly assembled computers to meet these specifications and shipped them directly to its customers.

What was it about Dell's concept that customers found so attractive? First, they could specify precisely

what they wanted—hard drive size, memory, modem or network card, and so on. Second, Dell's price/value offering was unbeatable—customers got more computer for their money. And, because Dell shipped quickly and offered strong service and support, albeit without local face-to-face handholding, these two major benefits—get exactly what you want, for less money—came without any significant drawbacks to its key target market, corporations.

SUSTAINABLE COMPETITIVE ADVANTAGE

Not only did Dell's direct business model offer tangible benefits to its target customers, it also brought Dell important advantages that gave it a real and—so far—sustainable edge over its competitors. Dell worked closely with its suppliers to arrange just-in-time delivery of parts for its custom-assembled PCs, communicating replenishment needs to key vendors on an hourly basis. By carrying, in 1996 for example, only 15 days of inventory on average, instead of 65 days for competitor Compaq, Dell not only saved carrying cost for its inventory, but it bought parts later, thereby benefiting from the fact that prices of components used to make PCs typically declined 25 to 20 percent per year. Additional savings from eliminating intermediaries in its distribution channel made Dell's cost advantage over its competitors a substantial one.

Given its lower cost structure than its competitors, Dell's custom-built, low-cost **positioning** in the marketplace allowed it to make an attractive strategic choice. Should it choose to reap higher margins than others in its industry, or should it keep prices low to gain market share? For much of its history, Dell made the latter choice, gaining share at the expense of its rivals.

THE HIGH-TECH RECESSION OF 2001

In 2001, a sharp recession in the high-tech economy caused computer sales to fall off a cliff. Earnings fell across most high-tech industry sectors, and PCs were no exception. Archrival Compaq lost $279 million on a 17 percent decline in sales in the second quarter of 2001. Dell's earnings slid too, falling 12 percent from second quarter 2000, though its sales were still up 10 percent over the prior year. Chipmaker AMD's earnings fell 92 percent from the prior year on a 16 percent decline in sales. How did Dell's positioning serve it in this challenging environment? Michael Dell didn't blink, announcing that Dell would seek to triple its share of the computer business to 40 percent, in spite of the slimmer profit margins it would endure. He figured his strong value positioning with customers would enable his company to grab market share from weaker rivals and his low-cost business model would give Dell the opportunity to tough it out profit-wise until conditions improved.

STRATEGIC CHALLENGES ADDRESSED IN CHAPTER 8

As Dell's story illustrates, the success of a product offered to a given target market depends on how well it is positioned within that market segment—that is, how well it performs *relative to* competitive offerings and to the needs of the target audience. **Positioning** refers to both the place a product or brand occupies in customers' minds relative to their needs and competing products or brands and to the marketer's decision making intended to create such a position. Thus, the positioning notion comprises both competitive *and* customer need considerations.

Positioning is basically concerned with differentiation. Ries and Trout, who popularized the concept of positioning, view it as a creative undertaking whereby an existing brand in an overcrowded marketplace of similar brands can be given a distinctive position in the minds of targeted prospects. While their concept was concerned with an existing brand, it is equally applicable for new products.[2] While typically thought of in relation to the marketing of consumer goods, it has equal value for industrial goods and for services, which require essentially the same procedure as consumer goods.[3] Because services are characterized by their intangibility, perishability, consumer participation in their delivery, and the simultaneous nature of their production and consumption, they are—when compared with products—more difficult for consumers to understand, to compare with competing products, to predict in terms of their performance, and, therefore, more difficult for marketers to position successfully.

In this chapter we take the final step in preparing the foundation on which effective marketing programs are based. Drawing on decisions made about target markets, as discussed in Chapter 7, we address the critical question, How should a business position its product offering—whether goods or services—so customers in the target market perceive the offering as providing the benefits they seek, thereby giving the product an advantage over current and potential future competitors? As marketing managers know, the positioning decision is a strategic one, with implications not only for how the firm's goods or services should be designed, but also for developing the other elements of the marketing strategy. Pricing decisions, promotion decisions, and decisions about how the product is to be distributed all follow from, and contribute to the effectiveness of, the positioning of the product in its competitive space.

> **STRATEGIC ISSUE**
>
> *The positioning decision is a strategic one, with implications not only for how the firm's goods or services should be designed, but also for developing the other elements of the marketing strategy.*

DIFFERENTIATION: THE KEY TO CUSTOMER PREFERENCE AND COMPETITIVE ADVANTAGE

Why do customers prefer one product over another? In today's highly competitive markets, consumers have numerous options. They can buy a personal computer from Dell, Apple, Compaq, or a host of other PC makers. They can choose from dozens of best-selling novels to take along on an upcoming vacation. They can buy the novel they choose from an online merchant such as Amazon.com, from large chain booksellers such as Barnes and Noble or their online counterparts, from book clubs, from a local bookstore, or in some cases from their nearby supermarket or mass merchant. They even can borrow the book at their local library and not buy it at all! Whether for goods such as computers or books, or services such as libraries, consumers make choices such as these nearly every day. In most cases, consumers or organizational customers choose what they buy for one of two reasons: what they choose is *better,* in some sense, or *cheaper.* In either case, the good or service they choose is, in some way, almost always *different* from others they could have chosen.

Differentiation is a powerful theme in developing business strategies, as well as in marketing. As Michael Porter points out, "A company can outperform its rivals only if it can establish a difference that it can preserve. It must deliver greater value to customers or create comparable value at a lower cost, or both."[4] Most of the time, differentiation is why people buy. They buy the latest John Grisham novel because they know it will be a page-turner, different from the last Grisham they read, and hard to put down. They buy it from Amazon.com because they know Amazon's selection is enormous, and its one-click ordering system takes only a minute. Or they buy it from the megastore because it's fun to browse there or from their local bookseller because they feel good about supporting their local merchants.

> **STRATEGIC ISSUE**
>
> *Differentiation is why people buy.*

They buy it at the supermarket because it's convenient. All these book-selling strategies are different, and they appeal to different consumers (i.e., different market segments) at different points in time, for different book-buying purposes. If these strategies did not vary, consumers would have no reason to use some of them, and they would buy their books where they were cheapest or most convenient, though even in such a case, the cheaper pricing or greater convenience would still constitute differences.

Differentiation in Business Strategies

Michael Porter's classic book on competitive advantage identified three generic strategies: cost leadership, differentiation, and focus, as shown in Exhibit 8.1.[5] These strategies,

Exhibit 8.1

GENERIC COMPETITIVE STRATEGIES

		Competitive Advantage	
		Lower Cost	Differentiation
Competitive Scope	Broad Target	**Cost Leadership Strategy**	**Differentiation Strategy**
	Narrow Target	**Focus Strategy (Cost-Based)**	**Focus Strategy (Differentiation-Based)**

Source: Adapted with permssion of The Free Press, a Division of Simon & Schuster, Inc. from *Competitive Advantage: Creating and Sustaining Superior Performance* by Michael E. Porter. Copyright 1985, 1988 by Michael E. Porter.

which differ in the scope of the target market and market needs they serve (broad or narrow competitive scope) and on whether they base their competitive advantage on low cost (lower prices to the customer for equivalent products) or differentiation (products that are superior on some important dimensions), represent distinctly different ways in which companies can compete for the minds and wallets of customers in their target markets. Porter argues that the worst strategy is to be "stuck in the middle," to be neither different nor lower in cost than one's competitors. Companies in such a position offer customers little reason not to take their business elsewhere. But customers don't really buy strategies. They buy specific goods and services and effective execution: on-time delivery, proper installation, responsive customer service, and so on. Thus, strategy is implemented at the product-market level, where differentiation lies at the heart of positioning.

Differentiation among Goods and Services

As we saw in the previous chapter, customers in one market segment have wants and needs that differ in some way from those of customers in other segments. Positioning allows the marketer to take advantage of and be responsive to such differences and position particular goods and services so as to better meet the needs of consumers in one or more of these segments. These differences are often physical. Dell's computers have exactly the features the customer wants, not a compromise based on what's available in the computer store. Nike's original waffle sole was a physical difference. But differences also can be perceptual, as with Nike's later products that benefited from endorsements by John McEnroe, Michael Jordan, and other famous athletes. Creating *both* physical and perceptual differences, using all the elements of the marketing mix—product, pricing, promotion, and distribution decisions—is what effective positioning seeks to accomplish.

STRATEGIC ISSUE

Creating both physical and perceptual differences is what effective positioning seeks to accomplish.

PHYSICAL POSITIONING

One way to assess the current position of a product offering relative to competitors is on the basis of how the various offerings compare on some set of objective physical characteristics. For example, an article in *The Wall Street Journal* discussed the pending battle in the 1996 season between the various brands of behemoth sport utility vehicles. It compared Ford's Expedition versus GM's Suburban on seating capacity, engine, city mileage, highway mileage, length, and price (see Exhibit 8.2).[6] In many cases a physical positioning

Exhibit 8.2

1996 FORD EXPEDITION VERSUS GM SUBURBAN ON A SELECTED NUMBER OF PHYSICAL DIMENSIONS

Feature	Expedition	Suburban
Seating capacity	9	9
Cargo capacity	115 cu. ft.	149.5 cu. ft.
Engine	4.6 liter, V-8	5.7 liter, V-8
City mileage	14 mpg	13 mpg
Highway mileage	18 mpg	17 mpg
Length	204.6 inches	220 inches
Price	$24–36,000	$24,682–38,000

Source: Aaron Lucchetti, "Ford's New Expedition Heads into Suburban's Terrain," *Wall Street Journal,* June 24, 1996, p. B1. Copyright 1996 by Dow Jones & Co. Inc. Reproduced with permission of Dow Jones & Co. Inc. via Copyright Clearance Center.

analysis can provide useful information to a marketing manager, particularly in the early stages of identifying and designing new product offerings.

Despite being based primarily on technical rather than on market data, physical comparisons can be an essential step in undertaking a positioning analysis. This is especially true with the competitive offerings of many industrial goods and services, which buyers typically evaluate largely on the basis of such characteristics. In addition, it contributes to a better marketing/R&D interface by determining key physical product characteristics; helps define the structure of competition by revealing the degree to which the various brands compete with one another; and may indicate the presence of meaningful product gaps (the lack of products having certain desired physical characteristics), which, in turn, may reveal opportunities for a new product entry.

Limitations of Physical Positioning

A simple comparison of only the physical dimensions of alternative offerings usually does *not* provide a complete picture of relative positions because, as we noted earlier, positioning ultimately occurs in customers' minds. Even though a product's physical characteristics, package, brand name, price, and ancillary services can be designed to achieve a particular position in the market, customers may attach less importance to some of these characteristics than, or perceive them differently from, what the firm expects. Also, customers' attitudes toward a product are often based on social or psychological attributes not amenable to objective comparison, such as perceptions of the product's aesthetic appeal, sportiness, or status image. Consequently, **perceptual positioning analysis**—whether aimed at discovering opportunities for new product entries or evaluating and adjusting the position of a current offering—is critically important.

PERCEPTUAL POSITIONING

Consumers often know very little about the essential physical attributes of many products, especially household products, and even if they did, they would not understand the physical attributes well enough to use them as a basis for choosing between competitive offerings. (For the major differences between physical and perceptual product positioning analyses, see Exhibit 8.3.) Many consumers do not want to be bothered about a product's

Exhibit 8.3

COMPARISON OF PHYSICAL AND PERCEPTUAL POSITIONING ANALYSES

Physical positioning	Perceptual positioning
• Technical orientation	• Consumer orientation
• Physical characteristics	• Perceptual attributes
• Objective measures	• Perceptual measures
• Data readily available	• Need for marketing research
• Physical brand properties	• Perceptual brand positions and positioning intensities
• Large number of dimensions	• Limited number of dimensions
• Represents impact of product specs and price	• Represents impact of product specs and communication
• Direct R&D implications	• R&D implications need to be interpreted

physical characteristics because they are not buying these physical properties but rather the benefits they provide. While the physical properties of a product certainly influence the benefits provided, a consumer typically can evaluate a product better on the basis of what it *does* than what it *is*. Thus, for example, a headache remedy is judged on how quickly it brings relief, a toothpaste on the freshness of breath provided, a beer on its taste, and a vehicle on how comfortably it rides.

The evaluation of many products is subjective because it is influenced by factors other than physical properties, including the way products are presented, our past experiences with them, and the opinions of others. Thus, physically similar products may be perceived as being different because of different histories, names, and advertising campaigns. For example, some people will pay considerably more for Bayer aspirin than for an unadvertised private label even though they are essentially the same product.

LEVERS MARKETERS CAN USE TO ESTABLISH POSITIONING

Customers or prospective customers perceive physical as well as other differences between goods or services within a product category, of course. Marketing decision makers seeking to win a particular position in customers' minds will seek to endow their product with various kinds of attributes, which may be categorized as follows:

- *Simple physically based attributes.* These are directly related to a single physical dimension such as price, quality, power, or size. While there is a direct correspondence between a physical dimension and a perceptual attribute, an analysis of consumers' perception of products on these attributes may unveil phenomena of interest to a marketing strategy. For instance, two cars with estimated gasoline mileage of 23.2 and 25.8 miles per gallon may be perceived as having similar gasoline consumption.

- *Complex physically based attributes.* Because of the presence of a large number of physical characteristics, consumers may use composite attributes to evaluate competitive offerings. The development of such summary indicators is usually subjective because of the relative importance attached to different cues. Examples of composite attributes are the speed of a Dell computer, roominess of a car, and a product's or service's being user friendly.

- *Essentially abstract attributes.* Although these perceptual attributes are influenced by physical characteristics, they are not related to them in any direct way. Examples include bodiness of a beer, sexiness of a perfume, quality of a French wine, and prestige of a car. All of these attributes are highly subjective and difficult to relate to physical characteristics other than by experience.

The importance of perceptual attributes with their subjective component varies across consumers and product classes. Thus, it can be argued that consumers familiar with a given product class are apt to rely more on physical characteristics and less on perceptual attributes than consumers who are less familiar with that product class. It also can be argued that while perceptual product positioning is essential for nondurable consumer goods, such is not the case for consumer durables (such as sport utility vehicles) and many industrial goods.

Even though there is considerable truth in these statements, perceptual attributes must be considered in positioning most products. One reason is the growing similarity of the physical characteristics of more and more products. This increases the importance of other, largely subjective dimensions. Consider, for example, whether Nike's Air Jordan basketball shoes would have sold as well without Michael Jordan's endorsement and his presence in their ads.

PREPARING THE FOUNDATION FOR MARKETING STRATEGIES: THE POSITIONING PROCESS

Positioning a new product in customers' minds or repositioning a current product involves a series of steps, as outlined in Exhibit 8.4. These steps are applicable to goods and services, in domestic or international markets, and to new or existing products. This is not to suggest that the determinant product attributes and the perceptions of consumers of the various competitive offerings will remain constant across countries or other market segments; rather, they are likely to vary with most products. After managers have selected a relevant set of competing offerings serving a target market (Step 1), they must identify a set of critical or determinant product attributes important to customers in that target market (Step 2).

Step 3 involves collecting information from a sample of customers about their perceptions of the various offerings, and in Step 4 researchers analyze this information to determine the product's current position in customers' minds and the intensity thereof (Does it occupy a dominant position?), as well as those of competitors.

Managers then ascertain the customers' most preferred combinations of determinant attributes, which requires the collection of further data (Step 5). This allows an examination of the fit between the preferences of a given target segment of customers and the current positions of competitive offerings (Step 6). And finally, in Step 7, managers write a concise statement that communicates the positioning decision they have reached.

A discussion of these steps in the positioning process takes up the remainder of this chapter.

Step 1: Identify a Relevant Set of Competitive Products

Positioning analyses are useful at many levels: company, business unit, product category, and specific product line or brand. At the company or business-unit level, such analyses are useful to determine how an entire company or business unit is positioned relative to its competitors. The results of such analyses are sometimes displayed graphically by plotting

Exhibit 8.4

STEPS IN THE POSITIONING PROCESS

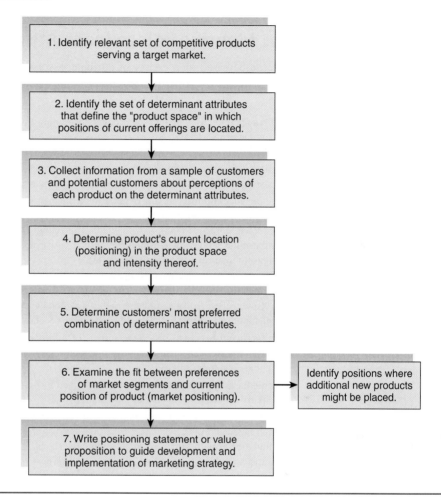

1. Identify relevant set of competitive products serving a target market.

2. Identify the set of determinant attributes that define the "product space" in which positions of current offerings are located.

3. Collect information from a sample of customers and potential customers about perceptions of each product on the determinant attributes.

4. Determine product's current location (positioning) in the product space and intensity thereof.

5. Determine customers' most preferred combination of determinant attributes.

6. Examine the fit between preferences of market segments and current position of product (market positioning).

Identify positions where additional new products might be placed.

7. Write positioning statement or value proposition to guide development and implementation of marketing strategy.

competing companies or businesses in their respective quadrants of the generic strategies grid shown in Exhibit 8.1. Larger or smaller dots or circles are used to indicate relative sizes of competing firms.

At the product category level, the analysis examines customers' perceptions about types of products they might consider as substitutes to satisfy the same basic need. Suppose, for example, a company is considering introducing a new instant breakfast drink. The new product would have to compete with other breakfast foods, such as bacon and eggs, breakfast cereals, and even fast-food drive-throughs. To understand the new product's position in the market, a marketer could obtain customer perceptions of the new product concept relative to likely substitute products on various critical determinant attributes, as we describe in Steps 3 and 4 of the positioning process (see Exhibit 8.4).

Once competitors introduce several brands into the category, a positioning analysis at the product or brand level can be helpful to better understand how various brands appeal to customers, to position proposed new products or brands or reposition current ones, and to identify where new competitive opportunities might be found.

At whichever level the positioning analysis is to be done, the analyst's choice of competing products (or product categories or firms) is critical. Marketers who omit important substitute products or potential competitors risk being blindsided by unforeseen competition.

Step 2: Identify Determinant Attributes

Positioning can be based on a variety of attributes—some in the form of surrogates that imply desirable features or benefits as a positioning base. The common types of bases are the following.[7]

- **Features** are often used in physical product positioning and, hence, with industrial products. An example of its use with a consumer good is Jenn-Air's claim, "This is the quietest dishwasher made in America." Amazon.com has a unique "1-click®" ordering system.

- **Benefits,** like features, are directly related to a product. Examples here include Volvo's emphasis on safety and durability and Norelco's promising a "close and comfortable shave."

- **Usage** includes **end use** ("If you've got it in the kitchen, it probably goes with pork"—a versatility claim); **demographic** ("Just because kids will be kids doesn't mean you can't have knock-down, gorgeous floors"—Congoleum); **psychographic or behavioral** (Ellesse positioning itself as producing a fashionable upscale active-wear line); and **popularity** (Hertz as the biggest rental car company in the world).

- **Parentage** includes who makes it (bottled by a French vintner; "At Fidelity, you're not just buying a fund, a stock, or a bond—you're buying a better way to manage it") and prior products ("Buying a car is like getting married. It's a good idea to know the family first," followed by a picture of the ancestors of the Mercedes-Benz S class model).

- **Manufacturing process** is often the subject of a firm's positioning efforts. An example is Jaeger-LeCoultre's statement about its watches: "We know it's perfect, but we take another 1,000 hours just to be sure."

- **Ingredients** as a positioning concept is illustrated by some clothing manufacturers saying their sports shirts are made only of pure cotton.

- **Endorsements** are of two types: those by experts ("Discover why over 5,000 American doctors and medical professionals prescribe this Swedish mattress"—Tempor-Pedic) and those via emulation as with Michael Jordan using Nike shoes.

- **Comparison** with a competitor's product is common ("Tests prove Pedigree is more nutritious than IAMS, costs less than IAMS, and tastes great, too"—Pedigree Mealtime).

- **Proenvironment** positioning seeks to portray a company as a good citizen ("Because we recycle over 100 million plastic bottles a year, landfills can be filled with other things, like land, for instance"—Phillips Petroleum).

- **Product class** as when freeze-dried coffee was introduced as a new and different product type versus regular or instant coffees.

- **Price/quality** is used in cases such as Wal-Mart successfully positioning itself as the lowest-price seller of quality household products.

- **Country or geographic area** (French wines, Russian vodka).

Theoretically, consumers can use many attributes to evaluate products or brands, but the number actually influencing a consumer's choice is typically small, partly because consumers can consider only attributes of which they are aware. The more variables used in positioning a given product, the greater the chance of confusion and even disbelief on the part of the consumer. The positioning effort must be kept as simple as possible and complexity should be avoided at all costs.

In using one or more attributes as the basis of a brand's positioning effort, it is important to recognize that the importance attached to these attributes often varies. For example, while the brands of soap or shampoo provided by a hotel may be an attribute that some consumers use in evaluating hotels, most are unlikely to attach much importance to it when deciding which hotel chain to patronize. Even an important attribute may not greatly influence a consumer's preference if all the alternative brands are perceived to be about equal on that dimension. Deposit safety is an important attribute to consider when choosing a bank, but most consumers perceive all banks to be about equally safe. Consequently, deposit safety is not a **determinant attribute:** It does not play a major role in helping customers to differentiate among the alternatives and to determine which bank they prefer.

Marketers should rely primarily on determinant attributes in defining the product space in a positioning analysis. The question is, How can a marketer find out which product dimensions are determinant attributes? Doing so typically requires conducting some kind of marketing research, using the marketing research process described in a previous chapter. This brings us to Step 3.

Step 3: Collect Data about Customers' Perceptions for Products in the Competitive Set

Having identified a set of competing products, the marketer needs to know what attributes are determinant for the target market and the product category under consideration. He or she also needs to know how different products in the competitive set are viewed on these attributes. Typically this market knowledge is developed by first conducting qualitative research, perhaps interviews or focus groups, to learn which attributes are determinant. Then quantitative research follows, perhaps a survey of consumers about their perceptions, to gather data on how competing products score on these attributes. Later in this chapter, we discuss several statistical and analytical tools that are useful in this portion of the positioning process.

Step 4: Analyze the Current Positions of Products in the Competitive Set

Whether the positioning process is directed at a new product not yet introduced or repositioning one that already exists, it is important to develop a clear understanding of the positioning of the products that have been determined to be in the competitive set (see Step 1). A useful tool for doing so is the **positioning grid,** also called a **perceptual map.**[8] The positioning grid provides a visual representation of the positions of various products or brands in the competitive set in terms of (typically) two determinant attributes. Where more than two attributes are to be considered in a positioning analysis, multidimensional grids, or multiple grids, are produced. But not all products or brands exist in the minds of most consumers.

A brand that is not known by a consumer cannot, by definition, occupy a position in that consumer's mind. Often the awareness set for a given product class is 3 or fewer brands even though the number of available brands is greater than 20. Thus, many if not most brands have little or no position in the minds of many consumers. For example, in the last 10 or so years, more than 200 new soft drinks have been introduced, most of which were not noticed or remembered by consumers. Thus, the first step in acquiring a distinct position for a brand is to build brand awareness. In doing so, the brand needs to be strongly associated with one or more concepts relating to the purchase decision. A distinct position is best obtained by developing a strong relationship between a brand and a limited number of attributes.[9] Determining the attributes on which the product's positioning will be based is a key outcome of the positioning process and a driver of the marketing communication strategy, as well as the marketing strategy overall, that will ultimately be developed. Without clear guidance about the intended position of the product, advertising agencies, salesforces, and others charged with building the awareness and recognition of the product in the marketplace will be ill-equipped to do this important job.

Building a Positioning Grid   An example of what can be done with data gathered in Step 3 is found in Exhibit 8.5, which shows the results obtained from a study done by Babson College that portrays how a sample of consumers positioned a number of women's clothing retailers in the Washington, D.C., area.[10] Respondents rated the various stores on the two determinant attributes of value and fashionability. Some stores, such as Nordstrom and Kmart, occupy relatively distant positions from one another, indicating that consumers see them as very different. Other stores occupy positions comparable to one another (Neiman Marcus, Saks) and thus are considered relatively alike, meaning the intensity of competition between these stores is likely to be considerably greater than for those that occupy widely divergent positions.

Exhibit 8.5

PERCEPTUAL MAP OF WOMEN'S CLOTHING RETAILERS IN WASHINGTON, D.C.

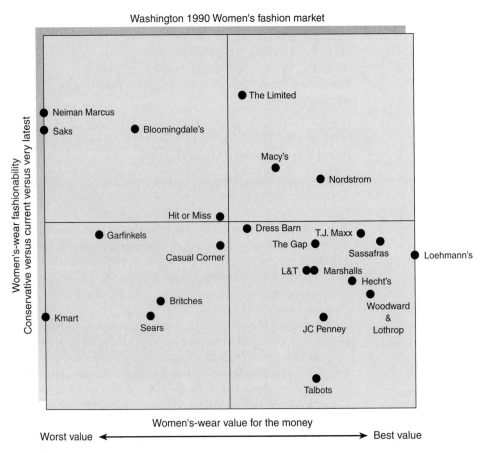

Source: Adapted from Douglas Tigert and Stephen Arnold, "Nordstrom: How Good Are They?" *Babson College Retailing Research Reports,* September 1990, as shown in Michael Levy and Barton A. Weitz, *Retailing Management* (Burr Ridge, IL: Richard D. Irwin, 1992), p. 205.

The store positioning shown in Exhibit 8.5 also provides useful information about possible opportunities for the launching of a new store or the repositioning of an existing one. Positioning for a new store could be done by examining the positioning map for empty spaces (competitive gaps) where no existing store is currently located. There is such a gap in the upper right quadrant of the "value/fashionability" map in Exhibit 8.5. This gap may represent an opportunity for developing a new entry or repositioning an old one that is perceived to offer greater fashionability than Nordstrom at a lower price. Of course, such gaps may exist simply because a particular position is either (1) impossible for any brand to attain because of technical constraints or (2) undesirable since there are few prospective customers for a brand with that set of attributes.

Marketing Opportunities to Gain a Distinct Position   In situations where one or a limited number of brands dominate a product class (or type) in the minds of consumers, the main opportunity for competitors generally lies in obtaining a profitable position within a market segment *not* dominated by a leading brand. Competing head-on against the leaders on the basis of attributes appropriated by larger competitors is not likely to be effective.

A better option is to concentrate on an attribute prized by members of a given market segment. Thus, Dell offers its customers a custom-built computer that has exactly the desired features, something its corporate customers value.

Constraints Imposed by an Intense Position   Although marketers should seek a distinctive and intense position for their brands, attaining such a position imposes constraints on future strategies. If shifts in the market environment cause customers to reduce the importance they attach to a current determinant attribute, marketers may have difficulty repositioning a brand with an intensely perceived position on that attribute. Repositioning carries with it the threat of alienating part or all of the product's current users regardless of success with its newly targeted group. Success in its repositioning efforts may well ensure losing its current group of users.

Another concern is the dilution of an existing intense position as a result of consolidation. For example, British Leyland was formed through a series of mergers involving a number of British car manufacturers. For years, the company did not have a clear identity because it was new and distributed a variety of brands, including Rover, Triumph, and Austin-Morris. Most Europeans had difficulty recalling spontaneously any British car manufacturer since once-strong brand names such as Austin and Morris had lost their identity and meaning.

Another danger associated with an intensely positioned brand is the temptation to overexploit that position by using the brand name on line extensions and new products. The danger here is that the new products may not fit the original positioning and the brand's strong image is diluted. For example, how many travelers know the difference between Holiday Inn, Holiday Inn Express, Holiday Inn Select, and Holiday Inn Garden Court?[11]

Limitations of Product Positioning Analysis   The analysis depicted in Exhibit 8.5 is usually referred to as *product positioning* because it indicates how alternative products or brands are positioned relative to one another in customers' minds. The problem with this analysis, though, is that it does not tell the marketer which positions are most appealing to customers.[12] Thus, there is no way to determine if there is a market for a new brand or store that might locate in an "open" position or whether the customers in other market segments prefer brands or stores with different attributes and positions. To solve such problems it is necessary to measure customers' preferences and locate them in the product space along with their perceptions of the positions of existing brands. This is called a **market positioning analysis.** We deal with this issue in Step 5.

Step 5: Determine Customers' Most Preferred Combination of Attributes

There are several ways analysts can measure customer preferences and include them in a positioning analysis. For instance, survey respondents can be asked to think of the ideal product or brand within a product category—a hypothetical brand possessing the perfect combination of attributes (from the customer's viewpoint). Respondents then could rate their ideal product and existing products on a number of attributes. An alternative approach is to ask respondents not only to judge the degree of similarity among pairs of existing brands but also to indicate their degree of preference for each. In either case, the analyst, using the appropriate statistical techniques, can locate the respondents' ideal points relative to the positions of the various existing brands on the product space map.

Another method of assessing customers' preferences and trade-offs among them is a statistical technique called conjoint analysis.[13] Customers are surveyed and asked their preferences among various real or hypothetical product configurations, each with attributes that are systematically varied. By analyzing the resulting data, the marketer can learn which of several attributes are more important than the others. These results then can be used in positioning analyses such as those described here.

Whichever approach is used, the results will look something like Exhibit 8.6, which shows a hypothetical cluster of ideal points for one segment of women's-clothing consumers. As a group, this segment would seem to prefer Nordstrom over any other women's clothing retailer on the map.

There are, however, several reasons not all customers in this segment are likely to prefer Nordstrom. First, the ideal points of some customers are actually closer to Macy's than Nordstrom. Second, customers whose ideal point is equidistant between the two stores may be relatively indifferent in their choice of which store to patronize. And finally, customers sometimes may patronize stores somewhat further away from their ideal—particularly when buying low-involvement, nondurable goods or services—to assess the qualities of new stores, to reassess older stores from time to time, or just for the sake of variety.

Using price as one dimension of a positioning grid, or as a key dimension on which a product is positioned, is typically not very useful unless price is a key driver of the marketing strategy. This is the case for two reasons. First, price is easily imitable by competitors. Unless the firm has a clear cost advantage over its competitors, by virtue of its processes or other sources of efficiency, using low price as a basis for positioning can be a fast road to a price war that no one (except consumers) will win. Second, claims that one's product—whether a good or a service—is low-priced are sometimes not very credible, because so many marketers make such claims. It is often better to position around more enduring differentiators, and let price speak more subtly for itself. Wal-Mart, an exception, has been able to sustain its low-price positioning in the United States because its costs, compared to those of its chief competitors, actually are lower. The same is true for Dell.

Step 6: Consider Fit of Possible Positions with Customer Needs and Segment Attractiveness

An important criterion for defining market segments is the difference in the benefits sought by different customers. Because differences between customers' ideal points reflect variations in the benefits they seek, a market positioning analysis can simultaneously identify distinct market segments as well as the perceived positions of different brands. When customers' ideal

Exhibit 8.6

PERCEPTUAL MAP OF WOMEN'S CLOTHING RETAILERS IN WASHINGTON, D.C., SHOWING THE IDEAL POINTS OF A SEGMENT OF CONSUMERS

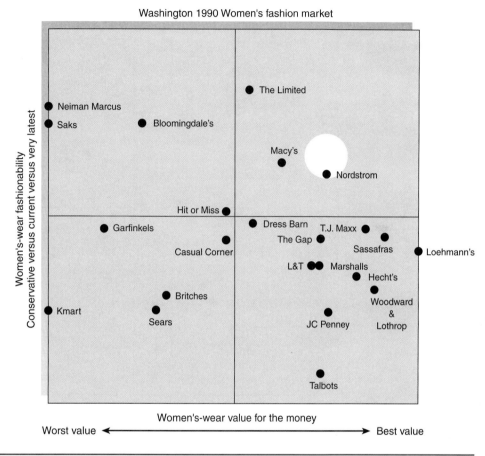

Washington 1990 Women's fashion market

Source: Adapted from Douglas Tigert and Stephen Arnold, "Nordstrom: How Good Are They?" *Babson College Retailing Research Reports,* September 1990.

points cluster in two or more locations on the product space map, the analyst can consider each cluster a distinct market segment.[14] For analytical purposes, each cluster is represented by a circle that encloses most of the ideal points for that segment; the size of the circle reflects the relative proportion of customers within a particular segment.

Exhibit 8.7 groups the sample of Washington, D.C., respondents into five distinct segments on the basis of clusters of ideal points.[15] Segment 5 contains the largest proportion of customers; segment 1, the smallest.[16] By examining the preferences of customers in different segments along with their perceptions of the positions of existing brands, analysts can learn much about (1) the competitive strength of different brands in different segments, (2) the intensity of the rivalry between brands in a given segment, and (3) the opportunities for gaining a differentiated position within a specific target segment.

Step 6 not only concludes the analysis portion of the positioning process and crystallizes the decision about the positioning a product should hold, but it also can uncover locations in the product space where additional new products could be positioned to serve

Exhibit 8.7

PERCEPTUAL MAP OF WOMEN'S CLOTHING RETAILERS IN WASHINGTON, D.C., SHOWING FIVE SEGMENTS BASED ON IDEAL POINTS

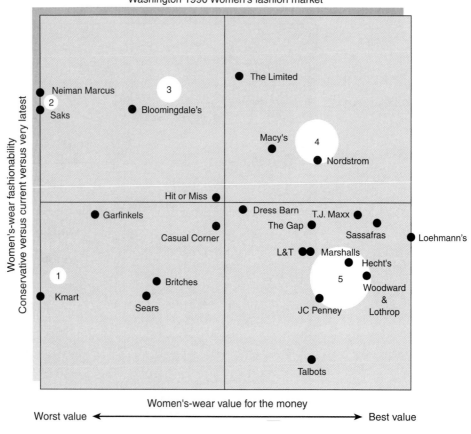

Washington 1990 Women's fashion market

Women's-wear fashionability
Conservative versus current versus very latest

Women's-wear value for the money

Worst value ← → Best value

Source: Adapted from Douglas Tigert and Stephen Arnold, "Nordstrom: How Good Are They?" *Babson College Retailing Research Reports,* September 1990.

customer needs not well served by current competitors. Thus, Exhibit 8.4 shows that a possible side benefit of the positioning process is recognition of underserved positions where additional new products might be placed.

Step 7: Write Positioning Statement or Value Proposition to Guide Development of Marketing Strategy

The final decision about where to position a new brand or reposition an existing one should be based on both the market targeting analysis discussed in Chapter 7 and the results of a market positioning analysis. The position chosen should match the preferences of a particular market segment and should take into account the current positions of competing brands.

It also should reflect the current and *future* attractiveness of the target market (its size, expected growth, and environmental constraints) and the relative strengths and weaknesses of competitors. Such information, together with an analysis of the costs required to acquire and maintain these positions, allows an assessment of the economic implications of different market-positioning strategies. Dell's belief that corporate customers, its principal target market, would value its custom-built, low-cost positioning and that competitors would have difficulty emulating its model has served it well through the ups and downs of the PC market.

Most successful products, like Dell computers, are positioned based on one or, at most, two determinant attributes, whether physical or perceptual. Using more simply confuses customers. Domino's Pizza, in its early days, focused its positioning solely on its fast delivery, since that was the principal dimension on which it established its competitive advantage. While there are many things Domino's could have said about the pizza itself, for example, it chose to focus its positioning on its key point of differentiation: fast delivery. Recently, when fast delivery became common in the pizza industry, Domino's added a heat retention device to its delivery containers and added a second positioning attribute: hot. Papa John's, a more recent entrant in the pizza business, positions its offering around a single attribute, the quality of its pizza, with its promotional phrase, "Better ingredients. Better pizza."

STRATEGIC ISSUE

Most successful products are positioned based on one or, at most, two determinant attributes.

Where there are no real product differences, as in so-called **me-too products,** or no differential benefits to the user, not only is success hard to achieve, but also ethical issues may arise. For an example of ethical issues involving positioning in the pharmaceutical industry, see Ethical Perspective 8.1.

Once the desired positioning for the product has been determined, it's a good idea to write it down so those charged with developing and implementing the marketing strategy have a clear understanding of what is intended for the product and where it will fit in its competitive set. Two approaches are commonly used for doing so. In the classical approach, a **positioning statement** is written. A more recent approach, one being adopted in a growing number of firms, involves writing a **value proposition** for the product.

Writing a Positioning Statement or a Value Proposition   A positioning statement is a succinct statement that identifies the target market for which the product is

---

ETHICAL PERSPECTIVE 8.1
The Case of TPA: Ethical Issues in Positioning Pharmaceutical Products

Given efforts on many fronts to hold down costs of medical care and health insurance, ethical questions have been raised about the positioning of new medications that sometimes perform no better than old treatments but at sharply higher prices. One example is the introduction of a drug called TPA (for tissue plasminogen activator) that helps break up blood clots in heart attack victims. The pharmaceutical firm that introduced TPA positioned the drug as the "newest treatment" and priced it at $2,500 per treatment compared to $220 for streptokivase, the traditional treatment.

Later research showed no significant difference in the effectiveness of the two drugs. Managers in pharmaceutical firms commonly face similar dilemmas, once the results of the clinical trials are in. Should they market a new drug that is little better than an old one, thereby (if the new drug is successful) enhancing shareholder value and providing funds for research that could lead to subsequent medical breakthroughs? Or should they write off their R&D investment, and devote their marketing efforts to drugs that really are better?

Exhibit 8.8

POSITIONING STATEMENT AND VALUE PROPOSITION FOR VOLVO AUTOMOBILES IN THE UNITED STATES

Positioning statement	Value proposition
For upscale American families, Volvo is the automobile that offers the utmost in safety and durability.	• Target market: Upscale American families • Benefits offered: Safety, durability • Price range: 20% premium over similar cars

intended and the product category in which it competes and states the unique benefit the product offers. An example of a positioning statement that reflects Volvo's marketing strategy in the United States is shown in Exhibit 8.8.

A value proposition is similarly explicit about what the product does for the customer (and sometimes, what it does not do) and typically also includes information about pricing relative to competitors. Both positioning statements and value propositions should reflect a **unique selling proposition** that the product embodies. In this sense, they reflect the basis on which the marketer intends to win sustainable competitive advantage by differentiating the product from others in its competitive space. In its shortest form, a value proposition typically looks like this:

- Target market
- Benefits offered (and not offered)
- Price range (relative to competitors)

Exhibit 8.8 also provides a value proposition for Volvo. More fully developed value propositions sometimes identify the best competing alternatives available to the customer and specify the benefits, in measurable terms, that the customer can expect to receive by using the proposed product.[17] Detailed value propositions such as these are particularly helpful in positioning industrial goods and services, where quantifiable customer benefits are often essential to make the sale.

It is important that the positioning statement or value proposition states **benefits** that the user of the product will obtain, rather than **features** or attributes of the product itself, or vague or ambiguous platitudes about high quality or excellent service. By benefits, we mean the resulting end-use measurable consequences that the user will experience through the use of the product, in comparison to others.

STRATEGIC ISSUE

It is important that the positioning statement or value proposition states benefits that the user of the product will obtain, rather than features or attributes of the product.

The marketer writes positioning statements and value propositions for use internally and by others, such as advertising agencies, engaged to develop the marketing strategy. They are short and succinct, and are typically *not* written in catchy consumer language, though catchy **slogans** and **tag lines** for communication with customers often follow. They are commonly written for a product line or a brand, as is the case in our Volvo example, but sometimes for a single product or for a business as a whole. For products or brands, they play several important roles. They provide direction for R&D and product development about what kind of attributes should be built into the product (side door airbags, for example, in Volvo's case). They provide direction for those who create advertising campaigns about what the focus of those campaigns should be (for example, Volvo's ads almost always focus on safety or durability, even though Volvo could say other things about its cars). The value proposition provides direction for pricing decisions. Thus, in a very real sense, the positioning statement or value proposition constitutes the foundation upon which the marketing strategy is built. More broadly, when used at the business level, as they sometimes are, these statements articulate the strategic direction toward which the company's activities in all arenas should be directed. Promising a certain sort of positioning, or value, to the target market is one thing. Delivering it is another. Clear and concise positioning statements and value propositions can play important roles in effectively executing the intended strategy.

Exhibit 8.9   Software Tools for Positioning Decision Making

Software tools useful for making positioning decisions include applications that identify important determinant attributes, as well as statistical applications that can plot positioning grids from market research data.

Conjoint analysis: As was mentioned in Step 5 of the positioning process, it is important to learn which key attributes are important to consumers. Conjoint analysis is one tool for doing so. Conjoint analysis determines which combination of a limited number of attributes consumers most prefer. The technique is helpful for identifying appealing new product designs and important points that might be included in a product's advertising. Although it can provide some insights about consumer preferences, it cannot provide information about how consumers perceive the positioning of existing products in relation to product dimensions. Conjoint analysis is one way to narrow down a set of product attributes to those most important to consider in product design and positioning decisions. Most often, it is used with physical attributes, not perceptual ones. Several widely used conjoint analysis applications are available from Sawtooth Software, Inc. (**www.sawtoothsoftware.com**).

Factor analysis and discriminant analysis: Factor analysis and discriminant analysis are two statistical techniques useful in constructing positioning grids based on actual marketing research data. They are included in most broad-based statistical packages, such as SPSS MR (**www.spss.com/spssmr**). To employ factor analysis, the analyst first must identify the salient attributes consumers use to evaluate products in the category under study. The analyst then collects data from a sample of consumers concerning their ratings of each product or brand on all attributes. The factor analysis program next determines which attributes are related to the same underlying construct ("load" on the same factor). The analyst uses those underlying constructs or factors as the dimensions for a product space map, and the program indicates where each product or brand is perceived to be located on each factor.

Discriminant analysis requires the same input data as factor analysis. The discriminant analysis program then determines consumers' perceptual dimensions on the basis of which attributes best differentiate, or discriminate, among brands. Once again, those underlying dimensions can be used to construct a product space map, but they are usually not so easily interpretable as the factors identified through factor analysis. Also, as with factor analysis, the underlying dimensions may be more a function of the attributes used to collect consumer ratings than of the product characteristics that consumers actually consider to be most important.

Multidimensional scaling: Unlike the other techniques in which the underlying dimensions identified depend on the attributes supplied by the researcher when collecting data, multidimensional scaling produces dimensions based on consumer judgments about the similarity of, or their preferences for, the actual brands. These underlying dimensions are thought to be the basic attractive dimensions that consumers actually use to evaluate alternative brands in the product class. Multidimensional scaling programs that use data on similarities construct geometrically spaced maps on which the brands perceived to be most similar are placed close together. Those that use consumer preferences produce joint space maps that show consumer ideal points and then position the most-preferred brands close to those ideal points.

Unfortunately, the underlying dimensions of the maps produced by multidimensional scaling can be difficult to interpret. Also, the dimensions identified are only those that already exist for currently available brands. This makes the technique less useful for investigating new product concepts that might involve new characteristics. Finally, the technique is subject to statistical limitations, when the number of alternative brands being investigated is small. As a rule, such techniques should be applied only when at least eight or more different products or brands are being examined.

ANALYTICAL TOOLS FOR POSITIONING DECISION MAKING

Throughout the positioning process, we have advocated collecting marketing research data so positioning decisions are anchored in solid evidence, not mere supposition or naive opinion. Advances in computing power and statistical techniques have made possible a broad range of tools to help the marketing decision maker make the best use of marketing research. We briefly outline a few of these tools in Exhibit 8.9. It is beyond the scope of this book to provide detailed instruction in the use of these and other statistical techniques. Texts on marketing research and new product development are good sources for additional depth in this area.[18]

TAKE AWAYS

- Clear and distinctive positioning that differentiates a product from others with which it competes is usually essential for developing a winning marketing strategy.

- The positioning process outlined in this chapter helps decision makers choose a position that maximizes their chance of establishing sustainable competitive advantage.

- Distinctive and intense positioning is best accomplished when based on one or at most two attributes. More are likely to be confusing to customers.

- Writing clear and succinct positioning statements or value propositions can play an important role in ensuring effective development and execution of a marketing strategy. This chapter provides templates for writing these materials.

- Self-diagnostic questions to test your ability to apply the analytical tools and concepts in this chapter to marketing decision making may be found at this book's website at **www.mhhe.com/walker**.

ENDNOTES

1. Based on Jan W. Rivkin and Michael E. Porter, *Matching Dell* (Boston, MA: Harvard Business School Publishing, 1999), and Ira Sager and Faith Keenan, "In Technology, the Mother of All Price Wars," *BusinessWeek Online,* July 30, 2001, at www.businessweek.com/magazine/content/01_31/b3743049.htm.

2. Al Ries and Jack Trout, *Positioning: The Battle for Your Mind* (New York: Warner Books, 1982).

3. For a discussion of the positioning of industrial goods, see Frederick E. Webster Jr., *Industrial Marketing Strategy* (New York: John Wiley & Sons, 1991), pp. 102–103.

4. Michael Porter, "What Is Strategy?" *Harvard Business Review,* November–December 1996, p. 62.

5. Michael Porter, *Competitive Advantage* (New York: Free Press, 1985).

6. Aaron Lucchetti, "Ford's New Expedition Heads into Suburban's Terrain," *The Wall Street Journal,* June 24, 1996, p. B1.

7. Adapted from C. Merle Crawford, *New Product Management* (Burr Ridge, IL: Richard D. Irwin, 1996), p. 348.

8. For a description of a perceptual mapping procedure that allows consumers to describe and rate the brands involved in their own terminology, see Jan-Benedict E. M. Steenkamp, Hans C. M. Van Tripp, and Jos M. F. Ten Berge, "Perceptual Mapping Based on Idiosyncratic Sets of Attributes," *Journal of Marketing Research,* February 1994, p. 15.

9. Jack Trout, *The New Positioning* (New York: McGraw-Hill, 1996), chap. 3.

10. Douglas Tigert and Stephen Arnold, "Nordstrom: How Good Are They?" *Babson College Retailing Research Reports,* September 1990.

11. Bruce Orwall, "Multiplying Hotel Brands Puzzle Travelers," *The Wall Street Journal,* April 17, 1996, p. B1.

12. Existing brands' attractiveness can be inferred from current sales volumes and market shares. The position occupied by the share leader is obviously more appealing to a greater number of customers than are the positions occupied by lesser brands.

13. See Paul E. Green, J. Douglas Carroll, and Stephen M. Goldberg, "A General Approach to Product Design Optimization via Conjoint Analysis," *Journal of Marketing Research,* May 1985, pp. 168–84; and J. Douglas Carroll and Paul E. Green, "Psychometric Methods in Marketing Research: Part I, Conjoint Analysis," *Journal of Marketing Research,* November 1995, p. 385.

14. When using preference data to define market segments, however, the analyst also should collect information about customers' demographic characteristics, lifestyle, product usage, and other potential segmentation variables. This enables the analyst to develop a more complete picture of the differences among benefit segments. Such information can be useful for developing advertising appeals, selecting media, focusing personal selling efforts, and designing many of the other elements of a marketing program that can be effective in appealing to a particular segment.

15. The sizes of the individual circles in Exhibit 8.7 are fictitious and designed for illustrative purposes only.

16. The map in Exhibit 8.7 shows five distinct preference segments but only one set of perceived product positions. The implication is that consumers in this sample were similar in the way they perceived existing brands but different in the product attributes they preferred. This is the most common situation; customers tend to vary more in the benefits they seek than in how they perceive available products or brands. Sometimes, however, various segments may perceive the positions of existing brands quite differently. They even may use different determinant attributes in assessing these positions. Under such circumstances, a marketer should construct a separate market-positioning map for each segment.

17. Michael J. Lanning, *Delivering Profitable Value* (Cambridge, MA: Perseus Books, 1998).

18. For extensive critical reviews of past marketing applications of these different approaches, see John R. Hauser and Frank S. Koppleman, "Alternative Perceptual Mapping Techniques: Relative Accuracy and Usefulness," *Journal of Marketing Research,* November 1979, pp. 495–506; John W. Keon, "Product Positioning: TRINODAL Mapping of Brand Images, Ad Images, and Consumer Preference," *Journal of Marketing Research,* November 1983, pp. 380–92; Paul E. Green, J. Douglas Carroll, and Stephen M. Goldberg, "A General Approach to Product Design Optimization via Conjoint Analysis," *Journal of Marketing Research,* May 1985, pp. 168–84; Thomas W. Leigh, David M. McKay, and John O. Summers, "Reliability and Validity of Conjoint Analysis and Self-Explicated Weights," *Journal of Marketing Research,* November 1984, pp. 456–63; Paul E. Green, "Hybrid Models for Conjoint Analysis: An Expository Review," *Journal of Marketing Research,* May 1984, pp. 184–93; Steenkamp, Van Tripp, and Ten Berge, "Perceptual Mapping," pp. 15–27; and Carroll and Green, "Psychometric Methods in Marketing Research: Part I, Conjoint Analysis."

SECTION THREE

FORMULATING MARKETING STRATEGIES

MARKETING STRATEGIES FOR NEW MARKET ENTRIES

Illinois Tool Works—New Nuts & Bolts to Fill Many Niches[1]

UNGLAMOROUS AND LOW-PROFILE, Illinois Tool Works makes a diverse array of products that typically are attached to, embedded in, or wrapped around somebody else's goods. It manufactures nails, screws, bolts, strapping, wrapping, valves, capacitors, filters, and adhesives—as well as the tools and machines to apply them.

Long known for superior engineering—and premium prices—in recent years the Chicago conglomerate has managed to develop and implement more cost-efficient manufacturing methods, become more price-competitive, and aggressively expand its global presence. More important, the firm has been extraordinarily innovative in a variety of mundane product areas. It is the inventor and world's largest producer of plastic safety buckles, a leading supplier of fasteners to General Motors, the inventor of the plastic loops that hold six-packs together, the maker of Zip-Pak resealable food packages, and the producer of painting equipment for Toyota's auto plants. ITW holds nearly 3,000 active U.S. patents, but the firm is so decentralized and has been so prolific that nobody at corporate headquarters can come up with an exact tally of how many products it makes.

How can a $10 billion company manage such diversity, reduce costs, and generate a constant stream of new products all at the same time? As we shall see in Chapter 13, the firm's organization structure and management policies have a lot to do with it. For one thing, the company is highly decentralized. Lower-level managers are given a great deal of authority to identify and pursue new products or new markets. This helps the firm maintain close contact and relationships with its many customers. And when engineers and marketers in one division develop and commercialize a successful new product, the company often spins off the product and the personnel as a new division. Consequently, the firm now has more than 500 separate divisions or business units operating in 40 different countries—each with its own marketing, R&D, and manufacturing operations—most of which are quite small and nimble, usually accounting for less than $50 million in annual sales.

While the company's divisions develop tons of new products every year, many are variations of existing products that are redesigned for new applications in new market segments. For instance, in the mid-1980s, an ITW researcher invented a durable safety-rated plastic buckle for a customer who makes life jackets. Now, the firm sells millions of dollars of buckles designed for packs, bicycle helmets, pet collars, and many other applications.

ITW is often the pioneer in developing new product-markets, but it does not always end up as the market share leader as those product categories mature. Instead, it tends to focus on, and often dominates, smaller market niches where competition is less intense and profit margins are higher. As one ITW manager says, "We try to sell where our competitors aren't."

Although the company is not the market share leader in all of its many businesses, its revenue growth and profitability over the past decade have been among the best in the United States. The firm has consistently been first or second among the most admired firms in the metal products industry on *Fortune*'s annual survey, and it achieved 14 percent growth in net income in 2000 despite a sagging U.S. economy.

STRATEGIC CHALLENGES ADDRESSED IN CHAPTER 9

Illinois Tool Works' success illustrates several important points about new product and market development. First, both sales growth and cost cutting can help improve profits. But while it is often easier to cut costs in the short term, revenue growth—particularly growth generated by the development of innovative new products—can have a bigger impact on a firm's profitability and shareholder value over the long haul. This point is confirmed by a study of 847 large corporations conducted by Mercer Management Consulting. The authors found that the compound annual growth rate in the market value of companies that achieved higher-than-average profit growth but lower revenue growth than their industry's average—companies that increased profits mostly by cutting costs, in other words—was 11.6 percent from 1989 to 1992. By contrast, companies that achieved higher-than-average profits as the result of higher-than-average revenue growth saw their market value jump at an annual rate double that—23.5 percent.[2]

Illinois Tool Works' history also illustrates that new product introductions can involve products that differ in their degree of newness from the perspective of the company and its customers. Some of the products developed by the firm, such as the first plastic safety-rated buckle, were new innovations in the eyes of both the company and its customers. But while many of the products ITW develops for new applications, such as buckles designed especially for bicycle helmets or pet collars, are new to the customers in those target niches, they are old hat to the company.

This chapter examines marketing strategies and programs appropriate for developing markets for offerings that are *new to the target customers*. Our primary focus is on programs used by the pioneer firm, or first entrant—into a particular product-market. Being the pioneer gains a firm a number of potential competitive advantages, but it also involves some major risks. Some pioneers capitalize on their early advantage and maintain a leading market share of the product category, earning substantial revenues and profits, well into the later stages of the product's life cycle.

STRATEGIC ISSUE

Being the pioneer gains a firm a number of potential competitive advantages, but it also involves some major risks.

Other pioneers are less successful. While ITW has pioneered many new product categories, for instance, it has not always ended up as the share leader in those categories as they grew and matured. In some cases this was a consequence of ITW's strategy of avoiding competition by focusing on specialized niche markets. But in other cases, followers have overtaken the pioneer by offering better products, superior customer service, or lower prices. This leads to an interesting strategic question: Is it usually better for a firm to bear the high costs and risks of being the pioneer in hopes of maintaining a profitable position as the market grows or to be a follower that watches for possible design or marketing mistakes by the pioneer before joining the fray with its own entry? We examine this question in the next section.

Not all pioneers are intent on remaining the overall share leader as the market grows. Some, like ITW, adopt a niche market strategy geared to making substantial profits from specialized market segments where they will face fewer large competitors. Others try to stay one jump ahead of the competition by introducing a constant stream of new products and withdrawing from older markets as they become more competitive. Which strategy is best? It depends on the firm's resources and competencies, the strength of likely future competitors, and characteristics of the product and its target market. Therefore, we will examine some alternative strategies that might be adopted by a pioneer and the situations where each makes most sense.

HOW NEW IS NEW?

A survey of the new product development practices of 700 U.S. corporations conducted by the consulting firm of Booz, Allen & Hamilton found that the products introduced by those firms over a five-year period were not all equally "new." The study identified six categories of new products based on their degree of newness as perceived by both the company and the target customers. These categories are discussed below and diagrammed in Exhibit 9.1, which also indicates the percentage of new entries falling in each category during the five-year study period. Notice that only 10 percent of all new product introductions fell into the new-to-the-world category.[3]

- *New-to-the-world products*—True innovations that are new to the firm and create an entirely new market (10 percent).
- *New product lines*—A product category that is new for the company introducing it, but not new to customers in the target market because of the existence of one or more competitive brands (20 percent).
- *Additions to existing product lines*—New items that supplement a firm's established product line. These items may be moderately new to both the firm and the customers in its established product-markets. They also may serve to expand the market segments appealed to by the line (26 percent).
- *Improvements in or revisions of existing products*—Items providing improved performance or greater perceived value brought out to replace existing products. These items may present moderately new marketing and production challenges to the firm, but unless they represent a technologically new generation of products, customers are likely to perceive them as similar to the products they replace (26 percent).
- *Repositionings*—Existing products that are targeted at new applications and new market segments (7 percent).
- *Cost reductions*—Product modifications providing similar performance at lower cost (11 percent).

A product's degree of newness—to the company, its target customers, or both—helps determine the amount of complexity and uncertainty involved in the engineering, operations, and marketing tasks necessary to make it a successful new entry. It also contributes to the amount of risk inherent in those tasks.

Exhibit 9.1

CATEGORIES OF NEW PRODUCTS DEFINED ACCORDING TO THEIR DEGREE OF NEWNESS TO THE COMPANY AND CUSTOMERS
IN THE TARGET MARKET

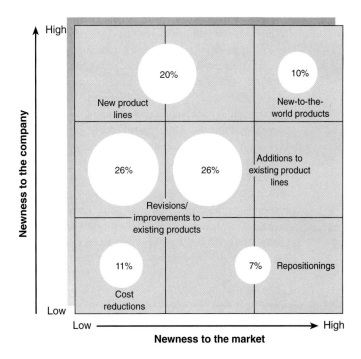

Source: New Products Management for the 1980s (New York: Booz, Allen & Hamilton, 1982). Reprinted by permission.

Introducing a product that is new to both the firm and target customers requires the greatest expenditure of effort and resources. It also involves the greatest amount of uncertainty and risk of failure because of the lack of information and experience with the technology and the target customers.

Products new to target customers but not new to the firm (such as line extensions or modifications aimed at new customer segments or repositionings of existing products) are often not very innovative in design or operations, but they may present a great deal of marketing uncertainty. The marketing challenge here—as with new-to-the-world products—is to build **primary demand,** making target customers aware of the product and convincing them to adopt it. We investigate this marketing problem in this chapter.

Finally, products new to the company but not to the market (such as new product lines, line extensions, product modifications, and cost reductions) often present fewer challenges for R&D and product engineering. The company can study and learn from earlier designs or competitors' products. However, these products can present major challenges for process engineering, production scheduling, quality control, and inventory management. Once the company introduces such a product into the market, its primary marketing objective is to build selective demand and capture market share, convincing customers the new offering is better than existing competitive products. We discuss marketing programs a firm might use to accomplish these objectives later in Chapter 10.

OBJECTIVES OF NEW PRODUCT AND MARKET DEVELOPMENT

The primary objective of most new product and market development efforts is to secure future volume and profit growth. This objective has become even more crucial in recent years due to rapidly advancing technology and more intense global competition. A steady flow of new products and the development of new markets, including those in foreign countries, are essential for the continued growth of most firms.

The ITW case illustrates, however, that individual development projects also may accomplish a variety of other strategic objectives. When asked what strategic role was served by their most successful recent new entry, the respondents in the Booz, Allen & Hamilton survey mentioned eight different strategic objectives. Exhibit 9.2 lists these objectives and the percentage of respondents that mentioned each one. The exhibit also indicates which objectives focused on external concerns (e.g., defending market share) and which were driven by a desire to improve or build upon the firm's internal strengths. Most respondents indicated their new entry helped accomplish more than one objective.

Exhibit 9.3 shows that different types of new entries are appropriate for achieving different strategic objectives. For example, if the objective is to establish a foothold in or preempt a new market segment, the firm must introduce a product that is new to that market,

Exhibit 9.2

STRATEGIC OBJECTIVES ATTAINED BY SUCCESSFUL NEW MARKET ENTRIES

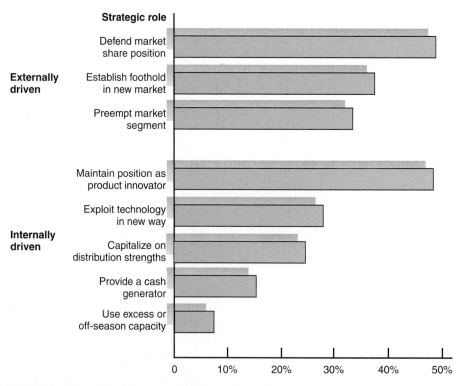

Source: New Products Management for the 1980s (New York: Booz, Allen & Hamilton, 1982), p. 11. Reprinted by permission.

Exhibit 9.3

TYPES OF NEW MARKET ENTRIES APPROPRIATE FOR DIFFERENT STRATEGIC OBJECTIVES

Objective	New entry
Maintain position as a product innovator	New-to-the-world products; improvements or revisions to existing products
Defend a current market-share position	Improvements or revisions to existing products; additions to existing product line; cost reductions
Establish a foothold in a future new market; preempt a market segment	New-to-the-world products; additions to existing product line; repositionings
Exploit technology in a new way	New-to-the-world products; new product line; additions to or revision of existing product line
Capitalize on distribution strengths	New-to-the-world products; new product line; additions to or revisions of existing product line
Provide a cash generator	Additions to or revisions of existing product line; repositionings; cost reductions
Use excess or off-season capacity	New-to-the-world product; new product line

although it may not be entirely new to the company. On the other hand, if the objective is to improve cash flow by adding another cash generator, simple line extensions or product modifications—particularly those that reduce unit costs—may do the trick.

A business's objectives for its new entries influence the kind of entry strategy it should pursue and the marketing and other functional programs needed to implement that strategy. For instance, if a business is pursuing a prospector strategy and its objectives are to maintain a position as a product innovator and to establish footholds in a variety of new product-markets, it should attempt to be the pioneer in as many of those markets as possible. As we saw in Chapter 3, successful implementation of such a strategy requires the business to be competent in and devote substantial resources to R&D, product engineering, marketing, and marketing research.

On the other hand, if the business is concerned primarily with defending an already strong market share position in its industry, it may prefer to be a follower. Usually entering new product-markets only after an innovator, a follower relies on superior quality, better customer service, or lower prices to offset the pioneer's early lead. This strategy usually requires fewer investments in R&D and product development, but marketing and sales still are critical in implementing it effectively. A more detailed comparison of these alternative new market entry strategies is the focus of the next section of this chapter.

MARKET ENTRY STRATEGIES: IS IT BETTER TO BE A PIONEER OR A FOLLOWER?

With products such as Word, Excel, and Powerpoint, Microsoft holds a leading share of most office application software categories. But in most of those categories, the firm was not the pioneer. Lotus 1-2-3 was the leading spreadsheet for many years, and WordPerfect and other programs led the word processing category. But as a follower, Microsoft developed improved product designs offering better performance, and it had superior financial resources to aggressively promote its products. Microsoft's Windows also held a commanding share of the operating systems market, a position the firm could leverage to convince personal computer manufacturers to bundle its applications software with their machines.

On the other hand, some of the software industry's pioneers have not fared so well in the marketplace. Lotus, for example, experienced financial difficulties and was ultimately acquired by IBM. While we have stressed the competitive importance of growth via the introduction of new products, the important strategic question is whether it always makes sense to go first. Or do *both* pioneer and follower market entry strategies have some particular advantages under different conditions?

Pioneer Strategy

Conventional wisdom holds that although they take the greatest risks and probably experience more failures than their more conservative competitors, successful pioneers are handsomely rewarded. It is assumed competitive advantages inherent in being the first to enter a new product-market can be sustained through the growth stage and into the maturity stage of the product life cycle, resulting in a strong share position and substantial returns.

Some of the potential sources of competitive advantage available to pioneers are briefly summarized in Exhibit 9.4 and discussed below.[4]

1.   *First choice of market segments and positions.* The pioneer has the opportunity to develop a product offering with attributes most important to the largest segment of customers or to promote the importance of attributes that favor its brand. Thus, the pioneer's brand can become the standard of reference customers use to evaluate other brands. This can make it more difficult for followers with me-too products to convince existing customers that their new brands are superior to the older and more familiar pioneer. If the pioneer has successfully tied its offering to the choice criteria of the largest group of customers, it also becomes more difficult for followers to differentiate their offerings in ways that are attractive to the mass-market segment. They may have to target a smaller peripheral segment or niche instead.

2.   *The pioneer defines the rules of the game.* The pioneer's actions on such variables as product quality, price, distribution, warranties, postsale service, and promotional appeals and budgets set standards that subsequent competitors must meet or beat. If the pioneer sets those standards high enough, it can raise the costs of entry and perhaps preempt some potential competitors.[5]

Exhibit 9.4

POTENTIAL ADVANTAGES OF PIONEER AND FOLLOWER STRATEGIES

Pioneer	Follower
• Economies of scale and experience	• Ability to take advantage of pioneer's positioning mistakes
• High switching costs for early adopters	• Ability to take advantage of pioneer's product mistakes
• Pioneer defines the rules of the game	• Ability to take advantage of pioneer's marketing mistakes
• Possibility of positive network effects	• Ability to take advantage of pioneer's limited resources
• Distribution advantage	
• Influence on consumer choice criteria and attitudes	
• Possibility of preempting scarce resources	

3. *Distribution advantages.* The pioneer has the most options in designing a distribution channel to bring the new product to market. This is particularly important for industrial goods where, if the pioneer exercises its options well and with dispatch, it should end up with a network of the best distributors. This can exclude later entrants from some markets. Distributors are often reluctant to take on second or third brands. This is especially true when the product is technically complex and the distributor must carry large inventories of the product and spare parts and invest in specialized training and service.

    For consumer package goods, it is more difficult to slow the entry of later competitors by preempting distribution alternatives. Nevertheless, the pioneer still has the advantage of attaining more shelf-facings at the outset of the growth stage. By quickly expanding its product line following an initial success, the pioneer can appropriate still more shelf space, thereby making the challenge faced by followers even more difficult. And as many retailers are reducing the number of brands they carry in a given product category to speed inventory turnover and reduce costs, it is becoming more difficult for followers with unfamiliar brands and small market shares to gain extensive distribution.

4. *Economies of scale and experience.* Being first means the pioneer can gain accumulated volume and experience and thereby lower per unit costs at a faster rate than followers. This advantage is particularly pronounced when the product is technically sophisticated and involves high development costs or when its life cycle is likely to be short with sales increasing rapidly during the introduction and early growth stages.

    As we shall see later, the pioneer can deploy these cost advantages in a number of ways to protect its early lead against followers. One strategy is to lower price, which can discourage followers from entering the market because it raises the volume necessary for them to break even. Or the pioneer might invest its savings in additional marketing efforts to expand its penetration of the market, such as heavier advertising, a larger salesforce, or continuing product improvements or line extensions.

5. *High switching costs for early adopters.* Customers who are early to adopt a pioneer's new product may be reluctant to change suppliers when competitive products appear. This is particularly true for industrial goods where the costs of switching suppliers can be high. Compatible equipment and spare parts, investments in employee training, and the risks of lower product quality or customer service make it easier for the pioneer to retain its early customers over time.

    In some cases, however, switching costs can work against the pioneer and in favor of followers. A pioneer may have trouble converting customers to a new technology if they must bear high switching costs to abandon their old way of doing things. Pioneers in the development of music CDs, for instance, faced the formidable task of convincing potential buyers to abandon their substantial investments in turntables and LP record libraries and to start all over again with the new technology. Once the pioneers had begun to convince consumers that the superior convenience, sound quality, and durability of CDs justified those high switching costs, however, demand for CDs and CD players began to grow rapidly and it was easier for followers to attract customers.

6. *Possibility of positive network effects.* The value of some kinds of goods and services to an individual customer increases as greater numbers of other people adopt the product and the network of users grows larger. Economists say that such products exhibit **network externalities** or **positive network effects.** Information and communications technologies, such as wireless phones, fax machines, computer software, e-mail, and many Internet sites, are particularly likely to benefit from network effects.[6] For instance, the value of eBay as an auction site increases as the number of potential buyers and sellers who visit and trade on the site increase. If the pioneer in such a product or service category can gain and maintain a substantial customer base before competing technologies or providers appear on the market, the positive network effects generated by that customer base will enhance the benefits of the pioneer's offering and make it more difficult for followers to match its perceived value.

STRATEGIC ISSUE

The value of some kinds of goods and services to an individual customer increases as greater numbers of other people adopt the product.

7. *Possibility of preempting scarce resources and suppliers.* The pioneer may be able to negotiate favorable deals with suppliers who are eager for new business or who do not appreciate

the size of the opportunity for their raw materials or component parts. If later entrants subsequently find those materials and components in short supply, they may be constrained from expanding as fast as they might like or be forced to pay premium prices.

Not All Pioneers Capitalize on Their Potential Advantages

There is some evidence to suggest that the above advantages can help pioneers gain and maintain a competitive edge in new markets. For instance, some research has found that surviving pioneers hold a significantly larger average market share when their industries reach maturity than firms that were either fast followers or late entrants in the product category.[7]

On the other hand, some pioneers fail. They either abandon the product category, go out of business, or get acquired before their industry matures. One study, which took these failed pioneers into account and averaged their performance together with that of the more successful survivors, found that pioneers overall did not perform as well over the long haul as followers.[8]

Of course, volume and market share are not the only dimensions on which success can be measured. Unfortunately, there is little evidence concerning the effect of the timing of a firm's entry into a new market on its ultimate profitability in that market or the value generated for shareholders.[9]

In view of the mixed research evidence, then, it seems reasonable to conclude that while a pioneer may have some *potential* competitive advantages, not all pioneers are successful at capitalizing on them. Some fail during the introductory or shakeout stages of their industries' life cycles. And those that survive may lack the resources to keep up with rapid growth or the competencies needed to maintain their early lead in the face of onslaughts by strong followers.[10]

Follower Strategy

In many cases a firm becomes a follower by default. It is simply beaten to a new product-market by a quicker competitor. But even when a company has the capability of being the first mover, the above observations suggest there may be some advantages to letting other firms go first into a product-market. Let the pioneer shoulder the initial risks while the followers observe their shortcomings and mistakes. Possible advantages of such a follower strategy are briefly summarized in Exhibit 9.4 and discussed below.

1. *Ability to take advantage of the pioneer's positioning mistakes.* If the pioneer misjudges the preferences and purchase criteria of the mass-market segment or attempts to satisfy two or more segments at once, it is vulnerable to the introduction of more precisely positioned products by a follower. By tailoring its offerings to each distinct segment, the follower(s) can successfully encircle the pioneer.

2. *Ability to take advantage of the pioneer's product mistakes.* If the pioneer's initial product has technical limitations or design flaws, the follower can benefit by overcoming these weaknesses. Even when the pioneering product is technically satisfactory, a follower may gain an advantage through product enhancements. For example, Compaq captured a substantial share of the commercial PC market by developing faster and more portable versions of IBM's original machine.

3. *Ability to take advantage of the pioneer's marketing mistakes.* If the pioneer makes any marketing mistakes in introducing a new entry, it opens opportunities for later entrants. This observation is closely related to the first two points, yet goes beyond product positioning

and design to the actual execution of the pioneer's marketing program. For example, the pioneer may fail to attain adequate distribution, spend too little on introductory advertising, or use ineffective promotional appeals to communicate the product's benefits. A follower can observe these mistakes, design a marketing program to overcome them, and successfully compete head-to-head with the pioneer.

Marketing mistakes can leave a pioneer vulnerable to challenges from later entrants even in product categories with substantial positive network effects. For example, Microsoft's Windows operating system was not the first user-friendly system on the market. However, Microsoft promoted and priced Windows very aggressively, it formed alliances with original equipment manufacturers (OEMs) in the personal computer industry to encourage them to install Windows on their machines, and it engaged in extensive licensing and cooperative agreements with other software developers. All these actions helped Windows capture a commanding share of the operating systems market, which in turn generated tremendous positive network effects for Windows and made it difficult for alternative systems to compete (perhaps *too* difficult, from the U.S. Justice Department's perspective).

4. *Ability to take advantage of the latest technology.* In industries characterized by rapid technological advances, followers can possibly introduce products based on a superior, second-generation technology and thereby gain an advantage over the pioneer. And the pioneer may have difficulty reacting quickly to such advances if it is heavily committed to an earlier technology. Consumer popularity of the newer VHS format, for instance, gave followers in the videocassette recorder market an advantage over pioneer Sony, which was locked in to the less-popular Beta format.

5. *Ability to take advantage of pioneer's limited resources.* If the pioneer has limited resources for production facilities or marketing programs, or fails to commit sufficient resources to its new entry, followers willing and able to outspend the pioneer experience few enduring constraints.

Determinants of Success for Pioneers and Followers

Our discussion suggests that a pioneering firm stands the best chance for long-term success in market-share leadership and profitability when (1) the new product-market is insulated from the entry of competitors, at least for a while, by strong patent protection, proprietary technology (such as a unique production process), substantial investment requirements, or positive network effects, or (2) the firm has sufficient size, resources, and competencies to take full advantage of its pioneering position and preserve it in the face of later competitive entries. Evidence suggests that organizational competencies, such as R&D and marketing skills, not only affect a firm's success as a pioneer, but also may influence the company's decision about whether or not to be a pioneer in the first place. Firms that perceive they lack the competencies necessary to sustain a first-mover advantage may be more likely to wait for another company to take the lead and to enter the market later.[11]

McDonald's is an example of a pioneer that has succeeded by aggressively building on the foundations of its early advantage. Although the firm started small as a single hamburger restaurant, it used the franchise system of distribution to rapidly expand the number of McDonald's outlets with a minimum cash investment. That expansion plus stringent quality and cost controls, relatively low prices made possible by experience-curve effects, heavy advertising expenditures, and product line expansion aimed at specific market segments (such as Egg McMuffin for the breakfast crowd) have all enabled the firm to maintain a commanding share of the fast-food hamburger industry.

On the other hand, a follower will most likely succeed when there are few legal, technological, or financial barriers to inhibit entry and when it has sufficient resources or competencies to overwhelm the pioneer's early advantage. For example, given Procter &

Gamble's well-established brand name and superior advertising and promotional resources, the company was able to quickly take the market share lead away from pioneer Minnetonka, Inc., in the plaque-fighting toothpaste market with a reformulated version of Crest.

A study conducted across a broad range of industries in the PIMS database supports these observations.[12] The author's findings are briefly summarized in Exhibit 9.5 and discussed below. The author found that, regardless of the industry involved, pioneers able to maintain their preeminent position well into the market's growth stage had supported their early entry with the following marketing strategy elements:

- *Large entry scale*—Successful pioneers had sufficient capacity, or could expand quickly enough, to pursue a mass-market targeting strategy, usually on a national rather than a local or regional basis. Thus, they could expand their volume quickly and achieve the benefits of experience-curve effects before major competitors could confront them.
- *Broad product line*—Successful pioneers also quickly add line extensions or modifications to their initial product to tailor their offerings to specific market segments. This helps reduce their vulnerability to later entrants who might differentiate themselves by targeting one or more peripheral markets.
- *High product quality*—Successful pioneers also offer a high-quality, well-designed product from the beginning, thus removing one potential differential advantage for later followers. Competent engineering, thorough product and market testing before commercialization, and good quality control during the production process are all important to the continued success of pioneers.
- *Heavy promotional expenditures*—Successful pioneers had marketing programs characterized by relatively high advertising and promotional expenditures as a percentage of sales. Initially the promotion helps to stimulate awareness and primary demand for the new product category, build volume, and reduce unit costs. Later, this promotion focuses on building selective demand for the pioneer's brand and reinforcing loyalty as new competitors enter.

The same study found that the most successful fast followers had the resources to enter the new market on a larger scale than the pioneer. Consequently, they could quickly reduce their unit costs, offer lower prices than incumbent competitors, and enjoy any positive network effects. Some fast followers achieved success, however, by leapfrogging earlier entrants. These followers won customers away from the pioneer by offering a product with more sophisticated technology, better quality, or superior service.

Exhibit 9.5

MARKETING STRATEGY ELEMENTS PURSUED BY SUCCESSFUL PIONEERS, FAST FOLLOWERS, AND LATE ENTRANTS

These marketers . . .	are characterized by one or more of these strategy elements:
Successful pioneers	• Large entry scale
	• Broad product line
	• High product quality
	• Heavy promotional expenditures
Successful fast followers	• Larger entry scale than the pioneer

	• Leapfrogging the pioneer with superior:
	    product technology
	    product quality
	    customer service

Successful late entrants	• Focus on peripheral target markets or niches

Source: 2001 Simmons Market Research Bureau. Reprinted by permission. www.smrb.com.

Finally, the author found that some late entrants also achieved substantial profits by avoiding direct confrontations with more established competitors and by pursuing peripheral target markets. They often offer tailor-made products to smaller market niches and support them with high levels of service.

Followers typically enter a market after it is in the growth phase of its life cycle, and they start with low market shares relative to the established pioneer. Consequently, our discussion in the next chapter of marketing strategies for low-share competitors in growth markets is germane to both fast followers and later entrants. Before focusing on strategies for followers, however, we should first examine strategies that might be successfully employed by the first entrant in a new product-market.

STRATEGIC MARKETING PROGRAMS FOR PIONEERS

STRATEGIC ISSUE

Success of a pioneering strategy depends on the nature of the demand and competitive situation the pioneer encounters in the market and on the pioneer's ability to design and support an effective marketing program.

The preceding discussion suggests that the ultimate success of a pioneering strategy depends on the nature of the demand and competitive situation the pioneer encounters in the market and on the pioneer's ability to design and support an effective marketing program. It also depends on how the pioneer defines *success*—in other words, the objectives it seeks to achieve. Thus, a pioneer might choose from one of three different types of marketing strategies: mass-market penetration, niche penetration, or skimming and early withdrawal. Exhibit 9.6 summarizes the primary objectives of each strategy and the circumstances favoring their use. While specific conditions may favor a given strategy, they do not guarantee its success. Much still depends on how effectively a firm implements the strategy. Also, it is highly unlikely that all the listed conditions will exist simultaneously in any single product-market.

Mass-Market Penetration

The ultimate objective of a mass-market penetration strategy is to capture and maintain a commanding share of the total market for the new product. Thus, the critical marketing task is to convince as many potential customers as possible to adopt the pioneer's product quickly to drive down unit costs and build a large contingent of loyal customers before competitors enter the market.

Mass-market penetration tends to be most successful when entry barriers inhibit or delay the appearance of competitors, thus allowing the pioneer more time to build volume, lower costs, and create loyal customers, or when the pioneer has competencies or resources that most potential competitors cannot match. Relevant competencies include product engineering, promotional and channel management skills, and the financial and organizational resources necessary to expand capacity in advance of demand. In some cases, though, a smaller firm with limited resources can successfully employ a mass-market penetration strategy if the market has a protracted adoption process and slow initial growth. Slow growth can delay competitive entry because fewer competitors are attracted to a market with questionable future growth. This allows the pioneer more time to expand capacity.

 Mass-market penetration is also an appropriate strategy when the product category is likely to experience positive network effects. Since the value of such products increases as the number of users grows, it makes sense for the pioneer to quickly capture and maintain as large a customer base as possible.

Exhibit 9.6

MARKETING OBJECTIVES AND STRATEGIES FOR NEW PRODUCT PIONEERS

Situational variables	ALTERNATIVE MARKETING STRATEGIES		
	Mass-market penetration	**Niche penetration**	**Skimming: early withdrawal**
Primary objective	• Maximize number of triers and adopters in *total market*. • Maintain leading share position in *total market*.	• Maximize number of triers and adopters in *target segment*. • Maintain leading share position in *target segment*.	• Recoup development and commercialization costs as soon as possible. • Withdraw from market when increasing competition puts pressure on margins.
Market characteristics	• Large potential demand. • Relatively homogeneous customer needs. • Customers likely to adopt product relatively quickly; short diffusion process.	• Large potential demand. • Fragmented market; many different applications and benefit segments. • Customers likely to adopt product relatively quickly; short adoption process.	• Limited potential demand. • Customers likely to adopt product relatively slowly; long adoption process. • Early adopters willing to pay high price; demand is price inelastic.
Product characteristics	• Product technology patentable or difficult to copy. • Substantial network effects; value increases with growth of installed customer base. • Components or materials difficult to obtain; limited sources of supply. • Complex production process; substantial development and/or investment required.	• Product technology offers little patent protection; easily copied or adapted. • Limited or no network effects. • Components or materials easy to obtain; many sources of supply. • Relatively simple production process; little development or additional investment required.	• Product technology offers little patent protection; easily copied or adapted. • Limited or no network effects. • Components or materials easy to obtain; many sources of supply. • Relatively simple production process; little development or additional investment required.
Competitor characteristics	• Few potential competitors. • Most potential competitors have limited resources and competencies; few sources of differential advantage.	• Many potential competitors. • Some potential competitors have substantial resources and competencies; possible sources of differential advantage.	• Many potential competitors. • Some potential competitors have substantial resources and competencies; possible sources of differential advantage.
Firm characteristics	• Strong product engineering skills; able to quickly develop product modifications and line extensions for multiple market segments. • Strong marketing skills and resources; ability to identify and develop marketing programs for multiple segments; ability to shift from stimulation of primary demand to stimulation of selective demand as competitors enter. • Sufficient financial and organizational resources to build capacity in advance of growth in demand.	• Limited product engineering skills and resources. • Limited marketing skills and resources. • Insufficient financial or organizational resources to build capacity in advance of growing demand.	• Strong basic R&D and new product development skills; a prospector with good capability for continued new product innovation. • Good sales and promotional skills; able to quickly build primary demand in target market; perhaps has limited marketing resources for long-term market maintenance. • Limited financial or organizational resources to commit to building capacity in advance of growth in demand.

Source: 2001 Simmons Market Research Bureau. Reprinted by permission. www.smrb.com.

Niche Penetration

Even when a new product-market expands quickly, however, it still may be possible for a small firm with limited resources to be a successful pioneer. In such cases, though, the firm must define success in a more limited way. Instead of pursuing the objective of capturing and sustaining a leading share of the entire market, it may make more sense for such firms to focus their efforts on a single market segment. This kind of **niche penetration** strategy can help the smaller pioneer gain the biggest bang for its limited bucks and avoid direct confrontations with bigger competitors.

A niche penetration strategy is most appropriate when the new market is expected to grow quickly and there are a number of different benefit or applications segments to appeal to. It is particularly attractive when there are few barriers to the entry of major competitors and when the pioneer has only limited resources and competencies to defend any advantage it gains through early entry. For example, the fact that the applications for many of Illinois Tool Works' products are highly specialized, its markets are fragmented, and it prefers to avoid direct confrontations with large competitors all help explain why the firm favors a niche penetration strategy.

Some pioneers may intend to pursue a mass-market penetration strategy when introducing a new product or service, but they end up implementing a niche penetration strategy instead. This is particularly likely when the new market grows faster or is more fragmented than the pioneer expects. Facing such a situation, a pioneer with limited resources may decide to concentrate on holding its leading position in one or a few segments, rather than spreading itself too thin developing unique line extensions and marketing programs for many different markets or going deep into debt to finance rapid expansion.

Skimming and Early Withdrawal

Even when a firm has the resources to sustain a leading position in a new product-market, it may choose not to. Competition is usually inevitable, and prices and margins tend to drop dramatically after followers enter the market. Therefore, some pioneers opt to pursue a **skimming** strategy while planning an early withdrawal from the market. This involves setting a high price and engaging in only limited advertising and promotion to maximize per-unit profits and recover the product's development costs as quickly as possible. At the same time, the firm may work to develop new applications for its technology or the next generation of more advanced technology. Then when competitors enter the market and margins fall, the firm is ready to cannibalize its own product with one based on new technology or to move into new segments of the market.

The 3M Company is a master of the skimming strategy. According to one 3M manager, "We hit fast, price high (full economic value of the product to the user), and get the heck out when the me-too products pour in." The new markets pioneered by the company are often smaller ones of $10 million to $50 million, and the firm may dominate them for only about five years or so. By then, it is ready to launch the next generation of new technology or to move the old technology into new applications.[13] An example of 3M's approach is described in Exhibit 9.7.

As Exhibit 9.6 indicates, either small or large firms can use strategies of skimming and early withdrawal. But it is critical that the company have good R&D and product development skills so it can produce a constant stream of new products or new applications to replace older ones as they attract heavy competition. Also, since a firm pursuing this kind of strategy plans to remain in a market only short term, it is most appropriate when there

The first water-activated synthetic casting tape to set broken bones was developed by 3M in 1980, but by 1982 eight other companies had brought out copycat products. The company's R&D people retreated to their labs and developed and tested 140 new versions in a variety of fabrics. In 1983, the firm dropped the old product and introduced a technically superior version that was stronger and easier to use and commanded a premium price.

Source: Christopher Knowlton, "What America Makes Best," *Fortune,* March 28, 1988, p. 45. © 1988 Time Inc. All rights reserved.

are few barriers to entry, the product is expected to diffuse rapidly, and the pioneer lacks the capacity or other resources necessary to defend a leading share position over the long haul.

Marketing Program Components for a Mass-Market Penetration Strategy

As mentioned, the crucial marketing task in a mass-market penetration strategy is to maximize the number of customers adopting the firm's new product as quickly as possible.

STRATEGIC ISSUE

The crucial marketing task in a mass-market penetration strategy is to maximize the number of customers adopting the firm's new product as quickly as possible.

This requires a marketing program focused on (1) *aggressively building product awareness and motivation to buy* among a broad cross-section of potential customers and (2) *making it as easy as possible for those customers to try the new product,* on the assumption that they will try it, like it, develop loyalty, and make repeat purchases.

Exhibit 9.8 outlines a number of marketing activities that might help increase customers' awareness and willingness to buy or improve their ability to try the product. This is by no means an exhaustive list; nor do we mean to imply that a successful pioneer must necessarily engage in all of the listed activities. Marketing managers must develop programs combining activities that fit both the objectives of a mass-market penetration strategy and the specific market and potential competitive conditions the new product faces.

Increasing Customers' Awareness and Willingness to Buy   Obviously, heavy expenditures on advertising, introductory promotions such as sampling and couponing, and personal selling efforts all can increase awareness of a new product or service among potential customers. This is the critical first step in the adoption process for a new entry. The relative importance of these promotional tools varies, however, depending on the nature of the product and the number of potential customers. For instance, personal selling efforts are often the most critical component of the promotional mix for highly technical industrial products with a limited potential customer base. Media advertising and sales promotion are usually more useful for building awareness and primary demand for a new consumer good among customers in the mass market. In either case, when designing a mass-market penetration marketing program, firms should broadly focus promotional efforts to expose and attract as many potential customers as possible before competitors show up.

Firms might also attempt to increase customers' willingness to buy their products by reducing the risk associated with buying something new. This can be done by letting customers try the product without obligation, as when car dealers allow potential customers to test-drive a new model, or when software developers allow customers to download a trial version and use it free for 30 days. Liberal return policies and extended warranties can serve the same purpose.

Exhibit 9.8

COMPONENTS OF STRATEGIC MARKETING PROGRAMS FOR PIONEERS

Strategic objectives and tasks	ALTERNATIVE STRATEGIC MARKETING PROGRAMS		
	Mass-market penetration	Niche penetration	Skimming: early withdrawal
Increase customers' awareness and willingness to buy	• Heavy advertising to generate awareness among customers in mass market; broad use of mass media.	• Heavy advertising directed at target segment to generate awareness; use selective media relevant to target.	• Limited advertising to generate awareness; particularly among least price-sensitive early adopters.
	• Extensive salesforce efforts to win new adopters; possible use of incentives to encourage new product sales.	• Extensive salesforce efforts focused on potential customers in target segment; possible use of incentives to encourage new product sales to target accounts.	• Extensive salesforce efforts, particularly focused on largest potential adopters; possible use of volume-based incentives to encourage new product sales.
	• Advertising and sales appeals stress generic benefits of new product type.	• Advertising and sales appeals stress generic benefits of new product type.	• Advertising and sales appeals stress generic benefits of new product type.
	• Extensive introductory sales promotions to induce trial (sampling, couponing, quantity discounts).	• Extensive introductory sales promotions to induce trial, but focused on target segment.	• Limited use, if any, of introductory sales promotions; if used, they should be volume-based quantity discounts.
	• Move relatively quickly to expand offerings (line extensions, multiple package sizes) to appeal to multiple segments.	• Additional product development limited to improvements or modifications to increase appeal to target segment.	• Little, if any, additional development within the product category.
	• Offer free trial, liberal return, or extended warranty policies to reduce customers' perceived risk of adopting the new product.	• Offer free trial, liberal return, or extended warranty policies to reduce target customers' perceived risk of adopting the new product.	• Offer free trial, liberal return, or extended warranty policies to reduce target customers' perceived risk of adopting the new product.
Increase customers' ability to buy	• Penetration pricing; or start with high price but bring out lower-priced versions in anticipation of competitive entries.	• Penetration pricing; or start with high price but bring out lower-priced versions in anticipation of competitive entries.	• Skimming pricing; attempt to maintain margins at level consistent with value of product to early adopters.
	• Extended credit terms to encourage initial purchases.	• Extended credit terms to encourage initial purchases.	• Extended credit terms to encourage initial purchases.
	• Heavy use of trade promotions aimed at gaining extensive distribution.	• Trade promotions aimed at gaining solid distribution among retailers or distributors pertinent for reaching target segment.	• Limited use of trade promotions; only as necessary to gain adequate distribution.
	• Offer engineering, installation, and training services to increase new product's compatibility with customers' current operations to reduce switching costs.	• Offer engineering, installation, and training services to increase new product's compatibility with customers' current operations to reduce switching costs.	• Offer limited engineering, installation, and training services as necessary to overcome customers' objections.

Finally, a firm committed to mass-market penetration might also broaden its product offerings to increase its appeal to as many market segments as possible. This helps reduce its vulnerability to later entrants who could focus on specific market niches. Firms can accomplish such market expansion through the rapid introduction of line extensions, additional package sizes, or product modifications targeted at new applications and market segments. Illinois Tool Works, for example, rapidly increased sales of its plastic safety buckle by modifying it for use with a variety of products, such as bicycle helmets, backpacks, and pet collars.

Increasing Customers' Ability to Buy   For customers to adopt a new product and develop loyalty toward it, they must be aware of the item and be motivated to buy. But they also must have the wherewithal to purchase it. Thus, to capture as many customers in as short a time as possible, it usually makes sense for a firm pursuing mass-market penetration to keep prices low (penetration pricing) and perhaps offer liberal financing arrangements or easy credit terms during the introductory period.

Pioneers introducing new information or communications technologies tend to be particularly aggressive in pricing their offerings for two reasons. First, as we have seen, such products often can benefit from positive network effects if enough customers can be induced to adopt them quickly. Second, the variable costs of producing and distributing additional units of such products are usually very low, perhaps even approaching zero. For instance, the costs of developing a new software product are high, but once it is developed, copies can be made and distributed over the Internet for next to nothing. These two factors mean that it often makes sense for pioneers in such product categories to set their price very low to initial customers—perhaps even to give away trial copies—in hopes of quickly building a large installed base, capturing more value from later customers with higher prices, and maximizing the lifetime value of their customers by selling them upgrades and enhanced versions of the product in the future.[14]

Another factor that can inhibit customers' ability to buy is a lack of product availability. Thus, extensive personal selling and trade promotions aimed at gaining adequate distribution are usually a critical part of a mass-market penetration marketing program. Such efforts should take place before the start of promotional campaigns to ensure that the product is available as soon as customers are motivated to buy it.

A highly technical new product's incompatibility with other related products or systems currently used also can inhibit customers' purchases. It can result in high switching costs for a potential adopter. The pioneer might reduce those costs by designing the product to be as compatible as possible with related equipment. It also might offer engineering services to help make the new product more compatible with existing operations, provide free installation assistance, and conduct training programs for the customer's employees.

The above actions are suited not just to the marketing of products; most are essential elements of mass-market penetration strategies for new service, retail, and even e-commerce websites as well. The marketing actions of an e-tailer such as Amazon.com, discussed in Exhibit 9.9, provide a textbook example of the elements of, as well as some of the risks inherent in, a mass-market penetration strategy.

Additional Considerations When Pioneering Global Markets   Whether the product-market a pioneer is trying to penetrate is domestic or foreign, many of the marketing tasks appropriate for increasing potential customers' awareness, willingness, and ability to buy the new product or service are largely the same. Of course, some of the tactical aspects of the pioneer's strategic marketing program—such as specific product features, promotional appeals, or distribution channels—may have to be adjusted to fit different cultural, legal, or economic circumstances across national borders. For Bausch &

| Exhibit 9.9 | Amazon's Mass-Market Penetration Strategy |

Founded in 1994 by Jeff Bezos as the first online bookstore, Amazon.com (**www.amazon.com**) has employed many of the marketing tactics we have listed as possible components of a mass-market penetration strategy. In the early days, the firm spent heavily on various promotional tools to attract buyers and build a base of loyal customers. In the late 1990s, the firm was spending an average of more than $50 for each new customer it attracted. The money was spent on banner advertising and alliances with other sites and Web portals, traditional media advertising, special consumer promotions, and an "associates" program through which sites that offer a link to Amazon get a cut of any sales they referred. As Amazon has built its customer base and increased public awareness, its acquisition costs per customer have declined substantially.

In the early years, many of Amazon's inventory storage and order fulfillment functions were outsourced, its fixed costs were low, and it had huge amounts of capital to play with. Consequently, it was able to attract customers from bricks-and-mortar bookstores by offering very low prices and a wide selection of titles.

To gain the loyalty of new customers it attracted, Amazon worked hard to constantly improve its customer service. It collected information from customers concerning their preferences, desires, and complaints, then launched a series of customer service innovations, such as one-click ordering and a popular bestseller list ranking sales on the site. More recently, it has invested hundreds of millions of dollars to build a network of company-owned distribution centers to better control order fulfillment and ensure quick and reliable delivery.

Finally, Amazon has greatly expanded its product lines over the years to include CDs, toys, electronics, tools, and a variety of other things. This move was motivated by the company's desire to become a one-stop shopping venue, and to increase the average annual revenues per customer.

By 2001 there were signs that Amazon's mass-market penetration strategy might succeed. Sales revenues were projected to grow to $4.5 billion in 2001 and $6.5 billion in 2002. More importantly, early customers were returning to make repeat purchases. Repeat customers accounted for 76 percent of revenues in 2000, and the average annual revenue per customer was projected to increase from $105 in 1998 to $135 in 2001.

But the firm was still experiencing operating losses in 2000. Cash flows were a negative $320 million in the first quarter alone, largely as a result of carrying costs and write-downs associated with excess inventory in the firm's new distribution centers. As a consequence Amazon's stock lost half its value between December 1999 and July 2000.

While analysts and investors were concerned that the firm might never be able to recoup the heavy expenditures and investments involved in its strategy, Bezos and the believers were confident that the firm's expanding customer base and its ability to increase the loyalty and lifetime value of those customers would eventually pay big dividends. It's too soon to know which side is right, but that is a very common state of affairs for any pioneering firm that opts to pursue a mass-market penetration strategy.

Source: Eryn Brown, "Nine Ways to Win on the Web," *Fortune,* May 24, 1999, pp. 112–25; and Robert Hof, Debra Sparks, Ellen Neuborne, and Wendy Zellner, "Can Amazon Make It?" *Business Week,* July 10, 2000, pp. 38–43.

Lomb to develop the Chinese market for contact lenses, for instance, it first had to develop an extensive training program for the country's opticians and build a network of retail outlets, actions that were unnecessary in more developed markets.

Unless the firm already has an economic presence in a country via the manufacture or marketing of other products or services, however, a potential global pioneer faces at least one additional question: What mode of entry is most appropriate? There are three basic mechanisms for entering a foreign market: exporting through agents (e.g., using local manufacturers' representatives or distributors), contractual agreements (e.g., licensing or franchise arrangements with local firms), and direct investment.

Exporting is the simplest way to enter a foreign market because it involves the least commitment and risk. It can be direct or indirect. The latter relies on the expertise of domestic international middlemen: **export merchants,** who buy the product and sell it overseas for their own account; **export agents,** who sell on a commission basis; and **cooperative organizations,** which export for several producers—especially those selling farm products. Direct exporting uses foreign-based distributors and agents or operating units (i.e., branches or subsidiaries) set up in the foreign country.

Contractual entry modes are nonequity arrangements that involve the transfer of technology or skills to an entity in a foreign country. In **licensing,** a firm offers the right to use its intangible assets (e.g., technology, know-how, patents, company name, trademarks) in exchange for royalties or some other form of payment. Licensing is less flexible and provides less control than exporting. Further, if the contract is terminated, the licensor may have developed a competitor. It is appropriate, however, when the market is unstable or difficult to penetrate.

Franchising grants the right to use the company's name, trademarks, and technology. Also, the franchisee typically receives help in setting up the franchise. It is an especially attractive way for service firms to penetrate foreign markets at low cost and to couple their skills with local knowledge and entrepreneurial spirit. Host countries are reasonably receptive to this type of exporting since it involves local ownership. U.S. companies have largely pioneered franchising—especially such fast-food companies as McDonald's, Pizza Hut, Burger King, and Kentucky Fried Chicken. In recent years foreign franchisers have entered the United States—largely from Canada, Great Britain, and Japan—in a variety of fields, including food, shoe repair, leather furniture, and wall cleaning.

Other contractual entry modes include **contract manufacturing,** which involves sourcing a product from a manufacturer located in a foreign country for sale there or elsewhere (e.g., auto parts, clothes, and furniture). Contract manufacturing is most attractive when the local market is too small to warrant making an investment, export entry is blocked, and a quality licensee is not available. A **turnkey construction contract** requires the contractor to have the project up and operating before releasing it to the owner. **Coproduction** involves a company's providing technical know-how and components in return for a share of the output that it must sell. **Countertrade** transactions include barter (direct exchange of goods—hams for aircraft), compensation packages (cash and local goods), counterpurchase (delayed sale of bartered goods to enable the local buyer to sell the goods), and a **buyback arrangement** in which the products being sold are used to produce other goods.

Overseas direct investment can be implemented in two ways: joint ventures or sole ownership. **Joint ventures** involve a joint ownership arrangement (e.g., one between a U.S. firm and one in the host country) to produce or market goods in a foreign country. Today, joint ventures are commonplace because they avoid quotas and import taxes and satisfy government demands to produce locally. They also have the advantage of sharing investment costs and gaining local marketing expertise. For example, Motorola had difficulty penetrating the Japanese market until it formed an alliance with Toshiba to set up a joint chip-making venture. In addition, Toshiba provided Motorola with marketing help.

A **sole ownership** investment entry strategy involves setting up a production facility in a foreign country. Direct investment usually allows the parent organization to retain total control of the overseas operation and avoids the problems of shared management and loss of flexibility. This strategy is particularly appropriate when the politics of the situation require a dedicated local facility. Firms using a direct investment strategy extensively include General Motors, Procter & Gamble, General Foods, Hewlett-Packard, and General Electric.

Exporting has the advantage of lowering the financial risk for a pioneer entering an unfamiliar foreign market. Unfortunately, such arrangements also afford a pioneer relatively little control over the marketing and distribution of its product or service—activities that are critical for winning customer awareness and loyalty in a new market. At the other extreme, investing in a wholly owned subsidiary typically makes little sense until it becomes clear that the pioneering product will win customer acceptance. Consequently, intermediate modes of entry, such as licensing or forming a joint venture with a local firm in the host country, tend to be the preferred means of developing global markets for new products. Joint ventures are particularly appropriate in this regard because they avoid quotas and import restrictions or taxes, and they allow a pioneer to share financial risks while gaining local marketing expertise.[15] Thus Bausch & Lomb established a joint venture with Beijing Optical as a basis for building contact lens factories in China and for gaining access to Chinese opticians. Consequently, the firm has been able to develop and maintain a leading market share in the world's most heavily populated country with a modest investment of only about $20 million.

Marketing Program Components for a Niche Penetration Strategy

Because the objectives of a niche penetration strategy are similar to but more narrowly focused than those of a mass-market strategy, the marketing program elements are also likely to be similar under the two strategies. Obviously, however, the niche penetrator should keep its marketing efforts clearly focused on the target segment to gain as much impact as possible from its limited resources. This point is evident in the outline of program components in Exhibit 9.8. For example, while a niche strategy calls for the same advertising, sales promotion, personal selling, and trade promotion activities as a mass-market program, the former should use more selective media, call schedules, and channel designs to precisely direct those activities toward the target segment.

Marketing Program Components for a Skimming Strategy

As Exhibit 9.8 suggests, one major difference between a skimming strategy and a mass-market penetration strategy involves pricing policies. A relatively high price is appropriate for a skimming strategy to increase margins and revenues, even though some price-sensitive customers may be reluctant to adopt the product at that price.[16] This also suggests that introductory promotional programs might best focus on customer groups who are least sensitive to price and most likely to be early adopters of the new product. This can help hold down promotion costs and avoid wasting marketing efforts on less profitable market segments. Thus, in many consumer goods businesses, skimming strategies focus on relatively upscale customers, since they are often more likely to be early adopters and less sensitive to price.

Another critical element of a skimming strategy is the nature of the firm's continuing product-development efforts. A pioneer that plans to leave a market when competitors enter should not devote much effort to expanding its product line through line extensions or multiple package sizes. Instead, it should concentrate on the next generation of technology or on identifying new application segments, in other words, preparing its avenue of escape from the market.

Now that we have examined some strategies a pioneer might follow in entering a new market, we are left with two important strategic questions. The pioneer is by definition the early share leader in the new market; hence the first question is, What adjustments in strategy might be necessary for the pioneer to *maintain its leading share position* after competitors arrive on the scene? The second is, What strategies might followers adopt *to take business away from the early leader and increase their relative share position* as the market grows? These two strategic issues are the focus of the next chapter.

TAKE AWAYS

- Being the pioneer in a new product or service category gains the firm a number of potential advantages. But not all pioneers are able to sustain a leading position in the market as it grows. A pioneering firm stands the best chance for long-term share leadership and profitability when the market can be insulated from the rapid entry of competitors by patent protection or other means and when the firm has the necessary resources and competencies to capitalize on its first-mover advantages.

- Evidence suggests that pioneers who successfully capitalize on their first-mover advantage and sustain a leading competitive position (*a*) introduce a quality product and pay careful attention to quality control, (*b*) have the capacity to enter on a large scale or the resources to expand rapidly as the market grows, (*c*) back the introduction with substantial promotion to build awareness and trial, and (*d*) rapidly expand the product line to satisfy multiple customer segments.

- Followers can trump the pioneer in a new product category if they can enter with more capacity backed by substantially larger marketing expenditures, or by leapfrogging the first mover with superior technology, product quality, or customer service.

- Not all pioneers attempt to penetrate the mass market and remain the share leader as that market grows. Some adopt a strategy geared to making profits from specialized niche markets where they will face fewer direct competitors. Still others try to stay one jump ahead of competitors by introducing a stream of new products and withdrawing from older markets as they become more competitive. The appropriate strategy to adopt depends on the firm's resources and competencies, the strength of likely competitors, and the characteristics of the product and its target market.

- Self-diagnostic questions to test your ability to apply the analytical tools and concepts in this chapter to marketing decision making may be found at this book's website at **www.mhhe.com/walker.**

ENDNOTES

1. This example is based on information found in Ronald Henkoff, "The Ultimate Nuts & Bolts Co.," *Fortune,* July 16, 1990, pp. 70–73; and I. Jeanne Dugan, Alison Rea, and Joseph Weber, "The Best Performers," *Business Week,* March 24, 1997, pp. 80–90; and at the Illinois Tool Works, Inc., website, www.itw.com.

2. These results are reported in Myron Magnet, "Let's Go for Growth," *Fortune,* March 7, 1994, pp. 60–72.

3. *New Products Management for the 1980s* (New York: Booz, Allen & Hamilton, 1982). More recent studies, though focusing on smaller samples of new products, suggest that the relative proportions of new-to-the-world versus less innovative product introductions have not changed substantially over the years. For example, see Eric M. Olson, Orville C. Walker Jr., and Robert W. Ruekert, "Organizing for Effective New Product Development: The Moderating Role of Product Innovativeness," *Journal of Marketing* 59 (January 1995), pp. 48–62.

4. For a more extensive review of the potential competitive advantages of being a first mover, and the controllable and uncontrollable forces that influence a firm's ability to capitalize on those potential advantages, see Roger A. Kerin, P. Rajan Varadarajan, and Robert A. Peterson, "First-Mover Advantage: A Synthesis, Conceptual Framework, and Research Propositions," *Journal of Marketing* 56 (October 1992), pp. 33–52; and David M. Szymanski, Lisa M. Troy, and Sundar J. Bharadwaj, "Order-of-Entry and Business Performance: An Empirical Synthesis and Reexamination," *Journal of Marketing* 59 (October 1995), pp. 17–33.

5. Thomas S. Gruca and D. Sudharshan, "A Framework for Entry Deterrence Strategy: The Competitive Environment, Choices, and Consequences," *Journal of Marketing* 59 (July 1995), pp. 44–55.

6. Carl Shapiro and Hal R. Varian, *Information Rules* (Boston: Harvard Business School Press, 1999), chap. 7.

7. For example, see William T. Robinson, "Market Pioneering and Sustainable Market Share Advantages in Industrial Goods Manufacturing Industries," working paper, Purdue University, 1984; and Robert D. Buzzell and Bradley T. Gale, *The PIMS Principles: Linking Strategy to Performance* (New York: Free Press, 1987), p. 183.

8. Peter N. Golder and Gerard J. Tellis, "Pioneer Advantage: Marketing Logic or Marketing Legend," *Journal of Marketing Research* 30 (May 1993), pp. 158–70.

9. Marvin B. Lieberman and David B. Montgomery, "First-Mover Advantages," *Strategic Management Journal* 9 (1988), pp. 41–59; and Michael J. Moore, William Boulding, and Ronald C. Goodstein, "Pioneering and Market Share: Is Entry Time Endogenous and Does It Matter?" *Journal of Marketing* 28 (February 1991), pp. 97–104.

10. Szymanski, Troy, and Bharadwaj, "Order-of-Entry and Business Performance."

11. Moore, Boulding, and Goodstein, "Pioneering and Market Share."

12. Mary L. Coyle, "Competition in Developing Markets: The Impact of Order of Entry," unpublished doctoral dissertation, University of Toronto, 1986. Also see Kerin, Varadarajan, and Peterson, "First-Mover Advantage."

13. George S. Day, *Analysis for Strategic Marketing Decisions* (St. Paul, MN: West, 1986), pp. 103–104.

14. Shapiro and Varian, *Information Rules,* chap. 2.

15. Franklin R. Root, *Entry Strategy for International Markets* (Lexington, MA: D. C. Heath, 1987). Also see Jeremy Main, "Making Global Alliances Work," *Fortune,* December 17, 1990, pp. 121–26.

16. This assumes that demand is relatively price inelastic. In markets where price elasticity is high, a skimming price strategy may lead to lower total revenues due to its dampening effect on total demand.

CHAPTER TEN

STRATEGIES FOR GROWTH MARKETS

Nike versus Vans: The Battle for Jocks' Hearts and Soles[1]

NIKE ATHLETIC SHOES began life in 1964—albeit under a different name—as a specialty product targeted at long-distance runners, a very narrow niche of the athletic footwear market. Phil Knight, a former distance runner at the University of Oregon, and his former coach Bill Bowerman believed that distance runners needed better shoes. With his wife's waffle iron and some latex, Bowerman developed the waffle outsole that would revolutionize the running shoe. Nike's new shoes were lighter and more flexible than competing shoes, with better lateral stability to protect against ankle sprains and more cushioning to help runners' bodies cope with miles and miles of repetitive impact.

The company struggled for years to strengthen its foothold in an industry dominated by much larger global competitors like Adidas. But in 1972 Nike finally gained the sporting world's attention when four of the top seven finishers in the Olympic marathon wore the firm's shoes. By 1974 Nike was America's best selling brand of training shoe, and the Nike brand was on the way to stardom.

Having become number one in training shoes, Nike set its sights on achieving share leadership in the entire industry. As a first step toward accomplishing that goal, the company invested heavily in new product R&D and design efforts to expand its product line with offerings tailored to the needs and preferences of participants in a wide variety of other sports. It held down costs by outsourcing production of the new lines to a number of offshore manufacturers. However, the firm maintained tight control over, and was much less frugal with, its marketing efforts. Nike spent heavily on endorsement deals with sport celebrities and on a series of stylish but edgy mass media ad campaigns to capture attention and build a strong brand image in its new target segments. It also constructed an extensive distribution network consisting largely of independent mass retailers and specialty chains like Footlocker.

In 1978, tennis great John McEnroe signed with the company and tennis shoes became a prominent part of the product line. In 1985, a promising Chicago Bulls rookie named Michael Jordan endorsed a line of Air Jordan shoes and apparel. By 1986, Nike's worldwide sales passed the billion-dollar mark and Nike had become the acknowledged technological leader in the footwear industry. Today, Nike offers a full line of shoes for virtually every athletic activity, it's the global leader in industry market share, and it dominates most segments of the market—with a few notable exceptions.

Boarders Are Bored with Nike

In 1995 Nike made a concerted run at capturing a dominant share of the shoe and apparel purchases of skateboarders, but stubbed its toe. These days, the brand of choice among boarders is tiny Vans Inc. The Santa Fe Springs, California, company pioneered thick-soled slip-on sneakers able to absorb the shock of a five-foot leap on wheels. The firm nurtures its cool image with an offbeat marketing program that forgoes media advertising and focuses instead on sponsorships, events, and other "experience" activities that fit the skateboard culture. The centerpiece of these marketing efforts is the elaborate skateboard parks Vans is building at malls around the country. The company also gets some broader media exposure by sponsoring events such as the Vans Triple Crown, a showcase for alternative sports ranging from skateboarding to BMX biking that is broadcast by NBC Sports. As Vans' CEO Gary Schoenfeld points out, "Our vision is not to hit our target audience over the head with ads, but to integrate ourselves into the places they are most likely to be."

Because the skateboarding craze was hot during the first years of the 21st century, Vans enjoyed heady growth. The company earned $15.5 million on sales of $336 million in its 2000 fiscal year, a 23 percent increase over the year before. True, that gives Vans less than 2 percent of an overall athletic shoe market that is half-owned by Nike, but the firm's focus on alternative sports fanatics has built an intensely loyal—and profitable—customer base.

While Vans would like to pursue growth by developing new products, it also wants to avoid offending loyal customers who love its maverick roots and outsider image. The company would rather preserve its dominance in a small but lucrative market niche than launch a risky and expensive battle for a bigger share of the entire market. Thus, the firm is experimenting with hiking boots, snowboard boots, and an expanded clothing line, but has steered clear of inline skates because skateboarders tend to see them as a wimpy offshoot.

Strategic Challenges Addressed in Chapter 10

While Nike was clearly not the pioneer of the athletic shoe industry, the firm's technical innovations, stylish designs, and savvy market segmentation strategy spurred a sustained period of market growth. Both conventional wisdom and the various portfolio models suggest there are advantages to be gained from a strategy of investing heavily to build and sustain a commanding share of a growing market, a strategy similar to Nike's. But a market is neither inherently attractive nor unattractive simply because it promises rapid future growth. And not all competitors have the resources and capabilities necessary to dominate an entire market, as Vans—with its limited marketing budget—seems well aware. Consequently, managers must consider how customer desires and the competitive situation are likely to evolve as a market grows, and determine whether their firms can exploit market growth to establish a sustainable advantage. Therefore, the next section of this chapter examines both the opportunities and competitive risks often found in growing product-markets.

The primary objective of the early share leader, usually the market pioneer, in a growth market is **share maintenance.** From a marketing perspective the firm must accomplish two important tasks: (1) retain repeat or replacement business from its existing customers and (2) continue to capture the major portion of sales to the growing number of new customers entering the market for the first time. The leader might use any of several marketing strategies to accomplish these objectives. It might try to build on its early scale and experience advantages to achieve low-cost production and reduce its prices. Alternatively, the leader might focus on rapid product improvements, expand its product line to appeal to newly emerging segments, or increase its marketing and sales efforts, all of which Nike employed in building global leadership in the athletic footwear market.

The second section of this chapter explores marketing strategies—both defensive and offensive—that leaders might use to maintain a dominant market share in the face of continuing growth and increasing competition.

A challenger's strategic objective in a growth market is usually to build its share by expanding its sales faster than the overall market growth rate. Firms do this by stealing existing customers away from the leader or other competitors, capturing a larger share of new customers than the market leader, or both. Once again, challengers might use a number of strategies to accomplish these objectives. These include developing a superior product technology; differentiating through rapid product innovations, line extensions, or customer service; offering lower prices; or focusing on market niches where the leader is not well established, as Van's has done in the skateboarding segment. The fourth section details these and other **share-growth** strategies that market challengers use under different conditions.

The success of a firm's strategy during the growth stage is a critical determinant of its ability to reap profits, or even survive, as a product-market moves toward maturity. Unfortunately, the growth stage is often short; and increasingly rapid technological change and market fragmentation are causing it to become even shorter in many industries.[2] This shortening of the growth stage concerns many firms—particularly late entrants or those who fail to acquire a substantial market share—because as growth slows during the transition to maturity, there is often a shakeout of marginal competitors. Thus, when choosing marketing strategies for competing in a growing product-market, managers should keep one eye on building a competitive advantage that the business can sustain as growth slows and the market matures.

OPPORTUNITIES AND RISKS IN GROWTH MARKETS[3]

Why are followers attracted to rapidly growing markets? Conventional wisdom suggests such markets present attractive opportunities for future profits because

- It is easier to gain share when a market is growing.
- Share gains are worth more in a growth market than in a mature market.
- Price competition is likely to be less intense.
- Early participation in a growth market is necessary to make sure that the firm keeps pace with the technology.

While generally valid, each of these premises may be seriously misleading for a particular business in a specific situation. Many followers attracted to a market by its rapid growth rate are likely to be shaken out later when growth slows because either the preceding premises did not hold or they could not exploit growth advantages sufficiently to build a sustainable competitive position. By understanding the limitations of the assumptions about growth markets and the conditions under which they are most likely to hold, a manager can make better decisions about entering a market and the kind of marketing strategy likely to be most effective in doing so.

Gaining Share Is Easier

The premise that it is easier for a business to increase its share in a growing market is based on two arguments. First, there may be many potential new users who have no established brand loyalties or supplier commitments and who may have different needs or preferences than earlier adopters. Thus there may be gaps or undeveloped segments in the market. It is easier, then, for a new competitor to attract those potential new users than to convert customers in a mature market. Second, established competitors are less likely to react aggressively to market-share erosion as long as their sales continue to grow at a satisfactory rate.

There is some truth to the first argument. It usually is easier for a new entrant to attract first-time users than to take business away from entrenched competitors. To take full advantage of the situation, however, the new entrant must be able to develop a product offering that new customers perceive as more attractive than other alternatives, and it must have the marketing resources and competence to effectively persuade them of that fact. This can be difficult, especially when the pioneer has had months or years to influence potential customers' decision criteria and preferences.[4]

The notion that established competitors are less likely to react to share losses so long as their revenues are growing at an acceptable rate is more tenuous. It overlooks the fact that those competitors may have higher expectations for increased revenues when the market itself is growing. Capital investments and annual operating budgets are usually tied to those sales expectations; therefore, competitors are likely to react aggressively when sales fall below expected levels whether or not their absolute volumes continue to grow. This is particularly true given that increased competition will likely erode the leader's relative market share even though its volume may continue to increase. As illustrated by the hypothetical example in Exhibit 10.1, the leader's market share might drop from a high of 100

Exhibit 10.1

MARKET SHARES OF THE LEADER AND FOLLOWERS OVER THE LIFE CYCLE OF A HYPOTHETICAL MARKET

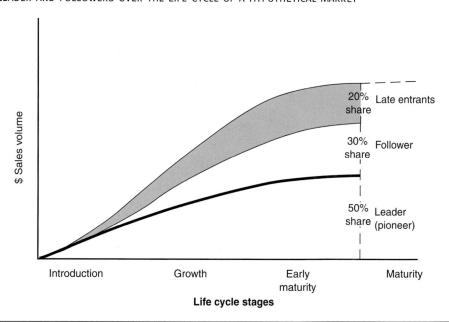

Source: From *Analysis for Strategic Market Decisions,* 1st edition, by G. S. Day © 1986. Reprinted with permission of South-Western College Publishing, a division of Thomson Learning. Fax 800-730-2215.

percent at the beginning of the growth stage to 50 percent by the maturity stage, even though the firm's absolute volume shows steady growth.

Industry leaders often react forcefully when their sales growth falls below industry levels, or when the industry's growth rate slows. For example, when growth in the personal computer market slumped in 2000 due to the dot-com crash and other factors, Dell Computer did not adjust its aggressive sales growth objective. Instead, it launched a brutal price war aimed at taking more business away from competitors in order to achieve its goal. Because Dell's focus on direct selling over the Internet, its build-to-order manufacturing system, and its tightly integrated supply chain made it the undisputed low-cost producer in the industry, Dell was able to slash gross margins from 21.3 percent in mid-2000 to 17.5 percent in mid-2001 and still make money. As a result, Dell's leading share of the global PC market increased from 10 percent to 13 percent by July of 2001. And while the firm earned $360 million in profits through the first half of 2001, its competitors suffered a total of $1.1 billion in losses.[5]

Share Gains Are Worth More

The premise that share gains are more valuable when the market is growing stems from the expectation that the earnings produced by each share point continue to expand as the market expands. The implicit assumption in this argument, of course, is that the business can hold its relative share as the market grows. The validity of such an assumption depends on a number of factors, including the following:

- *The existence of positive network effects.* As we saw in the previous chapter, pioneers in new product-markets enjoy several potential competitive advantages that they can—but don't always manage to—leverage as the market grows. For information-based products, such as computer software or Internet auction sites, one of the most important such advantage is the existence of positive network effects, the tendency for the product to become more valuable to users as the number of adopters grows. Such network effects increase the likelihood that an early share leader can sustain, and even increase, its relative share as the market grows. As Microsoft was able to license its Windows operating system to a growing number of computer manufacturers, for example, software developers created more and more applications to run on Windows, which made Windows even more attractive to later computer buyers and helped Microsoft expand its already commanding market share.

- *Future changes in technology or other key success factors.* On the other hand, if the rules of the game change, the competencies a firm relied on to capture share may no longer be adequate to maintain that share. For instance, Sony was the pioneer and early share leader in the videocassette recorder industry with its Betamax technology. But Matsushita's longer-playing and lower-priced VHS format equipment ultimately proved much more popular with consumers, captured a commanding portion of the market, and dethroned Sony as industry leader.

- *Future competitive structure of the industry.* The number of firms that ultimately decide to compete for a share of the market may turn out to be larger than the early entrants anticipate, particularly if there are few barriers to entry. The sheer weight of numbers can make it difficult for any single competitor to maintain a substantial relative share of the total market.

- *Future fragmentation of the market.* As the market expands, it may fragment into numerous small segments, particularly if potential customers have relatively heterogeneous functional, distribution, or service needs. When such fragmentation occurs, the market in which a given competitor competes may shrink as segments splinter away.

In addition to these possible changes in future market conditions, a firm's ability to hold its early gains in market share also depends on how it obtained them. If a firm captures share through short-term promotions or price cuts that competitors can easily match and that may tarnish its image among customers, its gains may be short-lived.

Price Competition Is Likely to Be Less Intense

In many rapidly growing markets demand exceeds supply. The market exerts little pressure on prices initially; the excess demand may even support a price premium. Thus, early entry provides a good opportunity for a firm to recover its initial product development and commercialization investment relatively quickly. New customers also may be willing to pay a premium for technical service as they learn how to make full use of the new product. In contrast, as the market matures and customers gain more experience, the premium a firm can charge without losing market share slowly shrinks; it eventually may disappear entirely.[6]

However, this scenario does not hold true in every developing product-market. If there are few barriers to entry or if the adoption process is protracted and new customers enter the market slowly, demand may not exceed supply—at least not for very long. Also, the pioneer, or one of the earliest followers, might adopt a penetration strategy and set its initial prices relatively low to move quickly down the experience curve and discourage other potential competitors from entering the market.

Early Entry Is Necessary to Maintain Technical Expertise

In high-tech industries early involvement in new product categories may be critical for staying abreast of technology. The early experience gained in developing the first generation of products and in helping customers apply the new technology can put the firm in a strong position for developing the next generation of superior products. Later entrants, lacking such customer contact and production and R&D experience, are likely to be at a disadvantage.

There is substantial wisdom in these arguments. Sometimes, however, an early commitment to a specific technology can turn out to be a liability. This is particularly true when multiple unrelated technologies might serve a market or when a newly emerging technology might replace the current one. Once a firm is committed to one technology, adopting a new one can be difficult. Management is often reluctant to abandon a technology in which it has made substantial investments, and it might worry that a rapid shift to a new technology will upset present customers. As a result, early commitment to a technology has become increasingly problematic because of more rapid rates of technological change. This problem is dramatically illustrated by the experience of Medtronic, Inc., as described in Exhibit 10.2.

Exhibit 10.2   Medtronic's Commitment to an Old Technology Cost It Sales and Market Share

The dangers inherent in being overly committed to an early technology are demonstrated by Medtronic, Inc., the pioneer in the cardiac pacemaker industry. Medtronic was reluctant to switch to a new lithium-based technology that enabled pacemakers to work much longer before being replaced. As a result, several Medtronic employees left the company and founded Cardiac Pacemakers Inc. to produce and market the new lithium-based product. They quickly captured nearly 20 percent of the total market. And Medtronic saw its share of the cardiac pacemaker market fall rapidly from nearly 70 percent to 40 percent.

Source: Reprinted from "Managing Innovation: Insights from the Cardiac-Pacing Industry," by Daniel H. Gobeli and William Rudelius, *MIT Sloan Management Review*, Summer 1985, pp. 29–43, permission of the publisher. Copyright 1985 by Massachusetts Institute of Technology. All rights reserved.

GROWTH-MARKET STRATEGIES FOR MARKET LEADERS

For the share leader in a growing market, of course, the question of the relative advantages versus risks of market entry is moot. The leader is typically the pioneer, or at least one of the first entrants, who developed the product-market in the first place. Often, that firm's strategic objective is to maintain its leading share position in the face of increasing competition as the market expands. Share maintenance may not seem like a very aggressive objective, because it implies the business is merely trying to stay even rather than forge ahead. But two important facts must be kept in mind.

First, the dynamics of a growth market—including the increasing number of competitors, the fragmentation of market segments, and the threat of product innovation from within and outside the industry—make maintaining an early lead in relative market share very difficult. The continuing need for investment to finance growth, the likely negative cash flows that result, and the threat of governmental antitrust action can make it even more difficult. For example, 31 percent of the 877 market-share leaders in the PIMS database experienced losses in relative share, and leaders were especially likely to suffer this fate when their market shares were very large.[7]

Second, a firm can maintain its current share position in a growth market only if its sales volume continues to grow at a rate equal to that of the overall market, enabling the firm to stay even in *absolute* market share. However, it may be able to maintain a relative share lead even if its volume growth is less than the industry's.

Marketing Objectives for Share Leaders

Share maintenance for a market leader involves two important marketing objectives. First, the firm must *retain its current customers,* ensuring that those customers remain brand loyal when making repeat or replacement purchases. This is particularly critical for firms in consumer nondurable, service, and industrial materials and components industries where a substantial portion of total sales volume consists of repeat purchases. Second, the firm must *stimulate selective demand among later adopters* to ensure that it captures a large share of the continuing growth in industry sales.

In some cases the market leader might pursue a third objective: stimulating primary demand to help speed up overall market growth. This can be particularly important in product-markets where the adoption process is protracted because of the technical sophistication of the new product, high switching costs for potential customers, or positive network effects.

The market leader is the logical one to stimulate market growth in such situations; it has the most to gain from increased volume, assuming it can maintain its relative share of that volume. However, expanding total demand—by promoting new uses for the product or stimulating existing customers' usage and repeat purchase rates—is often more critical near the end of the growth stage and early in the maturity stage of a product's life cycle. Consequently, we discuss marketing actions appropriate to this objective in the next chapter.

Marketing Actions and Strategies to Achieve Share-Maintenance Objectives

A business might take a variety of marketing actions to maintain a leading share position in a growing market. Exhibit 10.3 outlines a lengthy, though not exhaustive, list of such actions and their specific marketing objectives. Because share maintenance involves multiple objectives,

Exhibit 10.3

MARKETING ACTIONS TO ACHIEVE SHARE-MAINTENANCE OBJECTIVES

Marketing objectives	Possible marketing actions
Retain current customers by	
• Maintaining/improving satisfaction and loyalty.	• Increase attention to quality control as output expands.
	• Continue product modification and improvement efforts to increase customer benefits and/or reduce costs.
	• Focus advertising on stimulation of selective demand; stress product's superior features and benefits; reminder advertising.
	• Increase salesforce's servicing of current accounts; consider formation of national or key account representatives to major customers; consider replacing independent manufacturer's reps with company salespeople where appropriate.
	• Expand postsale service capabilities; develop or expand company's own service force, or develop training programs for distributors' and dealers' service people; expand parts inventory; develop customer service hotline or website.
• Encouraging/simplifying repeat purchase.	• Expand production capacity in advance of increasing demand to avoid stockouts.
	• Improve inventory control and logistics systems to reduce delivery times.
	• Continue to build distribution channels; use periodic trade promotions to gain more extensive retail coverage and maintain shelf-facings; strengthen relationships with strongest distributors/dealers.
	• Consider negotiating long-term requirements contracts with major customers.
	• Consider developing automatic reorder systems or logistical alliances.
• Reducing attractiveness of switching.	• Develop a second brand or product line with features or price more appealing to a specific segment of current customers (*flanker strategy*—see Exhibits 10.4 and 10.5).
	• Develop multiple-line extensions or brand offerings targeted to the needs of several user segments within the market (*market expansion*).
	• Meet or beat lower prices or heavier promotional efforts by competitors—or try to preempt such efforts by potential competitors—when necessary to retain customers and when lower unit costs allow (*confrontation strategy*).
Stimulate selective demand among later adopters by	
• Head-to-head positioning against competitive offerings or potential offerings.	• Develop a second brand or product line with features or price more appealing to a specific segment of potential customers (*flanker strategy*).
	• Make product modifications or improvements to match or beat superior competitive offerings (*confrontation strategy*).
	• Meet or beat lower prices or heavier promotional efforts by competitors when necessary to retain customers and when lower unit costs allow (*confrontation strategy*).
	• When resources are limited relative to a competitor's, consider withdrawing from smaller or slower growing segments to focus product development and promotional efforts on higher potential segments threatened by competitor (*contraction or strategic withdrawal strategy*).
• Differentiated positioning against competitive offerings or potential offerings.	• Develop multiple-line extensions or brand offerings targeted to the needs of various potential user applications or geographical segments within the market (*market expansion strategy*).
	• Build unique distribution channels to more effectively reach specific segments of potential customers (*market expansion strategy*).
	• Design multiple advertising and/or sales promotion campaigns targeted at specific segments of potential customers (*market expansion strategy*).

and different marketing actions may be needed to achieve each one, a strategic marketing program usually integrates a mix of the actions outlined in the exhibit.

Not all the actions summarized in Exhibit 10.3 are consistent with one another. It would be unusual, for instance, for a business to invest heavily in new product improvements and promotion to enhance its product's high-quality image and simultaneously slash prices, unless it was trying to drive out weaker competitors in the short run with an eye on higher profits in the future. Thus, the activities outlined in Exhibit 10.3 cluster into five internally consistent strategies that a market leader might employ, singly or in combination, to maintain its leading share position: a **fortress, or position defense, strategy; a flanker strategy; a confrontation strategy; a market expansion strategy;** and a **contraction, or strategic withdrawal, strategy.**

Exhibit 10.4 diagrams this set of strategies. It is consistent with what a number of military strategists and some marketing authorities have identified as common defensive strategies.[8] To think of them as strictly defensive, though, can be misleading. Companies can use some of these strategies offensively to preempt expected future actions by potential competitors. Or they can use them to capture an even larger share of future new customers.

Which, or what combination, of these five strategies is most appropriate for a particular product-market depends on (1) the market's size and its customers' characteristics, (2) the number and relative strengths of the competitors or potential competitors in that market, and (3) the leader's own resources and competencies. Exhibit 10.5 outlines the situations in

Exhibit 10.4

STRATEGIC CHOICES FOR SHARE LEADERS IN GROWTH MARKETS

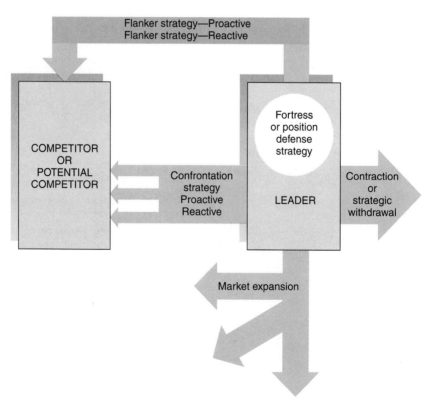

Source: P. Kotler and R. Singh Achrol, "Marketing Warfare in the 1980's," *Journal of Business Strategy,* Winter 1981. Republished with permission-EC Media Group, Eleven Penn Plaza, New York, NY 10001.

Exhibit 10.5

MARKETING OBJECTIVES AND STRATEGIES FOR SHARE LEADERS IN GROWTH MARKETS

SHARE MAINTENANCE STRATEGIES

Situational variables	Fortress or position defense	Flanker	Confrontation	Market expansion	Contraction or strategic withdrawal
Primary objective	Increase satisfaction, loyalty, and repeat purchase among current customers by building on existing strengths; appeal to late adopters with same attributes and benefits offered to early adopters.	Protect against loss of specific segments of current customers by developing a second entry that covers a weakness in original offering; improve ability to attract new customers with specific needs or purchase criteria different from those of early adopters.	Protect against loss of share among current customers by meeting or beating a head-to-head competitive offering; improve ability to win new customers who might otherwise be attracted to competitor's offering.	Increase ability to attract new customers by developing new product offerings or line extensions aimed at a variety of new applications and user segments; improve ability to retain current customers as market fragments.	Increase ability to attract new customers in selected high-growth segments by focusing offerings and resources on those segments; withdraw from smaller or slower-growing segments to conserve resources.
Market characteristics	Relatively homogeneous market with respect to customer needs and purchase criteria; strong preference for leader's product among largest segment of customers.	Two or more major market segments with distinct needs or purchase criteria.	Relatively homogeneous market with respect to customers' needs and purchase criteria; little preference for, or loyalty toward, leader's product among largest segment of customers.	Relatively heterogeneous market with respect to customers' needs and purchase criteria; multiple product uses requiring different product or service attributes.	Relatively heterogeneous market with respect to customers' needs, purchase criteria, and growth potential; multiple product uses requiring different product or service attributes.
Competitors' characteristics	Current and potential competitors have relatively limited resources and competencies.	One or more current or potential competitors with sufficient resources and competencies to effectively implement a differentiation strategy.	One or more current or potential competitors with sufficient resources and competencies to effectively implement a head-to-head strategy.	Current and potential competitors have relatively limited resources and competencies, particularly with respect to R&D and marketing.	One or more current or potential competitors with sufficient resources and competencies to present a strong challenge in one or more growth segments.
Firm's characteristics	Current product offering enjoys high awareness and preference among major segment of current and potential customers; firm has marketing and R&D resources and competencies equal to or greater than any current or potential competitor.	Current product offering perceived as weak on at least one attribute by a major segment of current or potential customers; firm has sufficient R&D and marketing resources to introduce and support a second offering aimed at the disaffected segment.	Current product offering suffers low awareness, preference, and/or loyalty among major segment of current or potential customers; firm has R&D and marketing resources and competencies equal to or greater than any current or potential competitor.	No current offerings in one or more potential applications segments; firm has marketing and R&D resources and competencies equal to or greater than any current or potential competitor.	Current product offering suffers low awareness, preference, and/or loyalty among current or potential customers in one or more major growth segments; firm's R&D and marketing resources and competencies are limited relative to those of one or more competitors.

which each strategy is most appropriate and the primary objectives for which they are best suited.

Fortress, or Position Defense, Strategy

The most basic defensive strategy is to continually strengthen a strongly held current position—to build an impregnable fortress capable of repelling attacks by current or future competitors. This strategy is nearly always part of a leader's share-maintenance efforts. By shoring up an already strong position, the firm can improve the satisfaction of current customers while increasing the attractiveness of its offering to new customers with needs and characteristics similar to those of earlier adopters.

Strengthening the firm's position makes particularly good sense when current and potential customers have relatively homogeneous needs and desires and the firm's offering already enjoys a high level of awareness and preference in the mass market. In some homogeneous markets, a well-implemented position defense strategy may be all that is needed for share maintenance.

Most of the marketing actions listed in Exhibit 10.3 as being relevant for retaining current customers might be incorporated into a position defense strategy. Anything the business can do to improve customer satisfaction and loyalty and encourage and simplify repeat purchasing should help the firm protect its current customer base and make its offering more attractive to new customers. Some of the specific actions appropriate for accomplishing these two objectives are discussed in more detail below.

Actions to Improve Customer Satisfaction and Loyalty   The rapid expansion of output necessary to keep up with a growth market often can lead to quality control problems for the market leader. As new plants, equipment, and personnel are quickly brought on line, bugs can suddenly appear in the production process. Thus, the leader must pay particular attention to quality control during this phase. Most customers have only limited, if any, positive past experiences with the new brand to offset their disappointment when a purchase does not live up to expectations.

Perhaps the most obvious way a leader can strengthen its position is to continue to modify and improve its product. This can reduce the opportunities for competitors to differentiate their products by designing in features or performance levels the leader does not offer. The leader might also try to reduce unit costs to discourage low-price competition.

The leader should take steps to improve not only the physical product but customers' perceptions of it as well. As competitors enter or prepare to enter the market, the leader's advertising and sales promotion emphasis should shift from stimulating primary demand to building selective demand for the company's brand. This usually involves creating appeals that emphasize the brand's superior features and benefits. While the leader may continue sales promotion efforts aimed at stimulating trial among later adopters, some of those efforts might be shifted toward encouraging repeat purchases among existing customers. For instance, it might include cents-off coupons inside the package to give customers a price break on their next purchases of the brand.

For industrial goods, some salesforce efforts should shift from prospecting for new accounts to servicing existing customers. Firms that relied on independent manufacturer's reps to introduce their new product might consider replacing them with company salespeople to increase the customer service orientation of their sales efforts. Firms whose own salespeople introduced the product might reorganize their salesforces into specialized groups focused on major industries or user segments. Or they might assign key account representatives, or cross-functional account teams, to service their largest customers.

Finally, a leader can strengthen its position as the market grows by giving increased attention to postsale service. Rapid growth in demand not only can outstrip a firm's ability to produce a high-quality product, but it also can overload the firm's ability to service customers. This can lead to a loss of existing customers as well as negative word of mouth that might inhibit the firm's ability to attract new users. Thus, the growth phase often requires increased investments to expand the firm's parts inventory, hire and train service personnel and dealers, and improve the information content on the firm's website.

Actions to Encourage and Simplify Repeat Purchasing   One of the most critical actions a leader must take to ensure that customers continue buying its product is to maximize its availability. It must reduce stockouts on retail store shelves or shorten delivery times for industrial goods. To do this, the firm must invest in plant and equipment to expand capacity in advance of demand, and it must implement adequate inventory control and logistics systems to provide a steady flow of goods through the distribution system. The firm also should continue to build its distribution channels. In some cases, a firm might even vertically integrate parts of its distribution system—such as building its own warehouses, as Amazon.com and several other e-tailers have done recently—to gain better control over order fulfillment activities and ensure quick and reliable deliveries.

Some market leaders, particularly in industrial goods markets, can take more proactive steps to turn their major customers into captives and help guarantee future purchases. For example, a firm might negotiate requirements contracts or guaranteed price agreements with its customers to ensure future purchases, or it might tie them into a computerized reorder system or a tightly integrated supply-chain relationship. Such actions are all aimed at increasing customers' repeat purchases and loyalty in order to maximize their lifetime value. While it makes good sense to begin building strong customer relationships right from the beginning, they become even more crucial as the market matures and competition to win over established customers becomes more intense. Consequently, we'll have more to say about building and managing customer relationships in the next chapter.

Flanker Strategy

One shortcoming of a fortress strategy is that a challenger might simply choose to bypass the leader's fortress and try to capture territory where the leader has not yet established a strong presence. This can represent a particular threat when the market is fragmented into major segments with different needs and preferences and the leader's current brand does not meet the needs of one or more of those segments. A competitor with sufficient resources and competencies can develop a differentiated product offering to appeal to the segment where the leader is weak and thereby capture a substantial share of the overall market.

To defend against an attack directed at a weakness in its current offering (its exposed flank), a leader might develop a second brand (a **flanker** or **fighting brand**) to compete directly against the challenger's offering. This might involve trading up, where the leader develops a high-quality brand offered at a higher price to appeal to the prestige segment of the market. This was Toyota's rationale for introducing its Lexus brand of luxury automobiles, for instance.

More commonly, though, a flanker brand is a lower-quality product designed to appeal to a low-price segment to protect the leader's primary brand from direct price competition. Pillsbury's premium-quality Hungry Jack brand holds the major share of the refrigerated biscuit dough market; however, a substantial number of consumers prefer to pay less for a somewhat lower-quality biscuit. Rather than conceding that low-price segment to competitors, or reducing Hungry Jack prices and margins in an attempt to attract price-sensitive consumers, Pillsbury introduced Ballard, a low-priced flanker brand.

A flanker strategy is always used in conjunction with a position defense strategy. The leader simultaneously strengthens its primary brand while introducing a flanker to compete in segments where the primary brand is vulnerable. This suggests that a flanker strategy is appropriate only when the firm has sufficient resources to develop and fully support two or more entries. After all, a flanker is of little value if it is so lightly supported that a competitor can easily wipe it out.

Confrontation Strategy

Suppose a competitor chooses to attack the leader head to head and attempts to steal customers in the leader's main target market. If the leader has established a strong position and attained a high level of preference and loyalty among customers and the trade, it may be able to sit back and wait for the competitor to fail. In many cases, though, the leader's brand is not strong enough to withstand a frontal assault from a well-funded, competent competitor. Even mighty IBM, for instance, lost 20 market-share points in the commercial PC market during the mid-1980s to competitors such as Compaq, whose machines cost about the same but offered features or performance levels that were better, and to the clones who offered IBM-compatible machines at much lower prices. Later, the firm's share of the PC market eroded further as companies such as Dell and Gateway introduced more convenient and efficient Internet ordering and direct distribution systems and cut prices even more.

In such situations, the leader may have no choice but to confront the competitive threat directly. If the leader's competitive intelligence is good, it may decide to move proactively and change its marketing program before a suspected competitive challenge occurs. A confrontational strategy, though, is more commonly reactive. The leader usually decides to meet or beat the attractive features of a competitor's offering—by making product improvements, increasing promotional efforts, or lowering prices—only after the challenger's success has become obvious.

Simply meeting the improved features or lower price of a challenger, however, does nothing to reestablish a sustainable competitive advantage for the leader. And a confrontation based largely on lowering prices creates an additional problem of shrinking margins for all concerned.[9] Unless decreased prices generate substantial new industry volume and the leader's production costs fall with that increasing volume, the leader may be better off responding to price threats with increased promotion or product improvements while trying to maintain its profit margins. Evidence also suggests that in product-markets with high repeat-purchase rates or a protracted diffusion process, the leader may be wise to adopt a penetration pricing policy in the first place. This would strengthen its share position and might preempt low-price competitors from entering.[10]

STRATEGIC ISSUE

Simply meeting the improved features or lower price of a challenger, however, does nothing to reestablish a sustainable competitive advantage for the leader.

The leader can avoid the problems of a confrontation strategy by reestablishing the competitive advantage eroded by challengers' frontal attacks. But this typically requires additional investments in process improvements aimed at reducing unit costs, improvements in product quality or customer service, or even the development of the next generation of improved products to offer customers greater value for their dollars.

Market Expansion Strategy

A market expansion strategy is a more aggressive and proactive version of the flanker strategy. Here the leader defends its relative market share by expanding into a number of market segments. This strategy's primary objective is to capture a large share of new customer groups who may prefer something different from the firm's initial offering, protecting the firm from future competitive threats from a number of directions. Such a strategy is particularly appropriate in fragmented markets if the leader has the resources to undertake multiple product development and marketing efforts.

The most obvious way a leader can implement a market expansion strategy is to develop line extensions, new brands, or even alternative product forms utilizing similar technologies to appeal to multiple market segments. For instance, although Pillsbury holds a strong position in the refrigerated biscuit dough category, biscuit consumption is concentrated among older, more traditional consumers in the South. To expand its total market, gain increased experience-curve effects, and protect its overall technological lead, Pillsbury developed a variety of other product forms that use the same refrigerated dough technology and production facilities but appeal to different customer segments. The expanded line includes crescent rolls, Danish rolls, and soft breadsticks. Similarly, Nike captured and has sustained a leading share of the athletic shoe market by developing a series of line extensions offering technical, design, and style features tailored to the preferences of enthusiasts in nearly every sport.

A less-expensive way to appeal to a variety of customer segments is to retain the basic product but vary other elements of the marketing program to make it relatively more attractive to specific users. Thus, a leader might create specialized salesforces to deal with the unique concerns of different user groups. Or it might offer different ancillary services to different types of customers or tailor sales promotion efforts to different segments. Thus, performing arts groups often promote reduced ticket prices, transportation services, and other inducements to attract senior citizens and students to matinee performances.

Contraction, or Strategic Withdrawal, Strategy

In some highly fragmented markets, a leader may be unable to defend itself adequately in all segments. This is particularly likely when newly emerging competitors have more resources than the leader. The firm may then have to reduce or abandon its efforts in some segments to focus on areas where it enjoys the greatest relative advantages or that have the greatest potential for future growth. Even some very large firms may decide that certain segments are not profitable enough to continue pursuing. For example, IBM made an early attempt to capture the low end of the home hobbiest market for personal computers with the introduction of the PC Jr. But the firm eventually abandoned that effort to concentrate on the more lucrative commercial and education segments.

SHARE-GROWTH STRATEGIES FOR FOLLOWERS

Marketing Objectives for Followers

Not all late entrants to a growing product-market have illusions about eventually surpassing the leader and capturing a dominant market share. Some competitors, particularly those with limited resources and competencies, may simply seek to build a small but profitable business within a specialized segment of the larger market that earlier entrants have overlooked, as Vans has done with great success in the skateboarder segment of the athletic shoe market. As we have seen, this kind of *niche strategy* is one of the few entry options that small, late entrants can pursue with a reasonable degree of success. If a firm can successfully build a profitable business in a small segment while avoiding direct competition with larger competitors, it often can survive the shakeout period near the end of the growth stage and remain profitable throughout the maturity stage.

Exhibit 10.6

Marketing objectives	Possible marketing actions
Capture repeat/replacement purchases from current customers of the leader or other target competitor by	

• Head-to-head positioning against competitor's offering in primary target market.	• Develop products with features and/or performance levels superior to those of the target competitor.
	• Draw on superior product design, process engineering, and supplier relationships to achieve lower unit costs.
	• Set prices below target competitor's for comparable level of quality or performance, but only if low-cost position is achieved.
	• Outspend the target competitor on promotion aimed at stimulating selective demand:
	    Comparative advertising appeals directed at gaining a more favorable positioning than the target competitor's brand enjoys among customers in the mass market.
	    Sales promotions to encourage trial if offering's quality or performance is perceptively better than target competitor's, or induce brand switching.
	    More extensive and/or better-trained salesforce than target competitor's.
	• Outspend the target competitor on trade promotion to attain more extensive retail coverage, better shelf space, and/or representation by the best distributors/dealers.
	• Outperform the target competitor on customer service:
	    Develop superior production scheduling, inventory control, and logistics systems to minimize delivery times and stockouts.
	    Develop superior postsale service capabilities. Build a more extensive company service force, or provide better training programs for distributor/dealer service people than those of target competitor.

• Technological differentiation from target competitor's offering in its primary target market.	• Develop a new generation of products based on different technology that offers superior performance or additional benefits desired by current and potential customers in the mass market (*leapfrog strategy*).
	• Build awareness, preference, and replacement demand through heavy introductory promotion:
	    Comparative advertising stressing product's superiority.
	    Sales promotions to stimulate trial or encourage switching.
	    Extensive, well-trained salesforce; heavy use of product demonstrations in sales presentations.
	• Build adequate distribution through trade promotions and dealer training programs.

Stimulate selective demand among later adopters by	
• Head-to-head positioning against target competitor's offering in established market segments.	• See preceding actions.
• Differentiated positioning focused on untapped or underdeveloped segments.	• Develop a differentiated brand or product line with unique features or prices that is more appealing to a major segment of potential customers whose needs are not met by existing offerings (*flanking strategy*). or • Develop multiple line extensions or brand offerings with features or prices targeted to the unique needs and preferences of several smaller potential applications or regional segments (*encirclement strategy*). • Design advertising, personal selling, and/or sales promotion campaigns that address specific interests and concerns of potential customers in one or multiple underdeveloped segments to stimulate selective demand. • Build unique distribution channels to more effectively reach potential customers in one or multiple underdeveloped segments. • Design service programs to reduce the perceived risks of trial and/or solve the unique problems faced by potential customers in one or multiple underdeveloped segments (e.g., systems engineering, installation, operator training, extended warranties, service hotline, or website).

Many followers, particularly larger firms entering a product-market shortly after the pioneer, have more grandiose objectives. They often seek to displace the leader or at least to become a powerful competitor within the total market. Thus, their major marketing objective is to attain *share growth,* and the size of the increased relative share such challengers seek is usually substantial. For instance, while Cisco Systems holds a dominant 80 percent share of the market for the routers that direct data to the right places on the Internet, it was a late entrant into the market for switching systems used by telephone companies to direct voice traffic. In 1999, Cisco held less than a 1 percent share of the $225 billion market for telephone equipment. Nevertheless, it announced its intention to become the global share leader in that market.[11]

Marketing Actions and Strategies to Achieve Share Growth

A challenger with visions of taking over the leading share position in an industry has two basic strategic options, each involving somewhat different marketing objectives and actions. Where the share leader and perhaps some other early followers have already penetrated a large portion of the potential market, a challenger may have no choice but to *steal away some of the repeat purchase or replacement demand from the competitors' current customers.* As Exhibit 10.6 indicates, the challenger can attempt this through marketing activities that give it an advantage in a head-to-head confrontation with a target competitor. Or it can attempt to leapfrog over the leader by developing a new generation of products with enough benefits to induce customers to trade in their existing brand for a new one. Secondarily, such actions also may help the challenger attract a larger share of late adopters in the mass market.

If the market is relatively early in the growth phase and no previous entrant has captured a commanding share of potential customers, the challenger can focus on *attracting a larger share of potential new customers* who enter the market for the first time. This also may be a viable option when the overall market is heterogeneous and fragmented and the current share leader has established a strong position in only one or a few segments. In either case, the primary marketing activities for increasing share via this approach should aim at *differentiating* the challenger's offering from those of existing competitors by making it more appealing to new customers in untapped or underdeveloped market segments.

Once again, Exhibit 10.6's list of possible marketing actions for challengers is not exhaustive, and it contains actions that do not always fit well together. The activities that do fit tend to cluster into five major strategies that a challenger might use singly or in combination to secure growth in its relative market share. As Exhibit 10.7 indicates, these five share-growth strategies are *frontal attack, leapfrog strategy, flanking attack, encirclement,* and *guerrilla attack.* Most of these strategies are basically mirror images of the share-maintenance strategies discussed earlier.

Which, or what combination, of these five strategies is best for a particular challenger depends on market characteristics, the existing competitors' current positions and strengths, and the challenger's own resources and competencies. The situations in which each strategy is likely to work best are briefly outlined in Exhibit 10.8 and discussed in the following sections.

Deciding Whom to Attack

When more than one competitor is already established in the market, a challenger must decide which competitor, if any, to target. There are several options:

Exhibit 10.7

STRATEGIC CHOICES FOR CHALLENGERS IN GROWTH MARKETS

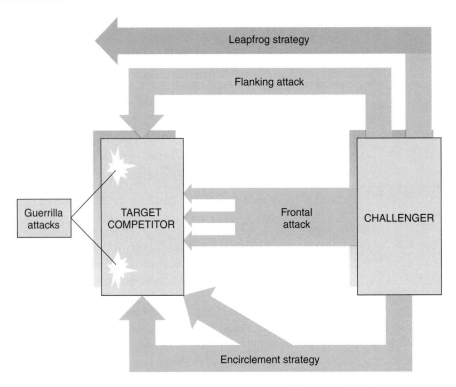

Source: P. Kotler and R. Singh Achrol, "Marketing Warfare in the 1980's," *Journal of Business Strategy,* Winter 1981. Republished with permission-EC Media Group, Eleven Penn Plaza, New York, NY 10001.

- *Attack the market-share leader within its primary target market.* As we shall see, this typi-cally involves either a *frontal assault* or an attempt to *leapfrog* the leader through the devel-opment of superior technology or product design. It may seem logical to try to win customers away from the competitor with the most customers to lose, but this can be a dangerous strat-egy unless the challenger has superior resources and competencies that can be converted into a sustainable advantage. In some cases, however, a smaller challenger may be able to avoid disastrous retaliation by confronting the leader only occasionally in limited geographic terri-tories through a series of *guerrilla attacks.*
- *Attack another follower who has an established position within a major market segment.* This also usually involves a *frontal assault,* but it may be easier for the challenger to gain a sus-tainable advantage if the target competitor is not as well established as the market leader in the minds and buying habits of customers.
- *Attack one or more smaller competitors who have only limited resources.* Because smaller competitors usually hold only a small share of the total market, this may seem like an ineffi-cient way to attain substantial share increases. But by focusing on several small regional competitors one at a time, a challenger can sometimes achieve major gains without inviting retaliation from stronger firms. For example, by first challenging and ultimately acquiring a series of smaller regional manufacturers, Borden managed to capture the leading share of the fragmented domestic pasta market.

Exhibit 10.8

MARKETING OBJECTIVES AND STRATEGIES FOR CHALLENGERS IN GROWTH MARKETS

SHARE-GROWTH STRATEGIES

Situational variables	Frontal attack	Leapfrog	Flank attack	Encirclement	Guerrilla attack
Primary objective	Capture substantial repeat/replacement purchases from target competitor's current customers; attract new customers among later adopters by offering lower price or more attractive features.	Induce current customers in mass market to replace their current brand with superior new offering; attract new customers by providing enhanced benefits.	Attract substantial share of new customers in one or more major segments where customers' needs are different from those of early adopters in the mass market.	Attract a substantial share of new customers in a variety of smaller, specialized segments where customers' needs or preferences differ from those of early adopters in the mass market.	Capture a modest share of repeat/replacement purchases in several market segments or territories; attract a share of new customers in a number of existing segments.
Market characteristics	Relatively homogeneous market with respect to customers' needs and purchase criteria; relatively little preference or loyalty for existing brands; no positive network effects.	Relatively homogeneous market with respect to customers' needs and purchase criteria, but some needs or criteria not currently met by existing brands.	Two or more major segments with distinct needs and purchase criteria; needs of customers in at least one segment not currently met by existing brands.	Relatively heterogeneous market with a number of small, specialized segments; needs and preferences of customers in some segments not currently satisfied by competing brands.	Relatively heterogeneous market with a number of larger segments; needs and preferences of customers in most segments currently satisfied by competing brands.
Competitor's characteristics	Target competitor has relatively limited resources and competencies, particularly in marketing and R&D; would probably be vulnerable to direct attack.	One or more current competitors have relatively strong resources and competencies in marketing, but relatively unsophisticated technology and limited R&D competencies.	Target competitor has relatively strong resources and competencies, particularly in marketing and R&D; would probably be able to withstand direct attack.	One or more competitors have relatively strong marketing, R&D resources and competencies, and/or lower costs; could probably withstand a direct attack.	A number of competitors have relatively strong marketing, R&D resources and competencies, and/or lower costs; could probably withstand a direct attack.
Firm's characteristics	Firm has stronger resources and competencies in R&D and marketing and/or lower operating costs than target competitor.	Firm has proprietary technology superior to that of competitors; firm has necessary marketing and production resources to stimulate and meet primary demand for new generation of products.	Firm's resources and competencies are limited, but sufficient to effectively penetrate and serve at least one major market segment.	Firm has marketing, R&D, and production resources and competencies necessary to serve multiple smaller segments; firm has decentralized and adaptable management structure.	Firm has relatively limited marketing, R&D, and/or production resources and competencies; firm has decentralized and adaptable management structure.

- *Avoid direct attacks on any established competitor.* In fragmented markets in which the leader or other major competitors are not currently satisfying one or more segments, a challenger is often best advised to "hit 'em where they ain't." This usually involves either a *flanking* or an *encirclement* strategy, with the challenger developing differentiated product offerings targeted at one large or several smaller segments in which no competitor currently holds a strong position. Thus, Vans has profited in the athletic shoe market by focusing on small alternative sports whose adherents do not find the "mainstream" image of Nike and other major brands very appealing.

Deciding which competitor to attack necessitates a comparison of relative strengths and weaknesses, a critical first step in developing an effective share-growth strategy. It also can help limit the scope of the battlefield, a particularly important consideration for challengers with limited resources.

Frontal Attack Strategy

Where the market for a product category is relatively homogeneous, with few untapped segments and at least one well-established competitor, a follower wanting to capture an increased market share may have little choice but to tackle a major competitor head-on. Such an approach is most likely to succeed when most existing customers do not have strong brand preferences or loyalties, the target competitor's product does not benefit from positive network effects, and the challenger's resources and competencies—particularly in marketing—are greater than the target competitor's. But even superior resources are no guarantee of success if the challenger's assault merely imitates the target competitor's offering.

To successfully implement a frontal attack, a challenger should seek one or more ways to achieve a sustainable advantage over the target competitor. As discussed earlier, such an advantage is usually based on attaining lower costs or a differentiated position in the market. If the challenger has a cost advantage, it can cut prices to lure away the target competitor's customers, or it can maintain a similar price but engage in more extensive promotion.

Challenging a leader solely on the basis of low price is a highway to disaster, however, unless the challenger really does have a sustainable cost advantage. Otherwise, the leader might simply match the lower prices until the challenger is driven from the market. The problem is that initially a challenger is often at a cost *disadvantage* because of the experience-curve effects established competitors have accumulated. The challenger must have offsetting advantages such as superior production technology, established relations with low-cost suppliers, the ability to share production facilities or marketing efforts across multiple SBUs, or other sources of synergy before a low-price assault makes sense.

A similar caveat applies to frontal assaults based solely on heftier promotional budgets. Unless the target competitor's resources are substantially more limited than the challenger's, it can retaliate against any attempt to win away customers through more extensive advertising or attractive sales and trade promotions.

One possible exception to this limitation of greater promotional effort is the use of a more extensive and better-trained salesforce to gain a competitive advantage. A knowledgeable salesperson's technical advice and problem-solving abilities can give additional value to a firm's product offering, particularly in newly developing high-tech industries.

In general, the best way for a challenger to effectively implement a frontal attack is to differentiate its product or associated services in ways that better meet the needs and preferences of many customers in the mass market. If the challenger can support those meaningful product differences with strong promotion or an attractive price, so much the better, but usually the unique features or services offered are the foundation for a sustainable advantage. For example, Dell has been successful as a follower in the PC market by offering *both* superior customer service and low prices. Customers can design their own computers on the company's website, get exactly the features they want, and have the equipment delivered to their doors in two or three days. Such excellent service is possible, in large part, due to the close coordination between Dell and its suppliers, coordination that minimizes inventories of parts and finished computers, thereby lowering costs and prices, and maximizes manufacturing flexibility and delivery speed. Dell's competitive advantage has proven to be sustainable, too, because its alliances with suppliers took years to develop and are hard for its competitors to match.

Variables that might limit the competitor's willingness or ability to retaliate can also improve the chances for successful frontal attack. For instance, a target competitor with a reputation for high product quality may be loath to cut prices in response to a lower-priced challenger for fear of cheapening its brand's image. And a competitor pursuing high ROI or cash flow objectives may be reluctant to increase its promotion or R&D expenditures in the short run to fend off an attack.[12]

Leapfrog Strategy

A challenger stands the best chance of attracting repeat or replacement purchases from a competitor's current customers when it can offer a product that is attractively differentiated from the competitor's offerings. The odds of success might be even greater if the challenger can offer a far superior product based on advanced technology or a more sophisticated design. This is the essence of a leapfrog strategy. It is an attempt to gain a significant advantage over the existing competition by introducing a new generation of products that significantly outperform or offer more desirable customer benefits than do existing brands. For example, the introduction of reasonably priced video cameras by Sony and other Japanese electronics manufacturers largely took over the market for home movie equipment and a large share of the market for Polaroid's self-developing photography equipment as well. And now digital cameras are doing the same thing to the video market.

In addition, such a strategy often inhibits quick retaliation by established competitors. Firms that have achieved some success with one technology—or that have committed substantial resources to plant and equipment dedicated to a current product—often are reluctant to switch to a new one because of the large investments involved or a fear of disrupting current customers.

A leapfrog strategy is not viable for all challengers. To be successful, the challenger must have technology superior to that of established competitors as well as the product and process engineering capabilities to turn that technology into an appealing product. Also, the challenger must have the marketing resources to effectively promote its new products and convince customers already committed to an earlier technology that the new product offers sufficient benefits to justify the costs of switching.

Flanking and Encirclement Strategies

The military historian B. H. Liddell-Hart, after analyzing battles ranging from the Greek Wars to World War I, determined that only 6 out of 280 victories were the result of a frontal attack.[13] He concluded that it is usually wiser to avoid attacking an established adversary's point of strength and to focus instead on an area of weakness in his defenses. This is the basic premise behind flanking and encirclement strategies. They both seek to avoid direct confrontations by focusing on market segments whose needs are not being satisfied by existing brands and where no current competitor has a strongly held position.

Flank Attack　A flank attack is appropriate when the market can be broken into two or more large segments, when the leader and/or other major competitors hold a strong position in the primary segment, and when no existing brand fully satisfies the needs of customers in at least one other segment. A challenger may be able to capture a significant share of the total market by concentrating primarily on one large untapped segment. This usually involves developing product features or services tailored to the needs and preferences of the targeted customers, together with appropriate promotional and pricing policies to quickly build selective demand. Japanese auto companies, for instance, penetrated the U.S. car market by focusing on the low-price segment, where domestic manufacturers' offerings were limited. Domestic car manufacturers were relatively unconcerned by this flanking action at first. They failed to retaliate very aggressively because the Japanese were pursuing a segment they considered to be small and unprofitable. History proved them wrong.

In some cases, a successful flank attack need not involve unique product features. Instead, a challenger can sometimes meet the special needs of an untapped segment by providing specially designed customer services or distribution channels. One major reason for the success of L'eggs pantyhose, for instance, was that it was the first brand to be distributed through an extensive channel of convenience goods retailers, such as grocery and drug stores, instead of more fashionable department and clothing stores. The greater shopping convenience provided by this new distribution channel appealed strongly to the growing segment of working women. More recently, as Exhibit 10.9 recounts, a small citrus farmers' cooperative has stolen substantial market share from much bigger competitors by delivering a high-quality product and emphasizing its folksy, common-man image.

Encirclement　An encirclement strategy involves targeting several smaller untapped or underdeveloped segments in the market simultaneously. The idea is to surround the leader's brand with a variety of offerings aimed at several peripheral segments. This strategy makes most sense when the market is fragmented into many different applications segments or geographical regions with somewhat unique needs or tastes.

Exhibit 10.9　A Small Citrus Juice Co-op Squeezes Big Rivals

When a little-known farmers' cooperative called Citrus World Inc. started to market its own brand of pasteurized orange juice, it looked like an improbable player in the $3 billion juice market. Citrus World, an 800-employee operation in rural Florida, was up against a couple of established giants: Seagram Co., owner of the Tropicana brand, and Coca-Cola Co., with its Minute Maid line.

But Citrus World knew exactly what to do: Squeeze that folksy image for all it was worth. To sell its Florida's Natural brand, it ordered TV commercials featuring sunburned farmers gulping down juice. In one ad, growers holding boxes of oranges hold a "stockholders' meeting" in the back of a truck. Other workers cut "overhead" by chopping a branch from an orange tree.

Thanks to catchy ads, a quality product, and aggressive pricing, Citrus World made a splash. In 1995 Florida's Natural knocked Minute Maid out of the number 2 spot in the rapidly growing market for "premium," or pasteurized, not-from-concentrate orange juice, and the brand experienced a larger percentage sales increase than Tropicana. While Citrus World attacked its larger rivals' exposed flanks, in part, by offering lower prices, its success also demonstrates that a substantial segment of consumers prefers to deal with what they perceive to be small, "underdog" companies.

Source: Yumiko Ono, "A Pulp Tale: Juice Co-op Squeezes Big Rivals," *Wall Street Journal,* January 30, 1996, p. B1. Copyright 1996 by Dow Jones & Co. Inc. Reproduced with permission of Dow Jones & Co. Inc. via Copyright Clearance Center.

Once again, this strategy usually involves developing a varied line of products with features tailored to the needs of different segments. Rather than try to compete with Coke and Pepsi in the soft drink market, for example, Cadbury-Schweppes offers a wide variety of flavors such as cream soda, root beer, and ginger ale—almost anything but cola—to appeal to small groups of customers with unique tastes. Similarly, Vans is trying to expand its foothold in the athletic shoe industry by targeting several niche segments of enthusiasts in other alternative sports—such as snowboarding—where the brand's youthful "outsider" image might be appealing and where the firm's larger competitors are not well established.

Guerrilla Attack

When well-established competitors already cover all major segments of the market and the challenger's resources are relatively limited, flanking, encirclement, or all-out frontal attacks may be impossible. In such cases, the challenger may be reduced to making a series of surprise raids against its more established competitors. To avoid massive retaliation, the challenger should use guerrilla attacks sporadically, perhaps in limited geographic areas where the target competitor is not particularly well entrenched.

A challenger can choose from a variety of means for carrying out guerrilla attacks. These include sales promotion efforts (e.g., coupon drops and merchandising deals), local advertising blitzes, and even legal action. Short-term price reductions through sales promotion campaigns are a particularly favored guerrilla tactic in consumer goods markets. They can target specific customer groups in limited geographic areas; they can be implemented quickly; and they are often difficult for a larger competitor to respond to because that firm's higher share level means that a given discount will cost it more in absolute dollars. For similar reasons, carefully targeted direct mail or Internet marketing campaigns also can be an effective guerrilla tactic, as illustrated by the dial-around companies described in Exhibit 10.10.

Exhibit 10.10 The Guerrilla Attack on AT&T

In the 1990s, kitchen phones across the United States sprouted little stickers with official-looking five-digit codes and slogans like "Dial & Save." They were evidence of a sneakily successful marketing campaign that took a $900 million bite out of AT&T and its major long-distance rivals. The stickers arrived in direct mail promotions by resellers of phone service known as *dial-around companies*. A customer could punch in the five-digit code when making a long-distance call and save from 10 to 50 percent over the undiscounted rates of the major long-distance companies.

Dial-around companies were mostly small, privately held firms that bought long-distance capacity in bulk from telephone giants and resold it at cut rates, routing calls through the switching equipment of other companies or their own. Their services were marketed under a variety of different brand names and promoted largely through direct mail campaigns. The mailings were usually targeted at customers whom AT&T and its rivals tended to neglect, such as older people. These consumers were often bargain hunters, yet typically they didn't use the phone enough to qualify for most long-distance savings plans.

How did dial-arounds gain so much ground without provoking a counterattack from AT&T? First, they focused on customers that the bigger firms did not deem very important or profitable. Second, many small companies were involved so it was hard for AT&T to retaliate against them individually. But as the volume of business of the dial-around companies continued to increase, the firm was eventually forced to react against them as a group. The firm instituted its One Rate plan, promising residential customers calls anywhere, anytime for 15 cents a minute.

Source: Henry Goldblatt, "The Guerrilla Attack on AT&T," *Fortune*, November 25, 1996, pp. 126–27.

In some cases the ultimate objective of a series of guerrilla attacks is not so much for the challenger to build its own share as it is to prevent a powerful leader from further expanding its share or engaging in aggressive actions to which it would be costly for the followers to respond. Lawsuits brought against the leader by several smaller competitors over a range of activities can effectively slow down the leader's expansionist tendencies by diverting some of its resources and attention.

Supporting Evidence

Several studies conducted with the PIMS database provide empirical support for many of the managerial prescriptions we have discussed.[14] These studies compare businesses that achieved high market shares during the growth stage of the product life cycle, or that increased their market shares over time, with low-share businesses. As shown in Exhibit 10.11, the marketing programs and activities of businesses that successfully achieved increased market share differed from their less-successful counterparts in the following ways:

- Businesses that increased the quality of their products relative to those of competitors achieved greater share increases than businesses whose product quality remained constant or declined.
- Share-gaining businesses typically developed and added more new products, line extensions, or product modifications to their line than share-losing businesses.
- Share-gaining businesses tended to increase their marketing expenditures faster than the rate of market growth. Increases in both salesforce and sales promotion expenditures were effective for producing share gains in both consumer and industrial goods businesses. Increased advertising expenditures were effective for producing share gains primarily in consumer goods businesses.
- Surprisingly, there was little difference in the relative prices charged between firms that gained and those that lost market share.

These findings are consistent with many of our earlier observations. For instance, they underline the folly of launching a frontal attack solely on the basis of lower price. Unless

Exhibit 10.11

STRATEGIC CHANGES MADE BY CHALLENGERS THAT GAINED VERSUS LOST MARKET SHARE

Strategic changes	Share-gaining challengers	Share-losing challengers
Relative product quality scores	+1.8	−0.6
New products as a percent of sales	+0.1	−0.5
Relative price	+0.3	+0.2
Marketing expenditures (adjusted for market growth):		
Salesforce	+9.0%	−8.0%
Advertising:		
Consumer products	+13.0%	−9.0%
Industrial products	−1.0	−14.0
Promotion:		
Consumer products	+13.0%	−5.0%
Industrial products	+7.0	−10.0

Source: Adapted with the permission of The Free Press, a Division of Simon & Schuster, Inc., from *The PIMS Principles: Linking Strategy to Performance* by Robert D. Buzzell and Bradley T. Gale. Copyright © 1987 by The Free Press.

the challenger has substantially lower unit costs or the leader is inhibited from cutting its own prices for some reason, the challenger's price cuts are likely to be retaliated against and will generate few new customers. On the other hand, frontal, leapfrog, flanking, or encirclement attacks based on product improvements tailored to specific segments are more likely to succeed, particularly when the challenger supports those attacks with substantial promotional efforts.

Regardless of the strategies pursued by market leaders and challengers during a product-market's growth stage, the competitive situation often changes as the market matures and its growth rate slows. In the next chapter, we examine the environmental changes that occur as a market matures and the marketing strategies that firms might use to adapt to those changes.

TAKE AWAYS

- If the market leader wants to maintain its number-one share position as the product category moves through rapid growth, it must focus on two important objectives: (1) retaining its current customers and (2) stimulating selective demand among later adopters.

- Marketing strategies a leader might adopt to defend its relative share as the product category grows include position defense, flanker, confrontation, market expansion, and contraction. The best one to choose depends on the homogeneity of the market and the firm's resources and competencies relative to potential competitors.

- For a challenger to increase its market share relative to the established leader, it must differentiate its offering by delivering superior product benefits, better service, or a lower price. Challenging the leader solely on the basis of price, however, is a good way to start a price war and can be a highway to disaster unless the challenger has a sustainable cost advantage.

- Smaller challengers often try to avoid direct confrontations with the share leader by pursuing flanker, encirclement, or guerrilla attack strategies that focus on market segments where the leader is not well established.

- Self-diagnostic questions to test your ability to apply the concepts in this chapter to marketing decision making may be found at this book's website at **www.mhhe.com/walker.**

ENDNOTES

1. Information to prepare this opening case was taken from the Nike, Inc., website at www.nikebiz.com/story/chrono.shtml, www.nikebiz.com/story/b_knight.shtml, and www.nikebiz.com/story/n_bowerman.shtml; and Arlen Weintraub and Gerry Khermouch, "Chairman of the Board," *Business Week,* May 28, 2001, p. 96.

2. Neil Gross, Peter Coy, and Otis Port, "The Technology Paradox," *Business Week,* March 6, 1995, pp. 76–84.

3. For a more extensive discussion of the potential opportunities and pitfalls of rapidly growing markets, see David A. Aaker and George S. Day, "The Perils of High-Growth Markets," *Strategic Management Journal* 7 (1986), pp. 409–21; and Myron Magnet, "Let's Go for Growth," *Fortune,* March 7, 1994, pp. 60–72.

4. Gregory S. Carpenter and Kent Nakamoto, "Consumer Preference Formation and Pioneering Advantage," *Journal of Marketing Research,* August 1989, pp. 285–98.

5. Andrew Park and Peter Burrows, "Dell, the Conqueror," *Business Week,* September 24, 2001, pp. 92–102.

6. In some rapidly evolving high-tech markets, price premiums can disappear *very* quickly, as pointed out in Gross, Coy, and Port, "Technology Paradox."

7. Robert D. Buzzell and Bradley T. Gale, *The PIMS Principles: Linking Strategy to Performance* (New York: Free Press, 1987), pp. 188–90.

8. For a detailed discussion of these strategies in a military context, see Carl von Clausewitz, *On War* (London: Routledge and Kegan Paul, 1908); and

B. H. Liddell-Hart, *Strategy* (New York: Praeger, 1967). For a related discussion of the application of such strategies in a business setting, see Philip Kotler and Ravi Singh Achrol, "Marketing Warfare in the 1980's," *Journal of Business Strategy,* Winter 1981, pp. 30–41.

9. Thomas T. Nagle, "Managing Price Competition," *Marketing Management* 2 (Spring 1993), pp. 36–45; and Akshay R. Rao, Mark E. Bergen, and Scott Davis, "How to Fight a Price War," *Harvard Business Review,* March–April 2000, pp. 107–16.

10. Robert J. Dolan and Abel P. Jewland, "Experience Curves and Dynamic Demand Models: Implications for Optimal Pricing Strategy," *Journal of Marketing,* Winter 1981, p. 52.

11. Andy Reinhardt, "Meet Mr. Internet," *Business Week,* September 13, 1999, pp. 128–40.

12. For a more extensive discussion of factors that can limit a leader's willingness or ability to retaliate against a direct attack, see Michael E. Porter, *Competitive Advantage* (New York: Free Press, 1985), chap. 15.

13. Liddell-Hart, *Strategy,* p. 163.

14. Robert D. Buzzell and Frederick D. Wiersema, "Successful Share-Building Strategies," *Harvard Business Review,* January–February 1981, pp. 135–43; Carl R. Anderson and Carl P. Zeithaml, "Stages in the Product Life Cycle, Business Strategy, and Business Performance," *Academy of Management Journal,* March 1984, pp. 5–25; and Buzzell and Gale, *The PIMS Principles,* chap. 9.

CHAPTER ELEVEN

STRATEGIES FOR MATURE AND DECLINING MARKETS

Johnson Controls: Making Money in Mature Markets[1]

AT FIRST GLANCE, JOHNSON CONTROLS INC. in Glendale, Wisconsin, appears to be the epitome of a staid, slow-growing, "old-economy" company. After all, the firm's success and future survival depend on several product and service categories that have not experienced very much growth in the domestic market in recent years. Johnson's major businesses include batteries, seats, and other internal components for automobiles; heating and cooling equipment for large commercial buildings and schools; and facilities management services.

But first glances can be deceiving. The firm's managers have developed a four-pronged strategy for making money in such mature markets. First, Johnson has acquired a number of weaker competitors in each of its product categories over the years in order to gain market share and remove excess capacity. Second, the firm has expanded sales volume by moving aggressively into global markets. The firm now operates in 500 different locations around the world.

Most important, the firm has nurtured close relationships with established customers such as General Motors, Ford, Daimler-Chrysler, BMW, and Toyota. Those relationships, in turn, have enabled Johnson to maintain solid profit margins by improving customer retention and gaining operating efficiencies via logistical alliances, just-in-time delivery systems, and other process improvements. Finally, the firm's close customer relationships have provided it with market intelligence and facilitated joint development projects, both of which have helped the firm gain additional revenue from the introduction of new product and service offerings targeted at those customers.

A strong balance sheet and a long-term perspective have helped Johnson build market share—and expand into foreign countries—through the acquisition of competitors. In some cases, the firm has snapped up firms with product or service offerings that complement and extend Johnson's own product line in one of its established target markets. For instance, the firm spent $167 million to acquire Pan Am's World Services division, a facility management operation that does everything from mow the lawn to run the cafeteria. That acquisition, when combined with Johnson's existing heating and cooling systems business and some new products and services developed internally, turned the company into a full-service facilities operator. Johnson can now manage a client's entire building while offering highly customized heating and cooling systems and controls that minimize energy use.

This combination of customized products and full service has both expanded the company's share of the commercial real estate market and enabled it to maintain relatively high margins in a highly competitive business.

In other businesses, Johnson has combined the economies of scale generated through savvy acquisitions with the knowledge gained from close customer relationships to both develop new products and drive down operating costs. For example, Johnson has become the leading worldwide supplier of automotive seating and interior systems, such as floor consoles and instrument panels, by assisting manufacturers with the design and development, as well as the manufacture, of such components. As one engineer at Daimler-Chrysler pointed out, "Johnson is able to completely integrate the design, development, and manufacture of [our] seats," and do it for less than the auto companies could. And by closely coordinating inventories and production schedules, Johnson has reduced costs even further for both its customers and itself. For instance, by locating its plants close to a customer's production facility, Johnson is able to assemble seats to order, load them on a truck in a sequence that matches the cars coming down the assembly line, and deliver them to the customer all in as little as 90 minutes.

Despite the maturity of its markets, Johnson's strategy is paying off, in terms of both revenue growth and profits. In recent years the firm has averaged nearly 30 percent annual growth, with sales increasing from about $10 billion in 1996 to more than $17 billion in 2000. At the same time, the firm has increased dividends paid to shareholders for 25 straight years, and in 2000 it earned a 20 percent return on shareholder equity.

STRATEGIC CHALLENGES ADDRESSED IN CHAPTER 11

Many managers, particularly those in marketing, seem obsessed with growth. Their objectives tend to emphasize annual increases in sales volume, market share, or both. But the biggest challenge for many managers in developed nations in future years will be making money in markets that grow slowly, if at all. The majority of product-markets in those nations are in the mature or decline stages of their life cycles. And as accelerating rates of technological and social change continue to shorten such life cycles, today's innovations will move from growth to maturity—and ultimately to decline—ever faster.

A period of competitive turbulence almost always accompanies the transition from market growth to maturity in an industry. This period often begins after approximately half the potential customers have adopted the product and the rate of sales growth starts to decline. As the growth rate slows, many competitors tend to overestimate future sales volume and consequently end up developing too much production capacity. Competition becomes more intense as firms battle to increase sales volume to cover their high fixed costs and maintain profitability. As a result, such transition periods are commonly accompanied by a **shakeout** during which weaker businesses fail, withdraw from the industry, or are acquired by other firms, as has happened to some of Johnson Controls' competitors in the United States and European automotive seat and battery industries. In the next section of this chapter we examine some strategic traps that can threaten a firm's survival during an industry shakeout.

Challenges in Mature Markets

Businesses that survive the shakeout face new challenges as market growth stagnates. As a market matures, total volume stabilizes; replacement purchases rather than first-time buyers account for the vast majority of that volume. A primary marketing objective of all competitors in mature markets, therefore, is simply to hold their existing customers—to sustain a meaningful competitive advantage that will help ensure the continued satisfaction and loyalty of those customers. Thus, a product's financial success during the mature life cycle stage depends heavily on the firm's ability to achieve and sustain a lower delivered cost or some perceived product quality or customer-service superiority.

Some firms tend to passively defend mature products while using the bulk of the revenues produced by those items to develop and aggressively market new products with more growth potential. This can be shortsighted, however. All segments of a market and all brands in an industry do not necessarily reach maturity at the same time. Aging brands such as Jell-O, Johnson's baby shampoo, and Arm & Hammer baking soda experienced sales revivals in recent years because of creative marketing strategies. Thus, a share leader in a mature industry might build on a cost or product differentiation advantage and pursue a marketing strategy aimed at increasing volume by promoting new uses for an old product or by encouraging current customers to buy and use the product more often. Therefore, in this chapter we examine basic business strategies necessary for survival in mature markets and marketing strategies a firm might use to extend a brand's sales and profits, including the strategies that have been so successful for Johnson Controls.

Challenges in Declining Markets

Eventually, technological advances; changing customer demographics, tastes, or lifestyles; and development of substitutes result in declining demand for most product forms and brands. As a product starts to decline, managers face the critical question of whether to divest or liquidate the business. Unfortunately, firms sometimes support dying products too long at the expense of current profitability and the aggressive pursuit of future breadwinners.

An appropriate marketing strategy, however, can produce substantial sales and profits even in a declining market. If few exit barriers exist, an industry leader might attempt to increase market share via aggressive pricing or promotion policies aimed at driving out weaker competitors. Or it might try to consolidate the industry, as Johnson Controls has done in its automotive components businesses, by acquiring weaker brands and reducing overhead by eliminating both excess capacity and duplicate marketing programs. Alternatively, a firm might decide to harvest a mature product by maximizing cash flow and profit over the product's remaining life. The last section of this chapter examines specific marketing strategies for gaining the greatest possible returns from products approaching the end of their life cycle.

SHAKEOUT: THE TRANSITION FROM MARKET GROWTH TO MATURITY

Characteristics of the Transition Period

The transition from market growth to maturity typically begins when the market is still growing but the rate of growth starts to decline. This slackening of the growth rate either sparks or occurs simultaneously with other changes in the market and competitive environment. As mentioned earlier, such changes typically include the appearance of excess capacity, increased difficulty of maintaining product differentiation, increased intensity of competition, and growing pressures on costs and profits. Consequently, weaker members of the industry often fail or are acquired by larger competitors during this shakeout stage.

Strategic Traps during the Transition

A business's ability to survive the transition from market growth to maturity depends to a great extent on whether it can avoid some common strategic traps.[2] Four such traps are summarized in Exhibit 11.1.

The most obvious trap is simply the failure to recognize the events signaling the beginning of the shakeout period. The best way to minimize the impact of slowing growth is to accurately forecast the slowdown in sales and hold the firm's production capacity to a sustainable level. For both industrial and consumer durable goods markets, models can forecast when replacement sales will begin to outweigh first-time purchases, a common signal that a market is beginning to mature.[3] But in consumer nondurable markets—particularly those where growth slows because of shifting consumer preferences or the emergence of substitute products—the start of the transition period can be nearly impossible to predict.

A second strategic trap is for a business to get caught in the middle during the transition period without a clear strategic advantage. A business may survive and prosper during the growth stage even though it has neither differentiated its offering from competitors nor attained the lowest-cost position in its industry. But during the transition period, such is not the case.

A third trap is the failure to recognize the declining importance of product differentiation and the increasing importance of price or service. Businesses that have built their

Exhibit 11.1

COMMON STRATEGIC TRAPS FIRMS CAN FALL INTO DURING THE SHAKEOUT PERIOD

1. Failure to anticipate transition from growth to maturity.
   - Firms may make overly optimistic forecasts of future sales volume.
   - As a result, they expand too rapidly and production capacity overshoots demand as growth slows.
   - Their excess capacity leads to higher costs per unit.
   - Consequently, they must cut prices or increase promotion in an attempt to increase their volume.
2. No clear competitive advantage as growth slows.
   - Many firms can succeed without a strong competitive advantage during periods of rapid growth.
   - However, firms that do not have the lowest costs or a superior offering in terms of product quality or service can have difficulty sustaining their market share and volume as growth slows and competition intensifies.
3. Assumption that an early advantage will insulate the firm from price or service competition.
   - In many cases, technological differentials become smaller as more competitors enter and initiate product improvements as an industry approaches maturity.
   - If customers perceive that the quality of competing brands has become more equal, they are likely to attach greater importance to price or service differences.
   - Failure to detect such trends can cause an early leader to be complacent and slow to respond to competitive threats.
4. Sacrificing market share in favor of short-run profit.
   - A firm may cut marketing or R&D budgets or forgo other expenditures in order to maintain its historical level of profitability even though industry profits tend to fall during the transition period.
   - This can cause long-run erosion of market share and further increases in unit costs as the industry matures.

success on technological superiority or other forms of product differentiation often disdain aggressive pricing or marketing practices even though such differentiation typically erodes as markets mature.[4] As a result, such firms may delay meeting their more aggressive competitors head-on and end up losing market share, as Hewlett-Packard and Compaq both discovered in the wake of Dell's aggressive pricing policies as the personal computer market slumped in 2000.

Why should a firm not put off responding to the more aggressive pricing or marketing actions of its competitors? Because doing so may lead to a fourth trap—giving up market share too easily in favor of short-run profit. Many businesses try to maintain the profitability of the recent past as markets enter the transition period. They usually do this at the expense of market share or by forgoing marketing, R&D, and other investments crucial for maintaining future market position. While some smaller firms with limited resources may have no choice, this tendency can be seriously shortsighted, particularly if economies of scale are crucial for the business's continued success during market maturity.

STRATEGIC CHOICES IN MATURE MARKETS

The maturity phase of an industry's life cycle is often depicted as one of stability characterized by few changes in the market shares of leading competitors and steady prices. The industry leaders, because of their low per-unit costs and little need to make any further investments, enjoy high profits and positive cash flows. These cash flows are harvested and diverted to other SBUs or products in the firm's portfolio that promise greater future growth.

Unfortunately, this conventional scenario provides an overly simplistic description of the situation businesses face in most mature markets. For one thing, it is not always easy to tell when a market has reached maturity. Variations in brands, marketing programs, and customer groups can mean that different brands and market segments reach maturity at different times.

Further, as the maturity stage progresses, a variety of threats and opportunities can disrupt an industry's stability. Shifts in customer needs or preferences, product substitutes, increased raw material costs, changes in government regulations, or factors such as the entry of low-cost foreign producers or mergers and acquisitions can threaten individual competitors and even throw the entire industry into early decline. Consider, for example, the competitive position of Timex, a brand that dominated the low-price segment of the American watch market in the 1970s. First the appearance of imported digital watches and later a shift in consumer preferences toward more fashionable and prestigious brands buffeted the firm and eroded its market share.

On the positive side, such changes also can open new growth opportunities in mature industries. Product improvements (such as the development of high-fiber nutritional cereals), advances in process technology (the creation of minimills for steel production), falling raw materials costs, increased prices for close substitutes, or environmental changes all can provide opportunities for a firm to dramatically increase its sales and profits. An entire industry can even experience a period of renewed growth.

Discontinuities during industry maturity suggest that it is dangerously shortsighted for a firm to simply milk its cash cows. Even industry followers can substantially improve volume, share, and profitability during industry maturity if they can adjust their marketing objectives and programs to fit the new opportunities that arise.[5] Thus, success in mature markets requires two sets of strategic actions: (1) the development of a well-implemented business strategy to sustain a competitive advantage, customer satisfaction, and loyalty and (2) flexible and creative marketing programs geared to pursue growth or profit opportunities as conditions change in specific product-markets.

Strategies for Maintaining Competitive Advantage

As discussed in Chapter 3, both *analyzer* and *defender strategies* may be appropriate for units with a leading, or at least a profitable, share of one or more major segments in a mature industry. Analyzers and defenders are both concerned with maintaining a strong share position in established product-markets. But analyzers also do some product and market development to avoid being leapfrogged by competitors with more advanced products or being left behind in new applications segments. On the other hand, defenders may initiate some product improvements or line extensions to protect and strengthen their position in existing markets, but they spend relatively little on new product R&D. Thus, an analyzer strategy is most appropriate for developed industries that are still experiencing some technological change and may have opportunities for continued growth, such as the computer and commercial aircraft industries. The defender strategy works best in industries where the basic technology is not very complex or is unlikely to change dramatically in the short run, as in the food industry.

Both analyzers and defenders can attempt to sustain a competitive advantage in established product-markets through *differentiation* of their product offering (either on the basis of superior quality or service) or by maintaining a low-cost position. Evidence suggests the ability to maintain either a strongly differentiated or a low-cost position continues to be a critical determinant of success throughout both the transition and the maturity stage. One study examined the competitive strategies pursued by the two leading firms (in terms of return on investment) in eight mature industries characterized by slow growth and intense competition. In each industry, the two leading firms offered either the lowest relative delivered cost or high relative product differentiation.[6] Similarly, more recent observations by Treacy and Wiersema found that market leaders tend to pursue one of three strategic disciplines. They either stress operational excellence, which typically translates into lower costs, or differentiate themselves through product leadership or customer intimacy and superior service.[7]

Generally, it is difficult for a single business to pursue both low-cost and differentiation strategies at the same time. For instance, businesses taking the low-cost approach typically compete primarily by offering the lowest prices in the industry. Such prices allow little room for the firm to make the investments or cover the costs inherent in maintaining superior product quality, performance, or service over time.

It is important to keep in mind, however, that pursuit of a low-cost strategy does not mean that a business can ignore the delivery of desirable benefits to the customer. Similarly, customers will not pay an unlimited price premium for superior quality or service, no matter how superior it is. In both consumer and commercial markets customers seek good *value* for the money, either a solid, no-frills product or service at an outstanding price or an offering whose higher price is justified by the superior benefits it delivers on one or more dimensions.[8] Thus, even low-cost producers should continually seek ways to improve the quality and performance of their offerings within the financial constraints of their competitive strategy. And even differentiated defenders should continually work to improve efficiency without sacrificing product quality or performance. This point is clearly illustrated in the diagram of the customer value management process in Exhibit 11.2, which shows that actions to improve customers' perceptions of quality (whether of goods

Exhibit 11.2

THE PROCESS OF CUSTOMER VALUE MANAGEMENT

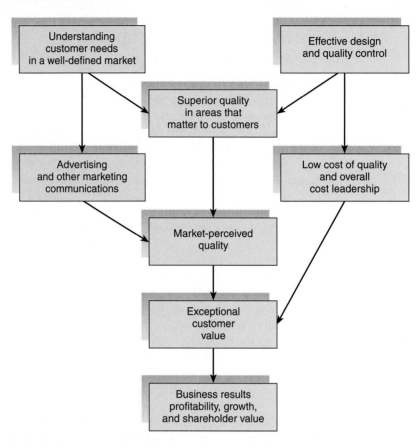

or service) and to reduce costs both impact customer value. The critical strategic questions facing the marketing manager, then, are: How can a business continue to differentiate its offerings and justify a premium price as its market matures and becomes more competitive? and How can businesses, particularly those pursuing low-cost strategies, continue to reduce their costs and improve their efficiency as their markets mature?

Methods of Differentiation

STRATEGIC ISSUE

Quality *and* service *may be defined in a variety of different ways by customers.*

At the most basic level, a business can attempt to differentiate its offering from competitors' by offering either superior product quality, superior service, or both. The problem is that *quality* and *service* may be defined in a variety of different ways by customers.

Dimensions of Product Quality[9]   To maintain a competitive advantage in product quality, a firm must understand what *dimensions customers perceive to underlie differences across products* within a given category. One authority has identified eight such dimensions of product quality. These are summarized in Exhibit 11.3 and discussed next.

Exhibit 11.3

DIMENSIONS OF PRODUCT QUALITY

• Performance	How well does the washing machine wash clothes?
• Durability	How long will the lawn mower last?
• Conformance with specifications	What is the incidence of product defects?
• Features	Does an airline flight offer a movie and dinner?
• Reliability	Will each visit to a restaurant result in consistent quality?
	What percentage of the time will a product perform satisfactorily?
• Serviceability	Is the product easy to service?
	Is the service system efficient, competent, and convenient?
• Fit and finish	Does the product look and feel like a quality product?
• Brand name	Is this a name that customers associate with quality?
	What is the brand's image?

Source: Reprinted from "What Does 'Product Quality' Really Mean?" by David A. Garvin, *MIT Sloan Management Review,* Fall 1984, pp. 25–43, by permission of publisher. Copyright © 1984 by Massachusetts Institute of Technology. All rights reserved.

European manufacturers of prestige automobiles, such as Mercedes-Benz and Porsche, have emphasized the first dimension of product quality—**functional performance.** These automakers have designed cars that provide excellent performance on such attributes as handling, acceleration, and comfort. Volvo, on the other hand, has emphasized and aggressively promoted a different quality dimension—**durability** (and the related attribute of safety). A third quality dimension, **conformance to specifications,** or the absence of defects, has been a major focus of the Japanese automakers. Until recent years, American carmakers relied heavily on broad product lines and a wide **variety of features,** both standard and optional, to offset their shortcomings on some of the other quality dimensions.

The **reliability** quality dimension can refer to the consistency of performance from purchase to purchase or to a product's uptime, the percentage of time that it can perform satisfactorily over its life. Tandem Computers has maintained a competitive advantage based on reliability by designing computers with several processors that work in tandem, so that if one fails, the only impact is the slowing of low-priority tasks. IBM had difficulty matching Tandem's reliability because its operating system was not easily adapted to the multiple-processor concept. Consequently, Tandem has maintained a strong position in market segments consisting of large-scale computer users, such as financial institutions and large retailers, for whom system downtime is particularly undesirable.

The quality dimension of **serviceability** refers to a customer's ability to obtain prompt and competent service when the product does break down. For example, Caterpillar has long differentiated itself with a parts and service organization dedicated to providing "24-hour parts service anywhere in the world."

Many of these quality dimensions can be difficult for customers to evaluate, particularly for consumer products. As a result, consumers often generalize from quality dimensions that are more visual or qualitative. Thus, the **fit and finish** dimension can help convince consumers that a product is of high quality. They tend to perceive attractive and well-designed products as generally high in quality, as witnessed by the success of the Krups line of small appliances. Similarly, the **quality reputation of the brand name,** and the promotional activities that sustain that reputation, can strongly influence consumers' perceptions of a product's quality. A brand's quality reputation together with psychological factors such as name recognition and loyalty substantially determine a brand's **equity**—the perceived value customers associate with a particular brand name and its logo or symbol.[10] To successfully pursue a differentiation strategy based on quality, then, a business must understand what dimensions or cues its potential customers use to judge quality, and it should pay particular attention to some of the less-concrete but more visible and symbolic attributes of the product.

Dimensions of Service Quality   Customers also judge the quality of the service they receive on multiple dimensions. A number of such dimensions of perceived service quality have been identified by a series of studies conducted across diverse industries such as retail banking and appliance repair, and five of those dimensions are listed and briefly defined in Exhibit 11.4.[11]

The quality dimensions listed in Exhibit 11.4 apply specifically to service businesses, but most of them are also relevant for judging the service component of a product offering. This pertains to both the objective performance dimensions of the service delivery system, such as its **reliability** and **responsiveness,** as well as to elements of the performance of service personnel, such as their **empathy** and level of **assurance.**

The results of a number of surveys suggest that customers perceive all five dimensions of service quality to be very important regardless of the kind of service being evaluated. As Exhibit 11.5 indicates, customers of four different kinds of services gave reliability, responsiveness, assurance, and empathy mean importance ratings of more than 9 on a 10-point rating scale. And though the mean ratings for tangibles were somewhat lower in comparison, they still fell toward the upper end of the scale, ranging from 7.14 to 8.56.

The same respondents also were asked which of the five dimensions they would choose as being the most critical in their assessment of service quality. Their responses, which are shown in Exhibit 11.5, suggest that reliability is the most important aspect of service quality to the greatest number of customers. Both service reliability and responsiveness are proving to be particularly important for, and the Achilles' heel of, many e-commerce sites. This point is dramatically illustrated by the experiences of Petopia.com Inc., described in Exhibit 11.6.

The key to a differentiation strategy based on providing superior service is to meet or exceed target customers' service quality expectations and to do it more consistently than competitors. The problem is that sometimes managers underestimate the level of those customer expectations, and sometimes those expectations can be unrealistically high. Therefore, a firm needs to clearly identify target customers' desires with respect to service quality and to clearly define and communicate what level of service they intend to deliver.

Exhibit 11.4

DIMENSIONS OF SERVICE QUALITY

•	Tangibles	Appearance of physical facilities, equipment, personnel, and communications materials.
•	Reliability	Ability to perform the promised service dependably and accurately.
•	Responsiveness	Willingness to help customers and provide prompt service.
•	Assurance	Knowledge and courtesy of employees and their ability to convey trust and confidence.
•	Empathy	Caring, individualized attention the firm provides its customers.

Source: Reprinted with the permission of The Free Press, A Division of Simon & Schuster, Inc., from *Delivering Quality Service: Balancing Custom Perceptions and Expectations* by Valarie A. Zeithaml, A. Parasuraman, and Leonard L. Berry. Copyright © 1990 by The Free Press.

Exhibit 11.5

PERCEIVED IMPORTANCE OF SERVICE QUALITY DIMENSIONS IN FOUR DIFFERENT INDUSTRIES

	Mean importance rating on 10-point scale*	Percentage of respondents indicating dimension is most important
Credit-card customers (n = 187)		
Tangibles	7.43	0.6
Reliability	9.45	48.6
Responsiveness	9.37	19.8
Assurance	9.25	17.5
Empathy	9.09	13.6
Repair-and-maintenance customers (n = 183)		
Tangibles	8.48	1.2
Reliability	9.64	57.2
Responsiveness	9.54	19.9
Assurance	9.62	12.0
Empathy	9.30	9.6
Long-distance telephone customers (n = 184)		
Tangibles	7.14	0.6
Reliability	9.67	60.6
Responsiveness	9.57	16.0
Assurance	9.29	12.6
Empathy	9.25	10.3
Bank customers (n = 177)		
Tangibles	8.56	1.1
Reliability	9.44	42.1
Responsiveness	9.34	18.0
Assurance	9.18	13.6
Empathy	9.30	25.1

*Scale ranges from 1 (not at all important) to 10 (extremely important).

Source: Reprinted with permission of The Free Press, a Division of Simon & Schuster, Inc., from *Delivering Quality Service: Balancing Customer Perceptions and Expectations* by Valarie A. Zeithaml, A. Parasuraman, and Leonard L. Berry. Copyright © 1990 by The Free Press.

When this is done, customers have a more realistic idea of what to expect and are less likely to be disappointed with the service they receive.

Improving Customer Perceptions of Service Quality The major factors that determine a customer's expectations and perceptions concerning service quality—and five gaps that can lead to dissatisfaction with service delivery—are outlined in Exhibit 11.7 and discussed next.

1. **Gap between the customer's expectations and the marketer's perceptions.** Managers do not always have an accurate understanding of what customers want or how they will evaluate a firm's service efforts. The first step in providing good service is to collect information—through customer surveys, evaluations of customer complaints, or other methods—to determine what service attributes customers consider important.

Exhibit 11.6   Petopia.com—Learning the Importance of Service Reliability and Responsiveness on the Web

At first, the people at Petopia.com Inc. thought it was time to break out the champagne: during the 1999 holiday season 160,000 customers clicked the pet supply site's buy button—four times the number it expected. But the flood of orders quickly overloaded its one distribution center, and thousands of complaints and questions poured in. And when customers couldn't get through, they blitzed Petopia with angry e-mails, many of which went unanswered for as long as four days.

It's the sort of nightmare that has plagued many e-tailers. The reason? Many sites, figuring the Web's self-service model could save them millions of dollars in customer service costs, didn't realize that was the last place they could afford to pinch pennies. Market researcher Datamonitor estimated that Web sales lost due to poor service could reach $11 billion in 2000. And studies conducted by Forrester Research, Inc., indicate that websites can get much higher sales gains by providing good service to existing customers and keeping them happy than by blindly seeking new ones. Their findings suggest that more than 90 percent of satisfied consumers say they'll visit a site again, and 87 percent will recommend it to others.

Some e-tailers are learning their lesson. The first thing Petopia did was apologize by sending a free gift to every customer who had a problem with an order. More importantly, the firm paid out $10 million in 2000 to expand its order fulfillment capabilities and install new customer service software. As a result, Petopia can now service twice as many people a day as it could in 1999, and it responds to all e-mail queries and complaints within 24 hours.

These improvements in Petopia's service reliability and responsiveness have begun to pay off. According to the research firm Gomez Advisors Inc., the firm now ranks tops in customer relations among pet sites, and 70 percent of its sales are now coming from repeat customers.

Source: Reprinted from Jeanette Brown, "Service, Please," *Business Week e.biz,* October 23, 2000, pp. EB48–50, with special permission. Copyright © 2000 by The McGraw-Hill Companies, Inc.

2. **Gap between management perceptions and service quality specifications.** Even when management has a clear understanding of what customers want, that understanding might not get translated into effective operating standards. A firm's policies concerning customer service may be unclear, poorly communicated to employees, or haphazardly enforced. Unless a firm's employees know what the company's service policies are and believe that management is seriously committed to those standards, their performance is likely to fall short of desired levels.

3. **Gap between service quality specifications and service delivery.** Lip service by management is not enough to produce high-quality service. High standards must be backed by the programs, resources, and rewards necessary to enable and encourage employees to deliver good service. Employees must be provided with the training, equipment, and time necessary to deliver good service. Their service performance must be measured and evaluated. And good performance must be rewarded by making it part of the criteria for pay raises or promotions, or by other more direct inducements, in order to motivate the additional effort good service requires.

4. **Gap between service delivery and external communications.** Even good service performance may disappoint some customers if the firm's marketing communications cause them to have unrealistically high expectations. If the photographs in a vacation resort's advertising and brochures make the rooms look more spacious and luxurious than they really are, for instance, first-time customers are likely to be disappointed no matter how clean or well-tended those rooms are kept by the resort's staff.

5. **Gap between perceived service and expected service.** This results when management fails to close one or more of the other four gaps. It is this difference between a customer's expectations and his or her actual experience with the firm that leads to dissatisfaction.

The above discussion suggests a number of actions management can take to close the possible gaps and improve customer satisfaction with a company's service. Some of those actions are nicely illustrated by the response of Petopia.com's managers to the firm's service problems,

Exhibit 11.7

DETERMINANTS OF PERCEIVED SERVICE QUALITY

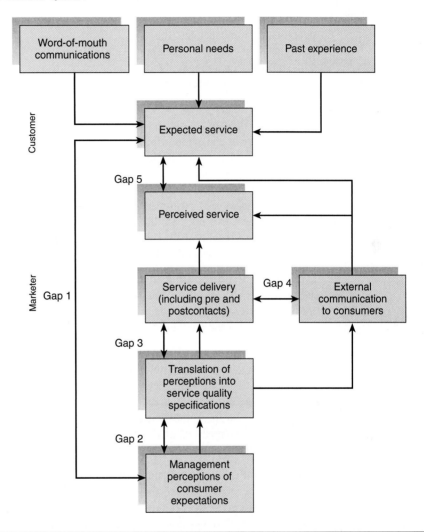

Source: Reprinted from A. Parasuraman, Valarie A. Zeithaml, and Leonard L. Berry, "A Conceptual Model of Service Quality and Its Implications for Future Research," *Journal of Marketing,* Fall 1985, p. 44. Published by the American Marketing Association. Reprinted with permission.

as described earlier in Exhibit 11.6. Achieving and sustaining high levels of service quality can present difficult implementation problems, however, because it usually involves the coordination of efforts of many employees from different functional departments and organizational levels. Some of these coordination problems are examined in Chapter 13.

Methods of Maintaining a Low-Cost Position

Moving down the experience curve is the most commonly discussed method of achieving and sustaining a low-cost position in an industry. But a firm does not necessarily need a large relative market share to implement a low-cost strategy. For instance, Johnson

Controls relies on close alliances with customers, as well as economies of scale, to hold down its inventory and distribution costs. And Michael Dell, as a small follower in the personal computer industry, managed to achieve costs below those of much larger competitors by developing logistical alliances with suppliers and an innovative, Internet-based direct distribution channel.

Some other means for obtaining a sustainable cost advantage include producing a no-frills product, creating an innovative product design, finding cheaper raw materials, automating or outsourcing production, developing low-cost distribution channels, and reducing overhead.[12]

A No-Frills Product   A direct approach to obtaining a low-cost position involves simply removing all frills and extras from the basic product or service. Thus, Suzuki cars, warehouse furniture stores, legal services clinics, and grocery stores selling canned goods out of crates all offer lower costs and prices than their competitors. This lower production cost is often sustainable because established differentiated competitors find it difficult to stop offering features and services their customers have come to expect. However, those established firms may lower their own prices in the short run—even to the point of suffering losses—in an attempt to drive out a no-frills competitor that poses a serious threat. Thus, a firm considering a no-frills strategy needs the resources to withstand a possible price war.[13]

Innovative Product Design   A simplified product design and standardized component parts also can lead to cost advantages. In the office copier industry, for instance, Japanese firms overcame substantial entry barriers by designing extremely simple copiers, with a fraction of the number of parts in the design used by market-leading Xerox.

Cheaper Raw Materials   A firm with the foresight to acquire or the creativity to find a way to use relatively cheap raw materials also can gain a sustainable cost advantage. For example, Fort Howard Paper achieved an advantage by being the first major papermaker to rely exclusively on recycled pulp. While the finished product was not so high in quality as paper from virgin wood, Fort Howard's lower cost gave it a competitive edge in the price-sensitive commercial market for toilet paper and other such products used in hotels, restaurants, and office buildings.

Innovative Production Processes   Although low-cost defender businesses typically spend little on *product R&D,* they often continue to devote substantial sums to *process R&D.* Innovations in the production process, including the development of automated or computer-controlled processes, can help them sustain cost advantages over competitors.

In some labor-intensive industries, a business can achieve a cost advantage, at least in the short term, by gaining access to inexpensive labor. This is usually achieved by moving all or part of the production process to countries with low wage rates, such as Taiwan, Korea, or Mexico. Unfortunately, because such moves are relatively easy to emulate, this kind of cost advantage may not be sustainable.

Low-Cost Distribution   When distribution accounts for a relatively high proportion of a product's total delivered cost, a firm might gain a substantial advantage by developing lower-cost alternative channels. Typically, this involves eliminating, or shifting to the customer, some of the functions performed by traditional channels in return for a lower price. In the consumer banking industry, for example, automated teller machines have helped reduce labor costs and investment in bricks-and-mortar branch banks. But they also have reduced the amount of personalized service banks provide to their customers, which may help explain why average customer satisfaction with banks fell by more than 8 percent from 1994 to 2000.[14]

Reductions in Overhead   Successfully sustaining a low-cost strategy requires that the firm pare and control its major overhead costs as quickly as possible as its industry matures. Many U.S. companies learned this lesson the hard way during the 1980s when high costs of old plants, labor, and large inventories left them vulnerable to more efficient foreign competitors and to corporate raiders.

Customers' Satisfaction and Loyalty Are Crucial for Maximizing Their Lifetime Value

Analyzer, and particularly defender, businesses are mostly concerned with protecting their existing positions in one or more mature market segments and maximizing profitability over the remaining life of those product-markets. Thus, financial dimensions of performance, such as return on investment and cash flow, are usually of greater interest to such businesses than are more growth-oriented dimensions, such as volume increases or new product success. Businesses can achieve such financial objectives by either successfully differentiating their offerings or maintaining a low-cost position.

While the primary emphasis in many businesses during the early 1990s was on improving efficiency through downsizing and reengineering,[15] there is substantial evidence that firms with superior quality goods and services also obtain higher returns on investment than do businesses with average or below average offerings.[16] The lesson to be learned, then, is that the choice between a differentiation or a low-cost strategy is probably not the critical determinant of success in mature markets. What is critical is that a business *continually work to improve the value* of its offerings—by either improving product or service quality, reducing costs, or some combination—as a basis for maintaining its customer base as its markets mature and become increasingly competitive.

Measuring Customer Satisfaction   To gain the knowledge necessary to continually improve the value of their offerings to customers, firms must understand how satisfied existing and potential customers are with their current offerings. This focus on customer satisfaction has become increasingly important as more firms question whether all attempts to improve *absolute* quality of their products and services generate sufficient additional sales and profits to justify their cost. This growing concern with the economic "return on quality" has motivated firms to ask which dimensions of product or service quality are most important to customers and which dimensions customers might be willing to sacrifice for lower prices. For instance, United Parcel Service recently discovered that many of its customers wanted more time to interact with the company's drivers in order to seek advice on their shipping problems, and they were willing to put up with slightly slower delivery times in return. Consequently, UPS now allows its drivers an additional 30 minutes a day to spend at their discretion to strengthen ties with customers and perhaps bring in new sales.[17]

Useful measures of customer satisfaction, then, should examine both (1) customers' *expectations and preferences* concerning the various dimensions of product and service quality (such as product performance, features, reliability, on-time delivery, competence of service personnel, and so on) and (2) their *perceptions* concerning how well the firm is meeting those expectations. Any gaps where customer expectations exceed their recent experiences may indicate fruitful areas for the firm to work at improving customer value and satisfaction. Of course, such measurements must be made periodically to determine whether the actions taken have been effective.[18]

Improving Customer Retention and Loyalty   Maintaining the loyalty of existing customers is crucial for a business's profitability. This is especially true as markets mature because loyal customers become more profitable over time. The firm not only avoids the high costs associated with trying to acquire replacement customers in an increasingly competitive market, but it also benefits because loyal customers (1) tend to concentrate their purchases, thus leading to larger volumes and lower selling and distribution costs; (2) provide positive word-of-mouth and customer referrals; and (3) may be willing to pay premium prices for the value they receive.[19]

Periodic measurement of customer satisfaction is important because a dissatisfied customer is unlikely to remain loyal over time. Unfortunately, the reverse is not always true: Customers who describe themselves as satisfied are not necessarily loyal. Indeed, one author estimates that 60 to 80 percent of customer defectors in most businesses said they were "satisfied" or "very satisfied" on the last customer survey before their defection.[20] In the interim, perhaps competitors improved their offerings, the customer's requirements changed, or other environmental factors shifted. Companies that measure customer satisfaction should be commended—but urged not to stop there. Satisfaction measures need to be supplemented with examinations of customer *behavior*, such as measures of the annual retention rate, frequency of purchases, and the percentage of a customer's total purchases captured by the firm.

Most important, defecting customers should be studied in detail to discover why the firm failed to provide sufficient value to retain their loyalty. Such failures often provide more valuable information than satisfaction measures because they stand out as a clear, understandable message telling the organization exactly where improvements are needed. The actions of MicroScan, as detailed in Exhibit 11.8, provide a good example of the intelligent use of such defector analysis.

Are All Customers Equally Valuable?[21]

While improving customer loyalty is crucial for maintaining market share and profitability as markets mature, an increasing number of companies are asking whether every customer's loyalty is worthy of the same level of effort and expense. In these firms, technology is creating a new business model that alters the level of service and benefits provided to a customer based on projections of that customer's value to the firm. With the development of extensive customer databases, it is possible for companies to measure what different levels of customer service cost on an individual level. They also can know how much business a particular customer has generated in the past, estimate what she or he is likely to buy in the future, and calculate a rate of return for that individual for different levels of service.

STRATEGIC ISSUE

An increasing number of companies are asking whether every customer's loyalty is worthy of the same level of effort and expense.

Exhibit 11.8   MicroScan Examines Defectors to Improve Customer Loyalty

The MicroScan division of Baxter Diagnostics, Inc., makes instruments used by medical laboratories to identify microbes in patient cultures. In 1990 MicroScan was neck-and-neck with Vitek Systems, Inc., for market leadership, but its management knew it would have to do better to win the race. The firm analyzed its customer base, highlighting accounts that had been lost as well as those that remained active but showed a declining volume of testing. MicroScan interviewed all the lost customers and a large portion of the "decliners," probing deeply for the causes underlying their change in behavior. They found that such customers had concerns about the company's instrument features, reliability, and responsiveness to their problems.

In response, MicroScan's management shifted R&D priorities to address specific shortcomings its lost customers had identified, such as test accuracy and time-to-result. It also redesigned customer service protocols to ensure that immediate attention was given to equipment faults and delivery problems. As a result, MicroScan's sales began to improve and it established a clear market-share lead within two years.

Source: Frederick F. Reichheld, "Loyalty and the Renaissance of Marketing," *Marketing Management* 2 (1994), pp. 10–21.

Exhibit 11.9   Pros and Cons of Varying Service Levels According to Customers' Profitability

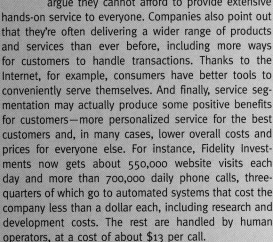

From a purely economic viewpoint, tailoring different levels of service and benefits to different customer segments depending on their profitability makes sense, at least in the short run. In an era when labor costs are increasing while many markets, especially mature ones, are getting more competitive, many firms argue they cannot afford to provide extensive hands-on service to everyone. Companies also point out that they're often delivering a wider range of products and services than ever before, including more ways for customers to handle transactions. Thanks to the Internet, for example, consumers have better tools to conveniently serve themselves. And finally, service segmentation may actually produce some positive benefits for customers—more personalized service for the best customers and, in many cases, lower overall costs and prices for everyone else. For instance, Fidelity Investments now gets about 550,000 website visits each day and more than 700,000 daily phone calls, three-quarters of which go to automated systems that cost the company less than a dollar each, including research and development costs. The rest are handled by human operators, at a cost of about $13 per call.

From an ethical standpoint, however, many people question the inherent fairness and potential invasion of privacy involved in using a wealth of personal information about individual consumers as a basis for withholding services or benefits from some of them, especially when such practices are largely invisible to the consumer. You don't know when you're being shuttled to a different telephone queue or sales promotion. You don't know what benefits you're missing or what additional fees you're being charged. Some argue that this lack of transparency is unfair because it deprives consumers of the opportunity to take actions, such as concentrating their purchases with a single supplier, switching companies, or paying a service fee, that would enable them to acquire the additional services and benefits they are currently denied.

From a strategic view, there are also some potential dangers in cutting services and benefits to customers who have not generated profits in the past. For one thing, past behavior is not necessarily an accurate indicator of a customer's future lifetime value. The life situations and spending habits of some customer groups—college students, for instance—can change dramatically over time. In addition, looking only at a customer's purchases may overlook some indirect ways that customer affects the firm's revenues, such as positive word-of-mouth recommendations and referrals to other potential buyers. And some customers may not be spending much with a company precisely because of the lousy service they have received as a result of not spending very much with that company. Instead of simply writing off low-volume customers, it may make more strategic sense to first attempt to convert them into high-volume customers by targeting them for additional promotions, by trying to sell complementary goods and services, or by instituting loyalty programs (e.g., the airlines' frequent-flier programs).

Finally, by debasing the satisfaction and loyalty of low-volume customers, firms risk losing those customers to competitors. In a mature industry, particularly one with substantial economies of scale, such a loss of market share can increase unit costs and reduce the profitability of those high-volume customers that do remain loyal. And a creative competitor may find ways to make other firms' cast-off customers very profitable after all.

 The ability of firms to tailor different levels of service and benefits to different customers based on each person's potential to produce a profit has been facilitated by the growing popularity of the Internet. The Web has made it easier to track and measure individual transactions across businesses. It also has provided firms with new, low-cost service options; people can now serve themselves at their own convenience, but they have to accept little or no human contact in return.

The end result of this trend toward individually tailored service levels could be an increased stratification of consumer society. The top tier may enjoy unprecedented levels of personal attention. But those who fall below a certain level of profitability for too long may face increased service fees or receive reduced levels of service and benefits. For example, some credit-card companies now charge higher annual fees to customers who do not rack up some minimum level of interest charges during the year. In other firms, call center personnel route customers to different queues. Big spenders are turned over to high-level problem solvers while less profitable customers may never speak to a live person. Finally, choice customers may get fees waived or receive promotional discounts based on the value of their business, while less valuable customers may never know the promotions exist.

The segmentation of customers based on projections of their value and the tailoring of different service levels and benefits to those segments raise both ethical and strategic questions, some of which are explored in Exhibit 11.9. One possible way for a firm to resolve some of the dilemmas involved in dealing with less profitable customers is to find ways to increase their lifetime value by increasing the frequency and/or volume of their purchases. This is one strategy examined in detail in the following section.

MARKETING STRATEGIES FOR MATURE MARKETS

Strategies for Maintaining Current Market Share

Since markets can remain in the maturity stage for decades, milking or harvesting mature product-markets by maximizing short-run profits makes little sense. Pursuing such an objective typically involves substantial cuts in marketing and R&D expenses, which can lead to premature losses of volume and market share and lower profits in the longer term. The business should strive during the early years of market maturity to *maximize the flow of profits over the remaining life of the product-market.* Thus, the most critical marketing objective is to *maintain and protect the business's market share.* In a mature market where few new customers buy the product for the first time, the business must continue to win its share of repeat purchases from existing customers.

In Chapter 10 we discussed a number of marketing strategies that businesses might use to maintain their market share in growth markets. Many of those same strategies continue to be relevant for holding on to customers as markets mature, particularly for those firms that survived the shakeout period with a relatively strong share position. The most obvious strategy for such share leaders is simply to continue strengthening their position through a *fortress defense.* Recall that such a strategy involves two sets of marketing actions: those aimed at improving customer satisfaction and loyalty and those intended to encourage and simplify repeat purchasing. Actions like those discussed earlier for improving the quality of a firm's offering and for reducing costs suggest ways to increase customer satisfaction and loyalty. Similarly, improvements to service quality, such as just-in-time delivery arrangements or computerized reordering systems, can help encourage repeat purchases.

Since markets often become more fragmented as they grow and mature, share leaders also may have to expand their product lines, or add one or more *flanker* brands, to protect their position against competitive inroads. Thus, Johnson Controls has strengthened its position in the commercial facilities management arena by expanding its array of services through a combination of acquisitions and continued internal development.

Small-share competitors also can earn substantial profits in a mature market. To do so, however, it is often wise for them to focus on strategies that avoid prolonged direct confrontations with larger share leaders. A *niche strategy* can be particularly effective when the target segment is too small to appeal to larger competitors or when the smaller firm can establish a strong differential advantage or brand preference in the segment. For instance, with only 36 hotels worldwide, the Four Seasons chain is a small player in the lodging industry. But by focusing on the high end of the business travel market, the chain has grown and prospered. The chain's hotels differentiate themselves by offering a wide range of amenities, such as free overnight shoeshines, that are important to business travelers. Thus, while they charge relatively high prices, they also are seen as delivering good value.

Strategies for Extending Volume Growth

Market maturity is defined by a flattening of the growth rate. In some instances growth slows for structural reasons, such as the emergence of substitute products or a shift in customer preferences. Marketers can do little to revitalize the market under such conditions. But in some cases a market only *appears* to be mature because of the limitations of current marketing programs, such as target segments that are too narrowly defined or limited product offerings. Here, more innovative or aggressive marketing strategies might successfully extend the market's life cycle into a period of renewed growth. Thus, *stimulating additional volume* growth can be an important secondary objective under such circumstances, particularly for industry share leaders because they often can capture a relatively large share of any additional volume generated.

A firm might pursue several different marketing strategies—either singly or in combination—to squeeze additional volume from a mature market. These include an *increased penetration strategy,* an *extended use strategy,* and a *market expansion strategy.* Exhibit 11.10

Exhibit 11.10

SITUATIONAL DETERMINANTS OF APPROPRIATE MARKETING OBJECTIVES AND STRATEGIES FOR EXTENDING GROWTH IN MATURE MARKETS

	GROWTH EXTENSION STRATEGIES		
Situation variables	Increased penetration	Extended use	Market expansion
Primary objective	Increase the proportion of users by converting current nonusers in one or more major market segments.	Increase the amount of product used by the average customer by increasing frequency of use or developing new and more varied ways to use the product.	Expand the number of potential customers by targeting underdeveloped geographic areas or applications segments.
Market characteristics	Relatively low penetration in one or more segments (i.e., low percentage of potential users have adopted the product); relatively homogeneous market with only a few large segments.	Relatively high penetration but low frequency of use in one or more major segments; product used in only limited ways or for special occasions; relatively homogeneous market with only a few large segments.	Relatively heterogeneous market with a variety of segments; some geographic areas, including foreign countries, with low penetration; some product applications underdeveloped.
Competitors' characteristics	Competitors hold relatively small market shares; comparatively limited resources or competencies make it unlikely they will steal a significant portion of converted nonusers.	Competitors hold relatively small market shares; comparatively limited resources or competencies make it unlikely their brands will be purchased for newly developed uses.	Competitors hold relatively small market shares; have insufficient resources or competencies to preempt underdeveloped geographic areas or applications segments.
Firm's characteristics	A market share leader in the industry; has R&D and marketing competencies to produce product modifications or line extensions; has promotional resources to stimulate primary demand among current nonusers.	A market share leader in the industry; has marketing competencies and resources to develop and promote new uses.	A market share leader in the industry; has marketing and distribution competencies and resources to develop new global markets or applications segments.

Exhibit 11.11

POSSIBLE MARKETING ACTIONS FOR ACCOMPLISHING GROWTH EXTENSION OBJECTIVES

Marketing strategy and objectives	*Possible marketing actions*

Increased penetration

Convert current nonusers in target segment into users

- Enhance product's value by adding features, benefits, or services.
- Enhance product's value by including it in the design of integrated systems.
- Stimulate additional primary demand through promotional efforts stressing new features or benefits:
  Advertising through selective media aimed at the target segment.
  Sales promotions directed at stimulating trial among current nonusers (e.g., tie-ins with other products).
  Some sales efforts redirected toward new account generation, perhaps by assigning some sales personnel as account development reps or by offering incentives for new account sales.
  Improve product's availability by developing innovative distribution systems.

Extended use

Increase frequency of use among current users

- Move storage of the product closer to the point of end use by offering additional package sizes or designs.
- Encourage larger volume purchases (for nonperishable products):
  Offer quantity discounts.
  Offer consumer promotions to stimulate volume purchases or more frequent use (e.g., multipack deals, frequent-flier programs).
- Reminder advertising stressing basic product benefits for a variety of usage occasions.

Encourage a wider variety of uses among current users

- Develop line extensions suitable for additional uses or applications.
- Develop and promote new uses, applications, or recipes for the basic product.
  Include information about new applications/recipes on package.
  Develop extended use advertising campaign, particularly with print media.
  Communicate new application ideas through sales presentations to current customers.
- Encourage new uses through sales promotions (e.g., tie-ins with complementary products).

Market expansion

Develop differentiated positioning focused on untapped or underdeveloped segments

- Develop a differentiated flanker brand or product line with unique features or price that is more appealing to a segment of potential customers whose needs are not met by existing offerings.

Or

- Develop multiple line extensions or brand offerings with features or prices targeted to the unique needs and preferences of several smaller potential applications or regional segments.
- Consider producing for private labels.
- Design advertising, personal selling, and/or sales promotion campaigns that address specific interests and concerns of potential customers in one or multiple underdeveloped segments to stimulate selective demand.
- Build unique distribution channels to more effectively reach potential customers in one or multiple underdeveloped segments.
- Design service programs to reduce the perceived risks of trial and/or solve the unique problems faced by potential customers in one or multiple underdeveloped segments (e.g., systems engineering, installation, operator training, extended warranties).
- Enter global markets where product category is in an earlier stage of its life cycle.

summarizes the environmental situations where each of these strategies is most appropriate and the objectives each is best suited for accomplishing. Exhibit 11.11 then outlines specific marketing actions a firm might employ to implement each of the strategies, as discussed in more detail in the following paragraphs.

Increased Penetration Strategy

The total sales volume produced by a target segment of customers is a function of (1) the number of potential customers in the segment; (2) the product's penetration of that segment, that is, the proportion of potential customers who actually use the product; and (3) the average frequency with which customers consume the product and make another purchase. Where usage frequency is quite high among current customers but only a relatively small portion of all potential users actually buy the product, a firm might aim at increasing market penetration. It is an appropriate strategy for an industry's share leader because such firms can more likely gain and retain a substantial share of new customers than smaller firms with less-well-known brands.

The secret to a successful increased penetration strategy lies in discovering why nonusers are uninterested in the product. Very often the product does not offer sufficient value from the potential customer's view to justify the effort or expense involved in buying and using it. One obvious solution to such a problem is to enhance the product's value to potential customers by adding features or benefits, usually via line extensions.

Another way to add value to a product is to develop and sell integrated systems that help improve the basic product's performance or ease of use. For instance, instead of simply selling control mechanisms for heating and cooling systems, Johnson Controls offers integrated facilities management programs designed to lower the total costs of operating a commercial building.

A firm also may enhance a product's value by offering services that improve its performance or ease of use for the potential customer. Since it is unlikely that people who do not know how to knit will ever buy yarn or knitting needles, for example, most yarn shops offer free knitting lessons.

Product modifications or line extensions, however, will not attract nonusers unless the enhanced benefits are effectively promoted. For industrial goods, this may mean redirecting some sales efforts toward nonusers. The firm may offer additional incentives for new account sales or assign specific salespeople to call on targeted nonusers and convert them into new customers. For consumer goods, some combination of advertising to stimulate primary demand in the target segment and sales promotions to encourage trial, such as free samples or tie-in promotions with complementary products that nonusers currently buy, can be effective.

Finally, some potential customers may be having trouble finding the product due to limited distribution, or the product's benefits may simply be too modest to justify much purchasing effort. In such cases, expanding distribution or developing more convenient and accessible channels may help expand market penetration. For example, few travelers are so leery of flying that they would go through the effort of calling an insurance agent to buy an accident policy for a single flight. But the sales of such policies are greatly increased by making them conveniently available through vending machines in airport terminals.

Extended Use Strategy

Some years ago, the manager of General Foods' Cool Whip frozen dessert topping discovered through marketing research that nearly three-fourths of all households used the product, but the average consumer used it only four times per year and served it on only 7 percent of all toppable desserts. In situations of good market penetration but low frequency of use, an extended use strategy may increase volume. This was particularly true in the Cool Whip case; the relatively large and homogeneous target market consisted for the most part of a single mass-market segment. Also, General Foods held nearly a two-thirds share of the frozen topping market, and it had the marketing resources and competencies to capture most of the additional volume that an extended use strategy might generate.

One effective approach for stimulating increased frequency of use is to move product inventories closer to the point of use. This approach works particularly well with low-involvement consumer goods. Marketers know that most consumers are unlikely to expend any additional time or effort to obtain such products when they are ready to use them. If there is no Cool Whip in the refrigerator when the consumer is preparing dessert, for instance, he or she is unlikely to run to the store immediately and probably will serve the dessert without topping.

One obvious way to move inventory closer to the point of consumption is to offer larger package sizes. The more customers buy at one time, the less likely they are to be out of stock when a usage opportunity arises. This approach can backfire, though, for a perishable product or one that consumers perceive to be an impulse indulgence. Thus, most superpremium ice creams, such as Häagen-Dazs, are sold in small pint containers; most consumers want to avoid the temptation of having large quantities of such a high-calorie indulgence too readily available.

The design of a package also can help increase use frequency by making the product more convenient or easy to use. Examples include single-serving packages of Jell-O pudding to pack in lunches, packages of paper cups that include a convenient dispenser, and frozen-food packages that can go directly into a microwave oven.

Various sales promotion programs also help move inventories of a product closer to the point of use by encouraging larger volume purchases. Marketers commonly offer quantity discounts for this purpose in selling industrial goods. For consumer products, multi-item discounts or two-for-one deals serve the same purpose. Promotional programs also encourage greater frequency of use and increase customer loyalty in many service industries. Consider, for instance, the frequent-flier programs offered by major airlines.

Sometimes the product's characteristics inhibit customers from using it more frequently. If marketers can change those characteristics, such as difficulty of preparation or high calories, a new line extension might encourage customers to use more of the product or to use it more often. Microwave waffles and low-calorie salad dressings are examples of such line extensions. For industrial goods, however, firms may have to develop new technology to overcome a product's limitations for some applications. For instance, Johnson Controls recently acquired Prince Automotive to gain the expertise necessary to develop instrument panels and consoles incorporating the sophisticated electronics desired by top-end manufacturers such as BMW and Mercedes-Benz.

Finally, advertising can sometimes effectively increase use frequency by simply reminding customers to use the product more often. For instance, General Foods conducted a reminder campaign for Jell-O pudding that featured Bill Cosby asking, "When was the last time you served pudding, Mom?"

Another approach for extending use among current customers involves finding and promoting new functional uses for the product. Jell-O gelatin is a classic example, having generated substantial new sales volume over the years by promoting the use of Jell-O as an ingredient in salads, pie fillings, and other dishes.

Firms promote new ways to use a product through a variety of methods. For industrial products, firms send technical advisories about new applications to the salesforce to present to their customers during regular sales calls. For consumer products, new use suggestions or recipes may be included on the package, in an advertising campaign, or on the firm's website. Sales promotions, such as including cents-off coupons in ads featuring a new recipe, encourage customers to try a new application. To reduce costs, two or more manufacturers of complementary products sometimes cooperate in running such promotions. A recent ad promoting a simple Italian dinner, for instance, featured coupons for Kraft's Parmesan cheese, Pillsbury's Soft Breadsticks, and Campbell's Prego spaghetti sauce.

In some cases, slightly modified line extensions might encourage customers to use the product in different ways. Thus, Kraft introduced a jalapeño-flavored Cheese-Whiz in a microwavable container and promoted the product as an easy-to-prepare topping for nachos.

STRATEGIC ISSUE

In a fragmented and heterogeneous market where some segments are less well developed than others, a market expansion strategy may generate substantial additional volume growth.

Market Expansion Strategy   In a mature industry with a fragmented and heterogeneous market where some segments are less well developed than others, a market expansion strategy may generate substantial additional volume growth. Such a strategy aims at gaining new customers by targeting new or underdeveloped geographic markets (either regional or foreign) or new customer segments. Once again, share leaders tend to be best suited for implementing this strategy. But even smaller competitors can employ such a strategy successfully if they focus on relatively small or specialized market niches.

Pursuing market expansion by strengthening a firm's position in new or underdeveloped **domestic geographic markets** can lead to experience-curve benefits and operating synergies. The firm can rely on largely the same expertise and technology, and perhaps even the same production and distribution facilities, it has already developed. Unfortunately, domestic geographic expansion is often not viable in a mature industry because the share leaders usually have attained national market coverage. Smaller regional competitors, on the other hand, might consider domestic geographic expansion a means for improving their volume and share position. However, such a move risks retaliation from the large national brands as well as from entrenched regional competitors in the prospective new territory.

To get around the retaliation problem, a regional producer might try to expand through the acquisition of small producers in other regions. This can be a viable option when (1) the low profitability of some regional producers enables the acquiring firm to buy their assets for less than the replacement cost of the capacity involved and (2) synergies gained by combining regional operations and the infusion of resources from the acquiring firm can improve the effectiveness and profitability of the acquired producers. For example, Heileman Brewing Company grew from the 31st largest brewer of beer in the mid-1960s to the 4th largest by the mid-1980s through the acquisition of nearly 30 regional brands. Heileman took control of strong regional brands such as Old Style, Carling, and Rainier, but because it had no dominant national brand it avoided antitrust opposition to its acquisition program. After acquisition, Heileman maintained the identity of each brand, increased its advertising budget, and expanded its distribution by incorporating it into the firm's distribution system in other regions. As a result, Heileman achieved a strong earnings record for two decades, until the firm was itself acquired by an Australian brewer.

In a different approach to domestic market expansion, the firm identifies and develops entirely **new customer** or **application segments.** Sometimes the firm can effectively reach new customer segments by simply expanding the distribution system without changing the product's characteristics or the other marketing-mix elements. A sporting goods manufacturer that sells its products to consumers through retail stores, for instance, might expand into the commercial market consisting of schools and amateur and professional sports teams by establishing a direct salesforce. In most instances, though, developing new market segments requires modifying the product to make it more suitable for the application or to provide more of the benefits desired by customers in the new segment.

One final possibility for domestic market expansion is to produce **private-label brands** for large retailers such as Sears or Safeway. Firms whose own brands hold relatively weak positions and who have excess production capacity find this a particularly attractive option. Private labeling allows such firms to gain access to established customer segments without making substantial marketing expenditures, thus increasing the firm's volume and lowering its per-unit costs. However, since private labels typically compete with low prices and their sponsors usually have strong bargaining power, producing private labels is often not a very profitable option unless a manufacturer already has a relatively low-cost position in the industry. It also can be a risky strategy, particularly for the smaller firm, because reliance on one or a few large private-label customers can result in drastic volume reductions and unit-cost increases should those customers decide to switch suppliers.

Global Market Expansion—Sequential Strategies

 For firms with leading positions in mature domestic markets, less-developed markets in foreign countries often present the most viable opportunities for geographic expansion. As discussed in previous chapters, firms can enter foreign markets in a variety of ways, from simply relying on import agents to developing joint ventures to establishing wholly owned subsidiaries—as Johnson Controls has done by acquiring an automotive seat manufacturer in Europe.

Regardless of which mode of entry a firm chooses, it can follow a number of different routes when pursuing global expansion.[22] By *route* we mean the sequence or order in which the firm enters global markets. Japanese companies provide illustrations of different global expansion paths. The most common expansion route involves moving from Japan to developing countries to developed countries. They used this path, for example, with automobiles (Toyota), consumer electronics (National), watches (Seiko), cameras (Minolta), and home appliances, steel, and petrochemicals. This routing reduced manufacturing costs and enabled them to gain marketing experience. In penetrating the U.S. market, the Japanese obtained further economies of scale and gained recognition for their products, which would make penetration of European markets easier.

This sequential strategy succeeded: by the early 1970s, 60 percent of Japanese exports went to developed countries—more than half to the United States. Japanese motorcycles dominate Europe, as do its watches and cameras. Its cars have been able to gain a respectable share in most European countries.

A second type of *expansion path* has been used primarily for high-tech products such as computers and semiconductors. For the Japanese it consists of first securing their home market and then targeting developed countries. Japan largely ignored developing countries in this strategy because of their small demand for high-tech products. When demand increased to a point where developing countries became "interesting," Japanese producers quickly entered and established strong market positions using price cuts of up to 50 percent.

A home market—developed markets—developing markets sequence is also usually appropriate for discretionary goods such as soft drinks, convenience foods, or cosmetics. Coca-Cola, for instance, believes that as disposable incomes and discretionary expenditures grow in the countries of South America, Asia, and Africa those markets will drive much of the company's future growth. Similarly, firms such as the French cosmetics giant L'Oreal have positioned a number of different "world brands"—including Ralph Lauren perfumes, L'Oreal hair products, and Maybelline and Helena Rubinstein cosmetics—to convey the allure of different cultures to developing markets around the world.[23]

STRATEGIES FOR DECLINING MARKETS

STRATEGIC ISSUE

The relative attractiveness of the declining product-market and the business's competitive position within it should dictate the appropriate strategy.

Most products eventually enter a decline phase in their life cycles. As sales decline, excess capacity once again develops. As the remaining competitors fight to hold volume in the face of falling sales, industry profits erode. Consequently, conventional wisdom suggests that firms should either divest declining products quickly or harvest them to maximize short-term profits. Not all markets decline in the same way or at the same speed, however; nor do all firms have the same competitive strengths and weaknesses within those markets. Therefore, as in most other situations, the relative attractiveness of the declining product-market and the business's competitive position within it should dictate the appropriate strategy.

Relative Attractiveness of Declining Markets

Although U.S. high school enrollment declined by about 2 million students from its peak in 1976 through the end of the 1980s, Jostens, Inc., the leading manufacturer of class rings and other school merchandise, achieved annual increases in revenues and profits every year during that period. One reason for the firm's success was that it saw the market decline coming and prepared for it by improving the efficiency of its operations and developing marketing programs that were effective at persuading a larger proportion of students to buy class rings.[24]

Jostens' experience shows that some declining product-markets can offer attractive opportunities well into the future, at least for one or a few strong competitors. In other product-markets, particularly those where decline is the result of customers switching to a new technology (e.g., more students buying personal computers instead of portable type-writers), the potential for continued profits during the decline stage is more bleak.

Three sets of factors help determine the strategic attractiveness of declining product-markets: *conditions of demand,* including the rate and certainty of future declines in volume; *exit barriers,* or the ease with which weaker competitors can leave the market; and factors affecting the *intensity of future competitive rivalry* within the market.[25] The impact of these variables on the attractiveness of declining market environments is summarized in Exhibit 11.12 and discussed below.

Conditions of Demand   Demand in a product-market declines for a number of reasons. Technological advances produce substitute products (such as electronic calculators for slide rules), often with higher quality or lower cost. Demographic shifts lead to a shrinking target market (baby foods). Customers' needs, tastes, or lifestyles change (the falling consumption of beef). Finally, the cost of inputs or complementary products rises and shrinks demand (the effects of rising gasoline prices on sales of recreational vehicles).

The cause of a decline in demand can affect both the rate and the predictability of that decline. A fall in sales due to a demographic shift, for instance, is likely to be gradual, whereas the switch to a technically superior substitute can be abrupt. Similarly, the fall in demand as customers switch to a better substitute is predictable, while a decline in sales due to a change in tastes is not.

As Exhibit 11.12 indicates, both the rate and certainty of sales decline are demand characteristics that affect a market's attractiveness. A slow and gradual decline allows an orderly withdrawal of weaker competitors. Overcapacity does not become excessive and lead to predatory competitive behavior, and the competitors who remain are more likely to make profits than in a quick or erratic decline. Also, when most industry managers believe market decline is predictable and certain, reduction of capacity is more likely to be orderly than when they feel substantial uncertainty about whether demand might level off or even become revitalized.

Not all segments of a market decline at the same time or at the same rate. The number and size of enduring niches or pockets of demand and the customer purchase behavior within them also influence the continuing attractiveness of the market. When the demand pockets are large or numerous and the customers in those niches are brand loyal and relatively insensitive to price, competitors with large shares and differentiated products can continue to make substantial profits. For example, even though the market for cigars

Exhibit 11.12

FACTORS AFFECTING THE ATTRACTIVENESS OF DECLINING MARKET ENVIRONMENTS

ENVIRONMENTAL ATTRACTIVENESS

Conditions of demand	Hospitable	Inhospitable
Speed of decline	Very slow	Rapid or erratic
Certainty of decline	100% certain, predictable patterns	Great uncertainty, erratic patterns
Pockets of enduring demand	Several or major ones	No niches
Product differentiation	Brand loyalty	Commoditylike products
Price stability	Stable, price premiums attainable	Very unstable, pricing below costs
Exit barriers		
Reinvestment requirements	None	High, often mandatory and involving capital assets
Excess capacity	Little	Substantial
Asset age	Mostly old assets	Sizable new assets and old ones not retired
Resale markets for assets	Easy to convert or sell	No markets available, substantial costs to retire
Shared facilities	Few, freestanding plants	Substantial and interconnected with important businesses
Vertical integration	Little	Substantial
Single-product competitors	None	Several large companies
Rivalry determinants		
Customer industries	Fragmented, weak	Strong bargaining power
Customer switching costs	High	Minimal
Diseconomies of scale	None	Substantial penalty
Dissimilar strategic groups	Few	Several in same target markets

Source: Reprinted by permission of *Harvard Business Review* from "End-Game Strategies for Declining Industries," by Kathryn Rudie Harrigan and Michael E. Porter, July–August 1983, p. 116. Copyright © 1983 by the Harvard Business School Publishing Corporation, all rights reserved.

shrank for years, there continued to be a sizable number of smokers who bought premium-quality cigars. Those firms with well-established positions at the premium end of the cigar industry have continued to earn above-average returns. And recently, the cigar market has been growing again.

Exit Barriers   The higher the exit barriers, the less hospitable a product-market will be during the decline phase of its life cycle. When weaker competitors find it hard to leave a product-market as demand falls, excess capacity develops and firms engage in aggressive pricing or promotional efforts to try to prop up their volume and hold down unit costs. Thus, exit barriers lead to competitive volatility.

Once again, Exhibit 11.12 indicates that a variety of factors influence the ease with which businesses can exit an industry. One critical consideration involves the amount of highly specialized assets. Assets unique to a given business are difficult to divest because of their low liquidation value. The only potential buyers for such assets are other firms who would use them for a similar purpose, which is unlikely in a declining industry. Thus, the firm may have little choice but to remain in the business or to sell the assets for their scrap value. This option is particularly unattractive when the assets are relatively new and not fully depreciated.

Another major exit barrier occurs when the assets or resources of the declining business intertwine with the firm's other business units, either through shared facilities and programs or through vertical integration. Exit from the declining business might shut down shared production facilities, lower salesforce commissions, damage customer relations, and increase unit costs in the firm's other businesses to a point that damages their profitability. Emotional factors also can act as exit barriers. Managers often feel reluctant to admit failure by divesting a business even though it no longer produces acceptable returns. This is especially true when the business played an important role in the firm's history and it houses a large number of senior managers.

Intensity of Future Competitive Rivalry   Even when substantial pockets of continuing demand remain within a declining business, it may not be wise for a firm to pursue them in the face of future intense competitive rivalry. In addition to exit barriers, other factors also affect the ability of the remaining firms to avoid intense price competition and maintain reasonable margins: size and bargaining power of the customers who continue to buy the product; customers' ability to switch to substitute products or to alternative suppliers; and any potential diseconomies of scale involved in capturing an increased share of the remaining volume.

Divestment or Liquidation

When the market environment in a declining industry is unattractive or a business has a relatively weak competitive position, the firm may recover more of its investment by selling the business in the early stages of decline rather than later. The earlier the business is sold, the more uncertain potential buyers are likely to be about the future direction of demand in the industry and thus the more likely that a willing buyer can be found. Thus, Raytheon sold its vacuum-tube business in the early 1960s even though transistors had just begun replacing tubes in radios and TV sets and there was still a strong replacement demand for tubes. By moving early, the firm achieved a much higher liquidation value than companies that tried to unload their tube-making facilities in the 70s when the industry was clearly in its twilight years.[26]

Of course, the firm that divests early runs the risk that its forecast of the industry's future may be wrong. Also, quick divestment may not be possible if the firm faces high exit barriers, such as interdependencies across business units or customer expectations of continued product availability. By planning early for departure, however, the firm may be able to reduce some of those barriers before the liquidation is necessary.

Marketing Strategies for Remaining Competitors

Conventional wisdom suggests that a business remaining in a declining product-market should pursue a harvesting strategy aimed at maximizing its cash flow in the short run. But such businesses also have other strategic options. They might attempt to maintain their position as the market declines, improve their position to become the profitable survivor, or focus efforts on one or more remaining demand pockets or market niches. Once again, the appropriateness of these strategies depends on factors affecting the attractiveness of the declining market and on the business's competitive strengths and weaknesses. Exhibit 11.13 summarizes the situational determinants of the appropriateness of each strategy. Some of the marketing actions a firm might take to implement them are discussed next and listed in Exhibit 11.14.

Exhibit 11.13

SITUATIONAL DETERMINANTS OF APPROPRIATE MARKETING OBJECTIVES AND STRATEGIES FOR DECLINING MARKETS

STRATEGIES FOR DECLINING MARKETS

Situational variables	Harvesting	Maintenance	Profitable survivor	Niche
Primary objective	Maximize short-term cash flow; maintain or increase margins even at the expense of a slow decline in market share.	Maintain share in short term as market declines, even if margins must be sacrificed.	Increase share of the declining market with an eye to future profits; encourage weaker competitors to exit.	Focus on strengthening position in one or a few relatively substantial segments with potential for future profits.
Market characteristics	Future market decline is certain, but likely to occur at a slow and steady rate.	Market has experienced recent declines, but future direction and attractiveness are currently hard to predict.	Future market decline is certain, but likely to occur at a slow and steady rate; substantial pockets of demand will continue to exist.	Overall market may decline quickly, but one or more segments will remain as demand pockets or decay slowly.
Competitors' characteristics	Few strong competitors; low exit barriers; future rivalry not likely to be intense.	Few strong competitors, but intensity of future rivalry is hard to predict.	Few strong competitors; exit barriers are low or can be reduced by firm's intervention.	One or more stronger competitors in mass market, but not in the target segment.
Firm's characteristics	Has a leading share position; has a substantial proportion of loyal customers who are likely to continue buying brand even if marketing support is reduced.	Has a leading share of the market and a relatively strong competitive position.	Has a leading share of the market and a strong competitive position; has superior resources or competencies necessary to encourage competitors to exit or to acquire them.	Has a sustainable competitive advantage in target segment, but overall resources may be limited.

Harvesting Strategy   The objective of a harvesting or milking strategy is to generate cash quickly by maximizing cash flow over a relatively short term. This typically involves avoiding any additional investment in the business, greatly reducing operating (including marketing) expenses, and perhaps raising prices. Since the firm usually expects to ultimately divest or abandon the business, some loss of sales and market share during the pursuit of this strategy is likely. The trick is to hold the business's volume and share declines to a relatively slow and steady rate. A precipitous and premature loss of share would limit the total amount of cash the business could generate during the market's decline.

A harvesting strategy is most appropriate for a firm holding a relatively strong competitive position in the market at the start of the decline and a cadre of current customers likely to continue buying the brand even after marketing support is reduced. Such a strategy also works best when the market's decline is inevitable but likely to occur at a relatively slow and steady rate and when rivalry among remaining competitors is not likely to be very intense. Such conditions enable the business to maintain adequate price levels and profit margins as volume gradually falls.

Exhibit 11.14

POSSIBLE MARKETING ACTIONS APPROPRIATE FOR DIFFERENT STRATEGIES IN DECLINING MARKETS

Marketing strategy and objectives	Possible marketing actions
Harvesting strategy	

Maximize short-term cash flow; maintain or increase margins even at the expense of market share decline.	• Eliminate R&D expenditures and capital investments related to the business.
	• Reduce marketing and sales budgets.
	  Greatly reduce or eliminate advertising and sales promotion expenditures, with the possible exception of periodic reminder advertising targeted at current customers.
	  Reduce trade promotions to minimum level necessary to prevent rapid loss of distribution coverage.
	  Focus salesforce efforts on attaining repeat purchases from current customers.
	• Seek ways to reduce production costs, even at the expense of slow erosion in product quality.
	• Raise price if necessary to maintain margins.

Maintenance strategy	
Maintain market share for the short term, even at the expense of margins.	• Continue product and process R&D expenditures in short term aimed at maintaining or improving product quality. • Continue maintenance levels of advertising and sales promotion targeted at current users. • Continue trade promotion at levels sufficient to avoid any reduction in distribution coverage. • Focus salesforce efforts on attaining repeat purchases from current users. • Lower prices if necessary to maintain share, even at the expense of reduced margins.
Profitable survivor strategy	

Increase share of the declining market; encourage weaker competitors to exit.	• Signal competitors that firm intends to remain in industry and pursue an increased share.
	  Maintain or increase advertising and sales promotion budgets.
	  Maintain or increase distribution coverage through aggressive trade promotion.
	  Focus some salesforce effort on winning away competitors' customers.
	  Continue product and process R&D to seek product improvements or cost reductions.
	• Consider introducing line extensions to appeal to remaining demand segments.
	• Lower prices if necessary to increase share, even at the expense of short-term margins.
	• Consider agreements to produce replacement parts or private labels for smaller competitors considering getting out of production.

Niche strategy	
Strengthen share position in one or a few segments with potential for continued profit.	• Continued product and process R&D aimed at product improvements or modifications that will appeal to target segment(s). • Consider producing for private labels in order to maintain volume and hold down unit costs. • Focus advertising, sales promotion, and personal selling campaigns on customers in target segment(s); stress appeals of greatest importance to those customers. • Maintain distribution channels appropriate for reaching target segment; seek unique channel arrangements to more effectively reach customers in target segment(s). • Design service programs that address unique concerns/problems of customers in the target segment(s).

Implementing a harvesting strategy means avoiding any additional long-term investments in plant, equipment, or R&D. It also necessitates substantial cuts in operating expenditures for marketing activities. This often means that the firm should greatly reduce the number of models or package sizes in its product line to reduce inventory and manufacturing costs.

The business should improve the efficiency of sales and distribution. For instance, an industrial goods manufacturer might service its smaller accounts through telemarketing or a website rather than a field salesforce or assign its smaller customers to agent middlemen. For consumer goods, the business might move to more selective distribution by concentrating its efforts on the larger retail chains.

The firm would likely reduce advertising and promotion expenditures, usually to the minimum level necessary to retain adequate distribution. Finally, the business should attempt to maintain or perhaps even increase its price levels to increase margins.

Maintenance Strategy   In markets where future volume trends are highly uncertain, a business with a leading share position might consider pursuing a strategy aimed at maintaining its market share, at least until the market's future becomes more predictable. In such a maintenance strategy, the business continues to pursue the same strategy that brought it success during the market's mature stage. This approach often results in reduced margins and profits in the short term, though, because firms usually must reduce prices or increase marketing expenditures to hold share in the face of declining industry volume. Thus, a firm should consider share maintenance an interim strategy. Once it becomes clear that the market will continue to decline, the business should switch to a different strategy that will provide better cash flows and return on investment over the market's remaining life.

Profitable Survivor Strategy   An aggressive alternative for a business with a strong share position and a sustainable competitive advantage in a declining product-market is to invest enough to increase its share position and establish itself as the industry leader for the remainder of the market's decline. This kind of strategy makes most sense when the firm expects a gradual decline in market demand or when substantial pockets of continuing demand are likely well into the future. It is also an attractive strategy when a firm's declining business is closely intertwined with other SBUs through shared facilities and programs or common customer segments.

A strong competitor often can improve its share position in a declining market at relatively low cost because other competitors may be harvesting their businesses or preparing to exit. The key to the success of such a strategy is to encourage other competitors to leave the market early. Once the firm has achieved a strong and unchallenged position, it can switch to a harvesting strategy and reap substantial profits over the remaining life of the product-market.

A firm might encourage smaller competitors to abandon the industry by being visible and explicit about its commitment to become the leading survivor. It should aggressively seek increased market share, either by cutting prices or by increasing advertising and promotion expenditures. It also might introduce line extensions aimed at remaining pockets of demand to make it more difficult for smaller competitors to find profitable niches. Finally, the firm might act to reduce its competitors' exit barriers, making it easier for them to leave the industry. This could involve taking over competitors' long-term contracts, agreeing to supply spare parts or to service their products in the field, or providing them with components or private-label products. For instance, large regional bakeries have encouraged grocery chains to abandon their own bakery operations by supplying them with private-label baked goods.

The ultimate way to remove competitors' exit barriers is to purchase their operations and either improve their efficiency or remove them from the industry to avoid excess capacity. With continued decline in industry sales a certainty, smaller competitors may be forced to sell their assets at a book value price low enough for the survivor to reap high returns on its investment, as Heileman Brewing Company did on its acquisitions of smaller regional brewers during the 1970s and 80s.

Niche Strategy   Even when most segments of an industry are expected to decline rapidly, a niche strategy may still be viable if one or more substantial segments will either remain as stable pockets of demand or decay slowly. The business pursuing such a strategy should have a strong competitive position in the target segment or be able to build a sustainable competitive advantage relatively quickly to preempt competitors. This is one strategy that even smaller competitors can sometimes successfully pursue, because they can focus the required assets and resources on a limited portion of the total market. The marketing actions a business might take to strengthen and preserve its position in a target niche are similar to those discussed earlier concerning niche strategies in mature markets.

TAKE AWAYS

- Strategic choices in mature, or even declining, markets are by no means always bleak. Many of the world's most profitable companies operate largely in such markets.

- A critical marketing objective for all competitors in a mature market is to maintain the loyalty of existing customers. To accomplish that goal, firms must pursue improvements in the perceived value those customers receive from their offerings—either by differentiating themselves on the basis of superior quality or service, by lowering costs and prices, or both.

- An important secondary objective for some firms, particularly share leaders, in mature markets is to stimulate further volume growth by taking actions to convert nonusers into users, to increase use frequency among current users, or to expand into untapped or underdeveloped markets.

- Declining markets can still offer attractive opportunities for sales revenues and profits. Their attractiveness—and the appropriate marketing strategy to follow—depends on, among other things, the pace and certainty of market decline, the presence of exit barriers, the firm's competitive strengths, and the likely intensity of future competition.

- Self-diagnostic questions to test your ability to apply the analytical tools and concepts in this chapter to marketing decision making may be found at this book's website at **www.mhhe.com/walker.**

ENDNOTES

1. This example is based on material found in Rick Tetzeli, "Mining Money in Mature Markets," *Fortune,* March 22, 1993, pp. 77–80; and in the *Johnson Controls Inc. 2000 Annual Report,* which can be found at the company's website at www.jci.com.

2. For a more detailed discussion of these traps, see Michael E. Porter, *Competitive Strategy* (New York: Free Press, 1980), pp. 247–49.

3. Fareena Sultan, John U. Farley, and Donald R. Lehmann, "A Meta-Analysis of Applications of Diffusion Models," *Journal of Marketing Research,* February 1990. pp. 70–77.

4. Ming Jer Chen and Ian C. MacMillan, "Nonresponse and Delayed Response to Competitive Moves: The Roles of Competitor Dependence and Action Irreversibility," *Academy of Management Journal* 35 (1992), pp. 539–70; and Hubert Gatignon, Eric Anderson, and Kristiann Helsen, "Competitive Reaction to Market Entry: Explaining Interfirm Differences," *Journal of Marketing Research,* February 1989, pp. 45–55.

5. Cathy Anterasian and Lynn W. Phillips, "Discontinuities, Value Delivery, and the Share-Returns Association: A Re-Examination of the 'Share-Causes-Profits' Controversy," distributed working paper (Cambridge, MA: Marketing Science Institute, April 1988). Also see Robert Jacobson, "Distinguishing among Competing Theories of the Market Share Effect," *Journal of Marketing,* October 1988, pp. 68–80.

6. William K. Hall, "Survival Strategies in a Hostile Environment," *Harvard Business Review,* September–October 1980, pp. 75–85.

7. Michael Treacy and Fred Wiersema, *The Discipline of Market Leaders* (Reading, MA: Addison-Wesley Publishing, 1995).

8. Rahul Jacob, "Beyond Quality and Value," *Fortune,* Special Issue, Autumn–Winter 1993, pp. 8–11.

9. The following discussion is based on material found in David A. Garvin, "What Does 'Product Quality' Really Mean?" *Sloan Management Review,* Fall 1984, pp. 25–43; and David A. Aaker, *Strategic Market Management,* 5th ed. (New York: John Wiley & Sons, 1998), chap. 9.

10. For a more extensive discussion of brand equity, see David A. Aaker, *Brand Equity* (New York: Free Press, 1991).

11. Valarie A. Zeithaml, A. Parasuraman, and Leonard L. Berry, *Delivering Quality Service: Balancing Customer Perceptions and Expectations* (New York: Free Press, 1990). See also Valarie A. Zeithaml and Mary Jo Bitner, *Services Marketing* (New York: McGraw-Hill, 1996).

12. For a more detailed discussion of these and other approaches for lowering costs, see Aaker, *Strategic Market Management,* chap. 10.

13. Akshay R. Rao, Mark E. Bergen, and Scott Davis, "How to Fight a Price War," *Harvard Business Review,* March–April 2000, pp. 107–16.

14. This percentage decline is based on the University of Michigan's annual poll of customer satisfaction among a sample of 50,000 consumers, as reported in Diane Brady, "Why Service Stinks," *Business Week,* October 23, 2000, p. 120.

15. Ronald Henkoff, "Getting beyond Downsizing," *Fortune,* January 10, 1994, pp. 58–64.

16. Robert Jacobson and David A. Aaker, "The Strategic Role of Product Quality," *Journal of Marketing,* October 1987, pp. 31–44.

17. David Greising, "Quality: How to Make It Pay," *Business Week,* August 8, 1994, pp. 54–59.

18. For a discussion of various approaches to measuring customer satisfaction, see J. Joseph Cronin and Steven A. Taylor, "Measuring Service Quality: A Reexamination and Extension," *Journal of Marketing,* July 1992, pp. 55–68; and Susan J. Devlin and H. K. Dong, "Service Quality from the Customer's Perspective," *Marketing Research* 6 (1994), pp. 5–13.

19. Frederick F. Reichheld, "Loyalty and the Renaissance of Marketing," *Marketing Management* 2 (1994), pp. 10–21. Also see Rahul Jacob, "Why Some Customers Are More Equal Than Others," *Fortune,* September 19, 1994, pp. 215–24.

20. Reichheld, "Loyalty and the Renaissance of Marketing." See also Thomas O. Jones and W. Earl Sasser Jr., "Why Satisfied Customers Defect," *Harvard Business Review,* November–December 1995, pp. 88–99.

21. The following discussion is largely based on Brady, "Why Service Stinks," pp. 118–28.

22. The following discussion of sequential strategies is based largely on material found in Somkid Jatusripitak, Liam Fahey, and Philip Kotler, "Strategic Global Marketing: Lessons from the Japanese," *Columbia Journal of World Business,* Spring 1985, pp. 47–53.

23. Gail Edmonson, "The Beauty of Global Branding," *Business Week,* June 28, 1999, pp. 70–75.

24. Jaclyn Fierman, "How to Make Money in Mature Markets," *Fortune,* November 25, 1985, p. 47.

25. Kathryn Rudie Harrigan and Michael E. Porter, "End-Game Strategies for Declining Industries," *Harvard Business Review,* July–August 1983, pp. 111–20. Also see Kathryn Rudie Harrigan, *Managing Maturing Businesses* (New York: Lexington Books, 1988).

26. Harrigan and Porter, "End-Game Strategies," p. 114.

CHAPTER TWELVE

MARKETING STRATEGIES FOR THE NEW ECONOMY

When Something Clicks: An Old-Economy Camera Retailer Gets Web-Savvy[1]

KOREAN-BORN JACK SHIN opened Camera World in a musty downtown location in Portland, Oregon, in 1977. By refusing to sell cheap "gray-market" goods (such goods are not meant by their overseas manufacturers to be sold in the United States and are generally not covered by manufacturers' warranties) that many dealers were pushing, Shin built close relationships with Fuji, Canon, Nikon, and other leaders in the photography world and parlayed those relationships into a thriving family business. By providing expert advice and first-rate customer service to retail and mail-order customers, Shin and his family made sure that customers who shopped at Camera World became repeat customers. In 1996, though, after struggling through several years of a flat camera market and worn out from the daily challenges every entrepreneur faces, Shin decided to sell his business.

Word of the availability of Camera World reached Alessandro Mina, a native Swede who, with two fellow European students in the MBA program at Stanford, had founded Sverica International, an investment vehicle designed to acquire and transform old-economy businesses into aggressive growth companies by taking advantage of new-economy technologies. Camera World "fit all our criteria," Mina recalls. "It was profitable. Sales were

stagnant, but there was a growth opportunity. The owner was retiring, and there was a successful mail-order business in place. It had a huge database of happy customers who came to Camera World in the same way people go to Amazon.com for books or Dell Computer for computers—they go there pretty much knowing what they want. I held the view that Internet and mail-order sales are basically the same that way, so I thought it had all the ingredients for a great Web business." The company even had a website, though visitors could not use it to make purchases.

TRANSFORMING THE BUSINESS

Mina bought the company and named its online arm Cameraworld.com. Fortunately, many of the key ingredients to build a new-economy business were already in place. The company already had figured out how to take orders, process and ship them, and process returns where necessary. It enjoyed long-established relationships with top-tier suppliers and had built innovative systems to provide customer service. Its phone lines were staffed by professional photographers (or photographers with day jobs) who knew their stuff. The key challenges that remained involved transforming the Web pages from simple brochures into a genuine transaction site and marrying the company's back-end systems to whatever happened on the Web. The toughest challenge, though, was time. Mina wanted his new company to become the leading online camera retailer before a competitor could.

Mina moved the company's distribution facility into a new and better-organized warehouse four times the size of its previous home, but with lower rent and reduced labor costs. "Because the warehouse was larger and better organized, we made more shipments on time"—within 24 hours instead of five days—"with fewer errors." Mina hired Web Northwest, the designer of the original Camera World website, to transform its 300-visitors-a-day site into a visually appealing, highly interactive one. He spent $20,000 on new servers to crank up the site's capacity. By early 2000, the Cameraworld.com site, which costs roughly $10,000 per month to maintain, was handling 15,000 visitors and 400 transactions per day. The site, now a full-fledged community for photo enthusiasts, offers a selection wizard to help customers choose the right camera, online chats with noted photographers, and an Internet telephony feature that lets customers talk online with the sales and support staff.

GROWING THE BUSINESS

Among Camera World's happy customers was an amateur wildlife photographer named Aneel Bhusri, whose real job was as a partner in Greylock, a Boston-based venture capital firm. In 1999, Greylock and five other venture capitalists invested $60 million to help Mina scale up the business. More online and offline ads, more sales and support staff, and a new CEO whom Mina helped find, Terry Strom, former CEO of Egghead Software, will take the company from an Internet start-up to an established e-commerce player, if all goes well. Mina, now living in Boston, is happy to let others grow the company. "I can go back to what I do best—finding good companies to invest in," Mina says. Investor Bhusri is thrilled at having an opportunity to play a leading role in an Internet company that, as he says, "gets it. If you look at what makes a website successful, most of it is logistics. Camera World had this figured out a long time ago. Why don't others? I honestly don't know the answer. These guys are rare. I think they can be the Dell of the camera business."

STRATEGIC CHALLENGES ADDRESSED IN CHAPTER 12

As the Camera World example shows, the opportunities presented by the Internet and other sectors of the new economy can transform old-economy companies and provide compelling opportunities for growth. Leaders of virtually every company today are, at a minimum, wondering what they should do about the Internet, the development of new communications media and technologies from broadband cable to mobile telephony, and other such developments. Some are committing significant resources in hopes of taking advantage of these new developments. But the optimal path through the new-economy maze is far from clear for most companies.

Thus, in Chapter 12, we address several timely and important questions that marketing strategists in today's companies and entrepreneurs must ask. Does the company need a new-economy strategy? Do the technological advances of the new economy represent threats or opportunities? Most importantly, how should marketers address the development of strategies to take advantage of—or defend against—the rapid pace of change inherent in the new economy: What marketing roles can the Internet and other recent and future technological developments play, and which of these should be pursued?

We begin by reviewing several trends that highlight the growing importance of the Internet and other new-economy technological developments. We then identify the key advantages and disadvantages inherent in new-economy phenomena, all of which every company must clearly understand. Next, we identify the marketing roles that new-economy technologies can plausibly play in marketing strategies, and we articulate a decision framework for managers to use to decide which of the growing array of new-economy tools their firms should employ—from Web-based marketing research to advertising on mobile phones to the delivery of digitized information, goods, and services over the Web. Finally, we examine what has gone wrong in the dot-com world to date, and we identify some key success factors in developing market offerings to successfully serve new-economy markets.

DOES EVERY COMPANY NEED A NEW-ECONOMY STRATEGY?

Like it or not, the **new economy** is here to stay. But exactly what do people mean by this ubiquitous phrase? By new economy, we mean the industries that fuel the development of or participate significantly in electronic commerce and the Internet, develop and market computer hardware and software, and develop or provide any of the growing array of telecommunications services. The obvious players are dot-com retailers such as Amazon.com, Web portals such as Yahoo! and America Online, companies such as Cisco and 3Com that make much of the hardware on which the Internet runs, software firms such as Netscape and Microsoft, and telecom companies such as AT&T, EchoStar, and Qwest whose communications networks permit the transmission of voice or data over various kinds of wire-line, wireless, and satellite networks. However, many formerly old-economy companies are making increasingly significant commitments to new-economy technolo-

gies. Longtime bricks-and-mortar retailers such as Gap and Wal-Mart, century-old manufacturing companies large and small whose electronic data interchange (EDI) systems are critical to their sourcing and/or selling, and service businesses such as Kinko's are all committed to the new economy in one way or another. These days, every company is asking itself, "Do we need an Internet (or other new-economy-based) strategy?"

The growing adoption in both consumer and commercial sectors of the Internet, wireless telephony, and other new-economy technologies is making this question an imperative one. The Gartner Group forecasts that by 2004 75 percent of U.S. households will have Internet access, of which 29 million households will be broadband-enabled.[2] Broadband, or high-speed, connections that permit data transmission dramatically faster than today's 56K modems will, according to Gartner, account for three-quarters of the $10,000 worth of goods and services that Gartner says will be bought online on average by each U.S. household in 2006. And the new economy is not just an American phenomenon. In 2000, nearly 400 million people worldwide had online access, of which only one-third were in the United States (see Exhibit 12.1).[3] Mobile telephones, more prevalent in Europe than in the United States, will soon surpass 100 percent penetration in some countries. New technologies will make many of these phones able to receive advertisements and will provide mobile access to the Web. Adding GPS (global positioning satellite) technology to the mix makes the possibilities even more intriguing, since marketers will know both *who* and *where* we are!

Exhibit 12.1

TOP 10 COUNTRIES IN INTERNET USE

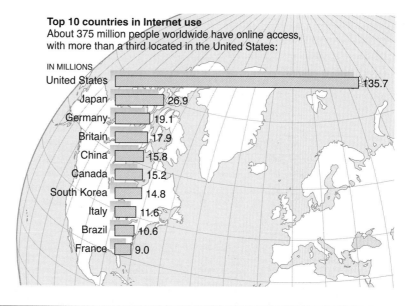

Top 10 countries in Internet use
About 375 million people worldwide have online access,
with more than a third located in the United States:

IN MILLIONS

United States	135.7
Japan	26.9
Germany	19.1
Britain	17.9
China	15.8
Canada	15.2
South Korea	14.8
Italy	11.6
Brazil	10.6
France	9.0

Source: "Internet Use," *Newsweek,* October 2, 2000, p. 74L. Copyright 2000 Newsweek, Inc. All rights reserved. Reprinted by permission.

Jupiter Research reports that online consumer spending in 1999 accounted for more than $1 billion in sales in at least four categories: air travel, hotels, personal computers, and books. Jupiter estimates that consumer spending online will grow from $17.3 billion in 1999 to $86.3 billion in 2003.[4] The same sort of growth is also happening in business-to-business e-commerce. While **B2B (business-to-business)** e-commerce accounted for only $215 million in 1999 (not counting business done via EDI channels), according to AMR Research Inc., or just 1.4 percent of all commercial transactions, it is expected to explode to $5.7 trillion by 2004.

What should marketers conclude from these trends? Notwithstanding the ups and downs of stock market valuations of new-economy companies, notwithstanding the difficulties many B2B and **B2C (business-to-consumer)** companies are having in developing business models that actually make money,[5] and notwithstanding the so-called digital divide, in which some segments of the population are dramatically underrepresented in the Internet population, the long-term prospects for doing business in the new economy are still enormous. Americans' love affair with entrepreneurs and the huge supply of available venture capital money (notwithstanding the industry downturn in 2000 and 2001),[6] combined with the growing market acceptance of and the inherent advantages brought by the Internet and other new-economy technologies, suggest that nearly every American company needs to examine how it will be affected by and can take advantage of these new technologies (see Exhibit 12.2). The rapid pace of Internet adoption outside the United States suggests that the same can be said in most other developed and developing countries.

The outcome of such an examination should be the development of one's own new-economy strategy in most companies of significant size or scope. The fact that one's competitors will surely develop and deploy such strategies is a further argument for doing so. But marketers should take heart, for the good news is this. "In the end, e-consumers and e-businesses aren't so different from traditional buyers and sellers after all. Customers are,

Exhibit 12.2

CONVERTING BROWSERS TO BUYERS IN ONLINE RETAILING

Big Spenders
While online retail sales are projected to grow (figures in billions)...

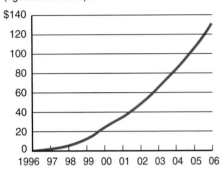

How Stores Score
The conversion rates of some big-name e-tailers.

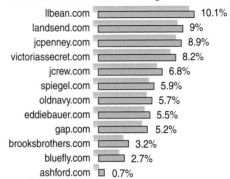

llbean.com	10.1%
landsend.com	9%
jcpenney.com	8.9%
victoriassecret.com	8.2%
jcrew.com	6.8%
spiegel.com	5.9%
oldnavy.com	5.7%
eddiebauer.com	5.5%
gap.com	5.2%
brooksbrothers.com	3.2%
bluefly.com	2.7%
ashford.com	0.7%

...But Few Spenders
...The percentage of browsers who actually buy something (the conversion rate) remains slim in most categories.

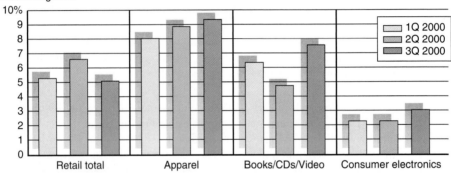

Source: Michael Totty, "Making the Sale," *Wall Street Journal,* September 24, 2001, p. R6.

by and large, pragmatists—whether they are individuals looking for a new shirt, or a big automaker looking for a new source of steel. When the e-way is easier, faster, and cheaper, it can win."[7] The promise of easier, faster, and cheaper is exactly what Alessandro Mina saw when he bought Camera World. Today's well-educated business students can bring the same insights—as well as new-economy expertise—to the companies they join.

THREATS OR OPPORTUNITIES? THE INHERENT ADVANTAGES AND DISADVANTAGES OF THE NEW ECONOMY FOR MARKETERS

What advantages do new-economy technologies provide to marketers and their customers? Seven potentially attractive elements characterize many new-economy technologies: the syndication of information, the increasing returns to scale of network products, the ability to efficiently personalize and customize market offerings, the ability to disintermediate distribution, global reach, round-the-clock access, and the possibility of instantaneous delivery.

The Syndication of Information[8]

Syndication involves the sale of the same good—typically an informational good—to many customers, who then combine it with information from other sources and distribute it. The entertainment and publishing worlds have long employed syndication, producing comic strips, newspaper columns, and TV shows that appear in many places at once. Without syndication, today's mass media would not exist as we know it. Though Internet marketers rarely use the word *syndication* to describe what they do, it lies at the heart of many e-commerce business models. Inktomi, an **originator** of syndicated content, provides its search engine technology to many branded search engine sites. Screaming Media, a **syndicator,** collects articles in electronic form and delivers relevant portions of this content to more than 500 sites, each of which appeals to a different target audience. E*Trade, a **distributor** of syndicated information, brings together from many sources content relevant to its investor clientele and packages it in ways useful to these clients. Cameraworld.com plays all these syndication roles, too, in different ways.

Why is syndication important? First, because syndication deals with informational goods (digitized text, music, photos, CAD/CAM files, and so on) rather than tangible goods, a company can syndicate the same informational goods or services to an almost infinite number of customers with little incremental cost. Variable costs approach zero. Producers of tangible goods and most services (candy bars, for example, or haircuts) must spend money on sugar and chocolate or labor for each additional candy bar or haircut sold. Not so for information producers, where sending a digital copy of a photo or an Internet news feature to one more recipient is essentially free. Second, the syndication process can be automated and digitized, enabling syndicated networks to be created, expanded, and flexibly adapted far more quickly than would be possible in the physical world.

Syndication via the Internet—and soon, perhaps, via mobile phones or other mobile devices—opens up endless opportunities for marketers. It replaces scarcity with abundance. Information can be replicated an infinite number of times and combined and recombined in an infinite number of ways. It can be distributed everywhere, all at once, and be available all the time. Taking advantage of this potential, however, requires new thinking. Companies need to identify and occupy the most important niches in syndication networks. These are the ones that maximize the number and strength of links to other companies and customers, though shifting market conditions inevitably mean that these links must change as markets evolve. Bloomberg, the provider of syndicated information to stock traders and analysts, is an example of a company that has positioned itself well; many of its clients now regard their Bloomberg terminals as indispensable. Thus, almost any company can think of itself as part of a larger, interconnected world and seek ways to occupy originator, syndicator, or distributor roles in an appropriate syndication network.

Increasing Returns to Scale of Network Products[9]

Any undergraduate economics student knows that an increased supply of a good leads to lower value, hence lower prices. But that was before fax machines, operating systems, and other products used in networks, where the second fax machine, for example, makes the first one more valuable, and so on. This characteristic of informational networks—a product becomes more valuable as the number of users increases—is often called a **positive network effect** or **network externality.** When combined with the syndication of informational products, this characteristic has led to the seemingly crazy strategy of giving one's Internet product away for free, often a strategy of choice for new-economy marketers! Hotmail, whose e-mail software costs users nothing, creates value for advertisers and others in the large network that it has created.

Companies that can identify and exploit opportunities where they can benefit from the **increasing returns to scale** that result from positive network effects can sometimes grow very quickly on relatively modest capital investment. If Cameraworld.com is successful in building a community of photo enthusiasts who share insights with one another—in chat rooms or other formats—via the Camera World website, the increasing returns of this growing community will benefit Camera World as well as its customers.

The Ability to Efficiently Personalize and Customize Market Offerings

Amazon.com tracks the books I buy and, using a technology known as **collaborative filtering,** is able to compare my purchases with those of others and thereby recommend to me books they think I would like, personalized to my taste and reading habits, as Amazon understands them (see Exhibit 12.3). If they do this well, my purchases go up, and I

Exhibit 12.3

PERSONALIZATION THROUGH COLLABORATIVE FILTERING

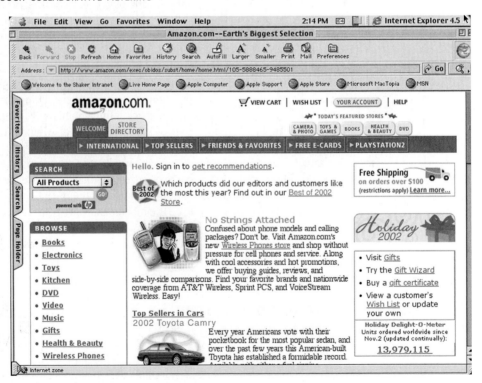

Source: www.amazon.com.

become a happier customer, because Amazon helps me find books I want to read. While collaborative filtering technology has a long way to go (the book I bought for my daughter when she was leaving for a semester in Ecuador does not make me a Latin American culture buff!), the potential of this and other new-economy technologies offers the promise of creating sharply targeted market segments—ultimately, market segments of one.

Collaborative filtering is but one way of personalizing a market offering to each customer. When formal decision rules can be identified in the way customers behave (for example, reminding customers of, or making special offers for, upcoming birthdays or offering supplementary items based on past purchases), **rules-based personalization** can be done. The most predictive rules, however, may require customers to divulge information that they do not want to take the time, or are not willing, to divulge.

Customization techniques, which are user-driven instead of marketer-driven (as we have seen for personalization approaches), allow users to specify the nature of what is offered to them. Several office supply firms, for example, now offer corporate users the ability to create customized office supply catalogs tailored to their company. Such catalogs simplify ordering procedures, save time and money in the purchasing department, and help control expense by offering to perhaps far-flung employees only what the purchasing department has approved in advance. Similarly, CDNow offers consumers the opportunity to order customized CDs consisting of only the songs the customer chooses. In today's highly competitive markets, personalization and customization can help build customer loyalty and make it less likely for customers to switch to other suppliers.

Disintermediation and Restructuring of Distribution Channels

Many goods and services are sold through distribution channels. The Internet makes it possible for marketers to reach customers directly, without the expense or complication of distribution channels, a phenomenon known as **disintermediation.** Best-selling author Stephen King sold his recent novel, *The Plant,* via the Web (see Exhibit 12.4), one installment at a time. King benefited by not having to share revenues with publishers and other distribution intermediaries, and King's fans benefited by paying only a dollar or two for each installment of the book and by getting instant delivery at any time, virtually anywhere in the world. More than 150,000 readers ponied up for the first chapter upon its release in July 2000 though interest in subsequent chapters dwindled.[10] Random House Inc. has announced plans to offer electronic versions of 100 classic works in its literary library, such as James Joyce's *Ulysses,* for as little as $4.95 online.[11] Rather than selling direct, however, Random House will sell through specialty sites, such as Shakespeare.com, as well as through some established online book retailers. Thus, rather than disintermediating its channel for these books, Random House is simply restructuring it to take advantage of the Web's increasing reach.

Deciding to disintermediate or restructure one's channel, however, should not be done lightly. Levi Strauss, the jeans maker, angered its existing retailers by offering custom-fit jeans direct to consumers via the Web. Ultimately, the company withdrew the offering due in part to the howls of protest it heard from its regular retail channel members. Similar concerns have arisen in the travel industry, as airlines and others have disintermediated travel agents by selling airline tickets and other travel services directly to consumers via the Web. Someone must perform the functions normally performed by channel members—taking orders, delivering products, collecting payment, and so on—so those who consider disintermediating their channels and selling direct must determine how they will perform these

Exhibit 12.4

AN EXAMPLE OF DISINTERMEDIATION IN BOOKSELLING

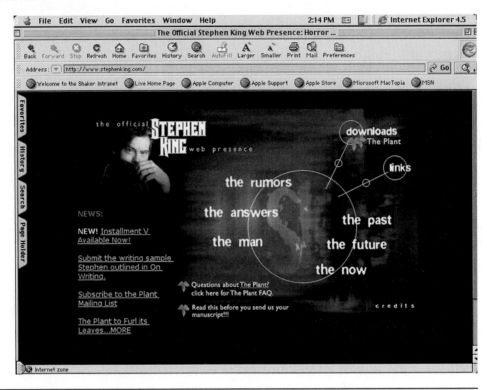

Source: www.stephenking.com.

functions and must evaluate whether doing so is more effective and efficient than using intermediaries.

Global Reach, 24×7 Access, and Instantaneous Delivery

With the Internet and other new-economy technologies, typically there is no extra cost entailed in making information, digital goods, or services available anywhere one can gain access to the Web—literally, **global reach;** making them available 24 hours per day, seven days per week, 52 weeks per year; and, in some cases, providing instantaneous delivery. In our increasingly time-pressed world, access and service like this can be of great value to customers. Camera World's online store, for example, is always open. Easy-Jet, a rapidly growing low-priced airline in Europe, sells a large proportion of its tickets on its own website, many of them to international travelers who reserve flights from afar, even from another continent. Flight confirmations are delivered instantly. Software vendors whose products may be purchased and instantaneously downloaded from the Web provide similar responsiveness. As mobile telephony and GPS technologies develop, similar benefits will be available to customers and marketers whose products are well suited to mobile media. Is anyone up for portable music downloaded to one's cell phone from the Internet?[12] How about a free salad with a pizza, today only, at the restaurant just around the corner?

ETHICAL PERSPECTIVE 12.1
Will E-Commerce Erode Liberty?

Cyberspace is evolving in ways that could threaten privacy and other constitutional rights. A vigorous debate has ensued over whether the government should put its finger in the Internet pie to protect these rights, or whether markets and consumers themselves are up to the task. To some, the Internet is a vast, out-of-control copying machine, spewing out an unlimited number of free copies of intellectual property rightfully owned by its creators. Further, they say, cyberspace is polluting households and schools with objectionable material too easily accessed by children. Others argue that the rapid progress in encryption technology will provide greater protection to copyright owners and families than has been available since Gutenberg's invention of the printing press. Whatever the outcome of the debate, there can be little doubt that the Internet has been an extraordinary boon to free speech—for better or worse—as anyone with Web access is free to disseminate his or her ideas, before regulators or other watchdogs even know what has appeared.

A number of possible solutions to these problems have been proposed. One is to provide filters so that Internet surfers can block speech or other material they dislike. But if such filtering is done upstream—by portals or others—it could become a powerful form of censorship. Another has to do with the increasingly rich trove of information on consumer surfing behavior. Optimists wonder whether firms will compete for customers by using such data to better serve customers, while respecting their privacy, perhaps by using reputable third parties to vouch for their practices. Is it Big Brother? Or is it customer service? Who will decide—government or the marketplace?

Source: Carl Shapiro, "Will E-Commerce Erode Liberty," *Harvard Business Review,* May–June 2000, pp. 189–96.

Are These New-Economy Attributes Opportunities or Threats?

Most marketers can choose to take advantage of one or more of the benefits offered by new-economy technologies, including those we have outlined above. To that extent, these technologies constitute opportunities available to marketers who employ them. Viewed differently, however, they raise complex ethical issues (see Ethical Perspectives 12.1 and 12.2) and they also present potentially significant threats.

First, the fact that the variable cost for syndicated goods approaches zero sounds like a good thing, until one realizes that for most products, price, over the long run, usually is not far from variable cost. If variable cost is zero, will prices drop to near zero, too? If so, such an outcome would represent disaster for information producers. Several companies once thought that providing lists of telephone numbers on CD-ROMs might be a good business. After all, it costs less than a dollar to produce a CD-ROM once the content is ready, and lists of phone numbers had already been compiled by the telephone companies. Alas for these marketers (but happily for consumers), numerous competitors rushed into the market, and with undifferentiated products they were soon forced to compete on price alone. Prices plunged. CD phone books, originally priced in 1986 at $10,000 per copy, soon sold for a few dollars in discount software bins.[13]

Selling music on the Internet also seemed like a good idea to music publishers and even to artists. Imagine getting $12 to $15 for the music on a CD, with no retailers or distributors to take cuts of the revenue, and no costs to pay for fancy packaging! Disintermediation sounds good, if you are a music publisher, but it's a threat if you're a music retailer, even a Web-based one like CDNow! But Napster, Gnutella, and others developed ways to enable consumers to share and download music—and other kinds of files—for free.[14] The music labels and artists, of course, were less than excited about Napster's delivery of their music to consumers for free, fearing that such delivery would eliminate the need for consumers to

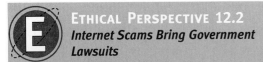

ETHICAL PERSPECTIVE 12.2
Internet Scams Bring Government Lawsuits

Miracle products that don't do what they promise. Credit-card theft. Pyramid schemes. Bogus vacation bargains. All these old tricks are finding new life on the Internet, changing the way law enforcement agencies and consumer protection groups do business. The U.S. Federal Trade Commission and other governmental agencies brought more than 250 lawsuits against online scam artists in 2000. To deal effectively with the global reach that the Internet affords such scams, the FTC is working to create an international network of consumer protection agencies, now comprised of more than 240 agencies around the globe. But differing laws in various jurisdictions make such efforts difficult. What's considered legal in one place may not be in another. But ethical? Who is to say? Jodie Bernstein, the FTC's director of consumer protection, is resolute in her efforts. "We want dot-con artists to know that consumer protection spans the globe, physically and in cyberspace," says Bernstein.

Source: Excerpt from Steve Raabe, "FTC Crackdown Details Internet Scams, Vows Crackdown on 'Dot-Cons,'" *Denver Post*, November 1, 2000, p. C1. Reprinted by permission.

buy CDs. Lawsuits ensued and Napster was required to remove copyrighted material from its site. While it is not clear at this writing how Internet distribution of music will play out, the fact that the variable cost of downloading the music on a CD is now essentially zero will likely have a profound effect on the pricing of recorded music in the long run, notwithstanding the current copyright laws that exist to protect the intellectual property of the musicians and songwriters.

Another threat to new-economy technologies is that there are few barriers to entry, and most Internet strategies are easily imitated. Numerous book retailers are challenging Amazon.com. Half a dozen e-tailers initially crowded the pet supplies business, though their numbers thinned fast. Unless one can patent one's method of doing business on the Web, as has Amazon with its 1-Click® ordering system or Priceline.com with its approach to selling cut-rate airline tickets online, it is likely that one's competitive advantage in the online space will not be sustainable. Even for Amazon and Priceline, long-term success is by no means assured.

Other threats include privacy and security issues, which can drive away customers rather than attract them if they are not handled with care. In Exhibit 12.5, we discuss the impact of the Internet's global reach on privacy issues. The most restrictive jurisdictions' privacy rules may eventually apply to Internet marketers anywhere. Privacy laws in Europe, compared to the United States, are substantially more strict, as is discussed in Exhibit 12.5.

Similarly for security, customers are wary of providing too much information to online marketers, even though that information might help the marketer tailor its offerings to the customer's benefit. Potential misuse of credit-card numbers and other personal information still concerns many users. The use of so-called **cookies,** electronic markers that enable websites to track whose computer visits them, for how long, and in what sequence, provides a wealth of consumer behavior data that marketers hope to use to personalize their offerings to customers. But how many customers want their **click-streams** tracked by an electronic Sherlock Holmes? Would a candidate for public office want the press to examine and make public his or her online shopping behavior?

Ultimately, a marketer's best defenses against these disadvantages are likely to take either of two forms. One defense is through the patent and copyright system, though as the Napster example shows, such protection may not be effective as new technologies are developed that make the protection of intellectual property problematic. A second defense is through what Carl Shapiro and Hal Varian call **versioning.**[15] Shapiro and Varian argue

Exhibit 12.5   The Impact of Global Reach on Internet Privacy

Stefano Rodata is Italy's top privacy cop. His job, as president of the Italian Data Privacy Protection committee, is to ensure compliance with Italy's strict privacy laws. "People have a right to be left alone," says Rodata. A recent and uneasy truce between European authorities and the United States, a so-called safe harbor agreement, provides a set of privacy guidelines that U.S. firms doing online business in Europe can follow to avoid European Union legal action when Europeans fill out registration forms or make purchases on U.S. websites. Exporting personal data in this manner to countries that don't meet EU privacy standards is unlawful in Europe. The draft agreement, along with other information, can be found at **http://europa.eu.int/comm/internal_market/en/media/dataprot/index.htm.**

In the United States, Internet privacy has been dealt with largely through market forces, whereby consumers are expected to avoid sites where privacy is not handled to their liking. As firms attempt to take advantage of the global reach afforded by the Internet, will they run afoul of privacy laws in countries whose consumers they serve? In what jurisdictions will complaints be heard and dealt with? Will the most restrictive countries end up ruling the roost? These privacy questions are far from settled.

Source: Thomas E. Weber, "Europe and U.S. Reach Truce on Net Privacy, But What Comes Next?" *Wall Street Journal,* June 19, 2000, p. B1. Copyright 2000 by Dow Jones & Co. Inc. Reproduced with permission of Dow Jones & Co. Inc. via Copyright Clearance Center.

that, even for information products whose variable cost approaches zero, the value of information to different kinds of customers is likely to vary substantially. Marketers who have the insight to determine which features will be valuable to some customers, but of little value to others, can package and repackage information differently and serve market segments with margins that need not fall to zero. Versioning can be done on many dimensions: time (which users value getting the information sooner than others?); convenience (can we restrict the place or degree of access to some users?); comprehensiveness (which users need detail? Which only need the big picture?); manipulation (which users want to be able to manipulate, duplicate, process, store, or print the information?); community (which users want to discuss information with others?); and support (who needs, and will pay for, support?). Other dimensions on which versioning can be based include freedom from annoyance, speed, user interfaces, image resolution (for visual images, such as stock photos), and more not yet imagined. By tailoring the same core information to the varied needs of different buyers, the unusual economics of information can work to the advantage of the seller, while providing excellent value to the buyer. Skills in market segmentation and targeting, differentiation, and positioning—skills developed earlier in this book—are needed to enable marketers to best take advantage of new-economy technologies and mitigate their disadvantages.

STRATEGIC ISSUE

Skills in market segmentation and targeting, differentiation, and positioning—skills developed earlier in this book—are needed to enable marketers to best take advantage of new-economy technologies and mitigate their disadvantages.

First-Mover Advantage: Fact or Fiction?[16]

In the Internet gold rush in the late 1990s, the key to Internet success was said to be **first-mover advantage.** The first firm to establish a significant presence in each market niche would be the one that succeeded. Thus, Amazon would win in books. EBay would win in auctions. Autobytel would win in the automotive sector, and so on. Later followers need not bother. As we saw at the beginning of this chapter, Alessandro Mina of Camera World appeared to hold this view. But is first-mover advantage real?

As we saw in Chapter 9, being the first mover does bring some potential advantages, but not all first movers are able to capitalize on those advantages. Thus, many are surpassed over time by later entrants. One thing a pioneer must do to hold on to its early leadership position is to continue to innovate in order to maintain a differential advantage over the many imitators likely to arrive late to the party but eager to get in.

Jim Collins, co-author of the best-sellers *Good to Great* and *Built to Last: Successful Habits of Visionary Companies,* is more blunt about the supposed rule that nothing is as important as being first to reach scale. "It's wrong," he says. "Best beats first."[17] As Collins points out, VisiCalc was the first major personal computer spreadsheet. Where is VisiCalc today? It lost the battle to Lotus 1-2-3, which in turn lost to Excel. What about the now-ubiquitous Palm Pilot? It came to market years after early leader Sharp and the Apple Newton. Palm Pilot's designers found a better way to design personal digital assistants—using one reliable script, instead of everyone's own script—and have sold 6 million units.[18] But its current advantage may not last, as Handspring and Blackbird are now nipping at Palm Pilot's heels. America Online, another new-economy star, got to its leading position by being better, not first. In the old economy, Wal-Mart didn't pioneer discount retailing. Nucor didn't pioneer the minimill for making steel from scrap. Starbucks didn't pioneer the high-end coffee shop. Yet all were winners, while the early leaders fell behind or disappeared. None of these entrants were first—they were *better.* Being first may help attract investors and may make some founders and venture capitalists rich, but it's hardly a recipe for building a great company. In his book *Digital Darwinism,* Evan Schwartz identifies seven strategies for surviving in the digital economy. Being the first mover is not among them.[19] Fortunately, with the dot-com crash in early 2000, investors seem to be catching on to the game.

STRATEGIC ISSUE

Being first may help attract investors and may make some founders and venture capitalists rich, but it's hardly a recipe for building a great company.

DEVELOPING A NEW-ECONOMY STRATEGY: A DECISION FRAMEWORK

Most companies of substantial size or scope will need to develop strategies to take advantage of new-economy technologies, but doing so is easier said than done. This is new ground in most companies. In several earlier chapters, we identified recent software applications with the potential for helping marketers be more effective and efficient in their marketing decision making and marketing activities. To some observers, such applications fall within the scope of the new economy. In this section, we examine areas in which even newer new-economy technologies have widespread marketing applications. While we recognize that other non-marketing applications also may be compelling for many companies, our focus remains on marketing, for which, as Peter Sealey points out, productivity gains have been hard to come by.[20] Sealey argues that major advances in marketing productivity will depend on the broader use of information. That will happen only when companies fully leverage the power of the Internet, he says. Thus, in this section we focus on how the Internet—and, for some applications, mobile telephony—can fruitfully be employed for marketing purposes.[21]

Marketing Applications for New-Economy Tools

In the first chapter of this book we pointed out that a number of activities have to be performed by somebody for an exchange transaction to occur between a selling firm and a potential customer. Retaining that customer for future transactions adds additional activities, such as providing effective and responsive customer service after the sale. From the customer's point of view, these necessary activities can be summarized in a six-stage **consumer experience process** that begins with communicating one's wants and needs to prospective sellers; moving through the awareness, purchase, and delivery processes; obtaining any necessary service or support after the purchase to support its use or consumption; and ultimately sometimes returning or disposing of the product (we identify the six stages from the marketer's perspective in Exhibit 12.6). Customers first provide information about their needs to sellers, whose **customer insight** permits them to develop goods or services intended to meet the customers' needs. This stage in the process requires that information flow from customer to seller, as shown in Exhibit 12.6. While there may be several back-and-forth iterations in the insight stage, as new product developers invent and refine their product ideas, ultimately some good or service is developed, and information about the new product—**promotion and brand building**—then flows to customers, to inform and encourage them to buy. If the customer likes what is offered, a **transaction** ensues, requiring that information about pricing, terms, delivery, and so on flow both ways. With a transaction consummated, **delivery** of the good or service is made, with the product flowing to the customer and money or other compensation flowing to the seller. But the seller's job is not yet done, for the customer may need some kind of **customer support or service** during use, in which case additional information may flow in either direction or additional goods or services may flow to the customer, possibly in exchange for additional revenue. Finally, the customer may need to **return, dispose** of, or discontinue use of the good or service, at which point the product may be returned to the seller, cash may flow back to the customer (as a result of the product's return or some kind of trade-in, perhaps), and another transaction—with this or another seller—may ensue, thereby repeating much of the process. The Internet and, to a more limited extent, mobile telephony offer applications at some or all of these stages. We now explore some of these applications, though in this fast-moving arena, new ones will undoubtedly arise before the ink is dry on this book. Then, in the next section, we set forth a decision framework to assist marketers in deciding for which of these stages, and with which applications, new-economy tools should become part of their strategies.

Internet Applications for Customer Insight   In Chapter 6, we discussed the role of marketing research in understanding customers and developing products—whether

Exhibit 12.6

A CUSTOMER EXPERIENCE MODEL FOR NEW-ECONOMY MARKETING DECISION MAKING

Stage in customer experience process from marketer's perspective	Direction of information flows	Direction of product flows (goods or services)	Direction of cash flows (revenue opportunities)
Customer insight	P ◄——— C		
Product promotion and brand building	P ———► C		
Transaction	P ◄———► C		
Product delivery		P ———► C	P ◄——— C
Customer support and service	P ◄———► C	P ———► C	P ◄——— C
Product return or disposal		P ◄——— C	P ◄——— C

P = Producer

C = Customer

goods or services—to meet their needs. Marketers rely on a flow of information from customers or prospective customers about their wants and needs, however latent these may sometimes be, to generate the insight essential to the development of compelling new products (see Exhibit 12.6). How might the Internet facilitate this process?

Pollsters and other marketing researchers are increasingly turning to the Internet to conduct marketing research. Why? Just as Alessandro Mina saw the potential for "easier, faster, and cheaper" in Camera World, so too do researchers when they consider the Internet. For example, in years past, when Hewlett-Packard wanted to know what customers thought about its printers, it sent thousands of surveys through the mail, either on paper or on a computer diskette. It was a cumbersome process and "very expensive," says H-P market analyst Anita Hughes.[22] Now, H-P sends customers to a website to gather feedback. The new approach saves time and money and allows greater depth in the research—targeting specific respondents with instant follow-ups, for instance, or showing product prototypes online. "The possibilities are just huge," says Hughes. H-P uses Greenfield Online, one of a growing number of firms that specialize in Web-based marketing research. In fact, some observers now view Internet-based quantitative research as the wave of the future, due to its cost-cutting, time-saving advantages over traditional telephone, mail, and mall-intercept surveys.[23]

Nonetheless, using the Web for research is not without controversy. Traditional researchers debate the Web's merits on a number of dimensions: in terms of representativeness of the current makeup of the Web audience, largely whiter, richer, younger, and more educated than the population as a whole; in terms of self-selection biases, where people volunteer to participate in Web-based polls; and in terms of the randomness, or lack thereof, of Web samples. But many of these problems are present in other forms of research, too, especially as more people refuse to answer mail or telephone surveys. Where random sampling is not an issue, such as for small-scale qualitative research such as focus groups, the Web may be particularly attractive. Greenfield Online recently ran an online focus group for Ford Motor Company in which 17 people who drive sport utility vehicles participated in three live chat sessions. Juli Caltrider, the Ford Expedition brand manager, followed the discussion from her own computer and occasionally interjected questions herself. Was the effort successful for Ford? "I got information faster, [and] I got additional depth in the information that I don't believe I would have gotten otherwise," Caltrider says. The downside was her inability to see facial expressions or read the participants' body language. Using Web-based research, for both qualitative studies like Ford's and for large-scale quantitative studies, is here to stay. The portion of total qualitative research done online could grow "to as high as 25 percent to 30 percent (of all money spent on qualitative research) in the future," says Bill McElroy, president of the New York-based Internet Marketing Research Organization (IMRO).[24] For demos of one provider's online research tools, see Interactive Tracking Systems Inc.'s website at **www.iTracks.com.**

STRATEGIC ISSUE

Using the Web for research is not without controversy.

New-Economy Applications for Product Promotion and Brand Building

There are three broad approaches for using the Internet to promote one's products or services, that is, to provide information about one's product to the intended target market and build brand awareness and equity (see Exhibit 12.6). One is to engage in **viral marketing,** whereby consumers are encouraged to spread the word about a Web-based marketer. Another is to place promotional content—**brochureware,** as it is sometimes called—on one's website and encourage customers to peruse it as they wish. A third approach is to place ads in various places on the Web.

Viral marketing was the way Hotmail.com, the largest free e-mail provider, won its success. It attached a message at the end of every e-mail sent by its users announcing its availability as a free provider. The more users sent e-mail, the faster the word about Hotmail spread. Viral marketing is a low-cost and potentially powerful technique for building brand awareness.[25]

Placing brochureware about a company's products, news development, and press releases, or about other things, on the Web is an easy and inexpensive first step toward a new-economy strategy. It provides answers to customer or prospective customer questions with global 24×7 access. It avoids looking technologically clueless: What company lacks a fax line or a website today? But it is not very proactive, and if a company doesn't otherwise promote the website where the information is placed, either on Web portals, on search engines, or in offline media, no one will know it is there. "The Web cliché, 'if you build it, they will come,' has lulled many online marketers into a false sense of security," says Charles Sayers, an Internet marketing consultant.[26] Unfortunately, brochureware also helps your competitors keep up with what you are doing.

To help customers find their websites, companies can use businesses such as Search Engine Watch to find software applications that help them appear among the first links the search engines return. Intelliquis is another such company. It is also a good idea to create so-called **hook pages** or **doorway pages.** These pages offer information on specialized subjects that consumers are likely to search for. E*Trade, for example, offers a hook page with free online stock advice and links the page to its own home page.[27] Another way to attract customers to one's website is to put together **affiliate deals,** in which owners of other websites are paid—in flat fees or commissions on whatever the referred customers buy—to send customers your way. The largest portals, such as America Online and Yahoo!, earn a substantial portion of their revenues this way.

Internet (and, perhaps soon, mobile telephony) advertising is a more proactive strategy, but deciding whether and how to use it is not easy. A simple way to advertise on the Internet is to take advantage of the shift in power from marketers to consumers brought about by easy access to comparative information by making available information for comparison purposes. The Web-based luggage retailer eBags.com, for example, provides charts to make it easier for customers to compare different garment bags and other products to find the one that's right for them. Automakers and other automotive sites provide similar comparative information to help consumers choose makes and models of cars that best suit their needs. Comparative sites are likely to turn up in virtually every product category over time, and having one's goods or services included among those described by such sites will likely turn out to be increasingly important. Of course, if one's goods or services do not pass competitive muster, being included on such sites can work the other way!

A more proactive advertising strategy is to place ads on the Web. In the early days, 4 percent to 5 percent of viewers of **banner ads,** the colorful strips of ad content splashed across the top of a Web page, would click on the banner to read the additional information that followed (see Exhibit 12.7). Today, as Web audiences widen beyond the early 'netheads who frequented the Web and such ads become more pervasive, the click-through rate has plummeted to 0.3 percent to 0.5 percent, according to Jupiter Research, far below

Exhibit 12.7

A TYPICAL BANNER AD

response rates for traditional direct mail, where about 2 percent of recipients respond.[28] Once touted as a way to build brands on the Internet, whether for online or offline companies, there's growing concern that banner ads may simply not work. By late 2001, amid an overall drop in ad spending across most media, online ad revenue had slid (see Exhibit 12.8) and the cost per thousand viewers for banner ads had dropped to about $10, about half the cost one year earlier.[29] By the first half of 2001, banner ads accounted for just 36 percent of online ad spending, down from 53 percent in the fourth quarter of 1999.[30]

Is advertising on the Internet dead? Probably not, as advertisers experiment with emerging formats for using this new medium (see Exhibit 12.8). Century 21, a real estate firm, has run humorous superstitials to promote its services that help homebuyers find new homes. Travelocity.com, the Internet travel agency, uses Internet ads for promoting specific travel offers. Consumer response is measured several times a day, and the message is changed if the ad isn't boosting sales.[31]

Exhibit 12.8

THE ONLINE PITCH

As Spending Eases...
Total internet ad revenue in millions has eased recently after years of explosive growth

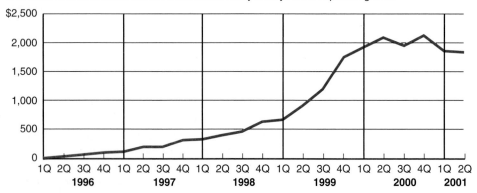

...Emerging Formats Gain
Internet ad revenue by format

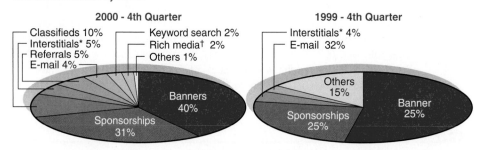

* Ads that appear between two content pages; also known as transition ads, intermercial ads, splash pages, and Flash pages.
† Generally includes a combination of animation, sound, video, and interactivity.

Source: Vanessa O'Connell, "The Best Way to Advertise," *Wall Street Journal,* November 12, 2001, p. R13.

The Century 21 and Travelocity ads reflect trends toward more compelling and, in some cases, more measurable ad vehicles. New techniques include **rich media** (short ads with video and sound), **cliffhangers** (rich media ads that leave the viewers "hanging" and direct them to a website to view the end of the ad); **superstitials** (rich media ads that show up unexpectedly on a viewer's screen); **streaming audio** (like a radio commercial); and vFlash (Consumers can choose to place a **vFlash** icon on their screen from, say Block-buster Video, which flashes when Blockbuster has an offer it wants to make. Clicking on a pop-up box then takes the viewer to the Blockbuster website, where the offer is pre-sented.). All these techniques, and new ones sure to be developed, hope to take advantage of growing Web penetration to reach consumers in new ways. If these approaches are not made more measurable, however, some observers say that big ad dollars are unlikely to flow their way.

There are several ways to use Internet advertising in a measurable manner. One way is to use **opt-in e-mail,** where consumers allow companies they are interested in to send them e-mail with new promotions. According to Seth Godin, such **permission marketing** (as opposed to interruption marketing, as Godin calls the current methods) offers the potential for companies to create trust, build long-term relationships with customers, and greatly improve their chances for making a sale.[32] By 2001, the average number of permission-based e-mails received by Internet users had increased to 36 per week, double the prior year figure.[33] For an example of how Harrah's, the resort casino operator, used e-mail mar-keting to fill its hotel rooms after the September 11, 2001, attacks on New York and Wash-ington, see Exhibit 12.9.

Another way to make Web advertising more measurable is to have advertisers pay for performance, rather than for placement, regardless of the type of ad employed. The adver-tiser might pay for click-throughs, for leads generated, even commissions for actual orders placed. Doing so, however, would require that extensive traffic data that follow a cus-tomer's **click-stream** be captured and analyzed. Jeff Forslund's job is to do just that for credit-card issuer NextCard, a major Web advertiser. For example, Forslund knows that a particular banner ad that appeared on Yahoo! on August 25, 2000, attracted 1,915 visits, 104 credit-card applications, and 22 approvals. He also knows that those 22 new customers transferred preexisting credit-card balances averaging $1,729 each.[34] With such data in hand, NextCard can determine the value of that banner ad and negotiate how much and on what basis—placement or performance—it is willing to pay Yahoo! to place another sim-ilar ad. Dan Springer, NextCard's chief marketing officer, believes that the Internet is bet-ter suited to getting measurable results than for branding efforts. He says current results indicate, however, that today's Web ad prices are too high.[35]

Exhibit 12.9   Harrah's Beats the House Odds to Fill Its Rooms

In the wake of the September 11, 2001, attack on Amer-ica, Harrah's Entertainment Inc. felt an immediate 25 percent downturn in its business in Las Vegas. Few peo-ple were in the mood to party, and fewer wanted to fly. By having already linked its 24 million-strong customer database with its website and e-mail marketing system, Harrah's was well positioned to counterattack. It tar-geted e-mails to customers it thought might want to take a trip to its tables and slot machines and, by the end of September, the hotel was back near 100 percent occupancy, filling almost 4,000 rooms that would oth-erwise have gone empty.

Source: David Rocks, "The Net As a Lifeline," *BusinessWeek,* Octo-ber 29, 2001, p. EB 16.

Additional factors, besides the high price for placing Web ads and the current lack of measurement capability for many of them are holding back development of the Web as a successful advertising medium. Two are privacy and security concerns, as mentioned earlier in this chapter. Consumer rights advocates are not certain that consumers want Jeff Forslund and others like him to have the click-stream data he needs to measure ad performance. What if someone's click-stream as he or she explores data about AIDS is gathered? Could such data be misused? Another deterrent is the glacial pace at which more interesting video and audio ads can download, given today's 56K modems. Many people won't wait for such ads to load. As faster broadband connections become more common, this problem will fade, but it's hard to tell just how quickly broadband will penetrate the market.

STRATEGIC ISSUE

The high price for placing Web ads and the current lack of measurement capability for many of them are holding back development of the Web as a successful advertising medium.

While Internet advertising now seems almost "old hat," advertising on mobile phones is about to emerge as a significant new vehicle for promotion, especially in Europe and Japan, where mobile phone usage and technological development are far ahead of the United States. As DoCoMo's iMode and other high-speed mobile phone technologies penetrate various markets, the installed base of web-enabled mobile phones will grow large enough that ads will begin to make sense. The issues surrounding the use and effectiveness of this medium will parallel those for the Internet, and the pace at which applications become user-friendly enough to be valued by customers will determine how quickly this medium develops. In Europe and Japan, and subsequently elsewhere, these developments bear watching.

New-Economy Applications for Conducting Transactions   If promotional activities do their jobs, the hoped-for consequence is that some customers will decide to buy. Can the Internet or mobile telephony help transactions occur? Several Web-based companies are in the business of enabling client websites to handle transactions. Making the transition to a transaction-capable website was among the first tasks Camera World's new owners had to do after they bought the business. BroadVision Inc. (**broadvision.com**), for example, offers a wide range of software products that enable clients to conduct B2B or B2C commerce on their websites or via kiosks or mobile telephones. Such products from BroadVision and others typically provide back-end systems and inventory control, prepare warehouse and ship documents, and bill the customer for the sale. Some such systems now allow companies to engage in **dynamic pricing,** a controversial system that gauges a customer's desire to buy, measures his means, and sets the price accordingly.[36] In this respect, target markets of one are now here, to the chagrin of some consumers!

Recent legislation in the United States has cleared the way for the use of **digital signatures** over the Web, and other countries may soon follow. Such digital authentication will pave the way for more efficient sale of insurance, mortgages, and other goods and services via the Web or mobile telephones. Imagine removing your car from your collision insurance policy when it's parked in the driveway for an extended period, and reinstating coverage with the click of a mouse. It also will lower the costs companies incur due to Internet fraud, which has been common, and thereby save consumers money. Brooks Fisher of Intuit Inc., a provider of a wide range of online financial services, says, "Less fraud means better pricing."[37]

More broadly, the Internet and wireless telephony are quickly removing constraints that limit sellers in terms of what they sell and how they sell it. Banks are moving all the transactions they can onto the Web, where a typical banking transaction costs just two cents, compared with 36 cents for an ATM transaction and $1.15 for a teller-assisted transaction.[38] In Scandinavia, 700,000 Finns use Sonera, the leading Finnish wireless carrier, to do everything from ordering chocolates from the back seat of a taxicab to getting a date. The 1999 mobile commerce and information revenues of Zed, a Finnish Internet site serving mobile phone users, totaled $126 million—in a country one-fortieth the size of the United States![39] Elsewhere, the Internet now offers buyers and sellers choices ranging from fixed-price online catalogs, to customer-tailored catalogs, to auctions, to negotiated prices, to Priceline.com's **demand collection system,** to barter and more.[40]

By enabling virtually frictionless movement among ways of doing business, these so-called **all-in-one markets** benefit both buyers and sellers. The trend toward multiple ways of transacting business on the Web runs counter to the conventional wisdom about e-commerce. Many observers had predicted that easy access to pricing information on the Internet would push all transactions toward a single mechanism—wide-open price competition in which the lowest-priced offer wins the order. For some commodity-like products that are easily compared—several Web **shopping bots** can tell a customer who has the lowest price on the latest Tom Clancy novel, for example—this may yet turn out to be the case. So far, however, this prediction has not come to pass.

New-Economy Applications for Delivering Digital Products   Many companies probably don't give much thought to it, but an increasing array of goods and services can be digitized and thereby delivered to customers via any digital medium, including the Internet, satellites, and digital telephones. Fifty years ago, the then-current technological miracle was the analog delivery of sounds and images to consumers via the newfangled invention called television. Today, as we have seen earlier in this chapter, books, music, and more can be delivered digitally any time, at any digitally connected place. In 2, 5, or 10 years, what else will be digitally deliverable? Psychotherapy, with or without a live therapist, and legal advice are now available online from numerous providers.[41] Online postage is available at several websites, including that of the United States Postal Service. Unfortunately for their investors, e-postage pioneers Stamps.com and E-stamp.com squandered millions in start-up capital to pursue this market, with little so far to show for their efforts.[42] One new company is even rumored to be developing technology for delivering scents online. Who knows what's next? Beam me up, Scotty![43]

New-Economy Applications for Customer Service and Support   An increasingly important application on the Internet is for various sorts of customer service, replacing more costly—and sometimes more inconsistent and error prone—human support. Companies from Dell to the Denver Zoo use the Web to provide answers to frequently asked questions, from technical ones in Dell's case to how to arrange a children's birthday party at the zoo. Savvy marketers know that, for all the hoopla about acquiring new customers, the real driver of the bottom line is the ability to profitably retain existing ones and that effective, responsive customer service is a key ingredient in doing so. They also know that **customer retention** is a competitive necessity. In nearly every industry, some company will soon figure out new ways to exploit the potential of the Internet to create value for customers. Without the ability to retain those customers, however, even the best-conceived business model on the Web will collapse.[44]

There are numerous examples of how Web-based customer service programs are providing customers with better service at lower costs, surely a win–win proposition. Michael Climo, purchasing director for e-tailer SmartHome.com, was seeking a supplier to provide fast delivery of its shipments to customers. United Parcel Service won the business not only by delivering SmartHome's parcels quickly, but also by cutting SmartHome's customer service costs while improving service. UPS helped redesign the SmartHome website so customers could track their shipments with a click of a mouse. SmartHome's call center now gets virtually no calls to check order status, down from 60 per day before the change, freeing its staff to make more sales calls. The Web-smart capabilities of UPS have made it the clear leader in delivering the $40 billion in merchandise bought online in 2000, with an estimated 55 percent of the business, compared to 10 percent for FedEx.[45] Attracting and retaining its business customers is what the UPS Web-based services are all about.

Benefits of an array of Web-based customer service applications are available to old- and new-economy companies alike, in both B2B and B2C contexts. Tracking shipments or answering other frequently asked questions is but one application. Building communities among users—using bulletin boards, chat rooms, or other e-techniques—is another one that can build customer loyalty and provide an important source of feedback on new product ideas, product problems, and other issues. Tom Lowe, founder of Playing Mantis, a maker of die-cast cars, plastic model kits, and action figures, credits his company's Web-based bulletin boards for feeding customer relationships that would be the envy of any company. As one customer posted to one of the Playing Mantis boards, "Polar Lights is very special to me. . . . You've rekindled the joy I once felt when buying these kits. . . . You're the ONLY company I feel a part of."[46]

The growing number of Web-based customer service applications offers the tantalizing combination of better service and significant cost savings. The trick is to focus on the customer service benefits first, rather than mere cost cutting. Customers are quick to discern when cost cutting takes precedence over genuine service responsiveness. Does anyone like the way call center software has changed the way consumers obtain phone numbers from directory assistance, or the fact that some banks won't provide bank-by-mail envelopes to those who prefer to do their banking the old-fashioned way?

One myth some companies have bought into is that the Internet is a self-service medium. They assume that they can let customers do all the work, but most customers really don't want to do more. One solution is **coproduction,** in which companies carefully consider which burdens they can remove from the customer, using new-economy technologies, and which customers can perform, assessing costs and benefits to both parties. Doing so can provide insights into new ways to serve customers better, as Charles Schwab now does when it e-mails customers to alert them to big moves in their stocks.[47]

New-Economy Applications for Product Return and Disposal   Customers' experiences with goods and some services do not end until the products are consumed, returned, or disposed of. Some companies have found ways to use new-economy technologies to facilitate these processes. Dell, for example, provides an Internet space where Dell customers can sell their old computers when they upgrade to a new one. Both old- and new-economy companies can avail themselves of similar applications. In retailing, many retailers with both online and offline stores accept returns at any location. Concerns related to returning online purchases (the inability to see and touch the goods before purchase and the inability to return goods easily) rank second and third on the list of factors that deter consumers from shopping online (see Exhibit 12.10).

Developing New-Economy Marketing Strategies: The Critical Questions

STRATEGIC ISSUE

Knowing what marketing arrows are available in one's new-economy quiver is one thing. Deciding which of these applications will deliver the most bang for the buck is quite another.

Knowing what marketing arrows are available in one's new-economy quiver is one thing. Deciding which of these applications will deliver the most bang for the buck is quite another. Our flow model of the customer experience process (see Exhibit 12.6) facilitates such decision making by raising six important questions that should be asked about whether to employ new-economy tools at any or all stages of the process. These

Exhibit 12.10

WHY SHOPPERS ARE WARY

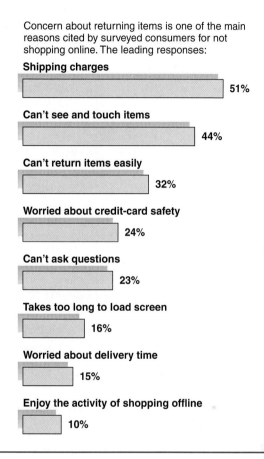

Concern about returning items is one of the main reasons cited by surveyed consumers for not shopping online. The leading responses:

Shipping charges
51%

Can't see and touch items
44%

Can't return items easily
32%

Worried about credit-card safety
24%

Can't ask questions
23%

Takes too long to load screen
16%

Worried about delivery time
15%

Enjoy the activity of shopping offline
10%

Source: Rebecca Quick, "Return to Sender," *Wall Street Journal,* July 17, 2000, p. R8. Copyright 2000 by Dow Jones & Co. Inc. Reproduced with permission of Dow Jones & Co. Inc. via Copyright Clearance Center.

diagnostic questions are shown in Exhibit 12.11. We address each of these questions in this section.

Can We Digitize Any or All of the Necessary Flows at Each Stage in the Consumer Experience Process?   At the heart of the new economy is the reliance on digital means of transmitting *information,* some of which is recomposed into *goods*—CDs, books, and more. In considering whether to employ new-economy technologies at any stage of the consumer experience process, a company should ask whether any of the flows—information, goods or services, or cash—can be digitized.

For cash, the answer is an automatic yes, via credit cards or other forms of electronic payment, except where currency issues pose problems, such as in some international settings. And new forms of electronic payment will soon enhance the security of cash flows over the Web.

For goods and services, the question is more difficult. Text, audio, and visual images (moving or still) can be digitized, as can books, music, photos, and, given enough bandwidth, movies and other videos. But at present, most tangible goods and many services cannot easily be transmitted digitally. For others, however, such as legal advice, therapy

Exhibit 12.11

DIAGNOSTIC QUESTIONS FOR NEW-ECONOMY MARKETING DECISIONS

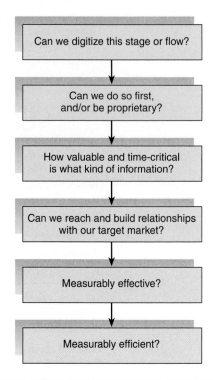

for mental health patients, and other goods or services that can adequately be represented in words, sounds, or images, the possibilities are endless. Will technology soon make possible the digital transmission of physical goods? Who knows? When it happens, the many sci-fi buffs around the world will not be surprised!

For information, text, audio, and images can be digitized. But what about the *soft hand* of a cashmere sweater? The *heft and balance* of a carpenter's hammer? The *taste* of fine European chocolate? The *fragrance* of a new cologne? Today, these important informational attributes of goods cannot be readily digitized. Tomorrow? Time will tell.

When any of the flows at any stage of the consumer experience process can, given sufficient information and ingenuity, be digitized, the remaining questions in Exhibit 12.11 should then be considered to decide whether or not new-economy applications for a particular flow should be implemented.

Can We Do So First, and/or in a Proprietary Way

 As we have seen, barriers to entry on the Web are low, and most good ideas can be quickly imitated. A key question in deciding whether or not to employ a new-economy application is whether one can do so in a proprietary way, thereby deterring imitation, or do so with a sufficient head start so that competitive advantage can be established before others follow. Amazon.com was early in the Internet retailing game and enjoyed a helpful head start. E-tailers of pet supplies, however, were not so fortunate, as half a dozen venture-capital-backed online pet stores battled for survival in 2000.[48] Without anything proprietary, and without a head start, most of these companies will likely fail and fail early, as some already have.

For old-economy companies, using the Internet for applications that do not reinvent the heart of the business as Camera World's new owners decided to do—for brochureware or customer service, for example—speed to market may or may not be critical, depending on how quickly others in their industry are likely to move into similar applications. As always, competitor intelligence, some of which can be gleaned from competitors' websites, is essential.

How Valuable and How Time-Critical Are What Kinds of Information to the Recipient?

For the informational flows in Exhibit 12.6, a key question in making resource deployments is the importance of various kinds of information to the recipient, either the company or the customer, depending on the direction of the flow. The more valuable and time-critical the information, the more sensible it may be to invest in new-economy applications to provide easy, timely, and 24×7 access to those who can benefit from the information. Wal-Mart, arguably an old-economy company that has long been an industry leader in its use of information technology, now posts on the Web password-protected, up-to-the-minute, store-by-store, SKU-by-SKU sales information that its key suppliers can access, thereby enabling them to better ensure that Wal-Mart's stores remain in stock on their merchandise.

Can New-Economy Tools Reach and Build Relationships with Customers in the Target Market?

Making information, goods, or services available on the Web is of little use if the people to whom those flows are directed lack Web access. As we have seen, some demographic groups are underrepresented on the Internet. Web-based services targeted at senior citizens may have difficulty, given the current paucity of seniors who have easy Web access, though the number of seniors on the Web is now growing rapidly. Similarly, people and businesses in the third world are also underrepresented. New-economy applications that make the most business sense will be those targeting groups for whom use of the Web is relatively widespread.

Simply *reaching* customers with new-economy tools may not be enough, however, especially for marketers of commodity-like products. Going beyond reach to build mutually beneficial *relationships* may be what is needed. Amazon.com has begun to build loyal relationships with its growing customer base by focusing its efforts on exceptional customer service. While book lovers often can find books for lower prices elsewhere on the Web, many of them simply return to Amazon's site, with its easy 1-Click® ordering, customer reviews, and other customer-friendly features. Using new-economy tools for building customer relationships may be their most important application in the long run.

Are New-Economy Tools Measurably *Effective* and *Efficient* Compared to Other Solutions?

Ultimately, given favorable answers to the first four questions in this section, deciding to invest in a particular new-economy marketing strategy or application comes down to two final questions. Is the new-economy solution effective, and is it more efficient than other solutions? As we have seen, UPS was able to sell SmartHome on its shipping because it was not only effective in getting SmartHome's parcels to their destinations on time, but also because SmartHome was able to improve on and save money on customer service at the same time.[49] Another example of using the Web for effectiveness and efficiency gains is the new Kinko's Internet order-taking system, Print to Kinko's. Customers can upload digital versions of documents to kinkos.com and have them delivered on paper at any Kinko's location within a few hours. Kinko's hopes the new system will capture some of the large market for corporate printing, thereby boosting sales, while enhancing productivity by reducing the error rate on printing orders from 10 percent to 1 percent, by cutting order handling costs, and by keeping Kinko's' copiers humming. Other dot-com printing players, such as iPrint and mimeo.com, were first to market, but Kinko's has the brand name and more than 1,000 stores. Will the digital strategy accelerate Kinko's' growth and increase earnings? CEO Joseph Hardin likes its potential. "We may be late to the market," he says, "but at the end of the day, he who executes wins."[50]

Marketers' concerns over the effectiveness and efficiency of their websites have led to the development of web analytics, software solutions that monitor and summarize website usage patterns. Web analytics is the equivalent of having a team of marketing researchers follow customers through a bricks-and-mortar retail store. The technology can uncover a variety of problems that can plague websites: cumbersome navigation, content that can't be easily found, underperforming search engine strategies, and unprofitable online marketing partnerships. The results of these analyses can improve customer satisfaction and response to the website, strengthen the marketer's hand in negotiating terms of partnership deals, and even identify new market segments that might be best served with tailored sites. "We're looking at the (Web analytics) every day, just like the guys on Wall Street look at daily stock quotes," says Jonathan Kapplow, corporate Internet marketing manager at Hanover Direct, a catalog and Web retailer of gifts and apparel.[51]

In the final analysis, setting clear SMART objectives that new-economy tools or activities are intended to meet—specific, measurable, attainable, relevant, timebound—and running cost–benefit analyses to assess their likely performance are necessary for making go/no-go decisions and for prioritizing which initiatives should be pursued first. Fortunately, the inherent measurability of many new-economy tools often provides clear and compelling feedback on whether they are meeting the objectives. In addition, attention must be given to a variety of business process issues that can get in the way of effective execution of even the best intentions for a new-economy strategy in an old-economy company. Recent research by Rosabeth Moss Kanter identified 10 common mistakes such companies commonly make (see Exhibit 12.12). Avoiding these errors is easier said than done, of course, but web analytics can help catch any errors that are made.

DEVELOPING STRATEGIES TO SERVE NEW-ECONOMY MARKETS

This chapter has, for the most part, addressed how companies of any kind, size, industry, or age can use new-economy tools and technologies for marketing purposes. No doubt, however, there are readers who see bigger fish to fry in the new-economy skillet. They see the new economy as offering the prospect for starting an entrepreneurial venture, in a new firm or within an existing one, to serve a market created by the advent of the Internet, wireless telephony, or other new or still-emerging technologies. Thus, in this final section, we address some lessons learned from the dot-com crash of 2000, we provide a framework for thinking about where and how revenues might be generated in the new-economy marketspace, and we examine what it is likely to take to create enduring success in the new-economy ventures of tomorrow.

What Lessons Can We Learn from the Dot-com Crash?

In April 2000 and the months that followed, the dot-com party ended. Many ventures with lofty market capitalizations stumbled and fell, in some cases losing more than 90 percent of their value by the end of 2000. Others shut their doors or were acquired, often on unfavorable terms. Venture capitalists slammed the funding window shut in some categories,

Exhibit 12.12

THE 10 DEADLY MISTAKES OF WANNA-DOTS

1. Sprinkle Internet responsibilities throughout the company—a little Web site here, a little brochure-ware there. Let them all go forward, as long as they stay small and innocuous. If any look like they have potential, raise skeptical questions at executive meetings and repeat frequently that the Internet is overhyped.

2. Form a committee to create a new corporate Internet offering, staff it with people from unrelated areas who are already doing five other things, and don't release them from their regular jobs. Give the leadership role to a bored executive as a reward for his years of loyal service. (Never mind that he has no Internet experience; he surfs the Web, doesn't he?)

3. Find the simplest, least-demanding thing you can do on the Web. Go for copyware that looks like what everyone else is doing. Instead of a killer app, create a "yawner app." (That will save time and money. And that way, you can cross the Internet off your to-do list quickly.)

4. To build the site, choose the vendors that are the most dismissive of your traditional business (they think you're dinosaurs) but whose abilities you're least capable of assessing. Then hand over the technical work to them (that way, nobody inside has to learn anything new) but refuse to take their advice about how the site should look (after all, you're the industry experts). Use more than one vendor—so you can have the fun of watching them slug it out.

5. Make sure what you do on the Web is exactly the same as what you do off-line: duplicate your traditional business assumptions on-line. (After all, the Internet is just a tool, isn't it?)

6. Insist that an Internet venture meet every corporate standard: cost controls, quarterly earnings, recruitment sources, compensation policies, purchasing procedures. Allocate just enough resources to keep it alive but not enough to risk its becoming an innovator—because that would require more investment.

7. Under the banner of decentralization and business unit autonomy, reward each unit for its own performance, and offer no extra incentives to cooperate in cyberspace. (Maintain your belief that conflict is a healthy spur to higher performance; let the victor get the spoils.) Keep reminding divisions that they are separate businesses because they are different, and that's that.

8. Compare your performance with your traditional industry competitors in the physical world. (That way you will always have someone to whom you can feel superior.) Dismiss on-line competitors as ephemeral fads. And don't even consider whether companies from unrelated industries could steal across the borders and poach your customers by using the Net. (Why worry about the hypothetical?)

9. Celebrate your conversion to e-business by giving people in the rest of the organization tools they are unable to use, requiring changes they are confused about making. Tell people this will help them do their work better. Schedule training classes at a distant location. Watch as the new tools take too much time and make it harder to get work done; then punish people for their resistance to make change.

10. And, last but not least, never forget that the company, not the customer, is in the driver's seat. The Internet is an opportunity for *us* to communicate with *them*.

such as e-tailing and e-hubs. With their coffers laden with money to invest, their focus moved to other more promising—or so they hoped—sectors.[52] What went wrong?

In a lengthy cover story in October 2000, *Fortune* magazine identified a dozen lessons to be learned from the dot-com crash.[53] The 12 lessons, shown in Exhibit 12.13, indicate collectively that many fundamental strategic marketing principles were ignored in the mad rush to what looked to be dot-com nirvana. Markets and market segments were not clearly identified and targeted. (Witness the Super Bowl ads for wedding announcements we saw in Chapter 7.) Low barriers to entry that made industries unattractive were ignored. (Venture capitalists tripped over one another in the mad scramble to fund seven pet portal companies over an eight-week span.[54]) First-to-market mania ruled, and the ability to sustain competitive advantage by offering better goods and services and better value often was overlooked. (Web latecomers such as Kinko's now appear to have an edge over their upstart net printing rivals.[55]) The basic economics of some businesses were ignored. (It can

Exhibit 12.13

LESSONS LEARNED FROM THE DOT-COM CRASH OF 2000

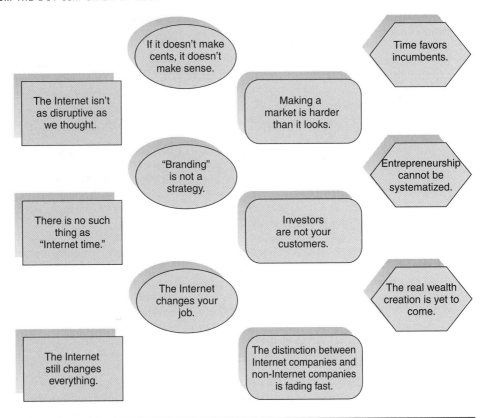

cost more to ship a bag of pet food than consumers typically pay for it.[56]) Acquiring (at reasonable cost) and retaining satisfied customers matter. Profitability and positive cash flow matter (sooner rather than later revenues should exceed expenses, including marketing expenses). Despite the carnage, however, *Fortune* concludes that, while the dot-com era is over, the Internet era is just getting started.

What Are the Key Success Factors in Serving the Dot-com Markets of Tomorrow?

What might tomorrow's entrepreneurs do to craft marketing strategies to serve these still enticing new-economy markets? For one, would-be Internet entrepreneurs should consider the various ways in which revenue can be generated on the Web or in other new-economy settings. Unless someone, a business or a consumer, is willing to fork over money for what a new business offers, its chances for success lie somewhere between slim and none. Exhibit 12.14 shows a number of ways in which revenue can be generated by Web-based businesses—from commerce, by selling content, by organizing communities, or from building the new-economy infrastructure. Understanding one's **business model** and being willing to change it as market and technological conditions warrant are essential.

Exhibit 12.14

E-BUSINESS MODELS

Commerce revenues	Description
Product sales	Sell or license physical or information-based products.
Commission, service, ice. or transaction fees	Charge a fee for services provided; can be a set fee or a percentage of the cost of a product or service.

Content revenues	Description
Subscription fees	Charge for receipt of updated information on a particular topic or a broad range of topics for a specified period (e.g., annual).
Registration or event fees	Charge a fee for attendance at an online event, workshop, or course.

Community revenues	Description
Advertising, slotting, affiliate, and referral fees	Collect a fee for hosting a banner advertisement or special promotion.
	Collect a fee for an exclusive or nonexclusive partnership relationship.
	Collect a fee each time a visitor clicks through from your site to another company's site.
Membership fees	Charge a fee to belong to a private group or service.

Infrastructure revenues	Description
Software/hardware sales	Sell or license a technology product.
Installation and integration fees	Charge either a set or variable fee for services provided; large-scale fixed-price projects are often broken into a series of discrete projects with well-defined time frames and deliverables; variable fees often are based on time, materials, and expenses incurred while working on a project.
Maintenance and update fees	Charge a fee for software/hardware maintenance and updates.
Hosting fees	Charge a fee for hosting a software application, website, data center, or network.
Access fees	Charge a fee for providing access to a network and/or to an Internet service.

Source: Lynda M. Applegate and Meredith Collura, *Overview of E-Business Models* (Boston: Harvard Business School Publishing, 2000).

Second, such entrepreneurs must ask not, What can I sell? but What do new-economy customers and markets need, whether through business-to-business (Grainger.com), business-to-consumer (Amazon.com or LandsEnd.com), consumer-to-consumer (eBay.com), or consumer-to-business (Priceline.com) business models, that my new company can provide better, easier, faster, or cheaper using new-economy tools and technologies? If a particular business idea does not fill some real, though perhaps currently latent, need identified by this question, there is no viable business.

Third, would-be entrepreneurs must now realize that barriers to entry are incredibly low in the new economy. For everyone who has the next latest and greatest Web-based idea, there are dozens of other prospective entrepreneurs likely to be exploring similar ideas concurrently. It's not really the ideas that count. As Bob Zider, president of the Beta Group, a Silicon Valley firm that develops and commercializes new technology, says,

"Many entrepreneurs make the mistake of thinking that venture capitalists are looking for good ideas when, in fact, they are looking for good managers in good industry segments."[57] What matters is the team that will execute an idea to deliver the performance and value that customers, whether businesses or consumers, want and will pay for. Only then will investors make money. Thus, execution is key, a truism we explore in greater depth in Chapters 13 and 14. As Intel's Andy Grove says about building the next wave of (it is hoped successful) Internet businesses, "It's work. Very unglamorous work . . . The heavy lifting is still ahead of us."[58] Much of this work is of the kind set forth in the first 12 chapters of this book: understanding customers and the markets they comprise; understanding industries and the competitors that do daily battle in them; and developing strategic marketing programs that can establish and maintain sustainable competitive advantage.

But there's also the work of strategy execution. In this chapter, we've explored the new economy and how both existing and new firms can find ways—measured in terms of effectiveness and efficiency—to take advantage of the promise it offers. In the two chapters that remain, we examine how best to organize for the effective implementation of, and control the results generated by, marketing strategies. "Give me 'A' execution of a 'B' plan over 'B' execution of an 'A' plan" is a common refrain heard from venture capitalists and other investors. Planning is important. But effective execution delivers the results, and results are what count.

TAKE AWAYS

- Seven potentially attractive elements characterize many new-economy technologies: the syndication of information, the increasing returns to scale of network products, the ability to efficiently personalize and customize market offerings, the ability to disintermediate distribution, global reach, 24×7 access, and the possibility of instantaneous delivery.

- First-mover advantage is simply wrong. Best beats first.

- Most observers now believe that the Internet is better suited for delivering measurable marketing results—as is direct marketing—than for brand building.

- Web-based customer service applications offer the tantalizing combination of better service and significant cost savings. The trick, of course, is to focus on the customer service benefits first, rather than mere cost

cutting, since customers are quick to discern when cost cutting takes precedence over genuine service responsiveness.

- Keys to success in tomorrow's new-economy ventures include clearly understanding one's business model (Exactly where will revenue come from: commerce, content, community, or infrastructure?), filling real (though perhaps latent) customer needs, and putting together the right management team that can deliver the performance and value that customers want and will pay for. Only then will investors make money.

- Self-diagnostic questions to test your ability to apply the analytical tools and concepts in this chapter to marketing decision making may be found at this book's website at **www.mhhe.com/walker.**

ENDNOTES

1. The information in this section comes from Bronwyn Fryer, "When Something Clicks," *Inc. Technology,* no. 1 (March 2000), pp. 62–72.

2. Allison Haines, "Gartner Says Consumers Will Spend 20 Times More on E-Commerce with Broadband Access," at www.gartner.com/public/static/aboutgg/pressrel/pr20001017a.html.

3. "The New Economy Goes Global," *Newsweek,* October 2, 2000, p. 74L.

4. Joseph B. White, "What Works?" *The Wall Street Journal,* October 23, 2000, p. R4.

5. Spencer E. Ante and Arlene Weintraub, "Why B2B Is a Scary Place to Be," *Business Week,* September 11, 2000, pp. 34–37.

6. William A. Sahlman, "The New Economy Is Stronger Than You Think," *Harvard Business Review,* November–December 1999, pp. 99–106.

7. Joseph B. White, "What Works?" *The Wall Street Journal,* October 23, 2000, p. R4.

8. This section is based on Kevin Werbach, "Syndication: The Emerging Model for Business in the Internet Era," *Harvard Business Review,* May–June 2000, pp. 85–93.

9. This section is based on Thomas Petzinger Jr., "So Long, Supply and Demand," *The Wall Street Journal,* January 1, 2000; and W. Brian Arthur, *Increasing Returns and Path Dependence in the Economy* (Ann Arbor, MI: University of Michigan Press, 1994).

10. Steven Levy, "The Book on the Future," *Newsweek,* August 28, 2000, p. 45.

11. Matthew Rose, "Random House Fires a Shot in E-Book Feud," *The Wall Street Journal,* November 1, 2000, p. B1.

12. Thomas E. Weber, "Web Music's Future: Turning Cell Phone into Wireless Walkman," *The Wall Street Journal,* July 10, 2000, p. B1.

13. Carl Shapiro and Hal R. Varian, "Versioning: The Smart Way to Sell Information," *Harvard Business Review,* November–December 1998, pp. 106–14.

14. Brad Stone, "Napster's Offspring," *Newsweek,* October 16, 2000, p. 58.

15. Shapiro and Varian, "Versioning: The Smart Way to Sell Information."

16. Much of this section is based on Jim Collins, "Best Beats First," *Inc.,* August 2000, pp. 48–51.

17. Ibid., p. 48.

18. Ibid., p. 49.

19. Evan I. Schwartz, *Digital Darwinism* (New York: Broadway Books, 1999).

20. Peter Sealey, "How E-Commerce Will Trump Brand Management," *Harvard Business Review,* July–August 1999, pp. 171–76.

21. For a broader look at Internet marketing, see Ward Hanson, *Principles of Internet Marketing* (Cincinnati: South-Western College Publishing, 2000).

22. Rebecca Buckman, "A Matter of Opinion," *The Wall Street Journal,* October 23, 2000, p. R46.

23. Steve Jarvis and Deborah Szynal, "Show and Tell: Spreading the Word about Online Qualitative Research," *Marketing News,* November 19, 2001, p. 1.

24. Ibid., p. 13.

25. Seth Godin, *Unleashing the Ideavirus* (New York: Do You Zoom, 2000).

26. Joe Dysart, "Sites That Sell Themselves," *Financial Times,* April 4, 2000, p. 19.

27. Ibid.

28. Jennifer Rewick, "Beyond Banners," *The Wall Street Journal,* October 23, 2000, p. R38; Suein Hwang and Mylene Mangalindan, "Yahoo's Grand Vision for Web Advertising Takes Some Hard Hits," *The Wall Street Journal,* September 1, 2000, p. A1.

29. Vanessa O'Connell, "The Best Way to Advertise," *The Wall Street Journal,* November 12, 2001, p. R13.

30. PricewaterhouseCoopers study for "Interactive Advertising Bureau (IAB) Reports Q1 & Q2 Internet Ad Revenue of $3.76 Billion in the United States," press release from IAB, September 24, 2001.

31. Ibid., p. R13.

32. Seth Godin, *Permission Marketing* (New York: Simon and Schuster, 1999).

33. "E-mail Is Growing as a Communications Channel for the Marketer and the Consumer," www3.doubleclick.net/market/1.htm.

34. Hwang and Mangalindan, "Yahoo's Grand Vision for Web Advertising Takes Some Hard Hits," p. A6.

35. Ibid.

36. David Streitfeld, "On the Web, Price Tags Blur," *The Washington Post Online,* www.washingtonpost.com/wp-dyn/articles/A_15159-2000Sep25.html.

37. Mark Wigfield, " 'Digital Signature' Bill Is Cleared by Congress," *The Wall Street Journal,* June 19, 2000, p. B12.

38. Youngme Moon and Francis X. Frei, "Exploding the Self-Service Myth," *Harvard Business Review,* May–June 2000, pp. 26–27.

39. Dennis K. Berman, "Killer Apps for a Wireless World," *Business Week e.biz,* September 18, 2000, p. EB 43.

40. Paul Nunes, Diane Wilson, and Ajit Kambil, "The All-in-One Market," *Harvard Business Review,* May–June 2000, pp. 19–20.

41. Rochelle Sharpe, "The Virtual Couch," *Business Week e.biz,* September 18, 2000, pp. EB 135–37; Richard B. Schmitt, "Lawyers vs. the Internet," *The Wall Street Journal,* July 17, 2000, p. B12.

42. Peter Gumbel, "Return to Sender," *The Wall Street Journal,* September 24, 2001, p. R19; Arlene Weintraub, "Dead Letter," *Business Week e.biz,* October 23, 2000, pp. EB 82–84.

43. From the science fiction movie *Star Trek,* in which it was routine to digitally transmit objects, including people, from place to place.

44. Frederick F. Reichheld and Phil Schefter, "E-Loyalty: Your Secret Weapon on the Web," *Harvard Business Review,* July–August 2000, pp. 105–13.

45. Charles Haddad, "Big Brown's Coup," *Business Week e.biz,* September 18, 2000, pp. EB 76–77.

46. Michael Warshaw, "The Thing That Would Not Die," *Inc. Technology,* no. 1 (March 2000), p. 89.

47. Youngme Moon and Francis X. Frei, "Exploding the Self-Service Myth," *Harvard Business Review,* May–June 2000, pp. 26–27.

48. Melanie Warner, "Fallen Idols," *Fortune,* October 30, 2000, pp. 108–21.

49. Haddad, "Big Brown's Coup."

50. Arlene Weintraub, "Late to the Party," *Business Week,* August 28, 2000, p. 254.

51. Steve Jarvis, "Follow the Money," *Marketing News,* October 8, 2001, p. 10.

52. Warner, "Fallen Idols."

53. Jerry Useem, "What Have We Learned?" *Fortune,* October 30, 2000, pp. 82–104.

54. Warner, "Fallen Idols."

55. Weintraub, "Late to the Party."

56. Ibid.

57. Bob Zider, "How Venture Capital Works," *Harvard Business Review,* November–December 1998, pp. 131–39.

58. Useem, "What Have We Learned?"

SECTION FOUR

IMPLEMENTATION AND CONTROL

CHAPTER THIRTEEN

ORGANIZING AND PLANNING FOR EFFECTIVE IMPLEMENTATION

Hewlett-Packard—Reorganizing to Implement a New Strategy[1]

THROUGHOUT MOST of the 1990s, Hewlett-Packard was one of the most successful and admired firm's in the computer industry. The firm's booming success in PCs and printers drove sales from $13 billion in 1990 to nearly $40 billion by 1996, with profits more than keeping pace.

A primary reason for HP's success during that period was its organization structure. The firm was managed like a conglomerate of small ventures, each responsible for its own success. More than 130 business units were focused on specific product lines such as UNIX computers or inkjet printers, each employing fewer than 1,500 people. And each SBU was granted substantial autonomy to pursue its own product and market development activities and to reinvest the capital generated by the unit.

Within HP's business units there was a heavy reliance on cross-functional teams. The PC unit, for example, was organized into small teams focused on different customer segments. The salesforce, too, was organized into teams focused on major accounts or application segments. HP's decentralized, team-based structure helped the firm stay in touch with changing customer needs and technical developments in each product category. And the SBUs were flexible enough to respond to those

changes quickly. The result was a constant stream of product improvements and line extensions. More than half of the company's sales in 1995, for example, came from products that were not in existence two years earlier.

THE INTERNET CHANGED THE FIRM'S MARKET ENVIRONMENT

 Paradoxically, the decentralized and flexible structure that enabled HP to be so successful at developing new generations of PCs and printers made it difficult for the firm to respond quickly to changes in the market environment brought about by the growing popularity of the Internet. For instance, as firms embraced the World Wide Web, system integration became critical. A company's computers, servers, routers, and software all had to be designed—often with the help of experienced consultants—to work together seamlessly, both internally and with the Internet itself. Unfortunately, while the narrow product focus and high level of autonomy of HP's business units had enabled them to move quickly and creatively when bringing out the next generation of offerings within their own product domains, it hindered their ability to coordinate efforts across product categories. Consequently, while old competitors such as IBM and new ones such as Sun Microsystems were designing and selling integrated e-business systems, HP lacked the internal coordination mechanisms necessary to do so.

The autonomy and financial independence of HP's many business units also caused difficulty in developing innovative new technologies not directly related to an existing product category. A decision to devote substantial resources to a technology that fell outside the domain of existing SBUs required the consensus of the various unit managers; and gaining that consensus could take months or years, thereby giving competitors a head start. Worse, some promising new Internet technologies were never developed because the necessary consensus was never achieved. For instance, HP researcher Ira Goldstein developed a prototype Web browser two years before Netscape Communications Corp. became the first Internet superstar with its Navigator browser. But the innovation was shot down by HP's computer division. "They just couldn't see how it would help them sell more computers," Goldstein says.

As a result of the firm's lack of coordination and strategic focus, HP missed much of the early growth in Internet hardware, software, and e-services markets that occurred in the late 1990s. Sales and profits began to stagnate, the firm's share price dropped dramatically, and management got the message.

REORGANIZING TO IMPLEMENT A NEW STRATEGY

One of the first steps toward correcting the problem taken by HP's board of directors was to bring in a new CEO from outside the company. Carly Fiorina was hired away from Lucent Technologies, where she had gained substantial experience developing and marketing gear for the new economy. Fiorina and other top managers quickly took several actions aimed at improving the coordination and sharpening the strategic focus of the company. They created four divisions—each headed by a divisional manager with CEO-like powers—to provide closer coordination and oversight for businesses making complementary goods and services without constraining their entrepreneurial spirit. For example, the UNIX computer and software and support units are now components of an Enterprise Computing Solutions Division, which is charged with combining computers and software into simple problem-solving packages for buyers, such as technology for helping small businesses set up shop on the Web.

Other steps aimed at improving the coordination of HP's Internet-related goods and services include increasing emphasis on e-commerce consulting services aimed at designing customized solutions for customers that utilize a wide range of HP hardware and software, changes in the compensation and reward system that increase the proportion of managers' pay tied to company sales and profit performance via bonuses and stock options, and a $100 million advertising campaign aimed at increasing customer awareness of the full range of Internet goods and services HP offers and improving the company's image as an e-commerce provider.

Finally, Fiorina created a new organizational entity, the E-Services Solutions Group, whose domain cuts across all of the other business units and divisions in the company. Its charge is to get the various business units to work in innovative ways with each other—and with outside partners—to develop new Web-based goods, services, and ways of doing business. The manager of the new group has been given $150 million in seed money and a lot of authority by top management to create, invest in, or acquire interesting Internet start-ups.

It's too soon to know whether Carly Fiorina's attempts to reorganize and reorient Hewlett-Packard and turn it into a major e-services provider will be entirely successful. The early results looked promising as revenues topped $48 billion and earnings reached nearly $3.9 billion in 2000. But sales and earnings were battered during 2001 due to slackening demand in many computer equipment and services markets and Dell Computer's attempt to capture market share through very aggressive pricing tactics. To complicate matters further, it was proposed in the fall of 2001 that HP merge with Compaq to create a new entity with revenues approaching $90 billion. The proposal was opposed by some of HP's board members and major stockholders, however, and as of this writing it is not clear whether the merger will occur. In any case, given the ongoing changes in HP's market, competitive, and internal environments, further adjustments in the firm's marketing strategies—and in the organizational structures needed to implement those strategies effectively—will likely be necessary.

STRATEGIC CHALLENGES ADDRESSED IN CHAPTER 13

Hewlett-Packard's fall from grace in the face of the dramatic Internet-driven shifts in its market environment and its subsequent attempts to remake itself into a major provider of e-commerce hardware and services illustrate that a business's success is determined by two aspects of strategic fit. First, its competitive and marketing strategies must fit the needs and desires of its target customers and the competitive realities of the marketplace. The emergence of the Internet increased companies' needs for closely integrated computer, network hardware, and software systems. Hewlett-Packard's balkanized approach of selling stand-alone products produced by many semiautonomous and entrepreneurial business units had once been extremely successful, but it was incapable of providing the integration customers were looking for in the Internet age. Consequently, the firm is scrambling to adjust its competitive strategy and product offerings to better fit the new realities of the marketplace.

But even if a firm's competitive strategy is appropriate for the circumstances it faces, it must be capable of implementing that strategy effectively. This is where the second aspect of strategic fit enters the picture. A business's organizational structure, internal policies, procedures, and resources must fit its chosen strategy or else implementation will fall short. Hewlett-Packard's highly decentralized structure and its policies of granting substantial control over financial resources to individual business units, for example, made it nearly impossible for the firm to implement a strategy of differentiating itself by providing tightly integrated and customized packages of Internet products and services to its customers. The company had to make major organizational changes to implement its new strategic direction. And it may have to make further changes to stimulate innovation or reduce costs in order to fend off Dell's aggressive compaign to capture market share.

Therefore, in the next section we examine several questions related to the issue of **organizational fit**—the fit between a business's competitive and marketing strategies and the organizational structures, policies, processes, and plans necessary to effectively implement those strategies.

STRATEGIC ISSUE

A business's organizational structure, internal policies, procedures, and resources must fit its chosen strategy or else implementation will fall short.

- For companies with multiple business units or product lines, what is the appropriate administrative relationship between corporate headquarters and the individual SBUs? How much autonomy should business unit managers be given to make their own strategic decisions, how much control should they have over the SBU's resources and programs, and how should they be evaluated and rewarded?

- Within a given business unit, whether it's part of a larger corporation or a one-product entrepreneurial start-up, what organizational structures and coordination mechanisms are most appropriate for implementing different competitive strategies? Answering this question involves decisions about variables such as the desired level of technical competence of the various functional departments within the business, the manner in which resources are allocated across those functions, and the mechanisms used to coordinate and resolve conflicts among the departments.

- How should organizational structures and policies be adjusted, if at all, as an organization moves into international markets?

However, even if a business has crafted brilliant competitive and marketing strategies, and it has the necessary organizational arrangements and wherewithal to implement them, implementation is unlikely to be very effective unless all of the business's people are following the same plan. This fact underlines the importance of developing formal, written marketing plans to document all the decisions made in formulating the intended strategy for a given good or service so it can be clearly communicated to everyone responsible for its implementation and to firmly establish who is responsible for doing what and when. And as we'll see in the next chapter, formal plans also establish the timetables and objectives that are the benchmarks for management's evaluation and control of the firm's marketing strategies. Thus, good planning is important.

Given the importance of formal plans as tools to aid implementation and control, we will return in the last part of this chapter to the planning framework we introduced briefly in Chapter 1. We will examine the content of effective marketing plans in more detail and review the many strategic decisions involved in formulating that content. The purpose of these strategic planning decisions is to lay a well-conceived foundation that permits effective implementation of the strategy. While good planning is important, effective implementation is crucial.

DESIGNING APPROPRIATE ADMINISTRATIVE RELATIONSHIPS FOR THE IMPLEMENTATION OF DIFFERENT COMPETITIVE STRATEGIES

In Chapter 3 we pointed out that businesses, whether small independent firms or units within a larger corporation, compete in different ways depending on their intended rate of new product-market development (i.e., prospectors versus analyzers versus defenders) and whether they seek an advantage by differentiating themselves via superior product or service quality or by being the low-cost producer. For example, during the mid-1990s many of Hewlett-Packard's business units could be characterized as differentiated analyzers. They were defending well-established share positions within their product domains by offering quality products while simultaneously investing in the development of more technically advanced product improvements and line extensions.

The chosen competitive strategy tends to influence the marketing strategies pursued by individual product offerings within the business unit, at least in the short term. The differentiated analyzer strategies of Hewlett-Packard's businesses, for instance, demanded a willingness to cannibalize existing products in order to ensure the future. Consequently, the advertising and promotion budgets for many older products were slashed as more technically advanced models were introduced.

Because the competitive strategies seek to satisfy customers and gain a sustainable advantage in varying ways, different organizational structures, policies, and resources are necessary to effectively implement them. For one thing, the administrative relationships between the unit and corporate headquarters influence the ability of SBU managers, including its marketing personnel, to implement specific competitive and marketing strategies successfully. This section examines three aspects of the corporate–business unit

Exhibit 13.1

ADMINISTRATIVE FACTORS RELATED TO THE SUCCESSFUL IMPLEMENTATION OF BUSINESS STRATEGIES

TYPES OF BUSINESS STRATEGY

Administrative factor	Prospector	Differentiated defender	Low-cost defender
SBU autonomy	Relatively high level	Moderate level	Relatively low level
Shared programs and synergy	Relatively little synergy—few shared programs	Little synergy in areas central to differentiation—shared programs elsewhere	High level of synergy and shared programs
Evaluation and reward systems	High incentives based on sales and share growth	High incentives based on profits or ROI	Incentives based on profits or ROI

relationship that can affect the SBU's success in implementing a particular competitive strategy:

1. The degree of autonomy provided each business unit manager.
2. The degree to which the business unit shares functional programs and facilities with other units.
3. The manner in which the corporation evaluates and rewards the performance of its SBU managers.

Exhibit 13.1 summarizes how these variables relate to the successful implementation of different business strategies. Analyzer strategies are not included because they incorporate some elements of both prospector and defender strategies. The administrative arrangements appropriate for implementing an analyzer strategy typically fall somewhere between those best suited for the other two types. To simplify the following discussion we focus only on the polar types—prospector, differentiated defender, and low-cost defender strategies.

Business-Unit Autonomy

Prospector business units are likely to perform better on the critical dimensions of new product success and increases in volume and market share when organizational decision making is relatively decentralized and the SBU's managers have substantial autonomy to make their own decisions. There are several reasons for this. First, decentralized decision making allows the managers closest to the market to make more major decisions on their own. Greater autonomy also enables the SBU's managers to be more flexible and adaptable. It frees them from the restrictions of standard procedures imposed from above, allows them to make decisions with fewer consultations and participants, and disperses power. All of these help produce quicker and more innovative responses to environmental opportunities.

One caveat must be attached to the above generalization, however. High levels of autonomy and independence can lead to coordination problems across business units. This can have a negative effect on market performance in situations where a firm's business units are narrowly defined and focused on a single product category or technology but the firm's customers want to buy integrated systems incorporating products or services from different units. This was the problem encountered by HP as the growing popularity of the Internet caused its customers to attach greater importance to system integration. One possible solution to this coordination problem is to redefine SBUs with a focus on customer or application segments rather than on narrowly defined product categories, as we discussed in Chapter 2. An alternative approach is to reduce the SBUs' autonomy somewhat by installing an additional level of managers—such as HP did with the appointment of divisional CEOs—responsible for coordinating the efforts of related business units. The risk inherent in this approach is that the essential flexibility and creativity of the individual business units may be compromised.

On the other hand, low-cost defender SBUs perform better on ROI and cash flow by giving their managers relatively little autonomy. For a low-cost strategy to succeed, managers must relentlessly pursue cost economies and productivity improvements. Such efficiencies are more likely to be attained when decision making and control are relatively centralized.

The relationship between autonomy and the ROI performance of differentiated defenders is more difficult to predict. On the one hand, such businesses defend existing positions in established markets and their primary objective is ROI rather than volume growth. Thus, the increased efficiency and tighter control associated with relatively low autonomy should lead to better performance. On the other hand, such businesses can maintain profitability only if they continue to differentiate themselves by offering superior products and services. As customers' wants change and new competitive threats emerge, the greater flexibility and market focus associated with greater autonomy may allow these businesses to more successfully maintain their differentiated positions and higher levels of ROI over time. These arguments suggest that the relationship between autonomy and performance for differentiated defenders (and probably for differentiated analyzers as well) may be mediated by the level of stability in their environments and by the proportion of offensive or proactive marketing strategies they employ. Units operating in relatively unstable environments and pursuing more proactive marketing programs (such as extended use or market expansion strategies) are likely to perform better when they have relatively greater autonomy.

Shared Programs and Facilities

Firms face a trade-off when designing strategic business units. An SBU should be large enough to afford critical resources and to operate on an efficient scale, but it should not be so large that its market scope is too broad or that it is inflexible and therefore cannot respond to its unique market opportunities. Some firms attempt to avoid this trade-off between efficiency and adaptability by designing relatively small, narrowly focused business units (as HP does), but then having two or more units share functional programs or facilities, such as common manufacturing plants, R&D programs, or a single salesforce.

Sharing resources poses a particular problem for prospector business units.[2] Suppose, for instance, a business wants to introduce a new product but shares a manufacturing plant and salesforce with other SBUs. The business would have to negotiate a production schedule for the new product, and it may not be able to produce adequate quantities as quickly as needed if other units sharing the plant are trying to maintain sufficient volumes of their own products. It also may be difficult to train salespeople on the new product or to motivate them to reduce the time spent on established products to push the new item. When Frito-Lay introduced Grandma's soft cookies, for instance, it relied on its 10,000 salty-snack route salespeople to attain supermarket shelf space for the new line. But because those salespeople were paid a commission based on their total sales revenue, they were reluctant to take time away from their profitable salty-snack lines to sell the new cookies. The resulting lack of strong sales support contributed to Grandma's failure to capture a sustainable share of the packaged cookie market.

One exception to this generalization, though, may be sharing sales and distribution programs across consumer package goods SBUs. In such cases, a prospector's new product may have an easier time obtaining retailer support and shelf space if it is represented by salespeople who also sell established brands to the same retail outlets. Similarly, as HP has recently discovered, sharing, or at least coordinating, sales, distribution, and customer service functions may be a good idea for business units that produce complementary goods or services that customers want to purchase as integrated systems rather than stand-alone offerings. In general, however, functional independence usually facilitates good performance for prospector businesses.

On the other hand, the increased efficiencies gained through sharing functional programs and facilities often boost the ROI performance of low-cost defender SBUs. Also, the inflexibility inherent in sharing is usually not a major problem for such businesses because their markets and technologies tend to be mature and relatively stable. Thus, Heinz, the cost leader in a number of food categories, uses a single salesforce to represent a wide variety of products from different business units when calling on supermarkets.

The impact of shared programs on the performance of differentiated defenders is more difficult to predict because they often must modify their products and marketing programs in response to changing market conditions to maintain their competitive advantage over time. Thus, greater functional independence in areas directly related to the SBU's differential advantage—such as R&D, sales, and marketing—tends to be positively associated with the long-run ROI performance of such businesses. But greater sharing of facilities and programs in less-crucial functional areas, such as manufacturing or distribution, also may help improve their efficiency and short-run ROI levels.

Evaluation and Reward Systems

Increasingly, U.S. firms are adopting some form of pay-for-performance compensation scheme. Some do it for individuals who meet specific goals (e.g., bonuses for salespeople who exceed their quotas), others on the basis of the performance of the SBU or the company as a whole (e.g., stock options). In either case, SBU managers are often motivated to achieve their objectives by bonuses or other financial incentives tied to one or more dimensions of their unit's performance. The question is, Which dimensions of performance should be rewarded?

For defender businesses in relatively mature markets, particularly those competing as low-cost defenders, operating efficiency and profitability tend to be the most important objectives, for reasons discussed in Chapter 3. Consequently, tying a relatively large portion of managers' incentive compensation to short-term profits seems sensible. This can be done either through bonuses based on last year's profit performance or economic value added (EVA) or through options keyed to increases in the firm's stock price.

In prospector businesses, on the other hand, basing too large a portion of managers' rewards on current profitability may cause problems. Such rewards may motivate managers to avoid innovative but risky actions or investments that may not pay off for some years into the future.[3] Even successful new product introductions can dramatically increase costs and drain profits early in the product's life cycle. By the time the new product starts contributing to the unit's profits, the manager who deserves the credit may have been transferred to a different business. Therefore, evaluation and reward systems that place relatively more emphasis on sales volume or market share objectives, or on the percentage of volume generated by new products, may be more appropriate for businesses pursuing prospector strategies. The 3M Company, for example, encourages innovation by tying a portion of every business unit manager's bonus to the goal of obtaining at least 30 percent of annual sales from products introduced in the past four years.

DESIGNING APPROPRIATE ORGANIZATIONAL STRUCTURES AND PROCESSES FOR IMPLEMENTING DIFFERENT STRATEGIES

Different strategies emphasize varying ways to gain a competitive advantage. Thus, a given functional area may be key to the success of one type of strategy but less critical for others. For instance, competence in new product R&D is critical for the success of a prospector business but less so for a low-cost defender.

Successful implementation of a given strategy is more likely when the business has the **functional competencies** demanded by its strategy and supports them with substantial **resources** relative to competitors; is organized suitably for its technical, market, and competitive environment; and has developed appropriate **mechanisms** for coordinating efforts and resolving conflicts across functional departments. Exhibit 13.2 summarizes the relationships between these organizational structure and process variables and the performance of different business strategies.

Functional Competencies and Resource Allocation

Competence in marketing, sales, product R&D, and engineering is critical to the success of prospector businesses because those functions play pivotal roles in new product and market development and thus must be supported with budgets set at a larger percentage of sales than their competitors. Because marketing, sales, and R&D managers are closest to the changes occurring in a business's market, competitive, and technological environments, they should be given considerable authority in making strategic decisions. This argues that bottom-up strategic planning systems are particularly well-suited to prospector businesses operating in unstable environments. Success here is positively affected by the extent to which customer orientation is an integral part of the unit's corporate culture.

In low-cost defender businesses, on the other hand, the functional areas most directly related to operating efficiency, such as financial management and control, production, process R&D, and distribution or logistics, play the most crucial roles in enabling the SBU to attain good ROI performance. Because differentiated defenders need to attain high returns on their established products, functional areas related to efficiency are also critical for their success. Similarly, such units also seek to improve efficiency by investing in process R&D, making needed capital investments, and maintaining a high level of capacity utilization. But because they also must maintain their differential advantage over time, functional departments related to the source of that advantage—the salesforce and product R&D for SBUs with a technical product advantage or sales, marketing, and distribution for SBUs with a customer service advantage—are also critical for the unit's continued success. For example, in an attempt to defend its leading share position, cement the loyalty of its growing customer base, and generate greater revenues from repeat purchases, Amazon.com has invested hundreds of millions of dollars to build its own distribution centers and improve the speed and reliability of its order fulfillment.[4]

Additional Considerations for Service Organizations

Given that service organizations pursue the same kinds of business-level competitive strategies as goods producers, they must meet the same functional and resource requirements to implement those strategies effectively. However, service organizations—and

Exhibit 13.2

ORGANIZATIONAL AND INTERFUNCTIONAL FACTORS RELATED TO THE SUCCESSFUL IMPLEMENTATION OF BUSINESS STRATEGIES

| | TYPE OF BUSINESS STRATEGY | | |
Organizational factor	Prospector	Differentiated defender	Low-cost defender
Functional competencies of the SBU	SBU will perform best on critical volume and share-growth dimensions when its functional strengths include marketing, sales, product R&D, and engineering.	SBU will perform best on critical ROI dimensions when its functional strengths include sales, financial management and control, and those functions related to its differential advantage (e.g., marketing, product R&D).	SBU will perform best on critical ROI and cash flow dimensions when its functional strengths include process engineering, production, distribution, and financial management and control.
Resource allocation across functions	SBU will perform best on volume and share-growth dimensions when percentage of sales spent on marketing, sales, and product R&D is high and when gross fixed assets per employee and percent of capacity utilization are low relative to competitors'.	SBU will perform best on the ROI dimension when percentage of sales spent on the salesforce, gross fixed assets per employee, percent of capacity utilization, and percentage of sales devoted to other functions related to the SBU's differential advantage are high relative to competitors'.	SBU will perform best on ROI and cash flow dimensions when marketing, sales, and product R&D expenses are low, but process R&D, fixed assets per employee, and percentage of capacity utilization are high relative to competitors'.
Decision-making influence and participation	SBU will perform best on volume and share-growth dimensions when managers from marketing, sales, product R&D, and engineering have substantial influence on unit's business and marketing strategy decisions.	SBU will perform best on ROI dimension when financial managers, controller, and managers of functions related to unit's differential advantage have substantial influence on business and marketing strategy decisions.	SBU will perform best on ROI and cash flow when controller, financial, and production managers have substantial influence on business and marketing strategy decisions.
SBU's organization structure	SBU will perform best on volume and share-growth dimensions when structure has low levels of formalization and centralization, but high level of specialization.	SBU will perform best on ROI dimension when structure has moderate levels of formalization, centralizaton, and specialization.	SBU will perform best on ROI and cash flow dimensions when structure has high levels of formalization and centralization, but low level of specialization.
Functional coordination and conflict resolution	SBU will experience high levels of interfunctional conflict; SBU will perform best on volume and share-growth dimensions when participative resolution mechanisms are used (e.g., product teams).	SBU will experience moderate levels of interfunctional conflict; SBU will perform best on ROI dimension when resolution is participative for issues related to differential advantage, but hierarchical for others (e.g., product managers, product improvement teams, etc.).	SBU will experience low levels of interfunctional conflict; SBU will perform best on ROI and cash flow dimensions when conflict resolution mechanisms are hierarchical (e.g., functional organization).

Source: Adapted from Orville C. Walker Jr., and Robert W. Ruekert, "Marketing's Role in the Implementation of Business Strategies," *Journal of Marketing,* July 1987, p. 31.

manufacturers that provide high levels of customer service as part of their product offer-ing—often need some additional functional competencies because of the unique problems involved in delivering quality service.

This is particularly true for services involving high customer contact. Because the sale, production, and delivery of such services occur almost simultaneously, close coordination between operations, sales, and marketing is crucial. Also, because many different employ-ees may be involved in producing and delivering the service—as when thousands of dif-ferent cooks prepare Big Macs at McDonald's outlets around the world—production planning and standardization are needed to reduce variations in quality from one transac-tion to the next. Similarly, detailed policies and procedures for dealing with customers are necessary to reduce variability in customer treatment across employees. All of this suggests that personnel management—par-ticularly the activities of employee selection, training, motivation, and evaluation—is an important adjunct to the production and marketing efforts of high-contact service organizations.

STRATEGIC ISSUE

Personnel management—particularly the activities of employee selection, training, motivation, and evaluation—is an important adjunct to the production and marketing efforts of high-contact service organizations.

Competence in human resource development is more crucial for service businesses pur-suing prospector strategies—and perhaps also for defenders and analyzers who differenti-ate their offerings on the basis of good service—than for those focused primarily on efficiency and low cost. In prospector service organizations, employees often play a criti-cal role in identifying potential new service offerings and in introducing them to potential customers. Consequently, the effective implementation of such a strategy requires employ-ees with superior communication and social skills and necessitates frequent employee retraining and performance feedback. For instance, banks pursuing a prospector strategy not only have more branches and engage in more market scanning, advertising, and new service development than those with other types of competitive strategies, but also devote more effort to screening potential employees and providing training and support after they are hired.[5]

Organizational Structures

Three structural variables—formalization, centralization, and specialization—are impor-tant in shaping both an SBU's and its marketing department's performance within the con-text of a given competitive strategy. **Formalization** is the degree to which formal rules and standard policies and procedures govern decisions and working relationships. **Centraliza-tion** refers to the location of decision authority and control within an organization's hier-archy. In highly centralized SBUs or marketing departments, only one or a few top managers hold most decision-making authority. In more decentralized units, middle- and lower-level managers have more autonomy and participate in a wider range of decisions. Finally, **specialization** refers to the division of tasks and activities across positions within the organizational unit. A highly specialized marketing department, for instance, has a large number of specialists, such as market researchers, advertising managers, and sales promotion managers, who perform a narrowly defined set of activities often as consultants to product managers.

Highly structured business units and marketing departments are unlikely to be very innovative or quick to adapt to a changing evironmental circumstance. Adaptiveness and innovativeness are enhanced when (1) decision-making authority is decentralized, (2) managerial discretion and informal coordination mechanisms replace rigid rules and poli-cies, and (3) more specialists are present. Thus, prospector business units and their mar-keting departments are likely to perform better when they are decentralized, have little formalization, and are highly specialized.

Differentiated defenders perform best when their organization structures incorporate moderate levels of formalization, centralization, and specialization. Those departments most directly related to the source of a differentiated defender's competitive advantage (sales, marketing, and R&D), however, should be less highly structured than those more crucial for the efficiency of the unit's operations (production and logistics).

Several common organizational designs incorporate differences in both the structural variables (formalization, centralization, and specialization) and the mechanisms for resolving interfunctional conflicts. These include (1) functional, (2) product management, (3) market management, and (4) various types of matrix organizational designs.

Functional Organizations   The functional form of organization is the simplest and most bureaucratic design. At the SBU level, managers of each functional department, such as production or marketing, report to the general manager. Within the marketing department, managers of specific marketing activity areas, such as sales, advertising, or marketing research, report to the marketing vice president or director, as shown in Exhibit 13.3. At each level the top manager coordinates the activities of all the functional areas reporting to him or her, often with heavy reliance on standard rules and operating procedures. This is the most centralized and formalized organization form and relies primarily on hierarchical mechanisms for resolving conflicts across functional areas. Also, because top managers perform their coordination activities across all product-markets in the SBU, there is little specialization by product or customer type.

These characteristics make the functional form simple, efficient, and particularly suitable for companies operating in stable and slow-growth industries where the environments are predictable. Thus, the form is appropriate for low-cost defender SBUs attempting to maximize their efficiency and profitability in mature or declining industries. For example, Ingersol-Rand, a low-cost manufacturer of low-tech air compressors and air-driven tools such as jackhammers, uses a functional structure.

The simplicity of the functional organization also makes it the most common organizational form among entrepreneurial start-ups, including many dot-com companies. Even

Exhibit 13.3

FUNCTIONAL ORGANIZATION OF AN SBU AND ITS MARKETING DEPARTMENT

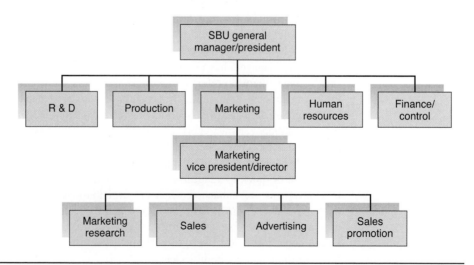

though the functional form is very hierarchical, such firms can still be nimble and innovative provided that (1) the company remains small enough that the entrepreneur can personally supervise and coordinate the various functions, (2) the firm is focused on a single product or product line targeted at one customer segment, and (3) the entrepreneur's personal vision is an adequate source of innovation to differentiate the entire company. As the start-up grows, its product offerings expand, and its markets fragment; however, it is usually wise to adopt a more decentralized and specialized organizational form. Unfortunately, some entrepreneurs find it difficult to delegate decision-making authority to their subordinates.

Product Management Organizations

When a company or SBU has many product-market entries, the simple functional form of organization is inadequate. A single manager finds it difficult to stay abreast of functional activities across a variety of different product-markets or to coordinate them efficiently. One common means of dealing with this problem is to adopt a product management organization structure. As Exhibit 13.4 illustrates, this form adds an additional layer of managers to the marketing department, usually called product managers, brand managers, or marketing managers, each of whom has the responsibility to plan and manage the marketing programs and to coordinate the activities of other functional departments for a specific product or product line.

A product management structure decentralizes decision making while increasing the amount of product specialization within the SBU. If the product managers also are given substantial autonomy to develop their own marketing plans and programs, this structure also can decrease the formalization within the business. Finally, although the product managers are responsible for obtaining cooperation from other functional areas both within and outside the marketing department, they have no formal authority over these areas. They must rely on persuasion and compromise—in other words, more participative methods—to overcome conflicts and objections when coordinating functional activities. These factors make the product management form of organization less bureaucratic than the functional structure. It is more appropriate, then, for businesses pursuing differentiated defender and analyzer strategies,

Exhibit 13.4

A MARKETING DEPARTMENT WITH A PRODUCT MANAGEMENT ORGANIZATION

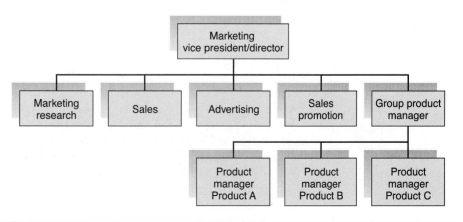

Exhibit 13.5   Ford Opts for Brand Management

Ford Motor Company's Ford division has joined the company's Lincoln-Mercury division and General Motors in adopting brand management. Driving this trend is intense global competition, which demands more distinctive products aimed at sharply defined segments and the need to react faster to changes in the marketplace. Both companies copy the organizations of such packaged household goods companies as Procter & Gamble in making a single executive responsible for all aspects relating to the marketing of a given brand.

The new Ford marketing organization means that the company will no longer distinguish organizationally between cars and trucks since consumers cross-shop these vehicles as follows:

Youthful vehicles—Aspire, Escort, Contour, and Ranger

Family vehicles—Taurus, Crown Victoria, and Windstar and Aerostar minivans

Sporting cars—Mustang, Probe, and Thunderbird

Expressive cars—Bronco, Explorer, and Expedition

Tough vehicles—F-Series pick-ups and the Econoline and Club Wagon vans

Ford brand managers will work closely with the company's global marketing plans unit, which, in turn, will work with five global vehicle development centers to design products. General Motors' brand managers, on the other hand, work directly with the engineer who oversees product design (called a vehicle line executive).

Source: Raymond Serafin, "Ford Puts Brands in the Driver's Seat," *Advertising Age,* October 8, 1995, p.3; Raymond Serafin, "Why GM Opted for Brand Management," *Advertising Age,* October 23, 1995, p. 3; Raymond Serafin, "Ford Taps Insiders as Brand Managers," *Advertising Age,* January 1, 1996, p.3; and Kathleen Kerwin and Joann Muller, "Reviving GM," *Business Week,* February 1, 1999, pp. 114–22.

particularly when they operate in industries with complex and relatively unstable market and competitive environments. See Exhibit 13.5 for why Ford opted for brand management.

When a firm targets a number of brands at different market segments, a product management organization typically includes one or more "group" or "category" marketing managers, on the level immediately above the product managers, who allocate resources across brands. Category management also provides an opportunity for the involvement of more experienced managers in brand management, particularly those concerned with coordinating pricing and other marketing efforts.[6]

Product management organizations have a number of advantages, including the ability to identify and react more quickly to the threats and opportunities individual product-market entries face; improved coordination of functional activities within and across product-markets; and increased attention to smaller product-market entries that might be neglected in a functional organization. Consequently, about 85 percent of all consumer goods manufacturers use some form of product management organization.

Despite its advantages, a product management organization has shortcomings. The major one is the difficulty of obtaining the cooperation necessary to develop and implement effective programs for a particular product given that a product manager has little direct authority. Also, the environment facing product managers is changing drastically. They increasingly must face the fact that customers can quickly compare products and prices—and even suggest their own price—over the Internet; that customers are becoming more price sensitive and less brand loyal; that competition is becoming more global; that rapidly changing technologies are providing new ways to improve production and distribution efficiency, but also shortening product life cycles; and that the power of large retailers and distributors has increased due in part to their ability to collect and control information about the marketplace. These environmental trends have led to an increase in the sales of private-label brands and more aggressive bargaining by distributors.[7] As a result of these trends and the inherent weakness of the product manager type of organization, many companies have undertaken two major types of modifications—market management and matrix organization—discussed next.

Market Management Organizations   In some industries an SBU may market a single product to a large number of markets where customers have very different requirements and preferences. Pepsi-Cola, for example, is sold through restaurants, fast-food outlets, and supermarkets. The syrup needed to make Pepsi is sold directly to institutions such as Kentucky Fried Chicken and Taco Bell. But marketing Pepsi to consumers for home consumption involves the use of franchised bottlers who process and package the product and distribute it to a variety of retail outlets. The intermediaries and marketing activities involved in selling to the two markets are so different that it makes sense to have a separate market manager in charge of each. Such a company or SBU might organize itself along the lines shown in Exhibit 13.6. Some SBUs have adopted a combination of product and regional market management organization structures. A product manager has overall responsibility for planning and implementing a national marketing program for the product, but several market mangers are also given some authority and an independent budget to work with salespeople and develop promotion programs geared to a particular user segment or geographic market. This kind of decentralization or regionalization has become popular with consumer goods companies in their efforts to increase geographic segmentation and cope with the growing power of regional retail chains.

Matrix Organizations   A business facing an extremely complex and uncertain environment may find a matrix organization appropriate. The matrix form is the least bureaucratic or centralized and the most specialized type of organization. It brings together two or more different types of specialists within a participative coordination structure. One example gaining increased popularity is the product team, which consists of representatives from a number of functional areas assembled for each product or product line. As a group, the team must agree on a business plan for the product and ensure the necessary resources and cooperation from each functional area. This kind of participative decision making can be very inefficient; it requires a good deal of time and effort for the team to reach mutually acceptable decisions and gain approval from all the affected functional areas. But once reached, those decisions are more likely to reflect the expertise of a variety of functional

Exhibit 13.6

A MARKETING DEPARTMENT WITH A MARKET MANAGEMENT ORGANIZATION

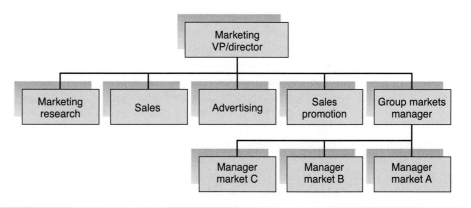

Exhibit 13.7   Using Teams to Get the Job Done

Pillsbury, which has recently merged with General Mills, replaced its traditional marketing department with multiple discipline teams centered around a product group (pizza snacks). Each involves managers from marketing, sales, and production. Lever Brothers restructured in a similar fashion. It reorganized its marketing and sales departments into a series of business groups and set up a separate customer development team responsible for retailer relations across all the various SBU brands.

Source: "Death of the Brand Manager," *The Economist*, April 9, 1994, p. 67.

---

specialists, to be innovative, and to be quickly and effectively implemented. Thus, the matrix form of organization particularly suits prospector businesses and the management of new product development projects within analyzer or differentiated defender businesses. For example, Pillsbury has relied heavily on cross-functional product management teams, as discussed in Exhibit 13.7.

Another form of matrix structure involves the creation of an additional organizational unit or managerial position responsible for coordinating the actions of other units within the firm. For example, nearly every business school has an MBA program director responsible for coordinating the courses offered by the functional departments in hopes of creating a tightly integrated and coherent curriculum. Similarly, Hewlett-Packard created an E-Services Solutions Group, a coordinating unit whose domain cuts across all the other SBUs and divisions in the company and who is charged with encouraging the other SBUs to work with each other and with outside partners to develop new Web-based goods and services.

Recent Trends in Organizational Design

As we have stressed throughout this book, the dynamics of the marketplace are forcing companies to respond more quickly to their opportunities and threats if they hope to survive and prosper. This has spurred a search for organizational structures that are flexible, responsive, able to learn, and market oriented.[8] While we are only just beginning to gain insights into organizational structures of the future, certain aspects seem reasonably clear. We briefly discuss the more important of these.

Organizations will increasingly emphasize the **managing of business processes** in contrast to functional areas.[9] Every business has about six basic or core processes, such as, for example, new product development and supply chain management. The former would be staffed by individuals from marketing, R&D, manufacturing, and finance. The latter would contain people with expertise in purchasing, manufacturing, order delivery, and billing.

Managing processes will make the organization essentially horizontal—flat and lean versus a vertical or hierarchical model. Thus, executive positions will no longer be defined in terms of managing a group of functionally oriented people; instead, executives will be concerned with a process that strongly emphasizes the importance of customer satisfaction.[10] Process management is quite different from the management of a function because, first, it uses external objectives, such as customer satisfaction versus simple revenues. Second, people with different skills are grouped to undertake a complete piece of work; their work is done simultaneously, not in sequence. Third, information flows directly to where it is used. Thus, if you have an upstream problem, you deal with people involved directly rather than via your boss.

Next, the use of **self-managing teams** is increasing. Regardless of the form of worker self-management, all are based on the concept of *empowerment*—the theory that those doing the work should have the means to do what it takes to please the customer. In turn, this requires that performance objectives and evaluation of activities be linked to customer satisfaction. Successful teams can dramatically improve productivity; for example, Boeing used empowered teams to reduce the number of hang-ups by half on its 777 jet.[11] But many teams have failed because management was not serious about its empowerment, team members were poorly selected, and the team was launched in isolation with little training or support.[12]

In the future many companies will use teams as the basis for collaborative networks that link thousands of people together with the help of a variety of new technologies. Such networks enable businesses to form and dissolve relations quickly and to bring to bear on an opportunity or a threat the needed resources regardless of who owns them.[13] For example, AT&T used Japan's Marubeni Trading Company as a means to link with Matsushita Electric Industrial Company to jump-start the manufacture of its Safari Notebook Computer, which was designed by Henry Dreyfuss Associates.[14]

But not all such collaborative networks are successful, especially those involving **joint ventures.** Partnering is at best a difficult and demanding undertaking requiring considerable managerial skills as well as a great deal of trust.[15] A major difficulty, especially for those involving companies from different parts of the world, is that "they cannot be controlled by formal systems, but require a dense web of interpersonal connections and internal infrastructures that enhance learning."[16]

Organizational Adjustments as Firms Grow and Markets Change

Managers often think of the design of their organization as stable and not subject to change. In rapidly growing entrepreneurial companies and in changing markets, however, such thinking can be dangerous. As the number of customers and the range of product lines grow, the best way to organize the marketing and sales functions should be subject to change.

An entrepreneurial start-up may begin with a simple functional structure, perhaps even simpler than that diagrammed in Exhibit 13.3. As it grows and its product offerings become broader and more complex, it may assign specialized product managers to coordinate the marketing efforts for the various products or product lines. Eventually, the firm might even split into several product divisions, each with its own sales and marketing departments. Or the firm's customers might fragment into a number of diverse segments with unique needs and requirements, favoring the adoption of a market management or matrix structure.

With each of these adjustments to a company's organization structure, however, comes added complexity and potential disadvantages. For instance, what if the new structure results in multiple salespeople, representing the company's different product lines, competing with each other for a customer's business? Such competition may be contrary to the company's self-interest as well as confusing and inconvenient for the customer. More importantly, such a lack of coordination would make it difficult to sell comprehensive solutions that cut cross the firm's product or divisional boundaries.

The above situation is where Hewlett-Packard found itself in 1999. Its various divisions, each with its own sales and marketing personnel, were ill-equipped to cooperate with each other or with outsiders to develop and market comprehensive systems and services geared to the new demands of the Internet, which HP viewed as crucial to its success. Consequently, new CEO Carly Fiorina reorganized the company and created the E-Services

Solutions Group, a new organizational entity whose domain cuts across all the other divisions. She tapped Nick Earle, HP's chief marketing officer for enterprise computing, to head the new unit and charged him with getting the firm's various businesses to work in innovative ways with one another and with other companies to create new Web *services,* a significant departure for the predominantly *goods*-oriented company.

How should managers decide when the time has come to restructure an organization, and what new structure should replace the old one? There are five key drivers in such decisions: (1) customer needs, (2) informational requirements of the sales and marketing personnel charged with meeting those needs, (3) ability of a given structure to motivate and coordinate the kinds of activities that market conditions require, (4) available competencies and resources, and (5) costs.

When customers all tend to use a narrow range of goods or services to satisfy similar needs, a simple functional structure may be sufficient. When customer segments use goods or services in different ways, either a product-focused or market-focused structure is likely to work well. If individual customers buy a broad range of the firm's goods or services, however, having multiple salespeople calling on those customers, unless they are organized into teams, is probably a bad idea. When a company's offerings are relatively simple and easy to understand, a single salesforce may be able to handle the entire line. But when products are technically complex or open to customization, each line may require its own specialized sales and marketing organization. When the firm is not well established or needs to educate potential buyers about the advantages of an innovative offering, it may need heavy incentives to encourage salespeople to expend the effort necessary to win new business. Under such circumstances, team-oriented selling arrangements are likely to be ineffectual. Finally, the fact that more highly specialized structures also tend to increase personnel and administrative costs should not be overlooked.

Thus, growing firms or those serving rapidly changing markets are likely to need to rethink—and perhaps change—the structure of their sales and marketing organizations frequently. Such changes can be disruptive to both internal and customer relationships, but as HP discovered, failure to adjust in the face of changing market conditions can make it impossible for the firm to implement its marketing strategy.

Organizational Designs for Selling in Global Markets[17]

An organization's complexity increases, often quite dramatically, as it "goes international" and especially so as overseas sales as a percentage of total sales increase. The issue is essentially one of deciding what organizational design is best for developing and implementing worldwide strategies while simultaneously maintaining flexibility with regard to individual markets. In evaluating the several types of international organizational structures discussed in this section, keep in mind two things: "first, that innovation is the key to success. An organization which relies on one culture for its ideas and treats foreign subsidiaries as dumb production-colonies might as well hire subcontractors."[18] Second, technology is making the world smaller.

Little or No Formal Organization   Early on in a firm's international involvement, the structure ranges from the domestic organization handling international transactions to a separate export department. The latter may be tied to the marketing department or may be a freestanding functional department.

An International Division   To avoid discriminating against international customers in comparison with domestic customers, an international division is often established to house all international activities, most of which relate to marketing. Manufacturing, engineering, finance, and R&D typically remain in their previous form to take advantage of scale effects. This type of organization serves best with a limited number of products that lack cultural sensitivity—for example, basic commodity types such as chemicals, metals, and industrial machinery.

Japanese firms have emphasized low-cost manufacturing coupled with quality assurance as the essence of their international competitive strategy. Both of these require strong centralized control and, thus, the use of an export-based organizational structure. In recent years, Japanese firms have become more interested in global structures based on products or areas.[19]

Global Structures   There are a variety of global types, of which the simplest replicates the firm's basic functional departments. A global company using the functional type of organization would have vice presidents (worldwide) for such areas as manufacturing, marketing, and finance—all reporting to the president.

By far the most common global structure is one based on products, which translates into giving SBUs worldwide control over their product lines. The main advantages of this type of structure are the economies derived from centralizing manufacturing activities and the ability to respond quickly to product-related problems originating in overseas markets. Marketing is localized at the country or regional level.

The *area structure* is another popular global organizational type and is especially appropriate when there is considerable variance across markets regarding product acceptance and marketing activities. Firms typically organize on a regional basis (North America, Latin America, Far East, Middle East, and Africa) using a central staff that coordinates worldwide planning and control activities.

Some companies use a hybrid organization that typically is some combination of the functional, product, or area types of structure. The global matrix is one such attempt. It has individual business managers reporting to both area and functional groups, or area managers reporting to business and functional groups, thereby enabling the company to balance the need for centralized efficiency and its responsiveness to local needs. But the dual reporting sets up conflicts and slows the management process to such an extent that many companies, including Dow and CitiCorp, have returned to more traditional organizational designs.[20]

Decision Making and Organizational Structure   Organization structures can be centralized or decentralized in terms of decision making. In the case of the latter, controls are relatively simple and relations between subsidiaries and headquarters mainly financial. The logic here is that local management is closest to the market and can respond quickly to change. But multinationals faced with strong global competition require more centralization, which calls for headquarters to provide the overall strategy that subsidiaries (country units) implement within a range agreed upon with headquarters.[21]

MARKETING PLANS: THE FOUNDATION FOR IMPLEMENTING MARKETING ACTIONS

As we pointed out in Chapter 1, preparation of a written plan is a key step in ensuring the effective execution of a strategic marketing program because it spells out what actions are to be taken, when, and by whom. Written plans are particularly crucial in larger organizations because a marketing manager's proposals must usually be reviewed and approved by higher levels of management, and because the approved plan then provides the benchmark against which the manager's and the marketing program's performances will be evaluated. Preparing formal, written marketing plans, however brief, is a useful

STRATEGIC ISSUE

A written plan is a key step in ensuring the effective execution of a strategic marketing program because it spells out what actions are to be taken, when, and by whom.

exercise even in small firms because the discipline involved helps ensure that the proposed objectives, strategy, and marketing actions are based on rigorous analysis of the 4 Cs and sound reasoning. Marketing plans can vary a good deal in content and organization, but they generally follow a format similar to the one outlined in Exhibit 1.10 and reproduced in Exhibit 13.8. To illustrate the kinds of information that might be included in each section of the plan, the contents of a marketing plan for a disguised Pillsbury refrigerated dough product are summarized in Exhibit 13.9.

Much of this book has focused on the planning process, the decisions that must be made when formulating a marketing strategy and its various components, the development of strategic marketing plans, and the analytical tools managers can use in reaching those decisions. Consequently, we will say little here about the processes or procedures involved in putting together a marketing plan. Instead, our purpose is to summarize how the topics we've covered can be integrated with a coherent marketing plan, and how the plan's content should be organized and presented to best ensure that the strategy will be effectively carried out.

Exhibit 13.8

CONTENTS OF AN ANNUAL MARKETING PLAN

Section	Content
I. Executive summary	Presents a short overview of the issues, objectives, strategy, and actions incorporated in the plan and their expected outcomes for quick management review.
II. Current situation and trends	Summarizes relevant background information on the market, competition and the macroenvironment, and trends therein, including size and growth rates for the overall market and key segments.
III. Performance review (for an existing product or service only)	Examines the past performance of the product and the elements of its marketing program (e.g., distribution, promotion, etc.).
IV. Key issues	Identifies the main opportunities and threats to the product that the plan must deal with in the coming year, and the relative strengths and weaknesses of the product and business unit that must be taken into account in facing those issues.
V. Objectives	Specifies the goals to be accomplished in terms of sales volume, market share, and profit.
VI. Marketing strategy	Summarizes the overall strategic approach that will be used to meet the plan's objectives.
VII. Action plans	This is the most critical section of the annual plan for helping to ensure effective implementation and coordination of activities across functional departments. It specifies • The target market to be pursued. • What specific actions are to be taken with respect to each of the 4 Ps. • Who is responsible for each action. • When the action will be engaged in. • How much will be budgeted for each action.
VIII. Projected profit-and-loss statement	Presents the expected financial payoff from the plan.
IX. Controls	Discusses how the plan's progress will be monitored; may present contingency plans to be used if performance falls below expectations or the situation changes.
X. Contingency plans	Describes actions to be taken if specific threats or opportunities materialize during the planning period.

Exhibit 13.9

SUMMARY OF AN ANNUAL MARKETING PLAN FOR A REFRIGERATED BREAD DOUGH PRODUCT

I. Analysis of current situation
  A. Market situation
   - The total U.S. market for dinner breadstuffs is enormous, amounting to about 10.5 billion servings per year.
   - Specialty breads, such as whole-grain breads, are growing in popularity, largely at the expense of traditional white breads.
   - Pillsbury's share of the total dinner breadstuffs market, accounted for by several brands including Crescent rolls as well as refrigerated bread dough, is small, amounting to only about 2 percent of the total dollar volume.
   - Since its introduction several years ago, refrigerated bread dough (RBD) has been able to achieve only low levels of penetration (only about 15 percent of all households have used the product) and use frequency (nearly two-thirds of the product's volume comes from light users who buy only one or two cans per year).
   - RBD consumption is concentrated in the northern states and during the fall and winter months (about 75 percent of volume is achieved from September through February).
   - Marketing research results suggest consumers believe RBD is relatively expensive in terms of price/value compared to alternative forms of dinner breadstuffs.
  B. Competitive situation
   - RBD's share of the total dinner breadstuffs category is likely to remain low because of the wide variety of competing choices available to consumers.
   - The largest proportion of volume within the category is captured by ready-to-eat breads and rolls produced by supermarket chains and regional bakeries and distributed through retail grocery stores.
   - RBD's major competition within the refrigerated dough category comes from other Pillsbury products, such as Crescent rolls and Soft Breadsticks.
   - There are currently no other national competitors in the refrigerated bread dough category; but Merico, a small regional producer, was recently acquired by a major national food manufacturer. Evidence suggests Merico may be preparing to introduce a competing product line into national distribution at a price about 10 percent lower than Pillsbury's.
  C. Macroenvironmental situation
   - Changes in American eating habits may pose future problems for dinner breadstuffs in general, and for RBD in particular:
     More meals are being eaten away from home, and this trend is likely to continue.
     People are eating fewer starch foods.
     While total volume of dinner breadstuffs did not fall during the 1990s, neither did it keep pace with population growth.
   - Increasing numbers of women working outside of the home, and the resulting desire for convenience, may reduce consumers' willingness to wait 30 minutes while RBD bakes, even though the dough is already prepared.
   - Because RBD does not use yeast as a leavening agent, Food and Drug Administration regulations prohibit the company from referring to it as "bread" in advertising or package copy, even though the finished product looks, smells, and tastes like bread.
  D. Past product performance
   - While sales volume in units increased only slightly during the past year, dollar volume increased by 24 percent due to a price increase taken early in the year.
   - The improvement to gross margin was even greater than the price increase due to an improvement in manufacturing costs.
   - The improvement to gross margin, however, was not sufficient to produce a positive net margin due to high advertising and sales promotion expenditures aimed at stimulating primary demand and increasing market penetration of RBD.
   - Consequently, while RBD showed improvement over the last year, it was still unable to make a positive contribution to overhead and profit.
II. Key issues
  A. Threats
   - Lack of growth in the dinner breadstuff category suggests the market is mature and may decline in the future.
   - The large variety of alternatives available to consumers suggests it may be impossible for RBD to substantially increase its share of the total market.
   - Potential entry of a new, lower-priced competitor poses a threat to RBD's existing share and may result in lower margins if RBD responds by reducing its price.
  B. Opportunities
   - The largest percentage of RBD volume accounted for by light users suggests an opportunity of increasing volume among current users by stimulating frequency of use.
   - Trends toward increased consumption of specialty breads suggests possible line extensions, such as whole wheat or other whole grain flavors.

Exhibit 13.9

(CONCLUDED)

C. Strengths
- RBD has a strong distribution base, with shelf-facings in nearly 90 percent of available retail outlets.
- RBD sales have proved responsive to sales promotion efforts (e.g., cents-off coupons), primarily by increasing volume among existing users.
- The fact that most consumers who try RBD make repeat purchases indicates a high level of customer satisfaction.

D. Weaknesses
- RBD sales have proved unresponsive to advertising. Attempts to stimulate primary demand have not been able to increase market penetration.
- Consumer concerns about RBD's price/value place limits on ability to take future price increases.

III. Objectives

A. Financial objectives
- Achieve a positive contribution to overhead and profit of $4 million in current year.
- Reach the target level of an average of 20 percent return on investment over the next five years.

B. Marketing objectives
- Maintain market share and net sales revenues at previous year's levels.
- Maintain current levels of retail distribution coverage.
- Reduce marketing expenditures sufficiently to achieve profit contribution objective.
- Identify viable opportunities for future volume and profit expansion.

IV. Marketing strategy
- Pursue a maintenance strategy aimed at holding or slightly increasing RBD volume and market share primarily by stimulating increased frequency of use among current users.
- Reduce advertising aimed at stimulation of primary demand/penetration and reduce manufacturing costs in order to achieve profit contribution objective.
- Initiate development and test marketing of possible line extensions to identify opportunities for future volume expansion.

V. Marketing action plans
- Improve the perceived price/value of RBD by maintaining current suggested retail price at least through the peak selling season (February). Review the competitive situation and the brand's profit performance in March to assess the desirability of a price increase at that time.
- Work with production to identify and implement cost savings opportunities that will reduce manufacturing costs by 5 percent without compromising product quality.
- Maintain retail distribution coverage with two trade promotion discount offers totaling $855,000: one offered in October–November to support peak season inventories and another offered in February–March to maintain inventories as volume slows.
- Reduce advertising to maintenance level of 1,100 gross ratings points during the peak sales period of September to March. Focus copy on maintaining awareness among current users.
- Encourage greater frequency of use among current users through three sales promotion events, with a total budget of $748,000, that will stimulate immediate purchase:
  One free-standing insert (FSI) coupon for 15 cents off next purchase to appear in newspaper on September 19.
  One tear-off refund offer (buy three, get one free) placed on the retailer's shelves during November.
  A $1 refund with proof of purchase offer placed in women's service books (i.e., women's magazines like *Good Housekeeping*) during March.

VI. Contingency plans
- Maintain the above marketing strategy and action plans without change during the planning period even if Merico (see item I.B) enters the market.
- If Merico enters, carefully monitor its pricing and promotion actions, sales results, consumer perceptions, and so forth, and prepare recommendations for next year's plan.

The success of a marketing plan depends on effective communication with other parts of the organizations (such as production, engineering, and R&D) and a variety of marketing units, especially those concerned with sales, advertising, promotions, and marketing research. By using the experience of others (as consultants) in preparing the action programs (for instance, in-store promotions), the planner not only benefits from the expertise of specialists, but also increases their buy-in to the overall marketing plan, thereby increasing the likelihood of its success.

The action programs should reflect agreements made with other departments and marketing units as to their responsibilities over the planning period concerning the product. For example, if a special sale is to occur in a given month, the production department must commit to making sufficient product available and to the use of a special package; the promotion group agrees to develop and have available for use by the salesforce in-store displays; the salesforce must allocate the time necessary to do the in-store work; and so on. Thus, the annual plan serves as a means of allocating the firm's resources as well as a way of assigning responsibility for the plan's implementation.[22]

The Situational Analysis[23]

While many marketing plans start with a brief executive summary of their contents, this is typically the first substantive section in which the marketing manager details his or her assessment of the current situation. It is the "homework" portion of the plan where the manager summarizes his or her analysis of current and potential customers, the competitive environment and the company's relative strengths and weaknesses, trends in the broader macroenvironment that may impact the product, and past performance outcomes for existing products. This section also typically includes estimates of sales potential, forecasts, and other assumptions underlying the plan. Based on these analyses, the manager may then call attention to one or more key issues, major opportunities, or threats that should be dealt with during the planning period.

Market Situation   Here data are presented on the target market. Total market size and growth trends should be discussed, along with any variations across geographic regions or other market segments. Marketing research information also might be presented concerning customer perceptions (say, awareness of the brand) and buying-behavior trends (market penetration, repeat purchase rate, heavy versus light users). As Exhibit 13.9 indicates, for instance, information about the market situation presented in the plan for Pillsbury's refrigerated bread dough (RBD) not only includes data about the size of the total market for dinner breadstuffs and Pillsbury's market share, but also points out the low penetration and use frequency of RBD among potential users.

Competitive Situation   This section identifies and describes the product's major competitors in terms of their size, market share, product quality, marketing strategies, and other relevant factors. It also should discuss the likelihood that other potential competitors will enter the market in the near future and the possible impact of such entry on the product's competitive position. Note, for instance, that while other Pillsbury brands are the primary competitors for RBD in the refrigerated dough category, the potential entry of a new low-cost competitor could dramatically change the competitive situation.

Macroenvironmental Situation   This section describes broad environmental occurrences or trends that may have a bearing on the product's future. The issues mentioned here include any relevant economic, technological, political/legal, or social/cultural changes. As Exhibit 13.9 indicates, for example, lifestyle trends leading to more meals being eaten away from home and increased desires for convenience pose a threat to future demand for Pillsbury's RBD.

Past Product Performance   If the plan is for an existing product, this part of the situation analysis discusses the product's performance on such dimensions as sales volume, margins, marketing expenditures, and profit contribution for several recent years. This

Exhibit 13.10

HISTORICAL AND PROJECTED FINANCIAL PERFORMANCE OF REFRIGERATED BREAD DOUGH PRODUCT

Variable	Last year	This year	Percent change	Next year	Percent change
Sales volume (cases)	2,290M	2,350M	3%	2,300M	(2%)
Net sales ($)	17,078M	21,165M	24	21,182M	0
Gross margin ($)	6,522M	10,787M	65	11,430	5
Gross margin/net sales	38%	51%	—	54%	—
Advertising and sales promotion ($)	11,609M	12,492M	+6	6,100M	(51)
Advertising & sales promotion/gross margin	178%	116%	—	53%	—
Net margin ($)	(5,087M)	(1,725M)	—	5,330M	—
Net margin/net sales	—	—	—	25	—
Product contribution ($)	(6,342M)	(3,740M)	—	4,017M	—

information is usually presented in the form of a table, such as the one for RBD shown in Exhibit 13.10. As the table indicates, even though RBD showed an improvement in gross margin due in part to reduced manufacturing costs, high advertising and sales expenditures prevented the product from making a positive contribution to overhead and profit.

The data contained in Exhibit 13.9 do not answer the question of whether the company's RBD prices and costs are competitive. Such information is critical since if a product's costs are not in line, then the product's market position is in jeopardy. This is especially true with commodity-type products, although even when products are differentiated it is essential that costs be maintained at competitive levels and any price premium charged provide a corresponding benefit to buyers.

The best way to determine a firm's relative cost position is to use the value chain concept, which identifies "the activities, functions, and business processes that have to be performed in designing, producing, marketing, delivering, and supporting a product or service."[24] The chain of value-creating activities starts with raw materials and continues on through parts and components production, manufacturing and assembly, wholesale distribution, and retailing to the ultimate end user of the product or service.[25] As would be expected, developing estimates for each value chain item is difficult and time consuming, especially so for estimating competitor's costs. Even so, it is well worth the effort.

Sales Forecast and Other Key Assumptions   Finally, the assessment of the current situation also typically includes estimates of sales potential, sales forecasts, and other evidence or assumptions underlying the plan. As we discussed in Chapter 6, such market measurements are particularly critical as the foundation for marketing plans for new goods or services where there is no past history to draw on. While the RBD plan does not explicitly report an estimate of total market potential, a sales forecast underlies the expected volume for next year, reported in the fourth column of Exhibit 13.10.

Key Issues

After analyzing the current situation, the product manager must identify the most important issues facing the product in the coming year. These issues typically represent either threats to the future market or financial performance of the product or opportunities to improve those performances. This section also should highlight any special strengths of the product or weaknesses that must be overcome in responding to future threats and opportunities. Some of the key threats and opportunities faced by Pillsbury's RBD, together with the product's major strengths and weaknesses, are summarized in section II of Exhibit 13.9.

Objectives

Information about the current situation, the product's recent performance, and the key issues to be addressed now serve as the basis for setting specific objectives for the coming year. Two types of objectives need to be specified. **Financial objectives** provide goals for the overall performance of the brand and should reflect the objectives for the SBU as a whole and its competitive strategy. Those financial goals must then be converted into **marketing objectives** that specify the changes in customer behavior and levels of performance of various marketing program elements necessary to reach the product's financial objectives.

The major financial and marketing objectives for Pillsbury's RBD are summarized in section III of Exhibit 13.9. Sales volume and market share are not expected to increase, but the product is expected to make a $4 million contribution to overhead and profit through additional cost reductions.

Marketing Strategy

Because there may be a number of ways to achieve the objectives specified in the preceding section, the manager must now specify the overall marketing strategy to be pursued. It is likely to be one, or a combination of several, of the strategies discussed earlier in Chapters 9, 10, 11, and 12. The chosen strategy should fit the market and competitive conditions faced by the product and its strategic objectives. It also should incorporate all of the necessary decisions concerning the 4Ps.

The RBD product manager recommends that a **maintenance strategy** be pursued. The intense competitive situation, uncertainty over the possible entry of Merico, and the past inability of primary-demand advertising to increase market penetration all suggest that it would be difficult to expand RBD's market by simply doing more of the same. Consequently, the recommended strategy seeks to maintain or slightly increase RBD volume and share primarily by stimulating repeat purchases among current customers. Reductions in advertising expenditures and continued improvements in manufacturing costs will be relied on to help the brand achieve its profit contribution objective. In addition, it is recommended that development and test marketing of several line extensions (for example, whole wheat and a French-style loaf) be initiated in an attempt to identify viable opportunities for future volume expansion.

Action Plans

The action plan is the most crucial part of the annual marketing plan for ensuring proper execution. Here the specific actions necessary to implement the strategy for the product are listed, together with a clear statement of who is responsible for each action, when it will be done, and how much is to be spent on each activity. Of course, actions requiring the cooperation of other functional departments should be included, but only after the product manager has contacted the departments involved, worked out any potential conflicts, and received assurances of support.

Here is where specific timelines and milestones are set forth. A variety of planning and project management tools—such at Gantt charts, stage-gate development processes, and others—may be used to illustrate and orchestrate the action steps entailed in the plan. Some of the action programs specified for RBD are outlined in section V of Exhibit 13.9.

Projected Profit-and-Loss Statement

The action plan includes a supporting budget that is essentially a projected profit-and-loss statement. On the revenue side, it forecasts next year's sales volume in units and dollars. On the expense side, it reflects manufacturing, distribution, and marketing costs associated with the planned actions. This budget is then presented to higher levels of management for review and possible modification. Once approved, the product's budget serves as a basis for the plans and resource allocation decisions of other functional departments within the SBU, such as manufacturing and purchasing, as well as other marketing units (e.g., marketing research). The projected financial results of RBD's annual plan are summarized in the second-to-last column of Exhibit 13.10.

Contingency Plans

Finally, the manager also might detail contingency plans to be implemented if specific threats or opportunities should occur during the planning period. The RBD product manager, for instance, recommended that no changes should be made in the product's overall marketing strategy nor in its pricing or promotion tactics in the event that Merico entered the national market. The rationale was that time should be taken to carefully analyze Merico's market impact and the magnitude of its competitive threat before crafting a response.

TAKE AWAYS

- While much of this book has covered the various analytical tools and frameworks necessary to develop effective marketing strategies, such strategies are worthless without good implementation. Therefore, marketing managers, and general managers concerned about marketplace issues, must attend to organizational design issues. A business's structure, policies, procedures, and resources must fit its chosen strategy or else implementation will fall short.

- For firms with multiple businesses or product lines, different administrative relationships between the business unit and corporate headquarters are appropriate for different competitive strategies. Prospector businesses perform better with high levels of autonomy, fewer shared resources, and more top-line focused reward systems than defender businesses.

- Within a given business—whether it's part of a larger organization or a one-product entrepreneurial start-up—

different functional competencies, levels of specialization, amounts of employee participation in decision making, and mechanisms for the resolution of internal conflicts are needed to effectively implement varying competitive strategies.

- Writing a formal marketing action plan is a key step toward ensuring the effective execution of a strategic marketing program because it spells out what actions need to be taken, when, and by whom. Written plans also provide the benchmarks by which the marketing strategy can be evaluated and controlled, as discussed in the next chapter.

- Self-diagnostic questions to test your ability to apply the analytical tools and concepts in this chapter to marketing decision making may be found at this book's website at **www.mhhe.com/walker.**

ENDNOTES

1. This example is based on material found in Alan Deutschman, "How H-P Continues to Grow and Grow," *Fortune,* May 2, 1994, p. 90; Wendy Zellner, "The Go-Go Goliaths," *Business Week,* February 13, 1995, p. 64; Anne B. Fisher, "America's Most Admired Companies," *Fortune,* March 4, 1996; Stratford Sherman, "Secrets of H-P's 'Muddled Team,'" *Fortune,* March 18, 1996; Peter Burrows and Peter Elstrom, "The Boss," *Business Week,* August 2, 1999, pp. 76–84; Eric Nee, "Hewlett-Packard's New E-vangelist," *Fortune,* January 10, 2000, pp. 166–68; Andrew Park and Peter Burrows, "Dell, the

Conqueror," *Business Week,* September 24, 2001, pp. 92–102; and the Hewlett-Packard website at www.hp.com.

2. Robert W. Ruekert and Orville C. Walker Jr., "The Sharing of Marketing Resources across Strategic Business Units: The Effect of Strategy on Performance," in *Review of Marketing* 1990 (Chicago: American Marketing Association, 1990).

3. Bernard J. Jaworski, "Toward a Theory of Marketing Control: Environmental Context, Control Types, and Consequences," *Journal of Marketing,* July 1988, pp. 23–39.

4. Robert Hof, Debra Sparks, Ellen Neuborne, and Wendy Zellner, "Can Amazon Make It?" *Business Week,* July 10, 2000, pp. 38–43.

5. Daryl O. McKee, P. Rajan Varadarajan, and William M. Pride, "Strategic Adaptability and Firm Performance: A Market-Contingent Perspecitve," *Journal of Marketing,* July 1989, p. 19. For an interesting discussion of recent developments in the implementation of strategies for service organizations, see James L. Heskett, W. Earl Sasser Jr., and Christopher W. L. Hart, *Implementing Strategy: Service Breakthroughs: Changing the Rules of the Game* (Cambridge, MA: The Mac Group, n.d.).

6. Michael J. Zenor, "The Profit Benefits of Category Management," *Journal of Marketing Research,* May 1994, p. 202.

7. Allen D. Shocker, Rajendra K. Srivastava, and Robert W. Ruekert, "Challenges and Opportunities Facing Brand Management," *Journal of Marketing Research,* May 1994, p. 149. Also see Donald R. Lehmann and Russell S. Winer, *Product Management* (Burr Ridge, IL: Richard D. Irwin, 1994) chap. 16.

8. For a discussion of firms as learning organizations and hence better able to cope with change, see "The Knowledge Firm," *The Economist,* November 11, 1995, p. 63; and Stanley F. Slater and John C. Narver, "Market Orientation and the Learning Organization," *Journal of Marketing,* July 1995, p. 63.

9. Some analysts believe this may lead to a strategic advantage. See David A. Garvin, "Leveraging Processes for Strategic Advantage," *Harvard Business Review,* September–October 1995, p. 77.

10. Rahul Jacob, "The Struggle to Create an Organization for the 21st Century," *Fortune,* April 3, 1995, p. 90; Thomas A. Stewart, "Planning a Career in a World without Managers," *Fortune,* March 20, 1995, p. 72; and John A. Byrne, "Management by Web," *Business Week,* August 21, 2000, pp. 84–96.

11. Brian Dumaine, "The Trouble with Teams," *Fortune,* September 5, 1994, p. 86.

12. Ibid.

13. Samuel E. Blucker, "The Virtual Organization," *The Futurist,* March–April 1994, p. 9; and Peter Coy, "The Creative Economy," *Business Week,* August 21, 2000, pp. 76–82.

14. John A. Byrne, Richard Brandt, and Otis Port, "The Virtual Corporation," *Business Week,* February 8, 1993, p. 98.

15. Rosabeth Moss Kanter, "Collaborative Advantage: The Art of Alliance," *Harvard Business Review,* July–August 1994, p. 97; and Ravi S. Achrol and Philip Kotler, "Marketing in the Network Economy," *Journal of Marketing* 63 (Special Issue 1999), pp. 146–63.

16. Kanter, "Collaborative Advantage," p. 97.

17. The discussion that follows draws heavily from Michael R. Czinkota, Pietra Rivali, and Idkka A. Ronkausen, *International Business* (New York: Dryden Press, 1992), pp. 536–45.

18. "The Discreet Charm of the Multicultural Multinational," *The Economist,* July 30, 1994, p. 57.

19. Christopher A. Bartlett and Sumantra Ghoshal, *Transnational Management* (Burr Ridge, IL: Richard D. Irwin, 1992) p. 520.

20. Ibid.

21. Czinkota et al., *International Business,* p. 545.

22. Donald R. Lehmann and Russell S. Winer, *Product Management* (Burr Ridge, IL: Richard D. Irwin, 1994), pp. 28–29.

23. While this example is based on the material contained in an actual marketing plan for a Pillsbury product, the name of the brand and some of the specific numbers included in this example have been disguised in order to protect proprietary information.

24. This section has benefited from the contents of chapter 4 in Arthur A. Thompson Jr. and A. J. Strickland III, *Crafting and Implementing Strategy* (Burr Ridge, IL: Richard D. Irwin, 1995).

25. Michael E. Porter, *Competitive Advantage* (New York: Free Press, 1985), chaps. 2 and 3; Robin Cooper and Robert S. Kaplan, "Measure Costs Right: Make the Right Decisions," *Harvard Business Review,* September–October 1988, pp. 96–103; and John K. Nrahk and Vijay Govindarajan, *Strategic Cost Measurement* (New York: Free Press, 1993), especially chaps. 2–6 and 10.

CHAPTER FOURTEEN

MEASURING AND DELIVERING MARKETING PERFORMANCE

Controls Pay for Wal-Mart[1]

WAL-MART IS A DISCOUNT general merchandise retailer with sales of over $165 billion and net income of over $5.5 billion in fiscal 1999. Founded less than 40 years ago, it is America's largest, most-profitable, and one of its most-admired companies. Over the past decade it has continuously ranked as one of the best companies in its return on stockholders' equity.

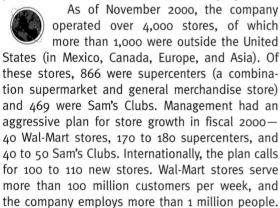 As of November 2000, the company operated over 4,000 stores, of which more than 1,000 were outside the United States (in Mexico, Canada, Europe, and Asia). Of these stores, 866 were supercenters (a combination supermarket and general merchandise store) and 469 were Sam's Clubs. Management had an aggressive plan for store growth in fiscal 2000— 40 Wal-Mart stores, 170 to 180 supercenters, and 40 to 50 Sam's Clubs. Internationally, the plan calls for 100 to 110 new stores. Wal-Mart stores serve more than 100 million customers per week, and the company employs more than 1 million people.

A major reason for Wal-Mart's success is its ability to control costs. In 1999 it was able to hold its operating, selling, and general administrative costs to 16.4 percent of sales. This was substantially below that of its closest competitor, Kmart, and explains, in part, the company's excellent profitability record.

In the 1960s when he had only 10 stores, Sam Walton realized he couldn't expand successfully unless he could capture the information needed to control his operations. He became, according to one competitor, the best utilizer of control information in the industry. By the late 1970s Wal-Mart was using a storewide computer-driven information system that linked stores, distribution centers, and suppliers. Kmart started using a similar system only in the early 1990s.[2] In the late 1980s Sam Walton tapped David Glass to take over as CEO. Now the company's chairman, Glass, more than anyone, successfully engineered the development of Wal-Mart's advanced distribution and merchandise-tracking system, which were needed to handle the enormous sales increases as the company's stores spread throughout the United States. "Wal-Mart's incomparable systems are a secret of its success—the unadvertised contributor to the stock's 46.8 percent average annual return during the decade before Sam's death."[3]

Today, the company can convert information into action almost immediately. To do so required a massive investment (over $700 million) in computer and satellite systems, which collectively generate the largest civilian database of its kind in the world. In addition to automated replenishment, the system provides up-to-the-minute sales of any item by region, district, and store. By looking at the computer screens in the satellite room, a manager can see systemwide data of the day's sales as they happen, the number of stolen bank cards retrieved that day, whether the seven-second credit card approval system is working properly, and the number of customer transactions completed that day.

Wal-Mart's philosophy has always been that its executives should spend part of their time in the field visiting with associates (employees) and customers. Thus, they board the company's prop planes in Bentonville on Monday each week, returning to share their findings with headquarters personnel and to prepare for a series of merchandise meetings Friday and Saturday. These are no-holds-barred sessions concerned with moving merchandise. For example, in one meeting it was suggested that Wal-Mart was missing a great business opportunity in street-hockey gear because of the in-line skate craze. Others agreed, and within a few minutes appropriate action had been taken, including the development of an eight-foot-long display section.[4] This was, and similar decisions will be, communicated to all store managers by the following morning at the latest using Wal-Mart's computer-driven communications system.

By merging state-of-the-art computer communications technology with hands-on management, Wal-Mart has developed a distribution system to the point stores should never be out of stock. Doing this better than its rivals has resulted in substantially more sales per square foot than competitors and, hence, a faster stock turn. This means less borrowing to carry fewer inventories and hence lower interest payments—several hundred million dollars lower than its nearest competitor. And lost sales because of stockouts are minimized.

STRATEGIC CHALLENGES ADDRESSED IN CHAPTER 14

In Chapter 13, we said that planning is important, and that effective implementation is crucial. The Wal-Mart example demonstrates how effective planning and implementation can play out in the performance of a company. Together, these two activities constitute the heart of most business endeavors. In the end, however, it is neither planning nor implementation that really counts. Results are what counts. Results are what managers and entrepreneurs are paid to deliver. Results are what attract investment capital to permit a company—whether a large public company such as Wal-Mart or an emerging dot-com start-up—to grow. Just watch what happens to a public company's stock price when the results are not what Wall Street expects. The share price plummets and, sometimes, heads roll. Weak sales and profit performance at Gap Inc. in late 1999 and 2000 cut Gap's stock price by half and led to a series of middle and upper management changes at the once high-flying retailer.[5] The focus on results is not restricted to for-profit organizations either. Exhibit 14.1 shows how some nonprofit organizations are measuring their success and winning increased funding from donors as a result.

In Chapter 14, we address several critical questions that provide the link between a company's efforts to plan and implement marketing strategies and the actual results that those strategies produce. How can we design **strategic control systems** to make sure the strategies we are pursuing remain in sync with the changing market and competitive environment in which we operate? How can we design systems of **marketing metrics** to ensure that the marketing results we plan for are the results we deliver? In other words, if the ship

STRATEGIC ISSUE

Results are what managers and entrepreneurs are paid to deliver. Results are what attract investment capital to permit a company to grow.

Exhibit 14.1   **Measuring and Demonstrating Results Attract Grants for Children's Services Agency**

Kingsley House, a children's services agency in New Orleans, has adopted specific, measurable goals for each of its programs, such as increased rates of employment and improved parenting skills for the client families it serves. It tracks and reports its results quarterly and shares them with its staff and the communication it serves. The agency credits its ability to demonstrate positive outcomes for its recent success in raising $4.7 million in grants and business donations, beating its fund-raising goal by $500,000. "Tracking outcomes leads to greater confidence that funded programs are effective, that they have the support of people in the community," says Martha Taylor Greenway, a senior director for United Way of America, one of Kingsley House's donors.

More than 150 local United Way organizations across the United States and more than 7,500 funded human services agencies have adopted models in which program outcomes are measured and assessed against specific goals. For United Way of the Piedmont (UWP) in Spartanburg, South Carolina, it is no longer enough to simply send money to popular causes. "We got out of the business of reviewing all the agencies that apply for funding and passing judgment on how they ought to be run," says UWP President Vince Pulskamp. "Their boards do that. We began to focus on how well they actually deliver results. Agencies receiving funding for their programs need to show that their customers are satisfied and that the program works, not just that their unit costs are in line. We treat our donor dollars as an investment with returns, so we can go back to the community and show how their money is spent and what was achieved."

Source: "Making Results Count," *Leader to Leader,* Summer 1997.

gets off course during the journey, either strategically or in terms of execution of the marketing strategy, how can we make sure that we know quickly of the deviation so that midcourse corrections can be made in a timely manner? In today's rapidly changing markets, even the best-laid plans are likely to require changes as their implementation unfolds.

We begin by developing a five-step process for evaluating and controlling marketing performance on a continuous basis. We then apply the process to the issue of **strategic control:** How can we monitor and evaluate our overall marketing strategy to ensure that it remains viable in the face of changing market and competitive realities? Next, we apply the process to tracking the performance of a particular product-market entry and to the marketing actions taken to implement its marketing plan, or **marketing performance measurement.** Are we meeting sales targets, in the aggregate and for various products and market segments? Is each element of the marketing mix doing its job: Which items in the product line are selling best, are the ads producing enough sales leads, is the salesforce generating enough new accounts, and so on? Finally, we show how **marketing audits** can be used periodically to link the control process—for both strategic control and for measuring current marketing performance—with marketing planning.

DESIGNING CONTROL SYSTEMS STEP BY STEP

As the Wal-Mart example demonstrates, a well-functioning control and reappraisal system is critical to the success of a business. To be successful, it should be well integrated with the other steps in the marketing management process: setting objectives, formulating strategies, and implementing a plan of action. The control system monitors the extent to which the firm is achieving its objectives. When it is not, the firm determines whether the

Exhibit 14.2

THE CONTROL PROCESS

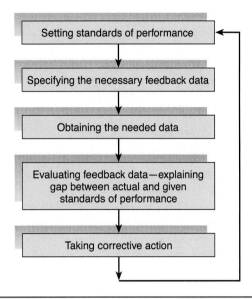

reason lies in the environment, the strategies employed, the action plans, the way the plans were being implemented, or some combination thereof. Thus, the control and reappraisal step is diagnostic, serving to start the marketing management process anew.

Control processes differ at each organization level. Thus, in a large diversified company, corporate management is concerned with how well its various SBUs are performing relative to the opportunities and threats each faces and the resources given them. Control here would be strategic. At the SBU level, or in smaller companies, concern is primarily with the unit's own strategy, especially as it pertains to its individual product-market entries. We will concentrate mainly on this latter organizational level since it constitutes the bulk of any control system.

Regardless of the organization level involved, the control process is essentially the same. It consists of five steps: setting performance standards, specifying feedback, obtaining data, evaluating it, and taking corrective action (see Exhibit 14.2). Although the staff organization is typically responsible for generating the control data, the line organization administers the control process. Certainly, this is the case with Wal-Mart, as seen in the involvement of regional vice president, district managers, store managers, and department heads in obtaining and processing control data as well as taking corrective action. More importantly, line managers need to be closely involved with the development of the control system, so that they can be assured of getting the performance data they need, on a timely basis, and in a format they can easily use to support their long-term and day-to-day decision making.

Setting Standards of Performance

These standards derive largely from the objectives and strategies set forth at the SBU and individual product-market entry level. They generate a series of performance expectations for profitability (return on equity or return on assets managed), market share, and sales. At the product-market level, standards of performance also include sales and market-share determinants such as percent effective distribution, relative shelf-facings, awareness, consumers' attitude change toward a given product attribute, customer satisfaction, and the extent of price parity.

Similarly, for every line item in a marketing budget—product development costs, advertising and promotional expenses, costs for salespeople, and so on—specific and

measurable standards of performance must be set so that each of these elements of marketing performance can be evaluated. We address the development of these standards later in this chapter. Without a reasonable set of performance standards, managers cannot know what results are being obtained, the extent to which they are satisfactory, or why they are or are not satisfactory. Performance-based control measures are often tied to the compensation of those individuals responsible for attaining the specified goals. Such a system can cause actions to be taken that in the short term may help attain the desired goals but in the longer term may be detrimental to the firm (see Exhibit 14.3).

Recent years have witnessed a shift from using primarily financially based performance measures to treating them as simply part of a broader array of measures. While the use of nonfinancial measures is not new, giving them equal or greater status is. Thus, more and more companies are turning to measures they feel better reflect how their managers think about what decision areas drive the firm's success, such as customer satisfaction, product quality, market share, and new product development. If the firm has set enhanced shareholder value as its ultimate objective, then it needs to change from the traditional ROI concept to one using a valuation model that focuses on the future cash flow trend, which is discounted at an appropriate discount rate adjusted for risk.[6]

The increasing use of cross-functional teams empowered to manage such processes as order fulfillment, major accounts, and new product introductions has required the development of a new set of imaginative control measures. In a similar vein, Robert Simmons believes that more managers are facing the problem of how to exercise control in organizational settings that require flexibility, innovation, and creativity. Employees are being asked to use initiative in servicing customer needs and seizing opportunities, and yet, in so doing, they may expose the company to substantial risk.[7]

To be of any value, performance standards must be measurable; further, they must be tied to specific time periods, particularly when they concern a management compensation system. The SMART acronym (specific, measurable, attainable, relevant, and timebound),

Exhibit 14.3   Blind Ambition at Bausch & Lomb

Bausch & Lomb, a large international firm known for its Ray-Ban sunglasses, contact lenses, and a wide array of eyewear products, has experienced serious financial problems. The emphasis on achieving double-digit annual profit growth caused managers to use short-term tactics that in the longer term would wound the company seriously. Favorite tactics were to give customers unusually long payment terms and threaten to fire distributors unless they took on large quantities of unwanted merchandise. They also shipped goods before they were ordered and booked them as sales.

According to some executives, division heads might receive a small bonus even if they fell 10 percent short of yearly earning targets, while an overage was handsomely rewarded. A small weight was assigned to such assets as receivables and inventories, but apparently one could miss the assigned asset objectives substantially and still get a big bonus. Customer satisfaction was given a small importance rating.

Source: Reprinted from Mark Maremont and Gail DeGeorge, "Blind Ambition," *Business Week*, October 23, 1995, p. 78, with special permission. Copyright © 1995 by The McGraw-Hill Companies, Inc.

to which we have referred when discussing the setting of objectives in earlier chapters, is a useful framework for setting performance standards. Generally, control systems at the product-market level operate on a monthly, quarterly, and annual basis, with the monthly and quarterly data cumulated to present a current picture and to facilitate comparisons with prior years. In recent years, the trend has been for control systems to operate over shorter periods (weekly and even daily) and for control data to be more readily available. Wal-Mart's inventory control system, for example, provides instantaneous up-to-date data. Strategic control tends to operate over longer periods.

Of particular importance is whether the business unit as a whole and its individual product-market entries have set forth milestone achievement measures. For example, in a three-year strategic plan, a given SBU might have 12-month milestones such as annual sales of $100 million, profits of $20 million, and a return on assets managed of 14.5 percent. At the product-market entry level, milestones include such measures as product sales by market segments, marginal contributions, and operating margins. At the marketing functional area level, examples of milestone measures for a consumer good are level of awareness, trial, repeat purchases (brand loyalty) among members of the target audience, reduction in marketing costs as a percent of sales, and percent of stores stocking (weighted by sales).

In recent years, major U.S. companies such as AT&T, DuPont, Ford, GM, IBM, and Motorola have used a new performance type of measure—benchmarking. What this means is that the firm's performance in a given area is compared against the performance of other companies. Thus, Wal-Mart regularly compares itself with its competitors on merchandise assortments, service quality, and out of stocks. The comparison does not, however, have to be with companies in the same industry. For example, Xerox benchmarked its order filling/shipping performance against L. L. Bean (a mail-order retailer catering to the outdoor set), which has a well-deserved reputation for fulfilling orders both quickly and accurately. A visit to Bean's warehouse revealed that workers could "pick and pack" items three times as fast as Xerox.[8]

Profitability Analysis   Regardless of the organizational level, control involves some form of profitability analysis. In brief, **profitability analysis** requires that analysts determine the costs associated with specific marketing activities to find out the profitability of such units as different market segments, products, customer accounts, and distribution channels (intermediaries). Wal-Mart does this at the department and individual store levels as well as for individual lines of goods within a department. More and more managers are attempting to obtain profitability measures for individual products by market segments.

Profitability is probably the single most important measure of performance, but it has limitations. These are that (1) many objectives can best be measured in nonfinancial terms (maintaining market share); (2) profit is a short-term measure and can be manipulated by taking actions that may prove dysfunctional in the longer term (reducing R&D expenses); and (3) profits can be affected by factors over which management has no control (the weather). For a discussion of the newly discovered profitability religion in the dot-com world, see Exhibit 14.4.

Analysts can use direct or full costing in determining the profitability of a product or market segment. In **full costing,** analysts assign both direct, or variable, and indirect costs to the unit of analysis. **Indirect costs** involve certain fixed joint costs that cannot be linked directly to a single unit of analysis. For example, the costs of occupancy, general management, and the management of the salesforce are all indirect costs for a multiproduct company. Those who use full costing argue that only by allocating all costs to a product or a market can they obtain an accurate picture of its value.

Direct costing involves the use of **contribution accounting.** Those favoring the **contribution margin** approach argue there is really no accurate way to assign indirect costs.

Exhibit 14.4   Is Profitability Important in the Dot-com World?

In the dot-com heyday of the late 1990s, it was said that profitability was not very important for dot-com companies. Other metrics, like first to market or first to scale, were thought to be sufficient. "We'll make money when we get big enough," said many a dot-com CEO. In April 2000, however, the sky-high dot-com stock market valuations came tumbling down, and the financing window for many dot-coms slammed shut. Suddenly, a newfound religion—profitability and positive cash flow—took its place on the dashboards of dot-com CEOs.

These CEOs found themselves thinking about more tangible, shorter-term performance metrics. The cost to acquire a customer was measured—and often found to be prohibitive—and new, lower-cost customer acquisition strategies were developed. The costs to deliver products sold in cyberspace but delivered on Maple Street were examined. Bags of dog food, for example, cost more to deliver one by one than most of them cost to buy in the first place. The efficacy and cost-effectiveness of banner ads for building brands was measured—and often found wanting—as we saw in Chapter 9.

In hindsight, most observers find these changes to have been healthy, in terms of directing investment capital to new-economy businesses that offer the potential to deliver real value for which customers are willing to pay. Is the frenzy over? Probably not. But today's dot-com entrepreneurs and those who fund them now know that measuring marketing performance and profitability is among the most important activities their firms undertake.

Source: Jerry Useem, "What Have We Learned?" *Fortune,* October 30, 2000, pp. 82–104; and Melanie Warner, "Fallen Idols," *Fortune,* October 30, 2000, pp. 108–21.

Further, because indirect costs are mostly fixed, a product or market may make a contribution to profits even if it shows a loss. Thus, even though the company must eventually absorb its overhead costs, the contribution method clearly indicates what is gained by adding or dropping a product or a customer. Exhibit 14.5 shows an example of full and direct costing. The difference in the results obtained is substantial—$370,000 using full costing versus $650,000 with the contribution method.

Contribution analysis is helpful in determining the yield derived from the application of additional resources (for instance, to certain sales territories). Using the data in Exhibit 14.6 we can answer the question, "How much additional profit would result from a marginal increase in sales of $300,000—assuming the gross margin remains at 19.62 percent and the only cost is $35,000 more in sales commissions and expenses?" As Exhibit 14.6 shows, the answer is a profit increase before taxes of $53,000.

Companies are increasingly turning from traditional accounting methods, which identify costs according to various expense categories, to activity-based costing (ABC), which bases costs on the different tasks involved in performing a given activity. ABC advocates have used it to improve product costing, thereby improving pricing parameters, providing better service, trimming waste, and evaluating quality initiative.[9]

Customer Satisfaction   So far, we have been discussing performance measures in essentially financial terms. But financial terms are insufficient since they fail to recognize the importance of customer satisfaction, which is an important driving force of the firm's future market share and profitability. As products and services become more alike in an already highly competitive marketplace, the ability to satisfy the customer across a variety of activities (of which the product is only one) will become an even greater success determinant. Thus, measures relating to customer preferences and satisfaction are essential as an early warning of impending problems and opportunities.

A multiproduct firm will need customer satisfaction measures for each of its different products even if they are sold to the same customer. This would especially be the case if

Exhibit 14.5

FINDING PRODUCT OR MARKET PROFITABILITY WITH FULL COSTING AND MARGINAL CONTRIBUTION METHODS ($000)

	Full costing	Marginal contribution
Net sales	$5,400	$5,400
Less: Cost of goods sold—includes direct costs (labor, material, and production overhead)*	3,800	3,800
Gross margin	$1,600	$1,600
Expenses		
Salesforce—includes direct costs (commissions) plus indirect costs (sales expenses, sales management overhead)†	510	450
Advertising—includes direct costs (media, production) plus indirect costs (management overhead)	215	185
Physical logistics—includes direct costs (transportation) plus indirect costs (order processing, warehousing costs)	225	190
Occupancy—includes direct costs (telephone) plus indirect costs (heat/air, insurance, taxes, building maintenance)	100	25
Management overhead—includes direct costs (product/brand manager and staff) plus indirect costs (salaries, expenses, occupancy costs of SBU's general management group)	180	100
Total	$1,230	$ 950
Profit before taxes	$ 370	
Contribution to fixed costs and profits		$ 650

*Production facilities dedicated to a single product.

†Multiproduct salesforce.

the choice criteria varied substantially between products, especially in terms of expectations regarding service (delivery, repairs, and availability of spare parts). Also, a firm needs to develop its own satisfaction measures with its various intermediaries (channel members) and major suppliers (advertising agencies).

Developing a meaningful measure of customer satisfaction requires the merging of two kinds of measures. The first has to do with an understanding and measurement of the criteria used by customers to evaluate the quality of the firm's relationship with them. Knowing the product/service attributes that constitute the customer's choice criteria as well as the relative importance of each should facilitate this task. These were developed in the process by which the firm identifies the target market for its product-market entries. Once these attributes are identified, they serve as the basis for developing **expectation measures.**

The second type of measurement is concerned with how well the firm is meeting the customer's expectations on an individual attribute as well as an overall basis. Thus, if the choice criteria of a cruiseline's target market included such attributes as food, exercise facilities, and entertainment, then a performance measure would be developed for each. By weighting these by the relative importance of each, an overall performance measure can be obtained. These two measures collectively serve as the basis for evaluating the company's performance on customer satisfaction.

Exhibit 14.6

EFFECT OF $300,000 INCREASE IN SALES RESULTING FROM INCREASED SALES COMMISSIONS AND EXPENSES OF $35,000
(SAME DATA AS IN EXHIBIT 14.5) ($000)

Net sales	$5,700
Less: direct costs (29.62%)	4,012
	$ 1,688
Expenses	
Sales commissions and expenses	485
Advertising	185
Physical logistics	190
Occupancy	25
Management	100
	$ 985
Contribution to overhead and profits	$ 703
Increase in profit (before tax) = $703 − $650 =	$ 53

In recent years more top-level executives are visiting their major accounts (whether they be end-use customers or intermediaries) to learn firsthand how to better serve them. Such visits frequently result in joint projects designed to reduce the costs incurred by both parties in the sale of a given set of products.[10]

Specifying and Obtaining Feedback Data

Once a company has established its performance standards, its next step is to develop a system that provides usable and timely feedback data on actual performance. In most cases someone must gather and process considerable data to obtain the performance measures, especially at the product-market level. Analysts obtain feedback data from a variety of sources, including company accounting records and syndicated marketing information services such as Nielsen. The sales invoice or other transaction records, such as those produced by retailers' point-of-sale systems, are the basic internal source of data because they provide a detailed record of each transaction. Invoices are the basis for measuring profitability, sales, and various budget items. They also provide data for the analysis of the geographic distribution of sales and customer accounts by type and size.

Another source, and typically the most expensive and time-consuming, involves undertaking one or more marketing research projects to obtain needed information. In-house research projects are apt to take longer and be more expensive than using an outside syndicated service. But there may be no alternative, as, for example, in determining awareness and attitude changes and obtaining data on customer service. Exhibit 14.7 gives an example of how Wal-Mart uses marketing research to help maintain its low-price image. A third source, and one we discussed above, involves the use of executives to gather information from their personal visits with customers.

Evaluating Feedback Data

Management evaluates feedback data to find out whether there is any deviation from the plan, and if so why. Wal-Mart does this in a variety of ways, including sending its regional vice presidents into the field on a regular basis to learn what's going on and why.

Exhibit 14.7   Wal-Mart Uses Marketing Research to Maintain Price Image

Wal-Mart makes every effort to keep its regular everyday prices lower than competitors' on a set of critical products. These "image items" are thought to be the basis of a customer's perception of how expensive a store is. Every few weeks Wal-Mart undertakes research to determine the prices charged by its major competitors for these same items. The company then makes sure that Wal-Mart has the lowest price. Even top management, including Sam Walton when he was alive, has been known to do comparison shopping.

Typically, managers use a variety of information to determine what the company's performance *should* have been under the actual market conditions that existed when the plan was executed. In some cases this information can be obtained in measured form; examples include a shift in personal disposable income (available from government sources), a change in the demand for a given product type (obtained when measuring market share), the impact of a new brand on market share (reported by a commercial source), or a change in price by a major competitor. Often, however, the explanation rests on inferences drawn from generalized data, as would be the case in attributing poor sales performance to an improvement in a competitor's salesforce.

At the line-item level, whether for revenue or expenses, results are compared with the standards set in step one of the control process. A merchandise manager or buyer at an apparel retailer such as Gap, for example, would track sales results of each style or merchandise category in terms of its selling rate (how many weeks' supply is on hand overall and in which stores?) and its gross margin performance. For a district sales team of an industrial goods manufacturer, salespeople might be measured on the number of sales calls they make per week, the number of new accounts they generate, their sales volume in dollars and units, their travel expenses, and a variety of other metrics. A stylist in a beauty salon might be measured in terms of the number or sales dollars of haircuts she produces per day or per hour.

Taking Corrective Action

The last step in the control process concerns prescribing the needed action to correct the situation. At Wal-Mart, this is partly accomplished at its various congresses held every Friday and Saturday when managers decide what actions to take to solve selected problems. Success here depends on how well managers carry out the evaluation step. When linkages between inputs and outputs are clear, managers can presume a causal relationship and specify appropriate action. For example, assume that inputs consisted of an advertising schedule that specified the frequency of a given TV message. The objective was to change attitudes about a given product attribute (the output). If the attitude change did not occur, remedial action would start with an evaluation of the firm's advertising effort, particularly the advertising message and how frequently it ran.

But in most cases it is difficult to identify the cause of the problem. Almost always, an interactive effect exists among the input variables as well as the environment. There is also the problem of delayed responses and carry-over effects. For example, advertisers can rarely separate the effects of the message, media, frequency of exposure, and competitive responses in an attempt to determine advertising effects. Even if the company could determine the cause of a problem, it faces the difficulty of prescribing the appropriate action to take. Most control systems are "based on the assumption that corrective action is known should significant variations arise. Unfortunately, marketing is not at a stage where performance deviations can be corrected with certainty."[11]

Sometimes the situation is so serious (shipping time lags competition by 30 percent) that radical change is needed. To more and more business managers this means "reengineering" or starting all over. This involves rethinking and redesigning the relevant business processes "to achieve dramatic improvements in critical contemporary measures of performance such as cost, quality, service, and speed."[12] A business process uses a variety of activities to create an output that is of value to a customer. For example, the order-filling process exists only to deliver the right goods to a customer in good shape and in the time promised.

Sometimes the outcome is greater or better than management had planned; for example, when sales and market share exceed the schedule. In such cases, the marketers still need an evaluation to find out why such a variance occurred. Perhaps a more favorable environment evolved because demand was greater than expected and a major competitor failed to take advantage of it. Or perhaps the advertising message was more effective than expected. These different reasons would call for different marketing responses to hold what had been obtained and to further exploit the favorable situation.

DESIGN DECISIONS FOR STRATEGIC CONTROL SYSTEMS

Strategic control is concerned with monitoring and evaluating a firm's SBU-level strategies (see Exhibit 14.8 for the kinds of questions this type of control system is designed to answer). Such a system is difficult to implement because there is usually a substantial amount of time between strategy formulation and when a strategy takes hold and results are evident. Since both the external and internal environments are constantly evolving, strategic control must provide some way of changing the firm's thrust if new information about the environment and/or the firm's performance so dictates. Inevitably, much of this intermediate assessment is based on information about the marketplace and the results obtained from the firm's marketing plan.

STRATEGIC ISSUE

Strategic control must provide some way of changing the firm's thrust if new information about the environment and/or the firm's performance so dictates.

Identifying Key Variables

To implement strategic control, a company must identify the key variables to monitor, which are the major assumptions (planning premises) made in formulating the strategy. The key variables to monitor are the two types: those concerned with external forces and those concerned with the effects of certain actions taken by the firm to implement the

Exhibit 14.8

EXAMPLES OF QUESTIONS A STRATEGIC CONTROL SYSTEM SHOULD BE ABLE TO ANSWER

1. What changes in the environment have negatively affected the current strategy (e.g., interest rates, government controls, or price changes in substitute products)?

2. What changes have major competitors made in their objectives and strategies?

3. What changes have occurred in the industry in such attributes as capacity, entry barriers, and substitute products?

4. What new opportunities or threats have derived from changes in the environment, competitors' strategies, or the nature of the industry?

5. What changes have occurred in the industry's key success factors?

6. To what extent is the firm's current strategy consistent with the preceding changes?

strategy. Examples of the former include changes in the external environment such as changes in long-term demand, the advent of new technology, a change in governmental legislation, and actions by a competitor. Examples of the latter types (actions by the firm) include the firm's advertising efforts to change attitudes and in-store merchandising activities designed to improve product availability.

The frameworks and analytical tools for market and competitive analysis that we discussed in Chapters 4 and 5 are useful in determining what variables to monitor in a strategic control system. Deciding exactly which variables to monitor is a company-specific decision; in general, it should focus on those variables most likely to affect the company's future position within its industry group.

Tracking and Monitoring

The next step is to specify what information or measures are needed on each of the key variables to determine whether the implementation of the strategic plan is on schedule—and if not, why not. The firm can use the control plan as an early-warning system as well as a diagnostic tool. If, for example, the firm has made certain assumptions about the rate at which market demand will increase, it should monitor industry sales regularly. If it has made assumptions about advertising and its effect on attitudes, it would be likely to use measures of awareness, trial, and repeat buying. In any event, the firm must closely examine the relevancy, accuracy, and cost of obtaining the needed measures.

The advent of e-mail, intranets, and other digital tools for disseminating information has made it easier for sometimes far-flung managers to monitor strategic developments. Critical strategic control information can now be monitored on a real-time basis anywhere in the world.

Strategy Reassessment

This can take place at periodic intervals—for example, quarterly or annually, when the firm evaluates its performance to date along with major changes in the external environment. It also can use the control system to alert management of a significant change in either or both its external/internal environments. This involves setting triggers to signal the need to reassess the viability of the firm's strategy. It requires a specification of both the level at which an alert will be called and the combination of events that must occur before the firm reacts. For example, total industry sales of 10 percent less than expected for a single month would not be likely to trigger a response, whereas a 25 percent drop would. Or a firm might decide that triggering will occur only after three successive months in which a difference of 10 percent occurred in each.

In the fast-changing dot-com world, strategy reassessment may happen much more quickly, as competitive and technological developments cause firms to quickly change their entire strategies and business models. Reasonware.com, an e-tailer of wireless telephone products and services, began in late 2000 to develop a new strategy focused on business services when it realized how difficult it was for most e-tailers to reach profitability.[13]

DESIGN DECISIONS FOR MARKETING PERFORMANCE MEASUREMENT

Designing control systems to measure marketing performance at the product-market and line-item levels involves answering four essential questions:

- Who needs what information?
- When and how often is the information needed?
- In what media and in what format(s) or levels of aggregation should the information be provided?
- What contingencies should be planned for?

In essence, designing a marketing performance measurement system is like designing the dashboard of a car. Such a system needs to include the most critical metrics to assess whether the car or the business is progressing toward its objectives. Thus, for a car, the dashboard includes a speed gauge and odometer to measure progress toward the destination, a fuel gauge, warning lights for engine and braking system malfunction, and so on, but it typically does not indicate how much windshield wiper fluid remains, how much weight the car is carrying, or other relatively nonessential indicators. The same holds true for a business: The "drivers" who are managing the business need to know certain essential information while the "car"—or strategy—is running, while other less crucial indicators can be omitted or provided only when requested. We now address the four key questions, or **design parameters,** of marketing performance measurement systems.

STRATEGIC ISSUE

In essence, designing a marketing performance measurement system is like designing the dashboard of a car.

Who Needs What Information?

Marketing performance measurement systems are designed to ensure that the company achieves the sales, profits, and other objectives set forth in its marketing and strategic plans. In the aggregate, these plans reflect the outcomes of the company's or the SBU's planning efforts, which have specified how resources are to be allocated across markets, products, and marketing-mix activities. These plans, as we noted in Chapter 13, include line-item budgets and typically specify the actions expected of each organizational unit—whether inside or outside the marketing function or department—and deemed necessary to attain the company's financial and competitive positioning objectives. The first and foremost objective for marketing is the level of sales the company or the product-market entry achieves.

Who needs sales information? Top management needs it. Functional managers in other parts of the organization—manufacturing, procurement, finance, and so on—need it. Marketing managers responsible for the various marketing-mix activities, from product design to pricing to channel management to selling and other promotional activities, need it.

Sales Analysis   A sales analysis involves breaking down aggregate sales data into such categories as products, end-user customers, channel intermediaries, sales territories, and order size. The objective of an analysis is to find areas of strength and weakness; for example, products producing the greatest and least volume, customers accounting for the bulk of the revenues, and salespersons and territories performing the best and the worst.

Sales analysis recognizes that aggregate sales and cost data often mask the real situation. Sales analysis not only helps to evaluate and control marketing efforts, but also helps management to better formulate objectives and strategies and administer such nonmarketing activities as production planning, inventory management, and facilities planning.

An important decision in designing the firm's sales analysis system concerns which units of analysis to use. Most companies assemble data in the following groupings:

- Geographical areas—regions, counties, and sales territories.
- Product, package size, and grade.
- Customer—by type and size.

- Channel intermediary—such as type and/or size of retailer.
- Method of sale—mail, phone, channel, Internet, or direct.
- Size of order—less than $10, $10–25, and so on.

These breakdowns are not mutually exclusive. Most firms perform sales analyses hierarchically; for example, by county within a sales territory within a sales region. Further, they usually combine product and account breakdowns with a geographical one: say, the purchase of product X by large accounts located in sales territory Y, which is part of region A. Only by conducting sales analysis on a hierarchical basis using a combination of breakdowns can analysts be at all sure that they have made every reasonable attempt to locate the opportunities and problems facing their firms.

Sales Analysis by Territory The first step in a sales territory analysis is to decide which geographical control unit to use. The county is the typical choice since it can be combined into larger units such as sales territories and it is also a geographical area for which many data items are available, such as population, employment, income, and retail sales. Analysts can compare actual sales (derived from company invoices) by county against a standard such as a sales quota that takes into account such factors as market potential and last year's sales adjusted for inflation. They can then single out territories that fall below standard for special attention. Is competition unusually strong? Has less selling effort been expended here? Is the salesforce weak? Studies dealing with such questions as these help a company improve its weak products and exploit its stronger ones. Category and brand development indices, such as those described in Chapter 6, are often used in assessing sales performance by territory.

Exhibit 14.9 illustrates a sales territory analysis. It shows that only one territory out of seven shown exceeded its 1999 quota, or standard of performance, and by just $18,112. The other six territories accounted for a total of $394,685 under quota. Territory 3 alone accounted for 55 percent of the total loss. The sales and the size of the quota in this territory suggest the need for further breakdowns, especially by accounts and products. Such breakdowns may reveal that the firm needs to allocate more selling resources to this territory. The company needs to improve its sales primarily in territories 3 and 5. If it can reach its potential in these two territories, overall sales would increase by $301,911, assuming that the quotas set are valid.

Exhibit 14.9

SALES ANALYSIS BASED ON SELECTED SALES TERRITORIES

Sales Territory	Salesperson	(1) Company sales 1999	(2) Sales quota 1999	(3) Overage, underage	(4) Percent of potential performance
1	Barlow	$552,630	$585,206	−$32,576	94%
2	Burrows	470,912	452,800	+18,112	104
3	White	763,215	981,441	−218,226	77
4	Finch	287,184	297,000	−9,816	96
5	Brown	380,747	464,432	−83,685	82
6	Roberts	494,120	531,311	−37,191	93
7	Macini	316,592	329,783	−13,191	96

Without a standard against which to compare results, the conclusions would be much different. Thus, if only company sales were considered (column 1), White would be the best salesperson and Finch the worst. By using sales quotas as a performance standard, White was not the best but the worst salesperson, with a 77 percent rating.

Sales Analysis by Product Over time, a company's product line tends to become overcrowded and less profitable unless management takes strong and continuous action to eliminate no-longer-profitable items. By eliminating weak products and concentrating on strong ones, a company can increase its profits substantially. Before deciding which products to abandon, management must study such variables as market-share trends, contribution margins, scale effects, and the extent to which a product is complementary with other items in the line.[14]

A product sales analysis is particularly helpful when combined with account size and sales territory data. Using such an analysis, managers often can pinpoint substantial opportunities and develop specific tactics to take advantage of them. For example, one firm's analysis revealed that sales of one of its highest-margin products were down in all the Asian sales territories. Further investigation showed that a regional producer was aggressively promoting a recently modified product with reduced prices. An analysis of the competing product revealed questionable reliability under certain operating conditions. The salesforce used this information to turn around the sales problem.

Sales Analysis by Order Size Sales analysis by order size may identify which dollar-size orders are not profitable. For example, if some customers frequently place small orders that require salesforce attention and need to be processed, order picked, and shipped, a problem of some importance exists.

Analysis by order size locates products, sales territories, and customer types and sizes where small orders prevail. Such an analysis may lead to setting a minimum order size, charging extra for small orders, training sales reps to develop larger orders, and dropping some accounts. An example of such an analysis involved a nationwide needlework product distributor, which found that 28 percent of all its orders were $10 and under. A study revealed that the average cost of servicing such orders was $12.82. The analysis also showed that the company did not break even until the order size reached $20. Based on these findings, the company installed a $35 minimum order, charged a special handling fee of $7.50 on all orders below $35, and alerted its field sales reps and telephone salespeople to the problem. As a result, the company increased its profits substantially.

Sales Analysis by Customer Analysts use procedures similar to those described earlier to analyze sales by customers. Such analyses typically show that a relatively small percentage of customers accounts for a large percentage of sales. For example, the needlework products distributor cited above found that 13 percent of its accounts represented 67 percent of its total sales. Frequently, a study of sales calls shows that the salesforce spends a disproportionate amount of its time with the small accounts as compared with the larger ones. Shifting some of this effort to the larger accounts may well increase sales.

Sales/Share Determinants Sales and market share are a function of a number of primary determinants. For a consumer product these include effective distribution, relative price, attitude maintenance or change toward one or more salient product characteristics relative to competition, and shelf-facings. These, in turn, are a function of secondary determinants such as number and frequency of sales calls, trade deals, and the effectiveness of the advertising message with a given reach and frequency schedule. An analysis of the share determinants should provide insights into presumed linkages between the firm's inputs and outputs: for example, number and frequency of sales calls and effective distribution. This, in turn, leads to a better understanding of the firm's marketing efficiency. Is the salesforce making as many calls per day as expected—and the right number of calls on target accounts to obtain a certain level of distribution?

Marketing research is usually required to ascertain the extent to which determinants are being attained. For example, consistently having a lower price on the same product relative to major competitors is an important determinant of sales. As in the case of Wal-Mart, interviewers would need to shop the targeted stores to obtain the desired price data.

Line-Item Margin and Expense Analysis   Sales data are not the only marketing performance information needed, of course. Gross and net margins must be tracked, and the effectiveness and efficiency of all line-item marketing expenses must be measured. The designers of marketing performance measurement systems must develop appropriate metrics to track the critical performance indicators for margins and expenses so that timely mid-course corrections can be made. Thus, the weeks-on-hand metric that tells a Gap sweater buyer how quickly each style is selling tells him or her whether to buy more of a particular style if it is selling well, or mark it down if it is not moving. Making such decisions on a timely basis can have a profound effect on gross margins. A not-so-pretty sweater may be more salable at 25 percent off before Christmas than at 60 percent off December 26.

Because budgets project revenues and expenses for a given time period, they are a vital part of the firm's planning and control activities. They provide the basis for a continuous evaluation and comparison of what was planned with what actually happened. In this sense, budgeted revenues and profits serve as objectives against which to measure performance in sales, profits, and actual costs.

Budget analysis requires that managers continuously monitor marketing–expense ratios to make certain the company does not overspend in its effort to reach its objectives. Managers also evaluate the magnitude and pattern of deviations from the target ratios. Managers of the various marketing units have their own control measures. For example, advertising managers track advertising costs per 1,000 target audience, buyers per media vehicle, print ad readership, size and composition of TV audiences, and attitude change. Sales managers typically track number of calls per salesperson, costs per call, sales per call, and new accounts. The major marketing expenses are those associated with marketing research, brand management, sales salaries, sales expenses, media advertising, consumer promotions, trade promotions, and publicity. Before taking corrective action on any of these expenses that are out of line, managers may need to disaggregate the data to help isolate the problem. For example, if total commissions as a percent of sales are out of line, analysts need to study them by each sales territory and product to determine exactly where the problem lies.

When and How Often Is the Information Needed?

Timeliness is a key criterion for the development of a marketing performance measurement system. As we have seen, Wal-Mart's systems provide sales information at the store and item level on an up-to-the-minute basis. More commonly, though, managers attend to performance information—whether for sales, margins, or expenses—on a periodic basis, since they don't have time or the need to assess the performance of every item at every minute of every day. Buyers and merchandise managers in retailing firms typically assess item and category sales performance on a weekly basis. In fashion categories, such as women's apparel, where timeliness is especially important, having sales information a couple of days, or even hours, ahead of competitors can make the difference between obtaining more of a hot-selling item or being left in a faster-moving competitor's dust. Store payroll expense, another key performance criterion for retailers that impacts both customer service and profitability, is typically measured on a weekly basis, though store managers may be encouraged to send employees home if business is unexpectedly slow on a given day or call in extra help when more is needed. The performance of industrial sales-people—in terms of number of sales calls, sales volume, expense control, and other indicators—is typically done on a monthly basis, though some firms may do so more or less frequently as they see fit. Strategic control indicators, such as changes in market share, macro trends, and so on, are likely to be measured and reported less frequently because these kinds of longer-term issues may not be readily apparent or may give false alarms at more frequent intervals.

In What Media and in What Format(s) or Levels of Aggregation Should the Information Be Provided?

Advances in information technology have made possible the measurement and reporting of marketing performance information with previously unheard-of ease of access and timeliness, without even printing the data! As we have seen, Wal-Mart's sales information is available on computer screens on an up-to-the-minute basis. In other companies, salespeople around the world now log on to company intranets to see the latest order status of a customer before they walk in the door on a sales call. But *having* good and timely information and *reporting* it in such a manner that it is easy and quick to use are different things. Imagine a Gap buyer having to manually add up the performance of various styles to determine how the category is performing. Reports should provide such aggregation, of course, but someone must decide what sort of aggregation is most useful for each information user.

STRATEGIC ISSUE

Having *good and timely information and* reporting *it in such a manner that it is easy and quick to use are different things.*

Even the format or medium in which performance information is presented can make a big difference to the manager using the data. Weekly weeks-on-hand sales reports that retail buyers and merchandise managers depend on are most usefully reported in order of how fast the styles are selling, rather than alphabetically or some other way. The styles at the top of the report (those with little stock on hand, as measured by their weeks-on-hand sales rate) are candidates for reorders. Styles at the bottom of the report (the ugly sweater in mid-November with 25 weeks of inventory on hand) are candidates for markdowns. The ones in between may need little attention. Once a season ends, a different report, aggregating styles by vendor, perhaps, might be useful to determine which suppliers have performed well and which have performed poorly across the assortment of styles they provide. Thoughtful attention to the format in which marketing performance information is reported, to the levels at which it is aggregated, for different kinds of decision purposes, and for different users, can provide a company with a significant competitive advantage. As we noted earlier in this chapter, it took Kmart many years to come close to Wal-Mart's system of tracking and reporting store and item sales performance.

What Contingencies Should Be Planned for?

Because all strategies and the action plans designed to implement them are based on assumptions about the future, they are subject to considerable risk. Too often, assumptions are regarded as facts; and little attention is paid to what action or actions can be taken if any or all of the assumptions turn out to be wrong.

Exhibit 14.10

THE CONTINGENCY PLANNING PROCESS

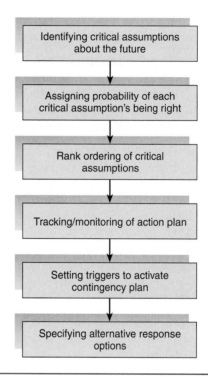

Managers, therefore, often follow a contingency planning process that includes the elements shown in Exhibit 14.10 identifying critical assumptions; assigning probabilities of being right about the assumptions; ranking the importance of the assumption; tracking and monitoring the action plan; setting the "triggers" that will activate the contingency plan; and specifying alternative response options. We discuss these steps briefly next.

Identifying Critical Assumptions   Because there are simply too many assumptions to track them all, contingency plans must cover only the more important ones. Assumptions about events beyond the control of the individual firm but that strongly affect the entry's strategic objectives are particularly important. For example, assumptions about the rate of market growth coupled with the entry's market share will strongly affect the entry's profitability objectives. The effect of a wrong assumption here can be either good or bad, and the contingency plan must be prepared to handle both. If the market grows at a rate faster then expected, then the question of how to respond needs to be considered. Too often contingency plans focus only on the downside.

Another type of uncontrollable event that can strongly affect sales and profits is competitive actions. This is particularly true with a new entry (when a competitor responds with its own new product), although it can apply with more mature products (competitor's advertising is increased). Assumptions about industry price levels must be examined in depth because any price deterioration can quickly erode margins and profits.

Assumptions about the effects of certain actions taken by the firm to attain its strategic objectives also need to be considered in depth. Examples include the firm's advertising objectives, which are based on assumptions about an improvement or maintenance of consumer attitudes toward the product's characteristics compared with competing brands, or the monies allocated to merchandising to improve the product's availability. Further, once the targeted levels of the various primary objectives are reached, there are assumptions about what will happen to sales and share.

Assigning Probabilities   This step consists of assigning to the critical assumptions probabilities of being right. These probabilities must be considered in terms of the consequences of being wrong. Thus, assumptions that have a low probability of being wrong but could affect the firm strongly need to be considered in depth (for instance, gas shortages or high prices or the demand for large luxury automobiles).

Rank Ordering the Critical Assumptions   If assumptions are categorized on the basis of their importance, the extent to which they are controllable, and the confidence management has in them, then the basis for rank ordering the assumptions and drafting the contingency plan has been set forth. Ordinarily, these criteria will have screened out those assumptions that need not be included—those with a low impact on objectives and those about which there is a high confidence they will not occur. Assumptions that relate to uncontrollable events should, however, be monitored if they strongly affect the entry's strategic objectives since the firm can react to them. For example, if the assumption about the rate of market growth is wrong, then the firm can either slow or increase its investments in plant construction.

Tracking and Monitoring   The next step is to specify what information (or measures) are needed to determine whether the implementation of the action plan is on schedule—and if not, why not. The contingency plan is, therefore, an early warning system as well as a diagnostic tool. If, for example, the firm has made certain assumptions about the rate of market demand increase, then it would monitor industry sales on a regular basis. If assumptions were made about advertising and its effect on attitudes, then measures of awareness, trial, and repeat buying would be likely to be used. Relevancy, accuracy, and cost of obtaining the needed measures must be examined in depth. Some of the information needed in the contingency plan might have been specified in the control plan, in which case it is already available.

Activating the Contingency Plan   This involves setting the "triggers" to activate the contingency plan. It requires a specification of both the level at which an alert will be called and the combination of events that must occur before the firm reacts. If, for example, total industry sales were 10 percent less than expected for a single month, this would not be likely to trigger a response, whereas a 25 percent drop would. Or a firm may decide the triggering would occur only after three successive months in which a difference of 10 percent occurred. Triggers must be defined precisely and responsibility assigned for putting the contingency plan into operation.

Specifying Response Options   Actually, the term *contingency plan* is somewhat misleading. It implies that the firm can know in advance exactly how it will respond if one or more of its assumptions go awry. This implication is unrealistic because there are a great many ways for critical assumptions to turn out wrong. To compound the problem, the firm's preplanned specific responses can be difficult to implement, depending on the situation and how it develops. This can lead to a set of responses that build in intensity. Thus, most firms develop a set of optional responses that are not detailed to any great extent in an effort to provide flexibility and ensure further study of the forces that caused the alert.

Global Marketing Control

Maintaining control over global marketing activities is more difficult than with domestic marketing, primarily because of the number of countries involved, each presenting a unique set of opportunities and threats. This makes it difficult to monitor simultaneously a variety of environments and to prescribe corrective action on an individual-country basis where appropriate. Differences in language and customs, accentuated by distance, further compound the control problem.

Keegan recommends that global companies use essentially the same control system format for both their domestic and foreign operations.[15] Report frequency and extent of detail would vary by the subsidiary's size and environmental uncertainties. The great advantage of using a single system is that it facilitates comparisons between operating units and communications between home office and local managers. On the surface, the use of electronic data interchange should simplify performance evaluation across countries. While this is true in terms of budget control, it leaves much to be desired in terms of understanding the reasons for any deviations.

The extent of control exercised over an overseas subsidiary is largely a function of its size, differences in the environment (including its stability), and the extent to which the company employs a standardized rather than a localized strategy.[16] The larger a company's international operation, the greater the likelihood that staff personnel specializing in control activities will be on-site, making the control system more elaborate and precise in its operation. Small overseas operations tend to involve fewer specialists and a less-intensive control system.

Another factor affecting the control system is the extent to which environmental differences exist. Ordinarily, the greater the differences between the home country and the foreign subsidiary, the more decision-making authority is delegated. Large multinationals compensate for these differences by clustering countries with similar environments into regions that have sufficient revenues to permit the use of a headquarters staff. When considerable environmental instability is present, it is difficult to employ a formal control system; the tendency is to delegate to local management the authority to make certain kinds of decisions without review and approval by the home office.

A third major factor affecting the international control system is the extent to which standardized strategy is used. The more standardized the strategy, especially with respect to the product, the greater the degree of control exercised over many activities, including purchasing raw materials and determining components, manufacturing, and quality specifications. Ordinarily, control over marketing activities is less stringent than with manufacturing. Other factors also affect control: the success of the subsidiary (the greater the success, the less the home office interference) and the physical distance separating the home office and the subsidiary (the greater the distance, the less frequently the subsidiary will be visited). Rapidly improving voice and data communication systems throughout the world have greatly improved the effectiveness of global managers, but many managers feel strongly that the personal touch is still important not only for control purposes but also to improve customer satisfaction.

A TOOL FOR PERIODIC ASSESSMENT OF MARKETING PERFORMANCE: THE MARKETING AUDIT

While marketing performance measurement systems are essential for tracking day-to-day, week-to-week, and month-to-month performance to see that planned results are actually delivered, it is sometimes useful to step back and take a longer view of the marketing performance of an SBU or of the entire company. Marketing audits are growing in popularity, especially for firms with a variety of SBUs that differ in their market orientation. They are both a control and planning activity that involves a comprehensive review of the firm's or SBU's total marketing efforts cutting across all products and business units. Thus, they are broader in scope and cover longer time horizons than sales and profitability analyses.

Our concern here is at the individual SBU level or the entire company, for smaller or single-business firms. Such an audit covers both the SBU's objectives and strategy and its plan of action for each product-market entry. It provides an assessment of each SBU's current overall competitive position as well as that of its individual product-market entries. It requires an analysis of each of the marketing-mix elements and how well they are being implemented in support of each entry. The audit must take into account the environmental changes that can affect the SBU's strategy and product-market action programs.[17]

Types of Audits

Audits are normally conducted for such areas as the SBU's marketing environment, objectives and strategy, planning and control systems, organization, productivity, and individual marketing activities such as sales and advertising. These areas are shown in Exhibit 14.11 with examples of the kinds of data needed and serve as the basis for the discussion that follows.

- The **marketing environment audit** requires an analysis of the firm's present and future environment with respect to its macro components, as discussed in Chapter 4. The intent is to identify the more significant trends to see how they affect the firm's customers, competitors, channel intermediaries, and suppliers.

- The **objectives and strategy area audit** calls for an assessment of how appropriate these internal factors are, given current major environmental trends and any changes in the firm's resources.

- The unit's **planning and control system area audit** evaluates the adequacy of the systems that develop the firm's product-market entry action plans and the control and reappraisal process. The audit also evaluates the firm's new product development procedures.

- The **organization area audit** deals with the firm's overall structure (can it meet the changing needs of the marketplace?); how the marketing department is organized (can it accommodate the planning requirements of the firm's assortment of brands?); and the extent of synergy between the various marketing units (are there good relations between sales and merchandising?).

- The **marketing productivity area audit** evaluates the profitability of the company's individual products, markets (including sales territories), and key accounts. It also studies the cost-effectiveness of the various marketing activities.

- The **marketing functions area audit** examines, in depth, how adequate the firm handles each of the marketing-mix elements. Questions relating to the *product* concern the attainability of the present product-line objective, the extent to which individual products fit the needs of the target markets, and whether the product line should be expanded or contracted. *Price* questions have to do with price elasticity; experience effects, relative costs, and the actions of major competitors; and consumers' perceptions of the relationship between a product's price and its value. *Distribution* questions center on coverage, functions performed, and cost-effectiveness. Questions about *advertising* focus on advertising objectives and strategies, media schedules, and the procedures used to develop advertising objectives and strategies, media schedules, and the procedures used to develop advertising messages. The audit of the salesforce covers its objectives, role, size, coverage, organization, and duties plus the

Exhibit 14.11

MAJOR AREAS COVERED IN MARKETING AUDIT AND QUESTIONS CONCERNING EACH FOR A CONSUMER GOODS COMPANY

Audit Area	Examples of questions to be answered
Marketing environment	What opportunities and/or threats derive from the firm's present and future environment; that is, what macro trends are significant? How will these trends affect the firm's target markets, competitors, and channel intermediaries? Which opportunities/threats emerge from within the firm?
Objectives and strategy	How logical are the company's objectives, given the more significant opportunities/threats and its relative resources? How valid is the firm's strategy, given the anticipated environment, including the actions of competitors?
Planning and control system	Does the firm have adequate and timely information about consumers' satisfaction with its products? With the actions of competitors? With the services of intermediaries?
Organization	Does the organization structure fit the evolving needs of the marketplace? Can it handle the planning needed at the individual product/brand level?
Marketing productivity	How profitable is each of the firm's products/brands? How effective is each of its major marketing activities?
Marketing functions	How well does the product line meet the line's objectives? How well do the products/brands meet the needs of the target markets? Does pricing reflect cross elasticities, experience effects, and relative costs? Is the product readily available? What is the level of retail stockouts? What percentage of large stores carries the firm's in-store displays? Is the salesforce large enough? Is the firm spending enough on advertising?

quality of its selection, training, motivation, compensation, and control activities. In some companies marketing audits cover additional areas including the two that follow.

- The company's **ethical audit** evaluates the extent to which the company engages in ethical and socially responsible marketing. Clearly this audit goes well beyond monitoring to make sure the firm is well within the law in its market behavior. If the company has a written code of ethics, then the main purpose of this audit is to make certain that it is disseminated, understood, and practiced.

- The **product manager audit,** especially in consumer goods companies, seeks to determine whether product managers are channeling their efforts in the best ways possible. They are queried on what they're doing versus what they *ought* to be doing. They also are asked to rate the extent to which various support units were helpful.[18]

TAKE AWAYS

- Most managers and entrepreneurs are evaluated primarily on the results they deliver. Effective design of control systems, whether for strategic control or for marketing performance measurement, helps ensure the delivery of planned results. A step-by-step process for doing so is provided in this chapter.

- Control systems that deliver the right information—in a timely manner and in media, formats, and levels of aggregation that users need and can easily use—can be important elements for establishing competitive advantage. Four key questions that designers of such systems should address are discussed in this chapter.

- From time to time, it is useful to step back from day-to-day results and take a longer view of marketing performance for a company or an SBU. A marketing audit, as outlined in this chapter, is a useful tool for conducting such an assessment.

- Self-diagnostic questions to test your ability to apply the analytical tools and concepts in this chapter to marketing decision making may be found at this book's website at **www.mhhe.com/walker.**

ENDNOTES

1. Based on "Briefly. . . ," *USA Today,* April 10, 1991, p. 28; Sam Walton, *Sam Walton: Made in America* (New York: Doubleday, 1992), pp. 85–86, 118, 212–27; David Smith, "One Step Ahead," *Arkansas Gazette,* September 30, 1991, pp. 7–9; Bill Saporito, "What Sam Walton Taught America," *Fortune,* May 4, 1992, p. 104; Wal-Mart's *1996 Annual Report;* Patricia Sellers, "Can Wal-Mart Get Back the Magic?" *Fortune,* April 29, 1996, p. 130; D. R. Stewart, "Wal-Mart Set to Open in China," *Arkansas Democrat-Gazette,* August 8, 1996, p. B1; and information from the company website at www.walmartstores.com.

2. For a discussion of Kmart's new centralized replenishment system, see "Remote Control," *The Economist,* May 29, 1993, p. 90.

3. Sellers, "Can Wal-Mart Get Back the Magic?" p. 132.

4. Bill Saporito, "A Week aboard the Wal-Mart Express," *Fortune,* August 24, 1992, p. 77.

5. Calmetta Coleman, "Gap Inc. Stumbles as Respected CEO Loosens Reins," *The Wall Street Journal,* September 7, 2000, p. B4.

6. Frances V. McCrory and Peter G. Gerstberger, "The New Math of Performance Measurements," *Journal of Business Strategy,* March–April 1992, pp. 33–38.

7. Robert Simons, "Control in an Age of Empowerment," *Harvard Business Review,* March–April 1995, p. 81.

8. Jeremy Mann, "How to Steal the Best Ideas Around," *Fortune,* October 19, 1992, p. 102.

9. Terrence P. Paré, "A New Tool for Managing Costs," *Fortune,* June 14, 1993, p. 124.

10. Carl Quintanilla, "More Top Executives Are Hitting the Road," *The Wall Street Journal,* January 12, 1996, p. B1.

11. Bernard J. Jaworski, "Toward a Theory of Marketing Control: Environmental Context, Control Types, and Consequences," *Journal of Marketing,* July 1988, p. 24.

12. "The Promise of Reengineering," *Fortune,* May 3, 1993, p. 94. This article is based on excerpts from Michael Hammer and James Champy, *Reengineering the Corporation: A Manifesto for Business Revolution* (New York: Harper Collins, 1993).

13. See the company's website at www.reasonware.com.

14. Activity-based accounting is particularly helpful to managers in determining product profitability since it allocates costs to products more accurately than traditional methods by breaking down overhead costs more precisely. See Paré, "A New Tool," p. 125.

15. Warren J. Keegan, *Global Marketing Management* (Englewood Cliffs, NJ: Prentice Hall, 1989), chap. 4.

16. Ibid.

17. Eric N. Berkowitz, Roger A. Kerin, Steven W. Hartley, and William Rudelius, *Marketing* (Burr Ridge, IL: Richard D. Irwin, 1994), pp. 630–32.

18. John A. Quelch, Paul W. Farris, and James M. Oliver, "The Product Manager Audit," *Harvard Business Review,* March–April 1987, p. 30. Based on their research, these authors conclude that product managers spend too much time on routine matters such as those relating to promotion execution and too little on product design and development.

Name Index

SUBJECT INDEX